Register Now for C
to Your B

SPRINGER PUBLISHING COMPANY
CONNECT™

Your print purchase of *Professional Coaching* **includes online access to the contents of your book**—increasing accessibility, portability, and searchability!

Access today at:

http://connect.springerpub.com/content/book/978-0-8261-8009-4 or scan the QR code at the right with your smartphone and enter the access code below.

FX0F048N

Scan here for quick access.

SPRINGER PUBLISHING COMPANY

View all our products at springerpub.com

Susan English, OSB, EdD, MCC, is cofounder and codirector of the Professional Coach Certification Program in the Palumbo Donahue School of Business at Duquesne University and has a private practice as a life and leadership coach. Susan has over 30 years of experience as a teacher, college professor, and supervisor and is an award-winning student mentor. She has worked in public, private, and prison school settings and has been an active leader in state and local professional and nonprofit organizations. Susan is a past president of the International Coach Federation (ICF) Pittsburgh and holds a doctorate in education from Indiana University of Pennsylvania. She has additional training in both internal family systems and emotional intelligence. As a coach, Susan's special interests are to improve communication skills, grow leadership abilities, increase emotional intelligence, overcome negative self-talk, enhance life balance, and triumph over roadblocks while finding joy and fulfillment in the process. She is a Benedictine Sister, daughter, mother, grandmother, and social justice advocate.

Janice Manzi Sabatine, PhD, PCC, is president of Avanti Strategies, LLC, a firm specializing in executive, leadership, and career coaching for academic physicians and scientists. She is a certified executive coach through the Pennsylvania State University Smeal College of Business and earned a BS in chemistry from the University of Notre Dame and a PhD in biochemistry from the University of Pittsburgh School of Medicine. With over 30 years of experience in biomedical research, she has been influential in the publication of over 50 journal articles and book chapters and nearly 30 funded grant applications. Recognizing the need among her technically trained peers for stronger leadership and interpersonal skills, Dr. Sabatine trained as an executive coach. In this role, she has helped numerous academic, scientific, and healthcare professionals become stronger, more effective leaders. A researcher by training, Dr. Sabatine relies on evidence-based methodologies to support her coaching and coach training activities. She is currently a recipient of an Institute of Coaching research grant to study the impact of a coaching-based career course supplemented with external coaching, entitled "The Impact of Developmental Coaching on Career Adaptability Capacity and Moderators of Sustained Career Development among Graduate Students." She is codirector of training in the Professional Coach Certification Program in the Palumbo Donahue School of Business at Duquesne University and is a past president of the Pittsburgh chapter of the International Coach Federation (ICF).

Philip Brownell, MDiv, PsyD, PCC, is a clinical psychologist licensed in North Carolina, Oregon, and Idaho. He has been in practice since 1998, but his experience working with people in various capacities, including full-time Christian ministry, dates to 1968, when he was a neuropsychiatric technician with the U.S. Navy. Dr. Brownell completed 6 years of formal training in gestalt psychotherapy, has written several books on the subject, and is involved in the global movement to establish a research tradition for gestalt therapy. He also completed the International Coach Federation (ICF)-accredited professional coach training program at Duquesne University. Currently, he works as the only psychologist for an integrated healthcare organization in southern Idaho, where he lives with his wife, 12 cats, one dog, two guitars, and a stack of books. At night from the deck around their house he can hear the roar of Shoshone Falls rising out of the Snake River Canyon.

Professional Coaching

PRINCIPLES AND PRACTICE

Susan English, OSB, EdD, MCC

Janice Manzi Sabatine, PhD, PCC

Philip Brownell, MDiv, PsyD, PCC

Editors

SPRINGER PUBLISHING COMPANY

Springer Publishing Company, LLC
11 West 42nd Street
New York, NY 10036
www.springerpub.com

Acquisitions Editor: Sheri W. Sussman
Compositor: Exeter Premedia Services Private Ltd.

ISBN: 9780826180087
ebook ISBN: 9780826180094

18 19 20 21 22 / 5 4 3 2 1

The author and the publisher of this Work have made every effort to use sources believed to be reliable to provide information that is accurate and compatible with the standards generally accepted at the time of publication. The author and publisher shall not be liable for any special, consequential, or exemplary damages resulting, in whole or in part, from the readers' use of, or reliance on, the information contained in this book. The publisher has no responsibility for the persistence or accuracy of URLs for external or third-party Internet websites referred to in this publication and does not guarantee that any content on such websites is, or will remain, accurate or appropriate.

Library of Congress Cataloging-in-Publication Data

Names: English, Susan (Life coach), editor. | Sabatine, Janice Manzi, editor.
  | Brownell, Philip (Clinical psychologist), editor.
Title: Professional coaching: principles and practice / [edited by] Susan
  English, Janice Manzi Sabatine, Philip Brownell.
Description: New York, NY: Springer Publishing Company, LLC, [2019]
Identifiers: LCCN 2018027692 | ISBN 9780826180087 | ISBN 9780826180094 (ebook)
Subjects: | MESH: Counseling—methods | Goals
Classification: LCC R727.4 | NLM WM 55 | DDC 362.1/04256—dc23
LC record available at https://lccn.loc.gov/2018027692

Contact us to receive discount rates on bulk purchases.
We can also customize our books to meet your needs.
For more information please contact: sales@springerpub.com

Publisher's Note: New and used products purchased from third-party sellers are not guaranteed for quality, authenticity, or access to any included digital components.

Printed in the United States of America.

Contents

PART III

Theories and Frameworks in Coaching

PART IV

Applications of Coaching

Contributors

Tim Anstiss, MB, Med, DOccMed, Academy for Health Coaching, UK

Jennifer Garvey Berger, EdD, Cultivating Leadership, Chief Executive, Paekakariki, New Zealand and London, UK

Richard Blonna, EdD, NCC, BCC, CHES, Professor Emeritus, William Paterson University, Marco Island, Florida

Richard E. Boyatzis, PhD, Distinguished University Professor, Professor, Departments of Organizational Behavior, Psychology, and Cognitive Science, H.R. Horvitz Chair of Family Business, Case Western Reserve University, Cleveland, Ohio

Vikki G. Brock, PhD, EMBA, MCC, International Coach Federation, Executive and Leadership Coach, former faculty University of Texas at Dallas Executive Coaching Certificate Program, former chief examiner CDI-Africa, Ventura, California

Philip Brownell, MDiv, PsyD, PCC, Psychologist, Family Health Services of Idaho, Twin Falls, Idaho; Principal Investigator for Spiritually-Integrated Processes in Gestalt Therapy, funded by the John Templeton Foundation and administered through Brigham Young University, Provo, Utah

John Campbell, BA, DipEd, MApp Sc, Executive Director, Growth Coaching International, Sydney, Australia

Stewart T. Cotterill, PhD, Head of School, School of Psychology, Sport and Physical Activity, AECC University College, Bournemouth, UK

Edward L. Deci, PhD, Professor, University of Rochester, Rochester, New York

Sharon Eakes, MA, BCC, International Coach Federation, Facilitator, Arbinger's Mastery Choice in Coaching Program, The Arbinger Institute, Farmington, Utah; Principal, Two Wise Women, Sewickley, Pennsylvania

Sean Esbjörn-Hargens, PhD, CEO of MetaIntegral, Sebastopol, California

Fran Fisher, MCC, International Coach Federation, Renton, Washington

Catherine Fitzgerald, PhD, MA, Principal, Fitzgerald Consulting, Petaluma, California

Lynn Grodzki, LCSW, MCC, International Coach Federation, Faculty, CoachU, Principal, Private Practice Success, Silver Spring, Maryland

Chad Hall, DMin, MCC, President, Coach Approach Ministries, Hickory, North Carolina

Liz Hall, BA Hon, Founder and Member of the Association for Coaching, Spain; Editor, Coaching at Work, Hitchin, UK; Founder, Liz Hall Coaching, Hove, UK and Alicante, Spain

Janet M. Harvey, MA, MCC, CEO and President, inviteCHANGE, Edmonds, Washington

Deborah Helsing, EdD, Co-Director, Minds at Work; Lecturer, Harvard Graduate School of Education, Boston, Massachusetts

Janet Keller, CPCC, PCC, Director of Certification, Coaches Training Institute, San Rafael, California

Jim Knight, PhD, Director, Kansas Coaching Project, University of Kansas Center for Research on Learning; Senior Partner, Instructional Coaching Group, Lawrence, Kansas

Hope Langner, MS, CPCC, MCC, Director of Faculty and Coach Training, Coaches Training Institute, San Rafael, California

James LoPresti, PhD, PCC, President, CohereUs Consulting Int'l; University of Colorado Denver, Denver, Colorado

Terrie Lupberger, MCC, Director of Coach Training, Newontology, Asia; Senior Director Women's Leadership, Altus Growth Partners, Boulder, Colorado

Marialexia Margariti, MSc, MA, ECP, PCC, Psychologist, Integrative Psychotherapist, Corporate Coach and Supervisor, EMCC Training Programs' Assessor (European Quality Awards), Vice-President Quality of International Executive Board (European Mentoring and Coaching Council), Founding Member and Former President of the Hellenic Coaching Association (EMCC Greece), Member of International Coach Federation, Member of European Psychotherapy Association, Athens, Greece

Margaret Moore, MBA, Founder/CEO, Wellcoaches Corporation, Wellesley, Massachusetts

Edward Mwelwa, PhD, CPsych, PCC, Member of the British Psychological Society, Member of the American Psychological Association, Member of the International Coach Federation, Teleos Leadership Institute Associate, Elkins Park, Pennsylvania

Keith Nelson, PGDip (Executive Coaching), PGDip (Coaching Psychology), BA, Director of Coaching Programmes, Møller Institute, Churchill College in the University of Cambridge, UK

Paddy Pampallis, D Prof, M Ed Psych, HED, Founder/CEO/Dean of Integral Africa & The Coaching Centre (Pty) Ltd, South Africa

Jonathan Passmore, D Occ, Psych, MBA, MSc, BA (Hons), BSc (Hons), MAC, FABPS, ACC, Henley Business School, University of Reading, Reading, UK

Jeremy Robinson, MSW, MFA, MCC, Faculty, iCoach New York; Founder and Dean, Executive Coach Academy, New York, New York

Amoráh Ross, MCC, CMC, CPC, International Coach Federation, Graduate of Academy of Coach Training/inviteCHANGE, Member of the International Coach Federation, Founder of Positive Life Works Coaching & Training Services, Woodinville, Washington

Richard M. Ryan, PhD, Professor, Institute for Positive Psychology and Education, Australian Catholic University, North Sydney, Australia

Janice Manzi Sabatine, PhD, PCC, President, Avanti Strategies, LLC, Co-Director, Professional Coach Certification Program, Duquesne University, Pittsburgh, Pennsylvania

Catherine Sandler, DPhil, DipCouns, Managing Director, Sandler Consulting Ltd, London, UK

Edmée Schalkx, MSc, PCC, aNDE Leadership Solutions on Demand and Founder and Past President, International Coach Federation, Dutch chapter, Rhenen, The Netherlands

Beena Sharma, President, Vertical Development Academy, San Jose, California

Doug Silsbee, PCC,[†] Founder, Presence-Based® Coaching, Asheville, North Carolina

Dorothy E. Siminovitch, PhD, MCC, Founder, Gestalt Coaching Program, Co-Founder and Director of Training, Gestalt Center for Coaching, Istanbul, Turkey and Toronto, Ontario, Canada

Nancy Smyth, MCC, Member, International Coach Federation, Director of Individual and Group Coaching; Facilitator, Arbinger's Mastery Choice in Coaching Program, The Arbinger Institute, Farmington, Utah; Principal, Two Wise Women, Sewickley, Pennsylvania

---

[†]Deceased.

Anne Starr, MBA, ACC, Principal, Annestarr.com, Somerville, Massachusetts, Partner, Systems Perspectives LLC, Certified Adult Development Coach and Scorer, Vertical Development Academy

Darlene Trandel, PhD, RN/FNP, MSN/CNS, PCC, NBC-HWC, Assistant Professor, Department of Partnerships, Professional Education & Practice, University of Maryland School of Nursing, Baltimore, Maryland; Faculty, Wellcoaches School of Coaching, Wellesley, Massachusetts

Christian van Nieuwerburgh, PhD, Professor of Coaching and Positive Psychology, School of Psychology, University of East London, London, UK

Steven Wendell, PhD, ACC, Assistant Professor, Pharmacology & Chemical Biology, University of Pittsburgh, Pittsburgh, Pennsylvania

Patrick Williams, EdD, MCC, BCC, Life and Leadership Coach, Author, and Speaker, Windsor, Colorado

Charles Wolfe, BA, MEd, ABD, CEO Charles J. Wolfe Associates, LLC, Leadership Consulting Firm, Simsbury, Connecticut, Nonprofit Community Radio Talk Show Creator and Host of "The Emotion Roadmap: Take the Wheel and Control How You Feel," Member of the Consortium for Research on Emotional Intelligence in Organizations

Preface

I don't remember when the light bulb went on for me. I would fly into Pittsburgh from Bermuda several times during that year. I would meet online in assorted discussion groups and webinars. Somewhere along the way in the course of completing my International Coach Federation (ICF)-accredited coach training program at Duquesne University, which was taught by Susan English and Janice Sabatine, I suggested to them that we create a really good reference book for the field of coaching. I had been writing for several years by that time, in the field of gestalt psychotherapy, and I knew that Springer Publishing had put out a reference book titled *Professional Counselor's Desk Reference*. So, that was the concept. We should edit a book titled the *Professional Coach's Desk Reference*. I asked Susan and Janice if they wanted to do that with me. The idea took hold with Springer; I had published three books with them already and contributed a chapter to the *Professional Counselor's Desk Reference*.

So, we all started down that bright, shining road. I would be the Executive Editor and Susan and Janice would be Associate Editors. It did not remain that way. A major, funded international research project on spiritually integrated processes in gestalt therapy almost literally fell in my lap. So, we reorganized.

Springer suggested a more appropriate title; so, we changed it to *Professional Coaching: Principles and Practice*. Susan took over the Executive Editor position. As it has worked out, both she and Janice have done the majority of the work, and I am happy for them to have this fantastic resource volume to their credit. I think it reflects the quality of their coach training program and represents Duquesne University well.

CONTENTS OF THE BOOK

I invite the reader to browse the table of contents. You will find that this book is a true reference book—a meaningful resource to professional coaches from a variety of fields. A reference book is like a novel; you don't usually sit down with it by the fire on a cold winter evening and read casually for the joy of putting cold winter, warm fire, and tantalizing read together in the same space. A reference book is usually something like a dictionary—a big, bulky thing that only nerds read for the fun of it. A reference book is a practical help. It gives specifics and it gives general descriptions in order for people to be able to contextualize and make sense out of the specifics. It suggests solutions and it provides answers. And, sometimes, it saves a semester by providing material for an assigned paper.

Our purpose in creating this reference book was to do those kinds of things for our colleagues in the field of coaching, broadly conceived. We hoped to bring together in one book the perspectives of expert coaches and experts on coaching.

The book is divided into parts that consider coaching from various perspectives. Each perspective is a way of seeing, a vantage point on the field of coaching. These are ways of organizing aspects of the field. There is a perspective of the field of coaching as a profession (six chapters). There are core considerations to practice within that field (11 chapters), and there are various professional perspectives on the practice of coaching (10 chapters). Last, there are eight chapters on the applications of coaching. All together there are 35 chapters and plenty to think about. Plenty to play with. Plenty to teach from if you are using this book as a text in a coach training program.

One of the benefits of this book, one that I had not foreseen, is that people writing about different things overlap one another, and that provides a depth to such issues. For instance, in Chapter 9, Sharon Eakes and Nancy Smyth introduce the importance of the coaching relationship. In Chapter 10, Keith Nelson describes relational dynamics in coaching and asserts that the coach creates a coaching environment through coaching presence—showing up as a real person. He also speaks of the ebb and flow of dialogue in the coaching relationship. In Chapter 11, Doug Silsbee speaks more directly about presence as a coaching meta-competency. He defines presence and depicts it as the individual and relational outcome of awareness in the current moment. In Chapter 12, Dorothy E. Siminovitch introduces the coach as an awareness agent, providing a process approach to building "awareness IQ." By the time the reader has reached my own chapter on hermeneutic coaching, the conversation is about making meaning out of the meeting between coach and coachee and using meaning-making to tap into values and motivation in the coaching relationship.

That is an example of the overlapping nature of these various chapters and the ways in which several complement one another.

HOW TO USE THIS BOOK

Succinctly, this is a learning and a teaching tool. It can be used as a textbook or basic text in coach training programs where groups of people interact around various chapters and discuss their contents. As such, it can provide a survey of the field that gives perspective and provokes a deeper understanding. However, the book can also be used by individuals as they seek to build on their basic training program—the kind of self-study that tracks a subject across several chapters and then looks up the resources and suggestion for further study. As such, it is one volume that enriches and enlarges a person, providing a rewarding investment.

WHO MIGHT BENEFIT MOST FROM THIS BOOK

Every person interested in finding out what professional coaching is, how it is done, what is involved in the profession, and who some of the leading lights in the field might be will benefit from this book. Trainers can use it in their training. Coaches can use it to improve their skills and increase their competence. It is a reference book, and I think it's fairly obvious how reference books can be used.

FINAL THOUGHTS FROM THE PERSPECTIVE OF A PEOPLE HELPER

I (Philip Brownell) have been involved as a people helper for a long time. I've worked line staff in residential treatment; done outpatient psychotherapy; coordinated multiple resource programs for children and families in what once was known as community mental health (but really was a mix of activism, organizational growth, and multi-systemic social services); organized, taught, and coached in two large, inner-city churches; and pastored small rural churches where one's field was not just the church but the whole community—back hills and creeks included. I was coaching before I knew what coaching was.

When I enrolled in the ICF-accredited coaching program at Duquesne University, I met Susan and Janice. I progressed through the program seeing similarities and overlaps with the form of psychotherapy that I utilize—gestalt therapy. I look forward to the day when the world of coaching does not have to flinch at the thought of working in tandem with the world of psychotherapy. Why is that? Because learning how to coach made me a better therapist. Conversely, I believe that learning from the world of psychotherapy would make coaches better coaches. As a clinical psychologist, I know there are times when I wish I could refer clients to a coach who could help clients make practical, concrete gains. As a professional people helper, I believe coaching to be one of the most efficient ways to bring about progress in a person's life.

I now identify as a coaching psychologist. There is a saying among my gestalt colleagues that goes like this: "There are as many versions of gestalt therapy as there are gestalt therapists." While it's not *quite* like that, it's close. Just so, there are many kinds of coaches, many approaches to coaching, and numerous applications or venues in which coaching can be utilized. You can see that in the pages of this book.

From the rim of the Snake River Canyon above Shoshone Falls
And the confluence of the Allegheny, Monongahela, and Ohio
Philip Brownell
with Susan English and
Janice Manzi Sabatine

The Profession of Coaching

1

Perspectives on the Definition of Coaching

Amoráh Ross

Since the mid-1990s, a still-emerging profession called *coaching* has been attracting thousands of practitioners all around the globe while rapidly evolving as a specific skill set and approach dedicated to stimulating increased excellence and goal attainment for individuals, teams, and organizations. To date, these coaching practitioners and the professional associations in which they participate have yet to collectively address and agree on a globally shared definition of coaching. Even without a consensus definition, however, coaching continues to serve a growing demand from individuals, teams, and organizations that want to engage with a coach as a partner in their pursuit of personal and professional goals.

The purpose of this chapter is to highlight the common elements of coaching and create an overall "framework of understanding" within which a coach, whether new to the profession or already a seasoned professional, can serve clients in a manner that is distinctly recognizable as coaching. Also included are some suggested best practices that support coaches in increasing their coaching expertise and proficiency.

ORIGINS OF THE WORD "COACH"

According to the *Online Etymology Dictionary* (n.d.), the word "coach" derived from the 1550s from a town called Kocs in northern Hungary where horse-drawn carriages were made. The meaning of "coach" as an instructor or trainer is purportedly from approximately 1830, when it was Oxford University slang for a tutor who "carried" a student through an exam. Around 1861, the term "coaching" was applied to improving the performance of athletes.

A well-known and highly respected pioneer of coaching, Brock (2014) offers a distillation of today's concept of coaching in her book *Sourcebook of Coaching History*, when she quotes Evered and Selman (1989): "Hence the root meaning of the verb 'to coach' is to convey a valued person from where he or she was to where he or she wanted to be" (Brock, 2014, p. 185).

Thus, the idea of coaching remained associated with academia and sports until the early 20th century, when it began to emerge in business as a tool for training employees.

EMERGENCE OF COACHING AS A WORKPLACE ACTIVITY

Because the actual history of coaching is presented elsewhere in this book, the following excerpts are offered as a timeline to highlight when the approach called coaching began entering the business world as a tool in the latter part of the 1930s. In researching her book, Vikki Brock reported that she found only nine references to coaching in human resource journals, three references in management journals, and one in a psychology journal, all between 1937 and 1959.

Coaching continued to develop in business over the next 30 years as evidenced in the following:

> David Megginson and Tom Boydell of the United Kingdom, in their 1979 coaching book for managers, stated that their definition of coaching at that time dealt with "a skill set to be used by a manager . . . we say that coaching is a process in which a manager, through direct discussion and guided activity, helps a colleague to learn to solve a problem or do a task better than would otherwise have been the case" (Megginson and Boydell, 1979). In 1989, Evered and Selman described coaching as an "action-oriented, results-oriented, and person-oriented relationship between coach and player/performer"; (Brock, 2014, p. 134).

DEFINITIONS FROM A SAMPLING OF GLOBAL PROFESSIONAL COACHING ASSOCIATIONS

As coaching gained momentum as a tool in organizational training and development, its practitioners began forming communities of practice to share experiences and further formalize, define, and hone this approach among themselves.

Association for Coaching (AC)

Established in 2002, the AC is based in the United Kingdom with members from over 60 countries and defines coaching in this way: "Coaching is a facilitated, dialogic and reflective learning process that aims to grow the individuals' (or teams') awareness, responsibility and choice (thinking and behavioural)" (AC, n.d.).

International Association of Coaching (IAC)

Founded in 2003 with members in 80 countries worldwide, the IAC claims that "coaching is a transformative process for personal and professional awareness, discovery and growth, and the expansion of possibilities" (IAC, n.d.).

International Coach Federation (ICF)

The ICF emerged in 1995 and is currently based in Lexington, Kentucky. The ICF is currently one of the oldest and largest professional coaching associations in the world. In 2006, the ICF defines coaching as "partnering with clients in a thought-provoking and creative process that inspires them to maximize their personal and professional potential" (ICF, n.d.).

A FRAMEWORK FOR UNDERSTANDING

Each of these professional organizations offers peer-reviewed credentialing processes, most of which demand that the individual coaches continuously expand their coach training and hone their skillset. In addition, each organization expects its member coaches to abide by a code of ethical conduct as a commitment to professional standards that support respect, responsibility, and integrity in their delivery of services. Common to professional standards across the global community of coaching associations are expectations that each coach will combine training and skillset with similar behaviors, qualities, and attitudes, such as:

- Developing a neutral and inquisitive mindset
- Committing to best practice and continuous improvement
- Clarifying and aligning with what the client wants to achieve
- Eliciting client-generated solutions and strategies
- Respecting the client as the expert in his or her life and work
- Perceiving every client as naturally creative, resourceful, and capable
- Developing the ability to use a range of tools and techniques resulting in positive outcomes
- Generating innovative and client-centered ways to shift perspective, thus expanding possibilities

Ultimately any definitions of coaching, combined with specific behaviors, attitudes, and standards, illustrate that what remains alive and well is the spirit contained in the origins of the word "coach": that a coach facilitates another's journey from where that person is in present time to where he or she desires to be in the future.

WHAT DISTINGUISHES COACHING FROM CONSULTING AND COUNSELING?

In addition to the different yet similar definitions of coaching, each of these organizations describes the skills and behaviors of coaching as an approach to human development that declares the client as the *expert* in the partnership and as being naturally resourceful. Alternatively, a consultant is expected to be an expert providing answers and solutions to the client, while the primary focus of a counselor is to "fix" or "heal" the client. Another difference is that the *status* of those engaged in a coaching partnership is designed to be equal and nonhierarchical, whereas status in a consulting or counseling relationship usually places the consultant or counselor as "one-up" from the client in terms of possessing specific areas of expertise or knowledge.

Key to these distinctions is that the coach brings to each coaching session a steadfast attitude or mindset that the client is the "smartest person in the room" concerning his or her life and work, and as such, is completely capable of sourcing solutions to challenges and sustaining momentum toward his or her goals. This mindset lays the groundwork for the coach to facilitate a process of discovery utilizing an *exploratory* conversation—one that allows clients to access knowledge and resources heretofore hidden or forgotten within their own experience, education, and training. It is a conversation designed to invite the clients to thoughtfully examine any attitudes and behaviors that affect their goals or current situations and to gain a different perspective from which to act.

This approach frees the coach to pose respectful yet evocative questions sourced from curiosity on behalf of the client to increase awareness, rather than "fixing" or "solving" via offering personal expertise. It also enables the coach to offer candid yet nonjudgmental observations about client behaviors, habits, or actions that may be impacting the client's progress—either positively or negatively—toward goal attainment. This process provides safety for clients to explore within themselves to reveal new perspectives and different choices than were previously accessible, thus opening new possibilities.

THE SPECTRUM OF COACHING

As the number of coaches continues to grow globally, most operate within the aforementioned context and framework that distinguishes coaching; however, there are differing philosophies about the *spectrum* of a coach's role in the partnership. In service to simplicity, that spectrum can range from "pure coaching" on one end and "coach-sulting" on the other, with infinite variations in between. Coach practitioners can choose a place on this spectrum in accordance with their personal conscience, sense of integrity, and professional code of ethics. Each coaching partnership defines its own uniquely tailored approach and structure, including the roles, expectations, and responsibilities of coach and client.

Pure coaching practitioners ask only questions and/or reflect the client's words, and rarely or never offer information or personal observations. "Coach-sultant" practitioners also ask questions and reflect the client's words, yet occasionally seek permission from the client to offer a personal experience, a piece of data, or relevant expertise *with the intent to fill a gap identified* during the coaching conversation.

Across the spectrum, the commonly held "agenda," explicit or implicit, for any coaching partnership is to collaboratively aim toward new awareness about existing client attitudes, beliefs, and behaviors that are overtly or covertly impacting a client's goals. The purpose for the conversation is to build on that new awareness to motivate client-generated strategies and action steps that clear the path to attaining them.

Regardless of where on the coaching spectrum a coach chooses to operate, the foundational bedrock that enhances trust and reinforces equality between partners in a coaching relationship is threefold: (a) The coach exercises restraint in the frequency of offering information, mentoring, or personal expertise; (b) the coach respects, elicits, and trusts the client's innate wisdom and abilities; and (c) the coach remains neutral and curious, listening deeply throughout the conversation. When this bedrock is comingled with the building blocks of evocative questioning and nonjudgmental observation, the client is motivated to follow through with self-directed momentum fueled by new insights.

BEST PRACTICES: CULTIVATING A COACH MINDSET

What uniquely identifies coach–client conversations as coaching, then, is an intentionally cultivated coach mindset of curiosity, neutrality, and trust in the client's innate wisdom, natural creativity, and resourcefulness. This mindset combined with full presence and keen listening allows the coach to serve the client as a curious questioner to elicit new perspectives, a neutral observer to reveal what may yet be hidden in a blind spot, a respectful challenger of current thinking, and a valuable resource.

Offered here are some simple best practices that can support and nourish this coaching mindset:

1. Remember that the client is naturally capable, creative, and resourceful; there is no need for "fixing" or "solving." This supports the coach's ability to remain neutral and curious as a coaching conversation unfolds.

2. Consistently engage in personal self-awareness activities to illuminate personal biases or blind spots. This enhances the coach's capacity to self-manage and maintain a neutral mindset if or when a client wants to explore something similar to what the coach may be facing personally.

3. Stay abreast of the most current data about human behavioral science, neuroscience, new tools and techniques, and so forth, related to personal and professional development. This broadens the coach's understanding of the "human operating system" and enhances the ability to identify and share currently invisible factors that may be impacting a client's progress.

CONCLUSION

As it continues to develop, coaching consistently reveals itself as a dynamic, evolving *process* of pursuing human behavioral changes and attaining goals that defies definition and resists containment. Within this process, an effective coach is a masterful facilitator who serves clients in moving from where they are to where they want to be—coming full circle back to the origins of the word "coach." May the journey ahead be filled with awe, revelation, and wonder as you continue to evolve your personal perspective, definition, and embodiment of coaching.

REFERENCES

Association for Coaching. (n.d.). Why coaching? Retrieved from http://www.association forcoaching.com/page/WhyCoaching

Brock, V. G. (2014). *Sourcebook of coaching history* (2nd ed.). Charleston, SC: CreateSpace Independent Publishing Platform.

International Association of Coaching. (n.d.). Certification and development. Retrieved from https://certifiedcoach.org/certification-and-development

International Coach Federation. (n.d.). Code of Ethics overview. Retrieved from https://coach federation.org/code-of-ethics-overview

Online Etymology Dictionary. (n.d.). Retrieved from http://etymonline.com/index.php?allowed_ in_frame=0&search=coach

2

The Roots and Evolution of Coaching

Vikki G. Brock

Coaching, as we know it today, emerged during the postmodern period of the late 20th century, born of a rapidly changing socioeconomic environment and nourished by root disciplines of philosophy, business, psychology, sports, and adult education. Now, over 25 years later, as we look at what's next for coaching, we can benefit from the perspective gained in its short yet explosive history. That history is characterized by the interaction between and the cross-disciplinary development of its root disciplines. It is compounded by the generational differences and varying professional backgrounds of its founders as well as the changing socioeconomic conditions of the times. Previously, coaches did not understand the rich and eclectic history of coaching. Instead they saw it as developing in the 1980s or 1990s. Its roots go back much further, some say, to the athletic coaches in ancient Greece who predated the birth of philosophy in the Western world.

The origin of the word "coach" came from Hungary during the 15th century in a city named Kocs, between Vienna and Budapest where a vehicle was created to take people between cities. This vehicle was named "kocsi szekér." This name "kocsi" gave rise to "kutsche" in German, "cocchio" in Italian, "coche" in Spanish, and "coach" in English to denote a type of carriage used to transport a valued person from where she or he is to where she or he wants to be. From the success merchants of the 1920s to the humanistic and transpersonal psychology of the 1960s, through the Human Potential Movement of the 1970s and into business in the 1980s—coaching still defies all attempts at definition and containment.

To help us understand coaching's complex, dynamic history, and ways in which that history informs coaching today, this chapter focuses on the influences of relevant root disciplines, impacts of influencers' backgrounds on the early discipline and its practices, and socioeconomic factors that led to the rise of coaching as a distinct discipline in the late 20th century. Five sections in this chapter address historical research observations (Brock, 2008), followed by a section on a possible future for coaching.

THE BROAD INTELLECTUAL FRAMEWORK OF COACHING

Coaching has a broad intellectual framework that contains the synergetic, cross-fertilized practices and theories of many disciplines. Individuals drawn to coaching came from a wide spectrum of disciplines and a rich heritage of life experience. The collaborative nature of the coaching field supported the cross-fertilization of such ideas and practices, customized to each coach and the person being coached, taking into account their environments and their specific needs and talents. This cross-fertilization was to some extent limited to coaching's earliest days as backgrounds of those who come to coaching today seem less varied, and forums where people once met are fewer in number (Brock, 2014). Simultaneously, cross-fertilization has continued both inside and outside coaching, with coaching drawing from its root disciplines and beginning to influence them as well.

A familiarity with the root disciplines of coaching is critical to understanding coaching's evolution, its present practice, and its future possibilities. Grounded by the major taproot of philosophy and minor taproot of the social sciences, coaching is an amalgam of a variety of disciplines and professions, some of them related and others entirely distinct.

Knowledge and root disciplines evolved from philosophy in the last 500 years. Natural sciences appeared in the early 1800s when curiosity about nature led to specialization. Social sciences including anthropology, linguistics, and psychology materialized in the mid to late 1800s when curiosity about people led to specialization.

Table 2.1 depicts the emergence of coaching root disciplines and some of their relationships, which clearly demonstrates interrelationships and influences among and between disciplines where coaching borrowed theories, models, and practices. Psychology appeared in 1879 (a mere 100 years before coaching) with subdisciplines splintering off in the early 1900s. Business disciplines of consulting, management, human resources, and training came about during the same period. Just after World War II, the Human Potential Movement, organization development, and adult education/development began (Brock, 2008).

Some coaching root disciplines, like philosophy, apprenticeships, mentoring, performing arts, and sports, have been in existence for many centuries. Others emerged more recently from the 19th century. Table 2.1 shows the emergence timeline of these newer root disciplines.

As demonstrated in Table 2.1, coaching is rooted in and influenced by multiple fields. Philosophy, psychology, and business have had the greatest influence on modern coaching, yet the contributions of sports and adult learning and development have also been significant. Examples of these are:

- Philosophy—mind/body connection, spirituality, elders around campfires, language, meaning and purpose, and 12-step programs

Table 2.1 The Emergence of Coaching Root Disciplines

General Category	Discipline (Year)
Natural Sciences	Biology (1800s) • Neuroscience (1890s)
Social Sciences	Education (before 1800) • Adult Education (1926) • Adult Development (1950s) • Adult Learning (1960s) Economics/Business (before 1800) • Management (19th century) • Consulting (late 19th century) • Personnel (1900) • Facilitation (1973) • Leadership (1977) Psychology (1879) • Psychodynamic Psychology (1890s) • Behavioral Psychology (1900s) • Cognitive Psychology (1950s) • Humanistic Psychology (1950s) • Transpersonal Psychology (1970s) Linguistics (1880s) Sociology (1838) Anthropology (1843) Human Resources (mid 1980s)
Other Influences	12-Step Programs (1935) Success Motivators (1937–1960) Human Potential Movement (1960s) New Age Movement (1970s) Organization Development (1930s–1950s) Vocational Guidance (1910s) Career Development (1980s)

- Psychology (clinical)—models and theories to change thinking and behavior applied to nonclinical populations, client-centered therapy, solution-focused therapy, Gestalt therapy, and Appreciative Inquiry

- Business—leadership development models, career counseling and entrepreneur life planning, organization development, systems perspective, and process consultation

The sports sector provided the field's fundamental model as well as the job description by which practitioners of the field became known. This sector also furnished a body of knowledge on motivation and a history of specialized, practical instruction. Sports offered valuable perspectives on differences between coaching individuals and teams, many of which were applicable in other sectors. Rounding out the root disciplines in the social sciences, adult learning offered coaching an abundant body of educational research, as well as a variety of practical methods drawn from the fields of training and career development. These disciplines feed into coaching with their own influences.

People entering the coaching field adapted theories and models from various fields to the normal population with a focus on potential for human growth and learning in the business and personal contexts. Early practitioners were consistent in taking key concepts, principles, and philosophical perspectives from their education and experience into coaching. Coaching models used research from academic disciplines and imported values, principles, and philosophical perspectives from nonacademic disciplines.

COACHING FILLED AN UNMET NEED IN THE WORLD

Coaching came into existence to fill an unmet need in a world of rapid change and complexity. That need, unsatisfied by traditional, pathology-centered therapy—an illness model—was met by the shift to a wellness model founded on the principles of humanistic psychology and the postmodern perspective of integral philosophy. While the advent of humanistic psychology was evidence of that shift, the illness model was still practiced by most clinical psychologists. By adding complementary practices from other fields, coaching did not have the constraints of traditional clinical practices. Instead, it become more interactive, client driven, and fluid.

The socioeconomic climate is an important part of setting the stage for the development of coaching. From about 1890 to 1950, the modern period was focused on the scientific worldview and on the illness or pathological model—taking care of your weaknesses and improving what was not working for you. This was the time of the Industrial Revolution. Instead of staying home, people went to work, which caused a separation of work and family. There was a shift from small isolated communities to a larger factory network where humans were economic units in the factory. During this time, humanity experienced two world wars that, along with transportation advances, hastened the shrinking of the world. In the late 1940s and early 1950s, political and economic attention turned toward rebuilding countries ravaged by war and on retooling the war economies of both the vanquished and the victorious.

The postmodern period emerged about 1950 and is characterized as a service society. One of the events that preceded this shift was the end of World War II, which brought many men back into the factories, displacing women who were fulfilling that role. Also, many items developed for war were brought into everyday civilian life as conveniences. Additionally, there was a growing interest in personal development that followed the Second World War. That interest was not confined to the business world where employees saw personal development as a means of getting ahead and management saw personal development as a way to improve the bottom line. This interest also extended to the suburbs, where personal development was considered a form of self-improvement. Fueling this emergence was "a shortage of listening in our modern society and a disconnection of the meaningful relationship between humans" (Patrick Williams, personal communication, 2006), as well as a yearning for more "heart connection" and fulfillment. When coaching emerged in the 1990s, there was nothing available that would meet this need.

We were not conscious that what was missing was our humanity—yet I maintain this was what was behind the emergence of coaching. Rediscovering, or reawakening, is about waking up to what we have forgotten or unearthing new dreams—it's about returning to awareness of something set aside in lack of time or motivation. This concept of coaching's true purpose came out of a conversation on September 30, 2016, with coaches in Hong Kong—that "rediscovering our humanity is the purpose coaching emerged at the time it did." In speaking with coaches around the world, this purpose resonates.

COACHING SOURCES AND RELATIONSHIPS

Coaching sprang simultaneously from several independent sources and birthplaces and spread through a series of complex and unpredictable relationships. As each source and birthplace came into existence, it sent branches out among existing professional relationships, spanned separate disciplines, and then reintegrated in ways no one could have foreseen. The initial stage occurred during the 1960s, an era of unprecedented personal and professional exploration and growth. The Human Potential Movement, a product of those times, gave us Esalen, the National Training Laboratory (NTL), Tavistock, and Findhorn, among many others. The rapid diffusion of coaching was fueled by a series of serendipitous, interdisciplinary gatherings in these venues. Key figures in those meetings connected through face-to-face conferences, workshops, and forums, long before technological advances made such interaction much easier. Once the information age dawned about 1995, the spread of coaching was put into hyperdrive by conferences, workshops, and forums, in both face-to-face and virtual environments.

Many key influencers and early coaches knew each other, even though they lived in different countries and worked in different fields. Various groups said, "We were the first" and that was not true. Several sources of connections that set the stage for coaching are:

- Success motivators out of the U.S. Depression—Dale Carnegie, Napoleon Hill, and Norman Vincent Peale among others.

- "T" and "S" groups flourished in Tavistock (UK), which spawned NTL (NTL – USA), where founders of Organization Development (OD) did their work.

- A similar connection existed between Esalen (humanistic psychologists Carl Rogers, Fritz Perls, Milton Erickson, Timothy Leary, and Tim Gallwey) and the rise of the Human Potential Movement.

- An interesting event that speaks to connections and relationships—in 1974 Sir John Whitmore (UK) brought spiritual and New Age aristocrats from the UK together with California Esalen hippies (including Werner Erhard of *est*). As a member of both groups, Sir Whitmore knew that similar ideas were being pursued.

- Large Group Awareness Training (LGAT) was the culmination of the shift to an awareness and responsibility perspective. Participants left meetings with limited support structures to change, though they had declarations, commitments, and enthusiasm.

These connections are part of a once-secret history, especially as they relate to Werner Erhard, who popularized personal growth and development in the 1970s through his LGAT, originally called *est*, and its numerous offspring. Many key pioneers in coaching participated in Erhard's programs and/or were his friends. For example, Tim Gallwey (*The Inner Game of Tennis*) coached Werner Erhard in tennis. Ken Blanchard (*The One Minute Manager*) and Peter Senge (*The Fifth Discipline*) were personal friends, and Warren Bennis (leadership guru and author of *On Becoming a Leader*) took *est* in 1979 in London and advised Erhard in the 1980s. Sir John Whitmore (*Coaching for Performance*, 1992) brought Erhard to the United Kingdom in May 1974. James Flaherty (1985 *est* training and follow-on book *Coaching: Evoking Excellence in Others*, and cofounder of New Ventures West) apprenticed to Fernando Flores (who collaborated with Erhard) as did Julio Olalla (1990 training Mastering the Art of Professional Coaching, cofounder of Newfield Network). When Thomas Leonard (founder of Coach U, International Coach Federation [ICF], CoachVille, and International Association of Coaching) worked as an accountant for Werner Erhard & Associates, he hired Laura Whitworth (The Coaches Training Institute and Professional Personal Coaches Association) to work there also. With several others, Jay Perry (coaching pioneer) started the Actors Information Project, a membership organization that focused on the business and career side of acting, which was informed by Erhard's concepts and work. Later, Henry Kimsey-House joined him as a member, then a business partner (The Coaches Training Institute).

So how did some of these people influence coaching?

- Fernando Flores contributed academic and philosophical grounding to coaching, and he was the first person to use the word "coach" as we know it today.

- Sir John Whitmore and Graham Alexander brought Tim Gallwey's Inner Game technology into business as coaching.

- Thomas Leonard popularized coaching by designing curricula to train coaches virtually.

- Laura Whitworth professionalized coaching by spearheading the Professional and Personal Coaches Association (PPCA).

Coaches who came from a psychology background worked as independents—and thus were harder to track down until after 2000 when coaching psychology appeared and many psychologists shifted to coaching. Some prominent psychologists who were early coaching influencers are:

- 1970s—Bob Witherspoon and Randy White of the Center for Creative Leadership were involved in the early days of 360-degree feedback and behavioral change.

- 1980s—David Peterson and Richard Kilburg were/are active in the American Psychological Association of Consulting Psychologists.

- Early 1990s—Frederic Hudson and Pamela McLean of the Hudson Institute shifted to coaching from mentoring based on adult development, psychology, adult learning systems, and developmental psychology.

- 1992—David Megginson and David Clutterbuck started the European Mentoring Council and expanded it in 2001 to include coaching.

MODERN COACHING PATTERNS AND PRACTICES ARE DYNAMIC AND CONTEXTUAL

Modern patterns and practices of coaching are neither uniform nor rigidly applied; instead they are dynamic and contextual. Megginson and Boydell (1979) defined coaching as "[a] skill set to be used by a manager, [that] by direct discussion and guided activity, helps a colleague to solve a problem or do a task better than would otherwise have been the case" (p. 1). Ten years later, Evered and Selman (1989) defined coaching as "action-oriented, results-oriented, and person-oriented relationships between coach and player/performer" (p. 9). In 1998, I defined coaching as raising awareness so each is at conscious choice. A general definition by Anthony Grant (Australia) is a "goal-directed, results-oriented, systematic process in which one person facilitates sustained change in another individual or group through fostering the self-directed learning and personal growth of the coachee" (Greene & Grant, 2003). To create a flexible, inclusive definition that encompasses the diversity of coaching, we can apply a range of continuum attributes adapted from the Chartered Institute of Personnel and Development, *Coaching and Buying Coaching Services Guide* (CIPD, 2006, p. 25) such as:

- Directive to facilitative

- Holistic to specific

- Short- to long-term

- Individual leads agenda to others leading the agenda

- High to low personal content

- High to low business content

- Developmental to remedial

In 2009, the ICF broadened its definition to "partnering with clients in a thought-provoking and creative process that inspires them to maximize personal and professional potential."

Whatever definition coaches use, they operate from an eclectic position, choosing compatible aspects of different definitions to explain and guide their coaching. Despite the difference in emphasis in definitions and the wide range of applications, core coaching constructs include:

- A collaborative and partnering rather than authoritarian relationship
- A focus on discovery and exploration rather than problem analysis
- The assumption of a normal population
- Collaborative goal setting and facilitating learning

Further, coaching is customized to the coach, the person being coached, the context, and the specific conditions that led to coaching. The fluid nature of the modern coaching environment requires every coach to rely on intuition, creativity, and flexibility, as well as a solid base of foundational knowledge. Each of us would likely approach the same client a bit differently and, if the client came to us with a different situation, then that would be another context. When people try to create a universal coaching definition and one standard way of doing coaching, there is the potential for loss of creativity, flexibility, and responsiveness.

COACHING RESULTED FROM AN INTEGRAL SOCIAL NETWORK OF DIVERSITY AND INCLUSION

Coaching came into being due to a newly open, integral social network characterized by diversity and inclusion. This first phase of coaching was one of exploration and inclusion and was about building relationships through mutual adaptation. Approaches were diverse, sharing and collaboration were celebrated, curiosity was abundant, and the social network was open and loose. For the earliest coaches, the goal was to contribute to the growth, happiness, and success of others.

Let's look at what happened with coaching from the 1930s to today. During the 1930s to 1950s, counselors, therapists, and organizational psychologists were counseling executives using practices similar to coaching. Sales coaching focused on how to be a better salesperson. Sporadic articles on coaching and performance improvement and management development appeared in journals.

In the 1960s to 1970s, coaching entered the business world where a leader's role in change was viewed from the intersection of organization development and psychology. Executive and business coaching emerged from leadership programs and assessment centers. Counselors, therapists, and organizational psychologists continued "counseling" executives. Seventeen articles on coaching were published in the 1970s along with four books on coaching by managers. Two of these books were *Performance Coaching for Managers* by Richard Fournies and *A Manager's Guide to Coaching* by David Megginson.

During the 1980s, the "Inner Game" approach to sports was adapted to business and called coaching. The first companies providing individual and business coaching services were founded in the United Kingdom and United States. Psychological consulting firms began providing services they called executive coaching. Sports coaches and business people identified common coaching principles across disciplines. In the United States and Europe, the first training schools were founded to deliver coach training to individuals and business. Coaching literature expanded with doctoral research, 29 journal articles, and five more published books that addressed coaching by supervisors to improve employee performance.

Rapid expansion began in the 1990s, with coach-specific training schools and programs growing to eight by 1995 and more than 100 by the year 2000 (Brock, 2008). Professional coach associations (and accompanying annual coach conferences) grew from zero to more than 10 during the same period. In the United States, consulting psychologists published three journal issues on executive coaching (Brock, 2008). The global spread of coaching was supported by virtual teleclass coach training and the first internal coaching assignments in companies were created. Seventy-nine coaching books were published during the 1990s, with 62% published from 1998 to 1999 (Grant & Cavanagh, 2004).

As we entered the 21st century, coaching exploded. Six peer-reviewed coaching publications began in 2001 or later in support of evidence-based coaching. Coaching psychology was identified as distinct in 2000, with special interest groups created in U.K. and Australian psychology associations. From 2000 to 2004, 153 coaching books were published, 132 coaching articles were published in business and psychological journals, and coaching culture became a common term in business (Grant & Cavanagh, 2004). This rapid growth has continued across the globe and coaching is reaching the mature stage in several countries (Bresser, 2013).

POSSIBLE FUTURE FOR COACHING

In the mid 1990s, coaching pioneers figured out how to train coaches and created standard competencies for coaching that made it a viable profession. In coaching's short and explosive history, there have been a number of significant achievements:

- Over 20 professional associations

- High standards of conduct and ethics, with increased industry alignment

- Over 500 coach-specific training organizations

- Academic education included coach-specific programs in schools of management, psychology, organization development, and others

- Harvard, with Harnisch Foundation, sponsors research grants while many other graduate programs also yield dissertation research in coaching

- Companies hiring their own internal coaches and over 50% using external coaches

- Coaching psychology as a subdiscipline as the fastest growing and most recent in the field

- Over 20 industry publications in various languages, television shows, YouTube, widespread use of "coach" in major industries

Coaching will likely increase as baby boomers mature and new leaders need to take their places and define what leadership looks like in the new business order. Just as demand will increase to meet the needs of emerging leaders, the supply of experienced semiretired executives and development professionals will increase. The market will mature further with customers looking for more robust coach credentials, simpler pricing structures, more common contracting procedures, and protocols to manage coaching interventions. There will be fewer independent coaches and more firms offering coaching, as consumers want one-stop shopping and a third party to watch over coaches' activities with clients. This will increase barriers to entry for executive coaches and encourage clearer definition between coaches who work in organizations and business systems and those who do life and career coaching with individuals. There will be greater networks among coaches using their alumni connections from coach training and working together in systems, so that collaboration and sharing of leads and opportunities are more likely. All of this speaks to consolidation of the field.

There will be more and better-trained internal coaches within companies, an increase in peer coaching among colleagues, group coaching sessions, and more virtual or phone/video conference coaching. There will be an increased drive to train and measure line managers on their coaching abilities as well. All these factors will drive prices down and make coaching more prevalent in organizations. Coaching, as we know it today, may continue to exist alongside other, more evolved forms of coaching.

Another trend that is sweeping the globe is the coach approach philosophy. Originally confined to professional coaching, it is an approach now used in leadership, parenting, and many other disciplines. The term philosophy represents two different things: a set of practices and a set of theories. What is happening is that there is a shift in perspective from coaching as a set of practices, to coaching as a worldview and advanced form of communication.

The coach approach has become an integral part of human development in a variety of organizational and nonorganizational contexts. The coach approach consists of:

- *Active listening*—seeking to understand before being understood

- Being curious and *asking open questions*—some call this beginner's mind as a coach does not walk in the client's shoes, so he or she is a beginner in this sense

- *Communicating directly*—through messages, challenges, and acknowledgment

According to Reinhard Stelter in *A Guide to Third Generation Coaching*,

the coach and coachee act as philosophers, their reflections sometimes shedding light on the big questions in life. Both take a wondering stance to essential human, existential and often value-oriented issues, and together with the coach the coachee explores new ways of understanding his or her existence and life. (Stelter, 2013, p. 51)

I take this one step further by stating that the coach approach has the potential for everyone to act as a philosopher and a coach. Professional coaches can support this trend by using a coach approach in all their interactions and teaching others the basics of the coach approach.

CONCLUSION

Today, coaching is woven into the tapestry of living in many parts of the world. In 1997, when coaching was new, the PPCA (a California-based professional coach association founded by graduates of early coach-training programs) held its second and final conference before it folded into the ICF. The conference theme, *Weaving Coaching into the Tapestry of Living,* had a vision that in 20 years:

> Coaching will become a universal language for all people, acting as a catalyst to ignite their lives in the direction of personal, cultural and hence, global fulfillment. Different people and professions. All vary in desire and purpose. Woven together they create the ever-evolving story of humanity. Life is a tapestry. The possibility for coaching is that it becomes an integral thread in the daily routine of all walks of life. Imagine the vibrancy of this global tapestry with the many textures and hues joined together with the common thread of coaching. A work of art begins with a dream and then a simple action. . .the thread! Come create the tapestry—the future of coaching and the world! (PPCA, 1997)

Twenty years later I checked back in with several 1997 PPCA board members who said they never could have imagined how much coaching would become woven into the culture and tapestry on a global scale. Already, coaching is accepted as a viable, impactful leadership development tool. We are seeing coach-like vocabulary appear in popular media and business and professional journals.

Coaching is a multidisciplinary field that, to be sustainable, must continue rapid innovation while encouraging diversity and inclusion and an integral balance within a loose, open social network. Coaching is a social phenomenon for the 21st century and beyond, and a catalyst to the next stage of human evolution. By choosing to be a role model for what we preach and by holding ourselves to the highest standards, coaches will continue to thrive and make a difference for the next 15 years and beyond.

REFERENCES

Bresser, F. (2013). *Coaching across the globe.* Cologne, Germany: Herstellung & Verlag.

Brock, V. G. (2008). *Grounded theory on the roots and emergence of coaching* (Unpublished doctoral dissertation). International University of Professional Studies, Maui, HI.

Brock, V. G. (2014). *Sourcebook of coaching history.* Charleston, SC: CreateSpace Independent Publishing Platform.

Chartered Institute of Personnel and Development. (2006). *Coaching and buying coaching services.* Retrieved from www.cipd.co.uk

Evered, R. D., & Selman, J. C. (1989). *Coaching and the art of management.* New York, NY: American Management Association.

Grant, A. M., & Cavanagh, M. J. (2004). Toward a profession of coaching: Sixty-five years of progress and challenges for the future. *International Journal of Evidence-Based Coaching and Mentoring,* 2(1), 8–21. Retrieved from http://ijebcm.brookes.ac.uk/documents/vol02issue1-paper-01.pdf

Greene, J., & Grant, A. M. (2003). *Solution-focused coaching: Managing people in a complex world.* Harlow, Australia: Pearson Education.

Megginson, D., & Boydell, T. (1979). *A manager's guide to coaching.* London, England: Broadwater.

Professional and Personal Coaches Association. (1997). *Weaving coaching into the fabric of living* (Conference binder). 2nd Annual Conference. Atlanta, GA: Author.

Stelter, R. (2013). *A guide to third generation coaching.* Copenhagen, Denmark: Springer.

3

The Business of Coaching Today

Lynn Grodzki

The early days of coaching were heady times for new coaches, like myself, who wanted to be in business. In 1996, I was in a CoachU class when Thomas Leonard, founder of both CoachU and the International Coach Federation (ICF), mentioned his simple formula for building a successful coaching practice. "Coach one hundred people, even if you do it for free. You will get known as a coach and your business will build naturally," he said. His idea, that the early adopters of coaching could find clients easily, just by word of mouth, turned out to be right—at least for me. That same year, I built my coaching business quickly. In 6 months, my part-time coaching practice paid for my entire coach training program and more, all without the usual drill of finding start-up funds or creating an actual business plan.

What a difference two decades can make. The business of coaching is much more difficult now than it was 20 years ago. Today, I am on the faculty of CoachU, teaching new coaches, and also have my own independent practice as a business coach, working with change agents: coaches, therapists, consultants, and other helping professionals. As such, I am in a position to hear from coaches across the globe who are trying to build a coaching business quickly or sustain an existing business. What I hear is that many coaches are struggling.

One newly minted coach tells me, "My business is constantly going up and down. I like going to amusement parks and riding the roller coaster, but this is not a good business model to have." In her busy metropolitan city, competition among coaches is fierce. She says there is a coach on every corner. She tries to define her niche, to help her stand out from those vying for the same contracts. Her colleagues, other coaches who are also trying to survive, are undercutting each other's fees in order to win clients. Trying to keep up with an uneven cash flow, a competitive market, and an ambiguous economic climate, she wonders: "Can a coach make it within a small business today?"

According to industry data and surveys about the coaching profession, this roller coaster experience may be the new normal. Market saturation and global economic uncertainty are two major challenges that coaches face today, that were not present when I started out. It's essential that coach training schools and organizations stay updated about the changing market for coaching services: What worked for coaches in prior decades is not necessarily working well anymore. The "good old days" of building or maintaining a coaching business based on word of mouth, without a business plan or any real business savvy, are probably best left to the past.

To survive and thrive in the business of coaching today, practitioners need to stay well informed. Coaches who own and operate a business must be knowledgeable—not just about the skills of coaching, but also about the best business strategies for keeping their business alive. This chapter offers a review of some business essentials, including:

- Being a coach-entrepreneur

- Global data about the current demand for coaching

- Anticipated coach earnings

- Business practices to help avoid unnecessary risk

- Marketing strategies that work best to attract clients

THE COACH AS ENTREPRENEUR

When you are a coach in business for yourself, you wear two hats: You are both a coach and an entrepreneur. You need to learn to be equally skilled and equally interested in both roles. The role of being the boss may be unfamiliar, even if you have worked in a business for others. Once you are in charge, you will find that you need a set of skills that you may not have acquired.

You are now a CEO, the visionary and strategist for your business, and the main marketer. You may work alone, or you might have a bigger venture in mind and will need to hire (and fire) staff. You'll have to attend to administration, no matter how much staff you have, since the owner needs to stay aware of daily business data. If you work solo, you will be doing a number of jobs beyond the ones mentioned including billing. The list of business tasks can feel endless.

Some new business owners have concerns about how much needs to get done. Maybe you feel that you are not as expert in some of these roles as you wish, and want to avoid them or hand them off to others. That is understandable, and if you have resources you certainly can bring in more staff, but you do best if you can learn the job yourself first. Fortunately, there is much that can help a new business owner: You can hire consultants, advisors, coaches, mentors, and rely on friends and family to help you understand what you need to do in order to accomplish your goals.

My advice is that you accept and embrace the role of being an entrepreneur with gusto. Read about business. Link with other business owners. Attend business conferences. The strongest position for a business owner is one of connection. In the same way that it takes a village to raise a child, it takes a community of professionals, advisers, and peers to grow a strong business. Get growing and build a circle of support around your coaching business now.

You will also need a way to stay focused. I like having a number of business mantras—short phrases that act as a shortcut and remind me how to keep moving forward. These four mantras are a few that I use when I need to stay on course.

SPEND TIME WORKING ON THE BUSINESS, NOT JUST IN THE BUSINESS

Michael Gerber, the author of *The E-Myth Revisited,* coined this helpful mantra. He urged entrepreneurs to go beyond seeing business as a job, and see it in a broader perspective. Consider the big picture needs of your business as being as important as the needs of your clients. Beyond the administrative tasks that you need to accomplish each week to keep your practice operating, give yourself 1 hour each week of CEO time to work on the business. Create a solid marketing plan on paper; gather your data into a financial report; develop a vision for the future.

INTEGRITY FIRST, NEEDS SECOND, WANTS THIRD

As mentioned, Thomas Leonard was one of my early teachers in the field of coaching. He used this mantra to prioritize problems. In business, integrity is what keeps you safe: your ethics, legality, and values. Fix these integrity breaks first. Next, attention goes to what your business needs to be profitable and viable. Needs include your goals: clients, income, business systems. Third, attention goes to your wants, those things that can make your business a pleasure to operate and own: a nicely decorated office, a refresher course in a method you like, a more recent picture of you on your website—things that are valuable and will help you feel happier about the state of your practice, but can wait a bit in the order of urgency.

FOCUS ON PROFIT, NOT GROWTH

Profit and growth are not the same thing. Keep your eye on your profit (your income minus your expenses) and make your existing business, large or small, as profitable as it can possibly be. Only then should you start to plan for growth. Even though you may be bored with the status quo or yearning for newness, you need to grow from a position of strength, not weakness. The best ways to improve profit include the following:

- Lower input costs: Negotiate to cut expenses.

- Increase productivity: Set boundaries on your unbilled activity. What will help you do more with less?

- Systemize: Organization is key in being more profitable. What can you clean out, fix up, delegate, and automate?

SMALL STEPS COUNT

In a small business, it's best to pace yourself and move forward with steady, small steps. A small increase in savings or a small reduction of spending can make a real difference. The addition of a few clients each week or each month can keep your practice humming. Small is beautiful. Let yourself think in short-term goals and outline immediate action steps. Avoid losing yourself in daydreams of big visions; keep your objectives specific and doable so that you don't get discouraged.

GLOBAL DEMAND REVISITED

Unfortunately, I find that too many new coaches do not have a realistic view of what to expect when they launch a coaching business. Some graduate from a coach training program filled with magical thinking about how easy or immediate it should be to make a lot of money. While a level of optimism and determination is necessary for any business owner, you need more than anecdotal evidence or wishful thinking in order to make good business decisions. You need good, solid, tangible information.

Without the right information, owning and operating a small coaching business can feel like you are wandering through uncharted territory. You may not know how to manage the landscape, or what hardships to anticipate on your journey. You may not be able to spot opportunities or profitable avenues. It helps to have a map. One map that I recommend is current industry data.

The coaching industry doesn't collect a lot of data about itself, but I have found some that I think are critical to consider. I appreciate the annual survey published by Sherpa Executive Coaching (a U.S. coach-training organization). For the past 12 years, Sherpa has invited coaches from dozens of countries to contribute to an anonymous survey. Sherpa's staff then carefully collects, compares, and publishes the survey findings in a free, online report of the state of coaching. Although Sherpa's primary focus is on executive coaching, the survey asks about and compiles data on other types of coaching, including life coaching.

In its March 2017 survey report, Sherpa suggests that times are tougher for many coaches than in the past: Global demand is falling, market saturation is rising, and market confusion (a lack of consumer understanding about coaching services) is also on the rise.

Perhaps what is most telling in the 2017 Sherpa survey is its Coaching Confidence Index (CCI), one that mirrors the way data are used in the U.S. Consumer Board's Consumer Confidence Index to measure consumer optimism (Sherpa Coaching USA, 2017). Sherpa developed its own CCI by combining data from its survey to offer a snapshot of several factors—those that may designate confidence—including:

- Perceived credibility of coaching in the marketplace

- Value ascribed to coaching from clients

- Optimism of coaches and clients about the future of coaching

- Any change in coach billing rates

- The level of coaches' workloads

- The state and direction of the general economy

Looking at these factors, Sherpa measures how coaching is perceived and accepted by both coaches working in the field and their clients, year by year. Here is the bad news: For the past 3 years, the Sherpa CCI has fallen to a negative level due to lower billing rates and reduced optimism from coaches and clients. This negative level of confidence reflects the worry that coaches express about the future of coaching.

Karl Corbett, Managing Director of Sherpa, is not as worried about the future as the survey might suggest. He gives the CCI data some context, saying, "Coaching is a stable industry and it will survive, but many coaches may go away." He means that the number of working coaches may dwindle over time, based on the competition and tougher road ahead to secure clients and contracts.

The Sherpa Survey CCI findings are echoed in a similar way when looking at data that are specific to life coaching. Journalist Elizabeth O'Brien, writing about life coaching for Marketwatch, explains that even as the number of life coaches has grown, demand for coaching, as measured by sales, has remained largely flat in recent years, according to data from within the self-improvement industry (O'Brien, 2014).

Even though the current global demand for coaching may not be increasing, it's important to remember that the overall coaching market is still substantial in terms of revenue. A report by the market research firm IBISWorld at the end of 2014 said coaching is a $1 billion industry in the United States alone (Milne-Tyte, 2016). The ICF estimates 53,000 coaches are working worldwide with a global revenue for all types of coaching at over $2 billion (International Coach Federation, 2016). This considerable level of revenue indicates that opportunities for coaches exist; the only question is how to tap into the revenue stream.

My personal research, from a variety of print and online coaching sources and interviews I have conducted with training directors at coaching schools, suggests to me that the next decade looks good for the coaching market, even if growth is slower than in the past. I see signs of strength in some key target markets such as wellness coaching, as medical insurers bring wellness coaches onboard in greater numbers to boost preventive medicine. I think that within corporate settings there is a strong commitment to executive and leadership coaching but predict it will result in more hires or training of primarily internal coaches. The U.S. federal government is continuing to hire external coaches to coach managers for performance improvement and, in some cases, for improving organizational morale; I think that engagement may continue, as long as coaching shows itself to be a good return on investment. Many training directors I spoke with think that coaching will stay strong and growing within international markets.

ANTICIPATED COACH EARNINGS

With so much coaching revenue in play, what do coaches actually earn today? The salaries and earnings of coaches are less than the big returns might suggest. Combining findings from a variety of recent surveys including the ICF, Sherpa Executive Coaching, and interviews with some coaching companies, the average reported coach earnings are as follows, in U.S. dollars:

- Executive coaches: $93,000
- Business coaches: $60,000
- Life coaches: $44,000

These earnings include those of coaches in business for themselves as well as those who work for coaching companies, or within corporations as executive or wellness coaches.

The reports of what a coach earns on an hourly basis vary widely, and there are no firm data in this regard. I queried senior coaches in each category and found that executive coaches make from $335 to $500 per hour and up. Executive coaching is often done by engagements and an average engagement may run for 6 months, for an average fee of $12,000 per person coached. Executive coaches report that their primary payers are corporate organizations; they are most often working with contracts, where the coaching for a director, executive, or manager is paid for by the company.

Business coaches who focus on performance and skills generally make $250 per hour and up. Life coaches make from $100 to $200 per hour or more, depending on their reputation and specialty. The lower fees make sense because most business and life coaches are working primarily with clients who pay them "out of pocket"—directly, without any job-related or corporate sponsorship. Julia Stewart (2012b), head of the School of Coaching Mastery and founding member of the International Association of Coaching (IAC), says that coaches worldwide average around $200 per coaching hour but adds a caveat: "Most discussions of coaching fees center around what coaches make per hour, during coaching sessions, but the truth is, most coaches don't sell their coaching by the hour. Rather, they charge a flat fee by the month or in multi-month blocks."

When working with new coaches to set their fees, Stewart (2012a) tells them to think about longer engagements, since virtually all clients need more than a month to see real progress. She suggests that coaches consider their business plan before setting a fee or monthly rate:

A great way to set your fee is to think about how many clients you want to have (5-10 is the norm), and how much money you want to make from them in three months. Divide the amount of money by the number of clients. Charge a bit more if your clients pay by the month. And remember, every coach is unique, so don't worry too much what others are charging. Charge what it's worth to you. Stewart (2012a)

I suggest that your fee be based on your business plan. Consider several factors including: your business vision and philosophy; market forces; the perceived value of your services; and your timeline to fill the business. Emotions such as fear and anxiety have no place in fee setting. Instead, be rational and use your fee as a way to accomplish your business goals.

Remember that it often takes 3 to 5 years to build a full coaching business with enough revenue to replace a previous full-time job. To boost earnings, you may want to diversify to create a stream of income from additional sources other than just coaching. Some coaches diversify their businesses by adding training, teaching, writing, organizational development, personal growth, or other types of healing and helping services.

BUSINESS PRACTICES TO AVOID RISK

The role of a small business owner always involves managing risk. In the United States, according to the Small Business Administration, half of all small businesses of all types fail every year. A coaching business is vulnerable to the same risks as any other small business, with at least one additional challenge: Coaching is still a new profession. Unless you are selling your services into a company or a setting where coaching is well understood, you will first need to educate a market about coaching benefits and outcomes, just in order to sell into that market. This combination of having to explain a service first, and then find those wanting to pay for the service, equates into a more complicated marketing activity.

The safest way to develop a business is with a plan. An informal business plan (vs. a formal written plan most often used when seeking funding) is a projection of what you expect will happen during the next 1 to 5 years in your business. The plan is for your use; it does not need to be fully written or explained, although most coaches find it is helpful to have it structured and available to read and reread. Your informal plan will help you to think through the major goals and needs of your coaching business and includes:

- Your legal structure

- Your business vision (the big picture of what you hope to achieve)

- Services you will offer and how you will charge for them

- Marketing ideas and a marketing plan

- A financial plan (your annual budget broken down month by month and a profit and loss statement of what you expect to earn and spend over the course of a year)

- Administration and management (how you will manage all the billing, paperwork, intakes, hiring of staff or advisors, etc.)

- Resources (a list of your strengths and assets that can help your business grow including who you know that can help you or offer advice)

- Projected results (a way to track and measure your progress over time)

The plan you develop today will change over the course of a year as you get feedback and results from your efforts. The best business plan is a living plan, one that changes and adapts as you and your coaching business grow.

For every business plan, you need to also consider risk assessment: How can you protect your business from harm? The first rule of business is to attend to client satisfaction. Your first defense against client unhappiness begins with the way you conduct your coaching business. Create clear guidelines around your coaching, so potential clients can easily understand what to expect when they hire you. Your clients need to know, ahead of time, what coaching is and is not; how to get their money's worth from the coaching experience; and all the rules and policies that make for an optimal coaching experience.

In an earlier book about the coaching profession, my coauthor, Wendy Allen, PhD, and I looked at guidelines for best business practices to avoid unnecessary risk (Grodzki & Allen, 2005). Here are a few do's and don'ts that can help you stay safe:

1. *Don't over-promise results.* Some coaches promise miracles, especially if you read their websites. This can invite a lawsuit if a client hires the coach and feels the promises were not met. Watch your written language. The bywords of a safe business are to under-promise and then over-deliver. Offer only what you are sure you can provide.

2. *Don't take on multiple roles.* Coaches do get sued for malpractice. Purchase liability insurance specific for coaching. To lessen your risk of liability, stay with one role. Be your client's coach. Don't take on conflicting functions, such as being both coach and close friend, or coach and financial planner to the same client. A good business practice is to keep your dealings with clients uncomplicated, transparent, and as professional as possible. Maintain professional boundaries. Avoid all situations that could lead to a conflict of interest. Define your coaching and business policies, make sure that they mirror the accepted coaching standards, and use a coaching contract with an informed consent section so that your clients understand what your coaching services and policies include.

3. *Do document your coaching sessions.* Some coaches feel that their discussions with clients are organic, that in session they simply follow a conversational flow, and as a result take few notes. But documenting what you do as a coach, especially since coaching is primarily a conversation between two people, protects you if a client distorts reality, makes false claims, or is not happy with the outcome. Create a system that allows you to take notes on each session easily. Date your files, and save copies of your notes on disks and store them safely. Track your results and have pre- and post-measures in place to help you define the efficacy of your engagements.

4. *Do maintain straightforward payment policies.* Coaching involves a fiduciary relationship, and it's safer and less risky to keep business finances uncomplicated. Some new coaches, hungry for business, accept bartering as a way to avoid losing a client who can't pay his or her fee. This is a bad idea. Resist temptation to try to equate your intangible coaching services with other,

more tangible services, to avoid feelings of resentment. Keep your dealings with clients legitimate. Don't set yourself up for a conflict of interest by investing with clients or complicate your fee with additional financial transactions outside the realm of coaching. Follow accepted billing and accounting procedures. Set a fee that you feel is fair and competitive within your niche, and stick with it.

MARKETING STRATEGIES

Most successful coaches target their market. They define a niche or specialty and build a reputation with a defined pool of people or organizations. Some new coaches in business ask: Why do I have to narrow my audience, rather than appealing to a broader market? What if by targeting my market I miss out on potential clients? It sounds counterintuitive to narrow your pool of clients just when you are desperate for clients, but targeting a market is actually the most effective way to build a coaching business because it helps you to conserve your energy, your costs, and your time. By targeting your market, you will achieve three key marketing objectives:

- *Focus:* New coaches make the mistake of trying to be all things to all people. This is understandable, because when you are new and hungry for clients, you fear rejecting any potential business. If, instead, you can get focused on one or two specific audiences, you will have a better chance to actually generate a steady flow of clients.

- *Research:* To build a receptive audience for your services, you need to really know your clientele. Even though you may have some degree of knowledge or awareness of your market, do you know the coaching services they want? It's easier to figure out the needs of the market if you narrow your approach, because if your market is too broad, the market research (understanding who your coaching clients are and what they will pay for) is too vast and daunting.

- *Ownership:* After you get focused and research the needs of your market, you are in a position to offer the right people the right services. Research the needs of that market carefully so that you offer the right products, services, and information for that small, targeted audience. Do this well and the market will recognize you as a credible coach, with needed expertise. Be the big fish in the small pond.

ATTRACTING CLIENTS

To be a coach in business, you need a steady source of paying clients. Since coaching is often short-term work, with clients staying for an average of 3 to 6 months, according to industry standards, you will need to be marketing as a coach, in one way or another, on a regular basis. Here are the top three strategies that I recommend.

NETWORKING

Networking is the least expensive, most effective strategy for finding clients, by developing relationships with those who can refer. Networking means meeting with other professionals, face-to-face when you can, and by phone or other outreach platforms when distance is involved. No matter how well the initial meeting goes, don't expect it to produce results. Referrals take time to develop. The average maxim in business and advertising is that it takes six contacts to produce results. That means you might need to connect well with a potential referral source six times before he or she will refer. You will need a strategic plan to do this in a way that is not overly promotional or pushy. When I work with coaches, we spend time preparing for all of these connections long before they occur.

Since coaching is an expensive service, most purchasers want to feel secure in who they have selected for coaching. This is why your reputation and connections can make a big difference in whether you will win a contract or if your name will be referred to a potential client. If you are in business, networking needs to be part of your continual business-building actions; networking activities should be on your calendar each month, whether you are full with client engagements or not.

ONLINE VISIBILITY

Few coaching client engagements come solely from the Internet, since most people prefer to have a direct connection with coaches prior to hiring them. But having a strong online presence is key for any coach in terms of marketing support. A good website gives you a platform for blogging or self-publishing articles. It also is a way to build an email list that can be used to advertise programs and any offers. Online marketing activities, such as composing and sending sales letters to an email and social media list to announce free programs, can develop a funnel of potential paying clients over time. Online marketing seems to be employed often by business coaches who sell performance-based skills, yet less successful for executive and leadership coaches, who look for longer-term contracts. Life coaches often make use of social media with Facebook pages, LinkedIn profiles, and website blogs to build a list of readers that may then become clients.

COMMUNITY BUILDING

As mentioned earlier, it takes a community to support the growth of a business. Your job as business owner is to join existing communities and/or build your own. These can be local existing communities (such as associations, clubs, industry-based groups) or national and international ones that you connect with virtually. To build community around your business, you will often use a "give to get" marketing strategy: You offer your time or expertise as a volunteer and add value to the community. Over time, you make connections, tap into advice and resources that help your business develop. Select a few communities that you want to be a part of. This marketing strategy is a long-term one and it helps for you to have the time and energy to fully engage with whatever communities you select.

A COACHING APPROACH TO BUSINESS

To sum up, just as Thomas Leonard inferred in his advice to me and others when I was a new coach, you have an undeniable business-building advantage: You are a coach. You are part of a profession whose goal is to help people improve and further their goals. Bring a coaching approach into all your public interactions. The more you can show others the value of your services, not by what you say but by who you are, the better your business will develop. In every interaction with potential referral sources—with advisors who you hire to help you grow, with all potential and existing clients—be a model of your services. Tackle all business issues with the positive attitude and solution-oriented vigor that you would suggest to clients. If you live the ideals of your profession, your persona and business will shine. Align your business with the approach that is the hallmark of our profession.

Building a business, any business, takes time, commitment, hard work, and a bit of luck. Learn to enjoy your business. Read and get educated. Stay current with coaching trends and global economic shifts. Draft a business plan that functions as your annual guide. Build your reputation by making an evidence-based difference in people's lives. Create a community around your business to support your efforts. Welcome to the business of coaching and the rich life of an entrepreneur.

REFERENCES

Grodzki, L., & Allen, W. (2005). *The business and practice of coaching* (pp. 188–193). New York, NY: Norton.

International Coach Federation. (2016). ICF Global Coaching Study. Retrieved from https://coachfederation.org/files/FileDownloads/2016GCS_FactSheet.pdf

Milne-Tyte, A. (2016). The business coaching industry is booming. *Marketplace.com*. Retrieved from https://www.marketplace.org/2016/02/25/world/business-coaching-business-booming

O'Brien, E. (2014). 10 things life coaches won't tell you. *Marketwatch.com*. Retrieved from http://www.marketwatch.com/story/10-things-life-coaches-wont-tell-you-2014-09-05

Sherpa Coaching USA. (2017). 2017 Sherpa Executive Coaching Survey. Retrieved from http://www.sherpacoaching.com/annual-executive-coaching-survey

Stewart, J. (2012a). *Life coach salary: 15 reasons your coaching fees are too low.* Retrieved from http://www.schoolofcoachingmastery.com/coaching-blog/bid/90425/Life-Coach-Salary-15-Reasons-Your-Coaching-Fees-Are-Too-Low

Stewart, J. (2012b). *Life coach salary: How much money do professional coaches make.* Retrieved from http://www.schoolofcoachingmastery.com/coaching-blog/bid/82347/Life-Coach-Salary-How-Much-Money-Do-Professional-Coaches-Make

4

Coach Training: Context, Competencies, Methodology, and Practice

Hope Langner and Janet Keller

Coaching is a broad river, fed by many streams. Some say it started just 30 years ago while others say it may have begun some 2,600 years earlier. The modern coaching industry is changing and growing and the same can be said for the training of coaches. Coach trainers are growing and developing the professional coach training industry as they engage in it.

THE CONTEXT OF COACH TRAINING

Coaching is a unique personal relationship that is focused on the person being coached (aka "the client") and his or her potential, rather than the client's presenting problem or situation. Coaching occurs in a clearly established partnership between the coach and the client. A coaching conversation is an intentional, purposeful, deliberately designed conversation within a consciously designed relationship. Coach and client have a clear agreement to focus on the growth and transformation of the client. Paradoxically, the conversation, while intentional and purposeful, will move and flow based on what is being discussed, as learning continually unfolds.

The coach is completely committed to the client's growth and transformation. The coach works with the client very closely, aiming to see the client's life through the client's eyes, while at the same time allowing enough distance to offer clear and unbiased observation of the client and the client's process. The closeness and the distance create a paradox that serves the client's learning. Coaching is both anchored in the present moment while at the same time coming from a high level perspective on the client and his or her life—without bias or attachment.

Much of the coach's work is intangible and may not always be visible. The conversation is about the human being who is the client, and not the client's circumstances. Something is happening in the client's world that gives rise to a topic, yet the coach's focus remains on the human being who is the client and how the client will grow and respond. A coaching conversation may feel chat-like, spacious, open, dreamy, yet there is always a thread of intentional energy running underneath the words—the coach's commitment to the client's transformation. Because of the depth and intimacy of coaching, it's crucial for the coach and client to establish trust and safety in their relationship. An agreement to hold confidentiality is key to this.

In addition to the qualities mentioned here, the coach will also be paying attention to the client's nonverbal communication and articulating what he or she is noticing about the client's energy level, changes in energy, emotion, physicality, tone of voice, and more. Sometimes the coach will be the client's witness, as the client recognizes something new or learns something deeper about himself or herself. Overall agreements and strategic goals for coaching over time are established at the outset of the coaching relationship. Specific topics and desired outcomes are reinforced or made explicit during each coaching session.

COACHING COMPETENCIES FOR COACH TRAINERS

Different accrediting organizations have developed frameworks for the competencies needed by an effective coach, and all accredited coach training programs are required to address the appropriate competencies (i.e., those identified by the organizations that accredit their coach training program). Here are two examples:

The International Coach Federation (ICF; n.d.) lists 11 coaching competencies.

1. Ethics and Standards—Understanding of coach ethics and standards and ability to apply them appropriately in all coaching situations

2. Establishing the Coaching Agreement—Ability to understand what is required in the specific coaching interaction and to come to agreement with the prospective and new client about the coaching process and relationship

3. Establishing Trust and Intimacy With the Client—Ability to create a safe, supportive environment that produces ongoing mutual respect and trust

4. Coaching Presence—Ability to be fully conscious and create spontaneous relationship with the client, employing a style that is open, flexible, and confident

5. Active Listening—Ability to focus completely on what the client is saying and is not saying, to understand the meaning of what is said in the context of the client's desires, and to support client self-expression

6. Powerful Questioning—Ability to ask questions that reveal the information needed for maximum benefit to the coaching relationship and the client

7. Direct Communication—Ability to communicate effectively during the coaching session, and to use language that has the greatest positive impact on the client

8. Creating Awareness—Ability to integrate and accurately evaluate multiple sources of information, and to make interpretations that help the client to gain awareness and thereby achieve agreed-upon results

9. Designing Actions—Ability to create with the client opportunities for ongoing learning, during coaching and in work/life situations, and for taking new actions that will most effectively lead to agreed-upon coaching results

10. Planning and Goal Setting—Ability to develop and maintain an effective coaching plan with the client

11. Managing Progress and Accountability—Ability to hold attention on what is important for the client, and to leave responsibility with the client to take action

The European Mentoring and Coaching Council (EMCC; 2015) lists these eight coaching and mentoring competence categories.

1. Understanding Self—Demonstrates awareness of the coach's own values, beliefs, and behaviors; recognizes how these affect his or her practice and uses this self-awareness to manage the coach's effectiveness in meeting the client's and, where relevant, the sponsor's objectives

2. Commitment to Self-Development—Explores and improves the standard of the coach's practice and maintain the reputation of the profession

3. Managing the Contract—Establishes and maintains the expectations and boundaries of the mentoring/coaching contract with the client and, where appropriate, with sponsors

4. Building the Relationship—Skillfully builds and maintains an effective relationship with the client, and where appropriate, with the sponsor

5. Enabling Insight and Learning—Works with the client and sponsor to bring about insight and learning

6. Outcome and Action Orientation—Demonstrates approach and uses the skills in supporting the client to make desired changes

7. Use of Models and Techniques—Applies models and tools, techniques and ideas beyond the core communication skills in order to bring about insight and learning

8. Evaluation—Gathers information on the effectiveness of the coach's own practice and contributes to establishing a culture of evaluation of outcomes

While these two organizations have different structures to their list of competencies, they cover very similar ground. So, essentially, a competent coach needs to be able to:

- Hold and apply a clear ethical stand as a professional coach
- Witness the client
- Create and be part of an intimate trusting relationship
- Recognize and work with the client's verbal and nonverbal communication
- Establish key focus areas for a coaching relationship and a specific topic of each coaching session
- Establish agreements for the work together (including strategic goals)
- Coach from a commitment to transformation for the client
- Be willing to risk and coach outside of the coach's own comfort zone
- Hold an intentional and purposeful conversation, with the ability to hold the unfolding learning in whatever form it emerges
- Have awareness of one's own biases, opinions, and skill level
- Self-manage

So the question before us is how do we train coaches? What is needed to instill the skills, tools, and know-how for someone to become a competent professional coach?

COMMON COACH TRAINING METHODOLOGIES

Coach training is offered in many formats: Most common are online, virtual courses by audio or video teleconference, one-to-one in-person training, and in-person group programs. Training programs and paths that include both in-person and distance learning options are most effective.

Although many beginning coaches are "naturals" at coaching, this natural talent is not always obvious or consciously available. Coach training helps coaches-in-training discover their natural ability and teaches them how to use their skills consciously and consistently. The skill and support of experienced coach trainers enable learner coaches to discover their own strengths and gifts and to practice their coaching skills and coaching presence with awareness. In order to support a student in accessing and releasing an inherent ability, a number of factors are worth considering, including:

- What type of training is most amenable to a student's learning style?
- How much focus does a student need on the being *and* on the doing of coaching?
- What are the skills and tools needed to become first a competent, then a master coach?

- How can coach training, mentoring, supervision, and practice support the development of the beginning coach?

In training environments, context creates an experience that leads to transformation. Coach trainers start with a script: a form, a timeline, a set of words on paper. The fixed timeline, and carefully designed structure of the training, is part of the context that must be created for a coherent and thoughtful experiential training program. However, each group and each delivery of the material is unique. This creates the magic of experiential learning and learning that leads to transformation: an awareness of who we are as coaches and our special gift for our clients and the profession. So, coach training is a paradox. Yes, it is formulaic. There are models, theories, skills, tools, and techniques to be taught, and a timeline to be delivered by the trainers. At the same time, effective training is deeply experiential, because all new coaches are bringing their own history, their own strengths and weaknesses, their own emotions into the art of their own very special coaching. This is the essence of experiential coach training: Trainers and students alike are transformed by experiential learning, mutual discovery, and deep practice.

Many coaching schools emphasize training that is focused on coaching skills, with a side benefit of personal development. This is true, as the teaching is focused primarily on specific coaching skills and techniques, firmly based on a theoretical foundation and laid out simply and powerfully in a coaching model. And yet, the learning will not last unless the student turns up with willingness, an open heart, and the courage to be fully open to learning, failing, and using the full power of their whole selves. Coach training is about who the coach is as well as what the coach does. The two are inextricably intertwined. Coach training teaches ethics, skills, and tools. From that platform, each coach develops into a unique coaching instrument, incorporating all that has been learned into the whole person that he or she is.

THE ROLE OF PRACTICE IN COACHING TRAINING

Coaches need practice, practice, and more practice to learn about themselves and their impact on others in order to serve coaching clients. And the best way to practice coaching is to practice coaching, then practice giving and receiving feedback on that coaching. There are a few standard ways of practicing. The first is in pairs, with one person as coach and the other as client. It helps to have a fixed and measured time allowance for each person to coach, in order to develop the discipline of running a professional coaching practice where sessions have a specific beginning and end. Students need to learn how to discover what the coaching topic is and to check during the session whether the coaching is on topic and serving the client's needs. They also need to learn how to draw out what the client has learned from the session and how to bring a coaching session to a timely end. Training also requires feedback. The coach in training needs to ask his or her practice clients about specifically what worked in the coaching, and what else would have been useful.

Both coach and client need to be fully present during the coaching practice. That requires trust, honesty, and courage. It also models one of the basic requirements of a good coach—the capacity to build a relationship. Confidentiality of the coaching content must be established from the start; it is essential that everyone in the training subscribes to the ethical stand of maintaining confidentiality. That confidentiality must be maintained when debriefing the learning from the practice sessions so an honest, authentic discussion of the skills and techniques used during the coaching may occur.

An even more powerful way of practicing is to work in threes, with each of the students taking a turn as coach, client, and observer of the process. The role of observer is a particularly valuable one because the observer can witness the whole relationship as it unfolds, noticing what the coach is doing and being, noticing how the client is reacting, and also observing the power of the relationship. The observer is then capable of giving valuable feedback to the coach about what worked well and what else would strengthen the coaching. That feedback allows the other two partners—the coach and the client—to step outside of their roles in the practice process and view the learning and growth more objectively. By the time each participant has had the chance to be coach, then client, then observer, there will be a strong partnership in the group and valuable insights on what is working in the coaching.

Practice, practice, and more practice affords the student a direct experience of skill level, growth, and personal style as a coach, coupled with a meta-view of what is happening in the coach/client process. A context of coaching, a personal and group experience of coaching, all leading to a transformation in the skills and ownership of the coach—that is the power of the experiential training of skills.

The relatively new theory of *deliberate practice* comes from *Peak: Secrets from the New Science of Expertise,* by Anders Ericsson and Robert Pool (2016). This pedagogical foundation can be seen in a good coach-training program offering coaching practice that leads to coaching competence, and then coaching mastery, by including the following elements:

1. *Good mental representations in order to catch mistakes and create better practice techniques.*Powerful coaching demonstrations, observed throughout the arc of a coaching program, can give students a helpful view of who they need to be and skills and tools they need to master in order to step more fully into coaching mastery.

2. *Trainers, mentors, and supervisors who are expert practitioners in the coaching field.* These master coaches can provide insights regarding their training methods, valuable feedback, and practice activities designed to help students improve their performance.

3. *Focus on the inquiry.* What's the *knowledge* you need to have and the *skill* you need to develop and the person you need to be to integrate the two?

Coach training should always include powerful demonstrations of masterful coaching. Trainers and facilitators should be open to their own growth, to their own vulnerability and their own strengths and weaknesses as coaches, not only to model the directly transferable skills of coaching but also to show how distinct and different each of us is as a coach. Good training should include some coaching demonstrations, using clients from the room who are willing and able to bring real coaching issues. Those demonstrations should have a clear outcome in demonstrating certain skills, but the overall pattern of the coaching is, by definition, uncertain because it should serve to demonstrate just how fluid and in the moment coaching needs to be. Good trainers need to be without ego when they demonstrate coaching. They should be prepared to fail and be prepared to celebrate failing and then use those failures as teaching points for the students. At the same time, they should be prepared to succeed, and then be prepared to use those successes as teaching points for students. Coaching demonstrations are no place for ego or for perfection. They are places for the trainer to show his or her full humanity as a coach, combined with clear demonstration of the underlying skills of coaching and a celebration that good coaching is never about the coach but about the client and the relationship.

Trainers should also be happy to be vulnerable, honest, transparent, and human by volunteering to be coached by students in front of the class. They need to be open and honest and bring real issues to show the impact of coaching. It is the place to be coached on real issues which are life-changing, and to rest in the confidence that even "poor" coaching by struggling learner coaches will provide value, both for the trainer and, most importantly, in service of the students.

When in a group learning to coach experientially, it can be a challenge for a learner coach to coach someone in front of colleagues and classmates. By having several students coach the same client in sequence, the training remains interesting and compelling, capitalizing on the learning opportunity to observe authentic coaching relationships that empower the client and lead to transformation.

The groundwork of coach training is to create the experience of being a coach while using the skills and tools of coaching. This groundwork is present in the many ways students are encouraged to practice their coaching—in twos, in threes, with a trainer as a client and as witness, and with an experienced coach trainer demonstrating effective coaching. Above all, coaching is an experiential process and the training helps students discover more fully who they are as individuals, who they are as coaches, in addition to what skills they need to learn.

While skills are the backbone of coaching, the flesh, the breath, and the life of coaching are the practice and experience of coaching. Without the backbone there is no structure. Without warmth, trust, challenge, safety, and the individual qualities of the coach, there is no flesh on that structure. So, what are the bones, or the skills that coaches all need to learn? Here are some examples.

Coaches need to learn how to ask powerful questions that are not seeking information or solving problems but are a way of opening up a client to his or her own exploration, awareness, and insight. The questions should be short, open, and take the client down an as yet unexplored path. Learning to avoid asking questions that can be answered by yes or no, or questions starting with *why* that often prompt justifications and storytelling, if not self-criticism, can be the first liberating step in becoming a coach. Asking powerful questions takes the coach out of the mode of *expert* and allows the client to discover his or her own answers and own paths to action and transformation. Letting go of solving the problem in favor of growing the client, can be the hardest first step in becoming a coach, especially those trained as teachers or managers, engineers or consultants, all of whom are paid to find and provide the right answers as quickly as possible.

Coaches need to learn how to listen in a different way, not just to their own internal chatter and opinions about what is good for the client or what they already know to be true. Coaches need to experience listening with full intention and direct focus on the client but also to listen to what is not being said, to the underlying emotions, to the body posture, and to movements—even to the temperature or the sounds of the environment in which they are coaching. All of those things, not just the spoken words, are invaluable sources of information. Listening in a different way is often a revelation to new coaches. It is hard to break the ingrained habits of a lifetime, but with gentle prompting from trainers comes a change in attention, a change of awareness, and the revelation that listening is not a chance to gather facts or to prepare the ground for solutions. Human beings notice so much more when they start noticing.

Powerful questions and intentional listening are the basis of a coachlike presence. A new coach learns and develops these abilities through experiencing them. Coaching presence, or the quality of simply being with a client from a fully authentic, courageous, and open place, is another competency of coaching that cannot be easily trained. Presence can be best learned by a coach in training having an experience of his or her own presence with a client. This is why practicing coaching and being coached are essential. The main job of a beginner coach is to discover his or her natural home base in behavior and impact, and then to expand the range.

When coaches learn more about themselves, they learn about their patterns and biases and how to let them go. Is the trainee a natural helper and comforter who sees all clients as in need of assurance and protection? Or is the trainee a natural challenger that sees all clients as in need of risk and growth? Or is the trainee hungry to dive deep into the emotions of the client, or more inclined to analysis and actions based on thought and planning? The exercises, group discussion, and practice coaching of the training course will all help trainees and their instructors to discover each coach's leanings and predilections.

At one level, coach training is just the transference of skills and tools. That is the context of the training course. We come together for a certain number of hours to follow a curriculum, to learn coaching skills, and to practice coaching. Those are the skills listed in the competencies of most coach training schools and international coaching organizations. But that is not enough. The skills are like musical notation or a recipe book. They need to be practiced and brought alive. Above all, coach training should be about experience. Who am I as a coach? What is my impact? What do I need to develop? What do I shrink away from? How do I expand my range so that I can coach a marine, a mother, a new employee, a grieving grandfather, a burned-out executive?

Finally, excellent coach training incorporates recent pedagogy on the very best ways to learn. Benedict Carey (2014), in his book *How We Learn,* highlights three critical elements of the learning process:

1. Move around—The use of embodiment is an important training methodology for creating deeper, more "in the bones" learning.

2. Mix it up—Excellent coach training uses many different pedagogical competencies as a way to create context for learning, and to allow students to use

and store material in a deeper way. The multiperspective, multirole coach training activities mentioned here are employed to create more transformative learning: discussions (live and virtual), observation (lectures and demos), solo contemplation, reading and research, paper writing, skill drills, doing actual coaching, being a client, receiving feedback from master coaches, and giving and receiving feedback with peers.

3. Space it out—Prospective students who wish to maximize the learning process will look for a 6-month to year-long program that will allow students time to evolve personally, time to integrate the learning, and truly acquire the ability to practice the art (or context) as well as the science (skills and tools) of coaching.

The true work of coach training is beyond a model, formula, timeline, or script. It is the magic that happens through experience, relationship, dedication, and the transformation that happens when we grow our awareness and make choices from our new growth. This growth process never ends, even for the most experienced of coaches. A humble and competent trainer is always learning, in service of trainee coaches who are on the way to being the powerful (and the very best) coaches they can be.

TYPES OF COACHING SCHOOLS

There are two major types of coaching programs: those housed in a dedicated coach training school or organization and those more academically oriented programs associated with a college or university. While programs of each type may be similar in terms of curricula and methodology, there are often marked differences in terms of academic rigor and programmatic expectations. For example, a university program will typically require more reading, research, and paper or thesis writing. Both types of coaching programs are instrumental to the growth and maturity of the coach training industry and to the coaching profession as a whole.

A current inquiry for the coach training industry is distinguishing between *coach training* and *coach education*. In general, coach training is the process of training people how to coach: learning concepts, tools, and skills, and applying those elements in coaching, while coach education (more typically practiced in programs that are connected to an academic institution) consists of research and study leading to new learning concepts and a deeper, richer understanding of the coaching and human transformation field.

REGULATING THE COACH TRAINING INDUSTRY

The coach training industry is self-regulated for the most part, so a prospective coach seeking quality coach training will need to research whether a particular coach training program maintains alignment with industry standards. The ICF is a global organization committed to advancing coaching in society and maintaining high standards in the profession. To that end, the ICF maintains a credentialing program for coaches and an accreditation program for coaching schools. The ICF currently offers three ways for schools to be accredited:

- Accredited Coach Training Program (ACTP): This is considered an all-inclusive program containing a minimum of 125 student contact hours. Coaches who complete an ACTP are eligible to apply for an ICF Associate Certified Coach (ACC) or Professional Certified Coach (PCC) credential via the ACTP path.

- Approved Coaching Specific Training Hours (ACSTH): These are a la carte programs that contain a minimum of 30 student contact hours. Coaches who complete the requisite ACSTH training are eligible to apply for an ICF ACC or PCC credential via the ACSTH path.

- Continuing Coach Education (CCE): These courses are designed to provide previously trained and credentialed coaches with ongoing training in the field. Coaches credentialed with the ICF must renew their credential every 3 years by completing 40 hours of training in Core Competencies and Resource Development.

In addition to the ICF, other important organizations dedicated to evolving excellence in the coach training industry are the Association of Coach Training Organizations (ACTO), the Graduate School Alliance for Education in Coaching (GSAEC), and EMCC.

CHOOSING THE RIGHT COACH TRAINING PROGRAM

One challenge for the prospective coaching student is choosing the right coach training program from the dizzying array of existing programs. Current estimates place the number of coach training schools and programs at over 500 and counting. The coach training arena is vast and growing and the number of choices can be overwhelming to the novice coach looking for a professional and comprehensive coach training program. Here are some criteria to use and questions to ask as you investigate a potential coach training program. Does the coaching school or program. . .

- Have a successful history of training coaches?
  - How many coaches have they trained?
  - How many coaches have they awarded a credential?
- Have a website that clearly states the following elements:
  - Full cost of the program?
  - Duration of the program?
  - Methodologies and pedagogy used in the courses?
- Are there various modes for content delivery: In-person? Virtual?

- What methodologies are used in the training process:
  - Instructor hours?
  - Mentoring?
  - Individualized coach supervision?
  - Instructor and peer coach practice sessions?
  - Discussions?
  - Coaching demos?
  - Background reading
  - Research and writing projects?
  - Homework?
  - Written and oral assessment?
- Are the faculty credentialed coaches who are gainfully employed in the coaching industry (either in private practice, inside an organization, or as brokered or external organizational coaches)?
- Is the training program accredited by a recognized accrediting body, like the ICF? Are the credits offered aligned with your professional and personal goals for your coaching practice?
- Does the program align with your professional and personal development needs? Should you be looking at a stand-alone coach training school or a coach training program associated with a college or university?
- Does the program emphasize the importance of transformational learning for students, and the integration of professional and personal growth?
- Does the program prepare you to apply for an industry-accepted credential?
- Does the school have a robust and active alumni network, both globally and locally?
- Is the school a member of ACTO and/or GSAEC?

INCLUSION AND DIVERSITY

At the growing edge of the coach training industry, a conversation is emerging regarding diversity and inclusion, specifically how the involvement of people of diverse backgrounds or characteristics, including culture, race, gender expression, and physical ability, enhances the learning experience for all and extends the reach of the coaching profession. Commitment to diversity offers us the opportunity to create a deeper experience of and appreciation for the wholeness of all learners. Broadening accessibility and creating greater inclusivity through the lens of wholeness opens up access within the coach training industry while deepening the impact of coaching and our very experience of how the human spirit expresses itself and finds ways to flourish.

THE FUTURE OF COACH TRAINING

Just as we hold that our clients are always evolving, the same is true for the coach training profession. As we look into the future, we see that insights in the fields of psychology, neuroscience, learning theory, quantum physics, leadership, and a multitude of other disciplines will continue to be integrated into coach training best practices. Coaches need to become experts at using the dynamics of each coaching moment to aid clients in their ongoing learning and growth. As coach trainers, we combine that critical context for the learning with a deep understanding of the content, curriculum elements, tools, and skills necessary to develop and demonstrate coaching excellence.

REFERENCES

Carey, B. (2014). *How we learn.* New York, NY: Penguin Random House.

Ericsson, A., & Pool, R. (2016). *Peak: Secrets from the new science of expertise.* New York, NY: Houghton Mifflin Harcourt.

European Mentoring and Coaching Council. (2015). EMCC Competence Framework V2. Retrieved from https://emcc1.app.box.com/s/4aj8x6tmbt75ndn13sg3dauk8n6wxfxq

International Coach Federation. (n.d.). Core competencies. Retrieved from https://coachfederation.org/core-competencies

5

Professional Standards: A Developmental Journey

Marialexia Margariti

I t is rather challenging to believe that one person—in this case myself, the author of this chapter—will be able to collect, digest, and appropriately reproduce all that has been happening during the last few decades around the globe on coaching and specifically on its definition of professionalization and standards. It has taken and continues to take a lot of time, effort, passion, and dedication from an extremely large number of experienced and hard-working practitioners who aim to establish all those frameworks, processes, procedures, and guides that would eventually lead to the personal development of professional coaches and to the professionalization of the coaching profession. I therefore only try to give a high level view of the key pillars of professional standards and to go, maybe, a bit further than that—as far as the total number of words of this chapter allows. It is certain that there are more details that could be given on each of the items that are highlighted in the next sections.

DEFINITIONS

A start to this introductory piece on definitions will be to define some key terms that will be used throughout this chapter. And in this case, an improvisation in defining Professional Standards will be avoided—there are formal definitions—and I intentionally refrain from using the definition of a single coaching professional organization. This chapter uses, where necessary, generic definitions found in glossaries or in the work of academics and experts in the field, which formulate in most cases the basis on which each professional organization defines these same terms. But before defining Professional Standards, it seems necessary to go a step back and see first what a Profession is. Looking, for example, onto the website of Professions Australia where the term "profession" is defined, we see that there are some core elements that define a profession and separate it from being just a practice. Those elements are (a) professional competencies (or "special knowledge and skills" as per the definition clearly identifiable for each profession, (b) dedicated training, and (c) a code of ethics that defines the appropriate code of conduct and ". . .practice beyond the personal moral obligations of an individual" (Professions Australia, n.d.). An important point to remember: All those core elements should be known to the general public and professional practice should be to the benefit of public interest.

We see, also, that the word "standards" is in the definition, among a few other key words, including the previously mentioned core elements, which will be the subjects of subsequent sections in this chapter: knowledge, skills, research, education, and training. All these under the overarching headline of "ethical" comprise, for me as a practitioner coach, the idea of professional standards. One could ask: "Why do we need professional standards in the first place?" My response is very simple: "We need them because we want to be called professionals!" Regardless of the diverse professional entities, this designation calls for exercising one's practice skillfully, diligently, and consistently, acting to the benefit of the client. Actually, professional standards should not be viewed as a requirement or an obligation, as this places them as something externally imposed on the practitioners. Standards are the backbone of our practice; they are an integral part of it.

The significance of establishing and holding professional standards is intensified from the fact that we, as coaches, are a rapidly growing community of practitioners with an increasing number of clients receiving our services. According to the International Coach Federation (ICF) in the *Executive Summary of the 2016 Global Coaching Study*, there were around 53,300 professional coaches worldwide as compared to 2,100 professional coaches in 1999. It is necessary, therefore, to safeguard the quality of services given, which is not only reassuring for the clients but also enables the sustainable growth of the discipline. As reported in the same Executive Summary, revenue from coaching services in 2015 was estimated as a global total of $2.356 billion, representing a 19% increase over the 2011 estimate. By our high quality standards today, we are basically building our professional future on solid ground so as to service effectively our clients and to establish a healthy business environment.

AT THE HEART OF PROFESSIONAL STANDARDS

As previously said, around the globe the coaching profession has been dynamically evolving through the years and a thousand valuable initiatives have been undertaken to further enhance professionalization of the profession by the independent bodies that exist. It is my belief and the outcome of my experience as a member of more than one professional coaching organization, that even if we do things differently, even if we are geographically apart, there are some core elements that underline professional standards that are "common." I place the word in quotation marks only because I would not like to be misinterpreted that what I said represents the official view of one or more organizations; it is clearly my own view even though I know that definitions, guides, and codes may vary from one professional body to the other.

CODE OF ETHICS

All professional bodies, like the Association for Coaching (AC), European Mentoring & Coaching Council (EMCC), ICF, International Association of Coaching (IAC), Worldwide Association of Business Coaches (WABC), and so forth, have defined a code of ethics to which their members abide, regardless of where they might be practicing in the world. Such a code provides guidance and a set of standards for members on their behaviors when working with clients. A code also defines the professional conduct with clients, colleagues, and the broader community and expresses the key elements—as per the definition—by each professional body for a fit-for-practice coach. The standards set in a code of ethics are enforceable, which means that in case of breaching any of those, a parallel Complaints and Disciplinary procedure exists to handle such incidents. At present, most of the independent professional coaching bodies have their own code of ethics that is posted on their websites' homepage or under a section dedicated to Ethics and Regulation or Professional Standards. There are also some initiatives from professional bodies to co-sign a single code of ethics. One of the first ones was, back in February 2016, when the AC and the EMCC signed a common Global Code of Ethics (GCoE). More recently, in May 2018, 5 professional organizations became co-signatories of the renewed version of the 2016 Global Code of Ethics. These organizations are AC, EMCC, Mentoring Institute University of New Mexico, Association for Professional Executive Coaching & Supervision (APECS), and Italian Association of Professional Coaches (AICP). This code can be accessed on a dedicated site (https://www.global-codeofethics.org/) and on the individual websites of all 5 organizations. The code of every single association is always downloadable so their members can educate clients or use it as an accompanying document to a contract of coaching services.

PROFESSIONAL CHARTER

Coaching, being a self-regulated profession—the word "profession" is not meant in a statutory sense—in the majority of countries where it is practiced (see more on regulation in the last section of this chapter), has to demonstrate to relevant regional and/or international authorities that are in a position to truly self-regulate. This can happen through the establishment of a professional charter that can be signed by more than one professional body and that encompasses all those items in the form of quality standards, rules, regulations, processes, and procedures that are in force by the signatories individually and collectively with the aim to ensure high quality standards and best practice sharing. A professional charter is meant to inform the professionals and also the general public that it is not replacing, in any way, the code of ethics or other regulatory procedures that the signatories hold individually but the charter is to be used in conjunction with those. To my knowledge, we have to date a Professional Charter for the coaching and mentoring professions that was prepared in 2011 by the EMCC and ICF as the first two signatories with AC joining in 2012 and Société Française de Coaching joining in 2013. This Charter was drafted according to European law requirements and it can be found in the publicly accessible Database on Self Regulation and Co-Regulation Initiatives of the European

Economic and Social Committee (EESC, n.d.) where all self-regulated initiatives are listed. Its main aim is:

> to establish a benchmark for ethics and good practice in coaching and mentoring, aiming to ensure that practising coaches and mentors conduct their practice in a professional and ethical manner, . . . to inform clients of coaching and mentoring, and to promote public confidence in coaching and mentoring as a process for professional and personal development. (Professional Charter for Coaching & Mentoring, 2011, p. 2)

DIVERSITY AND INCLUSION

Diversity and inclusion is for me, personally and professionally, a precious topic. I believe that it is found at the heart of the coaching profession because there is not much chance to be a successful and authentic coach unless one accepts the clients unconditionally and appreciates their separate, diverse, and very individual existence. This is just one part of the matter. The other is that in a global economy, most, if not all, of the independent professional bodies have a multiregional or global presence that immediately translates into members from different geographies, from diverse cultures and religions, from various belief and value systems, who speak hundreds of different languages and have as many views as many members there are! It is only through true-to-the heart openness to diversity and willingness to be really inclusive that the global coaching community can flourish and evolve and can serve its clientele best. This is the reason why this subject has a prominent position in the code of ethics or code of conduct of every professional body and there are a number of diversity and inclusion initiatives going on. As an example, EMCC's vision on Diversity and Inclusion (EMCC, 2018) highlights the significance of the subject: "As Coaches, Mentors, and Supervisors, we strive to embrace and respect the uniqueness of the individual, their talents and potential."

A JOURNEY TO INDIVIDUAL DEVELOPMENT

For the sake of being practical, it is key to see how professional standards translate for each professional coach; what is it that we can put our fingers on? One could argue that professional standards are and should be the responsibility of the independent professional bodies and indeed they are. There is tremendous work that is happening by all coaching bodies to establish standards, educate their membership on those, and communicate them to recipients and buyers of coaching services and, in some cases, to government bodies. However, it is each and every one of us in our professional capacity who brings these standards to life through our coaching practice and conduct with clients, sponsors, and colleagues—in short, through our personal brand. In my view at least, the individual who wants to be called *professional*, regardless of the profession held, has a responsibility to himself or herself and to the clients to continuously aim for personal growth and proficiency in their practice. And in order to build such a professional–personal brand characterized by high quality standards, there are some things that we can and should do.

Obtain Coaching Skills Training

Coaching is a profession and, as such, is characterized by competencies; it works on the basis of theories, models, and techniques that were invented by pioneers in the field like the late Sir John Whitmore. Can we get the books, engage in self-study, and be ready to work with our first coaching client? Apparently, some think they can and so they practice for years without having completed any coach-specific training. Their main reasoning is that they have robust working experience in various fields of business and perhaps they possess a degree or two in academic disciplines. It is exactly because of the fact that in coaching we are mostly transitioning from other disciplines that we need to ensure that we have built our coaching competencies and skills in a systematic and structured manner. A dedicated coach training would help us capitalize upon previous work experience and assist in channeling us in the appropriate direction while we preclude our diverse backgrounds from affecting our professional coach identity. For example, one could be helped to use one's previous experience in business appropriately when coaching someone, knowing how to avoid the trap of advice giving, or acting as a business consultant and not as a coach. The good thing is that these cases are reducing in number as coaching becomes better known, even to those newer to the profession and in newer markets. Since 2010, the Chartered Institute of Personnel and Development (CIPD) is advising the human resources community and the buyers of coaching services that *relevant qualifications and training* should be one of the criteria used to select the right coach because, as it can be read in the guide CIPD has published: "Coaches should be able to demonstrate that they are competent in the provision of coaching services. . . . The training of coaches should be fit for purpose. . . . Expertise will vary depending on the length of the course, level of qualification, depth of study" (CIPD, 2008, p. 36). One last remark on formal coaching skills training is that it is not a one off; there is the initial formal training to which I am mainly referring here, but refresher or upgrade courses to follow new developments in coaching or to enhance their skills are also necessary. The latter is the subject of the continuous professional development (CPD) plan to be discussed in a following section.

Become a Member of an Independent Professional Body

I am often asked by acquaintances, clients, or even coach or mentor colleagues whether I know a particular person who ascribes to being a coach in my country or in the region where I live and practice. My immediate answer, if I have not heard of that person before, is to check if that person is a member of any of the coaching professional bodies present in the region or country. Many more clients are now checking if a coaching provider is a member of a professional body. Membership is a piece of evidence for clients or buyers of coaching services that practitioners adhere to a code of ethics as this is mandatory by all professional bodies or that they have completed some form of formal coaching training. There are organizations like the ICF that require a minimum coach training of 60 hours for someone to become a member or bodies like the WABC that require five references from recipients of coaching services or clients for applicants of full membership. Of course, the benefit from being a member of a professional body is not only that it is checked by savvy clients. The most important benefit is that for the coach who leads a "lonely" professional life, membership gives a sense of belonging to a community where people share the same passions, the same anxieties, the same questions. Moreover, it is there where we can contribute to the evolution of our profession through project work and we can remain abreast of new developments via innovation and research.

ESTABLISH A PERSONAL DEVELOPMENT PLAN

We talk frequently about Continuous Professional Development (CPD) in the form of what is the best CPD activity in which to participate, and whether this covers the CPD hours requirement for individual accreditation. I am of the view that this way of thinking and acting on CPD reduces the developmental journey into a mere chase of hours that serves the purpose of ticking a box on a certification form. So I would propose to take a step back and talk about a Personal Development Plan that should guide our CPD activity choices. This plan is best established: (a) a few months after graduation from a coaching training program; (b) with real clients in the pipeline; and (c) with a supervisor to work in support of ongoing development. These three elements help with the developmental needs of a practicing coach and inform his or her personal plan. In a CPD guide we designed in 2017, with my colleagues in the EMCC—Hemmer, Margariti, Moral, Pinto Oliveira, and van Vlerken (2017)—we showed how the establishment of one's personal development plan enables us to explain the learning cycle we followed. We continued by explaining the stages of a learning cycle that should be owned by the coach and, if addressed in full, should enable personal and professional growth. This CPD guide outlines the following activities: (a) plan CPD activities and identify expected outcomes; (b) implement a CPD plan; (c) reflect on CPD outcome and experience; and (d) establish gains from the experience and incorporate them in new behaviors and practice (*Continuous Professional Development: Guide for Coaches, Mentors and Supervisors*, European Mentoring and Coaching Council [EMCC] Book Series). This way, the focus is on CPD activities, formal training or otherwise, that really answer an identified developmental need instead of a more unstructured sum of CPD activities geared only to cover the minimum CPD hours required of an individual accreditation or renewal process that often has minimum added value to the professional's coaching practice.

WORK WITH A SUPERVISOR

The importance of supervision, as part of a professional coach's CPD, has gained ground in the last few years with more specialized training programs and supervision accreditation products becoming available. Recently, the AC and then EMCC have published supervision guidelines for their members that can be found on their websites. The purpose of supervision is better described by the words of Peter Hawkins in his article "Coaching Supervision": Supervision "should be seen as a joint activity between coach and supervisor that ensures that the quality of practice constantly develops the capacity and capability of the coach and makes sure they are adequately resourced for the work they are undertaking" (Hawkins, 2010, p. 4).

The need for having a supervisor stems from the core of our profession—the establishment of a coaching relationship with another human being. It is the point where we find ourselves very close to other helping professions like counseling and therapy where supervision has been mandatory for decades now. The reason is that when we are interacting with people in any form of relationship, they evoke patterns in us and we are reacting to them even if it is only through reflections in our heads never expressed to our interlocutors. In order to keep our composure robust and the relationship with the client clear of interferences, these patterns and our reactions should be reflected upon and, on occasion resolved, in the safe space of supervision. I am not necessarily advocating supervision to become mandatory as it is in other helping professions. I only hope that the coaching community understands the significance of receiving support for the development of our skills and for reflecting and handling particular cases to the best interests of our clients and of our professional practice.

Become Accredited (or Credentialed or Qualified or Certified)

Professional bodies define in different ways the award of a qualification to an individual coach through an assessment process whereby the major milestones of the coach's professional journey are assessed. At ICF "*Credentials* are awarded to professional coaches and coach training programs are *accredited.* . ." (www.coachfederation.org). Both the AC (www.associationforcoaching.com) and the EMCC (www.emccouncil.org) award "accreditations" to individuals and training programs, as does the WABC (www.wabccoaches.com). The IAC (www.certifiedcoach.org), on the other hand, awards "certifications." Regardless of the different terminology, the value of becoming accredited lies with the fact that it is a proof of the high quality standards of your personal professional brand. It is the way to show commitment to ongoing development and continuous effort to become a better professional who is always fit for practice. It is evidence of one's willingness to put oneself through a stringent process of assessment of one's training qualifications, coaching experience and practice, and demonstrable mastery of coaching competencies—subject to each organization's accreditation requirements, as they tend to vary. Again, clients have started looking and checking the credentials of the coaches they are about to hire.

AN OVERVIEW ON REGULATION

This is a topic that requires a chapter in itself and even then, we wouldn't be able to incorporate the varying definitions of regulation of a profession around the globe nor to explain its different types and the role of local, regional, and international authorities on this subject. At present, the coaching profession is by and large self-regulated in most regions which in simple words mean that there is no license required to practice coaching and there are no governmental bodies that set the rules of practicing in this profession. A formal definition of self-regulation is the one provided by EESC and the Single Market Observatory. "Self-regulation is defined as the possibility for economic operators, the social partners, non-governmental organizations or associations to adopt amongst themselves and for themselves common guidelines at European level—particularly codes of practice or sectoral agreements" (European Economic and Social Committee, 2005, p. 8). If you think of other forms of helping professions like counseling, psychotherapy, psychology, and others, you will probably understand the difference as these professions are either fully regulated or co-regulated in most countries around the globe and sometimes the regulatory bodies are at regional level as, for example, in Europe. By being self-regulated, the professional bodies and the practitioners themselves are solely responsible both for the design and for the implementation of their codes of conduct, breaching procedures, membership criteria, and the like. They are also responsible for defining the set of professional competencies through which fit-for-practice is expressed and ensuring, through requirements and standards, that the professionals who claim coaching expertise are appropriately trained, assessed, and found capable of excellent practice.

That said, there have been attempts in the past at the country level—and some are currently still in discussions—to regulate fully or partially the coaching profession usually through efforts to define at the national level a coaching competence framework, which is directly affecting the educational aspect of coaching and the coach training program structures. On certain occasions, the local chapters or representatives of international professional bodies, like the EMCC or ICF, are consulted, while on others it is more of a national committee's decision. So what we have today might change in the future as there are obviously pressure groups that have a vested interest in seeing coaching become regulated. On the other hand, there have been initiatives like the Professional Charter that was submitted in the EU, cosigned by the AC, EMCC, ICF, and Société Française de Coaching, that show robust evidence of our ability to self-regulate through existing frameworks, codes, and procedures that cover the spectrum of professional requirements (competencies, codes of ethics, accreditation and credentialing products and services, research, membership rights, and obligations). In my view, our only real power to keep the profession self-regulated stems from all the items that were highlighted in this chapter. Only if each one of us continues to aim for high quality standards of practice, strives for excellent practice through a focus on personal and professional development, assists through individual work the efforts of the independent coaching bodies for professionalization, we can have more chances to keep coaching under a self-regulated structure.

CONCLUSION

Concluding at this point with an attempt to give an overview of factors that define and affect the idea of professional standards, I would probably repeat what I started with. The subject is important but is fairly large and multifaceted so it wouldn't be possible to include everything in this word limit. On top of this, I am aware of my own limitations as a single individual to have been able to even be remotely aware of every professional body and everything that goes on in the area of professional standards in the world. I am only hoping, therefore, that I managed at least to give you highlights of what currently exists and a taste of what you can do as a professional coach to further promote professional standards for our discipline. If these ideas have increased your appetite for searching more around this topic, then the mission of this chapter is accomplished. And for all that I might have not managed to include or have not given proper credit to, there will be surely a chance for more in the future.

REFERENCES

Chartered Institute of Personnel and Development. (2008). *Coaching and buying coaching services: A guide.* London, England: Author.

European Economic and Social Committee. (2005). *Current state of co-regulation and self-regulation in the single market.* Brussels, Belgium: Author. Retrieved from https://www.eesc.europa.eu/sites/default/files/resources/docs/2018_cahier_en_smo_def.pdf

European Economic and Social Committee. (n.d.). *The database on self- and co-regulation initiatives.* Retrieved from https://www.eesc.europa.eu/en/policies/policy-areas/enterprise/database -self-and-co-regulation-initiatives

European Mentoring and Coaching Council. (2018). Diversity and inclusion. Retrieved from https://www.emccouncil.org/quality/diversity

Hawkins, P. (2010). Coaching supervision. *The OCM Coach and Mentor Journal.* Deddington, England: The OCM Group Ltd.

Hemmer, N., Margariti, M., Moral, M., Pinto Oliveira, A., & Van Vlerken, A. (2017). *Continuous professional development: Guide for coaches, mentors and supervisors.* Brussels, Belgium: European Mentoring & Coaching Council.

International Coach Federation & PricewaterhouseCoopers LLP. (2016). *ICF Global Coaching Study* [Executive Summary].

Professional Charter for Coaching & Mentoring. (2011). Signatories: Association for Coaching (AC), European Mentoring and Coaching Council (EMCC), International Coach Federation (ICF), Société Française de Coaching.

Professions Australia. (n.d.). What is a profession? Retrieved from http://www.professions.com .au/about-us/what-is-a-professional

6

Coaching Research: A Critical Review

Stewart T. Cotterill and Jonathan Passmore

E vidence-based practice is crucial within professional disciplines, but this is particularly true of disciplines aligned with psychology. According to Grant, Passmore, Cavanagh, and Parker's (2010) review of coaching research, the study of coaching outcomes has been one of the most popular research issues in recent years. In general, the results from coaching research suggest that coaching offers a number of positive benefits including having a positive impact upon leadership (Thach, 2002); increasing self-efficacy (Baron & Morin, 2009; Evers, Brouwers, & Tomic, 2006); enabling previous classroom learning to be transferred to real work situations (Miller, Yahne, Moyers, Martinez, & Pirritano, 2004); improving behavioral learning (Passmore & Rehman, 2012); improving manager performance (Kombarakaran, Yang, Baker, & Fernandes, 2008; Luthans & Peterson, 2003; Smither, London, Flautt, Vergas, & Kucine, 2003); and increasing well-being, resilience, and goal attainment (Duijts, Kant, Brandt, & Swaen, 2008; Grant, Frith, & Burton, 2010).

We begin this chapter by reviewing the broader landscape of coaching research. We then explore the specific research underpinning a range of "key" factors relating to coaching including the coach, client, organizational clients, and the relationship between the coach and the client.

THE DEVELOPMENT OF COACHING RESEARCH

There has been an accelerating focus on research within the coaching domain over the last 25 years. From the first identified coaching study in 1937, development was initially slow, with limited empirical publications until the late 1990s (Passmore & Fillery-Travis, 2011). Indeed, Passmore and Fillery-Travis (2011) suggested that between 1937 and 1999 there were fewer than 100 research articles published. However, while there were an increasing number of publications toward the end of the 1990s, much research simply focused on coaching as a management skill. There were some quantitative studies (e.g., Olivero, Bane, & Kopelman, 1996), but this was not the norm. In Olivero et al.'s (1996) study, 31 managers underwent a conventional managerial training program followed by 8 weeks of one-to-one coaching. The authors reported a 22% increase in productivity after training and an 88% increase after coaching. While ground-breaking at the time for its attempt to assess the quantitative impact of coaching, a review of the article reveals significant weaknesses in its methodology.

Smither et al. (2003) used a quasi-experimental design that examined 1,361 managers who received multisource feedback; 404 of those managers worked with an executive coach to review their feedback and set goals. One year later, managers who worked with an executive coach were more likely than other managers to have set specific (rather than vague) goals, solicited ideas for improvement from their supervisors, and improved more in terms of direct report and supervisor ratings. Although executive coaching had a positive effect, the effect sizes were quite small. Bowles, Cunningham, De La Rosa, and Picano (2007) reported that middle (but not executive-level) managers who volunteered to receive 8 hours of formal training followed by 6 or 7 hours of coaching outperformed (e.g., achievement of quotas) managers who had not received the training and coaching. Bowles and Picano (2006) also reported that managers who more frequently applied coaching advice delivered by an external coach reported increased work satisfaction.

Contemporary research in coaching has also sought to understand the neuroscience of coaching (e.g., Dias et al., 2016). This interest in neuroscience has been further underpinned by the publication of numerous books on the topic (e.g., Brann, 2014; Brown & Brown, 2012). Jack, Boyatzis, Khawaja, Passarelli, and Leckie (2013) used fMRI technology to explore positive emotional attractor (PEA)- and negative emotional attractor (NEA)-related responses. Their data suggested that medial prefrontal regions and the right lateral prefrontal cortex showed greater activity in PEA conditions. The authors attributed these trends to sympathetic nervous system (SNS) activity, self-trait attribution, and negative effect.

There has been a further expansion of research focused on coaching approaches in recent years. For example, Jones and Spooner (2006) explored factors influencing the practitioner's ability to coach high achievers. The authors used semistructured interviews and concluded that more novel approaches are required and the development of a coaching relationship built upon trust and mutual respect is crucial.

The number of random controlled trial studies within the coaching domain has increased substantially in the period since 2000 (Grant, 2012; Grant, Passmore, Cavanagh, & Parker, 2010). Over a similar period of time, there has also been a broad range of qualitative literature reviews published that have sought to contextualize current understanding and future directions for research (e.g., Brock, 2008; Feldman & Lankau, 2005; Grant, Passmore, Cavanagh, & Parker, 2010; Kampa-Kokesch & Anderson, 2001; Passmore & Fillery-Travis, 2011; Passmore & Gibbes, 2007). Also, with the expanding evidence base relating to coaching interventions, a number of meta-analyses have emerged in the last decade. (e.g., De Meuse, Dai, & Lee, 2009; Theeboom, Beersma, & van Vianen, 2014). These meta-analytic reviews have highlighted the increasingly evidenced outcome that coaching as an approach can be an effective "change" methodology. Theeboom et al. (2014) reported that coaching has a significant positive effect on performance and skills (.60), well-being (.46), coping (.43), goal attainment (.74), and work/career attitudes (.54). Whereas De Meuse et al. (2009), in conducting their review, questioned the usefulness of the return on investment (ROI) index as an overall measure of effectiveness.

However, although a case for coaching as a change methodology has been cited, there is also a suggestion that evidence so far might have over-estimated or interpreted the emergent results from these studies. For example, the meta-analysis conducted by Theeboom et al. (2014) has suggested that the coaching literature and (meta-analytic) estimates of overall effectiveness could have been susceptible to publication bias (an over-representation of the studies that display significant positive results in the literature). Other more recent meta-analysis papers have reported low effect size data (De Meuse et al., 2009; Jones, Woods, & Guillaume, 2015; Sonesh et al., 2015; Theeboom et al., 2014). When compared with other interventions such as counseling, which has consistently shown effect sizes of 0.6 (see Cooper, 2008 for a discussion of effect sizes in counseling), a number of questions remain about these studies and the comparison with other parallel interventions.

THE KEY FACTORS

Executive coaching is frequently used by corporations to help executives develop their capacity to deal with change and to give them support in reaching their organizational or work-related goals (Goldsmith, 2009). The existing research that explicitly explores the effects of coaching during times of organizational change tends to be qualitative or exploratory. For example, Fahy (2007) presented an exploratory case study in which a grounded theory approach was used to examine the role that executive coaching played in the development of a senior leadership team as the team managed internal change. Also, Schnell (2005) presented a detailed case study of executive coaching as a support mechanism during a period of organizational growth and evolution. While such qualitative and exploratory grounded theory approaches can give rich insights into individuals' lived experiences, they fail to provide quantitative data often favored by organizations. Ideally, both qualitative and quantitative data are needed to comprehensively develop the knowledge base. Grant's (2014) within-subject study used both quantitative and qualitative measures to explore the impact of executive coaching during a period of organizational change on 31 executives and managers from a global engineering consulting organization. Participation in the coaching was associated with increased goal attainment, enhanced solution-focused thinking, a greater ability to deal with change, increased leadership self-efficacy and resilience, and a decrease in depression. The positive impact of coaching generalized to non-work areas such as family life.

COACH FACTORS

A key focus within the coaching psychology literature has been on understanding what factors and attributes differentiate the most successful coaches. Several studies (Hall, Otazo, & Hollenbeck, 1999; Kilburg, 1996, 2001) suggest that coaches should build their practice on a bedrock of counseling psychology. There is also a view that practical feedback from both coaches and coachees is beneficial in understanding what works. Hall et al. (1999) highlighted a range of key behaviors that appeared to be important in influencing how successful these interactions are. These behaviors included challenge, listening, reflecting back key information, and checking for understanding.

More recent research has also highlighted the importance of self-awareness, coaching competence, and an understanding of the coaching relationship (e.g., Dingman, 2004; Jarvis, Lane, & Fillery-Travis, 2006). Another factor that has been highlighted is the importance of recognizing and dealing with critical moments within the coaching process (De Haan, 2008a, 2008b).

An ongoing debate within the relevant academic literature relates to the training and development of coaching practitioners. One school of thought clearly recommends a basic need for a degree in psychology (Berglas, 2002; Dean & Meyer, 2002). However, it then becomes less clear regarding what the next step should be. There are advocates of clinical training, occupational training, and counseling training (Passmore & Fillery-Travis, 2011), while others have argued for neuro-linguistic programming (NLP) or more practice-based disciplines (Linder-Pelz, 2010). In seeking to understand what the client is looking for, Wasylyshyn (2003) suggested that a mixture of the following are important factors: training in psychology; experience in, or understanding of, business; established reputation as a coach; listening skills; objectivity; and professionalism as expressed by intelligence, integrity, and confidentiality. Research by the Institute for Leadership and Management (Passmore, Palmer, & Short, 2012) suggested 10 factors that clients should consider in making their coach selection including coach experience, understanding of the leadership or organizational environment, coach qualifications and training, ethical code, and supervision.

A number of recent studies have also explored the existence of personality type differences in coaching practitioners. For example, Passmore, Holloway, and Rawle-Cope (2010) used the Myers–Briggs Type Indicator® (MBTI®) type as a way to explore practitioner difference. The authors reported that coaches were more likely to have an intuitive (N) preference rather than a sensing (S) preference. There is increasing research exploring national and cultural difference in coaching (Passmore et al., 2012; Rossinski, 2003). There are also differences highlighted between psychologist and nonpsychologist coaches. For example, Bono, Purvanova, Towler, and Peterson (2009), in their survey of 428 coaches, highlighted that those coaches who were also psychologists tended to assess competencies (how competent an individual is at a given task), whereas nonpsychologists focused more on questioning competencies (which competencies might be being displayed by the individual).

Vandaveer, Lowman, Pearlman, and Brannick (2016) conducted a professional practice analysis for the Society of Consulting Psychology (SCP) and the Society for Industrial and Organizational Psychology (SIOP) to systematically investigate and identify the domain of knowledge, skills, abilities, and personal characteristics. The main findings reported that the top "critical success" factors were coach quality, the quality of the coaching relationship, and coachee readiness.

COACHEE FACTORS

Another fruitful avenue for research in recent years has been a focus on the impact that the client (coachee) and his or her behavior can have on the coaching process. There is a clear link highlighted in associated studies that the motivation levels of the client can have a significant impact on the effectiveness of the coaching interaction (Reynolds, Caley, & Mason, 2002). The importance of the "readiness to change" of the client has also been highlighted as being a critical factor (Dawdy, 2004; Singh & Vinnicombe, 2005). Lambert and Barley (2002) have also highlighted that the client's readiness was the most significant factor in bringing about change (accounting for 40% of the variation in outcomes).

McKenna and Davis (2009) suggested that coaching professionals had overlooked potentially important psychotherapy research for underpinning interactions with coachees. In particular, the authors suggested that an understanding of client/extra-therapeutic factors is of fundamental importance. In particular, motivation, acceptance of personal responsibility to change, readiness, and coping style were highlighted. A further factor highlighted as impacting the effectiveness of the coaching interaction is the wider support network of the coachee (McKenna & Davis, 2009). However, to date, there is limited research exploring the impact that managers, peers, friends, and partners can have in the process.

COACH–COACHEE RELATIONSHIP FACTORS

A number of authors have suggested that a key factor contributing to the success of the coaching engagement is the quality of the relationship between the coach and coachee (de Haan, Grant, Burger, & Eriksson, 2016; Passmore & Fillery-Travis, 2011).

However, there continues to be limited research exploring the coach–coachee relationship. Indeed, in their review of research into the coach–coachee relationship, de Haan et al. (2016) found only nine studies exploring this area. Within this domain, a number of studies have focused on personality-related factors. For example, Wasylyshyn (2003) conducted a survey of coachees and found the highest scoring characteristic of an effective coach was the ability to form a strong connection with the client. However, this study was limited as it was based on the clients of a single coach. Some subsequent studies have explored a similar line of research (Dingman, 2004; Thach, 2002).

Scoular and Linley (2006) explored how goal setting and personality fit (in terms of MBTI type) impacted perceived effectiveness. No differences were reported based upon goal setting style, but the greater the difference in MBTI type, the greater the reported effectiveness. Stewart, Palmer, Wilkin, and Kerrin (2008) explored how coach personality (as defined by the Big Five personality traits), and coachee self-efficacy predicted coaching effectiveness in 110 coachees. They reported moderate positive effects for conscientiousness, openness, emotional stability, and self-efficacy on perceived coaching effectiveness.

Baron and Morin (2009) reported that the coaching relationship (as measured by the Working Alliance Inventory) predicted coach effectiveness in terms of changes in coachee efficacy scores in a manufacturing company. Boyce, Jackson, and Neal

(2010) specifically explored the coach–coachee relationship in the context of the U.S. Military. The authors reported that relationship processes of rapport, trust, and commitment positively predicted coaching outcomes, including client and coach reactions, behavioral change, and coaching program results. These results echo similar findings in mentoring (Ragins & Kram, 2007).

Smith and Brummel (2013) explored the relationship between three active ingredients of therapy: the therapeutic relationship; expectancy, hope, and placebo effects; and theory and technique. The results of the study suggested that all three of these ingredients were significantly related to coaching success. The authors also reported that coachees who set developmental plans were more likely to experience competency improvement.

De Hann, Duckworth, Birch, and Jones (2013) explored the impact of a range of common factors on coaches. They reported that the working alliance, coachee self-efficacy, and perceptions of the coaching intervention influenced the coachees' perception of the outcome of the coaching process.

Grant (2014) explored the impact of the following four different aspects of the coach–coachee relationship on coaching success: autonomy support, the extent to which the coachee feels satisfied with the relationship, the degree to which the coaching relationship was similar to an ideal relationship, and a goal-focused coach–coachee relationship. The results suggested that a goal-focused coach–coachee relationship was the strongest predictor of coaching success.

Gessnitzer and Kauffeld (2015) adopted a different approach analyzing the working relationship of 31 videoed coaching dyads. The authors, using an interaction analysis and questionnaire-based approach, reported that coachee- (but not coach-) initiated goals were positively related to coaching success.

De Hann, Grant, Burger, and Eriksson (2016) sought to conduct a much larger scale study collecting data from 1,895 coaching pairs from 34 countries. The authors concluded that coachee perceptions of coaching effectiveness were significantly related to both coach and coachee ratings of the strength of the working alliance, and also to coachee self-efficacy. They further reported that effectiveness was not related to personality or personality matching.

Adopting a slightly different approach, Jowett, Kanakoglou, and Passmore (2012) explored the coach–coachee relationship as it emerges in organizations. The study used semistructured interviews with five coach–coachee dyads. The results highlighted the importance of the coaching relationship.

The studies reported here represent significant variability in terms of the design, population tested, and measures used. As such, the majority offers single perspectives. While encouraging, far more research is required to explore the real impact of specific factors on the coach–coachee relationship and perceptions of effectiveness.

TRIPARTITE RELATIONSHIP AND CLIENT FACTORS

There has been a shift in recent years to research focusing on the tripartite relationship among the client, the coach, and the organization (Correia, dos Santos, & Passmore, 2016; Jarvis et al., 2006; Passmore & Fillery-Travis, 2011). However, in order to understand these interactions, more complex research designs within the field of coaching have been required (Passmore & Fillery-Travis, 2011). There has also been increasing numbers of studies that have sought to understand the impact that each of these different factors can have. A meta-analysis by De Meuse et al. (2009) sought to understand the impact reported in other studies. The authors reported that ROI reported in previous studies have been over claimed, with studies reporting up to 5.7 (McGovern et al., 2001). The true effect size on ROI corrected for sampling error in the four studies analyzed was 1.27 compared with 0.6 for the effect size in "Other raters." However, a closer examination of the data shows wide variation between 1.98 and 0.02 for "Self-rated" improvement and for "Other raters" from 1.83 to 0.06. The variability between these reported scores is considerable and subsequent meta-analysis studies have built on these results.

There is now some evidence that coaching can create sustainable impacts over 6 months (Grant, 2012), 30 weeks (Green, Oades, & Grant, 2006), and 18 months (Libri & Kemp, 2006). However, there is no evidence regarding how this can be achieved. Mann (2016), author of the Ridler Report, highlighted that there is an expectation that the use of group coaching will increase within organizations in the next 5 years. The same report also questioned whether the use of internal or external coaches was more beneficial, and what the potential implications were on the tripartite relationship (Mann, 2016).

THE ROLE OF COACHING SUPERVISION

There has been limited research to date that has sought to explicitly answer the question of whether supervision has an effect on specific outcomes. But this issue is beginning to be addressed in the literature. Hodge (2016) explored the focus of the coaching supervision process by interviewing executive coaches ($n = 6$), and coaching supervisors ($n = 5$). The results advocated supervision as a way to facilitate coaches' reflection on their practice, well-being, and effectiveness. Hawkins and Turner (2016) conducted a UK survey of 717 coaches, 76 organizational representatives, and 61 individual clients. The authors reported that most organizations want supervision, but do not insist it takes place. They also report that many clients were unaware of whether their coach had a supervisor, which suggests some issues regarding practices of contracting and disclosure of this information to the client. This view that organizations feel that supervision is important was also highlighted by Mann (2016) in the Rider Report, with 88% of organizational responders stating that supervision is a fundamental requirement for professional executive coaches.

Passmore and McGoldrick (2009) adopted a grounded theory approach in seeking to explore the perceived benefits of the supervision process. The authors reported that from a sample of UK coaches, coaches expressed a belief that supervision offered benefits to them in their coaching practice, including raising awareness about their practice, increasing confidence, encouraging perseverance, and providing a sense of belonging. The study also highlighted the challenges facing coaching supervision as a result of the growing coaching industry and the lack of trained and experienced supervisors available to offer supervision services, while at the same time coaches in the study expressed a desire for trained supervisors with relevant contextual knowledge. There remains significant variation in supervision practice between the UK and United States, and across Europe.

METHODOLOGICAL APPROACHES IN COACHING

As the research field of coaching psychology matures, there is an increasingly broad range of methodologies and approaches being employed to develop a better understanding of the field and associated approaches. It is also true that these approaches are also becoming more complex to reflect the "real-world" complexity of the coach–coachee–environment interaction.

The dominant methodological approach within the coaching research literature has been positivist in nature: seeking to employ quantitative methodologies to better understand the interactions between the coach, coachee, and the environment. Randomized control trials (RCTs) were highlighted by Passmore and Fillery-Travis (2011) as being particularly important. However, Passmore and Theeboom (2016) suggested that there (at the time of writing) were less than 50 such studies. This compares with several hundred studies in parallel areas of practice-research, such as Motivational Interviewing (MI), which has developed over a similar time frame (Miller & Rollnick, 2012), although in MI's case predominantly within a healthcare context where RCT research is recognized as the gold standard of evaluation. Indeed, Grant (2012) stated that the small numbers of RCTs represented a major shortfall in the literature on coaching efficacy. We share this view and would argue for a greater focus on RCTs through collaborations between researchers and practitioners in coaching.

From a qualitative perspective, a range of contemporary methodologies have been employed including phenomenology and grounded theory. Examples of phenomenological studies include Correia, dos Santos, and Passmore's (2016) interpretative phenomenological analysis (IPA) study exploring how coaching processes psychologically operate. From a grounded theory perspective, Passmore (2010) explored the experiences of the coachee, highlighting implications for training and practice; while Passmore and McGoldrick (2009) focused on developing a grounded theory of the efficacy of coaching supervision. Duff and Passmore (2010) also conducted a grounded theory approach to understand decision making. One of the reasons for an increasing use of qualitative methodologies in recent years is because qualitative research methods and methodologies are especially suited for studying individualized interventions such as coaching (Passmore & Theeboom, 2016).

There has been far less use of mixed methods research within the coaching domain. Recent examples, though, include the studies undertaken by Passmore and Rehman (2012). The authors adopted a mixed methods approach utilizing an RCT with 208 participants and semistructured interviews with 11 participants. Grant (2014) also adopted a mixed methods design within-subject, using both quantitative and qualitative measures to explore the impact of executive coaching during a period of organizational change on 31 executives and managers from a global engineering consulting organization.

Finally, the last few years has seen the publication of a number of meta-analyses, which suggest a maturing of the coaching literature. Examples of meta-analysis studies include De Meuse et al. (2009), Theeboom et al. (2014), Jones, Woods, and Guillaume (2015), and Sonesh et al. (2015). De Meuse et al.'s (2009) analysis highlighted an initial 22 articles, though only six of these subsequently met the inclusion criteria of (a) intervention had to be focused on executive coaching; (b) the services of an external coach were used; (c) the design included both pre- and postcoaching ratings; and (d) statistics had to be reported in the article. Theeboom et al. (2014) screened 107 articles, with 18 matching the inclusion criteria of (a) quantitative data; (b) coaches were professionally trained; (c) and coachees belonged to a nonclinical population. Jones et al. (2015) outlined 54 studies of interest, with 17 meeting the inclusion criteria: (a) adequately described the coaching activity and evaluated its effectiveness; (b) studies focused on non-work outcomes or including line management were excluded; (c) had to use within- and between-subjects designs; (d) studies had to be conducted in an organizational setting; (e) studies needed to report sample sizes; (f) the dependent variable or coaching outcomes had to be measured at the individual level of analysis. As the coaching evidence base continues to expand further, well-defined and clearly articulated meta-analyses are required to provide a more detailed overview of current knowledge and understanding.

CONCLUSION

There are still significant gaps in understanding within the coaching literature. While there have been increases in the volume and quality of coaching-focused research studies, more needs to be done. Back in 2011, Passmore and Fillery-Travis challenged the field of coaching psychology to conduct 50 to 100 large-scale studies by 2021. In terms of future research, there are a number of key questions that need to be answered and areas that require further study. Passmore and Fillery-Travis (2011) suggested six core themes: the selection of coaching as an intervention; coaching cultures and organizational change; critical features of the coaching relationship; client readiness for change; coach development (through the coaching process); and coaching as an agent for social processes. Future research in coaching needs to address these issues while developing more representative methodologies to reflect the complex nature of coach–coachee and environmental interactions.

REFERENCES

Baron, L., & Morin, L. (2009). The coach-client relationship in executive coaching: A field study. *Human Resource Development Review, 20*(1), 85–106. doi:10.1002/hrdq.20009

Berglas, S. (2002). The very real dangers of executive coaching. *Harvard Business Review, 80*(6), 86.

Bono, J., Purvanova, R., Towler, A., & Peterson, D. B. (2009). Survey of executive coach practices. *Personnel Psychology, 62,* 361–404. doi:10.1111/j.1744-6570.2009.01142.x

Bowles, S., Cunningham, C. J. L., De La Rosa, G. M., & Picano, J. (2007). Coaching leaders in middle and executive management: Goals, performance, buy-in. *Leadership and Organization Development Journal, 28,* 388–408. doi:10.1108/01437730710761715

Bowles, S. V., & Picano, J. J. (2006). Dimensions of coaching related to productivity and quality of life. *Consulting Psychology Journal: Practice and Research, 58,* 232–239. doi:10.1037/1065-9293.58.4.232

Boyce, L., Jackson, J., & Neal, L. J. (2010). Building successful leadership coaching relationships: Examining impact of matching criteria in a leadership coaching program. *Journal of Management Development, 29*(10), 914–931. doi:10.1108/02621711011084231

Brann, A. (2014). *Neuroscience for coaches.* London, England: Kogan Page.

Brock, V. G. (2008). *Grounded theory of the roots and emergence of coaching* (Doctoral dissertation). Maui, HI: International University of Professional Studies. Retrieved from http://vikkibrock.com/wp-content/uploads/2008/11/brock-grounded-theory-roots-emergence-coaching-appendices-k-t-06-05-2008-v1.pdf

Brown, P., & Brown, V. (2012). *Neuropsychology for coaches.* Maidenhead, UK: Open University Press.

Cooper, M. (2008). *Essential research findings in counseling and psychotherapy.* London, England: Sage.

Correia, M. C., dos Santos, N. R., & Passmore, J. (2016). Understanding the coach coachee-client relationship: A conceptual framework for executive coaching. *International Coaching Psychology Review, 11*(1), 6–23.

Dawdy, G. N. (2004). Executive coaching: A comparative design exploring the perceived effectiveness of coaching and methods. *Dissertation Abstract International Section B: The Sciences & Engineering, 65*(5), 2674.

Dean, M. L., & Meyer, A. A. (2002). Executive coaching: In search of a model. *Journal of Leadership Education, 1,* 1–15. doi:10.12806/V1/I2/RF1

De Haan, E. (2008a). I doubt therefore I coach—Critical moments in coaching practice. *Consulting Psychology Journal: Practice and Research, 60*(1), 91–105. doi:10.1037/1065-9293.60.1.91

De Haan, E. (2008b). I struggle and emerge—Critical moments of experienced coaches. *Consulting Psychology Journal: Practice and Research, 60*(1), 106–131. doi:10.1037/1065-9293.60.1.106

De Haan, E., Duckworth, A., Birch, D., & Jones, C. (2013). Executive coaching outcome research: The contribution of common factors such as relationship, personality match, and self-efficacy. *Consulting Psychology Journal: Practice and Research, 65,* 40–57. doi:10.1037/a0031635

De Haan, E., Grant, A. M., Burger, Y., & Eriksson, P-O. (2016). Large-scale study of executive and workplace coaching: The relative contributions of relationship, personality match, and self-efficacy. *Consulting Psychology Journal: Practice and Research, 68*(3), 189–207. doi:10.1037/cpb0000058

De Meuse, K. Dai, G., & Lee, R. (2009). Does executive coaching work: A meta-analysis study. *Coaching: An International Journal of Theory, Practice, and Research, 2*(2), 117–134.

Dias, G. P., Palmer, S., O'Riodan, S., Bastos de Freitas, S., Habib, L. R., do Nascimento Bevilaqua, M. C., & Nardi, A. E. (2015). Perspective and challenges for the study of brain responses to coaching: Enhancing the dialogue between the fields of neuroscience and coaching psychology. *The Coaching Psychologist, 11*(1), 11–20.

Dingman, M. E. (2004). *The effects of executive coaching on job-related attitudes* [Unpublished Doctoral dissertation]. Virginia Beach, VA: Regent University.

Duff, M., & Passmore, J. (2010). Coaching ethics: A decision-making model. *International Coaching Psychology Review, 5*(2), 140–151.

Duijts, S., Kant, I., Brandt, P. A., & Swaen, G. M. (2008). Effectiveness of a preventative coaching intervention for employees at risk for sickness absence due to psychosocial health complaints: Results of a randomized controlled trial. *Journal of Occupational and Environmental Medicine, 50*(7), 765–776. doi:10.1097/JOM.0b013e3181651584

Evers, W. J. G., Brouwers, A., & Tomic, W. (2006). A quasi-experimental study on management coaching effectiveness. *Consulting Psychology Journal: Practice and Research, 58*(3), 174–182. doi:10.1037/1065-9293.58.3.174

Fahy, T. P. (2007). Executive coaching as an accelerator for whole system organizational change. *Dissertation Abstracts International Section A: Humanities and Social Sciences, 68*(3-A), 1066–1067.

Feldman, D. C., & Lankau, M. J. (2005). Executive coaching: A review and agenda for future research. *Journal of Management, 31*(6), 829–848. doi:10.1177/0149206305279599

Gessnitzer, S., & Kauffeld, S. (2015). The working alliance in coaching: Why behavior is the key to success. *The Journal of Applied Behavioral Science, 51,* 177–197. doi:10.1177/0021886315576407

Goldsmith, M. (2009). Executive coaching: A real-world perspective from a real-life coaching practitioner. *International Coaching Psychology Review, 4*(1), 22–24.

Grant, A. M. (2012). The efficacy of coaching. In J. Passmore, D. Peterson, & T. Freire (Eds.) *Wiley-Blackwell handbook of the psychology of coaching and mentoring.* Chichester, England: Wiley.

Grant, A. M. (2014). Autonomy support, relationship satisfaction and goal focus in the coach-coachee relationship: Which best predicts coaching success? *Coaching: An International Journal of Theory, Research and Practice, 7*(1), 18–38.

Grant, A. M., Frith, L., & Burton, G. (2010). Executive coaching during organisational change enhances goal attainment, resilience, wellbeing: A randomised controlled study. *The Journal of Positive Psychology, 4*(5), 396–407. doi:10.1080/17439760902992456

Grant, A. M., Passmore, J., Cavanagh, M. J., & Parker, H. M. (2010). The state of play in coaching today: A comprehensive review of the field. In G. P. Hodgkinson & J. K. Ford (Eds.), *International review of industrial and organizational psychology* (Vol. 25, pp. 125–167). Oxford, UK: Wiley-Blackwell. doi:10.1002/9780470661628

Green, L. S., Oades, L. G., & Grant, A. M. (2006). Cognitive-behavioural, solution-focused life coaching: Enhancing goal striving, well-being, and hope. *The Journal of Positive Psychology, 1*(3), 143–149. doi:10.1080/17439760600619849

Hall, D. T., Otazo, K. L., & Hollenbeck, G. P. (1999). Behind closed doors: What really happens in executive coaching. *Organizational Dynamics, 27*(3), 39–53. doi:10.1016/S0090-2616(99)90020-7

Hawkins, P., & Turner, E. (2016). Coming of age: The development of coaching supervision 2006-2014. *Coaching at Work, 11*(2), 30–35.

Hodge, A. (2016). The value of coaching supervision as a development process: Contribution to continued professional and personal wellbeing for executive coaches. *International Journal of Evidence-Based Coaching and Mentoring, 14*(2), 87–106.

Jack, A. I., Boyatzis, R., Khawaja, M., Passarelli, A., & Leckie, R. (2013) Visioning in the brain: An fMRI study of inspirational coaching and mentoring. *Social Neuroscience, 8*(4), 369–384. doi:10.1080/17470919.2013.808259

Jarvis, J., Lane, D., & Fillery-Travis, A. (2006). *Does coaching work?* London, England: CIPD.

Jones, G., & Spooner, K. (2006). Coaching high achievers. *Consulting Psychology, 58*(1), 40–50. doi:10.1037/1065-9293.58.1.40

Jones, R., Woods, S., & Guillaume, Y. (2015). The effectiveness of workplace coaching: A meta-analysis of learning and performance outcomes from coaching. *Journal of Occupational and Organizational Psychology, 89,* 249–277. doi:10.1111/joop.12119

Jowett, S., Kanakoglou, K., & Passmore, J. (2012). Application of the 3+1Cs relationship model in executive coaching. *Consulting Psychology Journal: Practice and Research, 64*(3), 183–197. doi:10.1037/a0030316

Kampa-Kokesch, S., & Anderson, M. Z. (2001). Executive coaching: A comprehensive review of the literature. *Consulting Psychology Journal: Practice & Research, 53*(4), 205–228.

Kilburg, R. R. (1996). Toward a conceptual understanding and definition of executive coaching. *Consulting Psychology Journal: Practice and Research, 48*(2), 134–144. doi:10.1037/1061-4087.48.2.134

Kilburg, R. R. (2001). Facilitating intervention adherence in executive coaching: A model and methods. *Consulting Psychology Journal: Practice and Research, 53*(4), 251–267. doi:10.1037/1061-4087.53.4.251

Kombarakaran, F. A., Yang, J. A., Baker, M., & Fernandes, P. B. (2008). Executive coaching: It works! *Consulting Psychology Journal: Practice and Research, 60*(1), 78–90. doi:10.1037/1065-9293.60.1.78

Lambert, M. J., & Barley, D. E. (2002). Research summary on the therapeutic relationship and psychotherapy outcome. In J. C. Norcross (Ed.), *Psychotherapy relationships that work: Therapist contributions and responsiveness of patients.* New York, NY: Oxford University Press.

Libri, V., & Kemp, T. (2006). Assessing the efficacy of a cognitive behavioral executive coaching program. *International Coaching Psychology Review, 1*(2), 9–20.

Linder-Pelz, S. (2010). *NLP coaching: An evidenced based approach for coaches, leaders and individuals.* London, England: Kogan Page.

Luthans, F., & Peterson, S. J. (2003). 360-degree feedback with systematic coaching: Empirical analysis suggests a winning combination. *Human Resource Management, 42*(3), 243–256. doi:10.1002/hrm.10083

Mann, C. (2016). *Ridler Report.* Ridler Co. Retrieved from http://www.ridler-report.com/ridler_ecom

McKenna, D., & Davis, S. (2009). Hidden in plain sight: The active ingredients of executive coaching. *Industrial and Organizational Psychology: An Exchange of Perspectives on Science and Practice, 2*(3), 224–260. doi:10.1111/j.1754-9434.2009.01143.x

McGovern, J., Lindemann, M., Vergara, M., Murphy, S., Barker, L., & Warrenfeltz, R. (2001). Maximizing the impact of executive coaching: Behavioral change, organizational outcomes, and return on investment. *Manchester Review, 6*(1), 1–9.

Miller, W. R., & Rollnick, S. (2012). *Motivational interviewing: Helping people change applications of motivational interviewing* (3rd ed.). New York, NY: Guildford Press.

Miller, W. R., Yahne, C. E., Moyers, T. B., Martinez, J., & Pirritano, M. (2004). A randomized trial of methods to help clinicians learn Motivational Interviewing. *Journal of Consulting & Clinical Psychology, 72*(6), 1050–1062. doi:10.1037/0022-006X.72.6.1050

Olivero, G., Bane, K., & Kopelman, R.E. (1996). Executive coaching as a transfer of training tool: Effects on productivity in a public agency. *Public Personnel Management, 26*(4), 461–469. doi:10.1177/009102609702600403

Passmore, J. (2010). A grounded theory study of the coachee experience: The implications for training and practice in coaching psychology. *International Coaching Psychology Review, 5*(1), 48–62.

Passmore, J., & Fillery-Travis, A. (2011). A critical review of executive coaching research: A decade of progress and what's to come. *Coaching: An International Journal of Theory, Practice & Research, 4*(2), 70–88. doi:10.1080/17521882.2011.596484

Passmore, J., & Gibbes, C. (2007). The state of executive coaching research: What does the current literature tell us and what's next for coaching research? *International Coaching Psychological Review, 2*(2), 116–128.

Passmore, J., Holloway, M., & Rawle-Cope, M. (2010). Using MBTI type to explore differences and the implications for practice for therapists and coaches. Are executive coaches really like counselors? *Counselling Psychology Quarterly, 23*(1), 1–16. doi:10.1080/09515071003679354

Passmore, J., & McGoldrick, S. (2009). Super-vision, extra-vision or blind faith? A grounded theory study of the efficacy of coaching supervision. *International Coaching Psychology Review, 4*(2), 143–159.

Passmore, J., Palmer, S., & Short, E. (2012). The Coaching Census—Building an understanding of coaching and coaching psychology practice in the UK. *Coaching Psychology International, 3*(2), 3–4.

Passmore, J., & Rehman, H. (2012). Coaching as a learning methodology–a mixed methods study in driver development–a Randomised controlled trial and thematic analysis. *International Coaching Psychology Review, 7*(2), 166–184.

Passmore, J., & Theeboom, T. (2016). Coaching psychology: A journey of development in research. In L. E. Van Zyl, M. W. Stander, & A. Oodendal (Eds.), *Coaching psychology: Meta-theoretical perspectives and applications in multi-cultural contexts* (pp. 27–46). New York, NY. Springer Publishing.

Ragins, B. R., & Kram, K. E. (Eds.) (2007). *The handbook of mentoring at work: Theory, research, and practice.* Thousand Oaks, CA: Sage.

Reynolds, J., Caley, L., & Mason, R. (2002). *How do people learn?* (Research report). London, England: CIPD.

Rossinski, P. (2003). *Coaching across cultures: New tools for leveraging national, corporate and professional differences.* London, England: Nicolas Brealey.

Scoular, A., & Linley, P. A. (2006). Coaching, goal-setting and personality type: What matters? *The Coaching Psychologist, 2,* 9–11.

Schnell, E. R. (2005). A case study of executive coaching as a support mechanism during organizational growth and evolution. *Consulting Psychology Journal: Practice and* Research, *57*(1), 41–56. doi:10.1037/1065-9293.57.1.41

Singh, V., & Vinnicombe, S. (2005, February). Creating momentum. *Public Service Review.*

Smith, I. M., & Brummel, B. J. (2013). Investigating the role of the active ingredients in executive coaching. *Coaching: An International Journal of Theory, Research and Practice, 6,* 57–71. doi:10.10 80/17521882.2012.758649

Smither, J. W., London, M., Flautt, R., Vergas, Y., & Kucine, I. (2003). Can working with an executive coach improve multisource feedback ratings over time? A quasi-experimental field study. *Personnel Psychology, 56,* 23–44. doi:10.1111/j.1744-6570.2003.tb00142.x

Sonesh, S., Coultas, C. W., Lacerenza, C. N., Marlow, S. L., Benishek, L. E., & Salas, E. (2015). The power of coaching: A meta-analytic investigation. *Coaching: An International Journal of Theory, Practice & Research, 8*(2), 73–95. doi:10.1080/17521882.2015.1071418

Stewart, L. J., Palmer, S., Wilkin, H., & Kerrin, M. (2008). The influence of character: Does personality impact coaching success? *International Journal of Evidence Based Coaching and Mentoring, 6*, 32–42.

Thach, E. C. (2002). The impact of executive coaching and 360 feedback on leadership effectiveness. *Leadership and Organization Development Journal, 23*(4), 205–214. doi:10.1108/01437730 210429070

Theeboom, T., Beersma, B., & van Vianen, A. E. (2014). Does coaching work? A meta-analysis on the effects of coaching on individual level outcomes in an organizational context. *The Journal of Positive Psychology, 9(1)*, 1–18. doi:10.1080/17439760.2013.837499

Vandaveer, V. V., Lowman, R. L., Pearlman, K., & Brannick, J. P. (2016). A practice analysis of coaching psychology: Toward a foundational competency model. *Counselling Psychology Journal: Practice and Research, 68*(2), 118–142. doi:10.1037/cpb0000057

Wasylyshyn, K. M. (2003). Executive coaching: An outcome study. *Consulting Psychology Journal: Practice and Research, 55*(2), 94–106. doi:10.1037/1061-4087.55.2.94

II

Core Considerations in Coaching

7

Ethics and the Professional Coach: Challenges and Best Practices

Patrick Williams

I n order to write a chapter for coaching and ethics in the global environment, one must be both generic and specific. There are principles of personal and professional ethics driven by common historical standards and ideals, and others specifically created for the profession of coaching. In this chapter, ethics is explored in both the historical context generally and in the professional context specifically. The historical contributions and challenges faced by the major coaching associations as they seek to uphold ethical practices for the profession are summarized. Then, after a review of the common ethical principles and guidelines, case studies to consider are offered. Finally, I commentary on privacy considerations when using the Internet is presented.

When I coedited *Law and Ethics of Coaching: How to Solve and Avoid Difficult Problems in Your Practice* in 2006, there were no other books on ethics in coaching. Now the profession has dozens of resources. These resources are especially important when ethical breeches by members, brought by consumers or colleagues, are being considered by an association's review board.

EVOLUTION OF A PROFESSION: COMPETENCIES, CREDENTIALING, AND ETHICS

As the profession of coaching has grown globally, its evolution includes a body of knowledge, evidence-based competencies, and ethical standards. These are necessary ingredients to be considered a true profession. The International Coach Federation (ICF), the largest association for coaches, and other established coaching organizations around the globe offer a place of community and training for members, but they also serve the role of creating the standards of competency and forming ethical guidelines and ethical review procedures.

The most visible coaching organizations worldwide that have ethical conduct standards are:

International Coach Federation (ICF)

European Mentoring and Coaching Council (EMCC)

Association for Coaching (AC)

International Association of Coaching (IAC)

Worldwide Association of Business Coaches (WABC)

Association for Professional Executive Coaching and Supervision (APECS)

Center for Credentialing and Education (CCE)

But if a coach is not a member of an association, there exists little recourse for any discipline or ethical mentoring or training. The dilemma in keeping coaching as an unlicensed profession is the fact that there exist no legal limits as to who is called a coach. Ideally, the buying public will become aware of what credentials and ethical practices to seek in someone they hire.

A problem develops when professional membership organizations connect credentialing to membership. The service of certification becomes monetized, creating a potential conflict of interest. I believe that, if coaching is to be a *profession* and not an industry, it would be better served to have certification of coaches done by a body separate from the membership organization. A more recent player in the field for creating a credential and a review process that is objective and solely involved in assessment of competencies with a testing and credentialing procedure is the Center for Credentialing and Education, which created the Board-Certified Coach credential in 2010. Also enhancing the body of knowledge, evidence, and credibility of this evolving profession are dozens of graduate schools that offer degrees or certificates in coaching as well as the growth of coach-specific research. All of this bodes well for a strong global profession to be highly regarded and self-regulated.

Coaching will, in addition, develop case law and references from the small percentage of coaches that will be sued or challenged in court for unethical behavior. This is how all professions evolve and distinguish professionals from unscrupulous opportunists. The decisions of ethical review boards will add to this body of knowledge. Not everyone reviewed by Ethical Review Boards will be found in breach of ethics but there must be a process to review any customer complaints. Being reviewed or interviewed by an ethics review board does not necessarily mean there has been an ethical breach; rather, this is sometimes a process for educating, clarifying, and informing both the coach and the complainant.

Ethics is usually a case of critical and informed thinking, but there will always be gray areas and the more case studies are available as examples, the more they are helpful. In the end, I believe the profession will gain the most credibility from coaches academically trained in both the art and science of coaching.

ETHICS IN A HISTORICAL VIEW

We can look back to the early theories of ethics from Socrates, Aristotle, and later Kant and others having to do with general moral and ethical behaviors for humans. And then, as businesses and professions began to evolve, there was the ethical practice of trades and professional societies (accountants, lawyers, etc.). These early considerations on ethics can be viewed as setting the stage for our current ethical guidelines (Carroll & Shaw, 2013). Five sources of ethical standards are commonly identified.

THE UTILITARIAN APPROACH

Some ethicists emphasize that the ethical action is the one that provides the most good or does the least harm, or, to put it another way, produces the greatest balance of good over harm. The ethical corporate action, then, is the one that produces the greatest good and does the least harm for all who are affected: customers, employees, shareholders, the community, and the environment. The utilitarian approach deals with consequences; it tries both to increase the good done and to reduce the harm done.

THE RIGHTS APPROACH

Other philosophers and ethicists suggest that the ethical action is the one that best protects and respects the moral rights of those affected. This approach starts from the belief that humans have a dignity based on their human nature per se or on their ability to choose freely what they do with their lives. On the basis of such dignity, they have a right to be treated as ends and not merely as means to other ends. Also, it is often said that rights imply duties—in particular, the duty to respect others' rights.

THE FAIRNESS OR JUSTICE APPROACH

Aristotle and other Greek philosophers have contributed the idea that all equals should be treated equally. Today we use this idea to say that ethical actions treat all human beings equally, or if unequally, then fairly based on some standard that is defensible. We pay people more based on their harder work or the greater amount that they contribute to an organization, and say that is fair. But there is a debate over

CEO salaries that are hundreds of times larger than the pay of others; many ask whether the huge disparity is the result of an imbalance of power and hence is unfair.

THE COMMON GOOD APPROACH

The Greek philosophers have also contributed the notion that life in community is a good in itself and our actions should contribute to that life. This approach suggests that the interlocking relationships of society are the basis of ethical reasoning and that respect and compassion for all others, especially the vulnerable, are requirements of such reasoning. This approach also calls attention to the common conditions that are important to the welfare of everyone.

THE VIRTUE APPROACH

A very ancient approach to ethics is that ethical actions ought to be consistent with certain ideal virtues that provide for the full development of our humanity. These virtues are dispositions and habits that enable us to act according to the highest potential of our character and on behalf of values like truth and beauty. Honesty, courage, compassion, generosity, tolerance, love, fidelity, integrity, fairness, self-control, and prudence are all examples of virtues. Virtue ethics asks of any action, "What kind of person will I become if I do this?" or "Is this action consistent with my acting at my best?" (Markkula Center for Applied Ethics, 2017).

Putting the Approaches Together

Each of these approaches helps us determine what standards of behavior can be considered ethical. There are still problems to be solved, however. For example, we may not agree on the content of some of these specific approaches such as human and civil rights. We may not agree on what constitutes the common good. We may not even agree on what is good and what is harm (Markkula Center for Applied Ethics, 2017). Further, different approaches may not all answer the question "What is ethical?" in the same way. Nonetheless, each approach gives us important information with which to determine what is ethical in a particular circumstance. Much more often than not, the different approaches do lead to similar answers.

MAKING DECISIONS

Making ethical decisions requires a trained sensitivity and a practiced method for weighing the considerations that should impact our course of action. When practiced regularly, the method becomes so familiar that we work through it automatically. The more novel and difficult the ethical choice we face, the more we need to rely on discussion and dialogue with others. Only by careful exploration of the problem, aided by the insights and different perspectives of others, can we make good ethical choices.

CRITICAL HISTORY IN THE DEVELOPMENT OF THE COACHING PROFESSION

To become a recognized profession, coaching must have professional standards, definitions, ethical guidelines, ongoing research, and credentialing. Beginning in the early 1990s, the coaching phenomenon saw the creation of several coach training schools and the creation of two major professional associations. In 1996, the Professional Coaching and Mentoring Association merged with the ICF, and the ICF led the way as the most recognized international association representing the coaching profession. Standards of practice, credentialing, and ethical guidelines were created. The goal was to maintain the profession of coaching as self-regulated.

Other organizations outside North America made efforts to create a global conversation about what was needed for coaching to be recognized as a profession with accepted standards of competencies, practice, and ethics. The Global Convention on Coaching at the Dublin Conference of 2008 began with the question: What's possible for coaching? This began a global dialogue with Europe, Australasia, South America, and North America

In addition to ethical guidelines, professional competencies, and certification, the coaching profession is witnessing a tremendous growth in academic research and graduate studies. This is a critical step. Research and training are necessary for developing a field of knowledge, theoretical orientations, and efficacy studies. Research on effectiveness and distinctions of skill sets and competencies, and the standardization of education and training is tantamount to any profession finding its place of acceptance in the private and corporate culture.

Historically, other major professions like psychology and counseling have written codes of ethics and professional standards. In addition, they typically are regulated by state licensing boards (at least in the United States) and government regulations. These government regulations usually deal with required training, practice laws, and legal requirements for maintaining a license. At this time, coaching is not regulated or monitored by a state agency or regulatory board. It is the current belief that the profession must monitor itself. However, some state mental-health regulatory boards think differently, as the following scenario demonstrates.

THE COLORADO CASE AND THE THREAT TO PRACTICING COACHES

In June 2001, the administrator of the Colorado Mental Health Board, Amos Martinez, wrote an opinion piece in the board newsletter entitled "Coaching: Is This Psychotherapy?" In this article, Martinez raised the idea that coaching, especially personal coaching, met the very broad definition of psychotherapy in the state of Colorado. Because of that interpretation, word began to spread that coaches in Colorado had to register as "unlicensed psychotherapists" and follow the regulations in the state's Mental Health Act that pertained to those individuals.

Immediately after reading that newsletter, Dr. Lloyd Thomas and I (Patrick Williams), both of us licensed psychologists and practicing coaches, drove to Denver and met with Dr. Martinez in an attempt to educate him and the board about professional coaching, the ICF, and standards of ethics. The meeting was cordial and Dr. Martinez sounded appreciative, but nothing changed in the next several months. The rumor began to spread across the globe that Colorado was "going after" coaches and that the profession was in danger of being lumped together with psychotherapy, a distinction most coaches were trying to clarify.

In the summer of 2002, the ICF Board of Directors chartered the Regulatory Committee with Patrick Williams (this author) and Diane Brennan as co-chairs. The goal was to research, monitor, evaluate, and proactively contribute to U.S. government and regulatory bodies in order to educate, articulate, and develop the growing coaching profession into a self-regulated profession.

In 2003, a case against a Colorado coach brought this discussion and the legal intrusion on the profession to a head. An ICF Master-Certified Coach who lived and worked in Colorado was charged with practicing psychotherapy without a license by the Department of Regulatory Agencies in Colorado. Although the charge was dropped as frivolous, Colorado was still forcing the coach to register as an unlicensed therapist which she refused to do. Hence, she closed her practice because she could not afford to hire an attorney to pursue the defense of her position.

That case led to a focused effort by the Colorado Coalition of Coaches to pursue changing the law, and the group hired a lobbyist to help with the effort. After 18 months of hard work by the Colorado Coalition and the lobbyist as well as grassroots support and donations by individual coaches, the ICF, the IAC, the WABC, and the Association of Coach Training Organizations (ACTO), the legislature agreed and approved an amendment to the Mental Health Act that exempted coaching from the legislature's oversight. Because coaching is an international profession, the ICF also began conversations about, and research on, any regulatory concerns or issues in other countries, but these concerns and issues have not warranted the same worldwide attention as those in the United States. The proliferation of government licensing and regulation of various professions seems to be unique to the United States. However, I want to point out here the importance of cultural sensitivity with regard to ethics. In reviewing the ethical guidelines of all the major professional bodies noted in the beginning of this chapter, the standards are all remarkably similar (Brennan & Wildflower, 2014)

ONGOING REGULATORY CHALLENGES AND ETHICAL MATURITY

The ongoing challenge continues to be how to distinguish the various niches of coaching (e.g., life and wellness coaching, relationship coaching, and health coaching) and how to distinguish coaching from the other helping professions. And yet, we all know that professional coaching uses some of the same skill sets and tools that arose from psychotherapy and counseling, but are applied in a different context. Skills, such as focused listening, rapport building, empathy, presence, evocative inquiry, and goal creation and planning are part of many other professions as well. Consultants, for example, are not licensed or regulated in most cases, and yet that profession, albeit contextually different from coaching, does not seem to attract the same level of scrutiny as does coaching from the various government agencies that regulate mental health services and from the professions of therapy and counseling, that may feel territorially threatened. One can find distinctions between coaching and therapy or counseling on the ICF website (International Coach Federation, 2017).

In my review of the current literature on ethics and coaching or other helping professions, there is wise guidance that ethical maturity and development come from training, practice development, collegial consultation, and continual critical thinking due to the individual uniqueness of what may arise in your role as a coach. In *Ethical Maturity in the Helping Professions: Making Difficult Life and Work Decisions,* Carroll and Shaw (2013) note strategies (p. 60) to save ourselves from being unethical:

- Do not think *I,* think *we.*
- Consider issues of power, domination, and privilege.
- Ask yourself if you would recommend what you are about to do.
- Try to look at the behavior, not the intention.
- Ask yourself how this might be perceived from the other's point of view.

AN ETHICAL FRAMEWORK FOR DECISION MAKING

I find the following framework for ethical decision making useful for exploring ethical dilemmas and choosing ethical actions. This framework is the product of dialogue and debate at the Markkula Center for Applied Ethics at Santa Clara University. It was last revised in May 2009. More information can be found on the Markkula Center website.

RECOGNIZE AN ETHICAL ISSUE

1. Could this decision or situation be damaging to someone or to some group? Does this decision involve a choice between a good and bad alternative, or perhaps between two "goods" or between two "bads"?

2. Is this issue about more than what is legal or what is most efficient? If so, how?

GET THE FACTS

1. What are the relevant facts of the case? What facts are not known? Can I learn more about the situation? Do I know enough to make a decision?

2. What individuals and groups have an important stake in the outcome? Are some concerns more important? Why?

3. What are the options for acting? Have all the relevant persons and groups been consulted? Have I identified creative options?

EVALUATE ALTERNATIVE ACTIONS

1. Evaluate the options by asking the following questions:

    - Which option will produce the most good and do the least harm? (The Utilitarian Approach)

    - Which option best respects the rights of all who have a stake? (The Rights Approach)

    - Which option treats people equally or proportionately? (The Justice Approach)

    - Which option best serves the community as a whole and not just some members? (The Common Good Approach)

    - Which option leads me to act as the sort of person I want to be? (The Virtue Approach)

MAKE A DECISION AND TEST IT

1. Considering all these approaches, which option best addresses the situation?

2. If I told someone whom I respect, or told a television audience, which option I have chosen, what would they say?

ACT AND REFLECT ON THE OUTCOME

1. How can my decision be implemented with the greatest care and attention to the concerns of all stakeholders?

2. How did my decision turn out and what have I learned from this specific situation?

A SIMPLE AND USEFUL VIEW OF ETHICAL DECISION MAKING: A LESSON FROM ROTARY

When we think of ethics, we may get lost in legalistic discussions of rules, rubrics, and detailed guidelines of how professionals should behave. Important as these are, simplifying the approach may help make the application of ethics easier and more practical. The first ethical standard embraced by the ICF is, "I will conduct myself in a manner that reflects well on coaching as a profession and I will refrain from doing anything that harms the public's understanding or acceptance of coaching as a profession." This standard and those that follow it should really be common sense, but as busy and distracted humans, reminders can help.

One of the world's most widely printed and quoted statements of business ethics is the Four-Way Test (Rotary International, n.d.), which was created in 1932 by

Rotarian Herbert J. Taylor (who later served as Rotary International president) when he was asked to take charge of a company that was facing bankruptcy.

Is it the *truth*?

Is it *fair* to all concerned?

Will it build *good will* and *better friendships*?

Will it be *beneficial* to all concerned?

The following coaching scenario exemplifies the application of ethical standard and illustrates use of the Four-Way Test of Rotary International.

Coach Carl has been coaching Client Carol for 3 months when Carol asks Carl if he has experience with reviewing business and marketing plans. She is at the point of her business where she feels she needs a coach or consultant to assist in the method and details required of such a formalized document. Carl is a competent life coach and has helped Carol immensely in designing her life and business to be more fulfilling, to have more balance over her time, and to delegate more in her business. However, Carl has neither formal experience nor training in designing business or marketing plans.

As an ethical coach, Carl tells Carol the *truth,* that while he can help her get clearer on her vision and long-term desired outcomes for her business, he would refer her to a business consultant who specializes in drafting business plans. He tells her that he can give her some referrals and encourages her to ask around in her community. Carl honestly tells her that even if she needs to stop the coaching relationship for a time so that she can focus her time and resources with a new consultant, it would be okay with him. His *fair* approach is to add that it is her decision if she can afford the time and money for both coaching and a business consultant. But, he says, his goal for her is to get what she wants and he does not have the specific expertise for what she is requesting. Carol thanks him and asks for referrals and says she will also ask around in her local group. Carl's actions create a stronger *friendship* with Carol and are *beneficial* not only to her and to his reputation as a coach, but they also build good will with the business consultants he recommends.

This approach by Carl is also a clear example of several of the ICF ethical standards regarding being honest about level of competence and not implying outcomes that the coach cannot guarantee. In the following case studies, observe how the application of the Four-Way Test and the other strategies and frameworks described in this chapter can impact your coaching effectiveness.

ETHICAL CASE STUDIES: WHAT TO KNOW AND DO TO AVOID "STICKY SITUATIONS"

These case studies are "sticky situations." Choose a code of ethics from one of the coaching associations and consider how you would handle each situation. What behaviors are questionable from an ethical point of view? What parts of the code of ethics apply to this issue? What would be your course of action?

CASE STUDY: THE NEW COACH

You are a relatively new coach who for the past year has regularly taken free online courses that claim to address professional coaching skills and provide participant group discussions about how best to coach clients. You have completed college, having earned a degree in English with a minor in television and film. You were drawn to coaching because of your fascination with people and what makes them tick. You began actually coaching people in a one-to-one format about 6 months ago, and you started to charge money for your services last month. You keep handwritten notes of your client sessions in a spiral-bound notebook that you keep in the bookshelf behind your desk for easy access. As you have gained more clients, you've begun noticing how hard it is to keep straight what each client expects to accomplish. On occasion, you've even accidentally written notes about one client in the section reserved for someone else (Williams & Anderson, 2006).

CASE STUDY: PRESSURE FROM ABOVE

The owner of a local company has engaged you to coach new Manager A. A very talented and effective individual contributor, Manager A has found the transition to management quite difficult at times. The owner believes that with some coaching, Manager A will make a fine leader. The owner makes it clear to you that she expects regular updates on Manager A's coaching and how he is responding. You have noticed that during the last two update sessions with the company owner, she has started pressing you for details regarding what Manager A has disclosed during your coaching sessions, stating that, "I just want to help. How can I help him if I don't know what his issues are?" Up until now, you've managed to successfully deflect her most pointed questions, but in today's session, she told you point blank that she wants you to give Manager A "a Myers–Briggs® test so that I can get a handle on this guy." She makes it clear that she expects you to share the results with her, stating, "I'm paying, so I'm playing!" You are not trained to administer the Myers–Briggs Type Indicator and what's more, you are not sure you will be able to avoid the owner's pointed requests for details of your coaching sessions much longer (Williams & Anderson, 2006).

CASE STUDY: LAYERS OF THE ONION

The CEO of a large corporation has retained you to enhance the performance of the Senior VP. Up until now, this VP has risen quickly through the organization, and came to the company with a demonstrated track record of incredible success. The CEO has noticed that her authoritarian management style, lack of empathy for other members of the organization, and lack of self-awareness have created havoc on the leadership team. He expects you to give him regular updates on how the coaching is going, as well as your periodic assessment of how the VP is responding to the coaching. During your most recent coaching session with the VP, she has shared with you that her marriage is floundering, and she feels an enormous sense of guilt that she spends very little time with her two young children. You also have begun to sense that she may have some issues with depression and anxiety, caused not only by her personal issues, but also by concerns she has voiced about being able to hit this quarter's sales goals. She has also confided that, to help cope, she has begun drinking more than she used to, including at lunch and behind closed doors in her office (Williams & Anderson, 2006).

CASE STUDY: COACHING AND PERSONAL ATTRACTION: STAYING OUT OF HOT WATER

Megan meets Derek at a networking event and gets excited about being coached by him. She really feels understood and believes he can help her in her business start-up. As her life begins to feel more energized and she feels full of passion for her work and her life, she also realizes she is feeling a personal attraction to Derek every time they meet. She believes after a few sessions that her business is on track but she likes spending time with Derek. She gets up the courage to share that with him; he feels similarly so they agree to end the coaching relationship and begin dating. Is this ethical or not? What assists in your critical thinking?

SIX DEGREES OF SEPARATION DILEMMA

Your coaching business has been growing steadily but the administration of your business is taking up too much time and energy from what you really love to do—coach. One day at the car wash, you see a business card for a virtual assistant (VA) and decide to try it out. You contact the VA who tells you how it works, what the fee is, and promises to send you a contract. She never mentions confidentiality and you never ask. You sign and mail the contract and once you start working with the VA you notice an immediate improvement to your business. It's hard to believe how much more focused you are now that you don't have to spend your time and effort on the administrative part of your business. A couple of months later, while trying to close a contract with a new sponsor company, the VP of HR discusses the company's confidentiality policy regarding coaching and asks you what your policy is. She states that she's extra aware now because her sister-in-law, who's a VA in your state, has shared some client stories and mentioned names that the VP recognized as their competitor's CFO and product manager. You explain your confidentiality policy and promise that nothing like that would ever happen with you. You add that as a member of the ICF, you uphold the highest ethical standards in coaching and that probably the other coach did not have as much experience as yourself in the business. Out of curiosity you casually ask who the VA is and to your horror, she mentions the name of your VA as well as the competitor's names of the CFO and product manager, both of whom are your clients (courtesy of the ICF Ethics & Standard Education Committee).

REFLECTIONS ON ONLINE SHARING AND SOCIAL MEDIA IN COACHING

All coaches should be aware of the pitfalls of online or Internet communication. For example, when I contract with corporate or government employees, I always ask what email they prefer me to use and which phone number as well. Our email communication is usually minimal unless the client has agreed to receive a report or data that may be shared with superiors as necessary or appropriate. And what about private clients who contract with you and pay with their own money? Both types of contracted clients need to know the safe and secure ways to communicate as email is not always safe, and some other methods, such as Skype, LinkedIn, and others, should be used cautiously. A good source of information about encryption, firewalls, and how to safely communicate in an online environment can be found on a website created by Kate Anthony and DeeAnna Nagel (Anthony & Nagel, 2017). This is a comprehensive site for ethical decision making and for developing an awareness related to the online or virtual environment of client services.

REFERENCES

Anthony, K., & Nagel, D. (2017). Ethical framework for the use of technology in coaching. *Online Therapy Institute.* Retrieved from http://onlinetherapyinstitute.com/ethical-framework-for -the-use-of-technology-in-coaching

Brennan, D., & Wildflower, L. (2014). Ethics in coaching. In E. Cox, T. Bachkirova, & D. Clutterbuck (Eds.), *The complete handbook of coaching* (2nd ed.). London, England: Sage.

Carroll, M., & Shaw, E. (2013). *Ethical maturity in the helping professions: Making difficult life and work decisions.* London, England: Jessica Kingsley.

International Coach Federation. (2017). Retrieved from https://coachfederation.org

Markkula Center for Applied Ethics. (2017). *A framework for ethical decision making.* Santa Clara, CA: Markkula Center. Retrieved from https://www.scu.edu/ethics/ethics-resources

Rotary International. (n.d.). Guiding principles: The Four-Way Test. Retrieved from https:// my.rotary.org/en/guiding-principles

Williams, P., & Anderson, S. (2006). *Law and ethics in coaching: How to solve and avoid difficult problems in your practice.* Hoboken, NJ: John Wiley & Sons.

8

Managing "Invisible" Cultural Issues to Create Partnerships That Work

Edmée Schalkx

In one of my first sessions after becoming a certified mentor coach, an American coach shared the frustrations she was experiencing with one of her coachees: "I am upset. I worked for almost 3 months with a French coachee, supporting him in finding a new job outside his current company because he did not like the company. And now he is telling me he accepted a promotion in that same company." In her opinion, the 3 months of work they had done together were a lost opportunity for the coachee. In her view, the coachee was compromising by accepting this position rather than moving forward. I asked her what she knew about the coachee and French culture. She told me that she knew very little. The subject of culture had never come up in their conversations. I was surprised. I wonder if the coach had been curious and had asked questions about French culture, would she have a different opinion about her coachee's decision?

As a third-culture child when growing up, and as an anthropologist and a professional coach, I approach my work with managers, organizations, and employees from a framework of safety, trust, and presence. This chapter covers the question of what is culture, how to create an ideal meeting space, and the areas of consideration when coaching and managing from this perspective.

I have always been fascinated by culture. I was born in Venezuela, to Dutch parents, although my mother was born in Indonesia. I attended a Venezuelan Catholic school where we spoke Spanish. Many of the students were also Venezuelans of Italian, Portuguese, or Spanish descent. But as soon as I left my Venezuelan school at 4 p.m., I became a Dutch girl in a Dutch world. At home we spoke Dutch, we ate Dutch food, and we were ruled by Dutch norms, values, and traditions (Sinterklaas, n.d.). Our family moved in very international circles. Many weekends were spent with the children of our parents' friends—Belgians, Dutch, Germans, Canadians, Polish, Norwegian, British. . . and we spoke a mix of English, Dutch, and Spanish. I realize now that I was brought up "between" cultures.

At the age of 8, my parents bought the entire set of *Encyclopedia Britannica*, all 24 volumes. As a bonus, they received a copy of *The Epic of Man*, a *Life* Magazine book about the evolution of man. I would spend hours with this big book on my lap, looking through the wonderful paintings and reading the short stories that accompanied them. From that moment, I knew I wanted to become an anthropologist. Before I even knew what culture was, I already knew it would be an important part of my future—part of who I am and what I do.

WHAT IS CULTURE?

In the words of anthropologist E. B. Tylor, culture is "that complex whole which includes knowledge, belief, art, morals, law, custom and any other capabilities and habits acquired by man as a member of society" (Tylor, 1907, p. 1785). Gilbert and Rosinski (2008) define culture as the features that make it possible to differentiate one group from another. According to Hofstede (1991), culture is an internal process that exhibits itself in the form of the obvious: artifacts, language, body gestures, social habits, and literature.

Within cultures there are subcultures—a cultural group within a larger culture, often having beliefs or interests different to those of the larger culture. Think of HispanoAmericans or Jewish American populations. Expatriates in a specific country can serve as a singular culture when considered as a large group or as distinct cultures by country. Different age or gender groups constitute different cultures and within those can be found further cultures; that is, a group of third-culture young men who identify as either punks, hardcore punks, or rappers. Companies have their own culture but it is possible that there are also differences among departments, which create their own subcultures.

I believe that the personality of an individual is partly made up of his or her cultural background: norms, values, beliefs, underlying assumptions, interests, experiences, upbringing, and habits that create a person's behavior. After high school, I went to Cambridge, UK, to study English. Afterward, there was a long waiting list to be accepted into the anthropology department, so I decided to study anthropology at the American University in Washington, DC, which led to pursuing a Masters in Cultural Anthropology at the London School of Economics. Soon after graduating I landed a job as an expert for the United Nations Development Programme (UNDP) and the International Labour Organization (ILO) in Honduras, Costa Rica, and Guatemala where people saw me as a hybrid, Latin-Dutch woman. As we were all from Latin America, I understood them, they understood me. My last assignment for ILO was in Italy, where I had a different life than the one I knew before. I was a single Dutch woman, and it seemed like my landlord adopted me with the signing of the contract. I often explained I was Venezuelan, I spoke Italian with a Spanish accent. The Italians saw me only as a smart Dutch lady who could speak many languages, which "of course all Dutch do." After I completed my work with the United Nations, I relocated to the Netherlands with the intention of securing a job somewhere else. I had known that the Netherlands was my parents' country, not mine.

For years I lived like I was just passing through, on my way to somewhere else. I was still working internationally, but my home base was Holland. I had never previously struggled with international moves, but I quickly found that living in my "home country" was unnatural. For the first time, people expected things from me: behave like them, talk like them, live like them. I look Dutch, I have a Dutch surname, and my parents were Dutch. So why was it so difficult to conform to life here and be Dutch?

At one point, I decided to work with a business coach to help me set up my business. In retrospect, even though I liked her very much, in some ways she oversimplified things. I now know why the program did not work: We were living in two very different worlds. She was not listening nor understanding my comments on how I felt like an outsider in the Netherlands. She knew my history, but even so, she was not able to connect to what I was feeling. She failed to create a *safe* and *trusting meeting space* where we could talk as two individuals with a different set of norms, beliefs, values, experiences, and perspectives. My coach, as well as the coach of the French coachee mentioned at the start of this chapter, had little exposure to working outside the United States, and missed the importance of the coachee's background and challenges.

WHEN WE LACK CULTURAL AWARENESS

With globalization and technological advances, such as the Internet and web-meeting platforms, people are crisscrossing through cultures all the time and are rarely aware of it. Coaches are increasingly using the Internet as their workspace to coach people from all over the world. While this has opened the door of opportunity for our businesses, it has also uncovered issues of which many coaches are not fully cognizant and are struggling to adapt.

If culture is an environmentally derived set of norms, values, and beliefs that strongly influence personality, then people, especially coaches, who work across cultures must develop a certain level of cultural sensitivity. When working with individuals from diverse backgrounds, there is a greater need to consider the impact of people's beliefs, norms, values, background, and experiences, including our own. Only then can we engage in a coaching relationship of equal partnership based on trust and safety.

Let's return to our French coachee: He spent a lot of money and energy working with his coach to assist him in his quest for the perfect job. When his employer offers him a promotion, he accepts it without much consideration of the work he has done with the coach. Why?

When I asked the coach what she thought had happened, although she had not asked the coachee directly, she assumed that the coachee lacked courage to pursue a career he really wanted and had chosen the "easy" way out. If she had dug deeper, she might have discovered other reasons for him to make the decision he did. If she had extended her questions to cover his cultural background, values, and beliefs, she might have uncovered very different motivations. In France, like in Japan, traditionally people do not tend to job-hop the way they do in the United States. Culturally, longevity is seen as loyalty. Employers perceive people working for the same company for long periods of time as loyal and trustworthy individuals. Employees get benefits when they have long working engagements. Had the coach been aware of this fact, the relationship could have developed in a very different tone. The coach could have asked the coachee how aware he was of the fact that he was accepting a new position in the same company for reasons of loyalty rather than the fulfillment of a new career.

CREATING THE IDEAL MEETING SPACE

Schein (2010) defines coaching as the behavior of the coach that helps the client find a new way of seeing, feeling, and behaving toward a troubling situation. The International Coach Federation (ICF, n.d.-b) defines coaching as partnering with coachees in a thought-provoking and creative process that inspires them to maximize their personal and professional potential. When attempting to use coaching in organizations to create culture change, Schein (2010) points out that culture change involves changing shared values and group behaviors when coaching is best used to change individual values and behaviors. This is a very interesting evaluation of how culture and coaching operate next to each other. Therefore, coaches and managers need to be aware when dealing with organizational cultural issues that they also need to look at the effect on the staff. As an example, similarly to a coach, a manager needs to keep both the individual cultural realities and the greater organizational culture in mind.

At the heart of coaching is a legitimate meeting. It is true that coaching offers tools, models, a language, and a worldview—yet it is the human connection, unfolding in the meeting space between coach and coachee, that is the most important factor for the success of coaching (Buber, 1958).

In a coaching relationship, the coach should be fully conscious, creating a spontaneous and intimate relationship with the coachee, and employing a style that is open, flexible, and confident. For this to occur, the coaches must be aware of their personal norms, values, and beliefs (including biases) so they can create a safe and trusting meeting space where coachees feel respected and considered an equal with their own norms, values, beliefs, and biases.

We all have a *set of norms* (standards of proper or acceptable behavior). These norms start to be embedded at birth and are ingrained within us during our developmental years. Family, environment, social status, and gender play a role in shaping these norms. These norms along with our religious beliefs and accepted social truths, form our personality. The *values* (commonly held beliefs about what is considered desirable and proper) have a major influence on a person's behaviors and serve as a broad guideline in social situations.

Each of us brings our unique set of values, norms, and beliefs into any relationship. In most cases, cultural awareness is implicit. During coaching, the coach needs to make cultural awareness/sensitivity explicit, bringing it forth into the conversation.

HOW DO YOU CREATE A MEETING SPACE?

Coaches who are members of ICF work with the coaching core competencies and a defined code of ethics (ICF, n.d.-a). At the top of the list are the essential competencies of creating the agreement, establishing trust, and adopting a coaching presence. These competencies are also of great importance when working across cultures. When a coach and a coachee are working together, there must be a meeting space that offers safety and trust and where both parties are willing to invest in being fully present and equally active members. A coaching meeting space needs to offer a place where respect, acceptance, and rules of engagement build constantly on trust and safety. To do this, the coach is curious, warm, and empathic, and offers genuine interest in the coachee as a person, embracing the latter's norms, values, biases, beliefs, and background.

ICF core competencies 7, Direct Communication, and 8, Creating Awareness, in particular, highlight the importance of integrating and accurately evaluating multiple sources of information and making interpretations that help the coachee to gain awareness and thereby achieve agreed-upon results. They also focus attention on what is important for the coachee, and to leave responsibility with the coachee to take action. These are essential elements if change and growth are to happen. They highlight how important it is to look at the multiple sources of information, make the interpretations necessary, and allow the client to take the necessary steps.

THE SAFETY, TRUST, AND PRESENCE APPROACH (STP): THREE ESSENTIAL ELEMENTS

For a successful relationship to begin and ultimately thrive across cultures, there are three equally important ingredients: *safety, trust,* and *presence* (STP). All factors are interdependent—each can only happen when the other two are present. This applies to one-on-one relationships or partnerships, work groups, and social engagements. These elements are even more important when people of different backgrounds come together. Filling in the thoughts of another's bias, that is, making incorrect interpretations as a result of coming from your own different reality, is an ever-present risk.

In a coaching relationship, the Coaching Core Competencies offer a rich coaching structure or framework for achieving STP. Below are the traits for each of the STP elements as I see them.

Remember our French coachee? The lack of cultural awareness got in the way of the coach asking the right questions, those questions where culture was the pillar of the coaching question. The coach missed the cultural value of loyalty and how important it was so that the client was willing to give up his dreams of a new career. And what about my own story? My coach missed that I was feeling unwelcomed and uncomfortable without realizing I was suffering from my own "invisible" culture shock. Coaches need to use the ICF core competencies in combination with cultural awareness and sensitivity. By applying the STP approach, the coach can explore cultural perceptions such as: the effects of single stories, sense of time, silence, and assumptions.

Safety Comes Through . . .	Trust Comes Through . . .	Presence Comes Through . . .

Respect
Emotional support
Presence
Empathy
Genuine interest
Listening
Keeping promises
Avoiding fixing or solving
Setting acceptable
  ground rules
Managing time and
  silence
	Respect
	Presence
	Interest
	Listening
	Understanding
	  background norms
	  and values
	Trusting with head or
	  heart
		Open communication
		Cultural awareness and sensitivity
		Trust
		Safety
		Curiosity
		Commitment
		Empathy
		Genuine interest
		Respect for different cultural
		  norms
		Strong sense of self
		Being engaging
		Being inviting
		Creating a common meeting
		  space
		Living by own norms
		Acting by values
		Evaluating own biases and
		  perspectives

THE DANGER OF A SINGLE STORY

Novelist Adichie (2009) tells the story of how she found her authentic cultural voice—and warns that if we hear only a single story about another person or country, we risk a critical misunderstanding. We all have stories to tell. Every story can be told in many different ways. Our lives, our cultures, are composed of many overlapping stories. The storyteller colors the story from his or her own perspective and experience. This is a real danger when a coach is in the meeting space with the coachee, listening to the coachee telling about a situation, and is not asking the right questions. Without probing deeper, the coach hears only a single side of the story and an incomplete one.

Presence is about staying in the moment with the coachee, offering a *safe* and *trusting* space where the coachee can tell his or her own story and where the coach can ask questions to uncover the many other sides of the story—including the cultural story—that might affect how the coach and coachee connect and stay attuned throughout the coaching relationship.

The effect of single stories can be influential and impactful. When a coach is supporting the coachee, the coach must integrate multiple sources of information and help the coachee gain awareness. For example, when new acquaintances learn that I speak five languages, the common reaction is: "Wow, you are clever!" On the other hand, when I say I am Dutch, the reaction is: "All Dutch people speak many languages." Different reactions, but in each, a single story. What people are not seeing are the many hours of school work, lonely hours at unknown places, and the hardships of starting over and over again in a new country. Any single story has the potential to be insensitive, naïve, and even demoralizing. The goal is to stay curious and discover the untold layers buried beneath.

SILENCE IS GOLDEN

Maintaining silence in a coaching session—or in any conversation—is difficult for some people. Speaking or staying silent is something we learn from the environment we live in. North American cultures tend to fill all the talking moments as a way to display how much they know and take control of the conversation. Asian cultures tend to keep silent because, on one hand, it is a sign of respect, and on the other hand, silence is a powerful skill. The more the other person is uncomfortable with silence, the more control the quiet person has (Bryant, 2017). In Latin countries (Italy, Colombia, Portugal, Mexico), people tend to answer questions fast. It's not because they are not listening, but because they do not want people to think they do not know the answer. Understanding the meaning of silence across cultures will help in creating a safe and trusting meeting space while being present in the moment. There is no right or wrong: It is the perception that one has and the space that one gives which is important.

TIME IS MONEY OR ISN'T IT?

The concept of time is an important cultural element. In business, but also in coaching, understanding the coachee's perception of time will support managing both process and accountability. The Lewis Model (Lewis, 1996) distinguishes cultures into three categories:

- Linear-actives—those who plan, schedule, organize, pursue action chains, do one thing at a time. Many Germans and Swiss are in this group.

- Multi-actives—those lively, loquacious people who do many things at once, planning their priorities not according to a time schedule, but according to the relative thrill or importance that each appointment brings with it. Italians, Latin Americans, and Arabs are members of this group.

- Reactives—those cultures that prioritize courtesy and respect, listening quietly and calmly to their interlocutors, and reacting carefully to the other side's proposals. Chinese, Japanese, and Finns are in this group.

When a coach has the expectation that the coachee will keep to an agreed schedule, they may find that time and accountability is a source of frustration. The coachee is going either too fast or too slow, and the coach has no grasp of the energy the coachee is investing. Not long ago, I was mentoring a Chinese coach and we started talking about the biggest frustrations he encountered when working with Europeans. He didn't understand why some people made plans and then did not keep them, while others moved so fast that they were missing essential learnings. He went on to tell me that a coachee's German boss complained that his coachee, a Greek, was not a good planner. Her activities seemed somewhat ad hoc and chaotic to her boss. In fact, she had put a lot of time and thought into the steps that needed to be taken. The German boss expected a written plan, while the employee was carefully revising her plan and activities every morning and proceeding accordingly. The employee was actually achieving great results, but the boss worked better when he could see the schedule.

There is also a big chance that the German boss thinks that all Greeks are messy, chaotic, and unstructured. This is an example of thinking from a single story, supported by a common bias.

Because it is so easy to cross borders, including virtual borders, there is an increase of coaches speaking only one language while coaching multilinguals. When language differences are present, these are to be addressed with respect and focus, always knowing that there will be cultural differences. Even if coach and coachee speak the same language, where they come from will influence the meaning people give to words and nonverbal communications. With globalization, we see many coaches coaching in their native language, paying little attention to coachees who might be bilingual or who may have a better grasp of the coaches' mother tongue than the coaches give them credit for. Language continuously evolves and is deeply affected by local environments: British English is not identical to American English; Dutch is not the same as Flemish, even if the root language is considered the same. The interpretation of words and meanings may change as a result of local customs, traditions, and situations. Research shows that language profoundly influences the way people see the world. Language is the verbal expression of culture. A simple example is the way people talk about colors, for some blue is just blue. For others blue can be celestial blue, cobalt blue, or indigo blue.

What Are Biases?

Biases are the result of skipping steps in an observation process. Based on limited inputs, you can form a perception or idea about a situation or person. Biases help us place thoughts and feelings into perspective. The primordial function of bias is to keep us safe. If we accept this to be true, then bias can have a positive or negative impact. The way you perceive something and what you do will result in certain emotions, negative or positive. While *single stories* involved looking at a situation from different angles or the way different individuals tell the story, biases have a lot to do with the individuals, emotions, and the attachments they give to the stories and how this affect them personally.

An example: You are an Human Resources (HR) manager and need to fill in some job vacancies. The first thing you do is make a list of the skills, knowledge, behaviors, background, and so forth, needed to do the job. Looking at, for example, background, you can name things like education, beliefs, gender, age, country of origin, and more.

This list by itself is a neutral one. But when you use it to disqualify people, it becomes a negative bias. When you write it down in the content of a job description, it is seen as "a qualification for the specific job," and then it is positive. Because biases are part of our process of measuring where we stand and how to act, they have an inherent effect on culture, communication, selection of friends, groups we are part of, and our choice of workplace.

Whenever I share this HR example, my American audience tells me this is an extremely bad example as legally HR people cannot mention age, gender, or religion in a job description. My European audience does not even flinch, as for us gender, religion, and age are options we may or may not address on our curriculum vitae or on the letter of interest. This is an example of cultural differences, as a European coach might find themselves walking into a field of landmines if they start addressing gender, age, or religion with an American coachee without being aware of the cultural and legal implications.

AREAS OF CONSIDERATION WHEN COACHING

Culture is everywhere, in all aspects of people's lives. Following are some backgrounds and/or situations where coaches should become more culturally competent when working with "global" people.

IMMIGRANTS

Immigrants are people who choose to move to another country with the intention to stay in the new homeland. Children are assimilated into the local culture but at the same time have their *own* ethnic subculture.

Issues to Take Into Consideration

Yearning for their old home country, being part of minority in the new country, looking physically different than locals, experiencing language issues.

EXPATRIATES

Expats are individuals who live outside their country. They usually stay for a couple of years in one country before moving to the next one.

Issues to Take Into Consideration

Partner gave up a job and cannot work in host country, children cannot adapt or are sent home to study, limited understanding of how local business works, safety concerns during political unrest in host country.

REFUGEES

These are individuals who leave their country to escape war, persecution, or natural disaster. Often people have traumas and might not stay permanently in a new country or region.

Issues to Take Into Consideration

Difficulty with integrating into host country, language issues, mental and physical traumas, experience with discrimination or misunderstanding by locals.

Third Culture Kids (TCKs) and Cross-Cultural People

These are individuals raised in a culture other than their parents' (or the culture of the country given on their passports where they are legally considered native) for a significant part of their early developmental years. They often have a *different* idea of their parents' homelands. Cross-cultural individuals have been brought up in the country of one parent and are influenced by the culture of the second parent who has a different homeland, including a second language and infusion of different norms, values, and beliefs.

Issues to Take Into Consideration

Big networks, no roots or sense of home, constantly on the move, flexibility, and adaptation are key words to survive, multilingual.

Language

In a multicultural environment, your coachee may have to deal with people talking different languages. Some people may be working using their mother tongue, while others will have to use a second language as the communication tool. This might bring confusion and misunderstandings, and translations might give different results than expected.

Issues to Take Into Consideration

Make sure there is a common understanding on language proficiency and cultural elements that might affect a conversation. A native speaker needs to create space and safety so a person expressing themselves in a language that is not the mother tongue can feel invited and listened to.

Written Communication

Cross-cultural communication might be a challenge. It is not only about language differences, but also the nonverbal communication is culturally determined. A lot of the original meaning can be lost during translation leaving people demotivated, confused, and at worst case insulted.

Issues to Take Into Consideration

Develop awareness on how to write emails and other communication forms and find out local customs. Written language is always received "harder" than spoken; therefore, take the time to write taking into consideration local and personal preferences.

Workplace

Corporate organizations have their own culture based on the products or services they offer including size, country, vision, and mission. Multinational and international organizations also have to take into consideration the needs of people buying the products. Coaches should be aware that many issues may arise, such as diverse teams, trust and safety, honor, local and global customs and traditions, conflicts management, age and sex education protocol, and just or unjust perspectives.

Issues to Take Into Consideration

Workplaces usually include cultural elements like local norms and values, how they perceive time, responsibility, ownership, local language, and customs. Cultures tend to look at power and hierarchy differently (Dutch people tend to have a "flat" management style, while North Americans often have a more top-down approach). Responsibility is usually determined by the cultural tendency of working together. In Latin America, people usually like to work together and share the responsibility as a group, while in Germany, people are often more individualistic and like having personal responsibility.

LOCATION

When coaching, it is important to be clear if the coachee is living in the country he or she is working in or is he or she just flying in (or meeting through the Internet). Whether a person is locally based or not might give the coachee some "power" or "acceptance" by the locals. I remember when I was working for a project in Armenia, my staff saw me as one of them and I could introduce unpopular decisions because they understood the ideas were not mine but came from the "big boss" in Germany. My staff felt they had to support me so I would not lose face, but as a team we could stand strong.

CONCLUSION

Culture is a concept that goes beyond countries; as coaches we need to become aware of the importance of developing the cultural competence to ensure a safe and trusting meeting space where the coach is present and culturally sensitive.
　　　　Edmée Schalkx (2017)

　　As we move into an increasingly globalized world, coaching across cultures is going to be the norm rather than the exception. Culture, based on norms, beliefs, and values, determines how we see, experience and relate to our environment, and to others. At the heart of coaching is an official meeting in which there are clear rules of engagement, designed to foster growth. Evolving in the meeting space of the coaching session is a partnership between coach and coachee that is the most important factor for the success of coaching. This partnership has to be based on *safety, trust, and presence*. Therefore, coaches need to understand the urgency and impact of developing their cultural competence.

　　Cultural competence is the ability to understand and interact effectively with people of all sorts of different backgrounds or attributes: gender, age, country, language, or experiences. Developing cultural competence is a complex and ongoing process where one must have open questioning of one's own norms, values, beliefs, and perspectives, and have a commitment to creating safe and trusting space. It takes time, curiosity, self-awareness, humility, and willingness to grow.

REFERENCES

Adichie, C. (2009). *The danger of a single story* [Video file]. TED Global. Retrieved from https://www.ted.com/talks/chimamanda_adichie_the_danger_of_a_single_story

Bryant, S. (2017). *Silence is golden, as the saying goes. But silence has many meanings in cross-cultural communication.* Retrieved from https://countrynavigator.com/blog/expert-view/cross-cultural-silence/

Buber, M. (1958). *I and thou.* New York, NY: Scribner Classics.

Gilbert, K., & Rosinski, P. (2008). Accessing cultural orientations: The online cultural orientations framework assessment as a tool for coaching. *Coaching: An International Journal of Theory, Research and Practice, 1*(1), 81–92.

Hofstede, G. (1991). *Cultures and organizations: Software of the mind.* London, England: McGraw-Hill.

International Coach Federation. (n.d.-a). Core competencies. Retrieve from https://coachfederation.org/core-competencies/

International Coach Federation. (n.d.-b). ICF definition of coaching. Retrieved from https://coachfederation.org/about/?navItemNumber=557

Lewis, R. (1996). *When cultures collide: Leading across cultures.* London, England: Hodder & Stoughton.

Schein, E. (2010). *Organizational culture and leadership.* San Francisco, CA: John Wiley & Sons.

Sinterklaas. (n.d.). Retrieved from http://www.holland.com/global/tourism/article/sinterklaas.htm

Tylor, E. (1871). The science of culture (p. 1). In *Primitive culture* (Vol. 1). London, UK: John Murray.

9

Honing the Ultimate Coaching Advantage: The Coach/Client Relationship

Sharon Eakes and Nancy Smyth

The ultimate coaching resource is a coach's ability to connect with and form meaningful relationships with clients. In this chapter, we explore an aspect of coaching deeper than technique or behavior. We identify the advantages of maximizing a robust coaching relationship with clients, because therein lies the active ingredient for best outcomes. We explore the coaches' way of being, which includes how they see and think, and the state of their hearts. We also examine how coaches can tap into their most authentic selves to facilitate success in the coaching relationship.

THE PRIMACY OF RELATIONSHIPS

Research shows that relationships are at the center of a fulfilled life. Relationships infuse our lives with meaning and purpose. The context for this chapter is an acknowledgment of how foundational relationships are to happiness and well-being. A 75-year study called the Harvard Study of Adult Development comes to the same conclusion (Waldinger, 2015). According to Waldinger, "Relationships are messy, and they're complicated. . . . Still, the clearest message that we get from this 75-year study is this: Good relationships keep us happier and healthier. Period." Seasoned coaches realize in their practice what research for decades has consistently demonstrated about therapy. As Castonguay, Goldfried, Wiser, Raue, and Hayes (1996) reported: "Relationship factors correlate more highly with client outcomes than do specialized treatment techniques" (p. 500).

We are social beings. Each of us is a wild story melded together from our relationships with others through all the years of our lives. Influences include family, schooling, fun, culture, values, beliefs, friends, trials and tribulations, successes and failures, and all the responses from and to everyone. Over time, we form our story and embellish it as we carry it with us. We treasure our story and see ourselves as unique, even though almost everything we experience is not unique and is common to us as people. The cultural mindset of our time supports an individualistic view. Self-help methods encourage us to focus on and work on ourselves to improve. However, we are never separate or apart from how we are in the world. We are part of something bigger. To be successful as a leader, politician, coach, employee, or parent, seeing and responding to the humanity in others are key.

In a talk on "Thriving in the Age of Acceleration," Friedman (2017) described having asked the U.S. Surgeon General, Dr. Vivek Murthy, about the most prevalent disease in America today. Is it cancer, diabetes, or heart disease? Dr. Murthy reported it is none of those; it is isolation. Friedman points out this irony: We live in the most connected age in history, and the most prevalent disease is isolation. Friedman (2017) states, "For many generations, we worked with our hands, then in the modern era we began to work with our heads, but in the age of acceleration, we are going to work more with our hearts. . . . Connecting hearts is going to be a very big career." Our coaching relationships provide an antidote to the dilemma of isolation. Through coaching, clients are encouraged to experience their role in a connected world.

Since the domain of relationships is paramount, it is worth exploring the significance of the coaching relationship from several perspectives: the client, the coach's relationship with self, the coach–client partnership, and how change takes place in the context of relationships.

THE CLIENT

In the early days of the coaching profession, people were referred for coaching when a big problem was identified. Coaching was often seen as remedial. The client might resist the intervention, feeling singled out or seeing coaching as punitive.

As the power of coaching to accelerate change and leadership development was recognized, coaches were engaged for high-potential employees and became an executive benefit. Organizational coaching is now standard. Additionally, individuals who identify areas they want to improve refer themselves. Prospective clients want to increase something, change something, or overcome a challenge in their lives and can't quite see the way forward. Often, even when it is not the presenting problem, there are problems in one or many relationships that contribute to the presenting problem.

Clients may need clarity around a situation to generate momentum or congruity. They know change is needed, but they feel stuck, experience frustration, inertia, overwhelm, inadequacy, or confusion. Clients may feel trapped or victimized and have trouble seeing how they contribute to the situation. They feel unsure how to proceed, or they need support to stay the course. Sometimes clients simply need a champion, someone who sees and appreciates them. It is from all these ripe places that a person engages a coach to get the desired results.

THE COACH–SELF RELATIONSHIP

We train as coaches. We are also human, with histories and struggles. Knowingly or not, we enter every coaching conversation carrying with us the entirety of our lives. Many of us were attracted to this profession because we like to help. Clients want help and come thirsting for answers. They want to know what to do or how to solve a problem. Quickly going to a solution has merit and can be exhilarating. However, taking the time to delve into the source of issues creates more sustainable results. From the latter perspective, the most important role we play as a coach is to develop relationships with clients that invite them to enter deeply into their inner wisdom.

Ongoing self-inquiry is necessary to refine our ability to connect with and invite clients into subtle contemplation. As coaches, we need to examine ourselves, genuinely asking ourselves questions similar to those we might ask clients: How open am I to knowing myself? Do I put on blinders, only seeing what I want to see? Do I settle for mediocre outcomes? Do I need to be seen as competent? If I become complacent, then how fully available am I for my clients? Will I have the capacity to expand clients' reality? Sometimes a client's presenting issue is also mine. Can I step into the opportunity to learn alongside my client?

- A client is struggling with a teenager, just as I am.

- Another client is not feeling appreciated by his peers, similar to how I struggle to feel equal to other coaches.

- My client wants to deliver dynamic presentations. So do I. Both of us have a long way to go.

Noticing challenges similar to those of my clients, how will I be available and effective? Do I get all wrapped up in myself? Am I able to meet clients where they are? Without careful observation, I can deny there is still much for me to learn. Above all, I am contracted to be a vehicle for the client's evolution and transformation, and need to fine-tune who and how I am to be the best for them.

Client change is inseparable from the coach's change. To continually open and live into my full capacity, I, too, must enter into the unknown. It isn't always comfortable. I must strive to be an eager companion with my client, vulnerable and willing to learn. I can never become smug about my awareness or attainment.

Self-awareness builds a strong self-relationship. Classical theories of self-awareness can be traced back to early social, clinical, and developmental psychology. Subsequent research by Sturm, Taylor, Atwater, and Braddy (2014) "repeatedly demonstrated that for self-awareness to successfully develop, individuals must have not only an understanding of themselves but also an understanding of and appreciation for others' perceptions of them" (p. 659). My growth as a human is inextricably tied to my effectiveness as a coach. As my self-awareness grows, I become whole and balanced as a coach. I see, soften, and reveal myself in relationship to others. I learn to accept my humanity, not needing to be perfect. Instead, I become real and authentic. I accept myself and acknowledge both strong and weak qualities, and simultaneously move toward more and more freedom from my limitations. My heart and mind become more astute, harmonious, and synchronized.

An excellent means to cultivate ongoing self-awareness is through a personal relationship with a coach or mentor. By being coached or mentored, I continue to face and embrace the changes I need to make. Relationships with my support team support my relationships with my clients. Another aid to hone the coaching relationship is to realize and implement all the processes and practices that bolster the coach's physical, mental, and spiritual energy. A strong sense of well-being is contagious and life-confirming for clients.

THE COACHING RELATIONSHIP

Years ago, when you told someone you were a coach, people often asked "What sport?" There is more widespread recognition of the coaching profession today. Nevertheless, great sports coaches can offer our profession wisdom. For example, by 2017, Coach Gregg Popovich of the San Antonio Spurs had helped the team win five NBA championships. Stallard (2015) reported that Coach Popovich develops in players what he calls "relationship excellence." He models and fosters caring and respect toward each player on and off the court. Because of the team's commitment to relationship excellence, the men play with the polish and precision of a space shuttle landing.

Living from an interrelated relationship space is potent. As coaches, we have the opportunity to spark excellence in clients' lives through the relationships we develop with them. From a connected place, clients access insights, energy, and fortitude to solve the toughest challenges. They are full of hope and creative possibilities, making choices that move them toward their goals and, as a bonus, help them create a better world.

THE RELATIONSHIP DYNAMIC

Coach and client engage to create a transformative dynamic. Both parties bring with them dreams, desires, histories, beliefs, cultures, abilities, and fears. Some are known, others are hidden from awareness. The fertile field of the coaching relationship allows both client and coach to uncover what is cloaked. The relationship is not static; it is a dynamic interplay of individuals growing in the presence of each other—each person influences the other.

The opportunity for growth is always available. It's surprising, then, how often we resist change. We want change and fear it. The coaching relationship provides clients with the safety to examine thoughts, deepen understanding, create clarity, test ideas, and have the confidence to take action. In our clients' presence we, too, get the chance to grow, to evolve, to create a deep connection with them and, through them, a link to our integrity and heart. We get to see and put down any inflexibility or judgment and open to learning.

When the coaching relationship is expertly engaged, penetrating below the surface layers of a situation to its roots, the client arrives at what is authentic and alive. The client no longer needs to leap like a frog, from lily pad to lily pad of discomfort, around a topic. Coaching, then, offers more than a quick fix or behavioral change. Clients make a shift back to wholeness. Situations don't seem so perplexing; the solution arises from a fresh awareness and is unexpected. Life feels different, freer than what clients previously experienced. It can be surprising to begin the coaching engagement with a specific goal in mind and discover instead that the client has made a paradigm shift that encompasses a much broader perspective. Each of these accounts illustrates a shift:

- One client came to coaching feeling the humiliation, frustration, and anger of being demoted from president of a company. He cleared these feelings. Then, he accepted a lesser position, and astonishingly, became the leader they had been looking for.

- A client transformed from always wanting others to change their behaviors to consistently helping people find the joy in creating great relationships.

How we, as coaches, show up in the coaching relationship is pivotal. When the coach leans entirely into the relationship, the client feels summoned to reciprocate. Both coach and client see more and are shaped by the experience. Let's consider this analogy: In a high-ropes course, there is an event called the xylophone. It is a V-shaped configuration of ropes. Two people on the high-ropes start at the V's point, leaning into each other. That is simple. They each take a step out and away from the point and lean in again. The two keep stepping, moving farther and farther away from each other as the ropes splay. The only way not to fall off the ropes is for the two people to lean in 100%/100%. When both client and coach are leaning in completely, the breadth of what is possible is astounding. It is up to us, as the coach, to fuel and enliven 100% participation—both coach and client fully engaged in relationship.

ESSENTIAL ELEMENTS IN THE COACH/CLIENT RELATIONSHIP

Bringing receptivity with us to each coaching session allows us to be amazed. We commit to seeing clients, wholly discovering who they are in the midst of their quest. We step beyond merely embarking upon the next project into the deepest core of what is meaningful and rooted within the client. Our full and heart-centered engagement, curiosity, and listening are required.

Listening and Curiosity

As coaches, we listen deeply and probe respectfully to help clients uncover or rediscover their inner wisdom and energy. It is like an exquisite dance, natural and unconstrained. Listening is a creative force. Thoughtfully, we receive the nuances below the surface of the client's words. Questions arise; we inquire. We discover what silence holds. We encourage the client to delve deeper into the essence of a concern, to ascertain and change the source, and feel empowered. In her book, Ueland (1993) wrote, "When we listen . . . there is an alternating current. . . ." (p. 205). The author suggests that being heard in the right way—"with affection and a kind of jolly excitement" (p. 207)—allows a truer conversation, the kind of pure conversation that invites the speaker to be most authentic. Ueland continues, "When we are listened to, it creates us, makes us unfold and expand" (1993, p. 205). Listening with this degree of rich interrelatedness in the coaching relationship is profound. Instead of dipping our toes in at the ocean's edge, we plunge into the ocean and serve the client's highest goals.

Heart-Centered Presence

Heart centeredness is central to the coaching relationship. Beneath whatever outcome clients want, they desire belonging, happiness, and fulfillment. These are issues of the heart. Therefore, the condition of the coach's heart matters. To the degree we are in touch with our pristine heart, we relate to our clients and the underlying aspects of their concerns. Our heart is a magnetic, cohesive force. It strengthens the relationship; our best emerges. For this reason, merging a powerful heart-energy with our mind and skill set provides support from our entire being and gives both our clients and us welcome benefits.

When our heart is engaged in the coaching relationship, we offer our full presence—clear-sighted, sincere, appreciative, free from resistance. We are authentic, trustworthy, and truthful. A harmonic milieu is established. When our heart is engaged, we invite the client to synchronize with our energy and access the whole of what is now possible between us. Meeting the client wholly—mind and heart—generates an exponential capacity, more than the sum of the two of us. The combined awareness—the client's and ours—illumines the source of the difficulty. Clarity emerges; solutions arise.

An authentic coaching presence is not bland; it is heart-centered. It has a rigor that is continuously adapting—sometimes acknowledging and encouraging, other times firm and fiercely challenging. We let go of being in control or having all the answers or striving to fix. Instead, heart-centered presence is an energetic force alive to whatever is needed for the client's best possible life and contribution to the world.

In the coaching relationship, heart-centered presence lays the foundation for trust and qualities of caring and safety so that clients can honestly share who they are, even in the messiest of places. They can accept difficulty with poise and discover they don't need to be stuck or confused. Friedman (2016) said, "When people trust each other, they can be adaptable and open to all forms of pluralism. When people trust each other, they can think long-term" (p. 359). Through our coaching relationship, a client's messy moments serve as transitional gateways to new possibilities. Clients can find themselves—their essence, courage, and strength—by reveling in the answers arising from their hearts. Sincere presence invites a metamorphosis. Our heart-centered relationship creates responsiveness in the client.

Now you may be thinking that speaking about heart sounds like sweetness and light—that we're talking only about children, family, and intimate relationships. Maybe your clients' challenges are professional, and this approach sounds weak, soft, or not for you. You may be thinking: "How could something like caring and the heart possibly be effective in a professional and competitive world?" The following are objections leaders might present:

- Solving relationship problems distracts and takes time.

- Increasing the bottom line is the company's goal.

- Professionals want answers, not processing.

Don't be fooled! The powerful energy of our hearts is like a laser beam that cuts through everything false to reveal the truth about what has been the cause of complications, disputes, or lack of productivity and revenue. Executives report that the job itself isn't usually the difficulty; it is the people. Here is a clear message to coaches to be cognizant of the relationships that are integral to every situation. People's hearts are at the center of every relationship, every interaction, every communication, every deal, and contract.

C. Otto Scharmer, the influential MIT business professor, supports that notion and so did his colleague, Bill O'Brien, the late CEO of Hanover Insurance. Scharmer (2015) reported that in an interview, O'Brien said, "The success of an intervention depends on the interior condition of the intervener." Scharmer continued, "We might say it this way: the success of our actions as change-makers does not depend on What we do or How we do it, but on the Inner Place from which we operate" (para. 3).

In the coaching relationship, there is a significant advantage in leading from the heart. When the mind and the heart are working together intimately, they shine as one clear source of light. We enter into and make available a realm of being beyond conscious thought—a zone of unimagined possibilities.

THE COACHING RELATIONSHIP POWERED BY WAY OF BEING

We are always both being and doing creatures. The principle we are emphasizing in this chapter is that the being part—the way we are at any given moment—has a significant impact on whatever we're doing. If we are fixing breakfast (doing) and we're feeling hurried, troubled, and resentful that we have to do it (being)—it affects how we feel inside and relate to people. Also, when our state is not good, our results are usually less than we hoped. Every minute of every day we make choices about *what* to do and *how* to do it, *what* to think and *how* to think, and literally, *how* to be with others. We need to see and understand the influence of our way of being.

A great deal of the focus of coaching is on changing behavior. That's the doing part. What we're suggesting is that in our coaching relationship the more time, attention, and focus we spend on cultivating the way of being—both ours and the client's—the more successful our coaching will be. Life is enhanced when, as the coach, our way of being is sprinkled generously with patience and compassion. These qualities are not soft, touchy-feely traits. They are full of power, energy, and life-force, able to transform the darkest circumstance. Situated in an authentic way of being, the coach's arrogance, inferiority, and self-focus are dismantled while turning humanness into a truly beneficial presence. As a coach, we hone our way of being in the service of our clients.

It is useful to teach clients this being/doing distinction as well. Most clients have already tried to change their *doing* selves before coming to coaching. In troubled projects or conflicts with others, clients may have:

- Resolved to say things with a better tone

- Left the room rather than escalating what is already contentious

It isn't that either of these things is wrong. Done respectfully, they may be a temporary fix. For a sustainable result, however, focusing on growing client awareness of their way of being is central. Consider: Are clients tuned in to their inner state? Are they aware how much their state impacts others and projects? Relationships always contribute to the presenting problem. Self-awareness about way of being stimulates understanding and generates choices that can transform clients' relationships. Clarity around the point in question follows naturally.

Since the quality of relationships determines the quality of life, it is hopeful to know that even our clients' most difficult relationships can change. Therefore, exploring a client's way of being in conflicted relationships is essential.

- In what ways does the client not respect or understand the other person?

- Is it possible that having to be right is getting in the way?

- In what ways might he or she be adding to the difficulty?

- How does he or she collect evidence to justify how he or she interacts?

- How might his or her way of being elicit resistance?

Resolving way-of-being issues improves relationships and paves the way to desired results. The coach doesn't get derailed by clients' limiting thoughts, beliefs, or justifications. Instead, maintaining a tranquil state, the coach sees the best in clients. The coach journeys with clients to draw out what is excellent in them by shining light where it is needed.

The coach needs that same degree of steadfast carefulness not to enlist into stories that clients are hoping to resolve. Without awareness, coaches' unresolved issues might blind them. Although a natural impulse, siding with clients might leave the clients feeling supported in what isn't working. We want to be compassionate, although what we intend as support can curtail growth and dishonor the relationship. Consider these narratives:

- The teenagers are out of control.

- A client complains about his excessive workload.

- A CEO sees how the Board of Directors does not have her back.

Rather than siding with clients when these issues provoke ours, we can help guide clients to discover and amend the underlying causes of the situation. If we collude with clients, how will they see what has previously been unnoticed in their way of being and stretch into a new level of competence? Helping clients resolve the source of the discomfort empowers their lives. The client creates a paradigm shift from a limited view to open-minded transparency. The advantages unlocked for both coach and client are these: meaning, fulfillment, excellence, and change. These rewards emerge in the coaching relationship.

Mindful of our way of being, coaching relationships gain depth and mutuality. When we simultaneously hold who the clients want to be, along with what they want to do, we help clients achieve freedom from all that has bound them and their energy. They begin to live in alignment with and realize their innermost desires.

MAXIMIZE CLIENT OUTCOMES: MERGE MIND AND HEART TO STIMULATE CHANGE

Imagine the place where two rivers meet and become one. It happens all over the world. In India, this confluence is considered sacred. In that same way, flowing together in one river needs to happen in the coaching relationship. It is the space of one-heart, one-mind. Regard it with reverence; this is where change occurs.

If I come to the coaching session tired, overwhelmed, with too detailed a plan in mind or attached to an outcome, I may not join the client at this confluence. I am involved in a river of thoughts, and my way of being is self-absorbed. I jump from shore to shore, not connecting. I talk. The client talks. I talk. The client talks.

But assume I am prepared—fully present, mind and heart—to swim with my client in our convergent river.

My client considers for the first time how her busyness, which she thought was moving her ahead, may be holding her back. We look at that possibility together. Even though she is the CEO, she doesn't feel she has influence. She asks how that could be possible. I ask what she wants more than anything. She tells me. Then she changes her mind. She's confused, and we swim together in the confusion, examining how she's feeling, what she sees, why it matters. With emotion, she shares that her busyness is hard on her husband and kids. I notice that her speech has slowed down.

She shares that she is breathing more deeply now. In fact, she continues by saying her busyness is also hard on work colleagues. She doesn't stop long enough to know them or hear their concerns. She doesn't feel connected. There are long silences now. I don't interrupt because I know we are in the river together and this is where change happens. She ends the silence by saying "This is huge. I knew this to be true, but I see now what I haven't been seeing." Acknowledging, I invite her to keep looking.

She dives deeper under the currents and notices that her busyness has revealed a hidden level—wanting to feel significant. Therefore, she never asks for help and feels the need to do it all—at work, at home, and in the community. Following my client's lead, I ask her more: What images of herself is she trying to protect? What might it be like for others to receive her busyness rather than a person? How does doing-it-all keep her focused on herself and separate from others? How does it prevent other people's growth? What is the difference she wants to make? Her answers are coming from a profound place.

We plunge deeper into the river together to explore her vision of life. She shares the preciousness of her relationships and what she desires for family and for the people she leads. As she ponders, she becomes lighter, more connected to herself and what really matters. More attuned to her heart, her way of being shifts. She has new eyes. It gives her the opportunity to see differently. Delighted, the client reports that her way out of busyness is now clear. She makes a commitment to leave work at a reasonable time, come home for dinner, and spend time with her husband and children on weekends.

Over time, my client has naturally become more patient with her children and appreciative of her husband, neighbors, and in-laws. She is embracing the people in her life. At work she notices herself in relationships and is more responsive. She came wanting a strategy and left with a heart full of gratitude that now guides her life. She has regained balance and respect for herself and the people in her life.

Change has happened in the coaching relationship. Neither of us saw exactly where the course of the river was going. We went together, bobbing and diving, surfacing and looking deeper. Change took place when the client forgot herself in response to the people in her life. Her resolve to be with family arose naturally from a shift that took place in her heart. With that inner opening, her follow-through was guaranteed.

Her shift of heart opened up a world of possibilities. At work, my client is more conscious of the rivers that her Board of Directors, colleagues, and direct reports occupy with her. She is slowing down enough to jump in the river with them—listening and engaging. The difference in her way of being is inspiring others. She has become a person in whose presence others can change. And to her amazement, having gotten much clearer about the importance of all her relationships, she is more efficient at work as well.

Inspired by my client's exploration, I have a reinvigorated sense of gratitude for the people in my life. I am connecting in more significant ways.

In the coaching relationship, close rapport, respect, and radical curiosity help clients navigate the river. When a shift in their heart occurs, the river opens wide and flows freely to the people in their lives, to their projects, and the world in meaningful ways.

CONCLUSION

To have the ultimate coaching advantage, refine the coaching relationship. Effectiveness in the relationship hinges on self-awareness and cultivating our way of being. As we open to fully *be* with our clients—mind and heart—in the deepest possible way, we facilitate clients' progress. Belief in who they are, grander than they ever dared to consider, invites them to actualize extraordinary possibilities not only in their projects but also in the relationships integral to the projects.

The coaching relationship is a reciprocal privilege. Our clients' transcendence sparks our excellence. Through alchemy, we both transform.

REFERENCES

Castonguay, L. G., Goldfried, M. R., Wiser, S., Raue, P. J., & Hayes, A. M. (1996). Predicting the effect of cognitive therapy for depression: A study of unique and common factors. *Journal of Consulting and Clinical Psychology, 64*(3), 497–504. doi:10.1037/0022-006X.64.3.497

Friedman, T. (2016). *Thank you for being late: An optimist's guide to thriving in the age of accelerations.* New York, NY: Farrar, Straus and Giroux.

Friedman, T. (2017). Thriving in the age of acceleration. *Intelligence Squared* [Podcast]. Retrieved from https://www.youtube.com/watch?v=_QOyKeEEU3Q&feature=em-subs_digest-vrecs

Scharmer, C. O. (2015). Theory U. Retrieved from https://www.presencing.org/#/aboutus/theory-u

Stallard, M. L. (2015). NBA's spurs culture creates competitive advantage. Retrieved from http://www.foxbusiness.com/features/2015/02/25/nbas-spurs-culture-creates-competitive-advantage.html

Sturm, R., Taylor, S., Atwater, L., & Braddy, P. (2014). Leader self-awareness: An examination and implications of women's under-prediction. *Journal of Organization Behavior, 35,* 657–677. doi:10.1002/job.1915

Ueland, B. (1993). *Tell me more on the fine art of listening from strength to your sword arm: Selected writings.* Duluth, MN: Holy Cow! Press.

Waldinger, R. (2015). *What makes a good life? Lessons from the longest study on happiness* [Ted Talk]. Retrieved from https://www.ted.com/talks/robert_waldinger_what_makes_a_good_life_lessons_from_the_longest_study_on_happiness

10

Interpersonal Approaches to Coaching

Keith Nelson

oaching creates an environment that enables the client to think more clearly, before moving on to consider and implement more effective choices than otherwise might have been the case, leading to enhanced performance and change. Without a coaching relationship, it is down to individuals to identify and work toward change and make improvements on their own. With a coach, the premise is that individuals not only change and raise performance more quickly and effectively, it also opens up new possibilities.

The platform for this raised performance can be found in the quality of the *coaching relationship* within the *environment* created and held by the coach. The foundations for this platform lie within the *coach's presence*: how the coach shows up in the coaching relationship. This chapter explores the ebb and flow of the dialogue between coach and client, within the context of the coaching relationship, coaching environment, and the coach's presence.

COACHING DEVELOPMENT

Professional coaches might recall that many coach training programs integrate the coach's role of "doing" within a broader philosophy of "being." This shifts the emphasis of coaching as something that the coach simply "does" to the client and gives greater prominence to how the coach is in the relationship. Stout-Rostron (2014) cited Spinelli's analysis: "No matter what model or methodology a practitioner uses, it is, according to Spinelli, 'the relationship' that affects the outcome of the coaching or therapy. It is the 'quality' of the relationship that is of importance" (p. 253). Gallwey (2000) described it as "a way of being" (p. 177).

Patterns within coaching relationships start to form at initial chemistry meetings and introductory sessions. Clarity over contracting and establishing the relationship provides a strong start. But it is only that. Preparing rich nutrients for the coaching journey as it unfolds is important work if the coach accepts Barrett-Lennard's (2013) perspective that a relationship is a "dynamic living system" with "its own emergent life" (p. 12). He continued that "human relationships are seen as engines of self-formation and as emergent from the association of selves" (p. 36).

Coaching provides a specialized, deeply personal, high quality relationship that offers the opportunity to generate both high levels of self-formulation and enables this emergence within the client. And the coaching journey follows a two-way street: not only does the client change, but so does the coach.

Facilitated effectively, a high quality, co-created reality becomes the oxygen for change and growth within the client. By contrast, a less effective co-created reality, with less oxygen, does not generate such an enabling opportunity. Both clients and coaches learn from, change, and grow within and through coaching relationships. The era of the coach brought in to fix the client—which reinforced the "doing" tendency—appears to be, thankfully, in decline. Coaching proposes a more optimistic view of human nature. Consider the words of Kahn (2014):

> In business coaching the focus is not about whether an individual is good or bad, healthy or sick, normal or abnormal. Rather, it is about the extent to which a particular individual in a particular organisational context creates [a] relationship in a way that works for the business. (p. 103)

The organizational context applies as much to the executive being coached as it does to the coach working with the client. Useful questions that the coach can ask himself or herself are these: How do you create coaching relationships? How might you expect the client to experience you as the coach?

COACHING PRESENCE

It is not unusual that the coaching environment becomes a unique space within the client's life to talk freely and without fear of judgment. This brings much responsibility for the coach if this is to remain effective and safe. When facilitated well, it enables significant growth for the client; at the opposing end of the spectrum the coach might stultify or, worse still, contaminate the conversation. Clients usually have enough of their own issues to work through without inadvertently being handed some more by their coaches.

Just as the coaches hold the mirror up to clients, good practice is to hold the mirror up to the coaches themselves: This is, after all, how they show up to clients. Yet presence goes much further than what's visible in the mirror. Leary-Joyce (2014) proposed that coaches "be as balanced and grounded as possible. You need to be equally aware of your perceptions, your emotional and physical feelings and your thinking" (p. 43).

The value of the coach's presence is described by Nelson (2010) and O'Neill (2007), while Joyce and Sills (2010) emphasized its importance for the counselor, who:

brings all of herself to the meeting and is willing to meet the client honestly and authentically. . . . She allows herself to be touched and moved by the impact of the client, to be *affected*. Sometimes this will mean being able to disclose her response in the service of the relationship. (pp. 45–46)

Allowing oneself to be touched, moved, and affected by clients becomes an intrinsic part of this dynamic and emerging relationship. The consequences of coaches not being touched might lead to them being experienced as uncaring; and the relationship is lessened as a consequence. Being affected affirms that coaching is less of the "doing" and more about bringing and embodying an interactive and authentic coaching presence. It then becomes valuable to consider how the coach is affected and then how this is introduced into the coaching relationship.

CASE STUDY

Felicity is the CEO of a business employing 1,500 people. The coaching session was being used to discuss and explore the company's need for a change of direction—and particularly the implications of these. The company's Board of Directors had decided to refocus the business in response to market pressures, yielding both good and bad news. Capital investment and brighter prospects on the one hand, 50 redundancies on the other.

Felicity used the coaching session to explore how and when to convey this mixed news. As she spoke, she described feeling upset about the redundancies. As the coach, my response was that it would help her to attend to her feelings regarding the redundancies and the tensions running through her regarding the good news and bad news for the business. I thought I perceived sadness in her. As she spoke, resting her head on her hand, I noticed her drop in energy. At the same time, I allowed myself to be touched by her: I noticed what I would describe as sadness settling in my chest.

I asked her to describe what she meant by feeling upset, which she did. I still felt there was more. So, I chose to disclose my response: that I thought I perceived sadness in her and was experiencing that too. That evoked a noticeable response in her. She thought the word "upset" was more appropriate. She described that she associated sadness with past experiences and feelings of decline and decay. It was a word that she wanted to disassociate herself from: It was replete with powerful and unpleasant meaning. Her strong reaction allowed us to hold a dialogue that explored the meaning and implications of both feelings as she portrayed and experienced them.

By the conclusion of the coaching session, I experienced Felicity as lighter. The inner had led to the outer. She had surfaced her feelings and chosen a course of action in a manner that allowed her to navigate a way of delivering the conflicting news to the staff.

THE COACH'S RESPONSE

When the coach selectively introduces a response in this manner, it is important to note the client's reaction: In this case, Felicity's marked aversion to sadness and why it had not been permissible for her to acknowledge her potential for sadness. The response opened the opportunity for exploring a new narrative.

Such exploration generates sense-making, even though it might entail wading through the deep undergrowth of ambiguity and uncertainty, experienced by both parties. There is no satellite navigation system here: This is a case of exploring the ground with the client. O'Neill (2007) considered clear coaching strengths in her book: *Executive Coaching with Backbone and Heart*: "Backbone means knowing and clearly stating your position, whether it is popular or not. Heart is staying engaged in the relationship and reaching out even when that relationship is mired in conflict" (p. 14).

This position requires the coach to retain an authentic stance while simultaneously engaging with the client. This is neither an objective nor neutral position. No coach can be fully objective. No coach is neutral. The coach experiences clients through all of the senses. These are filtered through their personal thinking processes, relationship patterns, emotional responses, life experiences, and knowledge, values, beliefs, and expectations. This reflects the value for the coach to be continually increasing self-awareness, to become more aware of patterns within self—as O'Neill (2007) proposed, to *respond* more and *react* less.

A well-honed presence is highly effective when the coach seeks to be fully present and is operating effectively in the here and now of the coaching. But if the ambiguity becomes too much, or if one of the coach's values is violated, then there is the risk that the coach's presence might be diminished and the coach's ability to work appropriately in the moment declines. If the temperature continues to rise, the coach might find that discomfort reaches alarming levels. The coach's internal self-talk might speculate if, indeed, the client is beyond (his or her) help. And the coach's feelings of being mired in helplessness may run parallel to those within the client. O'Neill (2007) stated: "Your job as a coach is to help the client strengthen his presence and lessen his reactivity" (p. 43). And to do that, coaches can continuously check in with themselves to monitor their responses throughout the session.

INTERPERSONAL SKILLS AND BEHAVIORS

An exercise I frequently run during coach training programs is to invite delegates to describe as many coaching skills and behaviors as they can. It took a recent group just a few minutes to generate the following:

> *aware of body language, boundaries, calmness, challenge, comfortable with silence, compassion, confident, confidential, effective questions, emotional intelligence, empathy, feedback, flexible, give undivided attention, integrity, listen deeply, observant, optimistic, outcome-focused, patience, positive approach, professional, rapport, reflect back, respectful, self-aware, self-manage, summarize, support, trustworthy, work in the here and now.*

There are many more that could be added to this list. Table 10.1 summarizes a few of these in the context of the coaching relationship. The first column describes the interpersonal quality; the subsequent columns suggest outcomes that might emerge if the coaching proceeds well or, alternatively, risks going off the rails.

Table 10.1 The Impact of the Coach's Interpersonal Coaching Qualities

The Coach's Interpersonal Qualities	When It Goes Well. . .	Look Out for. . .
High levels of empathy; experiences others' emotions	Client feels heard and understood.	Coach takes on and becomes overwhelmed by the client's emotions.
Excellence in cultivating warm relationships	Client feels strongly supported.	The conversation becomes too cozy.
An ability to challenge and hold clients to account	Client feels challenged; comfort zone is expanded.	Too much challenge; the client withdraws.
Deep rapport that builds a close relationship	Both parties get on very well together in the coaching.	Coach colludes with the client.
A focus upon outcomes and achieving goals	Client keeps focused upon achieving outcomes and achieving goals.	Insufficient exploration of the here and now and raising awareness.
Coach provides undivided attention	The client appreciates and benefits from the coach being present.	The client experiences high levels of scrutiny.
Structured coaching approach	The coaching session benefits from clear processes, leading to outcomes.	The coaching becomes overly rigid and insufficiently flexible in the moment.
The coach works in the here and now but with less focus on the outcomes	There is much energy in the here and now.	There are insufficient outcomes and change; client becomes frustrated.

As Table 10.1 illustrates, the different interpersonal qualities can have varying degrees of consequences for the client, for the co-created relationship, and for the coach. The coach who excels at building rapport might risk slipping into collusion with the client. The relationship becomes so strong that the coach's ability to stand back and challenge is diminished. Or the coach's challenge is too much for the client. The coach learns when it is timely to interject and when to hold back. Bluckert (2015) distinguished between "evocative" and "provocative" presence (p. 119)—at times a supportive presence may be what is required for the client; at other times, a more challenging presence becomes more valuable.

Providing support and challenge can sometimes be experienced by coaches as uncomfortable bedfellows. Many people who become coaches have a strong orientation to create warm relationships; they are caring individuals. This might play out in their relationships with clients—providing valuable support, but possibly struggling to provide greater challenge. Blakey and Day (2012) argued that coaches should go beyond the "zone of comfortable debate" and into the "zone of uncomfortable debate" (p. 21). They contended that "effective coaching is about challenging assumptions, examining habits, overcoming barriers and embedding change" (Blakey & Day, 2012, p. 23).

A coaching session might commence with warmth and support as the client relaxes into the coaching environment. As the session progresses—and depending upon the coach's sense of appropriateness of the client's readiness—then challenge can be introduced. Finally, as the session draws to a close and the session is wrapped up, then returning to positive and firm support becomes appropriate:

- How is this session leaving you?
- What are you going to do?
- What are you taking away?

Challenge is introduced nonjudgmentally. Modulating tone, appropriately selecting words, crafting questions, and being fully present are knitted together effectively. For some clients, being challenged rapidly becomes uncomfortable, while for others, it's an expectation. As is so often the case, the level of challenge depends upon the client. Every client is individual, every situation is fluid and emergent. In coaching "no one size fits all."

The coach who exudes high levels of empathy may find support comes easier than challenge. The coach with low levels of empathy might be experienced as a logical (if slightly remote) problem-solver, but who brings clear distance and detachment. As described in Table 10.1, a coach with high levels of empathy might run the risk of becoming overwhelmed by the tidal wave of the client's emotions. Contexts and individuals may be such that a detached, more distant presence is as appropriate as a warm, empathic presence. Effective coaching intuits the timeliness and appropriateness: It seeks to generate consistent, effective responses to the client's emerging wants and needs during the coaching session.

AWARENESS AND RESPONSIBILITY

Awareness and responsibility are twin principles that sit at the heart of coaching. In this context, responsibility is defined as what Perls (1969) described as *"response-ability*: the ability to respond, to have thoughts, reactions, emotions in a certain situation" (p. 85) and then to use those responses to consider options, make choices, and act upon them, and finally, to take responsibility for those actions.

Raising awareness is crucial before options are considered and choices made. Imagine, for a moment, the client is driving a car. The client has the control of the steering wheel and accelerator; the client is in control. Making choices without awareness could have catastrophic consequences—for example, approaching a bend too quickly when it's not safe to do so. The coach can help to de-mist the windscreen and enable a clearer view of the road ahead.

A process of raising awareness leading to change is described in Beisser's (1970) *Paradoxical Theory of Change*. "Change occurs when one becomes what he is, not when he tries to become what he is not. Change does not take place through a coercive attempt by the individual or by another person to change him" (p. 77).

This approach proposes that rather than trying to change, the client becomes just more aware. Rather than the coach trying to fix or change the client, the coach works with the aim, through dialogue, of continuously raising awareness. A useful mantra for the coach when things are not clear is to *just keep coming back to awareness.* It's where progress is made. A critical success factor in coaching is for clients to develop a clearer understanding of their realities, their situations, their contexts. If it's not making sense to the client, then the coach might experience puzzlement too. At these times, the coach's presence—and remaining fully present—is so important. These occasions can leave the coach grappling to comprehend what is going on. Putting to one side any inner need for certainty at such moments, the coach can simply listen and attend to the client and then choose to intervene. If it's not making sense to the coach, there's a reasonable chance it may not be making sense to the client. A useful, nonjudgmental intervention at this sense-making stage is to "drop-down" the discussion. A question is introduced to encourage the client to think further on the topic being discussed. Rather than chasing a goal or an outcome, a question is introduced into the here and now: "I'm not quite sure I'm fully grasping the point you are making right now. Can you tell me a little more about it?" Instead of chasing the outcome, the coach relaxes into—and explores further—the uncertainty, as illustrated in Figure 10.1.

In Figure 10.1, the journey from (A) to (B) demonstrates a frequently seen coaching journey: working with the client in position (A) to move toward and achieve the goal in position (B). In this instance, a goal has been agreed upon and the coaching is focused upon enabling the client to move toward this goal, shown by the central, horizontal line. But all is not yet clear for the client.

If the coach is aware of this, he or she can then drop-down the discussion, starting at position (A). This invites the client to reflect more fully. In Figure 10.1, the coach speaks from a nonjudgmental position of not fully understanding the client's story. The drop-down invites the client to restate the story, but in greater detail. The process from (A) to (C) provides the opportunity for the client to tell the story in greater detail and for the client to hear his or her own self talking about it out loud. The detail often leads to greater depth and allows the opportunity for exploration and dialogue in this newly revealed territory. Having reached (C), the coach can then engage with the client to move forward, perhaps to reach position (D). "As in all coaching conversations," wrote Gallwey (2000), "the point is simply that both client and coach become more conscious and more mobile" (p. 189).

The client's greater awareness heightens the prospect of more sustainable change and, significantly, the opportunity for transformational, rather than transactional, outcomes. Not only might the outcome have been achieved, but, through greater awareness and mobility, the client has changed too.

To summarize this through metaphor rather than trying to encourage the client to swim to the shore—to point (B)—the coach asks a question that encourages the client to remain in the same space. Rather than swimming, this might feel like treading water. The coach retains presence, remains patient, keeps comfortable with the confusion, and maintains trust in the coaching process. The coach keeps

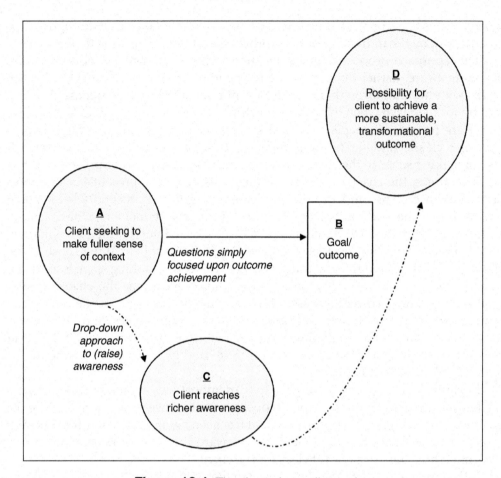

Figure 10.1 The drop-down discussion.

returning to awareness. It is a case of staying in the moment, in the confusion, to see what might emerge. Rather than the coach fixing or forcing, it offers the possibility for new awareness. This might seem counterintuitive for action-oriented coaches, but there's little point in starting to swim to the shore if it's out of sight and no one's clear exactly where it is.

CREATIVE APPROACHES

Inviting the client to explore further in this way encourages deeper reflection. But what happens if the client still struggles to articulate what is going on?

A "response-able" option in the midst of confusion is for the coach to shift the energy in the room. The coach might invite the client to draw a picture of what the topic would look like if sketched out on a piece of flipchart paper. Or create a constellation that maps out the topic on a table or on the floor. Or work dynamically and physically using the entire coaching room. Or act out roles. Or talk to empty chairs. The coach remains present in the moment and continuously reflects upon what might be usefully introduced within the here and now of the coaching session. What other resources might be to hand? Many are the coaching occasions when I have reached for tea bags, coffee and sugar packets, cookies, bottles, and glasses during coaching conversations. I like them because they're often close to hand and can be introduced in-the-moment and without formality. There is no "build-up" that might otherwise risk creating interference. Of course, these creative approaches can be introduced throughout the coaching session, not just at times of immobilization.

TRANSFERENCE AND THE LEADERSHIP CONTEXT

One of the tools in the coach's armory is the attendance toward what is being experienced between the coach and client. "Anyone hoping to make sense of interpersonal encounters at anything but an intuitive level needs to understand transference" wrote Kets de Vries (2006, p. 73).

Clients will often behave toward coaches in a way that they do with others. The client might unwittingly invite the coach to play a certain role in the relationship. Or the coach's stare might be experienced by the client as a criticism. A danger for the coach is being sucked into the client's repetitive patterns of communication that, rather than help, simply keep the client immobilized. It is a sobering and quite possibly a supervision-worthy moment when the client says: "That's what my father used to say."

Working with the transference as valuable data allows the coach to deepen understanding. What thoughts and emotions, what sense does the coach make while receiving transmissions from the client? How do these land with the coach? What feelings do these evoke within the coach? Experiencing these, remaining present, and maintaining presence is all part of the work.

As well as the impact within the relationship, the coach can attend to the transference themes that emerge from the client's stories. This is particularly noticeable when coaching leaders. Kets de Vries (2006) affirmed that "people in a position of authority have an uncanny ability—without conscious awareness—to reawaken transferential processes in themselves and others" (p. 76).

Leaders will invariably have expectations (leading to behaviors) of how they *should* behave in their leadership role. They will also have expectations of how their staff *should* behave. All of this provides valuable data for the coaches, who might also wish to reflect upon their personal perceptions around leaders' expectations and behaviors.

It certainly helps for coaches to become aware of their countertransference patterns. For example: "Some coaches may even experience an envy of high-flying executives who earn much more than the coach could ever command" (Peltier, 2001, p. 39). Awareness of transference and the potential for countertransference lessens the risk of the coach becoming entangled in the coaching relationship. Awareness is liberating in this context. It enables the coach to work more fully with what is said, how it is said, why it might be said, and what remains unsaid. Working above and below the surface, the coach draws together differing, complex strands within the coaching relationship. It is a curious state of being concurrently engaged and detached. Richer awareness of self and resilience as a coach provides a stable basis for managing self, responding to the client, and remaining present as the relationship emerges.

Nonjudgmentalism at such moments is vital. Rogers (1967) termed this unconditional positive regard, writing: "When someone understands how it feels and seems to be *me*, without wanting to analyze me or judge me, then I can blossom and grow in that climate" (p. 62). And Perls (1969) said that Gestalt therapists "do not analyze. We *integrate*" (p. 86).

ASSESSMENT TOOLS

In the middle and higher levels of organizations, coaches will encounter many leaders who have undergone, at various times, psychological profiles, 360-degree feedback, competency checks, and so on. They will have been measured, assessed, rated, described and possibly prescribed, and labeled accordingly. Coaches will do well to be aware not only the impact this has created in the arena in which they are working, but also their personal responsibilities regarding the application of such profiling tools. These assessments can be applied effectively and appropriately; on the other hand, they can be reductionist and, at their worst, risk leaving behind toxic atmospheres.

If a profiling tool—such as a personality profile or a 360-degree survey—has been applied, the results will have been documented; they will provide explicit information. What the coach can additionally bring to such explicit information (and the impact it has had) is a deep reservoir of tacit knowledge and understanding, garnered through the current (and previous) coaching interventions and life experiences. Using this tacit knowledge can then assist the client on the journey forward.

As the coaching conversation unfolds, what does the coach notice? A useful reflection point for coaches is to attend to what they notice. Or, to put it more starkly, what remains unnoticed. What the coach notices might be indicators of those triggers or transference patterns that the coach is attuned to. Yet what goes unnoticed? One practical methodology to explore this can be through attending group or peer supervision or to observe coaching practice (in groups). After the supervisee's or client's story has been told, each of the observers can note down what they noticed. Then they can attend to each other's observations.

COACHING RESPONSIBLY

Coaching is still finding its place as a developmental intervention. Rubbing shoulders with mentoring, consulting, counseling, and therapy, it continues to fill out its own emergent space.

Core skills such as building trust, promoting mutual respect, maintaining confidentiality, and acting with integrity are entry-level requirements. Joining a coaching association and following its code of ethics; continuously reflecting upon practice; and undertaking regular supervision are followed as the norm rather than the exception. Developing and being guided by an inner moral and ethical compass, and acknowledging and working within boundaries are all essentials for the coach who seeks to work safely and effectively.

A coaching session is not a therapy session. Coaches are not therapists. (Some coaches might possess counseling or therapy-based qualifications, but they have responsibilities to maintain boundaries between coaching and therapy practice.)

Coaching is about raising performance and bringing about change. Psychological factors underpin these. The realm of coaching encompasses cognition and emotion. Part of the coach's developmental journey is to increase competence in working with thoughts and feelings. To work with others in this way requires similar work on oneself. The coach can work within his or her boundary limits but at the same time seek to safely extend these. Pooley (2006) wrote that: "Coaches might be said to be working with 'dis-ease,' as opposed to with 'disease'" (p. 119). There is a lot of truth in the old adage that a problem shared is a problem halved: The simple coaching quality of really being listened to can feel therapeutic, but it is not therapy. It's difficult to underestimate the benefits offered by allowing someone just to talk and unpack his or her inner thoughts and feelings.

Within the coaching journey, paradoxically, it is often the case that, the less that coaches do, the more they do. Listening, selectively questioning, and intervening requires flexibility and an ability to remain present, even—and especially—in challenging times.

The coach's raft of interpersonal skills and behaviors are all deployed through the relationship. Just as the skilled pianist insists that the piano keys are finely tuned, so continuous practice and regular supervision help ensure the coach can seamlessly work safely, effectively, and appropriately within the co-created reality of the interpersonal arena.

REFERENCES

Barrett-Lennard, G. T. (2013). *The relationship paradigm: Human being beyond individualism.* Basingstoke, England: Palgrave Macmillan.

Beisser, A. (1970). The paradoxical theory of change. In J. Fagan & I. L. Shepherd (Eds.), *Gestalt therapy now: Theory, techniques, applications* (pp. 77–80). Gouldsboro, ME: Gestalt Journal Press.

Blakey, J., & Day, I. (2012). *Challenging coaching: Going beyond traditional coaching to face the facts.* London, England: Nicholas Brealey.

Bluckert, P. (2015). *Gestalt coaching: Right here, right now.* Maidenhead, England: McGraw Hill.

Gallwey, T. (2000). *The inner game of work: Overcoming mental obstacles for maximum performance.* London, England: Orion Business.

Joyce, P., & Sills, C. (2010). *Skills in gestalt counselling and psychotherapy* (2nd ed.). London, England: Sage Publications.

Kahn, M. (2014). *Coaching on the axis: Working with complexity in business and executive coaching.* London, England: Karnac.

Kets de Vries, M. (2006). *The leadership mystique: Leading behavior in the human enterprise* (2nd ed.). Harlow, England: Pearson Education.

Leary-Joyce, J. (2014). *The fertile void: Gestalt coaching at work.* St Albans, England: AOEC Press.

Nelson, K. (2010). *Your total coach: 50 ideas for inspiring personal and professional growth.* Oxford, England: Infinite Ideas Ltd.

O'Neill, M. B. (2007). *Executive coaching with backbone and heart: A systems approach to engaging leaders with their challenges* (2nd ed.). San Francisco, CA: Jossey-Bass.

Peltier, B. (2001). *The psychology of executive coaching: Theory and application.* New York, NY: Brunner-Routledge.

Perls, F. S. (1969). *Gestalt therapy verbatim*. Gouldsboro, ME: The Gestalt Journal Press.

Pooley, J. (2006). Layers of meaning: A coaching journey. In H. Brunning (Ed.), *Executive coaching: Systems-psychodynamic perspective* (pp. 113–130). London, England: Karnac.

Rogers, C. (1967). *On becoming a person: A therapist's view of psychotherapy*. London, England: Constable.

Stout-Rostron, S. (2014). *Business coaching international: Transforming individuals and organizations* (2nd ed.). London, England: Karnac.

11

Presence as Coaching Meta-Competency

Doug Silsbee[†]

P resence is, at core, the inner condition of being in the moment, creative, and resourceful. Presence is neither a coaching technique nor a methodology. It is a simple product of what we do with our attention, moment by moment.

Traditionally, presence has been thought of in the coaching world as a competency for coaches. This chapter expands this understanding to frame presence additionally as a crucial outcome for coaching clients that supports every other element of the coaching engagement. Presence is the very foundation for resilience, providing the inner conditions to access every other competency available to the client, regardless of the challenges that the client is facing. Presence also fosters the development of sustainable physiologically supported behavioral change and is thus a crucial meta-competency for the client as well as for the coach.

WHAT IS PRESENCE?

Presence is, in a sense, the experience of witnessing ourselves paying attention. We can learn to witness our thoughts, stories, and our relentless commentary on ourselves and on the world around us. We can witness our emotions and our moods as they arise and pass. We can witness our internal sensations: hunger, thirst, tension, breath, energy flow, stillness. And, as we witness our very experience, moment by moment, we come into the present.

[†]Deceased.

PRESENCE IS AN INTERNAL CONDITION

Presence is not a technique or a set of techniques. While presence can, of course, be accessed through techniques, it is the resulting state that is of most interest to us here.

Presence is the internal state of the awareness of immediacy, stillness, inclusive awareness and possibility (Silsbee, 2018). Presence is the actual experience of being open, available, and alert. Being present is observing the self, others, and the context as if from a balcony perspective, and having full awareness in the moment, rather than thinking about the future or rehashing the past. This experience of presence brings with it a palpable sense of clarity and intelligence and readiness for whatever might happen, and for whatever might be needed from us.

Practitioners with deep experience describe certain attributes that become reliably available by directing attention in this way (Davidson & Begley, 2012; Goleman & Davidson, 2017; Risom, 2010). These attributes, summarized in Table 11.1, are

Table 11.1 Attributes of Presence and the Implications for Coaching

Attribute	Coach/Client Experience	Implications for Coaching
Directed Attention	We focus and direct our attention, stabilizing and regulating state.	Supports impulse control. Stabilizes state independent of context. Staying present to action urge without acting is key to behavior change.
Clarity	Witnessing of thoughts, feelings, and sensations precisely as they arise without interpretation or judgment.	Identity needs and mental chatter have less grip. Present-moment experience can be externalized and included as coaching content.
Acceptance and Equanimity	Observation of self, others, and events as they are with neutrality and no judgment.	Produces a sense of safety, spaciousness, and unconditional positive regard. Supports facing the situation as it is.
Dis-identification	Conscious awareness that we are not our experience; experience of observing the self in action.	Witnessing makes us more self-aware, less entangled with our reactions, and with greater capability for behavioral choice.
Present-Moment Awareness	Precision and crystalline clarity.	A palpable sense of creativity, aliveness and resonance infuses the conversation. Fluidity and lightness provide ease.
Stillness and Timelessness	Awareness of the spaciousness available in this moment.	Presence expands the "space between stimulus and response," making available different choices in the moment.

characteristic of the experience of presence. They can be cultivated through attention practices done diligently over time. And, as we shall see, these attributes are highly relevant to us as coaches, to our clients, and to the generative capacity of the coaching relationship.

PRESENCE IS A DIRECT EXPERIENCE

While presence can be described, there is an inherent paradox in writing a chapter on presence. This chapter is essentially a linguistic and cognitive presentation on presence, yet presence itself is a whole-person subjective experience. By its very nature, presence is not reducible to cognition and language. Since I intend for this chapter to be a doorway into presence, your direct experience of presence will speak more loudly than could any set of words.

As a foundational experience, then, let us experiment. At the conclusion of this paragraph, please put the book down and close your eyes. As you close your eyes, bring your attention to the physical sensation of the breath moving in and out of your body: your chest rising and falling, or the coolness at the tip of your nose with your in-breath. Keep your attention on this precise physical sensation for a few seconds. . . . As you focus precisely on your breath, note the absence of words in this fleeting moment of stillness. For sure, your brain will soon generate additional words to fill the gap. But for a moment, a fleeting moment, as you wait expectantly for the next thought to come, you will reliably have a glimpse of the stillness that is presence.

Now try it. With this brief common experience to refer to, let's expand our notion of presence. I am hoping that you experienced at least a momentary cessation of the endless stream of thoughts that is the primary content of our awareness. If you did, that moment would have revealed a sense of timelessness, of stillness, of possibility.

Of course, this is just a moment. However, with some regular practice and consistency, these moments can be expanded in time. They can become embodied so that the inner condition of presence becomes increasingly available. And, as we shall see, the ready access to this inner condition is central to what coaching is all about.

PRESENCE EXTENDS AN INTERNAL CONDITION INTO A RELATIONSHIP

It is helpful to recognize presence both as an internal condition of the coach and as the extension of that internal condition into our relationships and conversations. As such, we can understand why the International Coach Foundation (ICF) has included coaching presence as one of the core competencies against which every credentialed coach is assessed (ICF, n.d.).

The use of certain modifiers with the word "presence" (e.g., "coaching presence" or "leadership presence") refers to the internal condition of one person being extended to others. This produces a sense of connectedness, intimacy, and resonance.

While coaching presence is underpinned by interpersonal neurobiological processes (Lewis, Amini, & Lannon, 2001; Siegel, 2012), the subjective experience of this connectedness, for both coach and client, is what is most germane for our purposes here. Our sense of resonance with our coaching clients is the very foundation for interpersonal trust, intimacy, and psychological safety. Presence produces the inherent neutrality in the coaching process that supports clients accessing their own resourcefulness.

PRESENCE REGULATES STATE

Presence, and specifically the process of directing our attention into our internal condition, stabilizes and regulates that inner condition. This is a profound realization, although not a new one. Mindfulness practitioners for millennia have recognized the power of directing attention inward.

When the nervous system is activated, because of chronic stress, immediate triggers, or a general reactivity to what is going on around us, directing attention into the breath or into the sensations of the body reduces the chatter of the mind and stabilizes and regulates the overall condition of the nervous system. Any number of simple practices, done over time, can help a person develop reliable access to a settled inner state and greater equanimity. The resulting inner state is less reactive, and more creative and resourceful.

The act of directing attention is always available. We see that directed attention is an inherent human capacity, allowing direct intervention through the vehicle of our attention into the very workings of our indescribably complex nervous system.

PRESENCE IS A DOORWAY INTO RESILIENCE AND CREATIVITY

Table 11.1 reveals some of the significant implications of presence for the coaching and development process. And the previous section offered the well-substantiated claim that attention itself changes the physiological condition of the nervous system. Access to the internal experience of presence, both for client and coach, supports a range of powerful capacities (Silsbee, 2018). These include:

- Consciously choosing among rich and complementary perspectives
- Recognizing and inhibiting reactive urges and impulsive actions
- Recognizing how challenges lead to defending identity
- Observing and self-regulating internal state at any moment
- Deepening resilience: the capacity to stay creative and resourceful no matter what's going on around you
- Directing attention into the commitments that matter most
- Deepening connectivity and relationships with others
- Tolerating strong emotional states in self and others
- Maintaining balance in complexity

Clearly these benefits from access to presence transcend the narrow roles of coach and coaching client. These are deeply human capacities, equally relevant for leaders, mothers, activists, business executives, and anyone else whose work in the world requires resilience and engagement with other human beings.

Every human possesses vast resourcefulness, including a wealth of behavioral and perspectival alternatives that are both real and potentially invisible to us in any given moment. In particular, when we are triggered in the heat of action by perceived threats to our identity or well-being, we tend to constrict, narrow, and default to behavioral strengths that may have worked well in the past but may not be optimal now.

A presence-based capacity for resilience is a powerful antidote to this trigger-induced narrowing of possibilities. Presence allows us to witness ourselves in the very process of being triggered, and then to regulate our state through directed attention. In short, the meta-competency of presence facilitates access to the myriad technical, interpersonal, and leadership skills that all of us possess.

PRESENCE IS A FOUNDATIONAL CONDITION FOR PHYSIOLOGICAL CHANGE AND EMBODIMENT

An exploding body of empirical research is establishing a better understanding of the neurobiology of learning and embodiment. It is clear that certain physiological conditions (described in Table 11.2) enable attention-directed neuroplasticity: the "rewiring" of crucial parts of the human nervous system (Claxton, 2016; Hanson, 2016). This rewiring literally changes the physiological substrate that gives rise both to our subjective experience and our spontaneous reactions to what is happening around us. Changing this physiological substrate changes the basis for our response capability as leaders and as humans. The implications of this for many fields, including coaching, are profound.

Table 11.2 Conditions for Presence-Enabled Embodied Learning

Condition	Coaching Process Design
Repetition	Design fieldwork that includes repetitive practices both of inner states and new behaviors
Presence and full attention	Develop immediacy and presence within sessions so that clients have the experience of presence to draw from in fieldwork
Emotional valence	Connect fieldwork and new behaviors to a sense of purpose
Healthy body	Support client's development of self-care around exercise, diet, and sleep that produce optimal physiological conditions for brain health
Whole-person engagement	Design fieldwork that includes cognitive, body-based, structural systems, and relational components so that the client's whole internal and external systems are engaged in learning

A coaching client, for example, can practice accessing the creative resourceful inner state of presence until this resilience becomes increasingly a default condition of this person's nervous system. Resilience has thus become embodied, making available the client's creativity and full range of skills despite external circumstances.

The meta-competency of presence directly supports every other behavioral and leadership outcome that a coaching client seeks to develop. Coaching interventions must be designed to foster embodiment if short-term insights are to translate into long-term capacities. Therefore, as part of the ongoing joint design process with clients, evidence-based coaching must include fieldwork practices that both cultivate resilient inner states and create the preconditions for neuroplastic change to take root. The result of leading-edge coaching process design is sustainable, physiologically supported change: embodied development.

IMPLICATIONS: PRESENCE AS COACHING COMPETENCY

Let's examine the implications of this more comprehensive understanding of presence for us as coaches. Here we look at what it means to practice presence as a coaching *competency*.

FLUIDITY AND STABILITY: THE INNER CONDITION OF THE COACH

Paradoxically, the capacity of the mind to self-regulate the nervous system serves multiple functions. Our directed attention can self-regulate and stabilize a ground and settled state in the midst of a client's strong emotional experience, or amidst the chaos and distractions of a reactive work environment. As we have seen, this grounded internal condition, by means of biological co-regulation and the relational field, serves the wonderful function of serving as a resource for the client's nervous system as well.

On the other hand, presence also supports fluidity of attention, which is seemingly the opposite of stability. The attributes of present-moment awareness and disidentification allow fast and fluid shifts of perspective and state. This fluidity, in which our attention can flit quickly over a wide range of ideas, perspectives, and experiences without attaching to any of them, can be quite enlivening. The resulting creativity and resourcefulness is wonderful for generating new ideas, thinking out of the box, and questioning long-held assumptions. (These, obviously, are also useful attributes for clients, as we shall see.)

AVAILABILITY OF THE COACH: SUSPENDING EGO TO SERVE CLIENTS' NEEDS

One of the ways in which the coaching process can become subverted is when the coach does not recognize his or her own biases, judgments, and attachments. These ego identifications can cause huge problems because coaching becomes co-opted by the coach's own unrecognized identity needs, rather than serving the client's learning process.

On the other hand, when the coach is present, the coach can directly experience the internal mobilization that precedes any behavior or action. With awareness, the coach can then inhibit previously automatic urges (e.g., to give advice) and, rather than acting on those urges, make himself or herself more available to the client. This means that the coaching conversation is more purely dedicated to emerging client needs and less driven by the coach's unconscious identity needs and resulting behavioral urges.

Thus, we are more resourceful as coaches when we are present. Being neutral, spacious, and available for whatever arises in the coaching conversation is an essential aspect of what makes the coaching relationship work.

RELATIONAL FIELD: QUALITIES OF THE FIELD

Presence also enables and supports the holding of a relational field: the felt container, palpable to both parties, within which a conversation takes place (Gilligan, 2004, p. 111). Often described through the metaphor of a "bubble," this field is the basis for resonance and connection.

Qualities of this field (such as compassion, neutrality, spaciousness, resonance, and unconditional positive regard; Silsbee, 2008) can be sensed by a coach who is present. These qualities are strengthened and reinforced through bringing them to the forefront of awareness; by extending the coach's attention toward the client; these qualities then become more available and palpable to the client as well.

BIOLOGICAL CO-REGULATION

The internal state of the coach can be available as a resource for the client's inner state. Inner states are contagious. If equanimity, groundedness, and optimism are essential qualities through which clients wish to engage with their challenges, it is exceedingly pragmatic when the coach can access and embody these qualities in service to the clients. When clients have difficulty generating these qualities on their own, the internal state of the coach can be transmitted through the process of biological co-regulation (Siegel, 2015; Silsbee, 2018), making that state more available for the clients.

All of us have witnessed biological co-regulation in play when the soothing presence of a mother settles a squalling baby, or when the calm voice of a firefighter reassures an accident victim that help is here. Clients who are triggered, anxious, or distracted will often not be able to resource themselves in the moment. A skillful coach can provide this same care, beneath the level of language, through the transmission of resourced inner states that then become increasingly available to the clients.

MODELING

The visible and palpable modeling of optimistic, resourceful, settled inner states is also a demonstration to the client that such states are possible. The coaches' witnessing of their own experience invites clients do this for themselves, increasing their own level of self-awareness during the coaching conversation. This modeling is part of the generation of resourcefulness in the moment.

IMPLICATIONS: PRESENCE AS COACHING OUTCOME

It is not conventional wisdom in the coaching field that presence is a crucial and reliable *outcome* of a coaching relationship. This reframed and deepened understanding of presence includes presence as a coaching competency and also expands it to claim, without hesitation, that presence is a client meta-competency essential to the success of the coaching enterprise.

Every one of the implications of the previous section on presence as a coaching competency also applies to clients. Clients' capacities to cultivate fluidity and stability of attention, to suspend their own identity needs in service to others, to attune to the relational field, to co-regulate with others, and to model presence in their own relationships are universally relevant skills.

Here we look at what it means, additionally, to practice presence as a coaching outcome for the client.

RESILIENCE OF THE CLIENT

Presence becomes a characteristic of the coaching conversation itself. Coaching is not simply talking in the abstract about the client's context, nor is it primarily a question of identifying solutions that can be applied after the session.

Rather, in addition to a conversation that takes place in language, coaching is an exchange between two nervous systems. In every coaching conversation, we are actively inviting the client to access and cultivate more resilient creative and resourceful inner states. This development of resilience, and presence as a meta-competency, makes the coaching conversation itself a real-time practice in building the foundation for effective action in the world. The coaching session is, in a sense, a laboratory for the cultivation of resilience itself.

A subtext of every coaching conversation is the inner state of a client. We pay attention to this as coaches when we invite clients to be present with themselves. We acknowledge and spotlight both the insights that coaching sometimes enables and also the inner state that enables the insights. Together, we tease apart how the client accessed this state, so that we can jointly design fieldwork that builds, over time, increasingly reliable access to resilience itself.

INCREASED ACCESS TO EVERY OTHER OUTCOME UNDER CULTIVATION

Resilience is not generally the reason people come to coaching. They come to coaching to envision new futures, increase their access to more effective behaviors, reduce the grip of old habits, and increase their capacity to lead a life of meaning and purpose. These broad coaching outcomes are underpinned by specific and observable competency-based coaching outcomes that clients develop over time. A coaching relationship is most obviously dedicated to supporting new meaning-making and behavioral outcomes.

What is less obvious is that the client's implementation of new behaviors is often impeded by unrecognized identity needs. The deeply worn neurologic grooves of old habits include both visible behaviors and the inner patterns of thinking and interpretation that are the underpinnings of the client's identity itself. Replacing old habits is not as easy as we might hope.

A client's resilient inner state reduces the grip of old habits. Resilience frees the tremendous capacity of the nervous system to reimagine futures and to find fresh perspective on the present. Resilience brings awareness into these subtle processes and illuminates choice points that might otherwise not be apparent. Resilience means the capacity to be creative and resourceful and capable of action regardless of what's going on around us. This directly translates to accessing the capabilities and skills that we sometimes forget in the frenzy of daily life.

Presence is an accelerant, a lubricant that greatly facilitates the client's liberation from old, worn habits and the availability of new possibilities and choices.

PRECONDITION FOR EMBODIMENT

Presence is also one of the preconditions for embodied learning. Research shows that focused and directed attention facilitates the formation of new neural pathways, and the reassignment of neural networks from old habits into the development of new, more effective and life-sustaining habits (Schwartz & Begley, 2003).

Coaching relationships integrate actual sessions and "fieldwork" done by the client between sessions. This real-world application provides a powerful chance to experiment with new behaviors, and to practice new capabilities that can lead, over time, to embodiment and ready access to a greater range of leadership moves. Presence supports this embodiment process, both within the coaching conversation itself and when integrated into fieldwork, as we discuss next.

APPLICATION

We have now described what presence is, and the implications for both client and coach. Now we will explore how to infuse the quality of presence into the coaching relationship by anchoring it in specific practices and behaviors.

A couple of years ago, I conducted an informal survey during an ICF webinar on mindfulness in coaching (ICF, 2015). Ninety-nine percent of the self-selected coaches from 30 countries on the webinar said they believed mindfulness was relevant and important in coaching. Seventy percent of these people had committed ongoing personal practices. Yet, only 50% actually included mindfulness or somatic methods in their coaching work itself! While surely a small sample, this reveals a startling gap between what coaches personally experience as effective and what they actually feel ready to bring into their coaching practices as an explicit part of their coaching model and process.

Table 11.3 reveals five distinct domains within which we can begin to infuse presence into the work we do with clients, in service to the ongoing development of the meta-competency of presence as a specific and pragmatic outcome throughout all of our coaching.

Table 11.3 Domains of Application for Presence in Coaching

Domain	Description
Ongoing foundational practice for the coach	Consistent and committed meditation and/or somatic practices that build a signature way of being
Session-specific presence techniques for the coach	Practices and methods that prepare and support the coach for self-regulation and presence during the coaching session
Presence-based and somatic methods used with client during sessions	Specific methods and techniques that build immediacy during the coaching session, and invite the client into presence and awareness. These methods build client self-regulation skills in the moment.
Specific practices and techniques incorporated into client fieldwork	Practices and exercises between coaching sessions that develop client capacity for presence and resilience
Ongoing foundational practices for client	Consistent and committed meditation and/or somatic practices that build a signature way of being

ONGOING FOUNDATIONAL PRACTICES FOR THE COACH[1]

Sit Regularly

Commit to a regular attention (sitting/meditation) practice. Even 10 minutes a day builds access, over time, to the reliable attributes of presence: directed attention, clarity, acceptance and equanimity, dis-identification, present-moment awareness, and stillness and timelessness. These attributes are fundamental to sustainable resilience and behavior change.

Do Somatic (Body–Mind) Practices

Engage the entire nervous system through awareness practices that involve the body. Sports, martial arts, yoga: almost any "physical" activity can be repurposed as a somatic practice when it is (a) coupled to a purpose, (b) done regularly, over time, and (c) done with presence and awareness.

Self-Observe and Reflect

Pay attention to your own internal experience during the course of your activities, including coaching. A structured self-observation practice builds on the essential presence experience of witnessing. Most often, this consists of a regular written reflection on your habitual behaviors, paying particular attention to the direct experience of the underlying drivers and the urges that precede these behaviors.

Inquire

Engage in regular inquiry practice. Inquire into your own experience, tracking sensation and thought, and reporting it to a partner, a journal, or an audio recording device. Inquiry is a wonderful way to keep you present in your experience and to follow it into deeper levels of understanding.

Do Psycho–Spiritual Work

Arrange for supervision, coaching, guidance, and/or other support in support of your own ongoing integration and development. Mindful attention reliably reveals the habits, rooted in our history, that reduce our flexibility and resourcefulness. However, recognizing and releasing the deeper levels of these triggers without outside support and perspective is difficult. (This outside resourcing, of course, is the premise of coaching in the first place! We need and deserve this ourselves.)

SESSION-SPECIFIC PRESENCE TECHNIQUES FOR THE COACH[1]

Center Yourself

Take a few minutes, every time, before your coaching sessions, to prepare yourself internally for the session. Center yourself, let go of whatever you were just doing, and align your attention toward this client and this moment.

Use Systematic Templates to Prime Your Attention

Create a system around your coaching sessions that encourages mindfulness. Build templates and processes for a consistent pre-session routine that helps you to:

- Clear your mind from distractions
- Orient to the client and set an intention
- Recognize and manage your mood and distractions
- Bring awareness to specific habits that you want to mitigate
- Focus on competencies that you want to develop

Stay Connected With Your Client

Build your coaching presence through consistent tracking of your own internal experience, of the client, and of the context throughout the session. Practice noticing the inevitable triggers and distractions, and build the competency of bringing your attention back, over and over.

Invite Biological Co-Regulation

Your own settled, mindful, centered inner state invites the same with your client. The condition of presence in your own nervous system has a biological regulating effect on that of your client. Think of your nervous system as a resource of great service to your client.

Commit to Regular Post-Session Self-Observation

Use a template for reflection after each session about your inner experience, habits that showed up, and triggers and distractions.

PRESENCE-BASED AND SOMATIC METHODS USED WITH CLIENT DURING SESSIONS[1]

Model and Disclose With Transparency

Model present-moment awareness through sharing your own internal experience, emotions, and so forth. While it is important to not make your own experience the focus, disclosing your own experience appropriately builds intimacy and safety, and models awareness for the client.

Request Client Self-Observation

Ask the client to observe and report on his or her inner experience, in the moment. Self-observation invites mindfulness and presence. This can be a request for the client's thoughts, what the client is feeling, or what body sensations the client is experiencing. Tracking and reporting on present-moment experience brings the client's attention into the moment.

Teach an Attention Practice

Provide live, real-time instruction with mindfulness, centering, or directing attention. Doing so builds skills during the coaching session and provides direct experience that can be built upon in subsequent sessions or in fieldwork.

Hold Space

Allow silence, maintaining your own presence during the silence. This deepens the sense of presence, encourages the client's own processing, and supports the client's capacity for attention to what might be emerging. The more profound your own internal silence, the more powerful the space that this silence introduces into the flow of the coaching conversation. Silence can deepen the relational field.

Direct Attention Into Sensation

Ask the client to report what the client is sensing in his or her body. Since sensations only exist in the present moment, asking the client to witness or self-observe what he or she is noticing internally brings the client into presence. In addition, tracking changes in these sensations over time refines the process of self-observation, and invites awareness of the shifts in state that often accompany self-observation.

Ground With Client's Strong States

Drop your attention and ground your own state when your client is having a strong experience (difficult emotions, energy release, feeling overwhelmed, etc.). Through the process of biological co-regulation, your stable dropped state serves as a resource to your client's nervous system during this strong experience. (Think of a crisis situation in which someone says, "I don't know how you stayed so calm when that happened, but your calmness helped me do what I needed to do.")

Offer Assessments, Followed by a Question

Reflect, through in-the-moment feedback, what you observe in language, in emotion, and/or in physical posture or other body-based observations. It is most helpful to follow the assessment with a question that invites the client to share what he or she is noticing, or to respond to how the assessment rings true (or not) for him or her. This resulting self-observation is a move toward presence.

Make Internal Processes Explicit

Ask the client to externalize internal experiences. When the client experiences a shift (increased energy, optimism, an insight, etc.), ask the client how he or she did it. By making the granular nature of this shift explicit, the client can learn how to replicate it. We reframe it from a surprising phenomenon to a cultivable skill that can be practiced.

SPECIFIC PRACTICES AND TECHNIQUES INCORPORATED INTO CLIENT FIELDWORK[1]

Include Attention Practices in Fieldwork

Incorporate a short, regular sitting practice into client fieldwork. Call it an "experiment," if that helps invite openness with your client. Even 10 minutes a day can have tremendous benefits. Providing a little research background on the health, psychological, and leadership payoffs will be helpful for those clients for whom this is new and different. Provide a narrative of relevance so that clients connect attention practice to a specific outcome that they care about.

Include Self-Observation Practices in Fieldwork

Design regular practices with your clients in which they pay rigorous attention to their inner experience during their daily activities. Structured daily reflections build clients' skills at witnessing the thoughts, emotions, and sensations that precede behavior. Over time, this builds client awareness and choice. Self-observations can be designed for clients for developing awareness around:

- Habitual and unconscious default behaviors that create problems
- Choice points that the client seems to override, falling into unhelpful patterns of thought or behavior
- New behaviors the client seeks to cultivate, but that don't come naturally

Include Somatic Practices in Fieldwork

Repurpose physical practices the client is already doing, or custom-design somatic practices that are particularly metaphorical for the client's coaching issue. Either way, engaging the client's entire nervous system in the change process greatly accelerates development. Emphasize the aspect of attention as the client does these practices and link the practices to neuroplastic change and the embodiment of new capabilities.

Invite Presence When Trying Out a New Behavior

Ask the client to couple presence and awareness with a new action or behavior that is part of the coaching fieldwork. Present-moment awareness as a new action is being taken helps loosen the grip of old habits and encourages the internalization and embodiment of new capacities.

Ongoing Foundational Practices for the Client[1]

When clients are at the developmental stage of being primarily focused on business results and leadership efficacy, they are unlikely to want a long-term practice for its own sake.

However, at later developmental stages, the client may begin to see resilience, mindfulness, and qualities of presence as foundational, and may seek ongoing presence practices that extend far beyond the initial coaching engagement. Clients who experience direct and pragmatic benefits from their cultivation of presence, both in their own sense of well-being and in their efficacy in their professional roles, will also probably have an investment in this continued development.

When clients are open to this, it can be a great service to connect the client to a teacher, class, books, videos, or other resources. Encourage your client to take on a regular practice of some sort, and/or commit to any of the strategies in the preceding section on foundational practices for the coach.

CONCLUSION

We have explored presence as a foundational competency for coaches and the numerous implications of this for the coaching process. Further, we have expanded our understanding of presence to include it as a coaching outcome for our clients.

The clear benefits of presence for deepening our coaching, and for supporting our clients' development of sustainable, physiologically supported behavior change, are neither automatic nor short term. Reading a book on coaching techniques is wholly insufficient. Further, using presence techniques without the spaciousness, ground, and unconditional positive regard that derive from our own presence as practitioners is likely to come across as shallow and even manipulative.

I believe it is imperative that coaching as a profession reframe presence as an essential outcome of the process. Coaches must actively develop their own access to presence. Only from that foundation can we then infuse presence and immediacy into our coaching conversations such that our world, in some small way, becomes a more resilient and life-affirming place.

NOTE

1. These sections are from Silsbee, D. (2016). Mindfulness and coaching: A primer. Retrieved from http://www.wbecs.com/wbecs2016/wp-content/uploads/2016/04/WBECS2016PreHandouts.docx.pdf

REFERENCES

Claxton, G. (2016). *Intelligence in the flesh: Why your mind needs your body much more than it thinks.* New Haven, CT: Yale University Press.

Davidson, R. J., & Begley, S. (2012). *The emotional life of your brain: How its unique patterns affect the way you think, feel, and live—and how you can change them.* New York, NY: Avery.

Gilligan, S. (Ed.). (2004). *Walking in two worlds: The relational self in theory, practice, and community.* Phoenix, AZ: Zeig, Tucker & Theisen.

Goleman, D., & Davidson, R. J. (2017). *Altered traits: Science reveals how meditation changes your mind, brain, and body.* New York, NY: Avery.

Hanson, R. (2016). *Hardwiring happiness: The new brain science of contentment, calm, and confidence.* New York, NY: Harmony.

ICF. (2015, September). Advance webinar: Science of coaching. Retrieved from https://www.coachfederation.org/events/landing.cfm?ItemNumber=3283&navItemNumber=3284

ICF. (n.d.). Core competencies. Retrieved from https://www.coachfederation.org/credential/landing.cfm?ItemNumber=2206

Lewis, T., Amini, F., & Lannon, R. (2001). *A general theory of love.* New York, NY: Random House.

Risom, J.-E. (2010). *Presence meditation: The practice of life awareness.* Berkeley, CA: North Atlantic Books.

Schwartz, J. M., & Begley, S. (2003). *The mind and the brain: Neuroplasticity and the power of mental force.* New York, NY: Harper Perennial.

Siegel, D. J. (2012). *Pocket guide to interpersonal neurobiology: An integrative handbook of the mind.* New York, NY: W. W. Norton.

Siegel, D. J. (2015). *The developing mind: How relationships and the brain interact to shape who we are* (2nd ed.). New York, NY: Guilford Press.

Silsbee, D. (2008). *Presence-based coaching: Cultivating self-generative leaders through mind, body, and heart.* San Francisco, CA: Jossey-Bass.

Silsbee, D. (2018). *Presence-based leadership: Complexity practices for clarity, resilience, and results that matter.* Asheville, NC: Yes! Global.

ADDITIONAL READING AND RESOURCES

Brown, K. W., Creswell, J. D., & Ryan, R. M. (Eds.). (2015). *Mindfulness in organizations: Foundations, research, and applications.* Cambridge, UK: Cambridge University Press.

Gunaratana, B. H. (2011). *Mindfulness in plain English.* Somerville, MA: Wisdom Publications.

Kabat-Zinn, J. (2013). *Full catastrophe living.* New York, NY: Bantam Books.

Presence-Based® Coach Training and Certification: presencebasedcoaching.com/training

Salzberg, S. (2010). *Real happiness: The power of meditation.* New York, NY: Workman Publishing.

Siegel, D. J. (2007). *The mindful brain: Reflection and attunement in the cultivation of well-being.* New York, NY: Norton.

Silsbee, D. (2010). *The mindful coach: Seven roles for facilitating leader development.* San Francisco, CA: Jossey-Bass.

Silsbee, D. (2018). *Presence-based leadership: Complexity practices for clarity, resilience, and results that matter.* Asheville, NC: Yes! Global.

12

The Coach as Awareness Agent: A Process Approach

Dorothy E. Siminovitch

No problem can be solved from the same level of consciousness that created it.
        —Einstein

Change and complexity define the 21st century. These challenges impose heightened urgency for leaders and their coaches being able to respond with strong awareness skills to access the self-knowledge, emotional and social intelligence, and creative adaptability necessary to meet those challenges. Awareness and the pursuit of awareness are referenced as early as the 2nd century BCE in the *Yoga-Sutras* of the great Indian sage Patanjali. His concepts of achieving awareness are still with us, augmented by later definitions and practices from divergent cultures and ideologies. The concept of awareness was the domain of a spiritualized, Eastern-oriented sensibility until it began to be translated into secularized Western paradigms, then introduced into leadership development programs and workplace environments. Awareness and awareness-based practices are now vital competencies to support leaders and their coaches, as traditional knowledge and skills are proving insufficient. We propose awareness development as the key component of successful 21st-century leadership. This chapter describes the essence of awareness, and practices for cultivating and using awareness strategically for ongoing learning and choiceful action.

BEING AWARE: THE NEW COORDINATES

It's important to understand that awareness is filtered by perception, which occurs through the experiential and phenomenological observations of our five senses of sight, hearing, taste, touch, and smell. These sensory data must be distinct enough to draw our attention as emergent awareness—an image, a sound, a taste, a scent, a visceral sense of touch. Becoming aware is the result of cognitively framing those data with a meaning interpretation. When something catches our attention or we experience a disruption—physical, emotional, or intellectual—we seek internal understanding by seeking more data, for better interpretation, and deciding whether to take action. Awareness is a complex phenomenon since there are multiple things competing for our attention. We develop an economy of what we will or will not pay attention to by establishing priorities and limits around what to attend to. The value of setting priorities and choosing constructive resistance about what not to pay attention to allows for discipline and self-preserving self-regulation. A dilemma occurs when resistance becomes overly habitual and awareness becomes restricted, such that important phenomena are missed. Awareness-raising techniques are then essential to promote contact with the internal or external data that may be relevant for alternative perspectives and choices. Heightening clients' awareness requires an interactive, collaborative process, where the coach offers the client data-based observations, questions, and feedback that may provoke new awarenesses for the client.

The increasingly fast-paced world has empowered process-oriented coaching approaches because awareness-heightening strategies can foster self-awareness, which strengthens self-development. The shift to awareness heightening in leadership development aligns itself with collaborative values and competencies of coaching. The coach is no longer the expert who tells clients what they need to know or how to put specific knowledge into practice. Today's coach is a *thought partner*, a *co-collaborator*, and an *experiential guide* who supports awareness practices for the client. In the moment when a person becomes aware, we often see a rapid self-initiated movement toward learning and self-identified opportunities.

Coaching for awareness can be described as a change from *horizontal* to *vertical* leadership development strategies (Petrie, 2014, p. 8). Horizontal learning is essentially technical training: a transfer of content—information, techniques—in focused areas, usually involving measurable behaviors or competencies. Its established role in virtually every organizational training program may explain the passion for accumulating official certifications as testaments to one's presumed development. The problem is that such learning isn't adequate to help leaders cope with the kind of unpredictable, ambiguous, and disruptive challenges now routinely encountered that cannot be answered by knowledge acquisition alone. The counterpart of horizontal development is vertical development, which highlights awareness development as a process that leads to an "ability to *think* in more complex, systemic, strategic, and interdependent ways" so that leaders can confidently negotiate from a position that is "equal to or superior to the complexity of the environment" in which these challenges occur (Petrie, 2014, pp. 8, 7; original emphasis). This requires that leaders have ways of perceiving and responding to their world informed by their capacity to be, and to stay, aware of themselves and their environment, and to use their awareness wisely to influence and effect positive change.

Horizontal development (knowledge acquisition) and vertical development (awareness development) are complementary, not competing, models. Vertical development strategies are best attuned to supporting leaders to meet contemporary challenges through awareness-driven processes. Awareness is a form of situational knowing, where there may be fresh information that was not previously available and requires the action of recognition or a promise for future action.

Facilitating clients' heightened or new awareness is a crucial intervention because it also makes obvious to clients the habitual processes that are out of their awareness. From this reawakened awareness, clients are enabled to be more consciously choiceful about their goals and decisions. Accessing one's awareness, in the moment when choice and action most matter, is strengthened by mindful processes that can improve with practice and experimentation. When we are distracted from the present moment—for example, committed to a predetermined course of action—it's easy to miss or dismiss pertinent data. The leader who insists on staying with an agenda when there are signs that no team coherence exists usually later confronts needless negative consequences. When important social cues affecting team members are missed or ignored because the leader was fixated on an agenda, the task of that agenda may be irreparably compromised.

We need to know what we are not aware of rather than staying asleep. Leaders especially need to become aware of and distinguish the signals of opportunity and threat. Coaches are responsible for creating conditions of trust that allow them to ask the probing, powerful questions that bring their clients to greater awareness. Awareness coaching requires comprehensive understanding of how to recognize awareness: the specifics and nuances of working with almost limitless aspects of awareness, recognizing lack of awareness, and knowing when resistance to awareness is functional.

In the vastness of working with awareness, *self-awareness, mindfulness,* and *emotional intelligence* have become touchstones in leadership development theory and its practitioners. Mindfulness and emotional intelligence are synergetic and powerfully beneficial for self-awareness development. Mindfulness is defined by Jon Kabat-Zinn as "paying attention in a particular way: on purpose, in the present moment, and non-judgmentally" (Kabat-Zinn, 1994, p. 4). Scientific research suggests that meditation—a form of practiced mindfulness—can actually change brain structure, improve concentration or focus, decrease anxiety, improve a sense of equanimity and well-being, and enhance interpersonal relationships. Google was among the first organizations to offer a mindfulness program for its leadership, conceived and directed by Chade-Meng Tan, who later founded the Search Inside Yourself Leadership Institute. Emotional intelligence (EI), popularized by Goleman (2005), has a profound impact on decision making and relational interactions, and has become a recognized competency in leadership development literature. Whether as coach or leader, the person who can best identify and read emotional reactions (in oneself and others) in the moment, who can defuse emotional distress and bolster emotional equanimity, and who is ethically responsible and accountable for his or her decisions in doing so, is one who has EI—one who can offer new perspectives, new possibilities, and re-energized commitment.

The power of the concepts of self-awareness, mindfulness, and EI lies in their ability to evoke self-directed change of who to be or who to become. Change that is self-initiated, coming internally from who we are and what we want, offers the most profound path to authentic transformation. Mindfulness strengthens one's mental focus, which further strengthens the indwelling power of awareness to promote compassionate discovery of what we are and are not paying attention to. Coaches use mindfulness techniques to focus attention, which facilitates client awareness in fresh and holistic ways by revealing habitual patterns and blind spots. Everyone has blind spots, things they're unable to see for themselves. Consider your car's rear-view mirrors, which broaden your typical range of vision so that you can see things you need to be aware of and pay attention to. Metaphorically, coaches are a kind of rearview mirror for clients, offering observations and questions that support clients to recognize their blind spots, empowering them to more choicefully decide which direction to take and how to better direct themselves.

AWARENESS IQ

Mindfulness and EI are part of the vertical strategies for self-awareness development. They both validate the Gestalt approach, which is rooted in awareness-enhancing methods. I have proposed the term *Awareness Intelligence,* or *Awareness IQ,* as an integrative model which incorporates the vertical development concept, the findings of neuroscience research on the impact and implications of awareness, and the foundations of the Gestalt approach (Siminovitch, 2017). Awareness IQ is an evolved and integrated concept that articulates a capacity to choicefully and masterfully use one's awareness, in the moment, to make the most effective decisions, leading to the greatest satisfaction and the least regret. Gestalt approaches make self-awareness the key to well-being, advocating its central role in self-empowerment and self-liberation, and practicing and teaching how to most effectively use self-awareness to initiate and guide change. Gestalt practice has been enriched through concepts like mindfulness and EI, through scientific research showing the positive impact that meditation practices make on the brain and on the body, and through emergent understanding of how self-awareness connects us with our heart and spirit.

Gestalt thinking and theory offer a time-tested, results-effective model of awareness-centered coaching. Awareness is the model, the method, and the goal for change, growth, and well-being. Gestalt practice was defined by one of its pioneers, Laura Perls, as "experiential, experimental, and existential" (cited in Rosenfeld, 1978, p. 24). Gestalt's foundations emerged from studies in phenomenology (how we perceive the world and make meaning of what we perceive); highlighted the need to experiment with our meaning-making processes in an environment of safety and trust; embraced existentialist premises (being responsible and accountable for our understanding of the world and the choices we make); and adopted wisdoms from Eastern philosophies (living in harmony with self, others, and the external world). The Gestalt approach continues to be vibrant, relevant, resonant, and adaptive in multiple disciplines and across all levels of system, whether for personal, team, or organizational coaching or consulting. The core concepts, principles, and models of Gestalt have proved insightful and meaningful in every so-called helping profession because they are rooted in organic, pan-cultural needs and wants.

People seek the services of coaches in pursuit of change. Gestalt coaching has a compelling understanding of what change entails and suggests appreciation for all patterns of behavior, even if those patterns no longer serve the person and the reasons for them have fallen out of that person's awareness. People tend to resist change, even when change is desired, because it's emotionally uncomfortable and behaviorally complex. For change to occur, one must first, with awareness, embrace existing perceptual and behavioral patterns. This deep insight, known as the paradoxical theory of change (Beisser, 1970), tells us first, that awareness in itself sparks change, and second, that change can only happen if one already fully embraces and accepts who one is. Gestalt practitioners reject the role of being change agents, who diagnose and fix what's presumably wrong. They instead take the stance of being *awareness agents* who offer astute observations and ask powerful questions to support clients to become more aware—to identify, especially, unaware patterns that sway clients perceptions and responses, their decision-making processes, and their relationships. Gestalt coaches seek to mobilize clients toward heightened or new self-awareness. When clients experience greater awareness, they also experience more personal power through expanded choices linked to that greater awareness, and therefore more possibility for moving forward toward desired goals.

PRESENCE AND USE OF SELF

In identifying awareness development as today's vital leadership competency, we encounter the issue of *presence* for coaches. Presence refers to the embodiment of identity—one's way of being in the world and one's impact on others. When we use our presence for decision making in the moment, or for resonant interpersonal relationships, that's an active, intentional *use of self*. When we miss an important awareness cue about a needed action, however small, we are left with some sense of regret. Awareness IQ is the integrative capacity to access the strengths of one's presence, when needed, and to act on one's awareness in ways that lead to satisfaction. Where presence is the domain of self-development, use of one's presence, or what we call use of self, is the way we intentionally use our resources to provoke an outcome that is needed, wanted, or missing.

The difference between presence and use of self is an important awareness. When we hear what we evoke in others, what we're hearing is an interior response to our being, our presence. When we hear what we did that provoked or influenced something, that impact is the result of our use of self. One satisfaction metric of use of self lies in the assessment question: Was there an adequate response to something that was needed, wanted, or missing? The answer we get is feedback about the effectiveness of our use of self. Awareness is needed to appreciate the distinction between evocation of one's presence and provocation regarding one's use of self. Understanding our presence and how this affects our use of self means understanding and being aware of the seven dimensions of presence that are available for our self-development and that influence how we respond in the world (Figure 12.1).

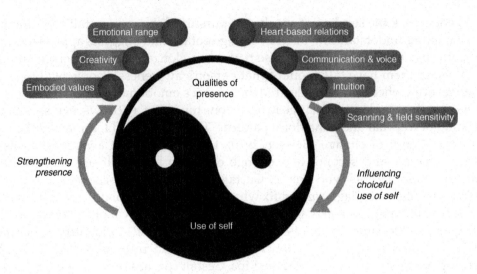

Figure 12.1 The dimensions of presence and use of self.

Source: Siminovitch, D. E. (2017). *A gestalt coaching primer: The path toward awareness IQ.* N.p.: Author.

THE SEVEN DIMENSIONS OF PRESENCE

Embodying One's Values and Beliefs

The ability to know and embody your values strengthens your presence, enhances perceptions of integrity, and engenders trust. Your presence is most immediately and memorably communicated to others somatically. When body language doesn't match words or demeanor, those watching and listening are distrustful or avoidant. The underlying strength of one's presence is congruence between body, mind, and spirit. When "our speech, facial expressions, postures, and movements align," this "internal convergence . . . is palpable and resonant. . . . We are no longer fighting ourselves; we are being ourselves" (Cuddy, 2015, p. 25). When leaders talk about what they value, they need to show up with the coherent embodiment that matches their message.

Creativity

Adaptability, resilience, and innovation are attributes of creativity. Creativity requires self-discipline to learn the horizontal information and skills associated with your profession, but vertical development is needed for originality, divergence, and conceptual flexibility. Creativity is not obstructed by failure but informed by those experiences in service of discovering what will be successful. The vacuum cleaner entrepreneur, James Dyson, had 5,126 failed attempts over 15 years before finally creating the model that made Dyson a multi-billion-dollar international company (Goodman, 2012). Creativity emerges from awareness, maybe in unexpected and unlikely moments, by being open to alternative ways of thinking or acting or being, and from calling upon all you know, have experienced, and can envision.

Emotions and Emotional Range

Recognizing, working with and using one's emotions wisely in the moment requires self-discipline. When coaches or leaders cannot access and use their emotions in the needed moment, to validate or to connect with others or to manage negative emotions, they lose a sense of personal presence. Along with our embodied values and beliefs, our emotional range and intelligence guides our choices about what we're willing to do and what we're not willing to do. A quote attributed to Viktor Frankl says, "Between stimulus and response there is a space. In that space is our power to choose our response. In our response lies our growth and our freedom." Our self-awareness about our emotions and emotional range gives us a power of nonreactivity in moments that have strong emotion. That stance gives us more options for an aware response, where we can take choiceful action and see more opportunities. Demonstrating emotional insight and emotional self-management further inspires trust in others.

Heart-Based Relations

Being seen, heard, and cared about are primary sources of resonance, generating hope and possibilities. Empathy, compassion, appreciation, passion, and courage are expressions of heart-based relations, both for oneself and for others. Research undertaken by the HeartMath Institute shows that the heart and brain are intricately connected physically, and that when the energetic heart and mind are in a state of coherence, we experience greater mental clarity, allowing for better communication, choices, and decision making (HeartMath Institute, n.d.). *Heart intelligence* is best expressed through value-laden actions that maintain personal health as well as support the welfare of others and our environmental fields. In 2015, Dan Price, a successful 31-year-old start-up entrepreneur, chose to give up 90% of his profits in order to guarantee each of his employees a $70K starting wage. He acted from his convictions—from an invested sense of personal psychological well-being and self-awareness, as well as from his sense of being invested in the welfare of others (Becker, 2017). The bond between coach and client, leader and follower, can often be traced to an aware sense of security and quality of care.

Communication and Voice

Being able to say what is needed in the moment is both skill and art, whether in writing, in person, or via audio- or video-recording. While presence is manifested most immediately through somatic cues, the words we choose and the characteristics of our voice are also key components. The quality of our words, the tone of our voice, and the congruence of both with our body language, touches others' minds and hearts. Many people, worldwide, know of Martin Luther King, Jr.'s "I Have a Dream" speech of 1963, and admire it not only for its historical significance, but for its rhetorical, emotional, experiential, and somatic coherence and authenticity. The goal is to clearly convey a message and a vision in a somatically coherent delivery, which moves people toward new perceptions and possibilities.

Intuition

Most people consider intuition a gift that is inborn and cannot be cultivated. Noted social scientist Herbert Simon, however, defined intuition as "subconscious pattern recognition" and "not associated with magic and mysticism" (cited in Frantz, 2003, p. 266). This recognition ability may be explained by the concept of *thin-slicing*, which refers to drawing "inference[s] about others from brief glimpses or 'thin slices' of behavior," that is, small and "random samples of the behavioral stream . . . that provide information regarding personality, affect, and interpersonal relations" (Ambady, 2010, p. 271). Dedicated meditators experience this power of thin-slicing intuition, as do those who are intensely trained and experienced in their given disciplines, such as some coaches. The International Coach Federation (ICF) introduces the relevance of intuition as a core competency of active listening at its highest credentialing level. The coach at this level

> recognizes both her and the client's ability of intuitive and energetic perception that is felt when the client speaks of important things, when new growth is occurring for the client, and when the client is finding a more powerful sense of self. (ICF, n.d.)

Scanning and Field Sensitivity

Scanning and field sensitivity refer to the capacity to recognize what is important as it is still emerging, almost unformed, in the purview of one's full awareness, drawing from one's knowledge, experience, and intuition. Leaders today are asked to navigate uncertain paths, yet must make effective decisions while the future continues to unfold. Those leaders who have a grounded sense of self, who are resonantly connected to others and open to new information, and who have a sense of safety around innovation and creative experimentation are most able to accurately scan their immediate and global environments to spot not just threats, but more importantly, opportunities and gifts. This capacity is most critical as we face continuous product and technological obsolescence, changing the criteria of business efficiency and customer service.

TWO TOOLS: COACHING FOR AWARENESS IQ

We offer two Gestalt-based coaching tools to work with awareness patterns. The *Cycle of Experience* (COE) serves as a process model of what one is aware of about oneself and one's environment, and how one acts on that awareness in relation to satisfying needs and wants. The COE's counterpart is the *Unit of Work* (UOW), a four-step model for orchestrating intentional awareness interventions. An issue is identified by the COE, and the UOW furthers the work by exploring that issue, which the client may have avoided or never adequately considered until his or her awareness was heightened and interest was generated to further explore it.

CYCLE OF EXPERIENCE

The COE is a process model built upon the concept of figure/ground. The figure/ground perceptual process refers to how external or internal sensations draw and focus our attention. What we pay attention to is the figure of interest that develops from among all the other available things in our environment, which is called the ground. A figure of interest emerges into awareness as a sensed need or want that we feel an urge to satisfy. If a figure is clearly identified and is compelling in terms of want or need or what is missing, we have an energetic response, which leads us to take action to satisfy the need or desire for that figure. Those action steps move us to make contact—to meet or create the conditions necessary to satisfy the need or want aroused. When contact happens, we feel a change in our energy. Having satisfied that particular figure, we feel a sense of closure, which allows that figure to fade back into the ground. The COE identifies need or want fulfillment processes across six points—sensation, awareness (figure of interest), energy (emotional investment), action, contact, and closure—which allow the coach to track and assess the client's awareness processes (Figure 12.2).

In terms of coaching for awareness development, the COE is the process lens for observing how clients satisfy or fail to satisfy their needs or wants, and is used to help clients become more self-aware of their own processes of scanning, meaning-making, and responsiveness. In keeping with being mindful, coaches track clients' COEs without judgment, looking only for observable sensory and verbal data. Clients usually think they already know and can articulate what they need or want, but may be unaware that their language, somatic cues, or behavior suggest otherwise. Focusing attention on what the client is thinking, feeling, and sensing is an important first step in data gathering in order to accurately identify what the client is experiencing. The move from sensation to awareness involves scanning both internal and external cues,

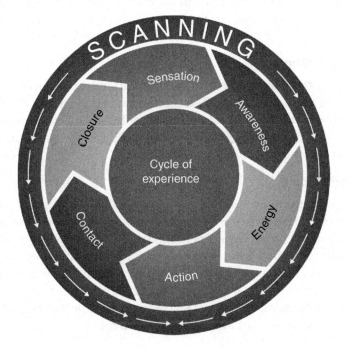

Figure 12.2 Cycle of experience.

Source: Siminovitch, D. E. (2017). *A gestalt coaching primer: The path toward awareness IQ.* N.p.: Author.

and identifying if the cues are in sync or misidentified. Whether the client can stay with the energy (physical, emotional, or cognitive) of the awareness, and whether he or she moves toward or holds back from taking action, are important awareness-based data. If the client makes contact, the client experiences a shift in energy, expressed verbally or somatically. If there is no visible shift, there is no change. If completion of the client's COE is satisfactory, that allows the client to move on to other figures of interest. If important COEs are left incomplete, these unfinished cycles can continue to impact the client by reducing his or her awareness and perceptions of other emerging issues.

Unit of Work

UOW is a process structure that intentionally orchestrates and facilitates client learning and change. The COE is always in some point of awareness, which can be mindfully described as data, not interpretation. The UOW draws from the awareness data of the COE and invites the client to engage in a learning experiment about the identified figure of interest that the client wishes to further explore. The UOW is a four-step structure.

Steps of the UOW

The "What Is" Process Analysis

The "what is" refers to a figure of interest which emerges from using COE—a need or want that attracts aware attention—in the client's current reality as he or she perceives and experiences it. The coach may suggest a figure drawn from mindful awareness observations of the COE, or the client may identify one.

Engaging in the Choice

The coach assists the client's choice of what to attend to and explore by offering observations and asking questions. The client is invited to choose whether to experiment with the primary figure of interest itself, or the client's resistance to that identified need or want, or the interplay between them. This is a bounded coaching agreement that sets the stage for experimentation.

Acting on the Choice

Once the issue is mutually defined, an experiential experiment, collaboratively designed, is offered. The client has to feel safe enough to proceed, but a sense of risk is essential for learning from experimentation and exploration. Too much calmness suggests that the identified issue is not sufficiently significant—it has no energetic charge or emotional risk, and invites no learning. Too much emotion suggests that fear will overwhelm curiosity about the unknown. The coach acts as a kind of ongoing barometer, discerning the client's tolerance for the vulnerability and risk involved. The experiments that are created need to bring the client in contact with a new awareness of the identified issue.

New "What Is"

Using the mindful data of the COE in this step, attention is paid to the somatic cues that signal awareness and learning shifts. Energy is focused now on inviting the client to integrate his or her new learning. One way of closing the experiment is to ask the client to name resultant learnings, and to invite reflection on insights and different possibilities in relation to the client's needs, wants, and goals. The successful closure of a UOW is the culmination of experiential learning that feels like an "aha moment" of awareness of freshly available choices and opportunities (Figure 12.3).

The UOW works thematically with awareness data revealed though the COE. Experimentation in the UOW deepens vertical development strategies, and illuminates potential positive shifts in perception, worldview, or behavior. Experimentation prompts surprising creativity and innovation that neither coach nor client could have predicted. Experimentation allows learning to occur from all opportunities. Success is when a new possibility is realized or even when a failure pattern is recognized that has thwarted client satisfaction. For example, if the COE reveals a place of "stuckness," in sensation or awareness or elsewhere in the cycle, one UOW could be to explore what is familiar about that stuckness and the cost of staying in that pattern. A UOW can be used to explore any challenge.

BEING AN AWARENESS IQ AGENT

We live in a world where what we know well, and are rewarded for knowing, can quickly become obsolete. The bias favoring technical competency is being displaced by a shift in the zeitgeist: a recognition of awareness as itself a powerful competency that promotes a capacity to confidently manage uncertainty and ambiguity, to be creative, to be adaptable. Awareness-based knowledge—once the domain of spiritual, philosophical, and mystic practices—is now the fundamental practical goal of many leadership development programs and much of leadership coaching. We offer Awareness IQ—an integration of seven awareness dimensions, the capacity to

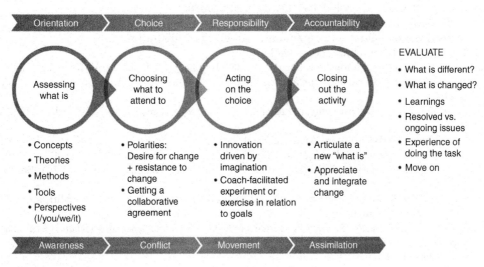

Figure 12.3 Unit of work.

Source: Siminovitch, D. E. (2017). *A gestalt coaching primer: The path toward awareness IQ.* N.p.: Author.

access those resources when needed, and the evidentiary support for the value of mindfulness and emotional intelligence—as a path toward personal and professional mastery.

In this time when information continually expands and knowledge needs to be constantly updated, being able to use one's awareness for vision, understanding, clarity, and agility is the fundamental competency. Coaching for awareness intelligence focuses on supporting leaders to look after their own well-being in synchrony with the welfare of others, and positioning leadership to better anticipate, compassionately manage, and ethically negotiate relentless organizational change and complexity in the moment that matters. Coaches who are privileged to support leadership in their vertical self-development are themselves supported by powerful awareness models, research, and tools.[1] Mahatma Gandhi wrote that "the future depends on what you do today." This is a fitting observation to close our discussion of developing self-awareness and using our awareness wisely. Coaches, and the leaders they work with, need to be skilled, and even artful, to recognize awareness moments that offer the inspiration, energy, and wisdom to respond effectively in the moment. Those moments are our portals into the future.

NOTE

1. With Barbara Singer, CEO of Executive Core, I have coauthored the Awareness 20/20™ 720° assessment tool for leadership awareness across the seven dimensions of presence.

REFERENCES

Ambady, N. (2010). The perils of pondering: Intuition and thin slice judgments. *Psychological Inquiry, 21*(4), 271–278. doi:10.1080/1047840X.2010.524882

Becker, S. (2017). The $70,000 minimum wage experiment reveals a dark truth. Retrieved from https://www.cheatsheet.com/money-career/the-70000-minimum-wage-experiment -reveals-a-dark-truth.html/?a=viewall

Beisser, A. (1970). The paradoxical theory of change. In J. Fagen & I. Shepherd (Eds.), *Gestalt therapy now: Theory, techniques, applications* (pp. 77–80). Palo Alto, CA: Science and Behavior Books.

Cuddy, A. (2015). *Presence: Bringing your boldest self to your biggest challenges.* New York, NY: Little, Brown.

Frantz, R. (2003). Herbert Simon: Artificial intelligence as a framework for understanding intuition. *Journal of Economic Psychology, 24*(2), 265–277. doi:10.1016/S0167-4870(02)00207-6

Goleman, D. (2005). *Emotional intelligence: Why it can matter more than IQ.* New York, NY: Bantam Books.

Goodman, N. (2012). James Dyson on using failure to drive success. Retrieved from https://www .entrepreneur.com/article/224855

HeartMath Institute. (n.d.). *The heart's intuitive intelligence: A path to personal, social and global coherence* [Video file]. Retrieved from https://www.heartmath.org/about-us/videos/the-hearts -intuitive-intelligence

International Coach Federation. (n.d.). Core competencies comparison table. Retrieved from https://coachfederation.org/app/uploads/2017/12/ICFCompetenciesLevelsTable.pdf

Kabat-Zinn, J. (1994). *Wherever you go, there you are: Mindfulness meditation in everyday life.* New York, NY: Hyperion.

Petrie, N. (2014). Vertical development leadership: Part I: Developing leaders for a complex world. Retrieved from http://insights.ccl.org/wp-content/uploads/2015/04/VerticalLeadersPart1 .pdf

Rosenfeld, E. (1978). An oral history of Gestalt therapy: Part one: A conversation with Laura Perls. *Gestalt Journal, 1*(1), 8–31.

Siminovitch, D. E. (2017). *A gestalt coaching primer: The path toward awareness IQ.* N.p.: Author.

13

Mindful Compassionate Coaching: An Approach Perfect for "VUCA" Times

Liz Hall

As the Zen saying goes, "relax, nothing's under control." Recent years have been punctuated by numerous reminders that this is very often—if not always—the case. Widespread political disruption, economic strife, terror attacks, environmental disasters—the list goes on. Mental ill health is on the rise, with anxiety and depression commonplace. The acronym VUCA (volatile, uncertain, complex, and ambiguous), coined by the U.S. Army decades ago to describe challenging situations on the battlefield, is increasingly used in business circles as shorthand for "It's crazy out there!" (Bennett & Lemoine, 2014).

Mindfulness, and increasingly compassion, has a vast and growing evidence base. Much of the research focuses on improvements to individuals' resilience and is compelling and relevant to all of us coaching in these VUCA times. However, research is highlighting many other benefits of developing mindfulness and compassion that are also pertinent to supporting clients to operate in today's world. These include increased adaptiveness (being better able to deal with complexity and ambiguity, to "dance in the moment"); improved emotional intelligence leading to greater capacity for collaboration; greater creativity and innovation; improved cognitive functioning; and enhanced ability for ethical and sustainable decision making and behavior.

At the same time as we see this shift in terms of application beyond stress management, we are seeing greater focus on collective mindfulness and compassion, and greater recognition of the benefits such a focus might deliver. Mindfulness-based interventions (MBIs) can be a positive tool for "building organizational readiness for change," supporting "innovative or disruptive ways of working," and helping organizations be "resilient and adaptable to the world's growing complexity" (Carter, Tobias, & Spiegelhalter, 2016).

In this chapter, I propose that mindful compassionate coaching (MCC), an approach underpinned by mindfulness, compassion, and body wisdom, is just what is needed to support individuals, teams, organizations, and society as a whole to not only cope, but to thrive and flourish in this VUCA world.

After defining key terms and touching on some relevant research, I lay out principles, behaviors, and practices for MCC, building on previous work (Hall, 2013, 2015a), grounded in awareness, body or somatic awareness and wisdom, and compassion (ABC [Hall, 2015a]). These include the FELT framework developed by this author (Hall, 2015a, updated here), and a practice I have developed for clients called SOAR (softening, opening, allowing, recharging), presented here for the first time. The chapter then concludes by exploring potential challenges to and solutions for working with MCC.

SETTING THE SCENE

Mindfulness has entered the mainstream thanks to pioneers including Jon Kabat-Zinn, creator of the Mindfulness-Based Stress Reduction (MBSR) program. Organizations adopting mindfulness include NASA, General Mills, and Google.

Increasing numbers of coaches are incorporating mindfulness into their practice. The literature on mindful coaching is still sparse albeit growing, and of course, much of the noncoaching-related research also has implications for coaching. It falls outside the scope of this chapter to explore previous literature relating to mindfulness and coaching but it is worth noting that it includes the work by Cavanagh and Spence (2013), Collard and Walsh (2008), Hall (2013, 2015a), Passmore and Marianetti (2007), Silsbee (2010), and Spence, Cavanagh, and Grant (2008).

DEFINITIONS

Mindfulness can be seen as a form of mind training, a way of being, and of doing, and of "paying attention in the present moment on purpose nonjudgmentally" (Kabat-Zinn, 1994). It is "a natural inherent human capacity akin to language acquisition" (Tobias, 2016).

Compassion can be defined as "basic kindness, with deep awareness of the suffering of oneself and other living beings, coupled with the wish and effort to alleviate it" (Gilbert, 2009a).

By somatic or body wisdom, I mean a "dual process of specifically paying attention to what's happening in the body and to what the body's telling us, as a source of information and wisdom, and where appropriate taking action to change the body shape, work with the breath and so on to promote healing and transformation" (Hall, 2015a).

THE COLLECTIVE

Research and practice in the mindfulness and compassion arena is moving beyond the individual to the collective, reflecting a similar shift in coaching. As mindfulness becomes more suitably adapted for specific contexts, it is becoming clearer that there is huge potential for positive application in teams, groups, organizations and beyond, not just with individuals. Research by Cranfield University and the Institute of Employment Studies (Carter, Tobias, & Spiegelhalter, 2016) looked beyond the value of mindfulness-based techniques and outcomes for individuals to consider their potential impact at a strategic level. It suggests that collective mindfulness is more than the sum of individual mindfulness, shaping interactions in all directions, and that mindfulness can be used to achieve successful change in organizations. It proposes a "multi-level" approach, applying mindfulness-based techniques (not solely meditation but other mindfulness-based tools and shared practices) at individual, team, and organization, or whole system levels. Coaching has much to offer as part of this collective approach.

One initiative with both mindfulness and coaching at its heart is being rolled out by Aberystwyth University in Wales, which is developing an innovative program with the Welsh Government to boost mindfulness, decision making, behavioral change, and systemic change in the public sector. The intervention, led mainly by Rachel Lilley and Professor Mark Whitehead, brings together mindfulness practice with decision making and behavioral theory, and coaching. It represents an integrative mindfulness intervention moving away from the standard MBSR and mindfulness-based cognitive therapy (MBCT) and adapted for specific workplace outcomes.

During her ongoing research, Lilley has found that although the participants are stressed, they are not vulnerable, so she can spend less time on basics and more on how mindfulness links with decision making, bias, how the mind creates its own reality and the lack of objective reality, and the central role of emotions. As Lilley suggests, this deeper understanding has profound implications for leadership in VUCA times, promoting agility and openness, and taking the leaders to a deeper level of mental capacity than MBSR and MBCT were designed to promote.

In addition to running traditional coaching alongside mindfulness training, I have proposed to combine them in MCC, as described in Table 13.1.

Let us explore some of the points mentioned in Table 13.1 in more detail, first looking at mindfulness for the coach.

MINDFULNESS FOR THE COACH

Even if we opt not to talk about mindfulness with our clients, practicing mindfulness will benefit us as coaches, helping us take care of ourselves, be more intuitive and more present.

Having our own mindfulness practice can help us be:

- *More resilient*—accessing more strategies and approaches to help us recharge and become more grounded

---

Table 13.1 Mindful Compassionate Coaching (MCC): Principles, Behaviors, and Aspirations

Generally
- Develop mindfulness, somatic awareness, and compassion daily for at least 10 minutes
- Explore the nature of the mind during your practice so you can lead others likewise
- Prepare mindfully for each coaching session
- Reflect mindfully after each session
- Seek out a coaching supervisor grounded in mindfulness or similar practices
- Consider various ways to combine mindfulness and coaching in myriad contexts

In coaching sessions
- Start with a mindfulness practice to help the client/s (and you!) arrive, become more open, and tune into what matters for them generally and in this session
- Become fully present
- Attend to what arises in the present
- Pay attention to and act upon the wisdom of the body
- Think systemically
- Aspire to adopt/model: nonjudgment; compassion/kindness; curiosity and openness; willingness to stay with ambiguity and acceptance of what is (where appropriate); turning toward "difficulty"; not being overly attached to outcomes
- Be prepared to sit with and in silence
- Encourage clients to explore who and what they are, including the nature of their minds
- Encourage the client to adopt mindfulness and self-compassion to quiet the inner critic
- Use mindfulness and self-compassion to help you self-regulate when "triggered"
- Share with the client any information you gather from being internally aware
- Share mindfulness practices in the session, or as homework (see Specific Practices later in this chapter)

- *More resourceful*—helping us be more creative and innovative as we become more open, more curious and less rigid, testing out assumptions and holding more possibilities

- *More emotionally intelligent*—better able to create rapport and trust in the relationship; to know ourselves, and self-manage; to know what's going on in our relationships, and to manage them

SUPPORTING THE CLIENT

We can support clients through mindfulness in a number of ways:

- Coaching them mindfully—implicitly or explicitly

- Drawing on specific models, frameworks, tools, and techniques to coach mindfully and compassionately, such as the FELT model (Hall, 2015a) outlined in a later section; ACT; Gestalt

- Highlighting benefits of developing mindfulness skills to the client, particularly in these challenging times (see Table 13.2)

- Imparting mindfulness skills directly in the session and/or as "home practice"—some specific practices are explored in the sections that follow

- Liaising with mindfulness trainers

- Weaving mindfulness into any leadership and other development programs that also have coaching at their core

The many benefits of coaching with mindfulness and compassion are outlined in Table 13.2.

SPECIFIC PRACTICES

We now explore what some of the well-known practices (easily accessible online or through the literature) might offer in coaching, and I introduce SOAR for the first time.

Table 13.2 Benefits of Explicitly Developing Mindfulness and Compassion in VUCA Times

- Improved mental and physical well-being, and resilience (Reitz, Chaskalson, Olivier, & Waller, 2016; Tobias, 2016)—mindful leaders are more resilient, more willing to stay put in the face of difficulty, and to proactively promote emergent, bottom-up decisions (Tobias, 2016). Clients are more able to "turn toward" whatever is difficult, including overwhelm and fear when faced with perceived threat and a greater ability to operate from an approach rather than avoidance state, allowing for increased resourcefulness and courage, and creativity.
- Greater self-awareness, including of the nature of mind—its tendency to make assumptions and be biased, particularly when under stress.
- Greater awareness in general, leading to more ethical and sustainable behavior (Amel, Manning, & Scott, 2009), and improving moral reasoning and increasing ethical decision making (e.g., Cavanagh & Spence, 2013; Hall, 2013).
- Improved cognitive functioning. Reduced tendency toward polarized thinking—more flexibility, openness, and curiosity about oneself and the surrounding environment.
- A realization by the client—and coach—that they cannot be in control of everything, and yet a growing sense of gaining "some control" by helping them choose how they respond.
- Increased ability to be comfortable with ambiguity and complexity, to better lead in complex conditions. Increased meta-capacities of metacognition (being aware of being aware), curiosity, and allowing (things to be as they are; Reitz et al., 2016).
- Improved relationships—more trust, collaboration (Reitz et al., 2016), and shared values. Increased awareness of the "interconnectedness" between the individual and the wider system, more systemic and strategic thinking and behavior. Heightened compassion to self and others.
- Enhanced body wisdom, leading to greater presence, attunement, and resonance (Hall, 2013), and more access to data.

THE BODY SCAN

Kok and Singer (2017) compared the effects ("fingerprints") of four common meditation practices, including the Body Scan, a well-known practice in MBSR and MBCT. The other practices were breathing meditation; Loving Kindness meditation (LKM); and observing-thought meditation (decentering—allowing thoughts to come and go without identifying with them).

The study found that all four increased positive emotions, energy, and present moment focus, and decreased thought distraction. But there were differences too. The Body Scan led to the greatest increase in interoceptive awareness (awareness of bodily sensations) and in metacognitive awareness ("being aware of being aware").

THE LOVING KINDNESS MEDITATION

Used in coaching, LKM helps coaches "quieten" their inner critic, be more present, and listen more deeply to their client (Heardman, 2017). Heardman's research found that practicing the LKM helped the coach create an environment that improved coaching outcomes, helping more transformational work take place.

PRESSING THE PAUSE BUTTON

It can be helpful to share with clients short practices they can easily do daily. Research (e.g., Reitz et al., 2016) indicates it is best to practice a little mindfulness daily—at least 10 minutes—than for long but infrequent periods. As well as building mindfulness capacities incrementally, short practices can be very helpful in the moment when clients are stressed. One such practice is SOAR, which helps clients pause quickly when they feel overwhelmed, or when they simply want to come back to themselves, to center, so they can be more resourceful. It can be done quickly, pretty much anywhere, standing up or sitting, with eyes open or closed.

SOAR

SOFTENING

As human beings, we tend to grasp after what we deem pleasant and push away what we deem unpleasant, and this tendency shows up in our bodies. We contract against pain, we hold onto things tightly, clench our jaws, hunch our shoulders, grimace, and so on. By starting this practice with the invitation to *soften*, we quickly let go of physical tension, and our tightness around thoughts, emotions, stories. We feel softening throughout our body—smiling, loosening our jaw, unhunching our shoulders, softening our belly, spreading this to incorporate our thinking, feelings, and mood.

OPENING

Having softened somewhat, we can now open to what life presents. We can sense this opening in our body, perhaps widening our shoulders, opening our arms, our hands, widening our stance. With openness comes curiosity about whatever has shown up in our inner and outer worlds. Without curiosity, we have no impetus for bringing our awareness into the present moment and staying with it.

ALLOWING

Next, we allow whatever is the case to be the case, meeting our experience with a spirit of openness and kindness, being less likely to criticize ourselves and others, which gets in the way of being mindful.

RECHARGING

Here we choose to tune in to whatever recharges us personally—feeling our feet on the ground, imagining we are a tree with roots going deep into the rich earth; tuning into God or some other deity; perhaps opening up to the energy of nature, to the beauty of our surroundings; maybe taking some deep breaths, connecting into the source of life. Most of us have a sense of what nurtures us, and here we quickly tap into that source.

THE FELT MODEL

If we choose to work explicitly with mindfulness, we may wish to lead our clients through mindful enquiry. The FELT model (Hall, 2015a) has been developed for this purpose and can be used to guide self-coaching, and to coach individuals, teams, and groups.

The FELT model can be particularly applicable during organizational restructuring or merger and acquisition by incorporating it into team or group coaching to help employees identify the emotional impact of the transition, what matters to them, what they find hard to let go of, next steps, and so on. Letting go and surfacing emotions in the process is hard, but not doing so can hinder organizational change programs.

It can also be applied when a client is struggling with "difficult" emotions in a relationship, or they wish to explore how to embody a new mindset.

FELT incorporates a number of key components (traits, aspirations, qualities, and behaviors) of mindfulness:

- Attention to the present moment
- Attentional control (where we intentionally direct our attention to a chosen object)
- Curiosity/enquiry
- Compassion (toward self and others)
- Non-judgment
- Acceptance
- Letting go

The coach may choose to move through the model in a linear fashion or fluidly between the different parts or stay within one or two parts of the model.

If you are working with an individual, you can offer the choice of working in silence as you guide him or her through the process, or they can share out loud what they are noticing as they go along. The idea is to help the individual stay in the mindful enquiry, not get caught up in cognitive processes such as interpretation. If your client does start doing the latter, gently guide him or her back to noticing bodily sensations. If you're working with a team or group, lead them through the process in silence.

In either case, you can debrief afterward.

Using the Model

Lead clients through a brief mindfulness practice, for example, inviting them to feel their feet on the floor and focus on the bodily sensations as they breathe. Then:

Focusing

Set the intention for example, to be curious, open, self-compassionate, or to park assumptions. Choose the focus of the enquiry, with an intention to focus steadily and with concentration, but with lightness of touch. For clients who struggle to be self-compassionate, you may like to separately do some compassion-building practices, such as developing compassionate imagery (Gilbert, 2009b).

Exploring and Embracing

Here, encourage the client to explore in a self-compassionate/kindly, curious, nonjudgmental way, just being open to whatever arises. We may stay with the original topic/object, or work with whatever else comes to light, exploring, without seeking to interpret or judge. We are seeking to activate the "approach system," associated with a number of benefits, including creativity.

Prompt them if you feel comfortable with the following questions (you may have your own). The idea is just to prompt further enquiry, not to take them away from their exploration. You will need to pay close attention to their body language so you don't keep interrupting their process. You might start by saying something like the following: (saying, for example, "turning" instead of "turn" feels more invitational and spacious): "Without seeking to change anything, and with curiosity and openness, self-compassion and nonjudgment, turning inward to explore what you've chosen to focus on. I might pose some questions with the aim of prompting your enquiry; they may or may not be appropriate."

Questions

- What is asking to be noticed?

- What are you noticing?

- Where are you feeling this in your body?

- Does whatever it is have a name?

- Does it have a color?

- Does it have a shape?

- What is it asking for?

- Is there any wisdom from your body that is making itself known?

Whatever comes up, suggest they sit with it, not grasping after it, nor turning away from it. . . cradling it, embracing whatever it is gently, perhaps. Here, while still maintaining focus and a sense of enquiry and exploration, we're turning toward *whatever* is there—unpleasant or pleasant, with nonjudgment and compassion or kindness, without grasping or pushing away. Vietnamese Buddhist monk Thich Nhat Hanh suggests imagining gently cradling a baby. So, for example, if anger arises, we turn toward and lightly embrace the anger, rather than moving to evaluate and criticize. We are working with acceptance. We might label whatever it is, thus creating some distance, so that we are gently embracing rather than identifying with it or creating an unhelpful storyline about it.

If clients find this exploration overly intense, guide them gently to pay attention to their breath. And of course if they want to stop at any time, that is fine. Remind them to be self-compassionate and nonjudgmental as best they can.

Letting Be, Letting Go, Letting In

Invite clients to just let whatever it is be (allowing them time to sit with this option), and then ask if there is anything that wants to be let go of (again, letting them sit with this), and then if there is anything they want to let in . . . and sitting with this. As coach, we can be led by what arises.

Transforming

Invite clients to sit with all that has arisen, noticing what is going on in their body— again any wisdom making itself known—and asking them if anything needs to transform. This might involve actively changing something, a behavior or mindset, or even a value but all coming from a place of wisdom, of compassion, of "knowing." This step can be about really taking time to embody a shift that has arisen from the exploration.

POTENTIAL CHALLENGES

Just as coaching is not a panacea for all ills, neither are mindfulness and compassion. Following are some potential challenges and potential solutions—with some examples—for introducing mindfulness into work with individuals and organizations.

The Type-A, highly driven and competitive client who embraces mindfulness as a wonderful technique to become even more focused and productive at work, who is at risk of becoming even more competitive, perhaps even ruthless, and of burning out.

What to Do: Challenge Type-A clients about wanting "more, more, more," helping them explore their meaning and purpose, and underlying values. Work with the LKM and other compassion-building practices to boost their self-compassion, and connection to others. Introduce short practices such as SOAR so they can press pause and recharge regularly.

The client who is already distant and unengaged for whom mindfulness becomes a way to disengage further.

What to Do: Work explicitly to build this client's body awareness and wisdom (e.g., through the Body Scan)—using the breath as an anchor, for example, to help the client stay grounded and connected.

Despite all the hype, there is a **lack of understanding of the term "mindfulness"** and what "mindful" looks like in practice leading to misunderstandings or misuse of MBIs, and mindfulness being reduced to a "generic tool to fix things, rather than a complex and context-sensitive embodied practice" (Carter, Tobias, & Spiegelhalter, 2016). There can be resistance too with mindfulness being seen as the latest fad.

What to Do: Explore mindfulness within group and team coaching, Action Learning Sets, and individual coaching sessions with leaders and human resources, organizational development, and learning and development professionals who can act as champions and enablers who can help dispel the myths, fuel momentum, and ground application in what is fit-for-purpose. Just as the Welsh Government is doing, enquiry can go way beyond stress management into the territory of exploring the nature of mind and can draw on many other disciplines and frameworks.

LANGUAGE AND CULTURE

What's in a name? Plenty when it comes to new approaches and behaviors being accepted. And as we know perhaps too well, the existing culture will often get in the way of both initial receptiveness to, and sustainability of, change. As Carter, Tobias, and Spiegelhalter (2016) point out, workplace cultures can be a barrier if success is seen to be at an individual, as opposed to team or business unit, level. Their research also highlighted as a barrier the wider culture outside work. Participants in their research said the wider culture is counter to that fostered by mindfulness, and is characterized by fear, reactivity, overload, short-termism, and a so-called "me" rather than "we" society. For some coaches, this may serve as a call to action in the same way that some feel called to support a shift away from traditional command-and-control organizational cultures to more coaching, affiliative, and empowering cultures.

In team coaching, we sometimes hit a brick wall because the culture is insufficiently open, likewise with mindfulness. According to Google's Project Aristotle, a 2-year study of 180 firms, the key drivers of a team's performance are trust and psychological safety. If the goal of a team coaching intervention is to improve performance, it thus makes sense to work on relationships. We know that mindfulness positively impacts relationships, boosting emotional intelligence, leading to less conflict in the workplace (e.g., Goleman, Boyatzis, & McKee, 2013), and helping people be more present, attuned to and resonant with others. So, it seems a no-brainer to bring mindfulness to any team coaching we do.

What to Do: With both individuals and wider systems, consider how mindfulness, and perhaps compassion, is labeled and presented. Frame interventions clearly according to potential benefits—stress management or improved emotional intelligence, for example.

Map with clients what they consider the hallmarks of a coaching leader and culture onto those they consider to be signs of a mindful leader and organization. When I explore this with participants on my mindfulness-at-work programs for coaches, Human Resources, and lead-ers, we find much common ground—including more openness, curiosity, and questioning of assumptions.

When working with teams, lead a mindful compassionate enquiry with team members individually and as a whole through the FELT model (Hall, 2015a) outlined in this chapter, weave mindfulness practices into team coaching and development days, including as "home-work," and role model mindfulness in encounters with client teams.

When supporting organizations to establish a coaching culture and become a mindful organization, join the dots, cross-fertilizing across the system. This might mean, for example, external coach consultants talking to those introducing mindfulness, and feeding back to the organization, weaving mindfulness into manager/leader-as-coach development programs, and into leadership coaching, as Unilever is doing.

SUSTAINABILITY

Many lament that the "McMindfulness" phenomenon in which mindfulness is seen as being co-opted by corporations is a superficial tool to increase productivity, or a sticking plaster for deep wounds in "toxic" workplaces, leaving employees highly vulnerable. The UK's Mindfulness Initiative (2016) highlighted concerns "that shal-low, introductory mindfulness is being used as a way to sustain unscrupulous work practices, and cover up unsustainable workload." Many organizational programs of course are set up with the best of intent; however, it can be hard to make a real dif-ference through mindfulness.

What to Do: In addition to supporting a widening of the potential remit of mindfulness, there is vast scope for coaching to enhance the "stickability" of mindfulness with individuals and in organizations.

Leadership buy-in is key to mindfulness benefiting the whole organization rather than remaining a nice-to-have for individuals, and coaching can offer vital support to help leaders shift mindsets and behaviors, which will then impact the rest of the organization. In many organizations, therefore, mindfulness is integrated into leadership development, and sup-ported by coaching. One example is the UK government's Project Leadership Programme, which seeks to improve management quality in senior civil servant leaders working on large and complex schemes, and which offers ongoing one-to-one coaching support as well as mindfulness e-learning and face-to-face modules.

In the Welsh Government program (referred to earlier), coaching—two individual coaching sessions per participant—was introduced in response to feedback that people were finding mindfulness useful personally but finding it harder to translate the learning into working practice. Allowing leaders to reflect in the coaching on the wider implications of their practice improved and accelerated the impact of the course on their work context.

Quaker Social Action's program also highlights how combining coaching and mindful-ness can make change stick. The charity offers a free program for local people on low income, consisting of three one-to-one life coaching and six sessions of group mindfulness training delivered by Rising Minds, a social enterprise that works with low-income people and front-line staff in stressful roles. The well-being of the participants before starting the program, measured using the World Health Organization's Wellbeing Index, averaged 8.5%, border-ing on clinically depressed. After the program, it averaged 15.2%. At Coaching at Work's annual conference in London in 2015, one participant said, "Mindfulness and life coaching have to go hand in hand. The life coaching gives you the direction, and mindfulness gives you the focus to stay there, and stay the course . . . mindfulness gives you tools for life." The participnt shared how she now had more *"focus, self-confidence, and motivation, and 'stick-to-it-ness.'"* The coaching helped her *"re-evaluate my values"* and the mindfulness helped her *"live daily and stick to my values."*

CONCLUSION

MCC offers a safe, gentle, yet powerful way to coach, promoting mental and physical well-being, enhancing emotional intelligence, creativity, cognitive functioning, compassion for self and others, and wisdom, all of which are particularly relevant in our VUCA world. It can support individuals, teams, organizations, and society as a whole, to turn toward and transform difficulties, including overarching crises for humanity such as excessive consumption, and unethical behavior, ultimately promoting a sustainable collective response to our pressing challenges.

REFERENCES

Amel, E. L., Manning, C. M., & Scott, B. A. (2009). Mindfulness and sustainable behavior: Pondering attention and awareness as means for increasing green behavior. *Ecopsychology, 1*(1), 14–25. doi:10.1089/eco.2008.0005

Bennett, N., & Lemoine, J. (2014). What VUCA really means for you. *Harvard Business Review, 92*(1/2). Retrieved from https://hbr.org/2014/01/what-vuca-really-means-for-you

Carter, A., Tobias, J., & Spiegelhalter, K. (2016). *Mindfulness in organisations.* Cranfield University, Institute for Employment Studies.

Cavanagh, M. J., & Spence, G. B. (2013). Mindfulness in coaching: Philosophy, psychology or just a useful skill? In J. Passmore, D. Peterson, T. Freire, J. Passmore, D. Peterson, & T. Freire (Eds.), *The Wiley-Blackwell handbook of the psychology of coaching and mentoring* (pp. 112–134). New York, NY: Wiley-Blackwell.

Collard, P., & Walsh, J. J. (2008). Sensory awareness mindfulness training in coaching: Accepting life's challenges. *Journal of Rational-Emotional & Cognitive Therapy, 26*(1), 30–37. doi:10.1007/s10942-007-0071-4

Gilbert, P. (2009a). *Overcoming depression* (3rd ed.). New York, NY: Basic Books.

Gilbert, P. (2009b). *The compassionate mind: A new approach to facing the challenges of life.* London, UK: Constable Robinson.

Goleman, D., Boyatzis, R. E., & McKee, A. (2013). *Primal leadership: Unleashing the power of emotional intelligence.* Boston, MA: Harvard Business Press.

Hall, L. (2013). *Mindful coaching: How mindfulness can transform coaching practice.* London, UK: Kogan Page Publishers.

Hall, L. (2015a). *Coaching in times of crisis and transformation: How to help individuals and organisations flourish.* London, UK: Kogan Page Publishers.

Hall, L. (2015b). Mindfulness in coaching. In J. Reb & P. W. Atkins (Eds.), *Mindfulness in organizations: Foundations, research, and applications* (pp. 383–408). Cambridge, UK: Cambridge University Press. 383.

Heardman, P. (2017). What's love got to do with it? *Coaching at Work, 12*, 3.

Kabat-Zinn, J. (1994). *Wherever you go, there you are: Mindfulness meditation in everyday life.* New York, NY: Hyperion.

Kok, B. E., & Singer, T. (2017). Phenomenological fingerprints of four meditations: Differential state changes in affect, mind-wandering, meta-cognition, and interoception before and after daily practice across 9 months of training. *Mindfulness, 8*(1), 218–231. doi:10.1007/s12671-016-0594-9

Passmore, J., & Marianetti, O. (2007). The role of mindfulness in coaching. *The Coaching Psychologist, 3*(3), 131–137.

Reitz, M., Chaskalson, M., Olivier, S., & Waller, L. (2016). *The mindful leader: Developing the capacity for resilience and collaboration in complex times through mindfulness practice.* London, UK: Ashridge Executive Education Hult.

Silsbee, D. (2010). *The mindful coach: Seven roles for facilitating leader development.* Hoboken, NJ: John Wiley & Sons.

Spence, G. B., Cavanaugh, M. J., & Grant, A. M. (2008). The integration of mindfulness training and health coaching: An exploratory study. *Coaching: An International Journal of Theory, Research and Practice, 1*(2), 145–163. doi:10.1080/17521880802328178

Tobias, J. (2016). *Building the case for mindfulness.* Sheffield, UK: The Mindfulness Initiative.

14

Successful Coaches Influence Emotions, Thoughts, and Behaviors

Charles Wolfe

The Chief Information Officer (CIO) was sitting in his office wondering why the leadership team meeting had been postponed. He had hoped to get an update today about two key projects. He also had a late meeting with his leadership coach and decided to see if Chuck could come earlier. As he was about to ask his administrative assistant to make the call, the Chief Executive Officer (CEO) knocked on his door and said, "Fred, I would like to talk. Is this a good time?"

Fred looked up and said, "Sure. What would you like to talk about?"

The CEO, Mark, was an intelligent man recently recruited from a competitor. He knew the industry and had a reputation for strategic thinking, blunt talking, and decisive action. People who worked for Mark found him driven, tough-minded, fair, but inflexible. Once he made a decision, there was little that could change it. Mark came into the organization 3 months ago. He spent the first 2 months talking with leaders in headquarters and in the field asking about the strengths and weaknesses of the company, their areas of responsibility, and other senior leaders. He analyzed what he learned and then made his decisions.

"Fred, after talking to company leaders, I decided to end your employment. Tomorrow Leslie from Human Resources will go over your severance package with you. I believe you will find it generous. As to why you are being let go, it is about teamwork. While some felt you were brilliant, a real asset, others found you extremely difficult to work with. Conversations were confidential so I won't say who I learned this from, but I heard you are often critical, sarcastic, and disrespectful. Your supporters pointed out when you dismissed others' ideas, you were probably right, but even they agreed your behavior shut down conversation. This

leadership group needs to become a team. It will happen quicker without you. So unfortunately, we need to part ways. I wish you well, and as you will see tomorrow, you have a generous severance package. Any questions, Fred?"

Fred, stunned, managed to say, "Mark, if I change to be more in line with what you are looking for, could I stay?"

"No. I made my decision. So long Fred. Good luck."

This chapter focuses on emotions of clients and coaches throughout the coaching process and includes examples of how emotions impact coaching individuals, teams, and organizations. Coaching is described and differentiated from consulting and therapy. And the Emotion Roadmap™ is introduced to help guide leadership coaches as they influence clients' emotions to achieve coaching goals.

This chapter opened with a real case with the permission of the client. Statements about each person's feelings and thoughts are based on conversations with my client. Throughout the chapter the case demonstrates how successful coaches influence emotions, thoughts, and behaviors.

Think about the importance of my client's feelings after the CEO's visit. What was he feeling? What help would he need from me? Shortly after the meeting Fred called and shared the news. If you were his coach, what would you feel, think, and do? What would you have as a strategic coaching goal for Fred?

In Boyatzis, Rochford, and Taylor's (2015) work on intentional change, they describe the key role of emotions in creating a compelling vision for the person being coached. In my coaching, I also find a key role for emotions. I assess clients' current emotions and identify specific emotions that will lead to an inspiring vision that will facilitate sustainable, lasting change.

I had begun coaching Fred 3 weeks before this meeting took place. Initially Fred's boss, the Chief Financial Officer (CFO), asked that I help Fred become a better team leader. We had met twice before Mark's meeting. The CFO did not know Mark intended to end Fred's employment. Since the coaching contract was paid, they allowed it to continue.

And while I had assessed Fred's initial feelings when we started, I now had to reassess Fred's current emotions and determine how to help him adapt. Initially I considered the patterns that emotions usually follow. For example, anger is associated with injustice. Would Fred think being terminated without a chance to correct his behavior was unjust and lead to anger? Would Fred feel embarrassed, shocked, or betrayed by colleagues? Would he want vengeance? I anticipated shock, anger, and betrayal and that he might blame others. Ultimately, he needed to be accountable, understand his role in what happened, and feel open to change.

My feelings were *concern* for Fred, *worry* regarding how he might react, and *confidence* I could help. As I listened to Fred, he did feel *anger, betrayal,* and *humiliation*. Given the intensity of emotions, he needed time to vent. As Mayer, Caruso, and Salovey (2016) point out, emotions impact cognition. Any effort to focus on rational next steps such as identifying what he might learn from what happened, or getting him to create a compelling vision of the future would have to wait for the negative emotions to dissipate. However, while Fred's case is powerful, most leadership coaching is not about explosive situations.

Coaching leaders is often about maximizing potential or helping them with projects like culture change, teambuilding, talent management, and reorganizations. When coaching leaders on change management, I use the metaphor of emotional land mines, that is, emotions that can be volatile and explode if not addressed as part of implementation strategy. I explain that the senior team worked months or years planning the change. They know what's coming and have time to emotionally prepare. Other organizational members hear rumors, worry about change, and experience fear and distrust leading to lost productivity and key people leaving. To defuse these emotional land mines, I suggest: (a) to address rumors, create an anonymous hotline via internal websites where questions can be raised and answered, and (b) to reassure key personnel to be retained a trusted leader should inform these employees that they are valued and that preferred opportunities will be available once change is implemented.

Some may argue leading change is about rational process. John Kotter, a leading change management expert, offers interesting insights. He has found that people try to deal with facts logically and plan rational responses when they identify problems. Yet a growing body of research by neurologists and psychologists suggests leaders can't just deal logically, they have to also deal with the unseen world of raging emotions. And yet strategic leaders have often been taught to discount feelings. Kotter (2008) suggests they do so at their own peril stating that "after three decades of studying great leaders who mobilize people to unexpected achievement by winning hearts over minds, I can say with some confidence that the leaders would side with the neurologists and the psychologists" (p. 56).

Leaders are not often trained in relationship skills, emotional intelligence, or organizational behavior. Occasionally, leaders are assigned coaches because they need "people skills." Some organizations create structured coaching programs where team members identified as high potential are taught competencies like leadership, strategic thinking, finance, conflict management, and risk-taking. A coach may teach these programs and then follow up to make sure learning is applied successfully.

Coutu and Kaufmann (2009) point out that Ram Charan, an expert coach, suggested coaching will increase because leaders will need constant coaching due to increased complexity and change. Ram described coaching as generally provided by entrepreneurs with backgrounds in consulting, psychology, or human resources. Ram feels coaching became popular because companies were concerned about losing highly talented team members and to emphasize their commitment to high-potential individuals they hired coaches. He feels business people often have coaches to help them with people-oriented skills. When Ram addressed coaching's future, he suggested we will see former CEOs, industry experts, and business-oriented faculty members engage in strategic, quantitative, and technical consulting to help clients deal with increased complexity and change. In these instances when the coach is the expert that the leader needs and wants, the emotions of coach and leader are aligned.

However, expertise-driven coaching still requires cooperation and personal chemistry. The coach's ability to manage emotions is critical when a conflict arises between coach and client. As anyone who has mentored or taught someone knows, there are moments when strong emotions surface unexpectedly and need to be managed successfully for learning to continue. Conflict leading to strong emotions can be generated by any number of situations. For example:

- The person being coached does not agree with the coach's approach. The coach may be highly structured and include steps the client feels are unnecessary. Or perhaps the client wants a curriculum with a clear beginning and end but the coach wishes to learn what is known so that coaching is customized and builds on existing knowledge.

- The person being coached may believe the coach lacks expertise. Perhaps the coach is a recent MBA graduate and even though part of a highly regarded firm, has little experience. Maybe the coach is a friend of someone high up, brought in as a favor, never coached before but wants to try it.

- The person being coached may feel the coach talks down and lacks respect.

- The person being coached does not feel comfortable sharing honestly because the coach will be reporting to senior leaders about their discussions.

Charan feels coaching goals are designed to influence how individuals act (Coutu & Kaufmann, 2009), and how an individual acts is based on that person's emotions and thoughts. Changes in client behavior follow changes in emotions and thinking. According to Daniel Goleman (1998), "Outstanding coaches and mentors get inside the heads of the people they are helping. . . . They know when to push. . . and when to hold back. . . . The way they motivate . . . [is to] demonstrate empathy in action" (p. 101).

At times, leadership coaches are asked to work specifically on team goals. The need for team leader coaching can occur at multiple levels within an organization. "A group. . . must. . . be mindful of the emotions of its members, its own group emotions. . ., and the emotions of other groups and individuals outside its boundaries" (Druskat & Wolff, 2001, p. 82). Identifying, using, understanding, and managing emotions effectively all contribute to strengthening relationships and achievement. To generate high levels of creativity and productivity, Druskat and Wolff (2001) found team members have to feel trust, belonging, and confidence:

- Trust in the team

- Belonging to a unique, worthwhile group

- Confidence that working together will accomplish more

.Regarding the senior team introduced at the beginning of this chapter, it might have turned out quite differently if the coach were also working with the CEO, Mark. What if by using the Emotion Roadmap (see Appendix at the end of this chapter) with Mark, the coach could demonstrate that terminating Fred was not his best choice. Remember all team members acknowledged Fred could be disrespectful, but many also recognized his value as a strategist.

- What if the coach asked the CEO, Mark, to consider retaining the strengths Fred brought by having Fred work on his relationship skills?

- What if Mark addressed the team with Fred present and let everyone know Fred wanted to correct any problem behaviors, and he wanted everyone to cooperate, and ended by appealing to heads and hearts by saying:

"Fred brings great strategic ability to the organization and a willingness to work on improving relationships. I want you all to feel, think, and behave in accepting and supportive ways. I want you to be able to disagree over facts, plans, and strategies, without being disagreeable. If we harness our talent, energy and passion, we can be very successful! And in encouraging you to support Fred, I hope you realize one day you may face a similar challenge and would want your colleagues' support. And Fred, our expectations are that you will continue to be critical when necessary, but the tone and delivery needs to be thoughtful and appropriate. Okay, now let's go to work."

Interestingly, if using the Emotion Roadmap was successful, the organization could have gained greater traction than what actually happened. As it turned out, many organization members were upset that Fred was terminated; they simply wanted a change in behavior. The team did not perform well after Fred left. The CEO was gone after 16 months. If the CEO had understood the implications from the research on teams, he would have known the importance of his team's feelings. After his decision to terminate Fred, the rest of the team felt distrustful, and members told me they were very guarded with what they shared with Mark.

If Mark had decided to work with Fred, he would have learned that Fred took an emotional intelligence assessment called the Mayer Salovey Caruso Emotional Intelligence Test (MSCEIT), which measures an individual's emotional abilities. It turns out Fred had what I call "emotional disabilities," which, in this instance, meant Fred is *unable* to identify or sense how people react to him (Wolfe, 2016).

When we see an individual who makes sarcastic remarks, we often correctly view the behavior as an attitude problem. But what if emotional disabilities prevent the individual from knowing how his behavior impacts others? What if the CEO learned that Fred does not have an attitude problem? Fred actually is *unable* to perceive how others feel. Once Fred found out how he was making others feel, he immediately wanted to correct this. Potentially, this changes how people view Fred. Instead of being angry, they are likely to be supportive!

For readers unfamiliar with the Ability Model of emotional intelligence, here is a brief explanation. If I asked you to identify how good your mathematical abilities are, you might say, poor, average, good, or great. That is a self–report. Instead, if I gave you a test on geometry, trigonometry, and calculus, we would have an assessment based on measurement. The MSCEIT measures a person's emotional abilities to identify, use, understand, and manage emotions. Based on MSCEIT results, it turns out Fred had high ability to understand emotions, but very limited ability to identify emotions and manage relationships with others. Typically, people might view Fred as a bully. However, if they knew he had no idea he was being hurtful, most people would feel differently about him. The more we delve into the role of emotions in coaching, the more important it seems, on multiple levels. At times, the coaching relationship even crosses over into personal aspects of clients' lives.

A Brazilian Company, Natura Cosméticos, engaged in coaching that was purposely more personal. CEO Alessandro Carlucci was concerned that senior managers competing with each other was hurting company prospects. He wanted senior leaders to collaborate more. He hired a coach to work with each manager and with them as a team. He felt this initiative led to their business growing by 21% in 2010. Carlucci explained. "It's not just talking to your boss or subordinates but talking about a person's life history, with their families; it is more holistic, broader, integrating all the different roles of a human being" (Ibarra & Hansen, 2011, p. 7). Discussing personal issues can become quite emotional. The coach needs to be extremely thoughtful about emotions when difficult situations from the past enter the dialogue. Consider the quote from Mr. Pedote, Natura's senior vice president for finance, IT, and legal affairs, who spoke about the emotions he and others experienced at Natura. "I think that the main point is that we are making ourselves vulnerable, showing that we are not supermen, that we have failures; that we are afraid of some things and we don't have all the answers" (Ibarra & Hanson, 2011, p. 7).

The question arises as to *when, if ever, does coaching become therapy*? What gets talked about in coaching sessions can border on what happens in therapy. Certainly, effective coaching may have a therapeutic impact on clients. However, it is critical to maintain focus on organizational goals and to refer serious mental health challenges to appropriate agencies and professionals. Coaching and therapy both focus on the past, present, and future, but therapy often focuses more on the past. The kind of coaching requested by Natura Cosméticos may purposely border on therapy. However, it isn't just when a company encourages this type of coaching that coaching can turn to troubling issues from the past.

Interestingly, most organizations don't hire coaches to deal with highly sensitive personal issues, but coaches report they often encounter them anyway. When coaches were asked if they were frequently hired to address personal issues, only 3% answered yes. However, when coaches were asked if they ever assisted executives with personal issues, 76% answered yes (Coutu & Kauffman, 2009).

In years past, people were told to leave emotions behind when they go to work. Somehow they were to simply turn off emotions and engage in rational planning, decision making, problem solving, and conflict management. This of course was a myth. In 1990 two psychologists, Jack Mayer and Peter Salovey, shed light on people's inner world of emotions and emotional abilities. They wrote a research paper that suggested there is an "emotional intelligence" unique and different than other intelligences. Their paper, along with Goleman's (1995) book, *Emotional Intelligence*, led to dialogue about emotions at work and to a greater focus on emotions in leadership coaching. Dan Goleman in a tweet referenced a study (Taylor, 2017) when he wrote ". . . adaptability is the EI competency that most predicts career success and happiness in life" (Goleman, 2017). This seems consistent with what Salovey and Mayer wrote in 1990: "People who have developed skills related to emotional intelligence understand and express their own emotions, recognize emotions in others, regulate affect, and use moods and emotions to motivate adaptive behaviors (Salovey & Mayer, 1990, p. 200).

In coaching, mentoring, supervising, and other forms of guidance, the goal is first to adapt, to accept the need for change, growth, goal setting, and goal achievement. The rate of change has gone from episodic to continuous and will only continue to accelerate, and those that adapt best will be those that survive and thrive (Kotter, 2008). If coaches are to influence clients' abilities to adapt, they need to know how to work with emotions. Let's return to Fred, the executive introduced at the beginning of this chapter, to consider how the Emotion Roadmap that I developed worked to help Fred.

As noted, Fred had unexpectedly been fired and as expected, he had a powerful emotional reaction. The Emotion Roadmap™ is a systematic, rational approach to managing emotions. Following is how it works in general and how it worked with Fred.

When smart people are stuck and uncertain about how to proceed, it is usually because strong emotions exist in them, or in people they are dealing with. Initially, I help clients identify any existing emotions negatively impacting their situation. Next, we explore what emotions would be more helpful, even ideal. Then together we plan how to change to the positive emotions. This constitutes an emotion roadmap. For Fred, anger and self-doubt first needed to be replaced with calmness and acceptance. Ultimately, he wanted to feel confident and successful.

The Emotion Roadmap comes from the creative integration of other theories and models. First is change management, taught to me by my mentor, Harvard professor, Anthony Athos, which requires:

1. High motivation to change based on pressure from environment or internal need

2. A compelling, inspiring vision of the future

3. Clear first steps that generate momentum

The idea for focusing change on emotions comes from working with Peter Salovey, Yale president, and his colleagues and their Ability Model of emotional intelligence. Once I understood how emotions influence thinking and behavior, and that specific emotions are best for particular tasks, I weaved this idea into the change process. After Fred became less angry, more calm, I asked him to consider what would be ideal to feel? If he could make magic happen and experience an ideal feeling, what would it be? He said he wanted to again feel *confident* and *successful*.

The next step in the Emotion Roadmap involves problem solving and appreciative inquiry; for example, how could Fred get from feeling angry and self-doubting to confident and successful? Problem-solving methodologies include identifying root causes, gap analyses, and ways to correct the situation. We traced the root cause for his current feelings to his inability to identify how people felt about what he said or how he acted. His sarcasm, which he intended for humor, was often interpreted as disrespectful. We considered ways Fred might disagree without being disagreeable. Before planned meetings, he would prepare ways to offer thoughtful comments where disagreement was likely. In unplanned meetings he would need to focus intently on others' emotional reactions. He also could assess people's feelings regarding what he was saying by asking, "What do you think?" By asking "What do you think?" people often respond with how they feel. What he would hear would guide what he would say next. We role-played and worked on these behavioral changes before he began interviewing for a new position.

When the time came to interview, Fred felt anxious and wanted to feel confident. This was new since he never felt much anxiety in a job interview before.

Knowing confidence was the goal, the ideal future emotional state, and anxiety the current state, I introduced appreciative inquiry, the methodology that uses existing strengths to handle challenging situations. I asked Fred if there had ever been a time when he felt anxious and managed somehow to become confident. Were there past times he could draw upon that might help now? He remembered in college a career counselor who prepped him on all he could do to ensure a positive outcome with potential employers. He had not thought about this for many years, but he remembered lessons learned and realized he had incorporated this knowledge, and he began feeling confident.

One concern, however, was how to discuss why he left his last job. Together we decided to describe what happened. A new CEO found Fred had some challenges with interpersonal skills and decided to move forward without him. Fred was comfortable talking about his excellent resume and strategic skill set, and that he had spent time working on improving relationship skills and was now ready to lead and work cooperatively.

In the Emotion Roadmap, the final step involves asking: Is the strategy one that Fred is capable of doing, and willing to do? These very different questions are equally important. Fred said he felt capable and willing and he began interviewing. In the second company he interviewed with, the CEO told Fred he had a similar experience and thought that the way Fred was handling the situation was great. He hired Fred. Fred has since shared that his new skills have resulted in his being happier both professionally and in his personal life. By using the template of the Emotion Roadmap a coach influences how the client feels, thinks, and behaves ultimately leading to success.

Fred's Situation and the Emotion Roadmap

Emotion Roadmap Current and Future Situations Involving Strong Emotions: Fred is fired and starts outplacement procedures.	
IDENTIFY (What is?) Current State	**Who are all the people involved? How is each key person feeling?** At this point, Fred and I are the only key people. Fred feels anger, betrayal, upset, and humiliation. I feel concern and worry about my client and how he will react. I also feel confident I can help.
USE (What is ideal?) Future State	**What feelings would be ideal for each key person?** Tactical level: Fred needs to vent, feel safe in letting his anger out without worrying about repercussions. I need to feel calm and focused as I listen without being judgmental and allow the anger to run its course. Strategic level: Fred needs to feel accountable, responsible, hopeful, and confident that he can learn and grow into a person who effectively manages relationships. I have to feel calm and patient as I coach him on how to improve relationship skills so he again feels confident and successful.

(continued)

Fred's Situation and the Emotion Roadmap (*continued*)

UNDERSTAND (Gap analysis) Problem Solving	How can we create the feelings we want for each key person?
	Once the anger dissipated, we began exploring the questions of what, why, and how. This took several months. At times we would step forward and then something would trigger an angry outburst and we took a few steps back. Throughout Fred needed to feel encouraged that we were progressing, and I needed to maintain patience.
	Over time, Fred understood and accepted that he had been responsible for alienating other team members. And while we both felt the CEO had been unfair, we accepted that life is not fair, and moved on to discuss what we learned and how we could make Fred's life better. Interestingly, the results of the emotional intelligence assessment became a key factor.
	Once Fred realized he was very poor at identifying what another was feeling, he felt less badly about what happened. He wished others knew his sarcasm had been intended as humor, but he came to accept that disparaging others' ideas was never going to be viewed as humorous by those who felt disrespected.
	Fred was weak in many emotional intelligence abilities but he had strength in understanding how emotions worked. I suggested a strategy for Fred. I said any time he said anything that could be perceived as negative that he try to be nonthreatening and, once finished, ask, "What do you think about that?" When asking what you "think," what you often hear is how people "feel." We discussed a number of ways Fred could use his great analytic ability and understanding of how emotions work to be proactive in finding ways to disagree without being disagreeable.
MANAGE (Execute and Modify)	What are we able to do? What are we willing to do?
	Over time, Fred became extremely well versed in his relationships with others by practicing these techniques and tactics.

The following comment shows the key result of coaching Fred using the Emotion Roadmap: After several years of employment in another setting, he called to tell me something that would never have been true before our work together. He said, "Chuck, I just had to tell you that I was called into the office today by my CEO, and he said, 'Fred, I just want you to know that I view you as the voice of reason in this company. And I am very glad you are here!'"

SUMMARY AND CONCLUSION

Emotions are somewhat similar to breathing. We don't often think about either, but they are both always happening. In the role of coaching, whether with an individual, team, or an entire organization, emotions are important in guiding thoughts and behaviors. While there are different models for understanding emotional intelligence, all of them can be assisted from a coaching perspective by using the Emotion Roadmap.

Coaching should not be about therapy, and yet personal situations constantly enter the dialogue. Some consider that coaching is only going to grow in importance and that key to leadership success is the ability to focus on emotions, to adapt, and to operate with a sense of urgency. Having a psychological background may not be necessary, especially for coaching that is technical or functional in nature, and yet, knowledge of emotions may determine whether even these types of coaching are successful. Successful coaches influence emotions, thoughts, and behaviors.

REFERENCES

Boyatzis, R. E., Rochford, K., & Taylor, S. N. (2015). The role of the positive emotional attractor in vision and shared vision: Toward effective leadership, relationships, and engagement. *Frontiers in Psychology, 6*, 670. doi:10.3389/fpsyg.2015.00670

Coutu, D., & Kauffman, C. (2009). What can coaches do for you? *Harvard Business Review*, 1–8. Retrieved from https://hbr.org/2009/01/what-can-coaches-do-for-you

Druskat, V., & Wolff, S. (2001). Building the emotional intelligence of groups. *Harvard Business Review*, 80–90. Retrieved from https://hbr.org/2001/03/building-the-emotional-intelligence-of-groups

Goleman, D. (1995). *Emotional intelligence: Why it can matter more than IQ*. New York, NY: Bantam Books.

Goleman, D. (1998). What makes a leader? *Harvard Business Review, 76*(6), 92–102.

Goleman, D. (2017). In a study, adaptability is the EI competency that most predicts career success and happiness in life [Tweet]. Retrieved from https://twitter.com/DanielGolemanEI/status/882948532575113216

Ibarra, H., & Hansen, M. T. (2011). Are you a collaborative leader? *Harvard Business Review*, 1–8. Retrieved from https//hbr.org/2011/07/are-you-a-collaborative-leader

Kotter, J. P. (2008). *A sense of urgency*. Boston, MA: Harvard Business Press.

Mayer, J. D., Caruso, D. R., & Salovey, P. (2016). The ability model of emotional intelligence: Principles and updates. *Emotion Review, 8*(4), 290–300. doi:10.1177/1754073916639667

Salovey, P., & Mayer, J. D. (1990). Emotional intelligence. *Imagination, Cognition, and Personality, 9*, 185–211. doi:0.2190/DUGG-P24E-52WK-6CDG

Taylor, M. (2017). How to coach for adaptability in leadership. *Key Step Media*. Retrieved from https://t.co/U7SUQh6F5H

Wolfe, C. J. (2016). Emotional intelligence: Emotion roadmap. *HR Director, 140*, 28–29.

Appendix

The Emotion Roadmap

Emotion Roadmap	Current and Future Situations Involving Strong Emotions	
Description **The Emotion Roadmap is an Emotion Based Planning & Problem-Solving Process which can be** 1. **Strategic:** Proactively preparing for change(s) 2. **Tactical:** Reactively dealing with difficult emotionally challenging situation(s). **As part of being both strategic and tactical, individuals need to pay attention to the science of how emotions work in general and to the unique characteristics of each key person.**	**IDENTIFY** **(What is)** **Current State**	**Who are all the people involved?** **How is each key person feeling?** (When smart people are stuck it is almost always because strong emotions are involved. Focusing on emotions can help create new options for moving forward.)
	USE **(What is ideal?)** **Future State**	**What feelings would be ideal for each key person?** (The science of emotional intelligence teaches that certain feelings are more ideal than others for particular tasks.)
	UNDERSTAND **(Gap analysis)** **Problem Solving**	**How can we create the feelings we want for each key person?** (This involves knowing why people feel the way they do and what it will take to make any necessary changes in feelings.)
	MANAGE **(Execute & modify)**	**What are you able to do?** **What are you willing to do?** (Once the problem solving takes place, you need to select the plan that you are both willing and able to do.)

Source: Wolfe, C. J. (2016). Emotional intelligence: Emotion roadmap. *HR Director*, 140, 28–29.

15

Hermeneutic Coaching

Philip Brownell

Frank walked into the living room. Sally was sitting on the couch with her legs apart, and Brenda, their daughter, was on the floor between them, facing away. Sally was braiding her hair.

Frank looked at them and said, "Wow."

There was something about the look on his face, the inflection of that word. "What does he mean?" Brenda wondered.

So often that is the question. What does one person mean by what they say, or don't say, or by what they do and how they carry themselves when they do it?

The meaning and the significance of any given word, action, incident, development, or situation are relative to given persons; so, the meaning is not the meaning for all people everywhere. It is the meaning and significance to this one here or that one there.

Hermeneutics is at the core of virtually every human interaction and search for understanding. What does a person mean by what they say? That's hermeneutics. This chapter defines the term, gives a brief history of its use, describes three key elements to a hermeneutic approach, and applies them to the field of professional coaching. Since we are concerned with an application of hermeneutics to working with people, and people have experiences, it is a certain kind of hermeneutics that we're concerned about here—hermeneutic phenomenology. "Hermeneutic phenomenology is consequently the study of experience together with its meanings" (Henriksson & Friesen, 2012, p. 1).

I believe hermeneutics is likely one of the more central concerns for coaching, because everything else we, as coaches, might do depends upon understanding and being understood. Therefore, gaining a model for how to appreciate and comprehend others can help coaches work more effectively.

DEFINING THE TERM

The word "hermeneutic" comes from the Greek word ἑρμηνεύω (hermeneuo). In classic Greek literature, it meant to translate, give the meaning, interpret, or explain. Hermeneutical principles have been the rules by which sacred texts are translated and elucidated. "In its most basic sense hermeneutics refers to the many ways in which we may theorize about the nature of human interpretation, whether that means understanding books, works of art, architecture, human communication, or even non-verbal bodily gestures" (Porter & Robinson, 2011, p. 1).

Hermeneutic coaching, then, would be the coaching process particularly focused on and utilizing the means by which the coach might understand the coachee and the coachee might understand the coach. As Porter and Robinson noted, we experience the meaning of any given figure of interest (such as a book held in the hands and the words on its pages) against the background, or the ground of the person's life as contextualizing life world. That would extend to the implications of whatever might emerge from that consideration—what is known as the intentionality, with the figure of interest being one's intentional object.

A VERY BRIEF HISTORY

There are simply too many people in the history of the development of hermeneutics to present here. A very simplified progression, however, can be traced from Friedrich Schleiermacher through Wilhelm Dilthey and Martin Heidegger to Hans-Georg Gadamer (Mantzavinos, 2016). Schleiermacher was a German pietist who took the rules for interpreting sacred texts and began applying them to the interpretation of experience. Dilthey continued that trend and made the process more explicit. Heidegger turned it into an ontology, and Gadamer turned to philosophy itself as his field of interpretation. From Kierkegaard in his criticism of stagnate Christianity, demanding "a halt from a distance," to Heidegger and a "critical turn against academic philosophy: the history of problems in Neokantianism and Husserl's transcendental phenomenology" came under his critical analysis (Gadamer, 1991, p. 15). The hermeneutic turn in philosophy was a turning toward understanding immediate, grounded experience of the life world. That is what the coach is after in the life of the client, but it cannot be attained apart from the interpretive experience found in the coaching relationship.

DESCRIBING THREE KEY ELEMENTS IN A HERMENEUTIC APPROACH

Three tenets crucial to a hermeneutic phenomenology, and thus hermeneutic coaching, are the hermeneutic circle, dialogue or immersion, and the fusion of horizons. While there are many things that could be said about hermeneutics, because whole volumes have been developed about hermeneutics, these three will suffice for the purposes of this chapter. It is simply impossible in the scope of one small chapter to do justice to the complexity of philosophical thought inherent to the subject of hermeneutics. This chapter has to be understood as a pointer for the interested reader and hopefully an encouragement to investigate the subject more.

THE HERMENEUTIC CIRCLE

The concept of a hermeneutic circle is gained by considering fluctuations between the perspective of a phenomenon as a whole and as something composed of individual parts. It's not just that familiar aphorism that the whole is larger than the sum of its parts. It's that the parts all, individually, as they are, contribute to make the whole what it is, even if the effect is larger than a simple sum of those parts.

> When the phenomenon is viewed as a whole, the integration of individual parts to create and define the entire experience is recognized. Conversely, when the phenomenon is considered in terms of individual parts, the importance of the whole in contextualizing or illuminating each piece is recognized. (von Zweck, Paterson, & Pentland, 2008, p. 119; see also Grondin, 2016)

In personal life, we all have experiences. Any one of them is a part of our whole life, our whole journey, and this current one, the "now," is only the latest part to emerge. The meaning of any experience along the way, including the current moment, must be understood by recourse to the whole journey (thus far). For instance, when I was 10 years old, I read a biography of Ernest Hemingway and decided I wanted to be a writer. Between then and now, I have had various opportunities to write. And now I am a published author. The significance of writing then as compared to writing now is different. Then it was an aspiration. Now it is an accomplishment. Then, it was what I wanted to be "when I grow up," but now it's what I grew up to become. Conversely, the whole journey cannot be appreciated; indeed it simply does not exist, but for the individual moments and experiences along the way. I wrote newspaper articles for the 4-H club when I was 10 years old. I wrote poems and song lyrics in high school. I wrote sermons as a pastor. I wrote daily conversations in email that went on for hours when the Internet was created. I wrote books, articles, and promotional pieces for professional audiences after I became a psychologist. I did not simply leap from the Hemingway biography to writing professional books. It was a journey of steps and so it has been a whole adventure, but it would not exist but for each moment along the way. I make sense of it through life review. I'm 70 years old now. I can look back and appreciate the vista from this vantage point, and with hindsight I revisit some of those "places," and the person I was then, and make sense of it with the whole in mind.

DIALOGUE/IMMERSION

"In hermeneutical dialogue, then, the general subject in which one is immersed— both the interpreter and the text—is the tradition, the heritage" (Palmer, 1969, p. 199). The terms "dialogue" and "immersion" are important.

Dialogue in this context is not simply a conversation between two people. It's more like one person digging in the dirt. This last weekend, I planted 20 trees on our property and I had a dialogue with the task, with the dirt, with the tools, with the landscape, and I went back and forth about how deep to dig the holes, how wide, what kind of soil preparation to use when I planted the trees, and so forth. As I interacted with the elements, I became immersed in the project. My hands and boots got muddy. And when I was done, I was exhausted, as if I'd been wrestling with someone quite larger and more powerful than myself.

An interpreter of texts digs into those texts and examines the cultures in which they originated. We are talking about the process of exegesis here (a bringing out of the meaning of a text, and so a hermeneutical consideration). The interpreter conducts a dialogical enquiry of the text. So, also one who seeks to understand another person must "dig into" the "stuff" of that person's life. They must get muddy with it. They will tire from the digging, because it takes patience, exhausting inquiry, the bracketing of assumptions and quick model-making, but they will persevere if they are to actually dialogue, if they are to immerse themselves in the process of finding out about the other person. And, yes, they will talk with one another too.

The Fusion of Horizons

A horizon in hermeneutic phenomenology is not the thin line way out where the sky meets the land. The horizon is everything that can be imagined, everything known or possible for a person in his or her life world. If something is not in a person's horizon, it never comes to mind. The horizon is the extent of the life world. With regard to interpreting a text, for instance, a sacred text, there are two horizons to consider: that of the reader and that of the culture in which the writer wrote and the original readers read. So, the fusion of horizons takes place when, as one dialogues with a text, with another person, with an event, and so forth, the meeting of two different perspectives takes place, and it's not just a literal line of sight that I'm talking about; it's everything attached to those relative perspectives. It is a collision of worlds. To a gestalt therapist versed in field theory, it is the way contact between the person and whatever is considered to be "other" generates a field of experience—a phenomenal field.

When horizons are in fusion, which is an event, they both question and are questioned. The fusion of horizons is not an easy thing. The unfamiliar calls for examination of all things previously known. It is an unsettling experience.

In talking about the process of meeting an other, for instance a client in therapy, I have often described the process of phenomenological investigation as beating a rug and watching the dust fly up and then resettle in a newly configured pattern. In the concept of a fusion of horizons, it's as if two rugs are beaten; their dust flies up, and when it resettles some of one rug's dust can be found on the other rug and vice versa.The fusion of horizons forms a mutuality. When we are talking about hermeneutic coaching, we are considering that kind of process. You can't come away from coaching without getting some of the client all over you.

APPLYING HERMENEUTICS TO COACHING

I want to bring this chapter now more deliberately into the practical for coaches. Learning to coach could be seen as the process of learning to ask cogent and important questions—questions that go to the vital places in the coachee's world, questions that dig up the pivotal, enduring themes in the coachee's life in order to link them to tangible goals and effective actions. That which is important and significant is what makes for motivated action. So, finding a way to understand the client is crucial.

May I suggest a way that incorporates the three tenets of hermeneutic phenomenology mentioned previously?

Imagine a literal circle drawn in the dirt of a dusty sandlot; call it the circle of meeting. The client stands inside. One must actually *meet* the other person before anything else can follow. So, step one is to enter that circle. So, the coach steps inside.

Step two is to look around and to notice the parts that comprise the whole. It is also to notice the whole that gives context to the parts. The coach must perceive those parts, observe their qualities, and the ways in which they function. So, there is the dusty dirt of the sandlot and the wind that whips up the dust. There is the circle drawn in the dirt, which is uneven, as if drawn with a blunt stick and a wavering intensity. There is the coach and the coachee. The coachee is barefoot, but the coach has tennis shoes on. The coach has no sunglasses and there is a hot, bright sun. The coachee wears his sunglasses loose on the bridge of his nose so that he can also peer slightly over the top of them. The parts are not simply a circle on the hot sandlot, but a situation in the afternoon heat. The parts contribute to the whole, but the whole interprets the parts.

Step three is to talk. The coach gives voice to what he or she observes, asks questions about the other, self-discloses how the other affects in return. The coach immerses himself or herself in the experience of the coachee. "What's it like for you not to have shoes?"

The coach makes himself or herself open, and therefore vulnerable as well to the impact, even the pointed questions of the coachee. "What's it like for you to not have sunglasses?"

"How can I help you take care of your burning feet?"

"I'm not here for my feet; I want to build an irrigation system for this sandlot."

"Oh!" Now there is surprise, unexpected difference, a clash of perspectives. Unless there is a fusion, these people will miss one another.

I do not mean to say there must be an enmeshment or a confluence (for that is where one gets lost in the other). My friends in the gestalt world understand contact to be the awareness of difference, and in this case, in the case of the fusion of horizons, what I mean is that it is a difference that hooks one and leads into the world of another. Without that kind of contact—a fusion of horizons—there is no practical perspective taking; one does not understand conceptually what the situation is like for the other, and one does not take the emotional perspective of the other in true empathy.

"Suddenly, it seems to me that this sandlot means more to you than I expected. How does this place fit into your life?"

Consider Table 15.1 showing hermeneutic principles (HP) and corresponding types of questions (TOQ) and self-disclosures (SD) coaches might find themselves presenting to the client:

As might be apparent from the table, you cannot appreciate the types of questions and the kinds of self-disclosures involved without getting into the details of the client's situation and the nature of the meeting between coach and coachee. If, while reading that list, you found yourself yearning for more detail, then that is what any given coach would sense and go for in the conversation.

That leads to another important point, and one covered by other writers in this book. The presence of the coach is absolutely essential. It is impossible to engage

Table 15.1 Principled Questions

HP	TOQ/SD
Hermeneutic Circle	• If your situation were a soup, what would be its ingredients? (TOQ) • Where are those parts located on the map of your life right now? (TOQ) • How would you describe the big picture of what's going on with you? (TOQ) • It seems to me that part of this situation that we have not talked about is _____. (SD) • When you go from the big picture to the small details how do you feel? (TOQ) • When you describe all the many details you're trying to handle, I feel _____ (full, overwhelmed, satisfied, lost, etc.) (SD) • Which of the details of your life right now are absolutely necessary to the big picture? (TOQ) • Which of the details of your life right now are not necessary? (TOQ)
Dialogue/ Immersion	• What's it like for you to be talking with me right now? (TOQ) • What would you like to ask me? (TOQ) • I am curious about _____. (SD) • What do you need at this moment to risk talking with me about things the way they really are? (TOQ) • That touches me. (SD) • I would like to know more about _____. (SD)
Fusion of Horizons	• How would you describe the two different worlds you and I come from? (TOQ) • When you say you want to achieve _____, it makes sense to me. (SD) • That would be about #10 for me, but for you it seems like it would be in the top five. (SD) • But where *would* you rank it? (TOQ) • How much do you think I get what you're trying to tell me? (TOQ)

HP, hermeneutic principles; SD, self-disclosures; TOQ, types of questions.

someone and find out what goal attainment would mean to them if one is not *there* to hear it, sense it, pick it up or stimulate its revelation to begin with. The coachee would not provide that information if he or she did not understand it was important to the coach. So, the coach must bring himself or herself *fully* into that circle of meeting. You will notice, for instance, that I placed self-disclosures in Table 15.1 and not just questions. The self-disclosure sets up a response; it is like a note left hanging between the coach and the coachee in which the coachee senses his or her response provides the resolving tone. Self-disclosure is a tool of coaching presence and can be considered a question in stealth mode. As such I like to think of coaching presence through self-disclosure as the most wide open of all open-ended questions. It also brings together dialogue or immersion and the fusion of horizons through a process of contacting.

That brings me to a true story. Once there was an art director for a thriving professional journal. Writers on staff would send him their articles and he would create graphics to illustrate them. Then, the world of graphic design was turned upside down by the advance of technology such that copious graphics could be found online and simply downloaded. Graphic programs made it possible for the average person to create and modify their own graphics. The art director lost his career and went back to school to become a counselor. He had to reinvent himself as the overall situation of his life demanded adjustment and new parts.

One day, in the life of the orthodox church he attended, it became necessary to create several life-sized icons.[1] He took this project on and gathered volunteers. Many of them had never painted before, let alone painted an icon. So, he coached them. He exhibited a gentle but serious attitude, because he believed one could not create something that would be used in worship without approaching it in a spirit of worship to begin with. He drew out the lines for the paintings and told them what colors belonged between which lines. He met with them in a studio where the necessary paint and brushes were made available, and he told them how to paint— not with quick, short and sketchy movements but with long, easy, continuously flowing movements. He put music on in the studio, and he encouraged the novice painters, telling them he thought they were doing well. He told them what to do. He told them how to do it, and he created an atmosphere, an attitude, and an example around what needed to be done. He was present. He brought the parts together to make the whole, but the whole defined and gave significance to the parts. He continuously interacted with novice painters to such a degree that the line between them blurred and they became members of one project. The novices never lost the fact that they were novices, but they knew they were working with a professional, and the professional realized that while he knew what he was doing, he not only needed the novices but also learned, as if all over again, the value of approaching a project with the wide-eyed excitement, if not the terror of having to create.

One of the things I'm trying to communicate with that story is that there is a "what" and a "how" to the process of hermeneutic coaching. It is impossible to capture the process with a description of principles and a chart of questions. There is an aesthetic to the whole thing, a sensory quality and an embodied process. So, there will be a felt sense to the meeting that the coach can learn to monitor. If the coach is actively working with the three principles mentioned earlier, then there will be a *swirling* going on.

What I mean is that the process cannot be understood to be simply linear. It might look something like shown in Figure 15.1.

Dialogue begins as two persons meet and they begin to discern the various parts to the whole situation. Indeed, the coach is doing an assessment to try to grasp the part-to-whole relationships that emerge from dialogue—which leads to more dialogue. As the process unfolds, and the coach and the coachee develop a working relationship, there emerges a growing fusion of horizons as each one affects the other. Not only do they begin to see things as the other sees them, but their own respective horizons expand. And that leads to the awareness of more parts, a new appreciation for the significance of the whole and so forth. Then it goes on and on from there, with a swirling that also meanders at times.

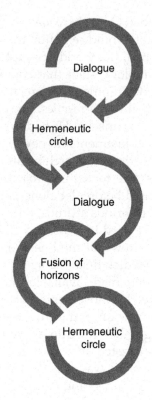

Figure 15.1 Swirling use of hermeneutic principles.

CASE EXAMPLE

See if you can find the hermeneutics at work in this case example.

I am a pastor who is also a clinical psychologist who is also a professional coach. Sometimes someone comes to me with a pastoral need (see Chapter 32 of this book). I don't send them down the line. If they want coaching, and if they cannot get help from their own pastor for whatever reason, I'll see what develops. So, one day Thomas[2] came to see me. He said he had been struggling with sin, a particular kind of sin. He wanted me to help him fix that.

We settled into chairs in my office. I invited him to look around and take notice of his surroundings. I ask him what he saw, what he noticed. He was puzzled with that.

He said, "I am struggling with sin. I feel defective. I feel like a bad Christian. Can you help me?"

I said, "I know what you said. Part of us working together, an important part, is getting used to one another and becoming comfortable paying attention to each other. Since you come here rather than me going to your house, I want you to start taking me in, looking around in my world, because I'm going to be looking around in yours. Does that make sense?"

He said, "I guess." Then he started looking around my office. He saw a picture of where I used to live in Bermuda, and he recognized where it was. He said, "That's Horseshoe Beach!"

"Right! Have you been to Bermuda?"

(continued)

CASE EXAMPLE (*continued*)

"My wife and I visited there once on a cruise. And we rented a couple of motorbikes and drove out to Horseshoe Beach. It was beautiful, and the water was so *warm*."

I smiled. I waited while he looked elsewhere in the office. There was silence. I reminded myself that sometimes silence is a good thing, but I always feel impatient with it. I remembered how many tourists died each year on those rented motorbikes when I was living in Bermuda. More time went by in silence. I felt the tension rising as I watched him look around. I heard a bird singing outside, and I forced myself back into the room. That bird was not an essential part of this situation. When I could stand it no longer, I leaned forward and asked, "How are things between you and your wife now?"

His countenance fell. His whole body sagged. He suddenly looked sad and exhausted. He said, "I am a sorry excuse for a husband. There must have been something terribly broken in my family when I was growing up, because I can't stop thinking about sex."

"Thomas," I said. "we have to decide down which road we are going to go with this." He looked puzzled.

"We can focus on your sin, and I can give you Bible passages to read, and we can go through the brokenness in your childhood and your current life, and all that would be counseling, or therapy. We would be two Christians doing Biblical counseling."

He interrupted me. He said, "No. I tried that. The guy listened to me cry and tell him how much I couldn't help myself, and then we turned to places in the Bible that related to slavery to sin and all, but I already knew I was enslaved to it. And reading those things just made me feel worse—more defective, more of a loser. I even stopped going to church because of it."

I said, "The other thing we can do is coaching. Coaching looks forward at what you want to accomplish, where you want to go, what you want to become. It is not focused on brokenness as such."

"But what about my sin?"

I said, "When the disciples were crossing the Sea of Galilee and Jesus came to them walking on the water, He told Peter to get out of the boat and come to him. So, Peter did, and while he was looking forward, toward Jesus, to where he was going, he was fine. But when he looked down and started dealing with the difficulty of walking on water, which he knew he was not capable of, he started to sink. The choice you have to make is between what you've been trying so far with a focus on what's not working and your enslavement and your brokenness and what is still out in front of you. It's a choice between counseling and coaching."

He pondered what I had said. "That's a different way of looking at it."

"When you think of these two different perspectives—the brokenness in which you came into my office and the forward-looking approach I'm suggesting, what comes to mind?"

"I wonder if it would be okay."

"It seems I'm not what you expected."

He laughed. "No. And this coaching thing seems a bit scary."

"Like maybe I'm a fallen pastor trying to recruit you to some kind of cult?"

He laughed. "Well, sorta."

"I guess that's something you'll have to think about."

CONCLUSION

Hermeneutic coaching is not some radically different kind of coaching that stands outside the box and is an entity all on its own. If you consider the various chapters in this book, you will see people using various techniques to help promote a sense of understanding. You will see them working with values in order to clarify what achieving various goals might mean or how pursuing a course of action might relate to who these people believe themselves to be. It all involves making meaning out of experience. It all involves hermeneutics. So, read some of the other chapters and use them as projects. Diagram them, looking for the hermeneutic circle, immersion, and the fusion of horizons. My bet is that you will be able to find these things everywhere. Further to that, you will be able to use them as a scaffolding upon which to hang several techniques and park various tools.

NOTES

1. An icon in the orthodox church comes from the Greek word εn ic (*eikōn*) meaning "image." Icons are religious works of art created and regarded reverentially.

2. This is a fictional name and some things are changed for purposes of confidentiality.

REFERENCES

Gadamer, H-G. (1991). Gadamer on Gadamer. In H. Silverman (Ed.), *Continental philosophy IV: Gadamer and hermeneutics* (pp. 13–19). New York, NY: Routledge.

Grondin, J. (2016). What is the hermeneutical circle? In N. Keane & C. Lawn (Eds.), *The Blackwell companion to hermeneutics* (pp. 299–305). Oxford, UK: Blackwell.

Henriksson, C., & Friesen, N. (2012). Introduction. In N. Friesen, C. Henriksson, & T. Saevi (Eds.), *Hermeneutic phenomenology in education: Method and practice* (pp. 1–14). Rotterdam, Netherlands: Sense Publications.

Mantzavinos, C. (2016). Hermeneutics. In E. N. Zalta (Ed.), *The Stanford encyclopedia of philosophy* (Winter 2016 ed.). Retrieved from https://plato.stanford.edu/archives/win2016/entries/hermeneutics

Palmer, R. (1969). *Hermeneutics: Interpretation theory in Schleiermacher, Dilthey, Heidegger, and Gadamer.* Evanston, IN: Northwestern University Press.

Porter, S., & Robinson, J. (2011). *Hermeneutics: An introduction to interpretive theory.* Grand Rapids, MI: William B. Eerdmans Publishing Company.

Von Zweck, C., Paterson, M., & Pentland, W. (2008) The use of hermeneutics in a mixed methods design. *The Qualitative Report, 13*(1), 116–134. Retrieved from http://www.nova.edu/ssss/QR/QR13-1/vonzweck.pdf

RECOMMENDED READING

Kahn, M. S. (2014). *Coaching on the axis: Working with complexity in business and executive coaching.* London, UK: Karnac Books, Ltd.

Knight, J. (2016). *Better conversations: Coaching ourselves and others to be more credible, caring and connected.* Thousand Oaks, CA: Corwin/Sage.

Zimmermann, J. (2015). *Hermeneutics: A very short introduction.* Oxford, UK: Oxford University Press.

16

The Coach's Imperative: Expanding Perspectives

Terrie Lupberger

The ability to perceive or think differently is more important than the knowledge gained.
      —David Bohm, American Scientist

We are human beings and therefore each see the world from a unique viewpoint that shapes the way we think, the way we behave, the actions we take and the results we get in life. A 30-something, Caucasian, male, oil rig worker from the Western part of the United States will have a different view of the world and how to navigate in it than a 57-year-old, unemployed widow from Delhi or an 18-year-old farm worker living with her parents in Nigeria.

Each of their unique ways of seeing and interacting with the world is not inherently right or wrong but they do affect the actions they see to take and the results they get. Their perspectives allow for what they think is possible and not possible and what they actually do or don't do as a result.

As human beings, we do not all see the same reality. Our perspective or lens of reality has been shaped by a multitude of factors. Our perspective has been shaped by our gender, age, race, geography. It's been influenced by the experiences we've lived so far. It's been shaped by the generation we are a part of and the thinking and norms of behaving that it elicits. It has been influenced by our families, by their beliefs and values and norms of behaving. Our thinking has been shaped by the cultural conversations we've been immersed in, consciously and unconsciously, and by the values and behaviors of the communities, organizations, and other contexts we've been a part of.

Regardless of whether you, as a human being, are aware of these influences, they do impact and shape everything you think and do. They have informed the person you are now and the way you think (including your beliefs, values, and judgments) as well as your behaviors.

Because of their influence, exploring the perspectives you hold is critical in revealing where they might be limiting your possibilities or keeping you stuck. Examining the observer you have become supports you to develop new awareness as well as new capacities for action; it supports you to better take care of the future you most want to create. It is, therefore, an imperative of good coaching.

A BRIEF DISCUSSION ABOUT SUBJECT–OBJECT THEORY

A useful way to think about shifting your observer or the lens you view the world through is offered by Dr. Robert Kegan, a pioneer in the field of human development, and author of many books including *In Over Our Heads* and *Immunity to Change*. He is probably best known for his work in subject–object theory and adult development theory (Kegan, 1994).

The simple but profound premise of subject–object theory is that we human beings are run by that which we are subject to; what we aren't aware of will have influence or control over us. Said in even simpler terms, you can't change what you can't see. Conversely, the more you can see, the more awareness you have, the more choice you have.

An overt example of what is meant by making something object that was once subject is that of Louis Pasteur, a French microbiologist from the 1800s who worked on germ theory. Before Pasteur, nurses and doctors didn't have awareness of germs; they were subject to them and their effects. Without that awareness, they didn't know that washing hands and sterilizing equipment would save lives. Pasteur and his colleagues were instrumental in making germs object for the medical field.

A relevant example for coaching is a senior female leader in healthcare that I worked with. Hands down she had the business acumen to run her operation very effectively. I shadowed her at a few of her executive staff meetings and noticed that her habit was to defer to the assessments and opinions of her new boss and the senior team, all of whom were men. The forthright and decisive leader I worked with in our one-to-one sessions wasn't the same woman that showed up in these meetings. In my 360° stakeholder interviews with her new boss, he told me he had reservations about her leadership abilities and wanted me to work with her on her assertiveness skills.

Armed with that feedback and my own observations, my client and I explored the underlying beliefs and emotions that led to her uncharacteristic behavior in those senior executive meetings. Up until that point, she had been subject to, or blind to, how her habit of reacting to the all-male team was impacting her behavior. With more awareness (and also some new practices), she had more choice to respond differently.

Another coaching example is that of a young man I worked with who was a partner in a successful start-up. He came to coaching looking to improve his relationship with his business partner who, fed up with my client's angry outbursts, was threatening to quit. With good conversation, exploration, and reflection, my client saw that his quick temper could cost him not only the business and the relationship with his partner, but his friendships and significant relationships outside of work. The observer he was up until the coaching—his overarching worldview and resulting way of being—was to be overly critical of everyone (and himself). He went quickly to anger with anyone who he assessed as incompetent or lazy. He saw that he was repeating the same behavior that was modeled by his father growing up. With growing awareness, he started seeing that he could practice choosing a different response to the circumstances that routinely triggered him. What he was subject to before the coaching was starting to become object, meaning it had less influence and control over his behavior.

Perhaps then, that is what coaching, at its best, can do for others. It can help make visible (and object) all the things our clients have been subject to, such as their beliefs, stories, assumptions, habits in thinking and behaving, emotional triggers, biology, and so forth. Coaching can point out how the observer that the client has become is impacting the outcomes he or she is seeking. It can point out blind spots that have been running the client and support him or her to practice new behaviors and take different actions. By questioning the unexamined assumptions our clients are living by, we can support them to expand their view of the world. We can support them to enlarge their possibilities for action and increase their effectiveness.

This quote, attributed to English psychoanalyst R. D. Laing and quoted by Goleman (1985), eloquently echoes this point:

> The range of what we think and do is limited by what we fail to notice. And because we fail to notice that we fail to notice, there is little we can do to change; until we notice how failing to notice shapes our thoughts and deeds. (Goodreads, n.d., para 10)

COACHING SUPPORTS OUR CLIENTS TO NOTICE

Until we notice that we fail to notice, we can't take new action. Without awareness, we will keep doing more of the same. By listening for what the clients may be subject to, by helping them notice what might be influencing their perspective that is limiting their results and possibilities, by helping them expand or shift perspective to include new thinking, the coach can support clients to be more at choice in what to do and how to move forward.

Supporting clients to see and shift the observer they are or the perspective they have is at the heart of the ontological approach to coaching. This approach to coaching calls into question the way the client frames issues and possibilities. It aims to shift the thinking from which the client's inaction or ineffective actions emerge so that, ultimately, the client's potential for action is enlarged.

A new team leader who is blind to how her own self-doubt is resulting in micromanaging her team will continue to behave the same way until she notices and shifts the beliefs she has about herself and her competency. A talented software engineer with aspirations to move into management will have to shift his constant, negative criticisms of the company to have any chance of promotion.

THE COACH'S BLIND SPOT

Having been an assessor and trainer of coaches for two decades, I still hear too many coaches falling quickly into problem solving with the client and missing the opportunity to question the worldview that is sourcing the client's ineffective actions or blinding them to new possibilities. Too many coaches only work at the surface of a client's presenting issue and fail to make visible what has been invisible or unavailable to the client.

It's not just an issue for coaches; it's an issue for us human beings. We still live, for the most part, under the illusion that the world can be perceived transparently and objectively; that through rational, logical analysis we can all see the same world and problem-solve the issues presented. We largely believe that more knowledge is the missing link to success. This is a belief that's been running in the background of our collective thinking for a very long time. It's like an old version of a computer operating system that we have been subject to (blind to) that is limiting what's possible and in desperate need of an upgrade.

Going as far back in history as the Greek philosopher Socrates, the Western world (especially but not exclusively) has held the belief that there's an objective world out there that is understandable through logic and reason. We have held the belief that human beings are fundamentally rational, reasonable beings who, by gathering as much information as they can about that objective world, can use it to understand and navigate in it.

While there were many philosophers, scientists, and scholars who influenced the thinking that we still operate with to this day, of note was René Descartes, French philosopher and physicist of the 1600s. Descartes postulated that knowledge of the world could be securely obtained with the powers of reason and this was further supported by scientist and physicist Isaac Newton's declaration that the world was linear, rational, predictable, and repeatable. While reason, rationality, and scientific knowledge is certainly one way to understand and navigate our world, it isn't the only one.

It's a fascinating history lesson in how we ended up privileging rationality and logic over other ways of knowing and, if you're interested in the topic, you would be interested to read *The Passion of the Western Mind* by Richard Tarnas. The more important point here is that most of us live our lives (and coach) from this unexamined belief system that makes the intellect king (Tarnas, 1991).

This cultural worldview has informed most of the systems we work within. To this day, most education is primarily about acquiring knowledge and information to produce effectiveness, regardless of our field of endeavor. That's good, but it only addresses part of what it means to be human. Often in adulthood, many of us find ourselves asking questions for which our intellect, knowledge, and our way knowing is woefully inadequate to address. Questions like these:

Why isn't the job fulfilling me? I love my partner so why do I have this longing I can't quite name? I really care about the environment, but what can I, as one person, do? I really dislike my boss, but how do I deal with these feelings so it doesn't derail my career? Within the confines of the organization's values, how do I take care of what matters to me? Where do I find the courage to be the kind of leader other people want to work for? I thought the promotion would make me happy, but

I'm really more miserable with the extra responsibilities, now what? Should I stay in this job for the sake of my family's security or should I follow my dream of being an artist? How do I manage through all the chaos and unpredictability I'm experiencing in the world? No one told me how hard parenting would be; I don't have any roadmap for how to do this right, what if I screw it up? What's meaningful and where do I put my attention and focus at this stage in my life?

Perhaps it's because of these kinds of questions, not addressed in other learning contexts, that coaching came into existence. These are normal and common questions that adults have about life, the meaning of it, and their place in it. Perhaps coaching is a conversational space for legitimizing and exploring these kinds of questions. Perhaps coaching showed up as an intuitive response to the fact that, even with all of our information and knowledge, it is still insufficient to address the more fundamental questions we have about our existence.

Please don't misinterpret that I'm saying knowledge, intellect, and rationality are not good or useful. On the contrary the rational, linear, analytical, scientific approach to life has generated countless positive outcomes. It's allowed us to build cities and spaceships to the moon and find cures for life-threatening diseases.

What I'm suggesting is that we've been subject to the collective thinking that we are detached observers looking at objective reality out there and through knowledge alone will learn how to better deal with that reality. This blind spot has led us to leave out many other key elements of being human that we need to reclaim and include in our daily living and in our work as coaches. It's caused us to put men on the moon but not figure out how to get along with others who have different worldviews or how to live a well-lived life.

HOW DO YOU SHIFT PERSPECTIVES?

What we are subject to—all the influences that shape our experience of the world and the choices we make—will have control over us until we notice them. Once we notice, we can then be more at choice about what to do with them. As a coach, there are specific things you can be listening for, specific areas or domains of being human that you can explore to help clients expand their perspective or see where their thinking is limiting them from achieving desired outcomes and results.

Based on my extensive training in an ontological approach to coaching, there are several key areas to consider to improve your coaching impact. We will explore three of them here. It might be helpful to think of these as doorways or pathways of exploration.

THE DOORWAY OF LANGUAGE

Because you are human, you live in language. Your words (whether spoken to others or internally thought to yourself) are what you use to make sense of your world, describe your reality, and create your future. You have narratives or stories about who you are, where you fit into the world, what you can accomplish, what you want, what they want, what you can't do, what you aren't good at, and so forth.

You constructed your narrative about the world and your place in it based on a multitude of influences we've spoken about (your family's beliefs, your age, your race, your gender, where you grew up, the communities you grew up in and the ones you now participate in, the collective conversations happening now, etc.). That's actually good news. That means there isn't some predetermined, finite, fixed perspective you were born with, like having green eyes, that you can't change. That means you can learn to change or expand your perspective. Once you are aware of the stories or narratives you tell, once you can see what thinking you are subject to, you can then change it; you'll have more choice and power over what you think, do, and become. What follows is just a sampling of some of the common narratives or stories my clients have told me over the years:

> I can't go back to school at this age.
>
> I'm married to someone who will never see me for who I am.
>
> I can't launch my new business in this economy.
>
> I'm just not as talented as they are.
>
> I don't have the time or the money to . . .
>
> It's my boss's fault. If he would have given me more opportunities, I would have been promoted a long time ago.
>
> My team just can't handle the pressure.
>
> If it's going to get done right, I have to do it.

Notice how each of these narratives reveals the speaker's perspective. Notice how the words used open or close possibilities for the speaker. Listen for what the speaker might be subject to. One way to think about what we do as coaches is that we are story busters. We listen for how our clients present their issue, challenge, or opportunity and we make it visible for them. We help them examine their unexamined and automatic thinking about their story. We listen for how they construct their reality, how they make meaning or sense of their world. We listen carefully to how they explain their world. Embedded within those explanations are the beliefs and assumptions that are impacting their behaviors and their results. It is in those explanations and narratives that the client's possibilities, and liberation, can often be found.

I had a client who, after several sessions, told me that his team was hopeless. I simply asked him, "So, do you have responsibility in the matter as the leader of your team?" That simple question was aimed to question his predominant narrative that it was his team's fault that they weren't performing well.

He needed a different narrative to move forward. If my client believed his team was hopeless, he (and the team members) had very little power—very few moves–to create a different outcome. If, however, he believed that as the team leader there were things he could and should do to positively impact the outcomes of his team, he would have a greater capacity for action and impact on the team results.

Of course, there is so much more to listen for in the client's language. A great resource on harnessing the power of language to generate desired outcomes is *Language and the Pursuit of Happiness* by Brothers (2005). It's based on the ontology of language that breaks the long-held assumption that language is simply a descriptor of how things are out there in the world. Through language, we actually create our reality and future with what we say, declare, request and offer to others and ourselves. Our narratives either open or close possibilities for ourselves or others. Therefore, the words we choose are not innocent. They have great power to create what we see and experience.

When it comes to the doorway of language, coaches can listen for the narratives, stories, and words the clients use. We can listen for how the client articulates or narrates his or her challenges and opportunities. We can listen for underlying beliefs. We can listen for the client's ability to say no, make powerful offers to others, make requests, ground opinions. By listening to the clients' language, we can help them discern what they may be subject to in their thinking that is limiting what's possible.

As coaches, we also have to watch for buying or believing the story presented by the client. While the client's explanation may be legitimate for him or her, it is also limiting. We can too quickly step over the client's explanations and rush to get them into action. In doing so, we miss the possibility to explore the kind of observer the client has become and how that observer impacts what the client can do.

THE DOORWAY OF EMOTIONS

As a human being, you have emotions and they are interwoven with your thinking and doing. Contrary to popular belief, you are always in an emotion (and often more than one). It's impossible to leave them at the door when you go to work, as was popularly touted in various management theories in the 1980s and 1990s.

A powerful way to think about emotions is that they are predispositions to action. If you are optimistic about a newly assigned project, you will be predisposed to take certain actions different than if you are feeling resentful about that project. If you are angry, your predisposition to take action might be to retaliate or to gossip or do damage to the reputation of someone. If you are feeling compassionate, your predisposition might be to forgive someone for perceived transgressions.

Emotions move us into actions or prevent us from taking actions. Fear of public speaking can immobilize you. Passion for your organization's mission can motivate you. Either way, emotions aren't neutral. Consider also that emotion is the power that connects human beings to what we care about. Without emotion we couldn't tell what is valuable to us; we wouldn't know how much time and effort we should spend trying to make something happen. Emotions serve a very important role in our lives. This goes against more than 2,500 years of history in the Western world believing that we can and should understand and operate in the world rationally and objectively and put our emotions aside. Historically we have dismissed and undervalued our emotions and the role they play in our success and failures.

It's only been in the last 20 or so years that we are acknowledging the influence that emotions have on our thinking. They influence what we say and don't say. They are reflected in our speaking and in the way we physically move in the world (you know, for example, that your spouse has had a rough day just by watching for body language as he or she comes through the front door). Emotions also create an important context for working with others.

Rather than being at the whim or mercy of our emotions, research on emotional intelligence and brain science is pointing to the fact that emotions can be learned. We are not doomed to repeat the emotional patterns that get in our way of generating desired outcomes. We can learn ambition if that is missing from our work life. We can learn to replace fear with enthusiasm. We can learn to be more tender and loving. As coaches, we can support our clients to learn new emotional habits that better serve what they want to achieve.

We can listen for the clients' emotions that are embedded in their stories and explanations of their challenge. We can listen for how those emotions influence their thinking, restrict their behaviors, shape their bodies (more on this in a moment), and ultimately impact results. At a minimum, we can listen for and acknowledge the emotions that our clients bring to the coaching—without judgment or without trying to rescue them. Our job is to make object—bring awareness to—any emotions or emotional habits that the client has been subject to.

THE DOORWAY OF THE BODY

As a human being, you have a body. It's not just something that carries around your brain and other organs. It is your vehicle for experiencing the world and for others experiencing you. Your beliefs, emotions, thoughts, behaviors are all carried in and revealed through your body. Your body influences your thinking and also is influenced by your thinking. Your body impacts your ability to get the results you want.

Have you ever made a poor choice that, in hindsight, was made when you were tired or stressed? Have you ever had your message misinterpreted even when you knew your words were well chosen? Did you ever watch someone nervously make a presentation and you found yourself getting uncomfortable watching them? Or did you ever lose the conviction in your voice when having a difficult conversation with someone? These are all examples of the body influencing your thinking and behaving.

It's only in the last few decades that we are starting to understand how our thinking as well as the actions we take are influenced by our own biology and physiological structure. We are starting to challenge the belief, as Descartes so famously postulated, that the body is separate from the mind, and that it is inconsequential, if not irrelevant, to our thinking and doing. We've been subject to how our body influences our thinking and doing but are starting to make it object. In coaching, we are transcending that traditional understanding that mind is separate from body and we want to work with the "whole" of the client.

A pioneer and expert in the field of coaching and the body is Richard Strozzi-Heckler, who teaches somatic coaching. Somatics is from the Greek word *soma*, which literally translates as "the living body in its wholeness" (Strozzi-Heckler, 2007). Somatic coaching supports the clients to notice all the ways that their thoughts, emotions, and behaviors are embodied—held and revealed by the body—and how that embodiment might be impacting their outcomes.

In coaching, we can work to support clients to change their embodiment, their presence, so that it is more aligned with who they want to be, how they want to show up for others. We can support clients to cultivate more and more versatility in their thinking and automatic responses and habits. Let me give you a simple example.

Imagine you are having a meeting with a colleague to discuss which strategic direction to take. You are angry because this colleague refuses to agree with your well-constructed arguments. The shape of your body in this conversation will correspond to your mood of anger. Your muscles will be tense and drawn tight. Your breathing will be more shallow than deep. Your movements will be sharper and more resolute. If you are sitting down, your body will likely be leaning forward. Your body will shape itself congruently to your thoughts and emotions.

Now, imagine having that same conversation with your colleague in a mood of curiosity. Instead of being angry that they refuse to see your point of view, you seek understanding. You become curious as to why they are taking their position and where you may be creating resistance in the other. In this mood, it's likely that your body will be more open and relaxed, your breathing will be deeper, your focus will be more expansive and inclusive and, if you are sitting down, your body will likely be less resolute.

Which body do you think your colleague will be more receptive to? Which one might they react to or defend against? Which one has the greater chance of having the impact you want? This is a simple example of how working with a client's physical presence might make a positive impact on the impact or outcomes they want.

As Strozzi-Heckler (2007) says: "It's important to understand that it is only through our bodies that we are able to be unwaveringly present to people and situations, a necessary requirement for exemplary leadership all but categorically denied by modern philosophy" (p. 88). The whole thrust of rationalism has been to play down the value and importance of emotions and body in the results we get and coaching is a way to recapture them for our learning and development. To leave out the body in coaching is to deny a huge influencer on our perspective of the world.

CONCLUSION

When we coach, we coach human beings. And, while perhaps obvious once stated, we have been subject to outdated beliefs and blind spots of this obvious fact. While we are uniquely different from each other, we also have in common what it means to be human.

We are individuals, responsible for our actions and our choices. At the same time, we are part of the whole and affected by a multitude of influences that include our families, communities, companies, countries, and so forth. We are part of a history, of traditions, of an era and epoch. We are part of a cosmology—a story about the universe and our place in it. We all communicate and coordinate actions with others through language; we have emotions; we have bodies. We are holistic and complex. We create meaning for our actions; assign purpose for our living. We are not neutral observers. The influences that shape our observer affect what we observe. We see the world not as it is, but as we are.

As a profession, we have a responsibility to listen for and appropriately challenge the multitude of influences that have shaped our clients' being, doing, and thinking in their lives, in the context of what they say they want to achieve. As a profession, we also have to challenge ourselves to root out where we have been blindly operating from outdated cultural assumptions. We need to make object that which we, as coaches, have been subject to.

This matters because, as many contemporary philosophers and great thinkers have been saying for decades, we human beings are arriving to the end of an era philosophically, ecologically, politically, psychologically, cosmologically, scientifically, and so forth. They conclude that we are witnessing a time on the planet where there are no simple problems left to address. The issues we are facing require new perspectives, new thinking. They require new awareness but also practice to embed and embody the new awareness.

We can certainly learn new skills or new knowledge but we also must become more socially adept, emotionally intelligent, somatically agile, and self-aware to navigate more and more complex and uncertain situations and environments. The more we can make object what was once subject, the more choice we have and that is the coach's imperative.

REFERENCES

Brothers, C. (2005). *Language and the pursuit of happiness.* Naples, FL: New Possibilities Press.

Goleman, D. (1985). *Vital lies, simple truths: The psychology of self deception.* New York, NY: Simon & Schuster.

Goodreads. (n.d.). R.D. Laing > Quotes. Retrieved from https://www.goodreads.com/author/quotes/4436873.R_D_Laing

Kegan, R. (1994). *In over our heads: The mental demands of modern life.* Cambridge, MA: Harvard University Press.

Strozzi-Heckler, R. (2007). *The leadership dojo.* Berkeley, CA: Frog, Ltd.

Tarnas, R. (1991). *The passion of the western mind: Understanding the ideas that have shaped our worldview.* New York, NY: Random House.

17

Evaluating Client Progress: A Developmental Approach — Beyond Convention

Paddy Pampallis

C oaching has moved beyond simply being a "tool" for enhancing performance. While it can be, its greater power lies in its creative potential in which to reflect on one's development and growth as a leader and a citizen of the world. The focus of an intervention may be specific to a topic, outcome, or need; in the hands of a skilled and trained coach it can also lead to paradigm shifts, with far-reaching impact beyond the life of a single individual that enables people to orientate through an increasingly complex world in which they often feel in over their heads (Kegan, 1994).

There is a need for the successful outcomes of coaching to be a shared responsibility of all the stakeholders to afford maximum success. This in itself is a shift in evaluation approaches from simply being in the hands of the coach or a single user of coaching. The last 14 years have seen the evaluation of client progress in the author's coach development programs take on dynamic progression from the groundbreaking doctoral research on developing a model for the supervision of executive coaches (Pampallis, 2005) to its current form. This evolved integral and developmental approach to learning, and assessment and evaluation of delegates, is aimed at deepening the transformative process for individual and collective growth and the value creation for individual and organizational clients. The Integral⁺ Practice of Leadership and Coaching™¹ is a unique adaptation of Ken Wilber's (2000b) integral framework and its application for leadership, coaching, and its concomitant development and training, and thus evaluation. This chapter looks at shifting a view on the practice of evaluation to go beyond convention to include and transcend it, into a more comprehensive approach.

EVALUATING CLIENT PROGRESS

Coaching can be transactional (skills- or information-based), transitional (role- or change-based), and/or transformational: leading to growth through expanding the meaning-making systems of the client along his or her development into maturity (Pampallis, 2005). The invitation is for people to examine their behavior and their thinking across a range of levels from simple to complex.

A less spoken about challenge is that coaching potentially, can be *dangerous*, for it can be *radically transformational*. Growth in awareness can challenge the status quo and disrupt the norms of the known fields of reality. Ironically, many organizations may not really want their people to grow in ways that are not within the parameters and goals of a particular mindset. The clarion call is *be better, more efficient at what you do, and faster*, and if a certain amount of psychological health comes with that, that is fine, but the latter is not the goal of say, business coaching (Kahn, 2014). The traditional need is still that an outcome can be conventionally and quantifiably measured. Measurement, however, presents a conundrum for defining the parameters of coaching as it is still an open field in terms of what is being evaluated.

SOME QUESTIONS TO CONSIDER

A question for us all to ask is: "What does evaluation actually serve to do?"

Coaches as *pattern explorers* offer the work of reflective and reflexive mirroring to their client's outer *and* inner worlds. This transformational aspect (shifting whole structures of mind and/or paradigms) gives another life to that which may lie dormant inside. When patterns that sit outside the frames of conscious insight are brought into conscious awareness (Kegan, 1994), it can wake us up to ourselves and to a greater capacity for "being" in the world. Until that moment of insight, we are limited in what our choices are or in what we can do with them (Pampallis, 2006).

If a coach can hold the space within a deeply embodied and holistic and integral framework of human experience, the coach is then able to use this frame to help the client make sense of a variety of possibilities, both tangible and intangible, personal and collective. The coach becomes both a powerful resource and evaluator (not judge) in this *exploration-in-action* with a client. This is not done in a vacuum, but in relationship with, and to, the cultural and systemic interconnections that the coach/client/stakeholders find themselves in. This increases the ability to see within, and beyond, the current narrative of a client's story in the context of the dynamic of the coaching relationship and position it in the world at large. The work can be to seek and surface the client's patterns, challenges, and growth points for which the coach may consciously, or unconsciously, be called to work with. Once insight is obtained, the client (and coach) can tap into that conscious choice, a fundamental power of the human experience, while also knowing that choices may have infinite consequences. The practice of intentional awareness that can come through coaching is that the minutest choices we make in the small moments of our everyday life can lead to the building of optimal life and leadership practices. While we can measure access to a framework and the impact of choice, there is no proof that we can put this in a basket for absolute evidence (Cox, Bachkirova, & Clutterbuck, 2018).

So then, how do we evaluate this practice, and its relevant fit for purpose? What is that basket and what is in it? Who is the coach and who is the client? How do we evaluate that quality that is the interior condition of the intervenor with an exterior signifier (Senge, Scharmer, Jaworski, & Flowers, 2004). What existential questions may arise that are not in the foreground of organizational coaching and the evaluation processes?

Some Thoughts

In a *world of fast*, coaching runs the risk of becoming yet another short-term solution, skill, or tool (though it is, in part) that is not sustainable, or capable of rising to its potential of transforming thinking to becoming more expansive and far-sighted, or of adding to the collective intelligence of an organization so that all may thrive! Baumol, a noted economist (Baumol & Bowen, 1967), called this a cost disease.[2] An important question is that if coaching falls into a labor-intense[3] category, then how does the cost of the service get justified according to the results it delivers and its direction, and ability to create *fields of learning possibilities*? Moreover, does evaluation need to take into consideration the definitions of coaching as an art, or a science, or a set of sequenced skills? Is it all three and more? Importantly, does economics as a primary consideration become coaching's limitation?

The challenge for evaluation is that it is a wide-open and complex space, with as many variables, as it is many things, models, and modes, to many people. For this reason, a *developmental and integral approach* (Pampallis, 2016) to evaluation, with an aim to make a distinction between conventional and post-conventional means of evaluation, is suggested as a useful distinction.

THE RISE OF RETURN ON INVESTMENT (ROI)

A key question asked in the rising market for the ROI of coaching, is whether the traditional/conventional methods of evaluation truly reflect the full impact of coaching? Coaching is both simple, and deep, and can be applied to many conditions, contexts, and for many reasons toward a variety of outcomes. Most evaluations to date ask: Were the objectives achieved? Did the client shift from A to B? Has the client improved along a range of indicators, and from what to what? What is the impact on the team and/or organization, and how does a scale of 1 to 5 indicate progress? At another level, some evaluation may seek to know whether coaching has contributed toward a culture change? Or has it improved leadership or performance? Coaching, unfortunately, is still often implemented as a stand-alone intervention and is not always well integrated into a long-term development learning plan.

FRAMING THE INTERVENTION

How the intervention is framed and thought about will direct the need and processes of evaluation. Without an integrated and robust multi-stakeholder engagement process for buy-in, as well as clear engagement from leadership, coaching as a valuable and necessary component of the development of people can be limited in its capacity for impact. Can the stakeholders be readied for something beyond objective, tangible outcomes? Are they ready to emerge "other" less conscious life of the client and organization to truly know what potential may lie dormant or seething in that unknown territory?

Coaching can fall into the trap of taking on a responsibility for performance management, and/or it can be used in an attempt to change what are essentially psychological, personality, and/or competency deficits. This is often not its primary function, though these may be unintended benefits. It may also, sadly, serve as a tick box on some organizational learning agenda.

CURRENT CONVENTIONAL EVALUATION

A survey of evaluations to date indicate that they have been fairly superficial. It is only over recent years that a concerted effort has been made to make this feature more robust. It is also difficult to manage this still very unregulated profession. Although there are many professional bodies and academics worldwide working toward standardization, qualifications, competencies, and ethics (Jarvis, Lane, & Fillery-Travis, 2006), the industry is still not sufficiently coordinated to draw on global trends. A further challenge is that the trend to differentiate the types of coaching into leadership, executive, business, or life, may require different outcomes, and evaluation would have to be designed to meet these needs. Research into leadership coaching (Kahn, 2014) made the points for the need for both formative and summative evaluations, which include the collection of multi-source data, and they went on to advocate for a systemic approach to evaluation.

Other challenges to evaluation are due to:

- A lack of sufficient accurate and complete information
- Anecdotal, self-reported, or superficial evaluations, for example, even when Kirkpatrick's (1959) measurement criteria are used, the focus is mostly on Level 1 of 4 criteria
- Unsystematic measures and designs
- Varied and diverse interventions

- Multiple stakeholders

- Varied motivations for engagement

- Long-term and short-term coaching mix

- Huge diversity in models, types, ways of coaching

- Large range of coaching background experience and training—if any!

Fillery-Travis and Cox (2017) state that researchers most often concentrate upon building a theory of how coaching is used, its utility and payback, and even how coaching can be improved for different purposes. They also state, however, that research is still relatively silent on a critical part of coaching practice—the intervention or what happens within the coaching relationship itself, and this is a critical consideration.

In a global study done among 28,000 employees in 10 major industry sectors, Right Management (2009, in Kahn, 2014) found there to be no robust proven methodology to measure impact because there is no algorithm or ROI calculation that can accommodate the enormous number of variables that will influence the impact of the coaching program. They argued that the only way to ensure an ROI on coaching is to factor in all stakeholders and related processes or systems, in addition to grounding the particular coaching objectives firmly in the business context and organizational capabilities (Kahn, 2014).

Kahn (2014) goes on to state that the study showed that quantitative measures (monetary returns, or statistical measures) need to be replaced with qualitative ones, and that "evaluation needs to occur across stakeholders which would include the client, the manager, perhaps the team, and any other relevant member of the system in which the client operates." This would result in more of an Return on Expectations (ROE) approach that could be facilitated through ongoing processes within the inter-subjective arena. This approach sits firmly on Kahn's axial approach that considers business coaching to be effective only when the client, the coach, and the organization speak to a systemic approach that engages in frequent and focused dialogue to ascertain success, not formal measurement indices attained. Kahn also mentions that well-being is not a focus for business coaching, and should be specific to the business needs, and not focused on personal development, though both may occur.

AN INTEGRAL⁺ APPROACH

A comprehensive integral approach, which I would call a *quad-axial* approach through the Integral⁺ Iceberg™ (see Figure 17.1; Pampallis, 2006), has both the conditions for engaging with assessment along "horizontal" (learning that adds on to what one already knows within a paradigm) and "vertical" (learning that shifts a whole worldview) planes of investigation. Pampallis has inverted Wilber's quadrant model to orientate topographically through the iceberg as an expression of the four key lenses onto human experience: the interior individual subjective lens and the inter-subjective lens that form the territory below the horizontal line of the iceberg,

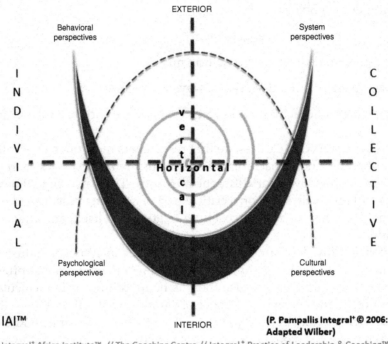

Figure 17.1 Integral⁺ Practice of Leadership & Coaching Process Diagram (2006).

and the objective individual and collective exteriors, which lie above. An integral approach to evaluation would include:

- Quantitative and qualitative evaluations

- Engaging the whole person, though a particular focus may be foregrounded

- Both vertical (unconscious to conscious progressions as per the iceberg quadrant model; Pampallis, 2005) and Cook-Greuter's (1985 ongoing) adult maturity framework and horizontal lenses of development and learning.

CONSCIOUS EVALUATION IN A CONSCIOUS BUSINESS

What is valuable is making a distinction between "functional and conscious business" and considering how it works as an integral system across the big four (quad-axial, Pampallis, 2005) domains of human experience (Wilber, 2000a), which include:

1. The worlds of inner subjective individual motivation, drive, and meaning-making

2. Individual's objective behavior

3. The subjective collective corporate culture and values

4. Its outer expression through its objective systems, and *flow patterns* (Pampallis, 2016), necessary to quality control into the market space.

To consider only one area of these four domains is to take a partial view on the full potential of the client and organization. Many businesses only consider the tangible outcomes as truly valid, which would engage mostly horizontal learning outcomes. A business that can see coaching and hence evaluation vertically, through all domains as active and intentional, acts to engage with itself as an organism that *invites people to be part of it in order to further serve the larger system in psychosocial, economic, and purposeful endeavors.* This is a huge mind shift for many, but one that is emerging as essential as people ask more from the workplace. The partial view of individuals limits integration across systems of thought, and a need of vertical learning considerations to enable levels of maturity and perspective to evolve is critical. Evaluation is thus useful whether one is setting out to evaluate a part, or the whole, and it will need to hold many polarities: seemingly opposing parts of a whole, in addition to an either/or analysis of finite benefits.

EVALUATING THE NEED FOR COACHING

To ascertain what needs to be achieved from the coaching, it is very important for the coach to do a preliminary evaluation of the needs, awareness, capacity, availability, and potency of the client, the stakeholders, the leadership and the organization as a whole. This will require not only an integral *mapscan* of the client, but also of the organization's ability to wake up, assimilate, and use the impact of coaching in its system as an ability to make meaning and grow maturity.

How the end game is evaluated, and from what level of complexity and maturity the evaluation is engaged with, is key to assessing its use. If leaders are invested in people growing into highly skilled, resourceful, and engaged members (not employees), they need to set up the conditions for the organization becoming a truly adaptive and agile living organism that is open to feedback and ongoing learning. We are then talking about vertical or transformational learning (Cook-Greuter, 1985; Kegan, 1994), learning that shifts the very way we think about and see the world, to include and move beyond.

CONVENTIONAL AND HORIZONTAL LEARNING AND EVALUATION

The more conventional approach to managing complexity would be to have the different aspects of a client's progress fit into discrete categories and along with it the need for a specific kind of tangible evaluation. This is not wrong, just partial and risks being reductionistic.

The role played by conventional evaluation methods is that it may come with the expectation that by doing the job faster and better, all ends will be achieved. This may be so on a manufacturing line, in a technical position, or administrative position. From this mindset, evaluation relies on a horizontal approach to learning, as progress along a specific line of inquiry, skill, or outcome, is part of the picture. Evaluation here would be about performance and spend, and the parameters would look at input, throughput, output, and outcomes that serve the purpose of the organization. If the individual happens to become a more responsive, conscious, engaged human being, this is usually considered a "nice to have" outcome, but is not a condition for success. In some cases, this can even contribute to the evaluation of the coaching as being a failure for a client may grow beyond the organization and the coach will not be considered a good fit for that organization at best, and a failed coach, at worst. Sadly, dysfunction often serves the needs of an organization better, so health is irrelevant in many instances—while performance to achieve profits is.

TRANSFORMATIONAL LEARNING

Kegan (1994) states that we actively organize our experience and meaning. This kind of knowing is not about cognition alone and he suggests that the subject–object distinction refers to the meaning given to what we consider to be subject: experience that is invisible and part of the self (below the iceberg), that is hard to reflect upon because it may not yet be conscious. Thus bias, assumptions, stereo-types, and interpretation of indicators for measuring can become challenging at this level.

Things that are object are those elements of our knowing that we can reflect on, look at, control, and by which we can relate to others. When the element of knowing is object, it is distinct enough from us that we can do something with it (Kegan, 1994) and it is here that evaluation may be more tangible and thus the easier option as experiences that are subject are equally valid and need to be factored in when assessing the value of an intervention. When that which has been subject becomes object and surfaces to our conscious experience sufficiently for us to be aware of it and thus reflect upon it, we can take intentional conscious action on it. If these moments are held out for examination long enough, they become more stable and can lead to whole paradigm shifts. Vertical and transformational learning (Kegan, 1994) can thus transform our thinking and move to another, broader, and more com-plex understanding of the world and of coaching per se. This journey of meaning-making is ongoing and not smooth. Cook-Greuter (1985, 1990) states that as a leader grows in maturity, the first part of this journey is about developing ego; once the individual reaches a second tier of conscious awareness and maturity, wisdom then becomes part of the make-up with which a leader can engage in problem solving and visionary thinking. Hence the question: What is being evaluated?

With the given crises in leadership and the levels of complexity and overload that have to be managed, it seems clear that one needs to cultivate new paradigms of thinking, and more expansive capacities with which to take new actions, manag-ing these challenges for which old thinking is no longer sufficient. Evaluation there-fore needs to consider developmental paths (leadership maturity) even though it may be more complex and require many more subtleties to the evaluation design and process. The work of a truly integrated evaluation process, therefore, will need to take into consideration both horizontal and vertical shifts.

When an organization can see itself as a living, learning organism (Senge et al., 2004) that is primarily there to work with and through its people to achieve agreed upon results, it is more likely to be open to less conventional methods of evaluation.

Optimally, a coaching intervention could provide multiple feedback loops and regenerative learning while also catalyzing and igniting the conditions that can enable a process for *liberating the multi-faceted intelligences* (Pampallis, 2005) of the client: It should not just be an event.

Any evaluation of progress as a result of coaching would be well placed if set along a developmental continuum upfront to satisfy the diverse needs that require specific interventions for particular outcomes with an individual client or team. One would need to consider not only what is being evaluated, but also from which level of thinking the evaluation arises. Perhaps the most critical aspect of taking a developmentally informed approach to the design, the people concerned, and the expected outcomes, comes from the fact that every person grows at a different rate and that learning cannot be confined to the limits of time, or a set style of intervention. Hence, the distinction between conventional learning and postconventional learning outcomes would, at the very least, need to be considered.

EVALUATION THAT IS DEVELOPMENTAL

Integral⁺ Practice™ provides individuals and organizations with a content-free framework that is suitable to a multitude of contexts. It is scalable and developmental and can be applied in minute detail as well as comprehensively. In order to meet the broad church of theoretical inputs and practices that exist in coaching, this framework according to Esbjörn-Hargens (2010) has capacity to draw on the most pertinent approaches and applications for understanding human experience: From this the practitioner can choose the most appropriate tools for assessment, taking action and finding solutions. The critical point here is that the *interior condition of the intervenor* (Senge et al., 2004), and thus evaluator, will determine how any information is perceived and made sense of. Conventional evaluators will measure conventional indicators: It needs this, and more. The *quad-axial* approach would need to be consulted when attempting to fully understand any situation, issue, or aspect of reality. If these are not considered, then the assessment/evaluation or solution is partial. What is key to working with these four domains is that each one simultaneously arises with the other and that to separate them creates massive compromise in assessment and solution-building. Many organizations will tend to work with that which lies above the iceberg in the tangible, scientific, and observable fields of inquiry and only touch on the below-the-line, intangible events, but because of their complexity, rule them out.

There is a large and growing community of integral and developmental practitioners who are critically evaluating the theory and practice. This active body of practitioners sees the value of the framework and its application into many fields of study. It acts as a navigational tool, a meta-paradigm for drawing together and holding separate paradigms into an interrelated network of approaches that are mutually enriching (Esbjörn-Hargens, 2010), as well as offers itself as a map for meaning-making. The rationale is multifold from both a coaching perspective and to ensure that coaching is situated within the global context of the world as we work in it. Esbjörn-Hargens (2010) states that due to us having to consider so many global worldviews (models and frameworks) that present huge challenges to our world and offer, at times, extreme perspectives on a multiple range of issues including radical fundamentalism, failing education systems, existential alienation, volatile financial markets, and socio-political chaos, it is extremely useful to have an *integral vision that is anchored in the minutiae of our daily lives' and holds the variety of valid perspectives towards collective solution building.*

Integral⁺ Inquiry and Evaluation (Pampallis, 2016) is the basis of the work being done in this field by this author. This integral framework has the facility to include competing approaches to coaching in its overarching and inclusive methodologies and can assist people in the context of our challenging lives. By considering the multiple intelligences, states of mind, body, systems in the context of the range and typologies of people and organizations, as well as the states, levels, and stages of development along the journey to maturity, it provides an encompassing scope for mapping the territory for evaluation and enabling it to name what it is and what it is not.

MANAGING COMPLEXITY

Understanding these dimensions and perspectives, however, both complicates and simplifies evaluation. Each of these dimensions has a developmental component with indicators for action-logic and levels of health. By utilizing these as measures of complexity thinking, one is able to fine-tune the graduations of measurement through both the tangible and intangible dimensions of both the individual and the collective while accessing the vertical line of development. It offers a place to reflect more closely the scope of human's capacity to grow up (vertical growth), as well as becoming more competent at a skills level (horizontal learning). There is a caution (Stern & Stout-Rostron, 2013) that when we measure development, we should frame things in terms of possible and preferable educational (learning) interventions. All measurement is open to error and in truth it becomes an indicator, a guide, a marker of possible factors that are currently alive in the system at that moment, and as such are not fixed characteristics of any one or any group but rather adaptations to the current field of experience and reality.

Existence is beyond the power of words
To define:
Terms may be used
But are none of them absolute.
In the beginning of heaven and earth there were no words,
Words came out of the womb of matter;
And whether a man dispassionately
Sees to the core of life
Or passionately
Sees the surface,
The core and the surface
Are essentially the same,
Words making them seem different
Only to express appearance.
If name be needed, wonder names them both:
From wonder into wonder
Existence opens.
—*Lao Tzu*
(*Esbjörn-Hargens, 2003, p. 319*)

While there is definitely a place for markers of success across a variety of criteria that are established upfront in the contracted agreements, there needs to be an openness to learning that goes beyond the markers and the scientific tangible evidence. If evaluation includes an integral and postconventional approach, it would take into consideration that any sort of evaluation is not static or linear; it is more of a spiral and is dynamic and ongoing. There is a fallacy that is set up by assessment and thus evaluative techniques, that there are fixed outcomes that are measurable and irrefutable as proof of success. This, however, stands as contradictory to the fundamental proposition of coaching as supporting growth and development, for this indeed is not fixed and is an ongoing, iterative process of life-long learning.

While tangible measurements may be useful, they are not complete without truly understanding that this process is mutable and ongoing, and a journey of getting it and then not getting it as one's mind and heart and actions, continue to learn, expand, and develop.

NOTES

1. The + after the word integral is symbolic of the framework and indicates the unique applications as adapted by P. Pampallis (2005, ongoing).

2. This refers to the tendency to take cost into primary consideration at the risk of the integrity of the product as with the arts.

3. The author is of the opinion is that coaching is labor intensive when one considers the thinking, preparation, reflection, stakeholder engagement, and often logistical considerations that need to be considered.

REFERENCES

Baumol, W. & Bowen, W. (1967). *Performing arts, the economic dilemma: A study of problems common to theater, opera, music, and dance.* New York, NY: Twentieth Century Fund.
Cook-Greuter, S. (1985). Nine levels of increasing embrace in ego development: A full spectrum theory of vertical growth and meaning making. Adapted and expanded from S. Cook-Greuter (1985). *A detailed description of the successive stages of ego-development.* Retrieved from http://www.cook-greuter.com/Cook-Greuter%209%20levels%20paper%20new%201.1'14%2097p%5B1%5D.pdf
Cook-Greuter, S. (1990). Maps for living: Ego-development stages from symbiosis to conscious universal embeddedness. In M. Commons, C. Armon, L. Kohlberg, F. A. Richards, T. Grotzer, & J. Sinnot (Eds.), *Adult development, 2: Models and methods in the study of adolescent and adult thought.* Westport, CT: Praeger (ABC-CLIO).
Cox, E., Bachkirova, T., & Clutterbuck, D. (Eds.). (2018). *Complete handbook of coaching* (3rd ed.). Thousand Oaks, CA: SAGE.
Esbjörn-Hargens, S. (Ed.). (2010). *Integral theory in action.* Albany, NY: SUNY Press.
Fillery-Travis, A., & Cox, E. (2017). *Researching coaching.* Manuscript in preparation.
Jarvis, J., Lane, D., & Fillery-Travis, A. (2006). *The case for coaching: Making evidence based decisions for coaching.* London, UK: Chartered Institute of Personnel Development.
Kahn, M.S. (2014). *Coaching on the axis: Working with complexity in business and executive coaching.* London, UK: Karnac Books.

Kegan, R. (1994). *In over our heads: The mental demands of modern life.* Cambridge, MA: Harvard University Press.

Pampallis, P. (2005). *Towards a theory of supervision: An integral approach* (Unpublished D Prof dissertation). London: Middlesex University. Retrieved from http://eprints.mdx.ac.uk/22177/

Pampallis, P. (2006). *Integral+ Practice of Leadership and Coaching*™ Diploma in Integral+ Practitioner Coaching, The Coaching Centre; TCC programme material. The Integral Africa Institute & The Coaching Centre. Retrieved from www.thecoachingcentre.co.za

Pampallis, P. (2016). *Coach evaluation: A developmental and integral approach.* Middlesex Coaching Conference Paper entitled a Developmental Approach to Coach Training Assessment: Paper being written.

Senge, P., Scharmer, C. O., Jaworski, J., & Flowers, B. S. (2004). *Presence: Exploring profound change in people, organizations, and society.* New York, NY: Currency/Doubleday.

Stern, L., & Stout-Rostron, S. (2013). What progress has been made in coaching research in relationship to ICRF focus areas from 2008-2012? *Coaching: An International Journal of Theory, Research and Practice, 6*(1), 72–96. doi:10.1080/17521882.2012.757013

Wilber, K. (2000a). *A brief history of everything.* Dublin: Colour Books.

Wilber, K. (2000b). *Integral psychology; consciousness, spirit psychology, therapy.* Boston, MA: Shambala.

III

Theories and Frameworks in Coaching

18

Coaching and Seeing Systems

Anne Starr

We live in a universe of nested systems that influence our individual, group, and collective experience. Yet we often don't see them. The following three stories illustrate aspects of systems at work in our internal, external, and interaction worlds. We experience these worlds as simultaneously inter-affecting us in our day-to-day living. They are separated here to illustrate coaching possibilities in each domain, and so that the reader may discern where they habitually focus and where they might be drawn to explore further.

JOHN'S STORY: TAKING A LESSON FROM HIS DAUGHTER— THE INTERNAL WORLD

Early on a spring day, I arrived at my client John's office and, as we settled in to work, I asked him how his weekend had been. "Well, on Sunday, out of the blue, my daughter decided she wanted to go to the track," he said, launching into a family story. "I haven't been able to run as much lately, so I was eager to go. As we headed over there, I started talking to her about pacing. I wanted to make sure she didn't burst out at the start and then exhaust herself. I didn't want her to have to quit before we finished the circuit and then be disappointed in herself and maybe give up. So, I was giving her tips.

When we started running, it was a beautiful day, and there were other people on the track too. We were chatting as we ran and I was encouraging her. Well, we kept going and then I started to feel winded and realized I was actually falling behind. She sailed right past me and just kept on going. By the end of the run, she'd completely left me in the dust! She was so far ahead of me it was comical."

He had a sheepish grin on his face and chuckled at the thought of being so clearly bested by his 11-year-old daughter. We both laughed at the perfect coming together of his humiliating defeat and the pride he felt as a father.

"Good for her for being such a spunky kid!" I said, "And for being willing to thumb her nose at you." I suddenly saw an opening into a subject I had not been sure how to broach with him. "I wonder whether the people who report to you feel they have that kind of latitude?"

It was still early in our coaching relationship. John had just sent me a series of email exchanges with a number of his direct reports. In each response, he was carefully advising or cautioning them on the possible negative ramifications of different ideas they had proposed.

"You said your original thought was to protect your daughter from disappointment, from a too early failure that might quash her wanting to run, right? I can see the love and care in that intention," I said. "But, also. . . .what you discovered in the end was that you really had no idea what she actually was capable of." John started scribbling notes, as he always did when he intended to work with an idea.

As our coaching continued over the next months, we focused on other, more pressing areas of concern that called for the ongoing practice of new behaviors. These were experiments with a close tracking of results that were then assessed and folded back into new experiments. Almost a year later, in a retrospective on our work, John stunned me by stating that he had taken that early insight and found ways to work with each of his people to support their aspirations. Though we had occasionally talked about issues with particular people, this was the first time we'd revisited the lesson from his daughter. Over time, he had found ways to loosen the reins that he had previously felt were necessary to protect his employees and the organization. He reported watching them each step into opportunities he couldn't have imagined them taking on before.

In addition, he found that his employees' increased autonomy freed up his own time. He could devote more of his attention to the strategic issues facing the organization, which was where his own gifts and aspirations were most useful. He reported the result as good for everyone: for his employees' development and morale, for the vitality of the organization, and for his own personal satisfaction and contribution to the company.

COMMENTARY

This simple story illustrates a number of basic systems principles. I knew John well enough to be concerned that attempting to address this problem head on might engender resistance. He had a long track record in the company and well-considered reasons for his behavior: Caution was prudent, justified and effective, in his mind, and necessary to his own ethical integrity. He set aside the noise of his staff's chronic frustration as an unfortunate part of the way things were at the moment, not something he could address within the constraints of the current situation. Instead, his reaction was to double down on his habitual patterns of thinking and behaving. His own deep personal story may have inclined him more toward exerting control, but, in this instance, by doing so he sacrificed autonomy—his own and his staff's. Like all mental models, these tendencies may have served him well enough in the past. Here they constituted a blind spot that caused him and his employees pain. I took his act of sharing the correspondence, however, as a call for help. It would have been easy for that experience to have remained a private memory, but the synchronicity of these events suggested the time was right for him to experience this learning.

John discovered that habits so ingrained we think of them as "the way things are," can sometimes give way easily when approached tangentially, especially through an emotionally potent experience. John did not think of himself as defended when it came to parenting his daughter, but rather, as her unalloyed champion, even if she did occasionally make him feel ridiculous. The juxtaposition of that exquisite moment and his thoughts about his staff allowed him to see instantly from an entirely new perspective. He recognized the burden his caution placed on the natural inclination to excel as counter to what he wanted for his staff—an unintended consequence. In that moment, he entered a new agreement with himself about how he was going to act with his employees.[1] This agreement made available new choices. He resolved to do what he could to open up possibilities, and his ongoing attention enabled him to support his staff in actualizing their aspirations. He learned that being able to modulate control and autonomy made for a more lively and resilient environment, which eventually provided more freedom and autonomy for himself as well as those he influenced.

Basic System Principles

System: A system is any group of interacting, interrelated, or interdependent parts that form a complex and unified whole that has a specific purpose (Kim, 1999). Living systems are self-organizing, perpetuate themselves, maintain stability through feedback, and tend to be self-corrective against change, as all who have tried to change habits can attest to (Bateson, 1972). The most successful complex adaptive systems are those that can accommodate multiple hypotheses and subject them to rapid and rigorous testing (Holland, 1995).

Mental Models. Everything we think we know about the world is a mental model (Meadows, 2008). To the extent our mental models are congruent with reality, they can serve us well as a critical shorthand in helping us choose effective action. Mental models are constructed from accrued information and experience, often long forgotten, and are strengthened and conserved by our habits. They can only selectively represent reality, are often flawed, and may lead to default behaviors that don't serve us. We are usually unaware of our mental models until we are challenged and have reason to question our assumptions. Others likely know our blind spots constituted by our mental models better than we do, as areas where we literally cannot see what does not conform to our habitual way of thinking. See Ladder of Inference (Argyris, 1990) as a useful tool in separating data from assumptions.

Story: A story is a deep personal system—a theme or plot that underlies the meaning one makes of one's experiences and actions, sometimes based in childhood experience and not explicitly remembered. Kegan and Lahey in *Immunity to Change* describe the difference awareness makes between "being had by" and "having" those stories. See Steven Ober's *Unleashing the Power of Your Story* (2014) for a rich resource on working with story in the work environment (Ober, 2014).

WHY THINK ABOUT SYSTEMS IN COACHING?

We and our clients are complex adaptive systems as individuals, wanting to act with integrity and intention within the larger family, friendship, team, organization, community, social, and natural systems in which we live and work. Though we all inhabit myriad systems, it is remarkably easy to lose sight of their influence on our perceptions, understanding, and decision-making processes. In the West, we live with a cultural habit of linear, cause-and-effect thinking—an "I-it" orientation that draws boundaries around what we consider consequential, ignores "externalities," and disregards more subtle interrelationships. We increase our effectiveness and choice when we can see clearly our deep internal systems, the forces acting upon us from the larger systems of which we are a part, and the quality of our interactions with individuals and groups.

The internal domain can include life experiences, cognitive skill, developmental stage, and psychological, emotional, and deep story systems. The external domain can include understanding the characteristics common to complex systems and specific to the client's group, organization, business, and marketplace. And the relationship domain includes awareness of the quality of our presence, as well as our ability to initiate and sustain constructive interactions. Clients who can understand and work with these three domains become skillful at aligning behavior with intention. They are better able to see systemic forces at play, depersonalize charged situations, exercise more choice in their behavior, and act in circumstances that otherwise might feel too challenging to address. Ideally, they carry this capacity with them far beyond the coaching relationship. What becomes possible when the system can see itself? This is a developmental journey taking us to an alive place where we can explore the edges of our knowing and not knowing, and remain open to the new possibilities that emerge there.

Systems theory emerged as its own discipline in the mid-20th century with the work of Weiner, Forrester, von Bertalanffy, and others, and quickly migrated from early work in cybernetics, organizations, social systems, and biology to psychology, medicine, urban policy, sociology, and more. Coaching is a natural beneficiary of the richness of this field, serving, as it does, at the nexus where individuals, groups, and organizations come together.

Agazarian's seminal Theory of Living Human Systems is being applied in the organizational sphere through Weisbord and Janoff's (2007) book, *Don't Just Do Something, Stand There!* and the many practitioners who apply her principles in their individual and group coaching. The large-scale Deep Democracy "processwork" from Mindell (2002) has been adapted by many who find their methods for dealing with polarizing issues to be powerful tools in their individual and group coaching. Hellinger's Family Constellations work has been applied and found valuable in individual, group, and organizational coaching work. Organizational and Relationship Systems Coaching (ORSC) interweaves a number of these systems disciplines in its trainings. Adult development coaches work with a theory that defines the pathway to maturity and the relationship between developmental stage and the degree of systems complexity we are able to see and work with (Cook-Greuter, 2010; Garvey Berger, 2013; Kegan & Lahey, 2009).

JOANNE'S STORY: PICTURING THE TROUBLE WITH HUMAN RESOURCES—THE EXTERNAL WORLD

Joanne was a Nursing Manager in a large VA hospital on the East Coast. She had a reputation as an effective manager and a high performer in that complex environment. Joanne's coaching relationship with my colleague Rick Karash was supported as part of a leader development program. Her objective for the coaching was to grow as a leader, particularly in her ability to deal constructively with operational challenges.[2]

Fairly early in the coaching relationship, Joanne voiced frustration with Human Resources (HR). Rick recounts this exchange in one of their coaching conversations:

"They're dropping the ball once again, just when I need them to perform. We're short on nurses, way below headcount. And I just heard they've got no one to send us. Everyone in my group is overworked." She clearly felt thwarted. "I need to lean hard on HR. I already have my boss involved and we'll likely have to bring in the Center Director to get any action."

"How long has this been going on?" Rick asked.

"Forever!" she exploded in exasperation. ". . . .and. . .yes, I've been here before." She paused. "I can see I'm about to do the same thing I've always done. . .and I'll probably get the same result."

"What are you really worried about here?" Rick asked.

"I guess the real worry is that this could get away from me," she said. "I'm handling it now. My people are terrific. They've been through this before. But if things get worse, it could be a downward spiral that spins out of control. That's what keeps me up at night."

"Let's get the key elements on the board." Rick said. He started with Headcount and handed the marker to Joanne (Figure 18.1).

Finishing the loop, she said, "That's the gist of it. When our headcount is down, overtime becomes a requirement. Then you start to see more turnover. That's the reinforcing loop—the downward spiral. You can see why I need to get the Center Director involved right now."

"I can see you're ready to take action," Rick said. "Let's wait, though. Let's keep looking at what's going on and why for a bit longer. What do you think is happening in HR?"

"Why should I care? That's their business!" she blurted. Then she paused, calmed herself and recollected something. "Well, they *did* just lose their best recruiter. And it takes a while for someone to come up to speed in this environment. That puts them behind. I know their morale is really bad. They're overloaded."

She grabbed the marker and went to the board (Figure 18.2).

"Their loop looks a lot like ours. . .which means they're in danger of the same downward spiral. If they implode, that's going to hurt us. . . . My putting pressure on them adds to their downward spiral. . . .I'm part of the problem!" she said, standing back. Then she re-approached the map. "I think the links between us would look something like this. . . ." Rick asked her to run him through her thinking as she was drawing (Figure 18.3).

"At the top, when they have recruiting success it adds to our headcount, making things better for us. That's when things are going well and the flow between us is

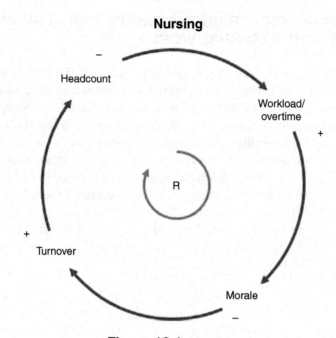

Figure 18.1 Nursing.
Source: Karash, R. (2018). *The trouble with HR*. Unpublished manuscript.

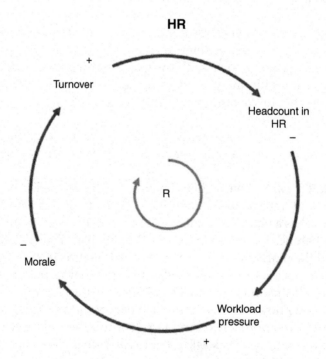

Figure 18.2 Human Resources (HR).
Source: Karash, R. (2018). *The trouble with HR*. Unpublished manuscript.

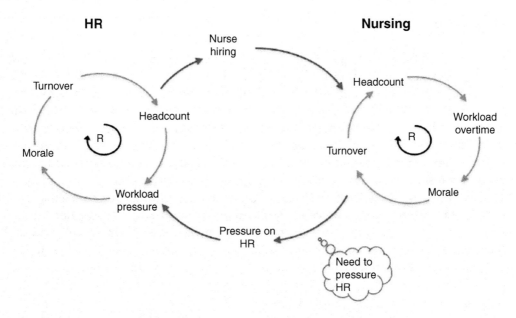

Figure 18.3 Agreements between Nursing and Human Resources (HR) help mitigate potential downward spiral.
Source: Karash, R. (2018). *The trouble with HR*. Unpublished manuscript.

balanced," she said. "The less they recruit, the worse off we get. Our staffing shortage increases their workload. When they've got too much on their plate, they miss follow-ups, get very inefficient, lose good candidates. I know it can be really demoralizing for them too."

She paused and sat down.

"You know, when I think about it, it's amazing how easy it is to want to think of them as the bad guys. Then I get to feel like a champion for my own people. It makes me feel better for a short while . . . like I'm actually *doing something!* But I see that when I ratchet up the pressure and try to pull out the big guns, it just makes it worse for them . . . and ultimately for my group too."

Rick listened.

"I can see it would be better for me to back off and let them get their house in order." She mused. "It sounds so crazy to hear myself say that! We've been so adversarial for so long. I'll have to get my boss on board. I'm going to schedule a meeting with the HR manager."

The **causal loop diagram** is a tool to stimulate exploratory conversation that questions, clarifies, and refines one's thinking and makes it visible. It can be done by an individual or with others in an individual coaching or group setting. A causal loop diagram helps us see more of the system and its variables and interrelationships, ask different questions, and try on different perspectives. It forces us to state our mental models explicitly and open them to question, testing, and revision. It shows reinforcing and balancing feedback and delays, all of which can otherwise be hard to see. And it gives us a chance to think about the unintended consequences that may arise from our actions.

COMMENTARY

Joanne had all the knowledge of the system and its interactions at her fingertips, but had not looked at it all at once. Drawing the situation in a simple causal loop diagram enabled her to step outside the heat of the experience and view it with more perspective. With a few well-placed questions from Rick, asking her to slow the action and then to expand her perspective, she could check her impulse to take action long enough to reflect on her habitual responses. As she kept revising her narrative about the dynamic, her thinking moved easily from the particulars of this event to considering the recurring pattern and larger context that kept it in place.

The drawing, though much simplified from reality, allowed her to see the reinforcing and balancing dynamics in the relationship with HR and how her actions were part of the problem. This insight produced compassion for herself and the other players in the system. She saw she had different choices. She could re-author a role for herself that felt at first counterintuitive, but which she thought might hold promise. She was energized by seeing the situation in a new light and left the meeting eager to explore new possibilities. Sometime after this session, she reported back to Rick that she and the HR manager had instituted some new agreements and practices and the hiring situation had improved—real progress from her perspective. What's more, she enjoyed a better relationship with him and felt liberated from the strong mental model that the only way to get results from HR was to apply more pressure.

JIM'S STORY: MASTER CRAFTSMEN ON THE MANUFACTURING FLOOR—THE INTERACTION WORLD

I was on assignment to shadow eight people leading a small manufacturing organization over a two and a half-day period. With no specific agenda, my job was to witness their meetings and be in conversation with each of them about what I'd seen. The next stop was with the Vice President for Manufacturing, and I stepped into his office with an open mind. It was a busy shared hub on the manufacturing floor, with people coming in and out, dealing with immediate technical questions or ideas for new products on the drawing board. Within moments Jim and I were seated across from one another and he raised an issue he was wrestling with.

He was looking at the path from entry-level position to Master Craftsman on the shop floor. He had clearly written descriptions of four levels that showed a logical progression one could expect to traverse. Yet, he'd found repeatedly that people aspiring to Master Craftsman could not see why they did not yet qualify. It was easily agreed that certain people were already Master Craftsmen. But those on the cusp of becoming masters often felt frustrated in their attempts to embody key distinctions that appeared to be spelled out clearly. Jim felt at a loss, and believed he needed to come up with a way to answer these people that acknowledged and encouraged their efforts while preserving the essence of what he felt defined the term "master."

This manufacturing operation existed within an organization which was intentional about supporting employees' growth. Employees were asked to take responsibility for the success of the company's clearly defined mission, however they saw their role relating to it. I asked Jim a few questions to clarify how he was thinking about this dilemma, and what ideas he'd already pursued. As we were talking, I suddenly felt my insides go cold.

The day before, as I'd sat in the airport awaiting my flight, I had received a call from a business colleague informing me that a close friend had just been promoted to partner, while I had not. At first, I was shocked, having not known that this change was in the offing. Very quickly, I was infuriated, questioning the rationale and feeling wholly stymied in my ability to address it. The call was necessarily brief as my plane was called for boarding. To make matters worse, I learned that I was the last of the group to be informed of this change. I was determined to manage my energy professionally for the duration of the assignment in front of me. I would deal with my own situation on my return home. I had effectively put it out of my mind.

Now here it was again, foremost in my awareness and reflected perfectly in my client's dilemma. The coincidence was too stark to ignore. I debated for an excruciating second about whether or not to reveal this to my client, wondering whether I might lose standing in his eyes. Then I took a deep breath and jumped.

"As a matter of fact, I'm having a similar experience of my own, just now," I said. "I was informed that a close associate made partner in a group I'm affiliated with, and I did not. It just happened, it's unresolved and it's really difficult for me to deal with."

There was silence in the room.

"So, I've got some fresh material to ponder about this for you." I knew I had a deeper inquiry in store for me. Over the next 2 days, I continued on with my meetings in the company and then returned home with much on my mind.

I initiated correspondence with Jim, which took place over the following month. I wrote that, in my experience, the "blind spot" he referred to signified the presence of a threshold that calls on us to step through it in a way that changes us from how we were before. That movement marks a center of gravity shift between the certainty of external reference and expertise, and a live, real-time exploration between Self and experience. This is a place of not knowing. While some sail over this threshold, it can challenge others who may experience unconscious forces marshalled to preserve the status quo, despite their conscious intention to advance. I referenced my own wrestling with this dilemma, where colleagues' explanations for not elevating me to partner did not feel useful in the least. I proposed that frustration and anger may be a necessary goad to summon the will to step over that threshold.

As it happened, I'd just read a passage in a Louise Penny (2008) mystery (*The Cruelest Month*) about the Emperor moth, which I quoted to Jim: "It takes years for the moth to evolve from an egg into an adult. . . . But it's not that easy. Before it can live as a moth it has to fight its way out of the cocoon. Not all make it. They need to fight their way out. . . It builds their wings and muscles. It's the struggle that saves them. Without it they're crippled. If you help an Emperor moth, you kill it."

I hypothesized that hardening the barrier might be productive for some, eliciting in them the will to step over. I also thought that each person's path was likely singular and had its own time and way. I wondered if mastery might require a piece of individual genius, and if inviting each person to imagine what his or her unique signature of mastery might be, how it would feel to express it, might help accelerate the process for others.

Jim responded that he had been hyperaware of thresholds in almost every aspect of his recent experience, and was fascinated by his sensing a web of interconnection between them. He also reported, surprisingly, that he had been noticing so many butterflies recently that it felt like the universe was conspiring to communicate something specifically to him. He went on to say that, as he saw it, the Master Craftsman represented a weaving of technical expertise, alignment of personal with company values, and an expression of personal gifts and unique voice that moved those around them to say, "There is a Master Craftsman." People grasped the technical aspects, he said, yet struggled with the rest. He thought an invitation for them to accept the challenge and take the first step worth a try. He told the story of a personal practice he had consciously undertaken some time ago, of "letting his light shine" to see what would happen. He described a liberation from his own fears and the surprising impact it had on those around him, as a personal threshold and probably his first experience of his own center of gravity shifting.

Hearing this, I sent Jim Elisabeth Sahtouris's description of the battle within the chrysalis between tiny newly forming "imaginal discs" that are at first snuffed out by the caterpillar's immune system. Eventually the number of discs so overwhelm the immune system that the caterpillar is reduced to a soup. The discs then turn into imaginal cells that build the butterfly by feeding on the pulpy mass. The butterfly has its own unique genome, which is carried by, but separate from, the caterpillar (Sahtouris & Lovelock, 2000).

COMMENTARY

In reflecting on these exchanges, I was struck by how Jim and I both stepped away from our standard roles to examine the raw materials of each of our experiences and together created ideas that might be useful to his dilemma.[3] Exploring together opened a rich stream of relating that otherwise would not have taken place. My decision to risk surfacing my own humiliating experience—and remain curious rather than defended—may have been an important step in my own passage over that threshold. The dilemma certainly was as alive in my field of awareness as it was in his, though from a very different vantage point.

Now, many years later, Jim reports that he has been holding open the space for people to identify and name what makes their work singular. He observed that though his Master Craftsmen perform similar roles, each describes his or her mastery differently. He said, "Each has a defining signature based on their gifts. It is this uniqueness that needs to be nursed to the forefront. These gifts are sometimes easier for others to see and define than for the person who possesses them." It was clear to him that the master craftsman, consciously or not, is aligned with his or her gifts and lives through them, as opposed to trying to live into them.

This whole exchange left me reverberating with the sense that we are all one system wanting to grow by informing itself about itself through our interactions with one another. The sense of synchronicity, as Jung defined it—"a *meaningful coincidence* of two or more events, where something other than the probability of chance is involved" (p. 104)—persisted in many aspects of our interaction.

CONCLUSION

In *Leading From the Emerging Future*, Scharmer and Kaufer (2013) quote Bill O'Brien, the late CEO of Hanover Insurance, as saying, "The success of an intervention depends on the *interior condition* of the intervener." As coaches, we take responsibility for knowing our own internal systems, for understanding and helping make visible our client's internal and external systems, and for modeling constructive interaction in the moment to the best of our ability. We are always attending to the self as instrument, cultivating a dynamic capacity to be fully present to what is happening in the environment and simultaneously within ourselves so that we are wholly available to act in the emerging moment. As we see systems and our clients see systems, we become instances of the system seeing itself, a fundamental requirement for transformation. Taking up the study and practice of working with systems can increase our capabilities, add to what we bring to our clients, and enrich what they take with them on their journey.

NOTES

1. Recognition of a formerly tacitly held agreement and shifting it in favor of an explicit new agreement that is aligned with currently held intentions for the future, is a fundamental *Harmonic Vibrancy move* described in Jim Ritchie-Dunham's book *Ecosynomics* (Ritchie-Dunham, 2014).

2. Story retold and causal loop diagrams recreated with permission from Richard Karash, independent consultant, Grantham, NH; richard@karash.com (Karash, 2018).

3. Comparing the raw data of our different experiences in this territory, sharing our insights, and constructing hypotheses is a small example of working with complex adaptive systems described in Marilyn Darling's Emergent Learning work (Darling, Guber, Smith, & Stiles, 2016). Jim completed the cycle by testing these hypotheses regularly with his people on the manufacturing floor, likely including input and hypotheses from all of them and many others, folding his learnings back into his thinking, and continually fine-tuning his approach.

REFERENCES

Argyris, C. (1990). *Overcoming organizational defenses.* New York, NY: Prentice-Hall.
Bateson, G. (1972). *Steps to an ecology of mind.* New York, NY: Ballantine Books.
Cook-Greuter, S. (2010). *Post-autonomous ego development.* Integral Publishers Dissertation Series.
Darling, M., Guber, H., Smith, J., & Stiles, J. (2016). Emergent learning: A framework for whole-system strategy, learning, and adaptation. *The Foundation Review, 8*(1), 59–73. doi:10.9707/1944-5660.1284
Garvey Berger, J. (2013). *Changing on the job.* Redwood City, CA: Stanford Business Press.
Holland, J. (1995). *Hidden order.* New York, NY: Perseus Books Group, Basic Books.
Jung, C. G. (1960). *Synchronicity.* New York, NY: Bollingen Foundation.
Karash, R. (2018). *The trouble with HR.* Unpublished manuscript.

Kegan, R., & Lahey, L. (2009). *Immunity to change.* Cambridge, MA: Harvard Business Review.

Kim, D. H. (1999). Introduction to systems thinking. *The Systems Thinker.* Retrieved from https://thesystemsthinker.com/introduction-to-systems-thinking

Meadows, D. H. (2008). *Thinking in systems.* White River Junction, VT: Chelsea Green Publishing Company.

Mindell, A. (2002). *The deep democracy of open forums.* Newburyport, MA: Hampton Roads.

Ober, S. P. (2014). *Unleashing the power of your story.* Retrieved from https://www.smashwords.com/books/view/463296

Penny, L. (2008). *The cruelest month.* New York, NY: St. Martin's Press.

Ritchie-Dunham, J. (2014). *Ecosynomics.* Belchertown, MA: Vibrancy Ins LLC.

Sahtouris, E., & Lovelock, J. (2000). *EarthDance: Living systems in evolution.* Santa Barbara, CA: Praeger.

Scharmer, O., & Kaufer, K. (2013). *Leading from the emerging future.* San Francisco, CA: Berrett-Koehler.

Weisbord, M., & Janoff, S. (2007). *Don't just do something, stand there!* San Francisco, CA: Berrett-Koehler.

ADDITIONAL READING

Agazarian, Y. M. (1997). *Systems centered therapy for groups.* New York, NY: Guilford Press.

Forrester, J. W. (1971). Counterintuitive behavior in social systems. *Technology Review, 73*(3), 52–68.

Garvey Berger, J., & Johnston, K. (2016). *Simple habits for complex times.* Redwood City, CA: Stanford Business Press.

Hellinger, B., Weber, G., & Beaumont, H. (1998). *Love's hidden symmetry.* Phoenix, AZ: Zeig Tucker.

19

Coaching With Intentional Change Theory

Richard E. Boyatzis

Coaching has been the primary form of development since humans began cooperating. It became formalized in the Ancient Eras and Middle Ages with apprenticeship to Master tradespeople as *the* way to learn a trade and enter a career. Within management, coaching has been used explicitly since the 1960s. Today, it is the fastest growing method of development, far surpassing the growth of training or education. The growing literature on effectiveness, roles, styles, and processes of coaching is helping sort the face-valid, well-marketed approaches from those approaches that might actually help others. The focus of this chapter is an evidence-based approach to coaching that helps others grow, learn, and develop.

With 39 longitudinal studies showing impact of a particular approach to coaching on behavior change and several neuroscience and psychophysiological studies showing how it works, coaching people with Intentional Change Theory (ICT) is one of the few evidence-based approaches to promoting sustained, desired change in others (Boyatzis, 2008). This chapter will describe how viewing coaching with ICT suggests techniques and an approach that can be more effective than typical approaches to problem-centered or person-centered coaching.

THE ROAD MAP FOR CHANGE: INTENTIONAL CHANGE THEORY

This approach comes out of ICT (Boyatzis, 2008), as shown in Figure 19.1. According to ICT, sustained desired change occurs when a person, or group, is moved along five discoveries, in sequence, and iteratively continues cycling through them. Each discovery is experienced consciously as an epiphany. It is a moment of discontinuous

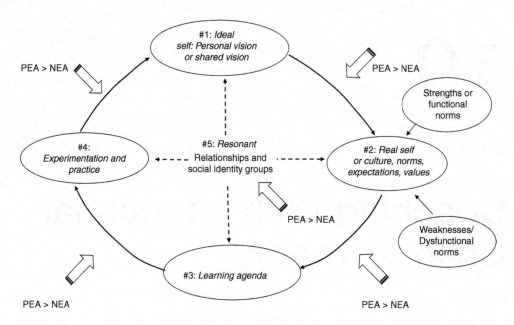

Figure 19.1 Boyatzis's Intentional Change Theory in fractals or multiple levels.

NEA, negative emotional attractor; PEA, positive emotional attractor.

Source: Boyatzis, R. E. (2008). Leadership development from a complexity perspective. *Consulting Psychology Journal: Practice and Research, 60*(4), 298–313. doi:10.1037/1065-9293.60.4.298; Boyatzis, R. E., & Cavanaugh, K. (2018). Leading change: Developing emotional, social, and cognitive competencies in managers during an MBA program. In K. V. Keefer, J. D. A. Parker, & D. H. Saklofske (Eds.), *Handbook of emotional intelligence in education: Integrating research with practice* (pp. 403–426). New York, NY: Springer.

awareness from which emerges a new way to looking at the future, the present, and possibilities. A person, or group, is moved from being in one discovery into the next through a tipping point. The tipping point is a psycho-physiological transformation from a person (or group) being in the negative emotional attractor (NEA) into the positive emotional attractor (PEA; Boyatzis, Rochford, & Taylor, 2015).

The PEA and NEA states are described in terms of three axes: (a) positive to negative affect; (b) neural activation in the default mode network (DMN) versus the task positive network (TPN); and (c) having a dominant hormonal arousal in the parasympathetic nervous system (PNS) versus the sympathetic nervous system (SNS). The DMN is the neural network that helps people be open to new ideas, others, and moral concerns (Boyatzis & Jack, 2018). The TPN is the neural network that helps people analyze things, make decisions, focus their attention on analytic matters, and solve problems. Together, the three components create a state of awareness that opens the person's perceptions and emotional considerations to new possibilities. They are more cognitively open and creative. They are more thoughtful and can see others around them. They are more considerate of moral concerns—what is fair and just (not the moralizing of right and wrong).

The first discovery is of the ideal self. The result is a personal vision. If the sustained, desired change is for a dyad, team, organization, community, or country, then the vision would have to be a widely shared vision to provide the growing awareness in discovery one.

The second discovery, only possible if the person (or group) has experienced the first and has some form of a personal vision, is an accurate image of their real self—the way they appear to others through their behavior. The immediate comparison to the ideal self results in the outcome of the second discovery, a personal balance sheet—a statement of strengths (places where the real and ideal self overlap) and weaknesses (places where the real and ideal self do not converge). Again, discussion with the coach is vital.

The coach helps to guide the person back into the PEA whenever he or she drifts into the NEA. It is inevitable that people examining their strengths and weaknesses will defensively focus on their weaknesses. In this phase, the coach is working hard to make the strengths the longer portion of the conversation and focus. In the context of a person's vision and strengths, the coach can guide a discussion of which of the person's weaknesses would be necessary to develop, helping to maximize the likelihood of deep commitment to the development process. To move ahead, the person not only needs awareness of his or her personal balance sheet, but must re-enter the PEA to move ahead. Discussion of the strengths often invokes the PEA.

The third discovery is awareness of the way forward in the form of a learning agenda that emerges from integration of the personal balance sheet and vision. It uses people's strengths to move closer to or maintain their vision, while identifying one or two weaknesses that can be developed. This is the basis for development of a learning, actionable plan. The learning plan will often consist of a set of learning goals and actions, anticipating obstacles and seeking sources of support and help, as well as indicators of progress along the way.

Discussion with the coach is again essential to help "reality test" the person's commitment to the learning goals, ease of engaging in the actions, and identifying possible obstacles that might be encountered. In addition to the usual ways people develop plans, our research suggests that consideration of the person's planning style would deeply improve the motivational power of the learning agenda (i.e., SMART goals are demotivating for approximately 75% of the professional and managerial workforce). Considering a person's preferred learning style enables people to identify actions that they are likely to enjoy and actually do, rather than commit to and never fulfill or sustain in the effort (Kolb, 2015).

Organizational life is filled with planning. Sadly, in development, most of the plans are done in service of someone else's goals, which invokes the NEA. The driving force behind the effort to drop performance appraisals is not the need for performance feedback but the feeble and dysfunctional latter aspect of these conversations—the "development plan."

Most people experience the developmental plan emerging in the latter portion of a performance review as a list of things the person "should do." The obligatory nature is likely to arouse the NEA. Many of the elements of it may come from the boss's perceptions and agenda (i.e., biases). My data over 45 years suggest that 70% to 80% of bosses are not adding much value: Who is to say that the boss's agenda is a good one or would help the person or unit be more effective?

This imposition, however well intended, is at the heart of what we call coaching for compliance. The intent is to have the person comply with the boss's view of how the former should act. The boss may be correct and the person has a serious, performance-threatening deficiency. In such a case, we contend that using a vision- and strengths-based approach may help the person change his or her views and con-sider change. Although at times necessary, the more NEA approach of coaching for compliance is more likely preparing the person for dismissal—not motivating change. The NEA is typically activated in problem-based coaching, or even at times in person-based coaching when the person is allowed to entirely frame or define the expectation or goal of the coaching. People will often come into coaching thinking they "should" fix some flaw in their behavior, feelings or thoughts.

The fourth discovery is the hard work of experimenting with new thoughts, feel-ings, and behavior. The mere exercise of self-control that is needed for change stimu-lates the SNS and is stressful. If the coach can keep the person reminded of his or her vision and using their strengths, the coach may periodically bring the person back into the PEA and restore the energy they need to continue the experimentation.

At some point, with practice, the new thoughts, feelings, or behavior may feel more comfortable, become habits, and are easier for the person to practice to the point of mastery. The image of the sports coach standing on the sidelines shouting at the person to keep him or her going may work in Hollywood, but is much less effective in real life. There are times the coach may need to help the person focus, which requires more NEA than PEA, but the better coaches know how to inter-sperse those moments with prolonged moments of encouragement, support, and reminders of the vision (i.e., PEA).

The fifth discovery is the quality of the relationship with a key other person. In this chapter, the relationship with the coach IS the fifth discovery if the coach is using this approach. If the coach is using harassment and intimidation, the efforts of the person are less sustainable, if at all, and drain energy from his or her commit-ment to pursue the learning agenda. More on this quality of the relationship is described in a later section of this chapter.

The fifth discovery introduces the importance of relationships in sustaining change and learning. Scholars have considered that people need multiple coaches or trusted advisors and helpers to move ahead in their career and life. Professor Kathy Kram called these "developmental networks." Professors Melvin Smith, Ellen Van Oosten, and the author featured this in their Massive Open On-Line Course (i.e., MOOC) on coaching as a person's Personal Board of Directors. Creating a personal board of directors becomes a major step in helping people continue to work on their change and learning for all the reasons described earlier—reality testing, support during stressful moments, overcoming obstacles, anticipating obstacles, knowing someone else cares, and people to whom you can report or check-in on progress. The actual exercises to help the person are in the study by McKee, Boyatzis, and Johnson (2005).

IT STARTS WITH VISION

Many approaches to counseling and coaching tell the novice to begin with the per-son seeking help. Ask the person what his or her issue or problem is. Then, stay focused on his or her framing of it. However, this is a problem-based approach to helping, not a person-based approach. Further, it often encourages people to dwell in the negative feelings they are having about themselves and others and feeling helpless.

As will be explained in more detail in a later section of this chapter, this approach focuses on what the person seeking help experiences as the NEA. It immediately results in a restriction of the person's ability to be open to new ideas, perceptual field of vision (the NEA invokes narrow vision), and dismissal of others as sources of help. It literally contributes to turning the person off to the very possibilities that could help him or her.

It would be odd to begin a coaching session or relationship without asking why the person is seeking help. But in a vision-based approach, after 5 to 10 minutes, the coach would swiftly move to defining the conversation as an opportunity to explore a bigger picture as the context of their own future. The specific "presenting issue" may be addressed but in the context of their personal vision—something that provides a far more sustainable context for learning and change.

Two research studies have shown that if a coach focuses the first third or more of their conversations on the person's personal vision of the future (i.e., literally, "If everything were perfect, absolutely ideal, what would your work or life be like in 10–15 years?"), this creates the context within which a person can explore change and learning (Howard, 2015; Passarelli, 2015). Behavioral, longitudinal studies have shown comparative impact of courses leading with vision coaching to have a positive impact on developing emotional and social intelligence (EI and SI) competencies shown to predict effectiveness in management and leadership of 11 times average impact in published studies in organizations—and 30 times the impact of above-average MBA programs (Boyatzis, 2008; Boyatzis & Cavanaugh, 2018).

Further research into the neural mechanisms that create this impact has shown that coaching to a person's vision (even 30 minutes of it) activates regions of the brain associated with visualizing, imaging, being open to new ideas and others, and the PNS. This is directly linked to cognitive creativity, complex thought, and openness to new ideas (Jack, Boyatzis, Khawaja, Passarelli, & Leckie, 2013; Passarelli, Jack, Boyatzis, & Dawson, in review). A mere 30-minute conversation about vision was so emotionally powerful that 3 to 5 days later, when answering questions about the experience while strapped into an fMRI scanner, the neural activation was strong, clear, and statistically significant.

Beginning coaching by asking the person to develop his or her personal vision or dream seems counterintuitive to most. They assume coaches should help to identify a problem and then help the person fix it. This approach to coaching, which we have called coaching for compliance (Boyatzis, Smith, & Beveridge, 2013), is an obligation to "fix" the problem. An approach that focuses on the desired context people have for their own future is more powerful. We call this approach coaching with compassion (Boyatzis et al., 2013).

For those of us who enter the helping professions, like coaching, we do so because we deeply want to help others improve their lives. If we see a way someone else can improve or "fix" a problem, we are eager to help. But as any of us trained in psychotherapy know, the sustainable impact comes from helping people discover their own solution and maybe even define the opportunity.

Our research moves this one step further to claim that the context or purpose for the helping is NOT to solve the immediate problem or fix the person. It is to help people find the big picture and deeper purpose for their future life and work. This becomes the context for resolving specific problems, deciding that they do not matter, or framing new opportunities. It provides a sustainable foundation and source of positive energy for the often long and grueling process of learning and change.

THRIVING VERSUS SURVIVING

The human body and mind needs stress (i.e., more than stress, we need the NEA) to survive, and the SNS provides for that quite well. But chronic, annoying stress, such as when your cell phone drops a call or you experience pressure from your manager or others to produce results, builds up and creates cognitive, emotional, and perceptual impairment (Boyatzis, Smith, & Blaize, 2006). For those in positions of responsibility, like managers, teachers, coaches, and even parents, the burden of responsibility adds a form of stress called power stress just because you are in the role without even any specific precipitating events. The body's antidote to this chronic annoying stress, role-related power stress, and occasional acute stress is the PNS. This part of the autonomic nervous system engages our immune system, fosters neurogenesis (growth of new neurons from brain stem cells), and invokes greater cognitive ability and openness to new ideas and people. This state, the PEA, can be called thriving (Boyatzis et al., 2015). This is when the human organism can flourish.

It is not surprising that negative emotions have been shown to be stronger than positive emotions. The body needs to have defense as its default. One cannot thrive and flourish if one is being eaten or has been killed. The challenge, therefore, is how to balance the onslaught of NEA and the SNS.

We know we need more than 1–1 correspondence to achieve a balance and the ability of a person to move back and forth between the NEA and PEA easily (Boyatzis et al., 2015). Fredrickson's (2009) extensive research shows that a ratio of 3 to 1 of positivity to negativity helps a person flourish and teams to be more effective in what she calls her "broaden and build" theory. Gottman, Murray, Swanson, Tyson, and Swanson (2002) have shown that stable, loving marriages have a 5 to 1 ratio of positive to negative exchanges between the couple even in brief conversations.

In one fMRI study of coaching, we found that two or three times the number of ½ hour PEA coaching sessions to each ½ hour NEA coaching session activates a part of the brain (i.e., the ventral medial prefrontal cortex) that is directly linked to activating the PNS (Passarelli et al., in review). In a related study of 49-year-old (average age) dentists, Howard (2015) showed that PEA coaching aroused far more positive affect than did NEA coaching. Passarelli (2015) showed a similar finding in work with graduate students in their mid-30s.

In earlier papers, we have suggested that stimulating the PEA multiple times a day, throughout the day, is more important for renewal and reversing the damage of chronic stress than one prolonged period of PEA. Coaching others with compassion arouses PEA in both the coach and the person being coached (Boyatzis et al., 2006). So if a person was doing coaching as a way to help balance his or her own system, the research suggests that coaching four or five people for 15 to 20 minutes each throughout the day is better than a 1 hour-long session for the coach's renewal and flourishing.

RELATIONSHIPS MATTER

People's relationships create their interpersonal environment. This environment both moderates and mediates everything that happens inside of us and outside forces as they affect our decisions and behavior. The quality of our relationships determines whether we feel isolated or a sense of belonging. In case of the former, we feel marginalized and often withdraw further. In case of the latter, the quality of the relationships affects how we view the world and what we see as appropriate behavior and attitudes.

Our relationships may contribute to our social identity—a key part of our ideal self or personal vision. Our approach to quality of relationships focuses on those characteristics most closely associated with PEA and renewal (Boyatzis, 2018). When we feel a sense of shared vision with others around us, we are in pursuit of common directions, purpose, and goals. When we feel a shared sense of compassion, we feel cared for and care for others. These two qualities define healthier, more positive relationships. When they occur, the interaction with others within these relationships arouse the PEA (Boyatzis et al., 2015).

The relationship with the coach can be a high intensity, emotional bond for a person seeking guidance and learning. Howard (2015) showed that PEA-oriented coaching for 49-year-old (average age) dentists resulted in dramatic increases in their positive affect and energy in pursuit of development as compared to coaching focusing more on problems and weaknesses (i.e., NEA approach). Passarelli (2015) showed a similar reaction with career professionals in their early 30s and PEA versus NEA approaches to coaching. Passarelli (2015) further showed that specificity of development goals and energy and commitment to work on them were significantly higher in people after a PEA coaching session than it was for the same people after an NEA coaching session. In assessing the quality of the link between large bank's executives' EI and SI competencies and their leadership effectiveness as well as engagement and satisfaction, Van Oosten (2013) showed that the stronger the relationship to the coach was in terms of shared vision and compassion, the greater the impact of the executives' EI and SI on their effectiveness, engagement in their work, and career satisfaction.

Resonant, trusting relationships are not only discovery five in ICT but also affect a person's movement and experience in each of the other stages of change. The relationships that help the most are characterized by shared vision and shared compassion (i.e., the PEA).

EXPANDING RESONANT RELATIONSHIPS TO PEER COACHING

Peer coaching has the potential to be the most important application of coaching to creating a culture of coaching in organizations and helping to create learning organizations (Parker, Kram, Hall, & Wasserman, 2017). Some of the people in one's personal board of directors may be peers. Or alternatively, a person may form a peer coaching or study group in addition to the personal board of directors. These discussions with peers have an additional benefit in that the others understand your work or life context. You do not need to spend time orienting them or explaining complex political social networks. They also might be sensitive to and help anticipate a problem that the person has not noticed or considered. It is believed that peer coaching groups, once begun, will spread organically as others learn of the benefits. When enough of them are functioning, the organizational norms may begin to change and develop a culture of coaching, caring, and learning (Parker et al., 2017).

Sustained, desired change at other levels of human groups, dyads, teams, organizations, communities, and countries, follow the same stages of ICT and each level can benefit from a coach. The difference is that each stage is a shared characteristic, like shared vision, or shared learning agenda. The PEA and NEA are still key tipping points that allow movement to the next stage. But now the state of being in PEA or NEA is a collective experience. The additional feature of human systems above teams is that resonant leadership relationships and social identity groups carry information and emotion across levels. Coaching these other levels, like teams and communities, would be the same process as explained in this chapter but with the various stakeholder groups within each level.

Coaching with larger groups involves working with modular units. That is, the coach would work with trios, departments, and so forth that constitute the large social organization. A common application is Team Coaching, which involves having the manager of a team along with direct reports engage in a leadership or professional development experience guided by a coach. It can also involve a group or team working with a coach around their individual development while simultaneously working on the team's development. The coach would seek to create opportunities for learning through sharing of new knowledge and frameworks and dialogue. The coach would seek more frequent and briefer opportunities than long meetings or retreats to maximize the likelihood of stimulating the PEA and not sliding into the NEA. You want people in such settings to look forward to the next session, not feel as if you had discussed the emotions or topics ad nauseam.

Large system interventions might require multiple coaches. In future research conferences or summits, there is often a team of facilitators who operate like coaches for varying levels of discussion groups. To be effective in using ICT in these settings, the coaches would emphasize a shared vision—either creating it together or conveying an existing one and establishing resonant relationships with many others. They would identify and enlist people who can or do build such relationships naturally. This forms an emotional pyramid or can be thought of as using emotional contagion positively in a multilevel marketing design, like Mary Kay Cosmetics has done so successfully over the decades in their "shows" and meetings. Once the large group processes begin, they have the potential of altering the organization's norms and culture. But it requires more than having an emotionally uplifting event. It requires coaches and leaders to remind people of their shared vision (i.e., common purpose). Through their resonant relationships, the leaders and coaches create a positive, magnetic pull toward these norms, which others in the organization witness—and some want to join or replicate in their part of the organization. In this manner, a culture of coaching and development organically emerges through more and more of the organization.

SUMMARY AND KEY LEARNING

ICT and the research over the last 30 years on coaching with it reveals that effective coaching can occur, with clear evidence of outcomes and understanding of the neural mechanisms. The lessons learned are:

1. Begin the coaching process with an in-depth discussion helping people identify and elaborate on their ideal future, including their passion, purpose and values, and personal vision. It should help to answer the question: What kind of person do I want to be? What do I want out of life and work?

2. Throughout the coaching process, emphasize the PEA state as much as possible or at least two to three times as often as the NEA is experienced by people. Inspire them to thrive as well as survive in their balancing of the PEA and NEA in their daily life and work.

3. Help people identify, value, and link their strengths to achieving or making progress toward their vision. If they are already in an ideal state, identify how their strengths can help them maintain it.

4. Help people identify one or two weaknesses that could be developed to help move closer to their personal vision. This would complete their personal balance sheet.

5. Guide people in developing a learning agenda (and some specific goals and actions) that they are positively excited about trying, eager to work on, and almost joyful in pursuit of the agenda.

6. Support them through efforts at experimenting with the new thoughts, feelings, or behavior, encouraging experimentation and novelty. Then, support them in practicing them to the point of mastery.

7. Build a resonant relationship with those being coached that maximizes their experience of hope and shared vision with the coach, compassion and shared caring, mindfulness, and playfulness with the coach.

8. When you can, expand the process to teams and entire segments of the organization helping to foster a culture of coaching and development.

REFERENCES

Boyatzis, R. E. (2008). Leadership development from a complexity perspective. *Consulting Psychology Journal: Practice and Research, 60*(4), 298–313. doi:10.1037/1065-9293.60.4.298

Boyatzis, R. E. (2018). Measuring the impact of quality of relationships through the positive emotional attractor. In S. Donaldson & M. Rao (Eds.), *Positive psychology of relationships* (pp. 193–209). Santa Barbara, CA: Praeger Publishers.

Boyatzis, R. E., & Cavanaugh, K. (2018). Leading change: Developing emotional, social, and cognitive competencies in managers during an MBA program. In K. V. Keefer, J. D. A. Parker, & D. H. Saklofske (Eds.), *Emotional intelligence in education: Integrating research with practice* (pp. 403–426). New York, NY: Springer.

Boyatzis, R. E., & Jack, A. (2018). The neuroscience of coaching. *Consulting Psychology Journal, 70*(1), 11–27.

Boyatzis, R. E., Rochford, K., & Taylor, S. N. (2015). The role of the positive emotional attractor in vision and shared vision: Toward effective leadership, relationships, and engagement. *Frontiers in Psychology, 6,* 670. doi:10.3389/fpsyg.2015.00670

Boyatzis, R. E., Smith, M. L., & Beveridge, A. J. (2013). Coaching with compassion: Inspiring health, well-being, and development in organizations. *Journal of Applied Behavioral Science, 49*(2), 153–178. doi:10.1177/0021886312462236

Boyatzis, R. E., Smith, M., & Blaize, N. (2006). Developing sustainable leaders through coaching and compassion. *Academy of Management Journal on Learning and Education, 5*(1), 8–24. doi:10.5465/amle.2006.20388381

Fredrickson, B. (2009). *Positivity: Top-notch research reveals the 3 to 1 ratio that will change your life.* New York, NY: Crown Publishing Group.

Gottman, J. M., Murray, J. D., Swanson, C. C., Tyson, R., & Swanson, K. R. (2002). *The mathematics of marriage: Dynamic non-linear models.* Cambridge, MA: MIT Press.

Howard, A. R. (2015). Coaching to vision versus coaching to improvement needs: A preliminary investigation on the differential impacts of fostering positive and negative emotion during real time executive coaching sessions. *Frontiers in Psychology, 6,* 455. doi:10.3389/fpsyg.2015.00455

Jack, A. I., Boyatzis, R. E., Khawaja, M. S., Passarelli, A. M., & Leckie, R. L. (2013). Visioning in the brain: An fMRI study of inspirational coaching and mentoring. *Social Neuroscience, 8*(4), 369–384. doi:10.1080/17470919.2013.808259

Kolb, D. A. (2015). *Experiential learning: Experience as the source of learning and development* (2nd ed.). Englewood Cliffs, NJ: Prentice-Hall.

McKee, A., Boyatzis, R., & Johnson, F. (2005). *Becoming a resonant leader: Develop your emotional intelligence, renew your relationships, sustain your effectiveness.* Boston, MA: Harvard Business School Press.

Parker, P., Kram, K. E., Hall, D. T., & Wasserman, I. (2017). *Peer coaching: Principles and practice.* Palo Alto, CA: Stanford University Press.

Passarelli, A. M. (2015). Vision-based coaching: Optimizing resources for leader development. *Frontiers in Psychology, 6,* 412. doi:10.3389/fpsyg.2015.00412

Passarelli, A., Jack, A., Boyatzis, R. E., & Dawson, A. J. (in review). *Neuroimaging reveals link between vision and coaching for intentional change.* Also presented at the Annual Meeting of the Academy of Management, 2015.

Van Oosten, E. (2013). *The impact of emotional intelligence and executive coaching on leader effectiveness* (unpublished PhD dissertation). Case Western Reserve University, Cleveland, OH.

20

Supporting Autonomy, Competence, and Relatedness: The Coaching Process From a Self-Determination Theory Perspective

Richard M. Ryan and Edward L. Deci

C oaching has matured into a vibrant discipline, one aimed at facilitating the development and wellness of both individuals and organizations. Increasing evidence has made clear that coaching can be a strong asset in both personal development and organizational performance. Nonetheless, in practice, coaching remains a synthesis of disciplines and strategies, with coaches drawing on multiple, and sometime disparate, bodies of knowledge.

In this chapter, we discuss self-determination theory (SDT; Ryan & Deci, 2017) as an approach of considerable utility to coaching. SDT is an empirically supported and yet highly practical framework that is focused on fostering high-quality motivation and performance, as well as psychological flourishing. It is especially concerned with the processes and conditions that facilitate or undermine people's self-motivation, optimal functioning, and well-being. It is thus not surprising that the constructs and practices within SDT's scope have become an increasingly integral part of discourse for many coaches, who must not only understand, but also catalyze, their clients' motivation, wellness, and growth.

SDT is particularly apt as a foundation for coaches, precisely because coaches must so often tread into different disciplines and domains of practice. SDT has been actively studied and applied across the fields of organizational psychology (Deci, Olafsen, & Ryan, 2017), counseling (Ryan, Lynch, Vansteenkiste, & Deci, 2011), and physical health (Ryan, Patrick, Deci, & Williams, 2008), among other areas of interest to coaches. In these areas, SDT details the specific types of motivational supports that facilitate engagement and thriving at work, and the principles of incentives and rewards that drive high-quality productivity. SDT also details the personal motivations behind health and ill health, and how to mobilize people to engage in healthier behaviors.

Yet as a translational science, SDT is also a source for guiding principles that inform counseling (e.g., Ryan et al., 2011) and behavior change interventions in work organizations (e.g., Deci, Connell, & Ryan, 1989; Hardré & Reeve, 2009) and healthcare (Ng et al., 2012). For coaches, who often work within organizations and are focused on both goal progress and wellness, these principles are of strong relevance and are a focus of this chapter.

SELF-DETERMINATION THEORY IN BRIEF

SDT began with two strong assertions: First, that motivation differs not only in amount, but also in its quality. Motivation can thus be differentiated into types. Within SDT, the primary differentiation is between autonomous motivation and controlled motivation, which have both different antecedents and different consequences. *Autonomous motivation* is characterized by people's experiences of willingness and volition as they are acting in accord with their interests and their deeply held values. *Controlled motivation*, in contrast, is characterized by the experience of pressure and obligation, commonly associated with acting because of external demands or inducements. As we explain, these different types of motivation have predicted both employee performance and wellness outcomes and have provided a focal point for SDT interventions.

A second SDT assertion is that a true motivation theory must pay considerable attention to the energy for action—to what it is that moves and sustains behavior. SDT addresses the energy issue primarily with the concept of *basic psychological needs*. These psychological needs are defined as the essential nutrients for effective behavior and wellness. In SDT, the fundamental psychological needs are those for autonomy, competence, and relatedness—needs understood to be relevant to functioning across gender, development, socioeconomic status, and cultures. Satisfaction of these needs is critical for self-regulation of daily behaviors and for positive experiences and life satisfaction (Chen et al., 2015; Ryan & Deci, 2017).

Together, these two assertions lead to the empirically based propositions that autonomous motivation is more effective for promoting high-quality performance and greater well-being than is controlled motivation, and that satisfaction of the three basic psychological needs promotes autonomous motivation and a range of positive consequences. Accordingly, we examine how these processes influence coaching.

Of immediate note, in this regard, is the emphasis shared between the coaching profession and SDT on the importance of both respecting and helping cultivate clients' autonomy. This is indeed a core focus of SDT, within which facilitating environments are specifically characterized as *autonomy-supportive*. As mentioned, autonomy is evident when a person acts with a full sense of volition and willingness and represents a high-quality form of motivation. Yet, supporting autonomy—that is, enhancing the processes through which people enter into a willing and collaborative effort—turns out to be a nuanced endeavor. SDT details the specific practices involved in this process, some of which we outline in the following.

Despite the crucial importance of autonomy support within SDT, autonomy support alone is insufficient for fostering high-quality motivation and wellness. To have high-quality motivation, one must also experience the confidence and competence to act. This aligns with the second central psychological need in SDT's process models, namely providing supports that help people satisfy their need for *competence*. Like autonomy support, facilitating feelings of competence turns out to be a multi-faceted endeavor, one in which goal setting, scaffolding, feedback, and coping strategies all loom large. SDT focuses particularly on the creation of *optimal challenges* (Ryan & Deci, 2017), which energize and sustain goal pursuits. Creating optimal challenges does not mean putting people at the edge of their skill set or pressuring them to learn. Rather, it means identifying capacities that clients will both value and can effectively master and expand.

The third basic psychological need within the SDT framework is that for *relatedness*. While every coach knows that creating rapport and collegiality is important to the process of change, SDT suggests specific elements of high-quality relationships that are important. Indeed, coaching depends on the cultivation of an open and authentic exchange between the coach and client. Yet how one fosters relatedness simultaneously with promoting change and goal progress has not always been an explicit focus of training or practice. SDT, with its focus on the three basic psychological needs, goes beyond other frameworks in specifying the ingredients of high-quality relationships in a coaching context (Ryan & Deci, 2017).

Finally, although autonomy, competence, and relatedness supports are core elements in SDT's application to coaching, the *content* of clients' aspirations and goals is crucial for coaches to consider. This is an issue especially salient to coaches and consultants, for they invariably work with clients whose agendas are often wide ranging or long term. Some clients are seeking more personal development, others are seeking organizational excellence, and still others are pursuing greater wealth and status. SDT research has provided an informative lens on such aspirations, showing how the life goals one pursues can differentially satisfy or frustrate basic psychological needs, thereby strongly affecting happiness and optimal functioning. For example, SDT research has shown that having one's goals and aspirations focused on money, status, or fame, which are referred to as *extrinsic aspirations*, are likely to affect well-being negatively, even when successfully attained. This occurs primarily from compromising basic psychological need satisfactions (e.g., Sheldon & Krieger, 2014). In contrast, the more one's goals are focused on giving to others or on personal growth, which are referred to as *intrinsic aspirations*, the more likely one is to be flourishing (Kasser & Ryan, 1996) and experiencing meaning in life. Intrinsic aspirations and goals yield deeper experiences of autonomy, competence, and relatedness, and thus their pursuit engenders greater wellness (Weinstein & Ryan, 2010). Accordingly, the concepts of *intrinsic and extrinsic aspirations* within SDT offer further guidance for coaches and their clients in terms of framing positive pathways for change.

There is now a large scientific literature supporting the motivational principles of SDT—including those related to types of motivation, basic psychological needs, and goal contents. We will not review that literature in this brief chapter, as that has been done quite comprehensively elsewhere (e.g., Ryan & Deci, 2017). Nonetheless, we still have a substantial agenda for this practically focused chapter. Our primary concern here is on SDT's view of a *facilitating environment*—one that provides support for autonomy, competence, and relatedness. Thus, we highlight some of the specific ways in which SDT maintains that these three basic psychological need satisfactions can be supported within coaching encounters, and in the client's independent actions within organizations and everyday life. In addition, we review how the contents of life goals affect well-being and ill-being, career commitment, and, ultimately, flourishing. We then discuss the role of mindfulness in promoting autonomous self-regulation, goal choices, and wellness. The central aim throughout is to highlight the empirically supported practice elements of SDT in areas relevant to the coaching endeavor.

THE FACILITATING RELATIONSHIP: SUPPORTING AUTONOMY, COMPETENCE, AND RELATEDNESS

Assumptions about development and change shape one's philosophy of how to coach or counsel others. One common view is that change is promoted from without, in which case the focus is on shaping, incentivizing, conditioning, training, instructing, or otherwise prompting behaviors in the direction of specific goal attainments. An alternative view is that sustainable development and change must come from within, in which case the focus shifts to supporting, facilitating, encouraging, and otherwise nurturing the processes of personal growth and learning. SDT has been particularly focused on the latter kind of *change-from-within*, because of the greater impact that results from internally initiated change. At the core of SDT's approach to creating a facilitating environment for growth is the practice of *autonomy support*.

AUTONOMY SUPPORTIVE TECHNIQUES IN COACHING

The concept of autonomy refers to the idea that a person's actions are willingly or volitionally engaged. To be autonomous means to feel self-regulating and authentic in acting—to both own and endorse what one does. When fully autonomous, one feels a sense of choice in one's behaviors. Autonomy does not mean doing whatever one feels like doing, but rather doing that which one reflectively sees as most valued. That is, it means engaging in behaviors fully supported by one's self.

In practice, autonomy support means trying to help identify and give voice to a person's most integrated and valued judgments, often by engaging in a process of exploration and reflection in a context that is completely without judgment or control. A truly autonomy-supportive person is not there to direct, but rather to nurture a process.

TAKING THE INTERNAL FRAME OF REFERENCE

At its most foundational level, autonomy support begins by embracing the perspective of the client—that is, *taking the internal frame of reference (IFOR) of the client*. Listening carefully and empathically to clients' viewpoints and experiences allows a fuller understanding of their situations, and the motives and values underlying their experiences. In taking a client's IFOR, a coach is nonjudgmentally and compassionately entering into the client's world, acknowledging feelings, values, and conflicts. Areas of possible ambivalence or perceived barriers to change are articulated and accepted. In listening with interest and compassion, the coach implicitly validates the client and energizes interest and insight into reasons for change.

Gaining access to the important experiences frequently involves focusing on emotions. Emotions are understood within SDT as neither good nor bad but, rather, as sources of *information*. This means that a coach's attending to them provides important inputs to help the client understand subjective reactions, threats, and desires. Taking interest in emotions, without judgment or control, can help the coach cultivate more disclosure and be more aware of obstacles or resistances to change.

PROVIDING A RATIONALE

Because change can often be threatening, it is especially important that coaches offer a *rationale* for any activity they suggest that a client might undertake. It is hard for people to be autonomously motivated unless they have clear reasons to act. Providing a rationale thus helps support autonomous motivation. Indeed, it is important that clients be encouraged to ask questions, give voice to ambivalence, and express doubts or confusions. Creating an atmosphere in which questions are prized and respected is a strong support for feelings of autonomy.

ACKNOWLEDGING FEELINGS OF RESISTANCE

Because coaching inevitably raises tough issues that can prompt resistance, moments of conflict and defensiveness are inevitable. Rather than either contradicting or downplaying such experiences, need-supportive coaches embrace and welcome their expression. Indeed, SDT research suggests better internalization when obstacles to change are acknowledged (e.g., Koestner, Ryan, Bierneri, & Holt, 1984). Responding with concern or compassion rather than judgment is truly connecting, especially in the face of distress and ambivalence, as well as unhappiness with change. Empathically embracing resistances is also strategic in that it often allows the strongest barriers to coaching work to become more fully expressed and understood. From the SDT perspective, if a client is balking at change, accepting and *moving toward* the resistance is critical in order to both grasp its significance and develop a collaborative effort to overcome it.

Providing Choice

The term "choice," as used in SDT, does not mean simply making decisions or having options. SDT interprets the term differently, as meaning that people optimally experience a sense of choice and endorsement about what they are doing—that is, they feel volitional when acting. Awareness is what allows people to make a decision that is a true choice. This implies, of course, that facilitating choice is not simply about offering options to clients; rather, facilitating choice means providing the support that allows clients to home in on what they value, and choose actions congruent with that awareness. Coaches and clients can collaboratively devise a course of action, review options, and openly embrace decisions, even decisions not to change.

Avoiding Controlling Pressures, Including Conditional Approval

Controlling motivational techniques undermine clients' autonomy and willingness to be engaged. Thus, in counseling or coaching others, any "rewards" that are employed should be minimal and symbolic—that is, focused on being informational and acknowledging progress rather than representing incentives or sanctions. Similarly, there are many interpersonal forms of control to be avoided. It is especially important for coaches to watch for statements conveying contingent approval or judgments. In other words, it is essential not to convey either disapproval or approval of a client based on what he or she does. Coaches can use informational statements focused on rationales for goals and affirmation of a behavior rather than statements that contain "oughts" or "musts" or that evaluate individuals. That is, by providing the empathetic perspective-taking of autonomy support rather than the positive guidance of direct support, coaches can promote autonomous motivation, greater goal attainment, and enhanced relationships. In short, when it comes to pursuing life goals, what most people want is autonomy support rather than direction, advice, or control.

Need-Supportive Limit Setting

There are cases in coaching situations in which setting limits is essential. Limits in coaching can involve time spent, boundaries of work, and demands from clients for help or support. Setting limits in these sensitive areas is important to a workable arrangement, but the way in which the limits are set is very important. Limits can be set in autonomy-supportive or controlling ways (Koestner et al., 1984). SDT articulates a multistep approach to limit setting that entails: (a) being clear about the limit; (b) providing a meaningful rationale for its imposition; (c) acknowledging and being empathic about conflicts with or resistance to the limit, and (d) providing options or choices. In other words, it proposes an autonomy-supportive approach to limit setting.

AUTONOMY SUPPORT ENCOURAGES INTEGRATION— EVEN OF DIFFICULT EXPERIENCES

Autonomy support is conducive to more integrative processing, encouraging the clients' use of their reflective capacities, emotional awareness, ownership of actions, and depth of processing. Illustrating this is a set of experiments in which Weinstein, Deci, and Ryan (2011) examined participants' autonomy in integrating past negative identities into their current sense of self. Participants were asked to recall two past identities—one a personal characteristic and the other a significant life event—with some participants being asked to recall positive past identities and some, negative ones. In *autonomy-supportive conditions,* participants were likely to be accepting of both positive and negative life events, to see these past characteristics as meaningful, and to be more prone to take a first-person or "ownership" perspective toward the events. In contrast, in the *controlled conditions,* participants were accepting of and took a first-person perspective only on events that were positive, and were more psychologically distanced from the negative characteristics. That is, they were much more defended against negative past material and were less able to integrate it into their current sense of self. There are considerable costs to such defensiveness. Weinstein et al. (2011) showed that greater integration of positive and negative past identities predicted more vitality, meaning in life, and satisfaction in relationships, as well as higher well-being, relative to a defensive focus only on the positive and away from the negative. Such findings highlight the intrapersonal conditions associated with integrative change.

RELATEDNESS-SUPPORTIVE TECHNIQUES

People are more willing to internalize ideas and inputs from people to whom they feel relatedness, and relatedness provides a sense of security for moving forward that is especially important in the often-rigid and conflicted areas of personal change. Of course, almost every school of coaching agrees that rapport and a therapeutic alliance are important, and SDT specifies how to foster such relatedness.

UNCONDITIONAL POSITIVE REGARD AND TAKING INTEREST IN THE PERSON

Unconditional positive regard (UCPR) is a concept that was originally introduced by Rogers (1957) as one of his "necessary and sufficient" ingredients in effective counseling. UCPR means that clients are accepted and valued non-contingently; they are positively valued regardless of what they experience. Studies in SDT on parenting have shown the importance of UCPR for the development of autonomous motivation (e.g., Roth, Assor, Niemiec, Ryan, & Deci, 2009). Similar patterns apply in counseling contexts. In fact, Zuroff, Koestner, Moskowitz, McBride, and Bagby (2012) showed that autonomy support, characterized by therapists' acceptance and empathy, fostered greater therapeutic alliance, and accordingly predicted greater gains in a study of therapists treating depression. UCPR facilitates not only autonomy satisfaction (because it is non-controlling) but also relatedness satisfaction, fostering a sense of caring and connection irrespective of outcomes.

Being interested in a client allows a coach to regard the client unconditionally and to relate to him or her more genuinely. Coaches who can be curious and engaged in the client's thoughts, perceptions, and experiences are likely to be met with more trust, more energy, and more satisfaction in the relationship.

AUTHENTICITY AND TRANSPARENCY

Coaches' authenticity within a coaching relationship is critical, but often misunderstood. Authenticity does not mean coaches share all their feelings with clients, but instead it means being honest when expressing concern, interest, and openness. It means reflectively sharing with the client perceptions and experiences that the coach judges to be important and meaningful for the client. It is also important that it be done in a way in which coaches *fully accept* their own experiences and do not blame the client for his or her own behaviors or feelings.

It is clear in discussing these relatedness-supportive elements in coaching that they overlap considerably with autonomy support. This, of course, goes back to our theory about relatedness satisfactions: They derive from the sense that another supports the person's self. When coaches are accepting of clients as the clients truly are, both autonomy and relatedness will be promoted.

COMPETENCE-SUPPORTIVE TECHNIQUES AND THE PROVISION OF STRUCTURE

Having feedback and guidance, rather than control or directives, can help a person feel more purposive and confident in bringing about potential changes. In contexts where the focus is on specific behavioral outcomes, skill building, as well as efficacy-relevant information and feedback, are nearly always useful. But presenting feedback can be precarious, especially to the extent that recipients experience being controlled or pressured. Accordingly, supports for the competence need must be provided within a context of autonomy support. Among facilitators of competence are the following.

IDENTIFYING BARRIERS AND OBSTACLES

Helping clients identify barriers to personal or professional change is critical to competence promotion. Sometimes the most formidable barriers are ones only vaguely understood by the client, so working to clarify and accept them as they are encountered is important and supportive. In the process, it is crucial that the coach be wholly accepting of the client's barriers so the client will gradually move toward the acceptance as a step in the direction of change.

GOAL SETTING: PROXIMAL AND DISTAL

Goal setting can be an important ingredient to motivating change, but only if: (a) the goals are truly self-endorsed or autonomous; and (b) the pathways to goal progress are clear, mapped out, and within reach. These latter aspects concern the implementation of *structure*, defined in SDT as clarity of goals and scaffolding of tasks such that success is an ongoing proximal outcome, and these proximal successes build toward distal goals and accomplishments.

Goal setting is particularly informed by the concept of *optimal challenges*. "Optimal" within SDT means challenges that are not trivially easy but can nonetheless be readily mastered with persistence. They are also not overly stressful or demanding. Accordingly, it is important for coaches to be attuned to the levels of challenge for which clients are ready, and accordingly to tailor interventions to the client's capacities. For clients lacking confidence, more proximal goals, reached through small, achievable steps, may help build perceived competence. For others, too easy or too proximal a goal set may leave them feeling underestimated or underchallenged, interfering with perceived competence. When goals are optimal, the client will have deliberated and made autonomous decisions about the goals and then considered how best to achieve them.

Promoting an Internal Locus of Evaluation

When clients are engaged in change-oriented activities, they can typically monitor their own progress, skill level, and performance. Being both the doer and the evaluator can be an empowering activity (because one is not being externally judged), and it is also a competence builder, because assessment involves observation and identification of both skill gaps and mastery. Done in a way that is autonomy-supportive toward oneself, self-monitoring is not *self-evaluative*—it is instead *self-informative*. When coaches maintain a non-judgmental, informational approach to feedback, they will be promoting informative self-monitoring by the clients.

Offering Rich, Clear, Effectance-Relevant Feedback

Expressing confidence in clients' accomplishments and efforts is useful, but beyond that, relevant and informational feedback (e.g., on goal progress) is especially important when specific behavior changes are a focus. Competence supports include communication of structure, strategy options, feedback, and clarity of limits. When feedback is provided, it is crucial that it be focused on behaviors and not persons. And to be effective, the feedback must not be imposed but rather offered by the coach or invited by the client. Reactions to feedback, which so often can engender internal criticism when negative, are specifically elicited and empathically considered. Any lack of success or progress is treated informationally—as revealing barriers or obstacles—rather than as a judgment on the client, and can be used to support the client's problem solving about how to handle such situations in the future.

Encouraging Reflection and Providing Relevant Information

Coaches appropriately examine, in a collaborative way, the costs and benefits of changes that the clients are considering. This means encouraging them to reflect authentically on their choices and behaviors. In so doing, coaches, as facilitators of change, may be "experts" who have important information relevant to the clients' goals. Coaches need not withhold such information, but they need to be cautious and thoughtful in providing it. Critical in this regard is the distinction between the *informational* and the *controlling* aspects of any feedback or inputs. The true intent of information is to enhance the person's authentic range of choices. That is, expert inputs are meant to inform rather than to lead. At the same time, they can support competence, helping the client to identify misconceptions about his or her situation or behaviors and to understand available options in an accessible, open-minded manner.

ORGANISMIC INTEGRATION

All of the techniques described above reflect SDT's basic assumption of an inherent developmental propensity, referred to as the *organismic integration process*, through which growth and well-being occur. SDT maintains that the interpersonal processes detailed throughout describe supports for effective organismic integration, leading to positive development over time.

BASIC PSYCHOLOGICAL NEED SATISFACTION AND FRUSTRATION IN EVERYDAY LIFE

Having talked about some of the critical need-supportive elements in the coaching relationship, we now elaborate some additional issues that are salient in the SDT approach. As noted earlier, SDT claims that "not all goals are created equal" (Ryan, Sheldon, Kasser, & Deci, 1996), for some are likely to fulfill basic psychological needs and promote well-being, whereas others, even when achieved, are likely to frustrate basic needs, and yield ill-being.

Paying attention to both the contexts of people's lives and the contents of their goals are key ways coaches can identify sources of both fulfilment and frustration. Where basic psychological needs are being neglected or thwarted in clients' work situations, lifestyles, close relationships, or habitual behaviors, it would be important for coaches to address it. For example, when people get caught up in extrinsic life goals such as the accumulation of wealth that do not satisfy basic psychological needs (Vansteenkiste & Ryan, 2013) as opposed to growth, intimacy, and generativity, there is likely work to be done. Listening to clients' aspirations and strivings can thus be helpful in supporting integration and wellness.

SDT also emphasizes that not only is the pursuit of extrinsic goals problematic, so can be their attainment. Exemplifying this was a recent large scale-study of lawyers in the United States by Sheldon and Krieger (2014). These investigators sampled thousands of lawyers and divided them into groups. One group was *service lawyers*, who pursued careers in law primarily to advocate for justice or social causes (i.e., intrinsic aspirations). A second group was the *money lawyers*, whose focus in practice was on attaining wealth and financial success (the extrinsic aspirations). Although service lawyers had much lower incomes, they also experienced greater well-being and less negative affect compared to money lawyers, and they drank less alcohol and did so less often than did money lawyers. Analyses showed that these effects were independent of income, years of work experience, class rank, and even self-rated values, suggesting that the job contexts, which differed in their intrinsic and extrinsic goal emphases, accounted for these results. The money lawyers may have gotten what they wished for, but it did not yield positive experiences and psychological well-being.

FOSTERING AWARENESS AND MINDFULNESS

Cultivating mindfulness, interest taking, and integrative processing of events is another key device in any coach's toolbox (Deci, Ryan, Schultz, & Niemiec, 2015). There are, of course, many techniques for raising awareness, some of which are basic, such as using reflection or mirroring the client's affect and content. When a coach uses closed questions (i.e., yes/no questions), it can make the coach seem like the person in control, but a coach using open questions accompanied by reflections offers more opportunities for deeper exploration. Further, encouraging *integrative processing* by guiding clients toward a nonjudgmental, curious, attention to internal and external events and experiences is likely to promote mindful interest-taking.

From the time we began developing SDT, we have argued for a strong role for relaxed and interested awareness in promoting autonomy and self-regulation. *Mindfulness* practices can be a route to developing such relaxed interest. Mindfulness is defined as the open, receptive awareness of what is occurring (Brown & Ryan, 2003). It allows people to contact information from both internal sources (perceptions, feelings, and values) and external events, and to use this information to come to a clear focus and gain a sense of what, all things considered, one would most value doing.

The power of mindfulness to clarify goals and support autonomous regulation has been confirmed in numerous studies. For example, Brown and Ryan (2003) found that people higher in mindfulness had better access to their emotional states, were more vital and autonomously motivated, and showed greater congruence between implicit and explicit emotions. Similarly, Niemiec et al. (2010) found that people with more mindful awareness responded less defensively to threats, suggesting that more mindful awareness can be considered an important underpinning for mental health and well-being.

Fostering awareness may be accomplished through mindfulness training by coaches. Yet even more often, awareness is facilitated by coaches or therapists being autonomy-supportive and encouraging clients' interest-taking in their own internal processes. By listening and eliciting, coaches increase clients' awareness and integrative spans. Mindful awareness, in turn, supports the organismic integration process by fostering a fuller acknowledgment of the often-divided feelings and goals one has, so the parts can be brought into coherence and harmony with one another.

AUTONOMY AS A GOAL FOR COACHING

Prescriptions from SDT that advocate providing autonomy support, fostering relatedness, and enhancing competence may sound either obvious or easy. Yet our involvement in counseling and coaching, as well as the supervision and training of many consultants and counselors, has taught us how hard it can be to be responsive to clients' basic psychological needs. To provide unconditional positive regard, for example, requires setting aside personal biases and agendas and, most especially, ego involvements in the outcomes of coaching.

Maintaining a freedom from controlling agendas and ego involvements is especially problematic within organizations in which specific outcomes *for the client or coach* are being contingently evaluated or controlled. The more a setting has high stakes and outcome pressures, the more likely it is that the coaches will themselves become outcome focused and then, all too often though not necessarily, more controlling in their approach. Practitioners have to be aware of and monitor their own goals, being sure they do not bring any pressures of their own into the relationships with their clients.

From the SDT viewpoint, the ultimate goal of coaching would never be simply attaining a specific behavioral benchmark or goal. Instead, the ultimate outcome is that of facilitating clients' abilities to make informed and reflective choices about their life challenges and aims. Supporting autonomy and competence is supporting the fundamental human capabilities for living a full life, within which a person effectively pursues what really matters to him or her. Through engagement in autonomy-supportive coaching, people re-evaluate, in a nonjudgmental atmosphere, what they are pursuing, and as a result they are likely to become even more self-motivated and integrated, and to experience their engagement as more authentic and vital.

TOWARD A CONCEPTION OF A FULLY FUNCTIONING PERSON

We began this discussion of SDT and coaching by highlighting their common aims: facilitating optimal functioning, better performance, and wellness. Coaching specifically aims at helping individuals maximally actualize their potentials both in work and in life. It is deeply allied with the goals of positive psychology that are not simply about remediating problems, but rather expanding competencies and satisfactions.

In SDT, there is a specific vision of what it means to be fully functioning. Whereas some psychologists have equated the idea of well-being with *happiness* (i.e., the presence of positive affect and the absence of negative affect; Kahneman, Krueger, Schkade, Schwarz, & Stone, 2006), SDT suggests that happiness and hedonic self-interest per se do not constitute a full definition of well-being (Ryan, Curren, & Deci, 2013). At the same time, we think that happiness is a *symptom* of wellness because it typically accompanies basic psychological need satisfaction, which is the basis for wellness (Ryan et al., 2013).

Critical to defining well-being in SDT is considering the functions and processes through which happiness might come about. For us, a truly good life, a *eudemonic* life, is to be found in the expression of human excellence and virtue. A good life is one in which the person does well at that which is *worth* doing (Ryan et al., 2013). What is interesting about this view is that it is critical: It says that some pathways of living will be more effective than others at yielding rich satisfactions. Living well—that is, experiencing eudaimonia—comprises a more fulfilling life, one likely to yield a sense of meaning and purpose, as well as happiness. In line with this, SDT emphasizes that living well satisfies the *basic psychological needs* necessary for *full functioning*, and that such living is characterized by vitality, awareness, exercise of capacities, and self-regulation. A fully functioning person is aware of both inner needs and outer circumstances and is open to, and welcoming of, change. When in need-supportive contexts, people will also tend to report more happiness, lower anxiety, depression, and defensiveness, and fewer somatic complaints.

Every individual faces a different set of obstacles in development, including both internal characteristics (e.g., temperament, disabilities) and external circumstances (e.g., social constraints, poverty). Although each of these issues can be considered in its own right, within SDT we focus on how such issues impact one's capacity to get core psychological needs fulfilled. This simply reflects the central proposition of SDT that *failure to satisfy any of these three needs results in diminished growth, integrity, and wellness.*

For example, consider a study of investment banking employees (Baard, Deci, & Ryan, 2004). In it we found that when these bank employees had higher levels of satisfaction of their autonomy, competence, and relatedness needs in the workplace, they also showed enhanced vitality and lower anxiety and somatization. As well, they performed better, adding to the profitability of their organizations.

Extending this idea, Ryan, Bernstein, and Brown (2010) obtained multiple daily reports from adult workers in various careers. When work experiences were associated with basic need satisfactions, multiple indicators of psychological wellness were enhanced—including positive affect and vitality, and lower reports of negative affect and physical symptoms of stress.

What is clear is that facilitating wellness involves finding ways to experience more autonomy, competence, and relatedness in everyday life, and engaging in the kinds of life goals and pursuits likely to yield these satisfactions. It also means gaining awareness of the ways in which these satisfactions are getting blocked or thwarted, so one can remove the obstacles to healthy functioning.

THE SDT MODEL FOR COACHING

To summarize, an SDT approach to coaching emphasizes that a facilitative coaching context can be created by supporting satisfaction of clients' basic psychological needs for competence, autonomy, and relatedness. These need supports help clients both reflect upon and then commit to goals they can most authentically pursue. We also discussed how relatively stronger intrinsic versus extrinsic aspirations can contribute to both more autonomous motivation and wellness outcomes. Each of these can contribute to autonomous motivation and fuller functioning. Both basic psychological need satisfaction and autonomous motivation account for independent variance in optimal outcomes, which include psychological wellness, effective behaving, enhanced mindfulness, more organizational citizenship, and satisfaction in one's job, relationships, and leisure activities, all of which constitute a more fully functioning life. This can be seen schematically in Figure 20.1.

We have provided but a bird's eye view of the SDT model and its applicability to coaching, but our hope is that the model will become further developed within the coaching profession to address both the abiding and varied issues and concerns faced in each project by coaches.

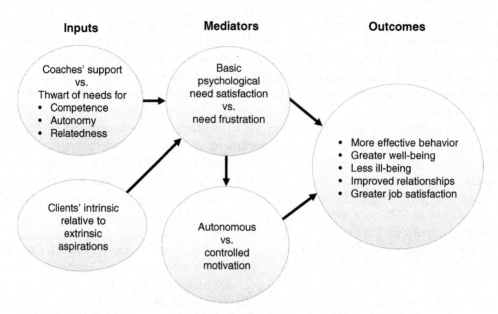

Figure 20.1 Self-determination theory (SDT) model of the processes of basic psychological need satisfaction/frustration and types of motivation that mediate the relations from contextual and individual difference inputs to coaching outcomes.

REFERENCES

Baard, P. P., Deci, E. L., & Ryan, R. M. (2004). Intrinsic need satisfaction: A motivational basis of performance and well-being in two work settings. *Journal of Applied Social Psychology, 34*, 2045–2068. doi:10.1111/j.1559-1816.2004.tb02690.x

Brown, K. W. & Ryan, R. M. (2003). The benefits of being present: Mindfulness and its role in psychological well-being. *Journal of Personality and Social Psychology, 84*(4), 822–848. doi:10.1037/0022-3514.84.4.822

Chen, B., Vansteenkiste, M., Beyers, W., Boone, L., Deci, E. L., Van der Kaap-Deeder, J., . . . Verstuyf, J. (2015). Basic psychological need satisfaction, need frustration, and need strength across four cultures. *Motivation and Emotion, 39*(2), 216–236. doi:10.1007/s11031-014-9450-1

Deci, E. L., Connell, J. P., & Ryan, R. M. (1989). Self-determination in a work organization. *Journal of Applied Psychology, 74*, 580–590. doi:10.1037/0021-9010.74.4.580

Deci, E. L., Olafsen, A. H., & Ryan, R. M. (2017). Self-determination theory in work organizations: The state of a science. *Annual Review of Organizational Psychology and Organizational Behavior, 4*(1), 19–43. doi:10.1146/annurev-orgpsych-032516-113108

Deci, E. L., Ryan, R. M., Schultz, P. P., & Niemiec, C. P. (2015). Being aware and functioning fully: Mindfulness and interest-taking within self-determination theory. In K. W. Brown, R. M. Ryan, & J. D. Creswell (Eds.), *Handbook of mindfulness*. New York, NY: Guilford Press.

Hardré, P. L., & Reeve, J. (2009). Training corporate managers to adopt a more autonomy support- ive motivating style toward employees: An intervention study. *International Journal of Train- ing and Development, 13*(3), 165–184. doi:10.1111/j.1468-2419.2009.00325.x

Kahneman, D., Krueger, A. B., Schkade, D., Schwarz, N., & Stone, A. A. (2006). Would you be happier if you were richer? A focusing illusion. *Science, 312*(5782), 1908–1910. doi:10.1126/ science.1129688

Kasser, T., & Ryan, R. M. (1996). Further examining the American dream: Differential correlates of intrinsic and extrinsic goals. *Personality and Social Psychology Bulletin, 22*(3), 280–287. doi:10.1177/0146167296223006

Koestner, R., Ryan, R. M., Bernieri, F., & Holt, K. (1984). Setting limits on children's behavior: The differential effects of controlling versus informational styles on intrinsic motivation and creativity. *Journal of Personality, 52*, 233–248. doi:10.1111/j.1467-6494.1984.tb00879.x

Ng, J. Y. Y., Ntoumanis, N., Thøgersen-Ntoumani, C., Deci, E. L., Ryan, R. M., Duda, J., & Williams, G. C. (2012). Self-determination theory applied to health contexts: A meta-analysis. *Perspectives on Psychological Science, 7*, 325–340. doi:10.1177/1745691612447309

Niemiec, C. P., Brown, K. W., Kashdan, T. B., Cozzolino, P. J., Breen, W. E., Levesque-Bristol, C., & Ryan, R. M. (2010). Being present in the face of existential threat: The role of trait mindfulness in reducing defensive responses to mortality salience. *Journal of Personality and Social Psychology, 99*(2), 344–365. doi:10.1037/a0019388

Rogers, C. R. (1957). *On becoming a person.* Boston, MA: Houghton Mifflin.

Roth, G., Assor, A., Niemiec, C. P., Ryan, R. M., & Deci, E. L. (2009). The emotional and academic consequences of parental conditional regard: Comparing conditional positive regard, conditional negative regard, and autonomy support as parenting practices. *Developmental Psychology, 45*, 1119–1142. doi:10.1037/a0015272

Ryan, R. M., Bernstein, J. H., & Brown, K. W. (2010). Weekends, work, and wellbeing: Psychological need satisfactions and day of the week effects on mood, vitality, and physical symptoms. *Journal of Social and Clinical Psychology, 29*(1), 95–122. doi:10.1521/jscp.2010.29.1.95

Ryan, R. M., Curren, R. R., & Deci, E. L. (2013). What humans need: Flourishing in Aristotelian philosophy and self-determination theory. In A. S. Waterman (Ed.), *The best within us: Positive psychology perspectives on eudaimonic functioning* (pp. 57–75). Washington, DC: American Psychological Association.

Ryan, R. M., & Deci, E. L. (2017). *Self-determination theory: Basic psychological needs in motivation, development, and wellness.* New York, NY: Guilford Press.

Ryan, R. M., Lynch, M. F., Vansteenkiste, M., & Deci, E. L. (2011). Motivation and autonomy in counseling, psychotherapy, and behavior change: A look at theory and practice. *The Counseling Psychologist, 39*, 193–260. doi:10.1177/0011000009359313

Ryan, R. M., Patrick, H., Deci, E. L., & Williams, G. C. (2008). Facilitating health behavior change and its maintenance: Interventions based on self-determination theory. *The European Health Psychologist, 10*, 2–5.

Ryan, R. M., Sheldon, K. M., Kasser, T., & Deci, E. L. (1996). All goals are not created equal: An organismic perspective on the nature of goals and their regulation. In P. M. Gollwitzer & J. A. Bargh (Eds.), *The psychology of action: Linking cognition and motivation to behavior* (pp. 7–26). New York, NY: Guilford.

Sheldon, K. M., & Krieger, L. S. (2014). Service job lawyers are happier than money job lawyers, despite their lower income. *Journal of Positive Psychology, 9*(3), 219–226. doi:10.1080/17439760.2014.888583

Vansteenkiste, M., & Ryan, R. M. (2013). On psychological growth and vulnerability: Basic psychological need satisfaction and need frustration as a unifying principle. *Journal of Psychotherapy Integration, 23*(3), 263–280. doi:10.1037/a0032359

Weinstein, N., Deci, E. L., & Ryan, R. M. (2011). Motivational determinants of integrating positive and negative past identities. *Journal of Personality and Social Psychology, 100*, 527–544. doi:10.1037/a0022150

Weinstein, N., & Ryan, R. M. (2010). When helping helps: Autonomous motivation for prosocial behavior and its influence on well-being for the helper and recipient. *Journal of Personality and Social Psychology, 98*(2), 222–244. doi:10.1037/a0016984

Zuroff, D. C., Koestner, R., Moskowitz, D. S., McBride, C., & Bagby, R. M. (2012). Therapist's autonomy support and patient's self-criticism predict motivation during brief treatments for depression. *Journal of Social and Clinical Psychology, 31*, 903–932. doi:10.1521/jscp.2012.31.9.903

21

Maturity Coaching: Enabling Vertical Development in Leaders

Beena Sharma

Coaching has undergone a rapid and astonishing revolution in the past few decades. The field has dramatically advanced in its power to help people reach what might have seemed impossible to them at the start of their journey toward becoming better leaders, parents, professionals, teams, and even organizations. The early practices of coaching can be traced to the long-established training of athletes, to children who struggled with math, and royalty needing personalized tutoring in public speaking. Today, coaching has transformed into a dizzying array of possibilities, serving many purposes in varied contexts. Coaching theories, their applications, the toolkits, and the competencies that coaches need to be effective in enabling individual and whole-system transformation have all multiplied exponentially.

One of the more recent evolutions in coaching practice relates to the number-one trend identified in the field of leadership for the next decade: *vertical development* (Petrie, 2011). This chapter focuses on the importance of including vertical development as a critical dimension in the current discourse around leadership learning and development. It makes a case for a new discipline in coaching, informed and guided by what we know about the evolutionary growth of adults through their lifetimes.

Research shows that adult development occurs in two fundamentally different ways: *horizontal* and *vertical* (Cook-Greuter, 2004). I imagine that coaches who can discern both of these processes in their clients are better equipped to enable transformative change. To help readers understand vertical development, I outline the Leadership Maturity Framework developed over the last five decades. I briefly describe "maturity coaching"—a comprehensive methodology that incorporates theory, measurement, and a well-developed practice with a distinct set of guidelines and interventions to facilitate greater maturity in adults. Maturity coaching can be applied as an advanced "lens," overlaid on any coaching methodology. When applied, it aims to address identity-related issues that can limit growth. It enables shifts in meaning-making that can also lead to further growth of perspectives, in line with the universally applicable evolutionary trajectory described by research.

This chapter discusses how a coach can facilitate greater maturity in adults by applying the knowledge of vertical development to *tailor* their coaching to the client's "stage" of development. I propose that *developmentally* informed coaching interventions can address deeper personality patterns, hidden aspects of inner life, belief systems, assumptions, and life stances that might escape other ways of coaching without this perspective. Additionally, I propose that coaches, aware of their own "level" of evolution in terms of their ability to observe their own hidden patterns, question their beliefs, and take larger perspectives, are likely to generate more powerful and compelling coaching experiences resulting in greater self-awareness and wisdom in their clients.

ABOUT VERTICAL DEVELOPMENT

Generally, evolutionary processes manifest through recognizable stages or levels of unfolding, where each stage can be distinguished from what came before and what comes after. Each movement is seen as part of a set of ordered dynamics based on an intrinsic logic of change, progress, advancement, or expansion. *The American Heritage Dictionary* ("Evolution," 2012) defines evolution as:

A gradual process in which something changes into a different and usually more complex or better form. (Copyright© 2012 by Houghton Mifflin Harcourt Publishing Company. Reprinted by permission of Houghton Mifflin Harcourt Publishing Company. All rights reserved.)

This is true of human development, as well (even as the criteria for what constitutes advancement change).

Multiple research studies show a gradual evolution of perspectives and maturity in adults throughout their lifespans (Cook-Greuter, 1999; Graves, 1981; Gilligan, 1982; Kegan, 1980; Loevinger, 1997).

As human beings grow, they go through fundamental shifts in how they comprehend and respond to life's challenges. These shifts occur in definable stages. With each stage, they learn wiser ways of being by expanding the depth and breadth of what they perceive and believe. Earlier stages are characterized by a narrow, static, constraint-driven, protective stance. As a result of formal and informal learning through life experiences, people develop new worldviews, each one a milestone in their development. A broader, more dynamic, context-driven, exploratory perspective characterizes the later stages of adult development. This process of growth into greater maturity is called "vertical development," and is a transformative process over the lifespan of an adult.

Horizontal development, in contrast to vertical development, relates to the acquisition and organization of knowledge and building new skills—without necessarily shifting one's mental models or level of self-awareness. In horizontal development, conditioned and chosen assumptions remain intact. Adults continue to learn and grow in diverse ways, without any fundamental shift in their identity or worldview. Responses to challenges follow tried and tested methods without any significant expansion of perspectives or modification of beliefs about self or others.

In general, before research revealed the structures underlying different stages of maturity, individual differences were usually understood to relate to different traits, preferences, strengths, competencies, and so forth, that were seen as different "styles" of behavior. No one style was seen to be better than another. It was important to be aware of one's style, to know how to interact optimally with other styles, how to be less fixed in one's style, and how to skillfully adapt one's style to context. With the advent of vertical development, we have a new set of differences to incorporate into our understanding. People are different not just in their style and skill, but also in their *stage* of development.

THEORIES OF VERTICAL DEVELOPMENT

Several theories describe this upward trajectory of human development. While each theory emphasizes different aspects, they are all based on research supporting the idea of development through an invariant sequence of stages. For example, Maslow's theory focuses on human needs (what do I *need*?), Kohlberg and Gilligan called out moral development (what should I *do*?), Piaget and Kegan explored cognition (what am I *aware* of?), and Graves explored the emergence of values over time (what do I *value*?). The various theories also differ in the number of stages delineated and where major milestones lie in the overall trajectory. Also, it is significant that not all theories have a current, peer-reviewed, validated, and evolving psychometric or measurement methodology that reflects the most up-to-date and theoretically sound descriptors for each stage of development.

For the past 14 years, I have focused on a particular theory of vertical development that strikes me as the most comprehensive, and that carries the most explanatory power. I work with ego development theory, which answers the questions: "Who am I?" and "What matters most?" Ego development theory is empirically based, and goes hand-in-hand with the most widely researched and validated measurement methodology—perhaps its greatest strength.

EGO DEVELOPMENT THEORY

Dr. Jane Loevinger first developed ego development theory in the 1960s, using the measurement called Washington University Sentence Completion Test (WUSCT; Loevinger, 1969). In the 1990s, Dr. Susanne Cook-Greuter considerably advanced the theory with the discovery of new stages at the higher end of the developmental spectrum (Cook-Greuter, 1999). Dr. Cook-Greuter built on the WUSCT and constructed new manuals, categories, and rules for rating with her updated instrument, the Maturity Profile (MAP). Multiple studies support the validity and reliability of this measurement methodology, which makes the MAP instrument currently the most reliable way to assess adult development.

Ego development theory describes how human beings construct their understanding of themselves and the world by making meaning of life experiences. The "ego" is a central construct in this theory, and is defined as the aspect of the self that constructs meaning by metabolizing life experiences. It then tells a story about the self and the world, which continues to evolve throughout life.

The ego's meaning-making process results in established beliefs and stories about the self, others, and the world that serve as orienting worldviews, providing clarity and certainty. Through new experiences that conflict with one's customary and long-held beliefs, new belief structures evolve to accommodate emergent realities. A newer worldview replaces the old, providing comfort and value in the light of new conditions. This new worldview now influences responses to current and future experiences. Research shows that across the lifespan of an adult, several such reorganizations can take place, where each stage of meaning-making is distinguishable from the next. Each stage of development offers broader perspectives, greater depth of mind and heart, and is more adequate to all of life than the one before. Each stage also presents new challenges including the loss of what was previously held dearly.

TENETS OF VERTICAL DEVELOPMENT

Studies of adult development from earlier to later stages of maturity reveal characteristics that apply to all vertical development, regardless of the particular theory:

- All human beings actively make sense of experience, establishing and operating from a worldview based on their sense-making.

- As adults continue to grow through a vertical development process, their worldviews evolve over time.

- These successive worldviews are described as "stages" of maturity, and follow a logical sequence, creating a hierarchy of stages over a lifetime.

- These worldviews are stable, but temporary, stations that evolve based on life conditions, internal resources, and external support.

- Not everyone grows through the full trajectory of development.

- People tend to "settle" into or "peak" at the stage of development most suitable for their internal world and external circumstances; this can become their permanent station in life.

- The stage sequence is invariant—no one can skip a stage of development.

- Earlier stages are characterized by a narrow, simple, concrete, static, constraint-driven, protective stance.

- Later stages are characterized by a broader, complex, abstract, dynamic, context-driven, exploratory stance.

- Those at earlier stages cannot understand later stages.

- Individuals at later stages can recognize and grasp earlier-stage perspectives; they may reject them or include them by choice.

• It can (and almost always does) take several years to move from one stage of maturity to the next, depending on internal and external support available.

THE MATURITY FRAMEWORK

We use the term "maturity" to describe the concept of expanding adult development. Our Leadership Maturity Framework defines and codifies the characteristics of maturity at various stages of adult development.

UNDERSTANDING THE STAGES OF MATURITY

The eight stages of the Leadership Maturity Framework, along with the key ego drivers at each stage, are given in Table 21.1.

To illustrate that each stage is more evolved than the previous, I offer one example describing how each stage answers the question "What matters most?" (Table 21.2). Clearly, each successive stage embraces greater complexity, depth, breadth, and dynamism.

MEASURING LEVELS OF MATURITY

The MAP instrument assesses a person's evolution of perspectives and overall maturity on a vertical transformation scale described by the Leadership Maturity Framework.

The MAP is a semi-projective written test—a kind of "verbal Rorschach," where the responses to sentence stems reveal a person's meaning-making. A certified scorer then interprets these responses and creates the client's unique developmental profile. The projective aspect of this psychometric instrument, where the respondent simply writes responses, has two benefits. One, it considerably reduces the risk

Table 21.1 Leadership Maturity Framework

Stage Number	Stage Name	Key Drivers at Stage
2/3	Self-Centric	Getting and Defending
3	Group-Centric	Conforming and Belonging
3/4	Skill-Centric	Comparing and Perfecting
4	Self-Determining	Analyzing and Achieving
4/5	Self-Questioning	Relativizing and Contextualizing
5	Self-Actualizing	Integrating and Transforming
5/6	Construct-Aware	Noticing Constructs and Ego Traps
6	Unitive	All-Embracing and Witnessing

Note: The numbers in Table 21.1 conform to the original numbering protocol used by Loevinger.

Table 21.2 What Matters Most?—Description by Stage

2/3	Own immediate needs, self-protection
3	Approval, acceptance; rules and norms
3/4	Craft expertise, procedures, and efficiency
4	Goal setting, achievement and effectiveness, objectivity, contractual agreements
4/5	Self-discovery, questioning system
5	Linking theory and principles with practice, dynamic systems interactions
5/6	Interplay of awareness, thought, action, and effects; transforming self and others
6	Nonevaluative, integrative witnessing of ongoing process of living

of exaggerated self-appraisal, a feature common in qualitative self-assessments. Two, by gathering spontaneous and unmediated projective responses, it eliminates interviewer bias that can color interpretations of the developmental stage.

Both the theory and the measurement instrument have a long research history and enjoy primacy in the field of constructive developmental theory by virtue of the rigorous scientific testing behind their creation (Loevinger & Wissler, 1978). Also significant is the ongoing statistical and qualitative analysis that continues to inform both the theory and the measurement methodology.

The MAP report provides the operating stage or "center of gravity" of the client and points out the unique aspects of the sentence structure, interprets major themes, preoccupations, and concerns expressed by the individual in a fine-tuned, tailored manner. The MAP is unlike some other development measures that equate higher development with people's increasing capacity for complex reasoning—which is only one aspect (although one of the core aspects) of human maturity. The MAP is unique in offering individuals a chance for deeper understanding of their meaning-making in multiple areas as an adult. It identifies the growth potential and expected challenges at each stage of the developmental journey.

MATURITY COACHING

All coaching can enable learning. However, not all coaching shifts meaning-making and leads to stage development.

With successful coaching using any of the multiple approaches available today, people can be helped to be more efficient and effective in their day-to-day functioning. They can gather new information, develop new skills, and do a better job. Yet, they may never get to challenge their assumptions, never get to question their own perspective, or realize their own conditioning. These aspects of growth are harder won. This kind of growth happens more deliberately as a result of coaching informed by ego development theory, which facilitates a level of self-questioning that goes beyond mere goal-setting and action-planning, and addresses sense-making. Real change becomes more accessible when an individual advances up the ladder of maturity. It increases the individual's level of self-awareness, enables him or her to acknowledge conditioning and to take a perspective on the story the individual tells himself or herself. The individual now has the inner resources to actively inquire into his or her identifications until they drop naturally as part of the process of growth. The individual arrives at a new temporary station.

Many factors influence the natural movement to greater maturity in adults. These variables include personality patterns and preferences; talent and attitude; one's needs, values, goals, and aspirations; early formative experiences; family, work, and life context; formal and informal learning; structured experiences such as workshops, individual therapy, or deliberate practices; and influence of significant relationships both positive or negative, supportive or limiting. Of these variables, the worldview is one of the most fundamental aspects because the ego is an organizing process that makes meaning of all the other variables. Thus, coaching at the ego level can be more liberating. It enables the client to walk away feeling more resourced to navigate life and leadership challenges. Developmental coaching ultimately equips the client to create a more nuanced, complex, integrated, and realistic map of meaning that enables them to better adapt to their increasingly complex external and internal world in an affirming and empowering way.

DEVELOPMENTAL MOVES

When we assess a client using the MAP, we determine, based on the client's responses, where the client is on the transformational trajectory. We distinguish different positions and moves within the ongoing process of development. To illustrate, here are four of the nine moves we identify.

Consolidation: The client needs to feel "at home," and to fully explore the current stage, or the new stage the client may have arrived at. That is, the client may need to "consolidate." Each new stage is an achievement over earlier ways of making sense. The maturity coach celebrates and validates the client's progress and helps the client transfer his or her knowing into new contexts, as well as to practice new skills and behaviors in the new action logic.

Transition: Here, the client may show signs that he or she is moving to the next stage. That is, the client may be in "transition" and may begin to explore a new stage inconsistently. The maturity coach supports the client with tools and practices most conducive to addressing anxiety and uncertainty concomitant with such transitions.

Transformation: Sometimes the client is in an active phase of radically shifting to the next stage—the process of transformation. During this particularly intense movement, which can be triggered by significant life events or critical situations, the maturity coach helps the client navigate the shift, and delve into questions that come with a new perspective—revealing both its advantages as well as new struggles.

Integration: Even with a stable sense of arrival at a stage, development can be a messy process. As a person grows and matures, material from earlier stages can be overlooked, bypassed, ignored, or neglected—that is, "unintegrated." Therefore, integration work is a crucial aspect of healthy vertical development. Unintegrated aspects of earlier stages can become barriers to greater wisdom and maturity.

We have identified several other micro movements; however, they lie beyond the scope of this chapter. Maturity coaching becomes more effective when the coach pays attention to these macro and micro movements—in addition to results from the MAP and framework.

MATURITY COACHING PRACTICE

The client's assessed developmental stage and the customized MAP commentary are used in the coaching process as a basis to explore how individuals see and present themselves in their personal and professional lives. The maturity coach builds on the recommendations in the MAP report, and offers coaching based on the client's trailing edge (aspects from earlier stages that may still limit the client) as well as the growing edge (aspects of impending growth into the next stage).

The framework offers a broad description of different stages within which individuals show pronounced heterogeneity. Two people can have a profile rooted in the same stage, yet share radically different narratives. They can operate within the same degrees of freedom with idiosyncratic outcomes. The later the stage, the more differentiated and distinctive the presentation generally is. The MAP offers the opportunity to create development plans tailored to the particular needs arising from their unique history and story. An ideal plan anchors horizontal consolidation, past integration, and vertical expansion—forming a heuristic triad that a coach can explore with each client.

The maturity coach prepares for the session by reflecting on the stage-related identifications observed in the client's responses. The coach tests the face validity of the profile, checking on how much the client feels "seen." During the session, the coach pays attention to assumptions, polarities, defenses, metaphors, and language patterns disclosed in the conversation. *Stage-related* polarities offer a highly effective and powerful way of shifting perspectives (Sharma & Cook-Greuter, 2010).

In the conversation, the client chooses to focus on specific personal, professional, or leadership challenges, and learns to make "object" (i.e., visible) what was previously "subject" (i.e., hidden). By naming and framing their thoughts, feelings, issues, desires, disorientations, and inclinations, they can begin to take a perspective on all of them. This gives them more options and brings them closer to a more realistic appraisal of their inner and outer life. It can also liberate energy blocked from trying to maintain one's belief structures despite inconsistent emergent data.

THE COACH'S MATURITY LEVEL AS RELEVANT

Given the significance of the stage framework and its centrality in human development, it may be obvious by now that the developmental stage of the coach also has a bearing on the coaching delivery. This is especially so when the coach remains unaware of his or her own worldview in relation to the maturity framework. Even if the coach has later-stage capacities, it remains possible that the coach may slip into an earlier mode when triggered by a specific context or situation. Here are some examples of what coaching operating from a particular stage might look like:

- An experienced coach, coming from the **Group-Centric** mindset, when hired by an organization with a strong culture and as part of a structured internal coaching program, may feel inclined to fit into the expectations of the program. The coach may be persuaded to deliver performance coaching or skill-based coaching to meet the goals and outcomes defined by the program or the hiring manager, when what the client could benefit from would be to reduce an over-focus on goals, and become more reflective, learning from mistakes or unanticipated outcomes. Coming from the Group-Centric stage, the coach might seek to encourage or cajole the client to be compliant, and meet program expectations.

- At the **Skill-Centric** stage, the coach tends to seek perfection in his or her chosen technique. A particular technology can quickly define coaches who have undergone a 1- or 2-year-long certification process. They implement their tool(s), sometimes arguing about their benefits in order to convince the client of the value. They set guidelines and process, ask the client to follow the steps and the process, without the ability or willingness to let go of their method. They tend to be identified by their specific approach, and other approaches are seen to compete with their own. (Of course, this aspect needs to be included and integrated by coaches—expertise is an important component of coaching, and also applies to expertise in maturity coaching.)

- Coaches at the **Self-Determining** stage will likely pay attention to contractual agreements, and encourage clients to make their own choices within a range of possibilities explored. They may follow their preferred method, while being open to experimentation and re-evaluation. They are drawn to different instruments to assess "as is" and "should be" scenarios, so they can plan for and track results. They emphasize measuring outcomes, and creating more comprehensive and longer-term plans to achieve desired outcomes. They "manage" client relationships to improve them by defining milestones.

Coaches who move past the Self-Determining stage are considered to have attained a major developmental milestone.

- At the **Self-Questioning** stage, coaches hold their chosen approach with greater nuance and allow a lot more space and attention for what emerges. The coach is now able to see that his or her understanding of the client's situation is only one interpretation, circumscribed by the coach's own biases, conditioning, and values. The coach can adapt the rules, ignore them when needed, vary what they offer depending on context, even co-create new practices with the client. The coach focuses on inquiry and reflection rather than trying to bring about predetermined changes. The coach also recognizes the impact of the coaching sessions on his or her own habits and patterns—and can walk away from the coaching session feeling personal shifts and appreciating the mutuality of the process.

- At the **Self-Actualizing** stage, the coach begins to appreciate the contribution of all the previous stage perspectives and is able to coach the client through a much broader range of options. The coach brings a truly systems view, seeking to integrate multiple contexts through higher-level principles that can benefit the client's organizational or family system. The client is encouraged to use feedback as a mirror to uncover blind spots not yet on his or her radar. The coach highlights exploring the correspondence between the client's inner and outer experience, stimulating inquiry, reflection, and ownership of unknown or hidden aspects of his personality.

PROFILE OF A MATURITY COACH

Coaching using the maturity framework is distinctly different from coaching approaches that don't use a developmental lens.

Depending on context and the client's objectives, the maturity framework can be used explicitly or implicitly. Employing the MAP as a basis for coaching is an example of explicit use. Explicit use of the framework also involves naming the stages and calling out stage-related beliefs held by the client. For clients at earlier stages of development, the MAP report provides structure, offers scientific evidence, and helps clients be more receptive to recommendations for future growth. Clients at more mature stages of development report being intrigued by the nuance and depth of self-understanding provided by the framework in conjunction with the MAP. They value the intelligence embedded in the framework itself. In a way, the more mature adults are, the more important a "map" becomes for their journey because the journey itself becomes more complex, nuanced, and variegated at later stages of sense-making.

A major difference between coaching using an evolutionary lens and coaching without one is that the developmental coach does not assume the client has Self-Determining capacity (Stage 4) . Most client-centered coaching schools assume that the client is empowered with self-determining choices, is self-reliant, and is free from the constraints of the earlier, more conforming stages. A maturity coach does not hesitate to bring instructional and directive tools to the coaching process if it is what the client needs as support, and will serve the client in transition to the next stage.

Coaches trained in various coaching methodologies—such as Neuro-Linguistic Programming (NLP) or mindfulness—can layer the adult stage-development viewpoint into their coaching, and tailor their existing toolkit to a specific developmental stage. Most coaching schools do not differentiate between concrete applications and more complex aspects of their approach, or know how to tailor their toolkit to clients at different stages of maturity. For example, polarity thinking is a tool that includes many elements and sophisticated principles. For an earlier-stage client who wants to achieve specific professional goals, the maturity coach can choose to present some practical, actionable aspects. In contrast, for later-stage clients, the coach can point out the more subtle and dynamic elements, challenge them to see interdependent truths within a polarity, and enable more fundamental internal shifts—that is, in their own mindset and attitude.

The maturity coach understands that there is no "race to the top" and takes great care not to use the maturity framework to pigeonhole or label the client according to the stage identified in his or her profile. Every stage is a triumph, so the coach is quick to affirm and appreciate the client's journey thus far, holding unconditional regard. Since later-stage clients have far greater ability to have their beliefs examined and even tested, the developmental coach can be quick to challenge the client when he or she determines that the client has the capacity to question and can handle potential disorientation. The coach is not in a hurry to provide solace, respite, relief, or comfort in an attempt to create ease for the client and resists problem solving for the client.

The maturity coach sees each stage as a constellation of identity-related tasks that need to be negotiated and mastered. While emphasizing vertical development, the coach also focuses on, facilitates, and furthers horizontal development as necessary. The coach can offer information, highlight skill gaps, provide tutoring, teach concepts, set milestones, and be directive about goals and tasks—with clarity on just how these steps would serve further growth. So integrating horizontal and vertical development is itself a distinguishing factor of maturity coaching. This approach can be particularly relevant in "performance improvement" coaching. Rather than assume the client has performance issues due to lack of competence or leadership skills, the maturity coach identifies, when applicable, the developmental barriers to performance. For example, a client may be identified as a "poor performer"; however, further exploration might reveal that the client identifies with being perfect and, as a result, is unable to complete tasks in pursuit of the ideal quality. Generally, this occurs at the Skill-Centric stage of development. The client has to learn to balance effectiveness with quality—a developmental task at the next stage.

The coach and his or her own unfolding is equally a part of the process of developmental coaching. The coach is aware of his or her own developmental journey and is able to track his or her own identifications, agendas, and preferences throughout the coaching engagement. The coach is able to pay attention to what arises within him or her that needs integration and notices when the coach uses his or her own preferences to guide the interactions. The coach is aware of how rigidly holding the framework can obscure what is needed, and can drop it as a filter when necessary. The coach has the capacity to say "no" to "Can I be of service at all, at this time?" and is aware of his or her own motivation to be a coach, and observes his or her own "need" to be seen as a resource. The coach uses the framework as an objective and powerful reference point, without undue attachment. The framework is an offering, not a compulsion. The coach is also able to take a perspective on the theory itself, holding it as one of many ways—albeit highly valuable—of seeing the client.

While the maturity coach includes himself or herself as part of the client system, the coach does not assume responsibility for the client's success. The maturity coach recognizes reciprocal impact and complexities of the coach system/client system interaction. The coach can often see how what emerged in the coaching process was exactly what was needed for his or her own development not just as a coach, but also as a human being.

Finally, the maturity coach maintains a stance of discovery and continually integrates new findings into an overall more real, more comprehensive, more dynamic awareness of day-to-day issues as well as the overarching secret, sacred path of human evolution. The coach can shape-shift his or her coaching guided by different metaphors: sometime "nurturing" as a gardener does, using different tools to tend, support, and prune, while at other times being present like water, taking the shape of the particular moment and flowing without resistance. The coach continues to notice his or her own assumptions and storytelling, and is able to let go of the developmental perspective when it doesn't serve the process. The coach recognizes that the maturity framework is just one story among so many stories we can tell about human learning and development.

ETHICAL CONSIDERATIONS IN MATURITY COACHING

The journey of each human being is larger than any theory or measurement. We apply our knowledge of adult development, based on research and personal experience, in an unconditionally ethical manner. Here are some principles we live by when we offer maturity coaching:

- We affirm the client's place on the universal path, wherever the client happens to be.

- We do not push the client to move to the next stage.

- We observe our own language when we refer to developmental stages. For example, we use the terms "earlier" and "later" stages, rather than "higher" or "lower."

- We do not label people with stage names; we refer to behavior or beliefs that come from a particular world-view.

- We never "stage" a person loosely or conversationally; we rely on a robust and scientifically validated instrument to gather evidence and use it to inform and support the client.

- We maintain strict confidentiality in handling sensitive data.

- We do not defend the measurement or collude with any defensiveness on the part of the client.

- We view later stages of development as outcomes of living and learning, not as a goal.

- We own that, however we see and interpret others, we are never free of our own worldview and meaning-making.

- We recognize that our particular framework of stages is one among many lights that illumine human nature and our evolution.

CONCLUSION

I hope this chapter has stimulated your interest—even fascination—for the adult's unfolding journey of meaning-making. I have outlined some of the many implications of this evolutionary lens for how we see, relate to, work with, and coach individuals toward a more capable, joyful, compassionate, and wiser way of being. I invite you to step into a review of your path so far, and what lies ahead for you, both as a coach and as a human being.

In conclusion, I call on all of us to explore the rich landscape that research has revealed about both our universal and particular developmental trajectories. In order to become adept at enabling vertical development, coaches are invited to delve into the intricacies of stage development, become deeply familiar with the rich textures of each worldview, observe and reflect on their own and their clients' responses to the infinite variety of life encounters, and practice guiding, challenging, and supporting themselves and their clients as they negotiate old and new territories of their evolving identities. May all beings evolve in their interiors and their exteriors, individually and collectively, sustaining self, other, community, nature, and spirit.

REFERENCES

Cook-Greuter, S. R. (1999). *Postautonomous ego development. A study of its nature and measurement* (revised ed., unpublished dissertation). Harvard University.

Cook-Greuter, S. R. (2004). Making the case for a developmental perspective. *Industrial and Commercial Training, 36*(7), 275–281.

Evolution. (2012). *The American heritage dictionary* (5th ed.). New York, NY: Houghton Mifflin Harcourt Publishing Company.

Gilligan, C. (1982). *In a different voice: Psychological theory and women's development.* Cambridge, MA: Harvard University Press.

Graves, C. W. (1981, May 20). *Summary statement: The emergent cyclical, double-helix model of the adult human biopychosocial systems.* Handout prepared by Chris Cowan for Dr. Graves's presentation in Boston, MA.

Kegan, R. (1980). Meaning-making: The constructive-developmental approach to persons and practice. *The Personnel and Guidance Journal, 58*, 373–380.

Loevinger, J. (1969). Theories of ego development. In L. Berger (Ed.), *Clinical-cognitive psychology: Models and integrations* (pp. 83–135). Englewood Cliffs, NJ: Prentice- Hall.

Loevinger, J. (1997). Stages of personality development. In R. Hogan, J. Johnson, & S. Briggs (Eds.), *Handbook of personality psychology* (pp. 199–208). San Diego, CA: Academic Press.

Loevinger, J., & Wissler, R. (1978). *Measuring ego development 1. Construction and use of a sentence completion test* (1st ed., second printing). San Francisco, CA: Josser-Bass.

Petrie, N. (2011). *Future trends in leadership development* [White Paper]. The Center for Creative Leadership. Retrieved from www.ccl.org

Sharma, B., & Cook-Greuter, S. R. (2010). *Polarity wisdom in ego development theory and developmental coaching.* Integral Theory Conference 2010.

ADDITIONAL READING

Fowler, J. W. (1981/1995). *Stages of faith: The psychology of human development and the quest for meaning.* New York, NY: Harper Collins.

Kegan, R. (1996). *In over our heads: The mental demands of modern life* (Third printing). Cambridge: Harvard University Press.

Kohlberg, L. (1969). Stage and sequence: The cognitive developmental approach to socialization. In D. A. Gosling (Ed.), *Handbook of socialization theory and research* (pp. 347–380). Chicago, IL: Rand McNally.

Loevinger, J. (1998a). History of the sentence completion test (SCT) for ego development. In J. Loevinger (Ed.), *Technical foundations for measuring ego development* (pp. 1–10). Mahwah, NJ: Lawrence Erlbaum.

Loevinger, J. (1998b). Reliability and validity of the SCT. In J. Loevinger (Ed.), *Technical foundations for measuring ego development* (pp. 29–40). Mahwah, NJ: Lawrence Erlbaum.

Lorry, M., & Manning, T. T. (1978). Measurement of ego development by sentence completion and personality test. *Journal of Clinical Psychology, 34,* 354–360. doi:10.1002/1097-4679(197804)34:2<354::AID-JCLP2270340217>3.0.CO;2-1

Manners, J., & Durkin, K. (2001). A critical review of the validity of ego development theory and its measurement. *Journal of Personality Assessment, 77,* 541–567. doi:10.1207/S15327752JPA7703_12

22

The Immunity-to-Change Process: When Change Is Hard to Make

Deborah Helsing

WHAT IS IMMUNITY TO CHANGE?

Seth is an engineer at a technology startup that has grown exponentially in recent years and has increasingly used collaborative teaming as a strategy to promote innovation, learning, and continued growth. While Seth enjoys the fast-paced, collaborative spirit of the organization, he dislikes spending so much of his time in team meetings. He feels that most are a waste of time and painful to sit through. For example, he notices that Jacinta, the team leader for a major project they have been developing, doesn't value his contributions. "Whenever I make any kind of suggestion at all, she just doesn't pick up on it," he explains. And since everything in the team seems to go through Jacinta, he isn't sure how he can productively participate. He is aware that he is beginning to become less engaged during meetings and cares less and less about what the team decides. At the same time, he knows that it's silly to sit there not saying anything, especially when he could be doing something else valuable during that time. But after repeated attempts to change his behavior and participate more fully in these team meetings, he finds himself only becoming more aware of his frustration with Jacinta and with himself. He doesn't like feeling that he's slacking off, and more importantly, he doesn't like the idea that Jacinta is disrespecting his ideas. After complaining about the situation to a colleague, Seth decides to approach Cheryl, a coach/consultant recently brought in to support the increased need for everyone in the organization to learn how to collaborate effectively.

Cheryl invites Seth to create an immunity-to-change (ITC) map to understand why he is having a hard time changing his behavior, despite his sincere attempts. She explains that an ITC map illuminates a hidden dynamic that impedes personal and organizational transformation. Once people see their "immune system," they understand why prior efforts have failed to create sustainable change, and new possibilities to move forward appear. Seth isn't sure he completely understands but agrees to give the ITC map-making process a try.

The ITC process has been successfully used nationally and internationally, with individuals and organizations in the professional sphere (Bowe, Lahey, Armstrong, & Kegan, 2003; Bowe, Lahey, Kegan, & Armstrong, 2003; *Business Digest*, 2009; Kegan & Lahey, 2009; Kegan, Lahey, Miller, Fleming, & Helsing, 2016; Markus, 2016), as well as in personal life (Brubach, 2009; Kegan, Lahey, & Helsing, 2016). This chapter illustrates the process using the example of Seth's work with his coach, but like Seth, you are likely to understand ITC best by trying it on for yourself. In order to experience the power of this exercise, you will need to fully engage in it with the expectation that you will uncover something intriguing and potent. Think carefully about each and every entry you make in your map, pushing yourself to be as honest and growth-oriented as possible. Here is a blank ITC map for you to fill out as you read. Or, if you don't want to write in this book, you can quickly re-create this simple table on your computer or on a piece of paper (Table 22.1).

Table 22.1 Blank ITC Map

1. Commitment (Improvement Goal)	2. Doing/Not Doing Instead	3. Competing Commitment	4. Big Assumption

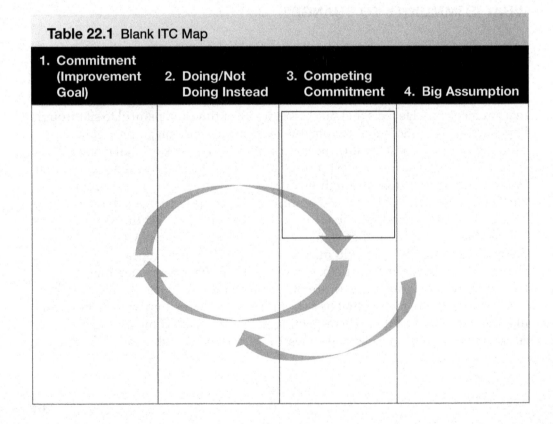

HOW TO MAKE AN ITC MAP

Column 1: Your Improvement Goal/Starting Commitment

To begin, you will need to make sure you are starting with an improvement goal that compels you. What do you most need to get better at? Is there something you, like Seth, have struggled to improve? That's a perfect place to start. Or if an improvement goal doesn't immediately come to mind, brainstorm a few possibilities from your professional life, as well as a few from your personal life. Ask for input from your supervisor, colleagues, direct reports, friends, and family.

As you narrow down your possibilities to one goal that feels powerful and is something you feel fully committed to improving, check to see that your starting commitment is:

- *To get better at* something, not to have the result or outcome. "Growing my coaching business" is not an improvement goal; it is a result or an outcome. "Getting better at networking" is an improvement goal (that could *lead to* growing your coaching business).

- *Stated affirmatively.* Instead of "getting better at being less anxious," choose an affirmative version like "getting better at calming myself."

- *Absolutely important to you*, so that achieving it will be very valuable and consequential.

- *Far from accomplished*—you recognize you have plenty of room for improvement and future growth.

- *Implicating YOU.* You (not someone else) must make some changes to the way you live, work, think, and act.

Seth's current frustration and dissatisfaction with his own attempts to improve his behavior led him to identify his goal quickly. "I am committed to getting better at contributing actively and consistently to team conversations," he told Cheryl and wrote this improvement goal down in the first column of his ITC map (Table 22.2).

Now it is your turn. Review your various commitments to choose one that meets all of these criteria. Write your starting commitment in the first column of your map. "I am committed to getting better at . . ." what?

Column 2: What You Are Doing and Not Doing Instead?

Now take a fearless inventory of all the *things you do* that work against your improvement goal, as well as the ways you are working against that goal by *what you are not doing*. In other words, we are asking you to tell on yourself —to be willing to fess up to your own "bad behaviors." Your list will show all the ways you are actually working against your improvement goal and you want to develop as robust, thorough, and accurate a list as possible. Again, draw on feedback from others to make sure you haven't overlooked anything important.

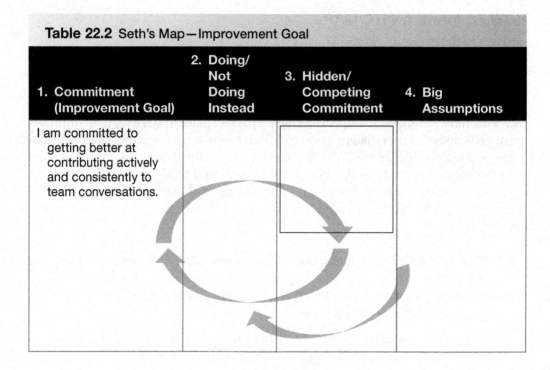

Table 22.2 Seth's Map—Improvement Goal

1. Commitment (Improvement Goal)	2. Doing/ Not Doing Instead	3. Hidden/ Competing Commitment	4. Big Assumptions
I am committed to getting better at contributing actively and consistently to team conversations.			

Make sure every item on your list is a behavior:

- **That works *against* your improvement goal.**
- **That is concrete.** For example, rather than writing "I don't like coaching people who are arrogant," write something like, "I stop listening when I think a client is bragging" or "I don't challenge arrogant client remarks." If you identify something that is more like a feeling or attitude, ask yourself, "What *do* I do (or what *don't* I do) that leads to these feelings or attitudes? What do I do (or not do) as a result of these feelings or attitudes?"

Seth did not enjoy making a list of the things that he was doing and not doing that undermined his improvement goal. The first things that came to his mind were all of the ways that *Jacinta* was making it harder for him to contribute more effectively. But Cheryl reminded Seth that he didn't need to wait for Jacinta to change in order for him to take personal responsibility for his own behavior. Agreeing that she had a point, Seth was able to come up with the list shown in Table 22.3.

Now enter all of *your* behaviors that work against your improvement goal in the second column of your map template. Although it may be tempting, *do not include* explanations for why you do things that work against your improvement goal or explanations of what you plan to do differently.

COLUMN 3 (TOP HALF): NAMING YOUR FEARS AND WORRIES

Something very intriguing starts to happen in Column 3 when the ITC dynamic that was previously hidden begins to emerge. Often, what people come to in this

Table 22.3 Seth's Map—Doing/Not Doing Instead

1. Commitment (Improvement Goal)	2. Doing/Not Doing Instead	3. Hidden/ Competing Commitment	4. Big Assumptions
I am committed to getting better at contributing actively and consistently to team conversations.	When Jacinta doesn't tell me explicitly what she thinks of my ideas, I withdraw, stop participating. I start ruminating about why she isn't commenting on my ideas, and I tell myself it is a waste of time to be on the team. I pay attention to how she responds enthusiastically to others' ideas. Because I am paying so much attention to how she is responding, I lose track of the substance of the conversation. I don't ask Jacinta what she is thinking or tell her that I'm upset with her.		

column feels unexpectedly potent and arresting. Because this part of the exercise is so important, we tend to complete Column 3 in two steps. First, look at the "worry box," the box that appears at the top half of Column 3. Now imagine yourself actually doing the *opposite* of each behavior you listed in Column 2. Try to come up with something that feels scary or a bit dangerous, something that you can feel in your gut.

When Cheryl asked Seth to identify his worries, he had an eye-opening experience. As he imagined what it would be like to continue to participate actively in conversations, regardless of how Jacinta responded, he felt a twinge of uneasiness. Cheryl gently directed him to create as vivid a picture as he could, and Seth imagined standing on the outside of a group of people who are all engaged in an animated conversation, trying to be seen and have his voice be heard with no effect. That mental image gave him a sinking, sick feeling of being disrespected, disregarded. He recognized that similar worries about how others viewed him were often operating as a kind of white noise in the background of his daily activity. They floated underneath much of his thinking, decisions, and actions at work. He was explicitly naming what had been obvious to him but also never acknowledged (Table 22.4).

Now imagine *yourself* doing (or even just trying to do) the opposite of each behavior you just listed in Column 2. What fears or worries arise for you? What might you really hate for others to see in you (that they might see if you were doing

Table 22.4 Seth's Worry Box

1. Commitment (Improvement Goal)	2. Doing/Not Doing Instead	3. Hidden/ Competing Commitment	4. Big Assumptions
I am committed to getting better at contributing actively and consistently to team conversations.	When Jacinta doesn't tell me explicitly what she thinks of my ideas, I withdraw, stop participating. I start ruminating about why she isn't commenting on my ideas, and I tell myself it is a waste of time to be on the team. I pay attention to how she responds enthusiastically to others' ideas. Because I am paying so much attention to how she is responding, I lose track of the substance of the conversation. I don't ask Jacinta what she is thinking or tell her that I'm upset with her.	Worries: Finding out I am not respected – I don't measure up to others' standards. My ideas are not respected. There will be more tension and conflict in our interactions.	

the opposite of what is in your second column)? What might be a way you would least like to see yourself (if you were doing, or even trying to do, the opposite of something in your second column)?

If you have identified something that feels only slightly worrisome, try to push more deeply. Ask yourself, "What would be *the worst thing* about that for me?" You want to experience yourself at risk, unprotected from something that feels dangerous to you.

COLUMN 3 (BOTTOM HALF): UNCOVERING YOUR HIDDEN COMMITMENTS

Identifying these fears and worries helps you discover what we call a "hidden competing commitment." The fears are the raw material for generating these commitments. Nobody wants to feel fear or worry. We don't generally enjoy experiencing ourselves as vulnerable, or in any danger. We defend ourselves from feeling that fear. We make sure that not only are we *not* standing on the edge of our own personal abyss of anxiety and danger, but that we are standing quite comfortably far, far away . . . far enough away so we don't even have to be consciously aware that the abyss is there. Hidden commitments are our (usually unconscious) mental strategies for standing far away from the abyss, our ways of staying far away from the things we fear.

What self-protective hidden commitment keeps you from feeling (or realizing!) your fears or worries? Take each one of your fears or worries and convert it into a "hidden competing commitment." Write your answer in the bottom half of Column 3 in your map template (underneath the worry box). Keep in mind:

- **The worst dread from the worry box should not disappear when you convert it into a hidden commitment; you should see how you are protecting yourself from danger.** Make sure you don't turn a worry into a noble hidden commitment. For example, "I fear others will think I'm a bad coach" should be converted to "I'm committed to others not thinking poorly of me" or "I'm committed to not being seen as incompetent" and **not** "I'm committed to others thinking I'm a good coach." You may need to use a clunky double negative in order to preserve the danger you are protecting yourself from, and that's fine!

- **Hidden commitments should show how the behaviors you have listed in Column 2 make perfect sense!** Powerful hidden commitments mean that those "bad behaviors" are also simultaneously very, very "good behaviors" if they keep you out of the danger you've now identified. The problem is that the perfectly sensible unconscious effort to take care of yourself is also guaranteed to keep you from accomplishing your goal!

Often, whatever you have listed as your worries in the top half of Column 3 can be rather directly converted into a hidden commitment. For example, Seth's main worry was that he would find out that he was not respected. So, Cheryl suggested he reword that worry as, "I am also committed to not finding out that I am not respected by others." Seth's worry about not measuring up to others' standards became, "I am also committed to not finding out that I don't measure up to others' expectations." And his worry about having more tension and conflict in his interactions became, "I am also committed to not having to deal with conflict or tension" (Table 22.5).

Table 22.5 Seth's Hidden/Competing Commitments

1. Commitment (Improvement Goal)	2. Doing/Not Doing Instead	3. Hidden/ Competing Commitment	4. Big Assumptions
I am committed to getting better at contributing actively and consistently to team conversations.	When Jacinta doesn't tell me explicitly what she thinks of my ideas, I withdraw, stop participating. I start ruminating about why she isn't commenting on my ideas, and I tell myself it is a waste of time to be on the team. I pay attention to how she responds enthusiastically to others' ideas. Because I am paying so much attention to how she is responding, I lose track of the substance of the conversation. I don't ask Jacinta what she is thinking or tell her that I'm upset with her.	Worries: Finding out I am not respected—I don't measure up to others' standards. My ideas are not respected. There will be more tension and conflict in our interactions. I am also committed to not finding out I am not respected by others. I am also committed to not finding out that I don't measure up to others' expectations. I am also committed to not having to deal with conflict or tension.	

THE IMMUNE SYSTEM

Once you have identified your own hidden commitments, you should now see a whole picture across your three columns, a picture of your personal immunity to change. The energy you are generating on your Column 1 starting commitment gets canceled by the energy you are generating to protect yourself on your Column 3 hidden commitments. For instance, you can see why Seth struggled to change his behavior on the team, even when he felt frustrated by it. Seth can't just *will* himself to participate more in team meetings because if he unconsciously senses he is in danger of not meeting others' expectations for him, he will work to protect himself from that possibility. It is as if he is sitting behind the wheel of a car with his right foot on the gas, without noticing that his left foot is also on the brake. His right foot is working on his improvement goal, the part of him that wants to engage more in team meetings. He steps on the gas, trying to speed up, to get more momentum going in the direction he'd like to be moving. He steps down even harder. The engine is revving. The car is even shaking as it holds this increased force. But the car isn't actually going anywhere because Seth's left foot won't let it move. The harder his right foot presses on the gas, the harder his left foot steps on the brake. The foot on the brake is working to make sure he does not run the risk of not being respected, of not meeting others' expectations, of having to deal with potential tension and conflict in his relationships. He is expending lots of energy but making no forward progress. And before he became aware of what is left foot is doing, he couldn't see why that was the case.

You should now also be able to see why you haven't been making progress on your improvement goal. While many people find mapping their immunity to change quickly gets them to a deep level of insight and awareness about how they are stuck, others need more time and help for their map to feel meaningful. If that's the case for you, what might help?

- If you can't see how your hidden commitments make your Column 2 behaviors look perfectly reasonable, that's a sign that you've gotten off track somewhere. Try to revise your hidden commitments or go back to your fears to see if you can clarify them.

- Make sure the fear, worry, or dread from the worry box did not disappear when you converted it into a hidden commitment. The danger your immune system has been protecting you from needs to be named in your hidden commitments. Ask yourself, "What is the danger lurking for me? In what way am I trying to protect myself?"

COLUMN 4: BIG ASSUMPTIONS

The most reliable route to ultimately disrupting the immune system begins by identifying the core assumptions that sustain it. Big Assumptions are basically beliefs we have about ourselves and about the world, but because we tend to take these beliefs as *truths*, as rules about how the world really is, we call them Big Assumptions. **When you look over all that you have uncovered, and especially your Column 3**

commitments, what does that suggest about your assumptions—the beliefs you hold about yourself and how things are—that connect to and support your immune system? Generate as many Big Assumptions as you can and write them into Column 4, remembering that:

- Some of your Big Assumptions may feel undeniably true. Some you may know aren't really true (although you act and feel as if they *were* true); and some you may feel are only partially or sometimes true. *All of these go in your fourth column.*

- *Big Assumptions show why one or more of your hidden commitments feel absolutely necessary.* You should be able to follow your map backward—to see how the Big Assumptions make your third column commitments necessary, how the third column commitments lead to your second column behaviors, and how these behaviors undermine your improvement goal.

- *Your Big Assumptions set clear limits on what you must do and what you must not do.* That is, you should be able to see that your Big Assumptions are rules you have for how to live your life, rules you must always follow if you want to avoid danger and disaster and defeat. But you might also be able to see (at least hypothetically) that these rules keep you living in a smaller world than might be necessary. These rules might actually be over-protecting you.

Looking at his third column commitments with Cheryl, Seth began to brainstorm all the possible assumptions he held. "What if I found out I wasn't respected by others, that I don't measure up to their standards and expectations? What if I did have to deal with conflict and tension?" Seth began to name the terrible things he was sure would result.

- If I am not respected by others, that means I am not smart enough or talented enough, and I'll be left behind as this company continues to grow.

- I assume that if others see I'm not smart or talented, they are right.

- I assume that if I have to deal with conflict or tension at work, I will be even less productive or effective.

- I assume that if I have to deal with conflict or tension at work, it is someone else's fault (i.e., Jacinta's).

He could also see that there was at least one other assumption that held his immune system together. For example, he knew that when he suggested an idea to his team, he immediately looked to see how Jacinta responded. That was the beginning of this whole issue for him. He now saw that he had been assuming that if someone did not praise his ideas, then that must mean the person did not value his ideas and did not respect him. "I realize that is a little illogical," Seth admitted to Cheryl. But making his map helped him see that he had been operating automatically as if that were true. When we treat an assumption as if it is the absolute truth, we allow it to rule our actions. We allow it to shape everything we see. We don't consider or explore any other possibilities, and so it continues to hold enormous power over us. That is why it is a ***Big Assumption*** (Table 22.6).

Table 22.6 Seth's Big Assumptions

1. Commitment (Improvement Goal)	2. Doing/Not Doing Instead	3. Hidden/ Competing Commitment	4. Big Assumptions
I am committed to getting better at contributing actively and consistently to team conversations.	When Jacinta doesn't tell me explicitly what she thinks of my ideas, I withdraw, stop participating. I start ruminating about why she isn't commenting on my ideas, and I tell myself it is a waste of time to be on the team. I pay attention to how she responds enthusiastically to others' ideas. Because I am paying so much attention to how she is responding, I lose track of the substance of the conversation. I don't ask Jacinta what she is thinking or tell her that I'm upset with her.	Worries: Finding out I am not respected—I don't measure up to others' standards. My ideas are not respected. There will be more tension and conflict in our interactions. I am also committed to not finding out I am not respected by others. I am also committed to not finding out that I don't measure up to others' expectations. I am also committed to not having to deal with conflict or tension.	If I am not respected by others, that means I am not smart enough or talented enough, and I'll be left behind as this company continues to grow. I assume that if others see I'm not smart or talented, they are right. I assume that if I have to deal with conflict or tension at work, I will be even less productive or effective. I assume that if I have to deal with conflict or tension at work, it is someone else's fault (i.e., Jacinta's). I assume that if someone doesn't explicitly comment and tell me my ideas are good, they do not respect my ideas.

WHAT COMES NEXT?

If you have been suspecting that Seth isn't the only one who has an immune system operating in ways that render his team less effective, you are right. And Cheryl was thinking the very same thing. She had been speaking recently with Jacinta, who had been a star performer in the sales department and, as the organization had grown, she had rapidly been promoted into a much larger leadership role. She confessed to Cheryl that she was experiencing lots of stress as she tried to take on new responsibilities and had begun to get feedback from others that they found her leadership style overly directive and sometimes abrasive. Cheryl suggested that they conduct a more formal 360-degree assessment, asking for feedback from Cheryl's supervisor, peers, and direct reports. The results reflected that Cheryl was in fact perceived as too quick to make decisions and too reliant on her own thinking. In particular, her respondents recommended that she work to improve her listening skills and slow down her decision-making process so as to draw more value from others' ideas and perspectives. Together, Jacinta and Cheryl used that feedback to draft Jacinta's own ITC map (Table 22.7).

After her session with Jacinta, Cheryl sat back and looked at Jacinta's ITC map again, this time putting it next to Seth's. She could clearly see how each person's immune system created a larger problematic dynamic. Jacinta couldn't fully consider Seth's ideas because that would lead her to feel worthless, empty, and depressed. But Seth wouldn't offer his ideas unless Jacinta praised them. No wonder this team had been struggling! Cheryl knew that if both Seth and Jacinta could begin to overturn their immune systems, they and the whole team would unleash more of their potential and increase their effectiveness. But she didn't want to move too quickly with Seth, who still seemed to be reeling a bit from the impact of identifying his immune system. So she asked him just to begin thinking about what it could look like if he were to make progress on his improvement goal by overturning his Big Assumptions.

> Imagine yourself, sometime in the future, actively contributing to team conversations, and you are no longer held back by your Big Assumptions! Can you generate a picture of what you would be doing, thinking, and feeling if that were the case? Let's begin to draft that vision next time. We'll be starting to make what is called an "ITC Continuum of Progress."

Cheryl could see that Jacinta was ready to move more quickly, and so she suggested they begin to design and run an "ITC Test of a Big Assumption." She asked Jacinta, "Which Big Assumption feels most powerful to you? Or, imagine finding out that one of these is not accurate, and so you can make real progress in overturning your immune system. Which assumption, if untrue, would really help you make that progress?" Jacinta chose: "If I start to question the value of my own ideas (start to question my value), I will feel worthless, flat and empty, totally depressed." "That one feels both terrible and consequential, but I'm also very curious to see if it's wrong," she explained. Cheryl suggested Jacinta consider, "What data would lead me to doubt the accuracy of that Big Assumption? And is there a safe way for me to seek out and collect that data?"

Table 22.7 Jacinta's ITC Map

1. Commitment (Improvement Goal)	2. Doing/Not Doing Instead	3. Hidden/ Competing Commitment	4. Big Assumptions
I am committed to getting better at listening to others' ideas and giving them my full consideration.	I talk more than others do. I don't respond to others' ideas before jumping in with my own. I provide explicit support to others who express ideas that are aligned with my own. I don't ask questions to understand others' ideas fully. I don't invite other people to comment, especially if I think they may disagree with what I am thinking.	Worries: My ideas will not be the ones that "win." I'll lose my mojo, be marginalized, not valuable, not the central player on this team. I am also committed to not questioning whether my ideas are the best and should win, whether I am the best and should win. I am also committed to not being marginalized, not valuable, or not central—committed to not being average, "just another player." I am also committed to not letting go of any of my power, my self-confidence.	If I start to question the value of my own ideas (start to question my value), I will feel worthless, flat and empty, totally depressed. I assume that leaders are valued for their individual contributions rather than their ability to bring out the best in others, despite whatever noble value people here espouse. If I am not always making my own individual contributions to our work, I will be marginalized or average (not the best). I am nothing. If I don't believe that I am the best, then I won't have the confidence and guts to make the tough decisions I need to make in this role. I assume that others want/need me to be confident, tough, and powerful in order to keep morale high and productivity high, especially when there is so much stress in this department.

An idea immediately came to Jacinta's mind. She knew that one of the most successful senior leaders in the organization was wonderfully open to and enthusiastic about others' ideas. Maybe Jacinta could interview him to learn how it is that he finds others' ideas so exciting, how he seems not at all threatened when the best ideas aren't his? Could she collect any data that would lead her to think that her own incomplete thinking was not so terrible but instead gave her the opportunity to find new and exciting ideas in others' thinking?

Cheryl suggested another possibility. Jacinta collaborated quite well with her former colleagues in the sales department. That might be the perfect context for Jacinta to begin exploring what happens in that context when she doubted whether her own ideas were as valuable as others. Jacinta agreed to consider both possibilities before her next meeting with Cheryl.

The ITC exercises (Helsing, Howell, Kegan, & Lahey, 2008; Helsing & Lahey, 2010; Kegan & Lahey, 2009; Kegan, Lahey, & Helsing, 2016), such as those on which Seth and Jacinta are about to embark, allow participants to explore whether and how their key Big Assumptions might not be accurate. Often, assumptions turn out to be distorted, overgeneralized, or completely wrong, and when we can replace or modify them, we are newly able to increase our effectiveness and develop a more expansive way of knowing (Kegan & Lahey, 2001, 2009). Although many personal and professional development approaches—and coaching methodologies—use words like *development* and *transformation* to describe their intentions and results, developmental psychologists (see, e.g., Kegan, 1982, 1994, 2000) use these terms to refer to very specific phenomena. Our way of knowing becomes more complex when we create a bigger internal system that incorporates and expands on our previous system. As the psychological demands of our increasingly challenging world call upon us to develop and exercise greater psychological complexity, immunity to change provides an answer to how we can develop the internal systems to best meet these challenges.

Cheryl was also thinking far beyond her next steps with Seth and Jacinta to imagine how the entire team, and eventually the entire organization, would undertake this same work. When the senior leaders had hired her, they asked her to help them each identify their own individual immunities and then those they collectively shared as a team. Their long-range goal was to have everyone in the organization identify a path for individual growth and continuous learning. In short, they hoped these initial steps were the first on a path to becoming a "deliberately developmental organization" (Kegan, Lahey, Miller, Fleming, & Helsing, 2016), a place where every individual could flourish and regularly experience their own further unfolding. They shared the belief that the excellence of the organization's work was the means to drive that development and to flourish as a result. Cheryl pictured Seth and Jacinta sharing their learning with each other, with their team, and with others in the organization, as the senior leaders were already beginning to do. She imagined making these explorations part of the work people do every day.

And what comes next for you? Are you eager to explore your own Big Assumptions and undertake personal transformation for yourself? For your clients? If you thrive on those moments when insight suddenly strikes and when new possibilities suddenly come into focus, the ITC process offers a methodology designed to engender those moments and to bring about lasting change. These individual transformations are accelerated further when they are collectively supported and enhanced. As organizations look to provoke and nourish insight, innovation, and continued development, ITC is a tool for transforming cultures in these directions.

ACKNOWLEDGMENT

The author expresses her gratitude to Lisa Lahey for devising the introductory conflict between Seth and Jacinta.

REFERENCES

Bowe, C. M., Lahey, L., Armstrong, E., & Kegan, R. (2003). Questioning the "big assumptions." Part I: Addressing personal contradictions that impede professional development. *Medical Education, 37*(8), 715–722. doi:10.1046/j.1365-2923.2003.01579.x

Bowe, C. M., Lahey, L., Kegan, R., & Armstrong, E. (2003). Questioning the "big assumptions." Part II: Recognizing organizational contradictions that impede institutional change. *Medical Education, 37*(8), 723–733. doi:10.1046/j.1365-2923.2003.01580.x

Brubach, H. (2009). You don't need more willpower. *The Oprah Magazine,* pp. 138–141.

Business Digest. (2009, June). Immunity to change: How to release the potential of individuals and organizations. Issue 197, pp. 1–9.

Helsing, D., Howell, A., Kegan, R., & Lahey, L. (2008). Putting the development in professional development: Understanding and overturning educational leaders' immunities to change. *Harvard Educational Review, 78*(3), 437–465. doi:10.17763/haer.78.3.888l759g1qm54660

Helsing, D., & Lahey, L. (2010). Unlocking leadership potential: Overcoming immunities to change. In K. Bunker, D. T. Hall, & K. E. Kram (Eds.), *Extraordinary leadership: Addressing the gaps in senior executive development* (pp. 69–94). San Francisco, CA: Jossey-Bass.

Kegan, R. (1982). *The evolving self: Problem and process in human development.* Cambridge, MA: Harvard University Press.

Kegan, R. (1994). *In over our heads: The mental demands of modern life.* Cambridge, MA: Harvard University Press.

Kegan, R. (2000). What "form" transforms? A constructive-developmental approach to transformative learning. In J. Mezirow (Ed.), *Learning as transformation* (pp. 35–69). San Francisco, CA: Jossey-Bass.

Kegan, R., & Lahey, L. L. (2001). The real reason people won't change. *Harvard Business Review, 79*(10), 84–92.

Kegan, R., & Lahey, L. L. (2009). *Immunity to change: How to overcome it and unlock the potential in yourself and your organization.* Boston, MA: Harvard Business School Press.

Kegan, R., Lahey, L., & Helsing, D. (2016). *Right weight, right mind: The ITC approach to permanent weight loss.* Cambridge, MA: Minds at Work.

Kegan, R., Lahey, L. L., Miller, M. L., Fleming, A., & Helsing, D. (2016). *An everyone culture: Becoming a deliberately developmental organization.* Boston, MA: Harvard Business Review Press.

Markus, I. (2016). Efficacy of immunity-to-change coaching for leadership development. *The Journal of Applied Behavioral Science, 52,* 215–230. doi:10.1177/0021886313502530

23

Internal Family Systems: Applications in Coaching

Margaret Moore

I n the 2015 Disney movie *Inside Out*, the 11-year old character Riley's "animated" mind was personified as five unique characters based upon primary emotions: Anger, Disgust, Fear, Sadness, and Joy (Disney, n.d.). This creative and much-loved movie brought to life the nature of the mind as multiple, having multiple subpersonalities that interact, are sometimes in conflict, and evolve together as the mind's internal family. The most developed model of multiplicity today is that pioneered by psychologist Richard Schwartz, who developed Internal Family Systems (IFS) as a therapeutic model now applied by thousands of psychotherapists and other practitioners (The Center for Self Leadership, n.d.). IFS practice assists clients in healing perturbations of the IFS that emerge from past adverse experiences and, as a thought process and a philosophy of living, has informed applications far beyond psychotherapy, including coaching and organizational development. In this chapter, we introduce multiplicity of mind models, describe the IFS model, and then focus on four coaching applications of IFS used by coaching thought leaders. We close with a discussion of new frontiers.

MULTIPLICITY OF MIND MODELS IN PSYCHOLOGY

The assertion of the existence of subpersonalities began early in the 20th century with Freud's description of the id, ego, and superego. John Rowan's book titled *Subpersonalities: The People Inside Us* (Rowan, 1990) explores the long history and diverse theories that support the existence of subpersonalities, thought to be enduring psychological structures that evolve over time. Subpersonalities integrate thoughts, emotions, needs, physiology, and behaviors. Rowan's working definition of a subpersonality is a semi-permanent and semi-autonomous region of the personality capable of acting as a person.

John Mayer's landmark paper in 1995 proposed a personality framework to organize 400 personality components described in 28 textbooks on personality psychology. The framework has four categories of personality components in a hierarchy (Mayer, 1995). Mayer's definition of an agency implies it operates like a subpersonality that integrates various components of a single personality:

1. Enablers—innately wired functions such as emotion, cognition, conation, consciousness

2. Establishments—self-concepts, world-concepts, self-in-world concepts

3. Themes—traits such as optimism or extraversion

4. Agencies—substantial subsets of a personality system that integrate enablers, establishments, and themes into their own agendas

While the existence of subpersonalities, both healthy and unhealthy, cannot be proven with today's research methods, approaching one's mind as multiple offers new paths to higher consciousness, along with healing, integration, growth, and thriving. The construct of multiplicity of mind aligns with the most advanced stage of adult development where one detaches from a dominant self-authored identity and welcomes an emergent, agile, and flexible identity, the self-transforming mind, which evolves moment to moment to adapt to the ever-changing inner and outer worlds.

INTRODUCTION TO IFS THERAPY

As mentioned, among the most active bodies of investigation and application of the concept of multiplicity of mind is the work of psychologist Richard Schwartz, leading the Center for Self Leadership, in developing the model of IFS practice, now supported by empirical evidence (Shadick et al., 2013). Applying radical empiricism as he puts it, Schwartz has devoted the past 30 years to exploring inner dialogues among *parts* (Schwartz, 1995). Schwartz, and thousands of therapists trained in IFS therapy, help people invite their *inner parts*, which are experiencing strong emotions, to a mindful, meditation-like sit-down. The therapy session follows a winding trail of parts to uncover small or large traumas and then unpack their interesting and often surprising stories. From the vantage point of a core Self, a state of wisdom inherent in all of us, the client sits compassionately with the suffering of the parts, and experiences a process designed to appreciate, accept and nurture, then heal and release the burdens of parts. These troubled parts get out of their place of exile below conscious reach and get onto a path of conscious actualization, *in which all parts are acknowledged and welcomed,* and are treated with acceptance, compassion, and benevolence.

One of Schwartz's empirical discoveries underlying the IFS is the concept of a central mindful *Self,* that is able to observe and accept without judgment or evaluation. Schwartz's Self construct is consistent with the *mindful* mind described in

Buddhist traditions and disseminated widely by Jon Kabat-Zinn (Kabat-Zinn, 2012). The mindful mind lives in a state described as meta-awareness, where one observes one's thoughts, feelings, and sensations in the moment and over time, as if watching a movie of one's life as a witness, rising above a narrative mode where one is the central character, embedded in the movie. Schwartz's Self is able to create a mental space between a mindful state and a cacophony of voices, emotions, and needs generated by an inner family of *parts*.

Beyond traditional models of mindfulness, Schwartz's Self not only observes and accepts the internal family, it also listens to and guides each part, and indeed the whole family of parts, toward a harmonious, balanced, resilient, and evolving system. In IFS therapy, the Self is also a compassionate force of healing for wounded parts, facilitated by guidance of a trained expert or self-reflection. Schwartz's Self acts as a conductor to elicit the unified sound of the inner orchestra made up of various instruments and players. The orchestral metaphor reminds us that without effort we don't hear the discrete voices. Led by a good conductor, the voices merge into a whole, harmonious sound. Self leads by integrating the best of the parts into daily functioning, moving from a *pause, observe, and reflect* state in mindful presence, to full focus and flow in intense activities, to sleep—allowing the lively night owl parts to act out in dreams.

Self at its best lives in a sophisticated orbital of mindfulness, emotional and social intelligence, self-compassion, and what Schwartz calls Self Leadership. It can reach what Vago and Silbersweig (2012) describe as the highest level of mindfulness, growing beyond self-awareness and self-regulation to self-transcendence, which could also be described as an optimal level of self-mastery.

Self in the IFS model also refers to an innate source of human wisdom and leadership available to every individual, manifesting important qualities, such as non-judgment, compassion, connection, and patience. These attributes and others represent our core human essence and are often blocked from being accessed by extreme beliefs, voices, points of view, behaviors, or other sensations that end up defining and controlling us. When these parts are acknowledged and accepted, a space naturally opens up allowing us to detach from their long-wired agendas, giving us greater clarity and perspective, as well as the ability to maintain compassion for ourselves and others. We can then be creative in facing difficult challenges or problems and find the courage to stay the course. The presence of Self helps us establish better connections within our own system of parts and with others. In fact, IFS is being applied to resolve conflict in relationships, families, and among cultural groups.

Let's explore four working models that apply IFS in coaching, created in the past few years by coaching innovators who completed IFS training, and that offer an entry point for coaches interested in the application of IFS in coaching.

STRENGTHS-BASED INNER FAMILY MODEL BY MARGARET MOORE

Moore's strengths-based multiplicity of mind or inner family model proposes the existence of a set of common primary subpersonalities, offering a tool for nontherapist coaches to help their clients access, discern, and learn from their distinct inner voices as widely recognized capacities. The model hypothesizes that over the course of evolutionary history, our ancestors developed a set of innate needs, which evolved into human needs, drives, values, capacities, strengths, or functions. These needs were probably important to survival from primordial times onward, and have recently been shown by scientists to be important factors in generating well-being and peak functioning. The most important of these needs or capacities may have manifested themselves as differentiated parts, states, aspects, or even subpersonalities. Essentially, these are distinct internal entities, with different agendas, desires, thoughts, emotional states, and voices (Moore, 2013; Moore, Phillips, & Hanc, 2016).

Emotions can be viewed as biological messengers sent by these discrete parts of the mind (Peil, 2014). Serving as a self-management or self-regulatory system, emotions signal our needs for self-preservation and self-development. What we often label as *negative* emotions may be messages alerting us that certain needs are not being met or values are not being served, while *positive* emotions tell us that certain needs are being met or values are being served. Decoding the emotional states of each part, or each inner family member, provides clues on how best to improve functioning and collaboration, and reduce inner tension, conflict, stress, and ambivalence. This can be done in a mindful roll call, calling on each part to share its emotions, needs, and requests.

Figure 23.1 displays the Mindful Self and the nine members of the inner family, who have been given names that describe their nature, at least in part: Autonomy,

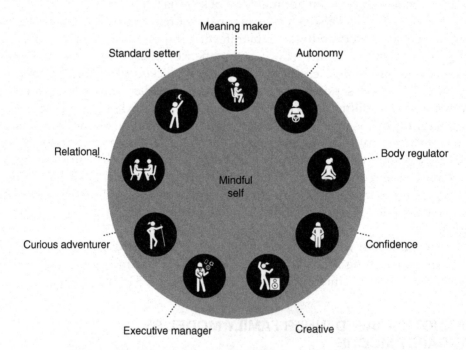

Figure 23.1 The mindful self and nine personality parts.
Source: Adapted with permission from Wellcoaches Corporation.

Figure 23.2 Moore's inner family.
Source: Adapted with permission from Wellcoaches Corporation.

Relational, Confidence, Body Regulator, Adventurer, Executive Manager, Standard Setter, Creative, and Meaning Maker. Figure 23.2 displays a cartoon of Moore's own inner family, who complete a daily roll call to explore and settle mixed emotions, and then access the wisdom of Self.

These personality parts have been synchronized to Carl Jung's eight cognitive processes: introverted and extraverted feeling, introverted and extraverted sensing, introverted and extraverted thinking, and introverted and extraverted intuition (Berens, 2000). Future developments include a mapping of the inner family members to other personality models including Myers–Briggs, Enneagram, VIA Character Strengths, and the Big Five Factor personality theory, which may lead to a theory of the personality, made up of universal parts that are assessed in different ways by different personality models.

MINDFUL SELF

The Mindful Self is the self-leader, the integrator or conductor of the inner family's performance in daily life, encouraging teamwork and harmonious interaction. Ideally, over a lifetime, the Mindful Self assists each inner family member or subpersonality in becoming whole, happy, and healthy, having its needs more fully met and manifesting its full potential within the Self.

AUTONOMY (JUNG—INTROVERTED FEELING)

In self-determination theory, psychologists Deci and Flaste (1995) describe autonomy as a primary organismic drive, a need that manifests as an independent voice, which wants freedom and authenticity and to march to its own drummer by aligning with core values and preferences. The Autonomy part has a sense of agency and wants meaningful choice. It acts in self-interest to avoid external control and it can be rebellious and resist following advice and rules imposed by others.

RELATIONAL (JUNG—EXTRAVERTED FEELING)

The Relational part serves others' needs and values first, ahead of self-interest. It is capable of being warm, loving, trusting, kind, and compassionate to ourselves and others, and seeks to belong and be in harmony with others. It serves others in the wide variety of roles one plays in life, from child to parent, colleague to boss, spouse, friend, and helping professional. The relational part also shows compassion to other members of the inner family.

BODY REGULATOR (JUNG—INTROVERTED SENSING)

The Body Regulator manifests as a voice with interests in equilibrium, self-care, and good health. It is grounded in our senses, in what is real, the nitty gritty details, the opposite of intuition. It seeks a balance of exertion with rest and recharge. It communicates via a wide range of bodily sensations, pleasurable or painful, to signal its needs. It strives for homeostasis, stability, and a healthy autonomic nervous system, balancing sympathetic (stress) and parasympathetic (rest and recover) activity.

ADVENTURER (JUNG—EXTRAVERTED SENSING)

The Adventurer wants to explore, savor pleasurable experiences, learn, and change. It seeks to be aroused and excited, and enjoys uncertainty, risk, and adventure. It is open-minded and curious, wondering what will happen next. Psychologist and curiosity researcher Todd Kashdan asserts that curiosity is a primary driver of human well-being and has recently published a new five-dimensional curiosity scale and four distinct types of curious people (Kashdan, Disabato, Stiksma, & Lazarus, 2017).

EXECUTIVE MANAGER (JUNG—INTROVERTED THINKING)

The Executive Manager seeks clarity and order, organizing the system to get things done efficiently, creating plans, goals, and to-do lists, and marshaling resources to accomplish tasks. It figures things out, thinks things through, using analytical, linear thinking processes. It directs focus and attention on the task at hand, a capable self-regulator setting aside disruptive emotions, impulses, and distractions. It wants to be productive. It would appear to be related to a brain capacity directing cognitive processes, called executive function, well-studied in the neuroscience literature (Banich, 2009).

STANDARD SETTER (JUNG—EXTRAVERTED THINKING)

The Standard Setter is concerned with performance and achievement, setting ambitious goals and meeting them. It measures and judges, setting internal standards and tracking external standards that determine self-esteem, to make sure we get respect, appreciation, and validation. It can be a hard taskmaster and a tough (inner and outer) critic. It is a source of grit, helping us persevere through ups and downs to accomplish big things. It cares about what others think and how we compare to others. It drives us to reach our potential, and often overworks in today's society-wide focus on achievement and accumulation of material resources.

Meaning Maker (Jung—Introverted Intuition)

The Meaning Maker engages in considering and answering overarching questions for Self, as well as connecting the dots and seeing patterns: what things mean, finding purpose in small and large domains, looking for the big picture, and encouraging growth. It is concerned with wholeness, peace, and harmony. It can incorporate a transcendent or spiritual capacity, connecting to the larger universe and thereby provide a larger meaning to one's life. It can be described as the inner coach, ready to reveal its quiet and profound wisdom when the mind is quiet.

Creative (Jung—Extraverted Intuition)

The Creative part is generative, imaginative, and spontaneous. It uses defocused nonlinear thinking processes, and enjoys brainstorming, humor, and being playful. When in full action, it produces deep flow states, a defocused state of mind when one loses a sense of self and is deeply absorbed in an activity. The inner Creative is the inventor and innovator, known for the ability to think outside the box and invent or design new ideas and technologies.

Confidence

The Confidence part is concerned with human behavior or action and is influenced by an internal assessment of competence—confidence leads to bold energy in action, self-doubt leads to hesitancy or procrastination. One's sense of strength, or empowerment, is a key determinant of behavior. There is extensive literature describing self-efficacy as a primary psychological construct, including Deci and Flaste's (1995) determination of competence as one of the three primary organismic drives (along with autonomy and relatedness) in Self-Determination Theory. The human desire to be strong, confident, and competent, and gain more knowledge, skills, and competence, is a primary need and capacity. One's level of confidence and the state of the Confidence part (strong or self-doubting) varies widely, and is domain-specific to myriad life activities, social environments, and demands of other capacities.

Coaching Using a Parts Model

This strengths-based model of inner family members offers coaches several insights and approaches. First, coaches can help clients activate a third-person or self-distancing perspective to improve objectivity and access wisdom, that is, a part of me is angry, not all of me (Kross & Ayduk, 2016). A second opportunity is for coaches to help clients become familiar with their own multiplicity of mind, and appreciate an inner family of parts. A coach can help a client decode met and unmet needs expressed by a client's emotions. A coach can also help a client decode conflicting perspectives on a decisional balance—which parts are promoting a change and why, and which parts are against the change and why. Then a client can identify ways to meet the unmet needs of the parts that are advocating against the change.

Coaches can also help a client conduct a roll call to get a variety of perspectives, or call on the perspective of one part to offer new insights. For example, a coach might ask: "If your body had a voice (Body Regulator), what would it advise?" Or "what wisdom does your Meaning Maker have to offer?" Or "what ideas would your Creative part bring?"

This model helps coaches and clients appreciate that internal conflict resulting from inbuilt conflicting needs and perspectives is normal and natural, that diverse perspectives are always available, and that the Meaning Maker as the inner coach is able to offer its intuitive wisdom needed most in any moment.

INNER TEAM COACHING AND IFS BY ISABEL D'ARENBERG

Barely keeping up with a world of accelerating change and overwhelming demands, coaching clients seek rapid solutions for a present challenge and desire short-term, laser-sharp interventions that deliver results quickly. They prefer solutions that add more skills and techniques to their self-management toolbox. Yet a client's "inner game," in the form of negative emotions, limiting beliefs, flawed thought patterns, and reactive behaviors, is often driving the outer game, holding back the client's ability to realize his or her full potential. Clients are often unaware of what is holding them back and that untapped resources lie within, and as a result prefer to not engage in deeper emotional or psychological work.

The ITC model was developed in Germany by Dr. Schulz von Thun, a communications psychologist, to help clients overcome fear and resistance to inner psychological work, develop self-leadership, and build a relationship with their personality parts daily (Lohnes-Fornoff, 2012). Clients become aware of being hijacked by agitated parts and then get centered to better navigate the inner game.

Both IFS and ITC help clients develop the *inner observer or witness*, the Self, that relates to different personality parts from a place of inner calm and strategic perspective, allowing clients to objectively decide how to proceed instead of being caught up in the story and emotional content of a part. ITC offers a solution-focused framework for addressing clients' concerns, helping them to become aware of and develop their resources, while applying the IFS technique of helping clients get in touch with their inner core, the Self, that radiates calm, connection, and compassion.

Similar to a meeting in an organization, where a manager convenes his or her team members to explore the issues at hand, a coach helps a client become aware of his or her parts/inner voices called "team members" (TMs) that arise when considering a specific issue. The coach helps the client disentangle from the TMs and take the stance of the Team Leader who acknowledges all TMs, mediates among them, and negotiates an agreement that takes into consideration their individual points of view.

To start, the coach helps the client identify and map all TMs that have something to say with respect to the client's concern. It is important that the coach evokes both the loud and preferred voices as well as those voices that are pushed into the background. The quieter voices when unheard will eventually find other ways to sabotage the client's progress to get attention, which can unintentionally impair mental, emotional, or physical well-being. Once a coach and client have understood the essence of a TM's concern, they summarize its intention in one sentence, give it a catchy name, find a symbol that further illustrates what it represents and draw it, for example, on a flip chart. Figure 23.3 shows a map for a client who has hired an unemployed friend. While the situation started out well, after some time the friend's bad moods were having a negative impact on workplace morale.

Next, the coach can map how the TMs relate to each other: identifying alliances, conflicts, and TMs that are pushed into the background. The coach looks for ways to reduce the number of TMs to a manageable size by grouping them by area of concern. Then the coach can suggest a way to proceed; for example, working with a TM that has a big emotional charge, engaging two that are in conflict, inviting differing opinions from several TMs, or recruiting a missing TM who might have needed resources (e.g., is there a part who can help bring wisdom?). In Figure 23.4, the dynamic among the client's inner team shows that there is a conflict of interest among several members (top part of figure) indicating that a team meeting is an appropriate way to proceed, asking each part for its perspective and suggestions for the way forward (bottom part of figure).

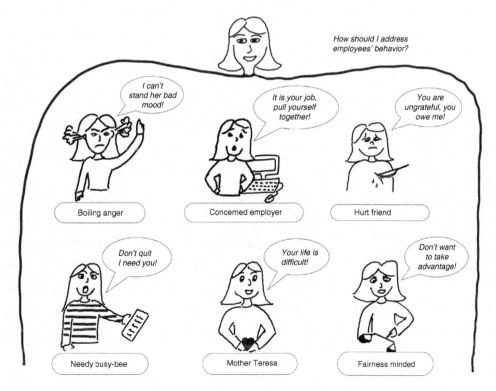

Figure 23.3 Map of client's inner team.
Source: Developed by Isabel d'Arenberg.

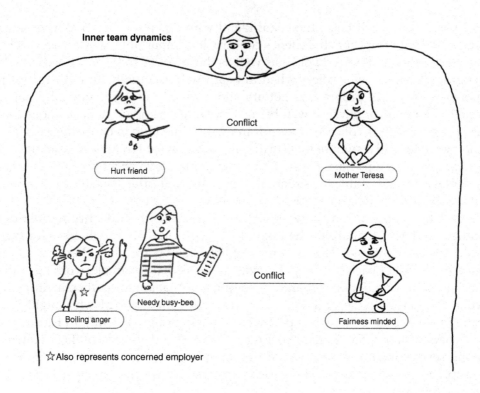

Figure 23.4 Inner team dynamics and inner team constellation.
Source: Developed by Isabel d'Arenberg.

One of the important benefits of ITC is the awareness and perspective a client gains on his or her internal motives, beliefs, emotions, and impulses. Mapping TMs, naming them, and distilling their key messages makes the client's inner dynamic more tangible. The client begins to use the part's creative name, recognize its voice, build a relationship, and identify the part more easily throughout the day. Often this level of awareness suffices to move toward a resolution of the situation. When clients become aware that some of their TMs are at the source of recurrent problems, they are more likely to engage in IFS therapy to heal and integrate the underlying dynamic.

CONCENTRATED COACHING MODEL BY MARK HURWICH

The Concentrated Coaching Model is a blend of coaching and IFS therapy and thus depends upon a coach completing a basic level of IFS training. The model supports clients who are stuck: holding themselves back for reasons they can't understand. They have sufficient skills to act, yet can't move forward or let go. An example is a serial entrepreneur whose company lost its funding and is unable to start another company. Another example is a well-published author who is stuck in a new book project, unable to move forward or give up. Third, an experienced business manager may invest heavily in consulting fees to develop elegant business strategies that then languish on a shelf. The logical mind wonders why logic cannot help highly effective people resolve illogical dilemmas. The IFS approach suggests that beneath the illogical behavior is hidden resistance, with sources below conscious awareness.

The first phase of the Concentrated Coaching Model focuses on strengthening the client's connection to a set of Core Intentions (Hurwich, n.d.) that generate a renewed sense of purpose and resourcefulness that were out-of-reach or hidden in the stuck state. A client may be able to identify five or more intentions. The next step is for the client to compare the current status to the core intentions and then explore his or her strengths and gifts available to assist in moving forward. A client also attunes to a deep sense of life meaning or purpose, the legacy and contribution his or her life is called to bring. A process of visualizing and experiencing an ideal future, using a time machine technique, is designed to help clients envision how their core intentions can manifest in the future to realize their life purpose and legacy.

The second phase deploys IFS techniques, with a focus on settling an internal civil war among the client's parts. This process may draw out some parts pounding the table to make progress, as well as other parts (which may have been previously hidden) that do not yet understand the merits of forward movement. The client is invited into his or her internal world, recalling the just-imagined future, guided by the coach; for example:

> *As you breathe, and focus within, recall the journey toward your future unfolding. Allow any parts of yourself that need to be heard or witnessed in any way to express themselves. You may notice feelings in your body, or perhaps you'll notice a phrase or hear something, or perhaps you'll get a sense of an image.*

As in IFS therapy, clients notice a sensation in or around their bodies, and the coach asks the client to describe the sensation fully, evoking its nature as a part. Then the coach guides the client to: *Notice how you are feeling toward this part of yourself.* If the client is feeling any agitation toward the part, rather than being open, calm, curious, and compassionate, that is a sign that other parts have emerged that are blocking access to the core, calm Self.

Usually, after a few minutes of mapping the parts that are present, the client will identify a part that signals a need for significant attention. The coach may ask the client to explore this part's identity, its role, needs, and fears. If it appears that the part is overworking as a protector of a deeper, wounded part, referred to as an exile in IFS, the coach facilitates the process for accessing and healing that exiled part. The IFS steps include witnessing the original wound, releasing the burden of the wounding experience created, connecting with blocked resources, and integrating the previously exiled part into a new, healthy state.

In a few Concentrated Coaching sessions, the client connects deeply with his or her core intentions and a future vision, while witnessing, healing, and integrating the parts that are troubled by change. The combination of drawing out strengths, desired intentions, and visualizing an ideal future, with a release of parts that might have seemed resistant, brings new awareness that is invigorating and transformational, allowing the client to flow forward in a healthier state.

WILLO3™: AN ORGANIZATIONAL MODEL BY TOUFIC HAKIM AND LAURA CRANDALL

The Willo3™ model (Hakim & Crandall, n.d.) emerged from an exploration of the application of IFS in an organizational context, in the context of curious questions: Is there an organizational equivalent to Self leadership? To what extent does an organization, as a collection of individuals, transcend the common phrase *greater than the sum of its individual parts*? If an organization then understood its culture in this way, would attributes of Self leadership translate in a usable way? And what would manifestations of individual Self attributes (i.e., compassion and calm) look like?

The Willo3™ model makes abstract ideas of organizational culture tangible, physically and visually in 3D. It is a conceptual framework, consistent with the constructs of IFS, to help organizations *make sense* of their complexity (systems of interacting systems) and use such learning to enhance flexibility, agility, and resiliency over time. Organizations, like individuals, have personalities commonly referred to as cultural norms (in Willo3: visual shapes). Awareness of these norms provides deep insight into an organization's own behavior, helping it to shift among shapes as needed. The Willo3 model brings three benefits:

a. An accessible conceptual framework that enables deep understanding of the culture from multiple viewpoints.
b. A 3D visual shape of organizational culture, both Present and Preferred, along with a colorful artifact to hold in one's hand.
c. A strategy to shapeshift between Present and Preferred states when desired in response to external conditions or internal needs.

The model's goal is to present an impartial view of an organization's culture that may be shared and refined with various stakeholders. Through a 3D lens—and "shape-awareness"—organizations see more clearly, become more nimble, and acquire sustainability over time through shape-shifting as needed. These outcomes are captured in the model's vision statement: *Perceiving their culture in 3D, organizations have the insight to shapeshift at will and to thrive.*

ARCHE-SHAPES

The model proposes seven predominant archetypes (cultural modes) that integrate three fundamental cultural aspects often aligned with collective organizational behavior. Organizations may rise above a *stuck* state in any mode if it is not serving their growth. Awareness of the Present mode, and why, combined with a view of a Preferred point in the future or vis-à-vis certain conditions, may reveal a pathway to shifting the mode/cultural shape—even if temporarily.

The model's 3DViewfinder™ extrapolates attributes of Self leadership, identifying cultural modes along three axes or dimensions, giving rise to seven predominant cultural archetypes called arche-shapes, based on the state of development of each fundamental mode (Figure 23.5). As a user-friendly, online assessment administered to various stakeholders, the tool allows an organization to identify its Present

Predominant shape	Predominant hue	Predominant modes	Sample driver	Sample attribute
	Red	EV	Accomplishment	Determination
	Purple	EV+LC	Growth	Competition
	Blue	LC	Knowledge	Studiousness
	Turquoise	LC+CH	Approval	Validation
	Green	CH	Fairness	Belonging
	Yellow	CH+EV	Improvement	Advocacy
	Full-Spectrum	EV+LC+CH	Integration	Hopefulness

Figure 23.5 Seven organizational arche-shapes.
CH, Community & Humanity; EV, Engagement & Vigor; LC, Learning & Creating.
Source: Copyright © 2017 Toufic Hakim and Laura Crandall.

and Preferred arche-shapes. Characterized by a special 3D shape, the volume and color represent the point of development along a given mode. Assessing its Present and Preferred shapes helps an organization begin to identify a path toward its Preferred Shape, as well as develop the ability to shapeshift over time.

Each shape indicates the particular, individual qualities that are positively reinforced in the organization. For example, in the Red Org, with Engagement and Vigor being predominant, persistence, confidence, and courage are reinforced. In the Green Org, compassion, presence, and connectedness are encouraged. In the Blue Org, creativity, curiosity, and openness are desirable individual qualities.

When aspects of culture are seen under a spotlight of color filters, "organizational consciousness," strategic understanding, and behavioral shaping can come to the forefront of planning and management. Willo3 presents a protocol guiding organizations to shapeshift. Arche-shapes represent positions in the organization's cultural map, shown in Figure 23.6, allowing intentionality of movement along pathways from one position to another to gain competence, agility, and resiliency.

The Willo3 process is collaborative, with multiple members/parts of an organization, external or internal, examining its culture visually, adopting common language, and ultimately sharing the same understanding. A strength of the model is its neutral view of the ideal organizational shape. There is no "right shape." Each arche-shape has strengths and benefits for different organizations and goals. Awareness of the shape, combined with the knowledge of what is Preferred and how to shift, can drive the shapeshifting process if or when needed.

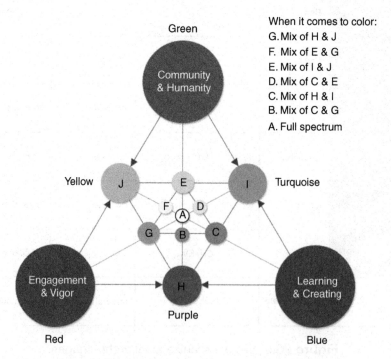

Figure 23.6 Organizational culture modes.
Source: Copyright © 2017 Toufic Hakim and Laura Crandall.

It is important to recognize how each person in an organizational system influences and is influenced by the current organizational strengths. Leaders, coaches, and employees bring their own personal arche-shapes and are influenced as well by the organizational arche-shapes. Last, the intent of the model is not to encourage static well-roundedness; the goal is for the organization to increase its capacity to self-assess, use its strengths, and flex its shape in response to circumstances.

CONCLUSIONS AND NEXT FRONTIERS

The four models of IFS in coaching that we explored in this chapter are novel and creative applications of IFS that serve as unique tools for cultivating human potential and thriving through personal and organizational transformation and *shape-shifting*. As coaches and psychologists continue to break new ground in applying the principles of IFS, beyond the healing process of IFS therapy, one can imagine future models that allow people to map their personalities or cultures, better understand and balance over-developed and under-developed capacities, and offer at-will tools for self-transformation, even daily. This work will then be ripe for continued research of outcomes and mechanisms. The applications of IFS in coaching are poised to unleash new levels of consciousness and wholeness within individuals and organizations heretofore not seen.

NOTE

The following were contributors to this chapter in the sections on IFS-based coaching models: Isabel d'Arenberg, Mark Hurwich, Toufic Hakim, and Laura Crandall.

REFERENCES

Banich, M. (2009). Executive function: The search for an integrated account. *Current Directions in Psychological Science, 18*(2), 89–94. doi:10.1111/j.1467-8721.2009.01615.x

Berens, L. (2000). *Dynamics of personality type: Understanding and applying Jung's cognitive processes.* West Hollywood, CA: Telos Publications.

Deci, E., & Flaste, R. (1995). *Why we do what we do: Understanding self-motivation.* New York, NY: The Penguin Group.

Disney. (n.d.). Inside Out gallery. Retrieved from http://movies.disney.com/inside-out-gallery

Hakim, T., & Crandall, L. (n.d.). What we do. Retrieved from www.willo3.com

Hurwich, M. (n.d.). *Core intention.* Retrieved from http://www.concentratedcoaching.net/training.html

Kabat-Zinn, J. (2012). *Mindfulness for beginners: Reclaiming the present moment and your life.* Boulder, CO: Sounds True.

Kashdan, T., Disabato, D., Stiksma, M., & Lazarus, R. (2017). The five-dimensional curiosity scale: Capturing the bandwidth of curiosity and identifying four unique subgroups of curious people. *Journal of Research in Personality, 73*, 130–149. doi:10.1016/j.jrp.2017.11.011

Kross, E., & Ayduk, O. (2016). Self-distancing: Theory, research, and current directions. *Advances in Experimental Social Psychology, 55*, 81–136. doi:10.1016/bs.aesp.2016.10.002

Lohnes-Fornoff, A. (2012). *"The Inner Team": A coaching tool to achieve authenticity* [Research Paper]. International Coach Academy. Retrieved from https://coachcampus.com/coach-portfolios/research-papers/annette-lohnes-the-inner-team-a-coaching-tool-to-achieve-authenticity

Mayer, J. (1995). The system-topics framework and the structural arrangement of systems within and around personality. *Journal of Personality, 63*(3), 459–493. doi:10.1111/j.1467-6494.1995.tb00503.x

Moore, M. (2013). Coaching the multiplicity of mind: A strengths-based model. *Global Advances in Health & Medicine, 2*(4), 78–84. doi:10.7453/gahmj.2013.030

Moore, M., Phillips, E., & Hanc, J. (2016). *Organize your mind, optimize your life.* Harvard Health books. New York, NY: William Morrow.

Peil, K. (2014). Emotion: The self-regulatory sense. *Global Advances in Health and Medicine, 3*(2), 80–108. doi:10.7453/gahmj.2013.058

Rowan, J. (1990). *Subpersonalities: The people inside us.* London, England: Routledge.

Schwartz, R. (1995). *Internal family systems therapy.* New York, NY: The Guilford Press.

Shadick, N., Sowell, N., Frits, M., Hoffman, S., Hartz, S., Booth, F., . . . Schwartz, R. (2013). A randomized controlled trial of an internal family systems-based psychotherapeutic intervention on outcomes in rheumatoid arthritis: A proof-of-concept study. *Journal of Rheumatology, 40*(11), 1831–1841. doi:10.3899/jrheum.121465. Retrieved from http://www.jrheum.org/content/jrheum/early/2013/08/10/jrheum.121465.full.pdf

The Center for Self Leadership. (n.d.). Retrieved from https://selfleadership.org/about-internal-family-systems.html

Vago, D. R., & Silbersweig, D. A. (2012). Self-awareness, self-regulation, and self-transcendence (S-ART): A framework for understanding the neurobiological mechanisms of mindfulness. *Frontiers in Human Neuroscience, 6,* 296. doi:10.3389/fnhum.2012.00296

24

Coaching for an Increasingly Complex World

Jennifer Garvey Berger and Catherine Fitzgerald

There is much written about volatility, uncertainty, complexity, and ambiguity (VUCA) that is becoming business as usual for leaders across industries and sectors around the world. Less is written about what those leaders should do about this shift. Perhaps even more unclear is how those of us who support leaders can change our own thinking and practices in order to help leaders learn not just how to handle the VUCA world, but how to thrive in it. We are hoping this chapter can help do just that.

WHAT IS COMPLEXITY ANYWAY?

Before we begin thinking about the ways coaches need to support leaders differently in times of complexity, we need a little background about complexity in the first place. There are lots of different frameworks that point to similar ideas: the distinction between technical problems and adaptive challenges, the difference between tame and wicked problems, the difference between those problems that are complicated and those that are complex (Camillus, 2008; Heifetz & Linsky, 2002; Snowden & Boone, 2007). The framework we turn to the most is Snowden's Cynefin[1] framework because it offers useful distinctions about how to recognize complexity and what to do about it. Cynefin highlights the difference between those things that are predictable (where patterns are straightforward enough to repeat time after time) and those things that are unpredictable (where patterns are created by such a wide variety of interacting forces that one cannot be sure that just because certain factors led to a particular outcome in one case, they will necessarily lead to the same outcome in the future).

In the predictable world, Snowden describes two different domains. Things are "Obvious" if the connection between cause and effect is repeatable and clear to all. Implementation is a technical issue, and people should readily agree on both the desired outcome and the desired pathway to get there. In the "Complicated" domain, there's a predictable and repeatable connection between the cause and the effect, but there's enough of a lag or enough different steps involved that you need experts to help figure things out. Different experts might disagree on exactly the right path (so you have to choose your experts carefully), but all of them should agree on the best outcome. The leaders we have worked with usually have this as their home base, the domain in which they are most comfortable. It is also our home base and the home base of most of the coaches with whom we have worked. This is not bad news: It is vital for us to handle complicated things well. The difficulty is that it can be hard to cross over into the complex space without some real effort.

That's because the rules change once the world becomes unpredictable. In the "Complex" domain, there are too many interacting forces to know what is going to happen next. Instead, we can only infer the causes after we see the effects. Much research has been done into complex events to try—misguidedly, as it turns out—to find the right answers that will help us predict and control the outcome the next time. We look at a company that has failed and try to understand the warning signs so that it will definitely not happen to our company; we look at a company that has done really well and we try to backfill our understanding of why it has been so successful. This can lead to interesting findings and helpful approaches, but we have to be careful to not slip into believing that simply because those things worked in the past, they will continue to work into the future in just this way[2].

Much of what leaders need to do is in the complex context. Marketplaces, business models, and business strategy are complex (although we often treat them as complicated and knowable). Just about everything to do with people and change—culture change, employee engagement, innovation, and so forth—is complex. It is not that *everything* leaders need to do is complex—lots of important work gets done in the obvious and complicated spaces—but every leader has key portions of his or her work that are complex.

The rules of thinking, acting, and being in complex contexts are fundamentally different from the rules that govern the more predictable world, so leaders need to be able to shift back and forth. Here, because there are so many interacting parts, you have to pay attention to the patterns in a system rather than following our more common cause-and-effect thinking and looking for single causes or anticipating single outcomes. In the complex world, there isn't a clear correlation between the size of an intervention and the size of the effect—which is why a massive roll out of a culture change program to get people to interact across silos sometimes changes virtually nothing (or makes things worse!), but a new app can spread like wildfire and change the way people communicate with each other across silos and around the world. Small strategic actions ("nudges") in particular directions allow leaders to watch for the emergence of new patterns so that they can encourage them (if they are going in a good direction) or discourage them (if they seem to be going the wrong way). Better than figuring out a single best answer or big bet, we should try small, safe-to-fail experiments[3] at first. In the complex domain, experimenting and then learning from the system as it changes is the best way to move in a desired direction.

Instead of trying to control or predict what will happen, we can observe, look for patterns, and intervene with an emergent, experimental approach. Understanding the fairly simple (but not easy) rules of complex systems means that leaders can use the complexity to their advantage instead of having it always be a force they are fighting against. But because the rules and practices that work in complex contexts are counterintuitive, leaders are likely to need support to get their heads and hearts and guts around them—and coaches are likely to need this support as well. It is just too easy to fall back into our more ordinary patterns, without noticing we are falling back into anything at all.

THE PERILS OF USING COMPLICATED APPROACHES FOR COMPLEX TIMES

Organizations have complicated approaches built into their DNA. Strategic planning, budgeting, risk management, performance management, compensation, innovation, culture change, leadership development—all of these systems generally operate with the fiction that we can predict and control the future—or at least that we should all look as if we can. Leaders are expected to know which moves to make to change the culture, to grow the business, to innovate. They are supposed to be able to create business cases and deliver outcomes and create stakeholder value and generally know how to make the world bend to their will. And when they do not know how to do this, we think they're incompetent. As Eric Beinhocker says,

> Corporate leaders are expected to be bold generals who forecast the future, devise grand strategies, lead their troops into glorious battle—and then [they] are fired at the first lost skirmish. It takes a courageous executive to push back against this mind-set, admit the inherent uncertainty of the future, and emphasize learning and adapting over predicting and planning. (Beinhocker, 2007, p. 347)

Taking a new approach to leadership is risky. Yet we know that for many leaders in many sectors, there is a choice between "deep change" or "slow death" (Quinn, 1996). We believe that while change is always perilous, never before has a status quo approach to leadership been so dangerous. We believe leaders who operate comfortably in the complex space think differently, engage differently, and act differently than leaders who operate in the complicated space (see Table 24.1).

THINK DIFFERENTLY

Leaders who deal well with the complex space think in different ways about people and problems. First, they recognize when they are dealing with a complex challenge and they distinguish it from obvious or complicated challenges for which different approaches are more helpful. They take a breath and redefine their sense of risk,

Table 24.1 Differences Among Thinking, Engaging, and Acting in a Predictable Versus Unpredictable, Complex World

	Predictable World	Unpredictable, Complex World
Thinking	Think about the future. Research, analyze, and plan carefully. Search for the root cause of the issue. Look to the past for an understanding of how the future will unfold.	Pay attention to the present, noticing patterns and connections. Notice what is at the center of the issue and stay away from that to find interventions at the edges where systems are more susceptible to change.
Engaging	Listen to others—particularly experts—and then decide best course. Work on your message to overcome the resistance of others and to align people.	Listen to others—particularly those who disagree with you—to find a wide and diverse set of possibilities you might build experiments around. Expect to give and receive feedback cleanly and well to focus on everyone's learning.[4]
Acting	Create interventions that attack the root cause of the issue. Solve problems one at a time with solutions that match the size and severity of the problems.	Create multiple, small, safe-to-fail experiments that seek to help shift the system and also learn from the system. Leaders are looking for the smallest interventions that might solve multiple problems as the whole system reorganizes to operate in more helpful ways.

knowing that in the complex space, it is never possible to know how something will turn out, so waiting for enough information to be sure is a losing strategy. This means that such leaders tolerate more uncertainty, ambiguity, and messiness while making decisions. These leaders stop privileging their logical minds that crave certainty and clarity. Instead they lead with their whole bodies, using their logic and also listening to their intuition and noticing and responding to their emotions.

ENGAGE DIFFERENTLY

Leaders who thrive in complexity understand that diversity of people and perspectives, while important across all domains, is critical in a complex context. They listen to people in different ways and to a different end—listening to learn rather than listening to convince others of their view. They hold different sorts of meetings, each of which is more likely to have a particular purpose rather than simply a recurring event with the same players and a similar agenda. They engage more of their stakeholders inside and outside the organization in more deeply inclusive, collaborative, emergent ways.

ACT DIFFERENTLY

In many leadership situations, like in carpentry, it pays to "measure twice and cut once"—know what you're doing and where you're going before you act. In complex situations, there's no way to measure twice before you cut—the context is moving so quickly that a precise measurement (or a piece of research or a committee recommendation) is too time consuming and may also lead to a false sense of certainty. Instead, in complex contexts, leaders try a number of experiments—interventions designed to be light and at the edges of the issue rather than using their root cause analysis to get straight at the heart of things (Schrage, 2014). This way the experiments are designed for maximum learning, and for the possibility that one of the experiments might have a much larger impact on the problem than anyone could have predicted.

HABITS OF MIND TO SUPPORT LEADERS IN COMPLEX SITUATIONS

If leaders need to shift the way they act, engage, and think, to these counterintuitive, complexity-friendly ways, they are going to need help. Over many years of research and practice, Berger and Johnston (2015) and our colleagues have found that there are particular habits of mind that, when we cultivate them, create a greater and greater level of success in complex times—and also create the conditions for leaders (and coaches) to experience complexity more as their home base rather than a foreign land where the language and customs are totally unfamiliar. These habits are: asking different questions, taking multiple perspectives, and seeing systems.

We know that these practices will not be wholly new to coaches. Really good coaching often focuses on these habits of mind, even if coaches may not have described them in this way. Yet we have found in our practice that encouraging a more explicit use of these different habits—in ourselves and in our clients—creates even more learning as well as creating more success in a complex world (see Table 24.2).

ASKING DIFFERENT QUESTIONS

As coaches, one of our central roles is to ask our clients questions that they may not have thought about themselves, which makes *asking different questions* a key coaching practice. We know that different questions open up different possibilities for our clients, and we tend to have a set of go-to questions we ask because we know those open up new insights or possibilities for our clients.

Whatever your personal set of powerful questions, complexity theories offer an expanded set of different questions that focus on the nature of the problem and on a leader's possible response to it. When coaching clients who are facing complex situations, one of the most helpful questions you can ask is simply whether the situation is complex or not. If the situation is complex, different questions can help shift clients from a focus on the destination to a focus on the direction, or from a focus on the future (or past) to a focus on the present.

For example, we[5] had a coaching client, Rochelle, a middle manager in a non-government organization, who had a practice of planning her 3- to 5-year goals each January. In our January coaching call, we learned that these goals, far from opening up clarity for Rochelle, were making her feel trapped and anxious. We asked

Table 24.2 Key Questions When Using the Habits of Mind

Habit in Complexity	Questions for Coaches to Ask to Support the Development of the Habit
Asking different questions	Is this an issue that repeats reliably (and so is predictable) or does it happen in a new way each time? Is the context changing such that what worked well in the past might not work so well now? Are you focused on a direction or a destination? Instead of creating an elaborate plan for change, what things are working well that you could enhance and build on, that you could "nudge"? What do you believe about this situation and how might you be wrong?
Taking multiple perspectives	What people and perspectives do you usually listen to about such topics and situations? How could you substantially expand the perspectives, information, and ideas that you are getting? What perspectives about this situation have you written off and what could you learn if you listened more deeply and more open-mindedly to these perspectives? How is that [obnoxious or annoying] person about whom you are complaining operating in good faith, with positive intentions (and being a hero in his or her own story)? If you listened to this person, what might you learn?
Seeing systems	Think about the boundaries of this issue. If you zoom out and consider a bigger picture (e.g., longer time period, more relationships, other parts of the business, other geographies), what do you learn? If you zoom in and consider a smaller definition of the issue, what do you learn? If you take your eyes off the search for the immediate root cause of this issue, what other contributing factors might be involved? Is there anything about this issue that reminds you of other past or current issues? Does connecting those issues show you any deeper patterns in your organization or give you any new insights or ideas? What dynamics do you see with this situation? If it is stuck, what factors/forces/relationships contribute to its stuckness? If it is spiraling, what factors/forces/relationships contribute to the spiral?

whether these goals were in the complicated, predictable space or the complex, unpredictable space and Rochelle saw that they were clearly in the complex realm. As Rochelle examined her goals, she noticed that all of the goals involved a single destination rather than a direction. She decided to reframe each of her destination goals (like "get into an MBA program") to a directional goal ("learn more about the scholarship of business so that I'm more prepared to successfully launch my own start-up"). This reframe not only changed Rochelle's feelings about her goals, but also opened up a huge new set of opportunities for meeting her goals that were more aligned with the direction of her life.

TAKING MULTIPLE PERSPECTIVES

People increasingly talk about leadership agility as a key driver of success in complexity. One key marker of that agility is the number of perspectives a person can hold simultaneously, while still holding on to his or her own perspective and without making any of the perspectives wrong or bad. This capacity is useful in many different sorts of situations because it enables leaders (and all of us) to not get stuck in a single perspective but to move fluidly across differences in order to find a better solution than the one that might have been most obvious.

You can see that this would be especially important in complex situations. In complexity, our own single perspective is always too small to fully understand an issue, so we require diverse perspectives—even those perspectives with which we disagree—because they help broaden our sense of the issue and the possibilities around it. They help us expand our set of possible safe-to-fail experiments to attempt to nudge the system and they make disagreement an asset rather than a liability as people disagree to expand what is possible rather than disagreeing about a single right answer.

While curiosity is helpful when employing all of the habits of mind, our ability to listen to one another is fundamentally shaped by our ability to open our minds to another person. In this case, the hope is to get your client really *curious* about what is going on for others. Without that curiosity, it is nearly impossible to listen well and to take perspective that is different from yours.

A key set of questions coaches can ask, then, will open leaders to the ways their perspectives are limited without having leaders judge their perspectives as wrong. Indeed, in complexity, all perspectives are necessarily limited, and even objectively wrong perspectives (where there is a mistake of fact, for example, or the repetition of a false rumor) can be helpful in unexpected ways.

Steve, the president of a large manufacturing company, was confused about employee engagement because the climate surveys and discussions with his senior managers tended to offer a picture that was more one-dimensional and uniform than he would have expected given the diversity of the work and the people in his global company. We helped him design meetings across the company, using "liberating structures," a set of highly interactive meeting designs,[6] to explore the topic without smoothing over the diversity of opinion into a single story (Lipmanowicz & McCandless, 2014). We also coached him to be able to hear even difficult perspectives without defensiveness and without the desire to leap to a solution immediately. As a result of these meetings, Steve and his senior leaders were able to gain a deeper understanding of the ways in which staff were and weren't feeling engaged, as well as many ideas about increasing engagement. What they hadn't expected as much was that the experience of the meetings themselves was an intervention into the engagement of the employees at many levels of the organization. People felt better just having had their say and been listened to so well, and their engagement and creativity increased. People throughout the organization also felt empowered to make small shifts in their work, which also increased their engagement and satisfaction.

SEEING SYSTEMS

Humans are wired to disentangle and categorize, to answer simpler questions when we think we are answering complex ones (Kahneman, 2013). We often make the mistake of looking at single events rather than understanding the ways things are interconnected with one another. Some of this is the "fundamental attribution error," which makes us likely to blame an outcome or an event on a person rather than on the circumstances, but it is also that the human brain automatically takes things apart and analyzes them.

In complexity, the connections are more important than the nodes, so it is more helpful to pay attention to the way things are connected and interacting than to pay attention to individuals or individual events. This means that we can ask questions that encourage our clients to focus on the interrelations and the forces in the issue rather than the particular people or events involved. We can draw clients' attention to particular patterns they see because observing the patterns will give them new places to push for experiments.

This is how we helped Richard, the Chief People Officer at a successful consumer goods company. Richard was frustrated that in two cases in a row, the external candidates who were appointed into senior leadership roles had stumbled and ultimately failed in their positions. He was looking for the root cause of the problem, which he figured was probably somewhere in the hiring process that selected these two individuals even though they were not a good fit for the organization. Because we know that in complexity there is no "root cause" (because there are too many factors interacting to have a sense of a single most important cause), we asked Richard questions about not just the two individuals and the hiring process, but also about the system of the organization into which they were hired. What were the many forces that contributed to the lack of success of these people? What were the patterns he had noticed over the past 10 new appointments into senior roles, whether they were successful or not? To what extent were leaders from outside the organization welcomed and supported?

As he looked at patterns, Richard continued to examine the hiring process, but he also turned his attention to the arrogance of the organizational culture that believed that homegrown talent was just more likely to "get it" than outsiders. He wondered about experiments he might try that would help him nudge his colleagues into curiosity about what "newbies" brought with them to the organization and how they might successfully change the organization rather than simply being a good fit from the beginning, or working hard in onboarding to become a good fit as quickly as possible. Looking at the system and a wider set of issues made it possible for Richard to see new possibilities for experimentation that might address not only this issue, but a whole suite of related issues as well.

COACHES FOR A COMPLEX WORLD

If you have been paying attention to the amazing number of ways our clients need to flex to operate well in the complex world, you might begin to wonder: "Dealing with complexity seems so hard for my clients—what are the implications for *me*?" We know that, throughout this chapter, we have suggested that you become a cultural guide to a land where you yourself are unlikely to feel entirely at home. Indeed, we have both been challenged over the last 15 years to make sense of the complex world around us and of the counterintuitive ways that we need to think, engage, and act as we alter our own habits of using complicated approaches to complex issues. This is just about the hardest work that either of us has ever done, and each day we are learning more, while continually bumping up against our own limitations. The better news is that starting to get our heads around the new rules for a complex world is also one of the most exciting and important ways of thinking we've ever encountered and, as a result, we have been able to support our clients in ways that they (and we) could not have previously imagined.

Like leading for complexity, coaching for complexity requires more than learning a new set of tools and approaches: It requires us to grow into a whole new way of seeing the world—both conceptually and instinctively. It requires us to redefine what coaching is and what expertise is. And it requires us to actually live these principles and ideas ourselves.

These changes are not just about *what we know* but about *how we understand the world*. This chapter offered a set of ideas, but these ideas cannot be put into practice without the mindsets and awareness to *live* them. Theories of adult development (Berger, 2012; Kegan, 1994; Torbert, 2004) give us one lens for understanding the way adults change and grow over time in their capacity to take multiple perspectives, see systems and interconnections, and cope with paradox and ambiguity. While there is not a straight line between a person's form of mind in an adult development sense and a person's capacity to cope well in complex situations, our hunch and experience is that these capacities are connected in some significant way. This means that, in our practice, a working knowledge of adult development and of the way coaches can support clients to grow developmentally is a key ingredient in the mix (Berger, 2012; Kegan & Lahey, 2009; Petrie, 2014). In other places, Jennifer has written more about the habits of mind that support leaders as individuals to stretch into these more complex ways of seeing and interacting with the world (Achi & Berger, 2015; Berger & Johnston, 2015). Familiarity with these ideas can be a valuable complement to an understanding of complexity.

Dealing with complexity is hard work, but our clients tend to find it exciting work; in fact, many clients have talked to us about the "redemptive power" of complexity. Although they can be frustratingly hard to encounter at first, the new perspectives and tools presented here have allowed leaders to make progress on challenges that have stumped them for years—without exhausting themselves by pushing harder and harder using the same tools and approaches they have used in the past.

The demands made on us as coaches, though, are at least as significant as the demands made on our clients, and we might find ourselves getting weary as well. As foreigners ourselves in this new land, we are challenged to work alongside our clients, to become co-explorers in this space, and to define and create a new way of working together with our clients and our colleagues.

And in many ways, this is the whole point. At its core, the call of complexity is to approach the world in more open and curious ways. It is about loosening our need for control and certainty, relinquishing our illusory image of our work and our lives as knowable and predictable. This is difficult work, but it is incredibly rewarding. As we become more agile at crossing between the complex and the complicated realms, we can flow with the currents of the water rather than fighting against them. We can begin to make use of the quickly changing, ambiguous world rather than wishing it would go away. We can also become more able to engage those best parts of our humanity—our compassionate, connected, and curious selves.

ACKNOWLEDGMENT

The authors would like to thank a fantastic set of colleagues for the comments that so improved this chapter: Amber Brooks, Carolyn Coughlin, David Kanter, Kate Sermanni, Keith Johnston, Michael Berger, Patrice Laslett, Wendy Bittner, and Zafer Achi.

NOTES

1. "Cynefin" is a Welsh word, meaning "habitat." It is pronounced "ken-EH-vin."

2. Snowden and Boone (2007) offer a fourth domain in the Cynefin framework— "Chaotic"—for those times when there is no pattern to follow and no relationship between cause and effect. Under those circumstances, the best thing a leader can do is act to stabilize the system, watch the way it responds, and shape your next set of actions in that way. There are many other subtleties to the Cynefin model that space does not allow us to cover here, but that are well worth your time to review.

3. Safe-to-fail experiments or "safe-to-fail probes" are aimed at learning more about a complex system while experimenting with intervening in the system.

4. See Jentz (2007, 2012) and Stone and Heen (2014) for ways to deal with differences in complexity-friendly ways.

5. We don't really coach together, of course.

6. This is a fabulous open source resource for meeting and decision making in complexity: www.liberatingstructures.com

REFERENCES

Achi, Z., & Berger, J. G. (2015). Delighting in the possible. *McKinsey Quarterly*. Retrieved from https://www.mckinsey.com/business-functions/strategy-and-corporate-finance/our-insights/delighting-in-the-possible

Beinhocker, E. D. (2007). *The origin of wealth: The radical remaking of economics and what it means for business and society*. Cambridge, MA: Harvard Business Review Press.

Berger, J. G. (2012). *Changing on the Job: Developing leaders for a complex world*. Stanford, CA: Stanford Business Books.

Berger, J. G., & Johnston, K. (2015). *Simple habits for complex times: Powerful practices for leaders*. Palo Alto, CA: Stanford Business Books.

Camillus, J. C. (2008). Strategy as a wicked problem. *Harvard Business Review*, pp. 99–106.

Heifetz, R. A., & Linsky, M. (2002). *Leadership on the line: Staying alive through the dangers of leading.* Cambridge, MA: Harvard Business Review Press.

Jentz, B. (2007). *Talk sense: Communicating to lead and learn.* Acton, MA: Research for Better Teaching.

Jentz, B. C. (2012). *EntryPlan Approach: How to start a leadership position successfully.* Leadership & Learning, Inc. Retrieved from www.entrybook.com

Kahneman, D. (2013). *Thinking, fast and slow.* New York, NY: Farrar, Straus and Giroux.

Kegan, R. (1994). *In over our heads: The mental demands of modern life.* Cambridge, MA: Harvard University Press.

Kegan, R., & Lahey, L. (2009). *Immunity to change: How to overcome it and unlock the potential in yourself and your organization.* Boston, MA: Harvard Business Press.

Lipmanowicz, H., & McCandless, K. (2014). *The surprising power of liberating structures: Simple rules to unleash a culture of innovation.* Seattle, WA: Liberating Structures Press.

Petrie, N. (2014). *Future trends in leadership development* (White paper). Greensboro, NC: Center for Creative Leadership.

Quinn, R. E. (1996). *Deep change: Discovering the leader within.* San Francisco, CA: Jossey-Bass.

Schrage, M. (2014). *The innovator's hypothesis: How cheap experiments are worth more than good ideas.* Cambridge, MA: The MIT Press.

Snowden, D. J., & Boone, M. E. (2007). A leader's framework for decision making. *Harvard Business Review*, pp. 69–76.

Stone, D., & Heen, S. (2014). *Thanks for the feedback: The science and art of receiving feedback well.* New York, NY: Penguin Books.

Torbert, W. R. (2004). *Action inquiry: The secret of timely and transforming leadership.* San Francisco, CA: Berrett-Koehler Publishers.

25

Acceptance and Commitment Therapy (ACT)-Based Coaching

Richard Blonna and Tim Anstiss

This chapter explores the key concepts, tools, and strategies for coaching people toward improved health, well-being, and performance using Acceptance and Commitment coaching (AC coaching), a holistic and multi-component coaching version of Acceptance and Commitment Therapy (ACT).

AC coaching is a pragmatic form of coaching, underpinned by functional contextualism and relational frame theory. The goal of AC coaching is to help clients increase their psychological flexibility—a state characterized by being clear about and living in harmony with one's values, spending time in the present moment, defusing and gaining separation from one's thoughts, accepting unwanted, unpleasant and unhelpful feelings and sensations, and cultivating the perspective of the observing self.

In contrast to much cognitive-behavioral coaching, rather than trying to alter the content of a client's thoughts (e.g., through inference chaining, error identification, disputation, behavioral experimentation), AC coaching emphasizes the importance of changing one's relationship with one's thought and thinking process, noticing and naming thoughts, beliefs and thinking patterns, and gaining some separation and distance from them. Clients are guided and encouraged to notice the rise and fall of unpleasant and unhelpful thoughts and feelings, and to "take them with them" as they go about living the kind of life they want for themselves. Indeed, experiential avoidance—struggling with and trying to avoid unwanted thoughts and feelings—is considered to be at the heart of many people's problems with living and can result in several health problems, especially when one tries to control one's feelings via eating, drinking, smoking, or other unhelpful behaviors.

In this chapter, we introduce the ramp model of AC coaching, emphasizing the need for clients to expend effort and take the time to practice (both within and between sessions), and to develop and regularly apply the skills that enable psychological flexibility and improved health, well-being, functioning, quality of life, and flourishing.

AC COACHING OVERVIEW

Coaching theory and practice revolve around helping motivate clients to achieve their values-based goals and live purposeful lives. Coaching theory assumes that clients are whole, functioning people who are looking to improve their lives.

Coaches assume that, given the right conditions, clients can often work out what is best for them, plan for the future, and solve their own problems. But when they present to the coach, they may be stuck in a rut and are not making progress at the rate they would like. They may also be experiencing unpleasant or unwanted emotions such as anxiety, worry, stress, anger, guilt, or shame and engaging in some unhelpful behavior patterns that contribute to them being stuck.

ACT-based coaching helps clients: (a) develop greater awareness regarding how their thoughts, feelings, and attempts to manage or control these contribute to their present state; (b) develop their psychological flexibility; and (c) become unstuck and move forward toward a more meaningful, engaged, and rewarding life. People experiencing a lack of psychological flexibility tend to:

- Lack clarity regarding their values, the things that really matter to them in life

- Take insufficient action in the direction of their values

- Fuse and become entangled with their thoughts, inner dialogue, memories, and images of the future and the past

- Avoid experiencing unpleasant or unwanted thoughts, feelings, and sensations (experiential avoidance)

- Lack contact with the present moment, the here and now, the direct sensations of their body

- Be over-attached to various stories, beliefs, rules, and assumptions about the self, their "conceptualized" or "narrative" self

These factors are represented in the Hexaflex model shown in Figure 25.1.

AC coaches use a wide range of coaching tools and strategies—including psycho-education, Socratic questioning, in-session skills practice, experiential learning, goal setting, modeling of helpful attitudes and behaviors, use of metaphor, values clarification, mindfulness and compassionate mind techniques, self-monitoring, active listening and homework assignments—to help clients develop greater psychological flexibility, get unstuck, move forward in the direction of valued life goals,

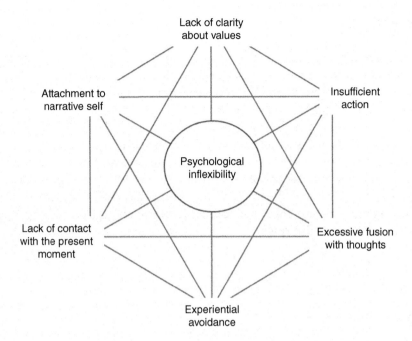

Figure 25.1 The Hexaflex model.

and experience improved quality of life and functioning in different life domains. Coaches also try to cultivate and maintain psychological flexibility in themselves. They specifically guide, encourage, and support clients to:

- Clarify what really matters to them, their values, and explore how they may manifest their values or live more fully in harmony with them over the coming weeks and months

- Take committed action toward important life goals that are in harmony with their values

- Accept, allow, tolerate, be willing to have, and make room for unpleasant thoughts, feelings, and sensations

- Notice their thinking and defuse from and gain separation and distance from their thoughts, seeing their thoughts as objects of consciousness that rise and fall, that come and go, and over which they have little control

- Pay attention with openness, flexibility, and curiosity to what is happening in the present moment

- Cultivate and view the world from the perspective of the observing self—that silent, quiet part of oneself that persists through time, observing and noticing change in the world, containing all the changes that go on inside a person's head but does not itself get caught up in those changes.

A NEW MODEL

The Hexaflex model is a very useful tool for visualizing and thinking about the different aspects or component processes of psychological flexibility. It also emphasizes the essential interrelationship and overlapping nature of these psychological processes or skills. It fails, however, to depict the need for effort and movement that is required for clients to make progress and move from being stuck and perhaps languishing in life toward being unstuck and flourishing in life.

This dynamic movement and process is an integral part of a new model developed by Anstiss and Blonna (2014) called the Ramp model (see Figure 25.2).

We also recast the six "Processes" that comprise psychological flexibility as skills and strategies to help them be more easily understood by coaching clients. We label these skills and techniques:

- Valued living

- Committed action

- Acceptance

- Disentanglement

- Contact with the present moment

- Observing self

From this perspective, the coach's role is to help the client make progress up the ramp toward his or her best possible life, learning about, practicing, and cultivating first one skill/strategy and then another, while helping the client see the overlap

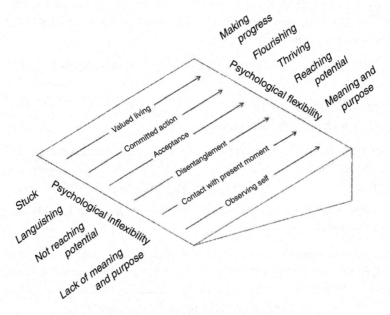

Figure 25.2 The Ramp model.

among these strategies and how progress with one will often aid progress with another. The skilled coach will be able to move backward and forward and side to side, helping the client to understand and apply the strategies and skills likely to be most helpful in making progress toward a vital, engaged, meaningful, and rewarding life. The Ramp model also suggests that:

- Effort is required to make progress (it won't happen spontaneously)
- Backsliding is not unexpected
- The coach cannot take the steps for the client or fix them
- "Insight" and self-understanding—the goals of some therapies—will only get the client so far
- There are multiple skills to be developed and practiced, not just one
- Everyone is somewhere on this journey toward improved quality of life
- Many people are "stuck" and unsure about how to make best progress

Let us now look at each of these skills and strategies.

VALUED LIVING

When clients are not clear about their values, they are like being in a sailboat without a rudder (Blonna, 2010). They find it very hard to stay on course, especially when navigating the rough seas of their lives. Values are the rudder that allow clients to steer their ship along the course they've set to reach their goals.

AC coaches help their clients clarify their values and see how moving toward and living more fully in harmony with their values will most likely result in more meaning, purpose, vitality, engagement, and well-being. Values are the things that are most important to us, which relate to and inform what we want our lives to be about. They inform and shape how we behave. Values are personally chosen, not imposed by others as "shoulds" or "musts." They can be considered compass points—providing a direction for our lives and enabling us to check, from time to time, if our lives are going in the right direction. Values are not goals. Goals are things that can be "reached" or "achieved." Values are things that can be "lived in harmony with," "expressed," "turned toward," or "moved in the direction of." The question "Am I done yet?" can be asked of goals, but not values (Hayes & Smith, 2005). Wilson and Murrell (2004) used the term "valued living," emphasizing that this is an ongoing process and not an outcome. Living in harmony with our values provides us with multiple and sustainable sources of positive reinforcement, provides us with both intrinsic and autonomous sources of motivation, and contributes to life satisfaction. AC coaches help their clients to see how clarifying and living more fully in harmony with their values can help them to flourish as human beings, to live the kind of life they want for themselves, and to reach their potential.

Values clarification may be one of the first things an AC coach does with a client, since until the coach knows what it is the client values, it can be hard to identify in what ways the client's psychological inflexibility and experiential avoidance are getting in the way. AC coaches have a range of tools and strategies to help clients clarify what is important to them, including:

- Selecting and prioritizing from a list of values

- Using a "values card sorting" exercise, placing different value cards into different piles according to their relative importance

- Visualization exercises, such as asking clients to describe what their life will be like when it is going well, or "attending one's own funeral" where clients are asked to describe their funeral; or the "writing one's own obituary" exercises. And inferring, from these, what are the most important things in life for the client

- Having clients talk about their values in different areas or domains of life

- Using the "values compass" exercise or worksheet

- Using a questionnaire such as the Valued Living Questionnaire, the Personal Values Questionnaire, or the Survey of Life Principles

The AC coach also touches on values from time to time during ongoing coaching—asking such questions as "Does this move you in the direction of your values, or away from the life you want to be living?" or "What would you like to do to take you in the right direction for a meaningful life for you?"

COMMITTED ACTION

Thinking and talking will only get the client so far—and perhaps not very far at that. For the client to make progress, he or she needs to act, to behave differently. Like many other coaches, the AC coach helps clients:

- Set long- and short-term goals in harmony with their values

- Make plans for new (values-consistent) behavior, so that it is more likely to occur

- Publicly commit to a particular course of action

- Do the required behaviors

- Be willing to experience uncomfortable thoughts, feelings, and sensations as they make behavior changes

Blonna (2010) describes willingness as the internal part of commitment, and a willing mind is one that understands the need to act while accepting that one cannot figure everything out in one's head in advance. The external part of committed action is the physical act of doing something constructive. Taking constructive action means behaving in value-congruent ways that help you meet your goals.

Some clients may need to develop or improve their skills in order to take committed action. For instance, a single person who values a warm, committed relationship may need to develop dating skills. A person who struggles with anger at work but values being a good colleague may need to develop anger management skills, and an overweight person who values independence may need to develop food selection, food preparation, and healthy eating skills, as well as the ability to tolerate any unpleasant feelings that may have historically triggered comfort eating.

It is important that clients do not feel overwhelmed by a commitment to live in harmony with their values. It is better that they realize that, regardless of recent or previous behavior, they can always choose—moment by moment—to turn toward their values, and have their values guide what they are going to do next. Like falling off a bicycle, the client can always choose to get back on and continue moving in a particular direction—toward a life that matters for them.

ACCEPTANCE

Acceptance involves a willingness to have what is being experienced right now—including uncomfortable thoughts, feelings, and sensations (Flaxman, Blackledge, & Bond, 2011). Willingness to have is not the same as wanting. For instance, anxiety is a painful feeling and not many people want it, but to be successful in different life areas a person may need to be willing to experience it from time to time, to tolerate this feeling. It is also commonly helpful to help the client make contact with the unpleasant emotion and experience it as if anew, locating it perhaps in the body, feeling it as it actually is and not as the mind says it is (e.g., awful, terrible, can't stand it; Forsythe & Eifert, 2007). Such experiential acceptance is the opposite of experiential avoidance and is an important strategy or skill in helping a person move forward toward a higher quality, engaged, and flourishing life.

Since avoiding uncomfortable experiences (anxiety, anger, sadness, shame, fast heart rate, unpleasant images, etc.) is natural and not always problematic, the AC coach may have to first explain to the client why learning to tolerate, be with, and accept these feelings may be a good idea. This can involve psycho-education about the fact that it is not the experience itself that is problematic and holding them back, but the things they are doing to avoid or attempt to control the experience. A range of metaphors exist to help the client "get" the importance of acceptance rather than avoidance, including:

- The "passengers on the bus" metaphor. The client is a bus driver, and whenever the client turns the bus in the direction he or she wants to go, passengers become noisy and come up to the front and threaten the driver, telling the driver to change direction. Often, the driver does what the passenger say, and turns the bus away from the direction he or she wanted to take it. But the passengers can never actually harm the driver. If the driver keeps going in the direction desired, the passengers will make some noise but will not ever touch or harm the driver. In this metaphor, the passengers are the client's thoughts and feelings, and the bus is the client's life, and the direction he or she wants to go is toward a better life in harmony with his or her values.

- The "unwanted visitor at a party" metaphor. You're having a party with friends, and an unpleasant neighbor turns up and barges in. You spend time trying to get the neighbor to leave, with little success. You get angry, spend less time with your friends, and begin to feel that the party is spoiled. Alternatively, you could choose to spend time doing what you want to do at your party with your friends, and just let the unwanted visitor be—not wanting the neighbor to be present but allowing him or her to be present, accepting and making space for him or her.

Once clients accept (or accept the possibility) that giving up their struggle with, and learning the skill of accepting and allowing, unwanted thoughts and feelings can help them get on with their lives, the AC coach helps them learn how to more fully notice, experience, take in, tolerate, and be with the unwanted feelings, using various mindfulness, visualization, and breathing exercises. The AC coach encourages clients to be open and curious about their inner experience and sensations, like a scientist—trying to locate in it their body, to describe it as a color or an object, to try to "breathe into" the sensation or experience, and to "soften" around it. This is a form of exposure therapy. Once clients are better able to accept and tolerate their unwanted experience, they are often able to see how they are now in a better position to get on with their lives—taking their unwanted experiences and sensations with them.

DISENTANGLEMENT

The AC coach uses a variety of tools and strategies to help their clients (and themselves) become less entangled and fused with unhelpful thoughts, beliefs, rules, sayings, words, phrases, images, and memories. Different metaphors are used to help clients get the idea of fusion—such as "radio doom and gloom" always playing in the background telling the client unhelpful stuff, or "getting hooked like a fish" in which the more the client struggles with a particular thought or belief, trying to change it, the more it hooks the client and prevents him or her from moving on. Some coaches invest in some Chinese paper finger traps. Once both index fingers are inserted, the more you pull your hands apart, the tighter they grip the fingers. In order to free yourself, you need to stop struggling and push the fingers toward each other so the grip lessens. Another experiential exercise to help clients get the importance of noticing thoughts rather than seeing the world through them includes having them write down some of the unhelpful thoughts and words they use about themselves on a sheet of paper. Then having them hold this piece of paper up in front of their face and asking them to walk around the room. They will, or course, experience some difficulty with this task as a result of having their view obstructed. Then ask the client to take the piece of paper away from their face and hold it lower down their body and perform the same task of walking round the room. Asking them what they noticed may evoke something like "well, it's a lot easier now"—and the parallel can be made with how holding onto our thoughts and beliefs too tightly and closely can lead to problems with navigating one's life and making progress in the world.

There are a large number of exercises the coach can use with clients to help them develop their skills in distancing and defusing from their thoughts and images, including:

- Leaves on a stream

- Viewing thoughts as if on a blank TV screen

- Singing the thoughts or saying them in a funny voice

- Repeating the word 50 times

- Thanking the mind for having the thought

- Saying "I'm having the thought that. . ."

(Stoddard & Afari, 2014)

Of course, the reason to help clients disentangle (defuse, separate) from unhelpful thoughts and beliefs is to increase their freedom to act in a desired way, to give them more control over the direction of their lives, and to give them more choice on a moment-to-moment basis. This helps them to more fully engage with the world as it is, directly experienced via the senses, rather than experiencing the world through filters of words, images, and other cognitions. Thoughts, images, and memories come to be seen as things that come and go, that rise and fall of their own accord and in their own time—rather than things to be struggled with, fought, suppressed, argued with, or blotted out.

CONTACT WITH THE PRESENT MOMENT

Unhelpful and unwanted thoughts and images are commonly about the past or the future—not about what is happening in the immediate moment. Many emotions and feelings have a past or future orientation—for instance, sadness, regret, anger, shame, guilt, bitterness, and hurt tend to be "backward looking" emotions, while anxiety, fear, and dread tend to be "forward oriented" emotions. But the past and the future have no independent existence outside of a human brain; they are not "real." By helping clients connect with, experience, and spend more time in the present moment, the AC coach helps reduce some of the power of the clients' recalled past and anticipated future. It also helps clients who are experiencing some anxiety or other intense unwanted feelings in the session become more grounded and less distressed and distracted.

Blonna (2010) outlines four aspects of mindful moments: (a) They focus on the present moment. (b) They are nonjudgmental and accept the present moment for what it is. (c) They are nonverbal (adding speech to describe the present moment adds a level of interpretation and is one step removed from the here and now). (d) They are nonconceptual. During mindful moments, nothing gets figured out, worked on, analyzed, or solved (Germer, Siegel, & Fulton, 2005).

The AC coach helps the client spend time in the present moment in a nonjudgmental, nonlabeling way—just paying attention to the raw sensations that change, rise, and fall both outside and inside their skin. Wilson et al. (2001) and others emphasize that evaluative language—our ability to label, rate, and judge things as good or bad, wanted or unwanted, acceptable or unacceptable, forgivable or unforgiveable, and so forth—is at the heart of much psychological distress, poor well-being, and poor performance in various life roles, but that none of these labels or judgments apply to the thing itself, as experienced through the senses of sight, touch, smell, hearing, or feeling. Focusing on the present moment puts one in closer contact with raw, unmediated sensations and can help clients to notice (and thus gain some separation from) the judgments, evaluations, commentaries, beliefs, and stories that they add to the mix, as these things come and go, rise and fall, appear and disappear.

Tools and strategies AC coaches use to help the client get in contact with the present moment include:

- Noticing one's hand. Have clients hold up their hand in front of them, and guide them for a few minutes to really pay attention to it in detail—the contour of the fingers, the patterns of any veins, the presence of any hairs, the nails, the lines, any scars that may be present, and so forth.

- Focusing on one's breath. Having the client pay attention to the breath coming in and the breath going out. What happens to the stomach and shoulders with each in breath and out breath? Noticing the sensation of the breath entering the nose or the mouth. Noticing any temperature difference between the breath coming in and the breath leaving.

- Listening to sounds. Have clients close their eyes and pay attention to the sounds in the room, to really listen for sounds and any sounds behind sounds. To notice them and how the mind tries to label them. And then to bring the mind back to just noticing the sounds. Sounds far way, sounds in the room, any sounds coming from the body.

OBSERVING SELF

The self is not a single thing. The self can be sensed or viewed from different perspectives including the "narrative" or "biographical" self (self as content), as well as the "observing" self (self as context). When viewing the world from the perspective of the narrative self, people see themselves as the same as their experienced thoughts, feelings, sensations, memories, stories, and images—including such adjectives, labels, and judgments as "bad," "unworthy," "unlovable," "selfish," "stupid," "weak," or "lazy." Viewing the world from this perspective can be associated with uncomfortable and painful private experiences, distress, avoidance, and difficulty in taking helpful actions toward valued living.

AC coaches help their clients adopt the perspective of the observing self, sensing and experiencing the part of themselves that is ever-present, the part of them that observes all kinds of experiences in the past, and the part of them that now notices the thoughts, feelings, sensations, memories, and images that flow in and out of awareness but is not changed by them. This "observing self" can be considered a kind of viewing or observation platform where the client can go to help them "defuse" or "disentangle" themselves from unhelpful, unwanted, or unpleasant thoughts and feelings, and increase their freedom to act in a more values-consistent manner.

Exercises and activities the coach might use to help clients experience and adopt the perspective of the observing self include having people notice their breathing and then to notice that they are noticing, or to notice the sounds present in the room and then to notice that they are noticing these sounds, and variations on these activities.

CONCLUSION

Much poor health, well-being, and performance can be attributed to the state known as psychological inflexibility. When in this state, clients are unsure about what really matters to them, take insufficient or insufficiently committed action in line with their values, spend excessive amounts of time thinking about and fused with thoughts relating to the past and the future, get tied up with unhelpful stories and beliefs about themselves, and do things to avoid experiencing painful or unwanted feelings—things like eating, drinking, smoking, avoiding social interaction, avoiding exercise, avoiding changing jobs, avoiding confronting unwanted behavior in other people. A coach can use the insights, tools, and strategies from ACT and AC coaching to help clients make better and more reliable progress in life, moving forward, get "unstuck," and take committed action toward important life goals that are consistent with the client's values. These approaches can help clients to spend more time in the present moment, noticing their thoughts, feelings, and sensations as they arise, stay for a while, and disappear without judging these thoughts and feelings or trying to control or avoid them. It can help them to judge and label themselves less, realizing that from one perspective they are the container of all these thoughts and feelings and emotions.

The skills and strategies we outlined in this chapter can also help coaches to become better coaches while making better progress with their own lives. This in turn will help them to better explain, model, and shape these behaviors and skills with their clients, in a virtuous circle of improvement.

REFERENCES

Anstiss, T., & Blonna, R. (2014). Acceptance and commitment coaching. In J. Passamore (Ed.), *Mastery in coaching: A complete psychological toolkit for advanced coaching*. London, UK: Kogan Page.

Blonna, R (2010). *Maximise your coaching effectiveness with Acceptance and Commitment Therapy*. Oakland, CA: New Harbinger.

Flaxman, P., Blackledge, J., & Bond, F. (2011). *Acceptance and Commitment Therapy: The CBT Distinctive Features Series*. London: Routledge.

Forsythe, J., & Eifert, G. (2007). *The mindfulness and acceptance workbook for anxiety*. Oakland, CA: New Harbinger.

Germer, C. K., Siegel, R. D., & Fulton, P. R. (2005). *Mindfulness and psychotherapy*. New York, NY: Guilford Press.

Hayes, S., & Smith, S. (2005). *Get out of your mind and into your life: The new acceptance and commitment therapy*. Oakland, CA: New Harbinger.

Stoddard, J., & Afari, N. (2014). *The big book of ACT metaphors*. Oakland CA: New Harbinger Publications

Wilson, K. G., Hayes, S. C., Gregg, J., & Zettle, R. D. (2001). Psychopathology and psychotherapy. In S. C. Hayes, D. Barnes-Holmes, & B. Roche (Eds.), *Relational frame theory: A post-skinnerian account of human language and cognition* (pp. 211–238). New York, NY: Kluwer Academic.

Wilson, K. G., & Murrell, A. R. (2004). Values work in Acceptance and Commitment Therapy: Setting a course for behavioral treatment. In S. C. Hayes, V. M. Follette, & M. Linehan (Eds.), *Mindfulness and acceptance: Expanding the cognitive-behavioral tradition* (pp. 120–151). New York, NY: Guilford Press.

26

Executive Coaching: A Psychodynamic Approach

Catherine Sandler

M *iles* was the recently promoted managing director of an underperforming division of a large insurance company. He had been chosen for his strategic skills and inclusive management style. Despite understanding how to turn the business around, he struggled to deal decisively with underperforming colleagues. *Francesca* faced a different challenge. The talented creative director of an advertising agency, she had a reputation for being difficult to work with. Easily frustrated, her angry outbursts were an increasing concern. Francesca attempted to curb her temper, but the outbursts continued. *David* also struggled with a behavioral issue. Financial controller in a manufacturing business, his interests lay in his technical area but the organization needed him to invest time in building his team. David understood that his failure to do this was resulting in low morale and high turnover, yet little changed.

Miles, Francesca, and David are based on composites of real coaching clients. Their issues illustrate the core challenge of executive coaching—how to help clients relinquish longstanding but unhelpful patterns of leadership behavior in favor of more effective strategies. By explaining the emotions that lie outside our conscious minds, but so often drive our behaviors, the psychodynamic model offers coaches the depth of understanding needed to help clients like these achieve transformational change.

THE PSYCHODYNAMIC MODEL

The psychodynamic approach has traditionally been the preserve of psychotherapists and psychoanalysts. Yet practitioners in the field of leadership development can benefit hugely from the insights it provides into the client's inner world. Over the past 25 years, I have used it as part of my executive coaching practice and shared it with other coaches and allied professionals through teaching, writing, and supervision (Sandler, 2011). World-class institutions such as the Tavistock Clinic and Tavistock Institute in the UK and INSEAD's Centre for Global Leadership also use a psychodynamic perspective, as do a number of other organizations, consultants, and coaches worldwide. As there is considerable variation in emphasis and style between practitioners, please note that this chapter describes my own practice.

KEY CONCEPTS

Psychodynamic theory derives from the ideas of Sigmund Freud but has been significantly developed over the past century. This chapter highlights those concepts that are most relevant to coaching. There is an extensive literature available for those readers who wish to explore the model and its evolution.

Emotions, the Unconscious Mind, and Psychological Defenses

The psychodynamic model highlights the role of emotion in human functioning. It suggests that we experience painful and uncomfortable feelings such as anger, jealousy, envy, guilt, insecurity, sadness, and loss more frequently than we realize or acknowledge. Programmed from birth to seek psychological as well as physical safety, we attempt to protect ourselves from intolerable thoughts and feelings by pushing them outside conscious awareness. We use a range of unconscious *psychological defense mechanisms* to do this, including:

- *Repression.* When whole aspects of our emotional experience are deeply buried

- *Denial.* When we resist acknowledging aspects of our emotional experience

- *Rationalization.* When we use logical explanations that ignore underlying emotional reasons for our behavior

- *Intellectualization.* When we distance ourselves from emotional discomfort by taking refuge in theories and data

- *Displacement.* When we focus on one problem to avoid a different, more emotionally challenging one

- *Splitting, idealization, and demonization.* When we see people as unrealistically and entirely either good or bad

- *Projection.* When we attribute unwelcome qualities or behaviors in ourselves to others, and then criticize them

- *Projective identification.* When we not only project part of ourselves onto another person but evoke in them a response that confirms the projection, for example, when someone expects their boss to be critical and unconsciously invites criticism by subtly provoking them

Psychological defenses are entirely normal. They help us to cope with difficult experiences and inner conflicts. However, this comes at a price. Defenses can lead to "blind spots" and the emotions we have "exported" can become invisible drivers of unhelpful, irrational, or self-destructive behavior. Even when we see that these patterns no longer serve us well, they are usually deep-rooted, familiar, and difficult to shift.

Our Characteristic Patterns

Several factors influence how we use psychological defenses. These factors both reflect and mold our character. Psychodynamic theory emphasizes the quality of early relationships in determining how we develop. The degree to which our emotional needs are met in our first years has a huge impact on how we relate to others and deal with setbacks throughout life. The importance of a child's relationship to its main caregiver has been convincingly reinforced by attachment theory. Research has also revealed the powerful influence of genetics on character, showing that qualities like shyness, competitiveness, and empathy are at least partly inherited. It has become clear that we are shaped by the interaction between our innate temperament, talents and inclinations, and our life experiences.

To illustrate the contrasting ways in which the same experiences can generate different patterns, we can imagine a child who struggles with a difficult emotional conflict when growing up. When hurt or upset, this child wants to be comforted but also badly wants the approval of parents who regard this "neediness" as babyish and unacceptable. This creates *anxiety* as the child wrestles with feelings of distress, anger, fear of rejection, and shame. Depending on the child's temperament, he or she may follow one of several different paths in attempting to resolve the conflict. These could include:

- Remaining angry at the parents' lack of empathy and becoming resentful and demanding

- Suppressing distress, identifying with the parental viewpoint and becoming critical of "weakness" in others

- Attempting indirectly to meet his or her needs by becoming a compulsive carer

- Distancing himself or herself from emotional intimacy and become fiercely self-reliant

Each strategy involves denying a part of the child's emotional self in order to restore a sense of safety.

The patterns we develop become part of us, deep-rooted and familiar. Some individuals, especially those who have experienced traumatic events, develop highly rigid, dysfunctional defenses, while others use defenses more flexibly, with fewer negative consequences. The term "psychodynamic" reflects Freud's view that our urges, thoughts, beliefs, feelings, and fantasies move between the conscious and unconscious parts of the mind. This indicates the human capacity, over time, to gain insight, tolerate thoughts and feelings previously suppressed, and develop new ways of handling difficult situations. However, our individual ability to do this varies significantly. The coaching client's underlying capacity for greater self-awareness is a key factor in their ability to achieve positive behavioral change.

Transference and Countertransference

The twin concepts of transference and countertransference have important implications for any practitioner–client relationship. The psychodynamic model suggests that we unconsciously tend to transfer aspects of significant past relationships to figures in the present. For example, individuals brought up by highly critical parents may fear being belittled by their coach while those with more nurturing parents may arrive with positive expectations. This means that observing the client's interaction in the "here and now" of the coaching relationship provides valuable insight into how the client might relate to others at work.

Countertransference refers to the practitioner's subjective response to the client. A coach who finds himself or herself feeling especially protective, for instance, may be responding to a need being subtly (often unconsciously) signaled by the client. This can provide helpful insight into the client's inner world. However, this demands a high level of self-awareness on the part of coaches so they can distinguish between a characteristic reaction of their own and a dynamic relating to the specific coachee.

APPLICATION TO COACHING

In my role of coach using a psychodynamic approach, I regard the coach–client relationship itself as central to the change process. It is essential to create a secure partnership that includes a genuine emotional connection with the client if a safe framework for reflection and risk-taking is to be provided. The coach must be able to see the world through the client's eyes and convey commitment to the client's well-being while, simultaneously, retaining an objective perspective and a determination to help the client address leadership issues. A strong relationship will enable the client gradually to develop a personal "inner coach"—an internal voice that will provide guidance and support when the external process ends.

To help clients become more aware of their blind spots and conflicting feelings, I take a more proactive approach than many coaches. I offer observations, thoughts, and suggestions when coaching and move flexibly among support, exploration, and advice. As mentioned already, good self-awareness is essential to using this approach. Regular coaching supervision can help coaches learn to recognize how they typically respond to different types of client, what makes them anxious, how they might respond, and the possible implications for their practice.

Even then, it is vital to proceed with care. Coaches are not therapists. Our role is to help clients develop their leadership effectiveness within a practical framework and achieve their goals. The psychodynamic model is an invaluable tool for understanding the client but sharing unfiltered hypotheses or using technical terms would be unhelpful and inappropriate. Coaches must separate what they think from what they say. We should never challenge the client's defenses head on. Instead, we must build a bridge to the client, using everyday language and deploying tact and sensitivity to ensure that our interventions are experienced as helpful and not undermining. Throughout the process, even while holding coachees to account, we must protect their self-esteem and avoid triggering their defenses.

UNDERSTANDING THE CLIENT—IDENTIFYING PATTERNS

As I start coaching a new client, I use three sources of information to help me identify the individual's emotional and behavioral *patterns:*

The Client's Material

This is what clients tell me about their role and organization, their successes and failures, and their current leadership challenges. I listen carefully to what they choose to share and the language they use, note their nonverbal behavior and observe what they convey, explicitly or implicitly, about their emotional experience of the events they describe.

Third-Party Perceptions

Briefings from the line manager or Human Resources, 360-degree feedback, annual reviews, or psychometric assessments provide vital information about how the client is seen by others.

How the Client Relates to Me and the Coaching Process

This can be an invaluable source of data, providing clues about how the client relates to other people, especially in new situations when he or she may be feeling anxious. Learning how the client manages the coaching boundaries is also highly revealing. These boundaries include communication (do they answer email promptly or need chasing), arranging meeting dates (is this straightforward or do they frequently cancel or reschedule), time management (are they often late for sessions), and payment (do they ensure that invoices are paid on time). The client's way of managing these boundaries will reflect behavioral patterns that almost certainly exist outside the coaching relationship.

Having identified patterns based on these data, I develop *working hypotheses* as to what might lie behind them, modifying, abandoning, or confirming them as more evidence emerges. We shall return to the case studies to illustrate my first experience of each of the three clients.

FIRST ENCOUNTERS—FRANCESCA, MILES, AND DAVID

Francesca was sent for coaching by her boss to address her aggressive behavior. Having postponed our meeting twice, she arrived late, blaming our map. She began the session by saying that she wanted to give me "the real picture." She felt that, having head-hunted her, the advertising agency where she worked had failed to set her up for success. Her team was low-caliber and she worked excessively long hours so it was not surprising that she sometimes lost her temper. Behind this tirade, I sensed Francesca's distress. Insisting she was a "good person," her voice faltered. A high achiever who drove herself extremely hard at work and outside (she competed in triathlons on weekends), Francesca's intentions seemed good. Yet her failure to manage her emotions and her habit of blaming others was damaging her effectiveness and potentially her career.

Miles came to coaching for help with his transition to Managing Director. A large, loose-limbed man, he was friendly and engaging. He outlined the challenges facing his business, which included long-standing problems with several members of his team. I was impressed by Miles's commitment to addressing these issues but struck by how long it was taking to resolve them. He seemed to be spending a disproportionate amount of time on multiple meetings, going over the same ground. Describing a troublesome individual who had been "tolerated for years," I noticed that Miles described his behavior as "entirely unacceptable" but also insisted he must "be given every chance to improve." He seemed reluctant to deliver firm messages or take prompt action if things did not improve and preferred lengthy attempts to persuade, even when this strategy was not working.

David came to coaching to improve his management style. Neatly dressed, punctual, and polite, he offered little small talk. His boss wanted him to spend more time on the "people side" of his role. While accepting the need to develop his team, he did not see how he could add much value. He viewed them as "intelligent adults who should just get on with the job." When describing his direct reports, David talked mainly about their tasks. Asked about difficult issues, he mentioned an individual who had recently returned to work following a miscarriage. He acknowledged her upsetting experience but felt unsure how to support her. He also mentioned a manager who became frustrated when Finance had difficulties caused by other departments, describing his "emotional rants" as "childish and pointless." Despite his doubts, I respected David's honesty and calm manner and his willingness to give coaching a try.

THE EMOTIONAL PROFILES TRIANGLE—
FIGHT, FLIGHT, AND FREEZE

To help identify a client's pattern of leadership behavior, I have developed a model called the Emotional Profiles Triangle (Sandler, 2012). This is concerned with understanding what makes individuals most anxious and how they respond when triggered into self-defense mode. The amygdala is the area of our limbic brain that scans the environment for danger. When it perceives a threat, we switch involuntarily into survival mode. Our bodies release adrenaline and other chemicals and our prefrontal cortex—the rational, thoughtful part of our brain—partially shuts down. At these moments, our behavior is driven by powerful forces beyond our conscious control. The Triangle model is based on the observation that leaders fall primarily into one of three categories that reflect their strengths, their triggers, and their characteristic mode of self-defense. It suggests that:

- Task-focused, high-energy leaders tend to go into *fight* mode when their sense of competence and control are threatened.

- People-focused, emotionally warm leaders tend to go into *flight* mode when interpersonal harmony and relationships are threatened.

- Task-focused, lower-energy leaders tend to go into *freeze* mode when other people's emotions threaten to overwhelm them.

This model can helpfully be applied to understanding the clients in the case studies.

HYPOTHESES—FRANCESCA, MILES, AND DAVID

Francesca was a passionate and task-focused leader who easily became angry and critical. It seemed that she was frequently triggered into *fight*. Although from the outside this did not look like a defensive maneuver, I hypothesized that Francesca suffered from a persecuting "inner critic"—an internal voice that condemned her whenever she failed to meet her own high standards. She worked exceptionally hard to avoid mistakes but when even small things went wrong, her sense of competence and control were threatened and she lashed out, for example when she furiously berated her assistant in an open office after discovering an error in her slides for a Board presentation. Already anxious about the presentation, this incident activated her defensive reaction. In the moment, Francesca *experienced the other person as the aggressor* and felt justified in hitting out. Afterward, however, having calmed down, she felt guilty and remorseful. This helped to explain the gap between Francesca's intentions and her behavior.

Miles was, in contrast to Francesca, a relationship-focused leader with a warm, empathic approach. This strength generally served him well yet his excessively patient approach when handling difficult colleagues was ineffective. It seemed that what would seem fair and reasonable to most people apparently felt aggressive, even abusive, to him. He had told me that he feared being "dictatorial" or "harsh," when in fact he was clearly the opposite. His view of what was appropriately firm appeared skewed. My hypothesis was that situations of potential conflict caused him significant anxiety and triggered a defensive *flight* response. I also suspected that, as is often the case with *flight* leaders, he was suppressing his own anger and projecting it onto others, whose aggressive reaction he then feared. Further sessions confirmed this view and became the focus of our work.

David presented a different dynamic. Calm, controlled, and task-focused, I sensed his discomfort at getting too close to people, especially if they risked becoming angry or upset. This hypothesis was supported by a recent crisis that David admitted he had not handled well. It concerned a major accounting error that escalated to Board level, causing considerable stress in the Finance Department. Instead of involving his team, David withdrew from his colleagues. His failure to communicate caused great frustration in his team and his attempt to deal with the problem alone slowed its resolution. This illustrated his tendency to go into *freeze* and disengage from relationships when the emotional temperature rose. I hypothesized that David feared being overwhelmed, both by others' emotions and his own. Distancing himself was a defensive maneuver designed to restore a feeling of safety. Clearly, if David was to become more effective at leading others, this key issue needed to be addressed.

COACHING INTERVENTIONS

As well as shedding light on the client's inner world, the psychodynamic approach also underlines how sensitively we need to handle the coaching conversations. During the process, we need always to hold in mind the client's need for psychological safety. However accurate our hypotheses, if we push too hard and trigger the client's defenses, the relationship will be damaged and learning will close down. To create and maintain trust, it is vital that the coach chooses words, tone, and timing with great care.

BUILDING THE COACHING PARTNERSHIP

How the coach handles the first encounter with a potential new client is particularly important. Both coach and client are likely to be feeling some anxiety about this meeting. There is a risk that the coach will focus more on establishing his or her credibility than on the client's needs. Even highly motivated clients will come with mixed feelings. After all, developing new skills involves recognizing potential deficits or weaknesses. Many clients fear being judged, criticized, or exposed, particularly if they have been "sent" for coaching; others fear revisiting painful experiences or being disappointed if the coach proves unable to help them. I find the following techniques helpful in reducing the client's anxiety and building rapport, trust, and confidence in the coaching process:

> *Provide a containing environment.* I offer a warm, calm, and attentive presence and a confidential space in which to work.

> *Get the client talking.* Avoid explaining the coaching process at the outset. The anxious client will be far more available to hear this at the end of the session.

> *Do not be distracted or provoked.* The client's anxiety can often emerge in the form of complaints, criticism, or challenging questioning. If gently deflected, they usually disappear once the work has started.

> *Empathize.* Actively convey your understanding of the client's experiences and emotions.

> *Normalize difficult thoughts, feelings, or behavior.* Show you regard them as natural. This helps reduce embarrassment and the fear of being judged.

> *Affirm strengths.* This also dispels fear of being judged and builds rapport. How much I do this reflects my sense of the client's personality.

> *Begin coaching.* Through insightful questions, links, and observations, you can establish credibility and demonstrate from the outset how coaching can help. In each of the case studies, I adapted my style to the client, holding his or her different needs in mind.

EARLY INTERVENTIONS — FRANCESCA, MILES, AND DAVID

Francesca needed to stop behaving in a way that was inappropriate and damaging to herself and others. However, I started building our partnership by acknowledging her good intentions and how hard she worked to deliver results. This was crucial in helping her feel less judged and shamed and so more able to take responsibility for her behavior. I also suggested that she was extremely hard on herself and empathized with how persecuting this could feel. She agreed and visibly relaxed. I proposed two related coaching goals. One was learning to manage her anger; to achieve this, I also wanted to help her develop a more compassionate attitude *toward herself*. She needed to ensure her own needs were met in order to feel less threatened and become less blaming when things went wrong.

Miles was determined to address his inherited people-problems and I started by praising this and noting the emotional toll of this task. I suggested that although he tried hard to achieve harmonious resolutions, this might not always be possible. I offered to help him learn to bring these situations to a timely close rather than remaining mired in endless discussions with a handful of "squeaky wheels." This would allow him to concentrate on more strategic issues. I added that developing a slightly more authoritative style of leadership generally would serve him and the business well in the future. Miles responded positively and we agreed to work on these issues.

David clearly felt uncomfortable talking about himself; to give him a sense of control and reassure him that his privacy would be respected, I matched his low-key style. I checked my understanding of what he had told me and shared some information about the business benefits of actively developing one's team members. I empathized with his reluctance and validated his willingness to push himself outside his comfort zone but felt that affirming his strengths more explicitly might feel too personal at this stage. I underlined the potential benefit of coaching by providing data about the results achieved by managers with the same agenda. David listened carefully and agreed that coaching was "worth a try."

PROMOTING INSIGHT AND POSITIVE BEHAVIORAL CHANGE

As coaching proceeds, I help clients make "quick wins" by exploring current work issues and generating practical ways of addressing them more effectively. I also focus on enabling them to gain insight into their behavior and their underlying thoughts and feelings. I share my observations and viewpoints, including my thoughts on how their behavior could become more effective, but always with empathy and tact to avoid raising their defenses. For example, I might explain that *a weakness is a strength taken too far*. This simple but effective technique helps clients accept their shortcomings without feeling attacked by linking a weakness to a positive attribute. In the case studies, for example, I pointed out that—if taken too far—Francesca's high standards could lead to impatience, Miles's empathy to conflict-avoidance, and David's calm, considered approach to emotional detachment.

Once clients gain insight, they need encouragement to try out new behaviors. However motivated they are, anxiety nonetheless remains high and most struggle to abandon old, familiar patterns. Some hesitate on the brink, fearing a "slippery slope" that could force a level of change they dread. When this happens, I often use the *spectrum technique,* pointing out that the client's current behavior is at one end of a spectrum and the shift he or she needs to make will only move the client a short way along it. For instance, I had a client who needed to raise her profile to achieve promotion but feared that taking more credit for her achievements would turn her into a self-promoter of the kind she despised. By pointing out that the behavior she described was at the opposite end of the scale to her own and that a 20% shift would transform her impact yet keep her firmly in the "nonpolitical" camp, I was able to reduce her fear of change.

Interventions such as these are designed with the client's emotional vulnerabilities and inner conflicts in mind. Throughout the coaching process, I aim to "get alongside" the client, offering encouragement and support combined with a consistent focus on coaching goals. Together we apply the client's learning to specific situations so that new strategies can be discussed, implemented, and reviewed. My aim throughout is to help the client grow in self-awareness, confidence, and skill and develop behaviors that will lift his or her leadership to the next level.

INTERVENTIONS AND OUTCOMES—FRANCESCA, MILES, AND DAVID

Francesca found the Emotional Profiles Triangle, which outlines the fight, flight, or freeze stress responses, very helpful in understanding the defensive nature of her aggressive behavior (Sandler, 2012). It emerged that the situations in which Francesca became angry were usually preceded by a sense of being let down by others. Yet she rarely asked for help, preferring to redo substandard work herself rather than insisting on improvement. Privately fuming, eventually a "final straw" would trigger an explosion. This dynamic reflected the considerable insecurity that lay beneath Francesca's apparent self-confidence. It fueled her drive for control and the intolerable vulnerability she experienced when exposed. As Francesca gained insight into this dynamic, we worked on how she could better meet her needs before a crisis arose. This involved setting firmer boundaries, delegating more, and holding others to account as well as building closer relationships with her staff. She also became able to notice the warning signs of "the volcano starting to rumble" and learned to use breathing techniques to calm down.

On checking with Francesca's boss, it seemed her behavior had greatly improved. There had been a couple of relapses but she had apologized afterward. Her colleagues appreciated the change though it took time to rebuild trust. As Francesca became more tolerant of herself—and others—her self-esteem and confidence improved. In due course, the outbursts became a thing of the past and she became quite an inspirational leader.

Miles acknowledged early on his dislike of tough conversations but deeper insight occurred when I asked about previous experiences of conflict. It seemed he came from a family where anger was unacceptable. The behavior of his autistic younger brother was difficult, sometimes violent, yet Miles was expected to be patient and understanding. He remembered when, provoked beyond endurance, he had "blown up" and retaliated. His parents' distress was clear and Miles had felt guilty and ashamed. This was a breakthrough moment. Miles realized that alongside his conscious preference for harmony lay a deep fear of other people's anger and disapproval and a terror of becoming enraged himself and losing control. These fears were inhibiting his ability to deal with others in a clear and straightforward way.

This enabled us to focus on new behavior. We explored different influencing styles, which helped Miles widen his repertoire to include insistence as well as persuasion. We rehearsed strategies for specific situations and he learned assertive techniques for delivering difficult messages with calm confidence. Acutely uncomfortable at first, he implemented this new approach and was delighted with how quickly most situations were resolved. Feedback from Miles's stakeholders affirmed his new behavior. Miles' enjoyment of his role increased. He spent more time playing to his strengths, coaching his new team, and forging a new strategy for his division that went on to deliver excellent results.

David found an understanding of personality types particularly useful. Our work on this enabled him to appreciate the needs of people different from himself, for example, those with higher relationship or recognition needs, while gaining insight into his own preference for an unemotional, self-contained approach. We discussed the likely motivators, strengths, and weaknesses of each of David's team members and identified what practical steps he could take to engage and develop them. An important moment came when he realized that they valued his *attention*— he did not always have to provide solutions. Instead, he could use open questions and active listening to learn what would help individuals feel more satisfied and improve their performance.

As David's self-awareness increased, he became more attuned to what made him anxious and the negative consequences of isolating himself when others needed his empathy and presence. We explored techniques such as mindfulness that helped him tolerate emotional situations without feeling overwhelmed. David determinedly put what we planned into practice. As he saw the impact of his new approach, he became convinced of its value for the team and department. David also became more relaxed. His emails had a warmer tone and he now chatted more freely. Feedback from senior management was good. His team's morale had noticeably improved and a key individual who had been planning to leave decided to stay with the company. While remaining naturally self-contained, David had mastered a significant shift in how he managed others.

CONCLUSION

The three senior executives described in this chapter came to coaching to address aspects of their leadership that were not serving them well. Yet none was in touch with the deep-rooted, unconscious fears that drove their problematic behavior. The psychodynamic model enabled me to make sense of their difficulties and to help them relax the rigid defensive patterns that were holding them back. While their personalities remained intact, their leadership behavior was transformed by new levels of self-awareness, emotional resilience, and new skills. I hope their stories have illustrated the value that psychodynamic concepts and techniques can offer and will encourage you to discover more about this powerful and fascinating approach.

REFERENCES

Sandler, C. (2011). *Executive coaching: A psychodynamic approach.* Maidenhead, UK: McGraw-Hill.
Sandler, C. (2012). The Emotional Profiles Triangle: Working with leaders under pressure. *Strategic HR Review, 11,* 65–71. doi:10.1108/14754391211202116

ADDITIONAL READING

Freud, S. (1991). *The essentials of psycho-analysis: The definitive collection of Sigmund Freud's writing.* London, UK: Penguin.
Gay, P. (1995). *The Freud reader.* New York, NY: W. W. Norton.
Gerhardt, S. (2004). *Why love matters: How affection shapes a baby's brain.* Hove, UK: Brunner-Routledge.
Holmes, J. (1994). *John Bowlby and attachment theory.* London, UK: Routledge.
Sandler, C. (2009). The psychological role of the leader in turbulent times. *Strategic HR Review, 8,* 30–35. doi:10.1108/14754390910946558

27

Integral Coaching: Whole Person Development in a Complex World

Sean Esbjörn-Hargens and Beena Sharma

T he field of professional coaching has expanded exponentially in the last 20 years. Dozens of distinct schools of personal and business coaching have emerged focused on various niches such as psychology, family, wellness, life skills, relationships, career, performance, and professional skills. There are well over 100 different types of coaching certifications in the marketplace and more than 70 coaching models to consider (e.g., Gribben, 2016). One reason so many different approaches to coaching exist is because human beings are multifaceted and different types of coaching serve different human needs. In addition to different schools based on niches, different schools also adhere to different philosophies or worldviews. A few unique schools have emerged in the last decade or so that take an integrated approach to human development.

Integral approaches are distinct from "holistic" approaches to coaching, which can be eclectic in their orientation, drawing on multiple tools and techniques in an unsystematic way. Integral approaches to coaching, by contrast, are guided by a metaview of reality and human beings and can combine insights from multiple other approaches in a systematic, coherent, and well-informed way.

This chapter offers an introduction to integral coaching. We begin by providing an overview of the theoretical basis for integral coaching. We then look at Integral Theory, a metatheory that informs many approaches to integral coaching.

Next, we discuss Constructive Developmental Theory and the concept of "vertical development." Having presented the theoretical basis, we then highlight what makes integral coaching unique and sets it apart from other schools. Then we discuss the Theory of Change that informs integral approaches and briefly discuss four schools of integral coaching. Last, we reflect on the future of integral coaching.

OVERVIEW OF INTEGRAL THEORY

Integral Theory has been developed largely by Ken Wilber, an American philosopher, and its origins are associated with the 1995 publication of Wilber's magnum opus *Sex, Ecology, Spirituality*. Integral Theory is an integrative metatheory, which means that it attempts to explain all of reality through the integration of data and theories from all major domains of human inquiry, including the hard sciences, social sciences, humanities, and arts (Wilber, 1995).

One of the main features of Integral Theory is its use of five major elements to analyze and interpret topics from an integral perspective: quadrants, levels, lines, states, and types. Each of these elements represents a core pattern found in reality that Wilber contends is necessary to include to have a complete picture of some topic or phenomenon.

Of the five elements mentioned, the *quadrants* and *levels* have come to iconically represent Integral Theory's "All-Quadrant, All-Level" (AQAL) approach. We briefly describe both in this section and then go deeper with levels in the next section.

Quadrants result from two overlapping primary polarities: *individual-collective* and *interior-exterior*. Together, these polarities create the four quadrants (Figure 27.1).

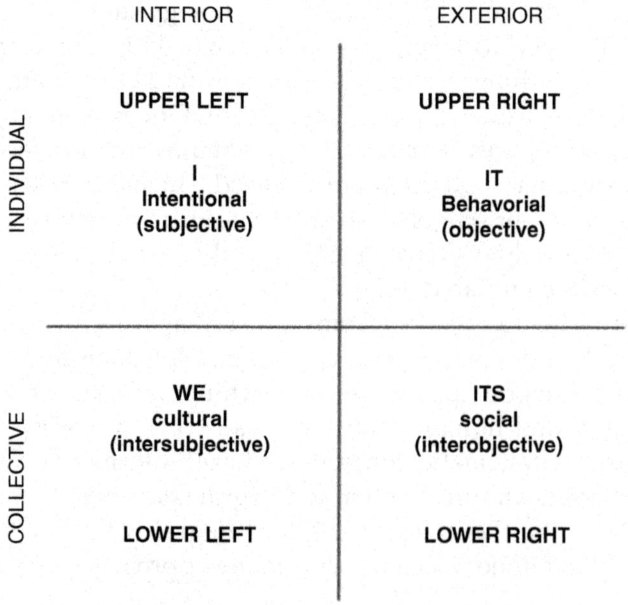

Figure 27.1 Wilber's four quadrants.

POLARITY WISDOM EMBEDDED IN INTEGRAL THEORY

A polarity is a pair of interdependent values or elements, where both are needed for a more complete approach (see Johnson, 2014). This significant principle underpins Integral Theory—polarities need to be integrated to facilitate ongoing evolution and human development. In fact, important polarities can be found in all five of Integral Theory's elements (e.g., quadrants, levels, lines). Privileging one pole of a polarity over the other leads to observable gaps in understanding people and situations completely, and therefore inhibits development. Thus, we can say that one fails at being integral when the polarities in any situation are not identified and engaged in a balanced/integrative fashion.

The four resulting domains of the quadrants are often referred to as *Intentional* or the "I" domain (individual-interior), *Behavioral* or the "It" domain (individual-exterior), *Social* (or Systems) or the "Its" domain (collective-exterior), and *Cultural* or the "We" domain (collective-interior). These four quadrants are a powerful diagnostic tool that helps professionals look at a unit of analysis from the insights associated with each quadrant and the associated fields of study.

Here is a simple example. An individual begins working with a coach to improve her leadership skills. She wants to focus on becoming a better team leader, and to create a cohesive team, where each member is empowered to lead and learn, and she wants to improve collective performance. From an integral four-quadrant perspective, coaching will necessarily include the following four dimensions:

- **I: Intentional/Psychological** (*Individual-Interior*):
  - Reflect on one's internal beliefs and worldview that impact the team.
  - Identify one's own strengths and values that benefit the team.
  - Define one's personal vision or blueprint as a leader.
  - Review patterns from the past that need to be dropped (such as holding the strategy and assuming the team simply needs to focus on operations).
  - Integrate polarities to be more effective (e.g., consciously integrating the polarity of directive leadership and shared leadership).

- **It: Behavioral/Physiological** (*Individual-Exterior*):
  - Observe one's behaviors and actions (recognizing gaps between intent and action and integrating that polarity).
  - Reflect on how one behaves during meetings (how one responds to conflict or differences of opinion).
  - Engage posture, body language, and energy management to enable new behaviors and quality of somatic presence.
  - Learn to change one's actions to be more accessible more often (e.g., create an open-door process, so team members can interact and be supported more easily).

- **We: Cultural/Relational** *(Collective-Interior)*:

  ○ Reflect on the team culture, and define the shared values that are *operating*, not just desired.

  ○ Create space for interpersonal dialogue—for example, using Bohmian dialogue that allows the team to reflect collectively, and create shared understanding of their inner landscape as a team. This harmonizes the polarity of collective reflection and participatory dialogue.

  ○ Design more effective one-on-one conversations with team members and continually attend to explicit and implicit contracts (another polarity) with each person. Revisit agreements periodically and attend to the contracts.

  ○ Plan for a quarterly team night with dinner and games to generate team spirit.

- **Its: Social/Systemic** *(Collective-Exterior)*:

  ○ Think through needed team processes that contribute to high performance—such as using after-action reviews and managing their frequency, integrating the polarity of action and reflection.

  ○ Design the structure of specific meetings to enable shared leadership.

  ○ Plan resource management and advocate for infrastructure or restructure existing resources for optimal benefits (e.g., downsize physical space, rotate work at home between team members, use funds released for learning or other needs).

In this example, one can see in a simple and clear way how adding all the various elements based on the four-quadrant approach results in a more "integral" development where clients intentionally explore the four dimensions and achieve more comprehensive solutions to their problems and dilemmas.

Another quick example that illustrates the value of a four-quadrant approach: Many coaching topics benefit from engaging all four domains. For example, if a client wants to work on communication with colleagues, this might at first appear as a topic largely related to the "We" quadrant. However, typically it will require the coach to work with the following aspects of the client in some combination: expanding the client's capacity for self-reflection and presence ("I" quadrant), shifting how the client holds his or her body during interpersonal interactions ("It" quadrant), engaging the way the client manages his or her busy schedule ("Its" quadrant), as well as exploring how the client does or does not seek other perspectives and demonstrates (or not) understanding other viewpoints ("We" quadrant).

In addition to using the quadrants for individual coaching, we find them to be a particularly powerful model for understanding the field of coaching itself. For example, some schools focus on *behavior* as the core area of change. Some focus on *psychology*. Some focus on *language*. And some focus on the *role fit* of a person with his or her job in a work environment. Thus, an integral approach to coaching includes a theory of change that recognizes the importance of each of these domains to human transformation and development (see Hunt & Divine, 2008).

Going further, it is worth noting that each quadrant and its associated domain can be examined from two main methodological approaches—an inside and outside approach. Integral Theory refers to the resulting eight methods as Integral Methodological Pluralism (IMP). This is a useful distinction for coaching in that it helps coaches design practices and interventions. For example, drawing on the client topic of "developing leadership skills" noted earlier, we would want to consider the following two aspects of the "I" quadrant:

- **Inside approach**: How do I think and feel? What is my subjective experience? What do I want and need? What are the contents of my ongoing stream of awareness and self-identity?

- **Outside approach**: How do I assess my strengths? What evaluation tool will help me see things I don't see? What underlying structures of my personality or awareness inform my thoughts and actions?

Integrally informed coaches can apply the inside/outside approach to each of the other quadrants to invite greater depth and richness of exploration.

One important fact about all four quadrants is that they each contain increasing levels of complexity and depth. For instance, in the *individual-interior* quadrant a general movement of increasing depth of awareness within self-identities goes from egocentric to ethnocentric to sociocentric to worldcentric. Similarly, in the *individual-exterior* quadrant, a progression of complexity occurs within organisms—from atoms to molecules to organs. These levels of complexity and depth are important in a coaching context.

This brings us to the other main element of Integral Theory we want to discuss: *levels*. We provide a brief description of levels here, and then in the next section go into greater depth regarding a particular approach to coaching with levels of self-identity described by *constructive developmental psychology*.

Just as different coaching approaches emphasize different quadrants in their methodology of change or transformation, the same dynamic and differences occur with levels: different coaching schools approach coaching from their own implicit worldviews, which are often associated with various developmental levels. Each level of development carries its own worldview; hence, one could say that different theories of how a coaching client changes emerge from different worldviews associated with developmental theory. For example, using the Maturity Profile (MAP) distinctions between levels, we observe at least four different developmental expressions to coaching. First, coaching that focuses on skill development to achieve performance goals comes from the **Skill-Centric** stage (competency-based leadership coaching). Second, client-centered coaching emerges from the self-authoring (Kegan) or **Self-Determining** (Cook-Greuter) stage of development, where it is assumed that the client is in charge and has the capacity to take self-directed action. Third, a co-created experience in the coaching process holds interpersonal dialogue and reflective action inquiry as central to enable change: the **Self-Questioning** stage approach to coaching (e.g., Gestalt coaching). Fourth, at the **Self-Actualizing** stage, the coach uses the self as instrument, and acknowledges being one element in a system of multiple elements that facilitate the transformation of both the client and the coach (Integral and Developmental Coaching; see Chapter 21 for more details and descriptions of the specific stages.)

Using only the elements of *quadrants* and *levels*, we can start to get a sense of what makes an integral coach: someone who includes all four quadrants in his or her approach to change and transformation, and who recognizes that any of the quadrants can be a starting point for an intervention depending on the client and his or her circumstances. Integral coaches also notice patterns in their client's quadrant preferences, and this can help the coach and client to see the client's natural tendencies (see Hunt & Divine, 2008). The coach can help the client to augment the client's frames of reference by including quadrants he or she typically tends to neglect or ignore. Integral coaches can also move across the levels, within and across the quadrants. This informs how the coach shows up; in one moment the coach might be an expert; in another, a solicitor of inner wisdom; and so forth. Thus, an integral coach works with multiple quadrants and levels (and the polarities within them) in an ongoing and dynamic way to best serve the client. Integral coaches are also aware of their own quadrant and level preferences, and use this awareness to minimize their own coaching biases.

Because working with developmental levels in the "I" quadrant is one of the things that sets integral coaching apart from other approaches, we now turn our attention there. Of course, all the elements of Integral Theory can be used in a diagnostic fashion.

AN OVERVIEW OF CONSTRUCTIVE-DEVELOPMENTAL THEORY AND VERTICAL DEVELOPMENT

Constructive Developmental Theory holds that meaning is actively constructed by individuals in response to the need to understand the world. This meaning-making is an orienting process and results in beliefs, conclusions, and stories about oneself and the world. As one continues to make sense of past and new experiences, fresh conclusions are drawn, new beliefs evolve, new stories are told . . . until a whole new worldview is constructed that enables one to have a greater sense of safety, comfort, and value in life. This occurs more forcefully when a dissonance or contradiction happens between what one predicts or believes and what one experiences as reality. When these contradictions occur, one must then reconstruct one's belief or ideas in order to include or contain the new dissonant experience. This alters previously held beliefs, which are now seen as assumptions that have been tested by reality and seen to be false, giving way to a new mental-model. This new worldview now influences what one can see, describe, and change.

This process is called *vertical development* (and sometimes *vertical learning*) and can be distinguished from "horizontal" growth or learning. Horizontal development is defined as acquiring experience and knowledge, as well as new skills and competencies. While important, horizontal development does not lead to shifts in how one sees the world and engages with its challenges. Vertical development does just that: It fosters the growth of new perspectives and a greater ability to handle difficult problems. Vertical development takes place when people learn to question prior beliefs and assumptions. In today's increasingly complex work and life contexts, vertical development becomes essential. Research over the last four decades has shown that vertical development can be traced as a logical sequence of stages through which leaders can interpret and gain insights about themselves, others, and the world around them. And today, fortunately, we can measure how an individual grows through these stages of maturity.

Several different models within Constructive-Developmental Theory explicate different levels of adult development. Two primary models are Kegan's (1995) five orders of consciousness and Cook-Greuter's (1999) nine levels of ego development. While significant differences exist between these two theories, they share the description of a sequential development of stages that become progressively more complex and involve a more dynamic and systemic understanding of oneself and the world.

The Leadership Maturity Framework from Cook-Greuter's theory and research describes stages of vertical development based on empirical evidence gathered since the 1960s. Each stage is generally more effective, flexible, and insightful than the previous one. The framework identifies the strengths and vulnerabilities of each stage. It pinpoints factors that promote or impede growth at each successive stage. With each new level, individuals can become more nuanced, integrated, and flexible in their thinking. In other words, they become significantly more capable of functioning at optimum levels and with more ease in our ever-more-rapidly changing and ambiguous environment. Each successive stage of vertical development is more capable and satisfying because we discern more and can make subtler distinctions. As a result, we can then articulate what we notice and make it an object of awareness. (For more information on vertical development, see Chapter 21.)

When coaching is delivered using the lens of vertical development, clients can be supported in more powerful ways. With level-informed coaching, clients can learn to see situations, goals, and people with new eyes and a broader perspective. They gain a balcony or helicopter view instead of being in the middle of it all. A focus on vertical development encourages fundamental shifts in making sense of life events and relationships, and can result in stage transitions, not just horizontal adaptation. It expands a person's depth and breadth of understanding. It enables individuals to comprehend and respond to leadership challenges in more complex, effective, and wiser ways. They can see new opportunities and possibilities. Overall, coaching for later stages of development expands leaders' inner and outer resources, enabling greater effectiveness and impact.

Linking this discussion to our previous section on quadrants, it is important to point out that vertical development is supported by an integral coach's engagement with all four quadrants. In other words, integral coaching supports vertical development by working with the polarities associated with all four quadrants. This makes for more comprehensive client development. Because it inherently includes both the individual *and* the collective polarity and the interior *and* the exterior polarity, integral coaching enables a more mature, broad, inclusive, and integrative development. Thus, quadrant-based coaching supports vertical development and vertical development-based coaching supports integration across the quadrants.

WHAT IS UNIQUE ABOUT INTEGRAL COACHING?

A number of features are unique to integral coaching. Earlier in the chapter, we focused on its use of quadrants and levels. In this section, we now summarize those unique features, as well as highlight other ways integral coaching is unique.

QUADRANTS

Integral coaching involves some version of the 4Qs or working with what is sometimes called the "Big Three": *subjective* (first person), *intersubjective* (second person), and *objective* (third person). Thus, these coaches manage multiple polarities, such as between self and other and between coach and client. They understand that transformation and change come from engaging and being aware of the influence of each quadrant.

DEVELOPMENTAL LEVELS

Integral coaching is keenly aware of human development and the full spectrum of stages of consciousness and the dynamics within them. It addresses levels of complexity. Integral coaching can help clients develop to the highest stages of human possibility—moving from linear thinking to systems thinking to advanced systems thinking, and eventually to principled/integrated thinking.

TYPES, LINES, AND STATES

While outside the scope of this chapter, types, lines, and states bear mention. Integral coaches often include their understanding of various typologies (e.g., Enneagram, The Big Five) in service of more effective coaching outcomes. They help clients see their deeper patterns as objects of awareness, hold them lightly, and create space for greater adaptability and, therefore, for greater maturity. An integrally informed approach includes observing and integrating various lines of development (e.g., emotional, kinesthetic, moral), with an appreciation of levels of development along each line, as well. When a client wants to explore state experiences (either in the context of spiritual development or how they fulfill their life purpose), the integral coach can offer the space and practices that help the client experience a more unified and fulfilling life experience across contexts and roles.

POLARITY WISDOM

Harmonizing polarities can be viewed as the concrete and granular "mechanics" of being integral. Inclusiveness is the essence of being integral—where all truths are seen as partial and need to be included in service to the whole. We are all socialized through formal and informal education to solve life's problems by finding the right answer, which involves "either/or" thinking. The integral approach is unique because it embeds, teaches, facilitates, and equips us to do "both/and" thinking, itself a marker of later-stage development.

INTEGRAL PSYCHOLOGY

Integral coaches have an integral view of human beings and draw on multiple schools of psychology to understand what makes people act the way we do and how can we change. Of the many schools of psychology, three stand out as primary: somatic psychology, developmental psychology, and transpersonal psychology. Integral coaches also understand different states of consciousness—both ordinary and nonordinary—and use multiple approaches to personality structures and typologies (see Wilber, 2000).

OPERATING AT THE INTEGRAL LEVEL AS A PERSON

Integral coaches adopt many perspectives. They are acutely aware of themselves and their biases and use the integral model to see this. They also use it to see the client and to design practices for the client. Integral coaches manage multiple polarities and perspectives and can move across quadrants and levels fluidly and not get stuck in one spot. They have a four-quadrant theory of change and draw on the best practices of other coaching approaches. They bring later stage-related worldviews to bear on their coaching as well as dealing with their clients' challenges. They are able to hold complexity and coach at a systemic level, seeing the client as a self-system as well as part of a larger organizational or social system. Integral coaches recognize their own preferences and assumptions, and are willing to acknowledge themselves as only one part of the larger forces that determine their clients' evolution.

INTEGRAL COACHING SCHOOLS AROUND THE GLOBE

Over the last 20 years, a number of schools of coaching have emerged that can be described as "integral coaching" or that contain important elements of integral coaching. The following four schools all provide certification programs accredited by the International Coach Federation (ICF).

The most prominent integral coaching school is Integral Coaching Canada (ICC), based in Ottawa. They explicitly use Wilber's Integral Theory as the core architecture of their approach and methodology (see Hunt & Divine, 2008). They have one of the most rigorous and lengthy certification programs of any coaching institution. It often takes individuals 2 to 3 years to complete. For a comprehensive overview of their approach, see the special issue of the *Journal of Integral Theory and Practice* listed in the References section. One of the features of ICC is their use of metaphors to describe the client's current way of being and future way of being. They do not personally deliver any assessments for stages of development, and advocate that coaches select from a variety of instruments. They use all five elements in a diagnostic way, which is part of their unique coaching methodology.

Another integral coaching school is New Ventures West (NVW) based in San Francisco, California. The work of Flaherty (2011) draws on Integral Theory as well as other complementary approaches, such as ontological coaching, which emphasizes the power of language and conversations to catalyze transformation in clients.

Like ICC, they use the label "integral coaching" to describe their work. Like ICC, they use the five elements associated with Integral Theory as well. However, their "levels lens" appears to be primarily based on the phases of transformation clients travel through in their coaching process rather than on a developmental sequence as described by constructive developmental theory. Their coaches also use narrative metaphors to describe past and future ways of being.

In Australia, Newfield is arguably *the* leading school exemplifying ontological coaching. While Newfield might not self-identify as being a school of integral coaching, its approach includes many of the characteristics associated with integral coaching. For example, ontological coaching emphasizes language and culture (the "We" quadrant), moods and experience (the "I" quadrant), and behavior and the body (the "It" quadrant). Thus, they include an equal emphasis on first-person, second-person, and third-person realities of the client (i.e., the four quadrants of Integral Theory). In fact, Sieler (2005, 2007, 2012) has published an impressive three-volume description of this triadic approach called *Coaching to the Human Soul*. Each volume covers one of these three dimensions. Furthermore, Newfield is known for its focus on a client's "way of being" (à la Heidegger) and this focus in many ways has been a foundational influence of both NVW and ICC and their own integral approach to a client's way of being.

More recently, Mark Divine, a retired Navy Seal Commander based in Encinitas, CA, has created an integral coaching program based on his SEALFIT and Unbeatable Mind approach (see Divine 2015, 2016). This program is currently being reviewed for ICF accreditation. Divine's Unbeatable Mind philosophy and subsequently his coaching program draw heavily on Wilber's Integral Theory. This is most noticeable in his use of the "Three Spheres" (i.e., I, We, and It), based on the four quadrants and their five levels of development, which they call "Plateaus." These two elements (three Spheres and five Plateaus) form the basis of the integrative training approach for "climbing" the Five Mountains: the Physical Mountain, the Emotional Mountain, the Mental Mountain, the Intuitional Mountain, and the Kokoro (a Japanese word for heart/mind or spirit) Mountain. One of the unique aspects of the Unbeatable Mind Coaching Program is its emphasis on physical fitness and wellness—significantly more than the other three approaches previously discussed. Coaches certified for Unbeatable Mind often have a background in nutrition, physical fitness, and wellness, and this shows up prominently in their coaching work with clients.

For a deep focus on the levels of development, we have VeDA—Vertical Development Academy (USA)—that has developed a robust, well-defined coach certification program. This program is ICF accredited and provides CEUs. VeDA operationalizes Dr. Cook-Greuter's theory and measurement methodology, with a deep commitment to an ethical holding of the work, given that ego- and identity-related assessments are highly sensitive. Their coaching methodology uses the MAP explicitly, and the Leadership Maturity Framework both explicitly and implicitly. Their Developing Leadership Maturity Program includes demonstrations and practice coaching sessions at each level of development from Group-Centric to Construct-Aware. Certified coaches gain membership to a global cadre of certified coaches that form an active learning community and advance the collective knowledge.

Other valuable vertical developmental systems that use Robert Kegan's approach include Kegan's Deliberately Developmental Organizations (DDO), and Jennifer

Garvey Berger's Cultivating Leadership. William R. Torbert's Collaborative Developmental Action Inquiry (CDAI) is another vertical development framework that also uses a version of the Sentence Completion Test developed by Dr. Cook-Greuter. Finally, we have the Lectica system, based on Kurt Fischer's Hierarchical Complexity and Skill Theory.

The integrally inclined coach has many vertical development resources available.

CONCLUSION: THE FUTURE OF INTEGRAL COACHING

The field of coaching is evolving. A proliferation of philosophies, approaches, theories, frameworks, methodologies, models, and tools all attempt to understand the evolving human and support that evolution in meaningful ways. This proliferation will continue—likely at breakneck speed. Thus, it seems logical that an overarching theory of the human being as described by Integral Theory can and should be applied to the field of coaching. This can allow us to create a comprehensive map of the different coaching schools and how they address the various dimensions of the human being revealed to us through the past centuries of philosophical, scientific, and artistic endeavor. As more and more coaching schools differentiate from each other and attempt to specialize in different aspects of the human experience, we believe that an integral view, from which to understand this process, will be increasingly important.

We also believe that while only a half dozen or so notable integral coaching schools currently exist, more will emerge in the coming years. We anticipate more coaches will draw on, and be based in, Integral Theory. These new integral approaches to coaching will play an important role in further contributing to the definition and expression of what integral coaching is and how it is expressed.

We feel that one of the most exciting contributions of the emerging field of integral coaching to coaching in general is that it helps to develop a more rigorous approach to measuring and understanding the transformative results of a coaching engagement. Integral coaching's use of vertical development can do much to further the scientific basis of coaching efficacy.

In conclusion, we believe that the various approaches to integral coaching offer a powerful way of supporting whole-person development in a complex world. By being intentionally attentive to the quadrants and levels of clients and their realities, integral coaches have a transformative methodology and set of lenses with which to navigate the emergent complexity of the human condition.

REFERENCES

Cook-Greuter, S. R. (1999). *Postautonomous ego development: A study of its nature and measurement.* Doctoral dissertation. Cambridge, MA: Harvard Graduate School of Education.

Divine, M. (2015). *Unbeatable mind* (3rd ed.). San Diego, California: Create Space Independent Publishing.

Divine, M. (2016). The way of the SEAL. *Reader's Digest.*

Flaherty, J. (2011). *Coaching: Evoking excellence in others* (3rd ed.). London: Routledge.

Gribben, S. (2016). *Key coaching models.* New York, NY: Financial Times Publishing.

Hunt, J., & Divine, L. (2008). Integral coaching special issue. *Journal of Integral Theory and Practice*, 4(1).

Johnson, B. (2014). *Polarity management.* Amherst, MA: HRD Press.

Kegan, R. (1995). *In over our heads.* Boston, MA: Harvard University Press.

Sieler, A. (2005). *Coaching to the human soul: Vol. I: The linguistic basis of ontological coaching.* Australia: Newfield.

Sieler, A. (2007). *Coaching to the human soul: Vol. II: Emotional learning and ontological coaching.* Australia: Newfield.

Sieler, A. (2012). *Coaching to the human soul: Vol. III: The biological and somatic basis of ontological coaching.* Australia: Newfield.

Wilber, K. (1995). *Sex, ecology, spirituality.* Boston, MA: Shambhala.

Wilber, K. (2000). *Integral psychology.* Boston, MA: Shambhala.

ADDITIONAL READING

Cook-Greuter, S. (1990). Maps for living: Ego-development stages from symbiosis to conscious universal embeddedness. In M. L. Commons, C. Armon, L. Kohlberg, F. A. Richards, T. A. Grotzer, & J. D. Sinnott (Eds.), *Adult development: Vol. 2, Models and methods in the study of adolescent and adult thought* (pp. 79–104). New York, NY: Praeger.

IV

Applications of Coaching

28

Leadership Coaching as a Growth Cycle: From Transition to Transition

James LoPresti and Edward Mwelwa

*You cannot teach a man anything. You can only help him to discover it
within himself.*
—Galileo Galilei

Coaching is, when done well, a growth cycle process for both the client and the coach. The cycle we propose starts in transition: an impulse, compulsion, or recommendation to seek change. From there, the relationship moves to the real job of coaching: the transformational work toward the client's goal or objective. Working in close collaboration, the coach and client create a shift in the coaching dynamic from "I" to "We" through the evolving dialogue (Glaser, 2016). Our primary focus in this chapter is on individual coaching rather than team coaching.

If the client and the coach do their work well, the resulting leadership transformation in the client—improved skills, enhanced competencies, behavioral changes—should naturally lead to a new transition to a higher level of leadership capability and, perhaps, even promotion. Transformation for the coach, on the other hand, may be a new insight into the use of intuition in his or her questioning methodology, a deeper sense of vocational purpose, or, perhaps, a new or renewed sense of accomplishment and pride in a job well done. The coach's transformation, therefore, can become his or her next step, or transition, toward greater effectiveness and efficiency in the coach's practice.

In short, what we wish to emphasize in this discussion is that not only is the leadership coaching engagement a cycle of growth, from transition to transformation and back to transition, but that it also can and should be a reciprocal one for both client and coach.

TRANSITION

Life is pleasant. Death is peaceful. It's the transition that's troublesome.
    —Isaac Asimov

Transition is defined as "change or passage from one state to another; the period of time during which something is changed from one state to another." The leadership coaching growth cycle begins at some point of transition for the client. Typically, clients find themselves stuck in an uncomfortable place or stage in their career. They may be stagnating in their position, or they may have lost their initiative or sense of purpose for the work they have been doing for decades or merely a couple of years. They wake up one morning to the hard reality that they need to make a change. Sometimes the need for change is recommended by a boss or Human Resources. In these cases, coaching has to be owned by the client for it to be meaningful. We, as coaches, always find our clients at some level of transition, eager, sometimes desperate, to move *from* somewhere, *to* somewhere. The destination may not always be crystal clear for the client, but the impulse to begin the journey, to change, is strong and motivating. The coach's job is to be a catalyst for effective and actionable change for each individual with whom he or she engages.

Coaching is not mentoring, nor is it counseling or training. Occasionally, in the client development process, a coach may act as trusted advisor or counselor. That, however, is the exception and not the rule. The coach's primary objective is to facilitate the client's transition. Fortunately, there is consensus among most in the professional coaching community about what a coach is not:

- Directive advisor: This takes away control from the client and creates dependence on the coach.

- Cheerleader: The client fails to develop self-motivation and relies on an external source of drive: the coach's praise and accolades.

- Therapist: It is clearly not a coach's role to resolve the client's past, unresolved emotional issues.

- Evaluator: This approach has a judgmental function associated with it and can hinder the development of trust between coach and client.

- Inauthentic: Lack of transparency from the coach can create mistrust and interfere with the coaching process.

On the other hand, what a coach *is* can be summed up as someone who rigorously practices self-awareness (Siminovitch, 2017). Great coaches are continually assessing and evaluating their skills, challenges, strengths, and personal goals through a reflective practice, such as journaling or routine discussions with another or other coaches. Great coaches are emotionally intelligent and genuinely curious about the world around them. They are nonjudgmental, caring and compassionate, build strong relationships, listen acutely, know their own boundaries and respect those of others. More importantly, they use their intuition and presence to help guide the incisive questions they ask their clients. These qualities are a result of their keen and constant focus on their own personal growth and development. In essence, that personal growth is a transition in the coach's skill and competency level.

What a coach needs to fully comprehend is that even if he or she is coaching two CFOs from the same industry, with the same issue of being stuck in the same job for 8 years, and possessing the same goal to move to the next level, clients are unique and distinct as individual human beings and in what they bring to coaching. Yes, they are both at a transitional point in themselves and their careers, but that is where the similarity ends. Although the methodology the coach uses will be fairly standard—probing questions; intuitive responses; deep, active listening—the process itself will be continually shaped and reshaped by the depth of connection and interaction between client and coach, as well as by the emotional, spiritual, intellectual, and physical uniqueness of each client. For the coach, every client and every client session is a transition to a unique experience of a particular mood, energy level, commitment, focus or distraction, and so forth, that is wholly distinct within that encounter.

Therefore, it is incumbent on the coach to be clearly aware of not only the discrete differences between clients, but also between each session with the same client. In other words, even though we begin to identify and develop a history with the client—opinions, insights, assumptions, educated guesses about him or her—we must be careful not to fall into a coaching routine that recycles old questioning and methodologies that may be of no further practical use. Each session has the potential to be a breakthrough experience with a transformative quality, transitioning the client and the coach, perhaps, to a whole new level of engagement.

CLIENT TRANSFORMATION

*Transformation does not happen by learning new information. It
happens when you change how you view and react to other people,
events, and things around you.*
        —Med Jones

Transformation is defined as "a change in form, appearance, nature, or character; a change or alteration, especially a radical one." Clearly, the heart and soul of coaching is realistic and sustainable change. The coach and the client begin the process by exploring the local habitation of the client:

- Where are you right now, in your career, in your mission, in your vision, in your professional cycle, as well as in your personal life?

- What is the pain point, frustration, apprehension, fault or flaw, or aggregate of some or all of these that compel you to seek change?

- Why the change now?

- Where, through this journey of change, do you want and need to find your-self at the end?

Once the client has decided that he or she can no longer accept the status quo, and answers the questions with honesty, candor, insight, and integrity, the transition toward transformation can begin.

As coaches, we ask probing questions that help us to gain insight into where our clients have been, where they are now, and where they wish to be. We explore their professional personas, their achievements, their promotions, their political gains and sacrifices. In short, our questions should promote deep reflection within our clients, encouraging them to appreciate and value who they really are, including recognizing vulnerability as a source of strength with the potential to influence others positively. In the beginning, we just get a peek at the man or woman behind the professional curtain—the mother or father, son or daughter, the husband or wife. The details are always different, but the situation is overall the same. Everything that encompasses who the client is—his or her beliefs, values, aspirations, dreams, hopes, fears, and challenges—are brought to the coaching experience for deep and meaningful exploration. Therein lies the power of coaching, and coaches have a tremendous influence on their clients' lives (not to mention organizations) because they stimulate clients to deeply reflect, reframe, and adjust behavior to the realities of the current situation. In terms of the coach/client relationship, coaches become trusted partners with their clients and their work occurs at the client's most vulnerable times when he or she could be highly influenced by the coach's ideas.

Therefore, coaches need a good dose of humility and a deep understanding of their power to influence. The coach's responsibility is considerable, yet many coaches are not well trained or up to the task of skillfully supporting an executive's discovery of his or her own resources. At the end of the day, executive leaders need coaches who are very smart, intuitive about business and interpersonal dynamics, have done their own personal development work, are neutral in their assessment of their client, and can tailor the coaching to individual needs—there are no canned approaches in effective leadership coaching.

Executive coach Angus McLeod emphasizes the equal importance of both the personal and the professional qualifications of the coach. McLeod observes:

> We should consider not only the coach's professional coaching background and aspects including certifications, but also their life and work experience in a holistic framework of coaching capability. As coaches, we should consider: what were the coach's own transformative learning experiences and can they apply to the coach's insight and skill set? Have they "walked in the shoes" of their clients to understand client's challenges and the organizational and people dynamics, which affect their client's leadership effectiveness? (McLeod, 2017, p. 17)

McLeod, like many other professional coaches, clearly understands the real work that coaches do—to deftly facilitate achievement of the leader's desired objective(s). More importantly, he also clearly articulates the critical work that coaches must do on themselves. There is a genuine need for not only well-trained, certified coaches, but for coaches who have done much of the self-awareness work on themselves that they are facilitating with their clients, as pointed out earlier. The burgeoning number of coaching certification and training programs in the mainstream marketplace need to be facilitating and strongly encouraging their coaching protégés to be actively working on their own personal growth. As recent research has pointed out:

> Executive coaching, both in the United States and abroad, is experiencing explosive growth. What began as developmental counseling in the 1960s . . . evolved into its present-day form. The International Coach Federation reports an excess of 15,000 members. Beyond its own ranks the federation estimates over 30,000 practitioners in the business of executive coaching. . . . (Bartlett, Boylan, & Hale, 2014, p. 75)

It is quite possible that many coaching programs may not see the urgent need for the coach's personal development as the demand for executive/leadership coaching rapidly increases. That would be a grave mistake and disservice to aspiring coaches and their future clients.

Several years ago, a Stanford University study identified a big gap between the number of executives who want coaching and the number who actually get it. Gretchen Gavett points out that "two-thirds of CEOs shared that they don't receive any outside advice on their leadership skills, and yet almost all would be receptive to suggestions from a coach" (Gavett, 2013, p. 8). Forty-three percent said they would be very receptive, while 57% shared that they would be receptive. These statistics are from a Stanford University/The Miles Group survey, mentioned earlier in this section, released in August 2013, which asked 200 CEOs, board directors, and other senior executives, questions about how they receive and view leadership advice. What is most important to note from this survey, in our opinion, is that virtually all executives admitted or realized that coaching can be a "transformational experience that carries the potential to change not only themselves, but their organizations in a meaningful way" (Gavett, 2013, p. 10).

Of course, the potential for leader and organizational transformation is very real and the Stanford/Miles Group's findings are very encouraging for all executive coaches, executives, and organizations. The professional relationship created during the coach–client pairing forms a microcosm of the work relationships an executive creates in the larger organization. Therefore, a trusting coaching relationship provides a model for the executive to emulate and to use as a lens through which to see and create professional relationships in the wider work context. Since executives work with a wide variety of people, relationship issues can hinder the effectiveness of a leader's influence within his or her organization. One likely cause of this problem is that most leadership development focuses solely on performance or career advancement, particularly skill development and strategic planning. As useful as these activities are, outcomes may be superficial or fleeting unless development also includes a deeper focus on professional relationship management (Boyatzis &

McKee, 2005). When leaders intentionally focus on developing their relational skills, they are afforded the opportunity to:

- Live their values and have an impact on purpose and meaning at work.

- Focus their vision on the future with hope and optimism.

- Create professional relationships that are caring and supportive and an organizational culture where employees feel respected, acknowledged, and appreciated by their leaders.

- Foster a climate where employees feel trusted, happy, and look forward to going to work.

It is important to note the undervalued benefits of hope, optimism, and happiness not only for the leader, but also for his or her organization (Sappala & Cameron, 2015). As "happiness at work" guru Annie McKee points out in her book *How to Be Happy at Work*,

> When we feel hopeful, we are more open and willing to consider our own and others' strengths, our dreams, and a desired vision for our collective future [of the organization]. Hope affects both our brains and our hormones in a way that changes our perceptions of the events around us. We are more likely to see people's actions as positively motivated and to view difficulties through the lens of problem-solving. (McKee, 2017, p. 31)

Coaching is never impersonal or just focused on work goals or performance. As we have stated, it is a growth process that promotes intimacy as a result of the deep connection and trust that develop between coach and client. Additionally, every person inside the company has an agenda of some sort that adds to the complexity of being a leader in an organization. This makes the coaching environment a rare and safe place in which to explore, receive honest feedback, experiment, and take safe risks while thinking through what is in the executive's best interest as a leader in order to guide the organization more effectively in the face of competing agendas (Siminovitch, 2017). The coach is not only concerned with the executive's personal transformation, but also with the transformation of the executive's organization.

Remember, transformation, as we have defined it here, implies not just change, but radical change—change that is observable and sustainable. To achieve this kind of radical change, a coach, in our opinion, needs to be cognizant of a systems approach to leadership coaching. In her book, *Executive Coaching with Backbone and Heart*, Mary Beth O'Neill observes:

> A systems perspective is highly relevant to executive coaches. When you focus too narrowly on your client alone—his personal challenges, the goals he has for himself, and the inner obstacles that keep him from being successful—you miss the whole grand "ecosystem" in which he functions. (O'Neill, 2000, p. 127)

People working together on a regular basis create a social interactional field. That field is a unitary whole in which everything affects everything else and influences should be understood as multiple, mutual, and complex. Executives act and react within this field, along with everyone else they lead. If coaches fail to see how the system affects their clients, coaches will not understand why their interventions are sometimes ineffective. The client is both influencing and being influenced by a broad network of interrelationships in and around his or her organization. Add to that network external contexts, such as the national and global economy and the natural environment, and the field of interrelated connections widens exponentially. "By taking a systems perspective, the coach can avoid pointing to one person or element within the organization as the root cause of a thorny problem" (O'Neill, 2000, p. 129).

A PLAN TO TRANSFORM

Transformation is not automatic. It must be learned; it must be led.
   —W. Edwards Deming

Real and sustainable change takes time and should not be rushed. Most of us may be familiar, at least in the Western world, with "the New Year's resolution" and what happens after a few days or weeks (Goleman, Boyatzis, & McKee, 2002, p. 49). Too often, as with the New Year's resolution, coaching leads with the creation of a plan. But many plans fail because they are not taken seriously enough by the client or the client perceives, usually erroneously, that he or she doesn't have the time to commit regularly to a plan. But this is when the real work starts and when a good coach can be most valuable. The trusting, professional relationship that coach and client both honor is critical to the success or failure of the engagement. A plan focused on the client's successful achievement of his or her goal (Boyatzis & McKee, 2005) is facilitated more effectively and efficiently by the coach when he or she provides the following as a manner of course:

- Emotional support when change is hard or when failure looms

- Energy by emphasizing the lessons learned from failure (and success)

- Shared resilience by encouraging the cultivation of optimism

- A place where a client can feel safe enough to mourn failures, be vulnerable, and truly celebrate success

What is key to these coaching best practices is that executives must know unequivocally that these are the behaviors that they can depend on when their resolve or optimism begins to wane.

So, we have established that coaching supports both personal and professional development in the leader. We have also established that good coaches facilitate and witness deep exploration of purpose, hope, and relationships at work with their client. Now it is time to plan. A plan is necessary because it provides a road map or direction for coaching and makes it possible to measure the progress being made during the coaching journey. As client and coach assess their progress, they can shape and alter the path to the goal(s) as appropriate. In this sense, the plan is organic and changes as new insights surface through the coaching cycle without losing focus on the end goal or objective.

One approach helpful in supporting the creation of an effective transformation plan is a visioning process referred to as *intentional change* discussed in *Resonant Leadership* by Richard Boyatzis and Annie McKee. The visioning is a result of extensive research in how adults learn and change in meaningful and sustainable ways. Their research concluded that there were five main steps that form a realistic and sustainable change process once the client has established a firm desire and momentum for change. *Intentional change* is an awareness of the need to change or improve behavior and then *intentionally* applying oneself to the following steps:

- The dream—visioning

- The reality—the current situation

- Gaps and learning plan—the difference between vision and reality

- Experimentation—practicing new behavior and receiving feedback

- "Board of Directors"—significant peers and colleagues who support my success

> The coach and client spend a good deal of time embellishing the elements of *intentional change*, especially the visioning component (step one), so that the client thinks and feels that he or she is "living the dream" (Boyatzis & McKee, 2005). This is the opportune time for the client to predict and design the future that he or she wants. Visioning taps into the brain's pre-frontal cortex to stimulate creativity in shaping the future. (Glaser, 2016, p. 52)

Extended focus on visioning is time well spent and reaps great dividends. Too often the visioning concept is shortened by a desire to go rapidly to achieve faster results, as if a person were a machine that can be programmed to achieve behavior change at the speed of light. What is achieved by going through this phase slowly is a deeper, meaningful, and reflective exploration of the inherent capabilities that are dormant within the client.

When visioning is done well and is followed by exploration of one's current reality (step two), noticing the gaps between current leadership and desired leadership as envisioned becomes easier. Creating a plan for getting to the desired future state from the current one moves more smoothly, since the leader's requirements can be seen, felt, and understood more clearly.

Once a plan is created (step three), the leader starts to practice and implement the plan (step four). Putting the plan into practice, the leader gathers data about potential obstacles to new, desired behavior(s). As the obstacles are brought into the coaching discussion, the coach supports refining or altering the plan to minimize or eliminate the obstacles to the plan's realization. The leader is, therefore, encouraged and coached to continue to practice the new behavior(s).

Finally, enlisting of board of directors (step five) comes into play as the leader asks for support from trusted colleagues and others for feedback as he or she practices new behaviors. The coach checks in with the client during the coaching sessions on how implementation of the new behavior is progressing. *Intentional change requires practice for a dedicated period of time for new behavior(s) to become the norm and for others to notice and believe in the behavior change exhibited by the executive.* A period of extended coaching becomes very necessary and helpful in supporting the leader to embed the new behaviors into his or her routine so that they become the new, preferred way of behaving.

COACH TRANSFORMATION

Transformed people transform people.
—Richard Rohr

The demands on, and responsibilities of, a coach are not to be taken lightly and require that the coach continually hone his or her coaching skills. Beyond basic executive coaching training, coaches need to be continually learning and challenging themselves to be better people, as we have already noted. By refining and reinforcing their emotional intelligence competencies, they create their own rich emotional reserve for reference. Angus McLeod notes that good coaches can facilitate the transformative process of their clients through informed questions:

> When coaches learn to ask questions that are designed to help the coachee learn, those coachees invariably become interested and excited to learn more about themselves; they become more engaged and committed to the coaching process and to real personal development. (McLeod, 2017, p. 24)

Shouldn't we say the same thing here about coaches? The more they engage themselves in deep, authentic self-awareness, the more they become "engaged and committed to the coaching process and to real personal development."

We have found, through discussions with other executive coaches, that the coach's process of personal development can include a wide variety of different practices, interests, and engagements. One of the more common methods, we have discovered, is peer support from other coaches. Some coaches organize peer support groups that meet once a month or so to discuss hard topics in coaching or "case study" issues about which a coach may wish to solicit other coaches' perspectives. Of course, many successful coaches have their own coach with whom they do their own development work.

In addition, as executive coaching has become more mainstream, countless books, videos, and articles have been published on a broad range of coaching topics.

Finally, there are the questions we need to ask ourselves. No series of questions fits all coaches, of course. But there are certain foundational queries that, we believe, need to be on every coach's list. These include:

- What is your life's purpose?

- What are your personal/professional relationship needs?

- What is your passion as a person? As a professional?
- What are your demons?
- What are your thoughts and feelings on power and diversity?
- Why do you want to be a coach?

As we have already noted, executive coaches themselves have a wonderful opportunity in their coaching experience to professionally and personally grow. Once the coach has begun and continues to explore his or her own self-awareness and personal development rigorously, as already suggested, what he or she brings to and takes away from the coaching engagement can be quite substantive on a number of levels. On a professional level, a coach may help facilitate not only a transformation in an executive leader, but also within his or her organization. One's enhanced coaching skills have the potential to affect many lives, not just the one in the "C" suite.

For one of these authors, 8 months of coaching an executive at a small to midsize organization resulted in tangible, sustained behavioral changes in the executive. In turn, the executive's organization of just over 500 employees reaped the benefits of the leader's changes in the observable culture change within the organization. People were happier, more productive, more collaborative, and more comfortable in communicating their needs and feedback in the new "safe" environment. For this coach, the experience was transformational in how it underscored executive coaching's potential power to affect an organization in a systemic fashion. In addition, the author came away with a more fulfilled sense of accomplishment and several additional "intuitive" tools to apply to future coaching engagements. This experience recalls an observation by Warren Bennis on leadership: "It is important that the quality of our lives is dependent on the quality of our leadership. Only when we understand leaders will we be able to control them" (Peltier, 2010, p. 26).

On a more economic level, one highly effective coaching engagement can lead to a word-of-mouth expansion of one's practice. Executives talk with other executives. If one finds high value in your coaching skills and competency, he or she will tell other executives.

On the personal level, many coaches relate stories of subsequent friendships that evolved from the coaching relationship after the engagement had ended. Both authors of this chapter have established long-term friendships with several clients as a consequence of the strong coaching relationships we cultivated. Additionally, a good coach has the potential to take away lessons learned about himself or herself in any particular session. Often, the client may mirror our own fears, challenges, needs—as well as our strengths, core values, and insights. When we bring our intuition to the coaching session, our questions may not only be intended for the client's growth, but for our own, albeit unconscious and inadvertent, personal development.

TRANSITION, AGAIN

A transition period is a period between two transition periods.
—*George Stigler*

When the time comes when both coach and client agree that their work together is complete, both experience a transition. In a best-case scenario, the client has achieved his or her objective(s). The root cause of the initial discontent has been identified and the client has a plan in place to address the issue(s) and is intentional in his or her commitment to change. If the coach and client have worked well together, the client is now unstuck and on a new level of leadership awareness and action. Gone is the dysfunctional behavior(s) that initially prompted the pursuit of coaching support and the repetitious patterns of poor judgment, weak communication, indecisiveness, or strained relationships. Or perhaps the client engagement was not focused on dysfunctional behavior(s), but on strengthening particular skills. Nevertheless, the client has transformed himself or herself with the deft guidance of the coach, perhaps transitioning to a new role in the organization, or transforming his or her old role into one more in tune with his or her core values, vision, and dreams of a better future for the organization.

The coach, too, is in transition from the role of coach, confidant, and trusted advisor for one client to his or her next executive engagement with a new client. Coaches may also transition to new tools or insights in their practice from the previous engagement that they think and feel may be useful to future clients.

CONCLUSION

Each thing is of like form from everlasting and comes around again in its cycle.
  —*Marcus Aurelius*

As we have tried to point out, executive coaching is a cyclical process that engages both client and coach in a reciprocal relationship of give and take, where both parties benefit from an objective- or goal-driven relationship between coach and client. It is a co-creation process that ends with the client being less dependent on the coach and the implications of the conclusion of the engagement are explored, discussed, and next steps are identified and planned. For simplicity's sake, it is a process starting in transition, moving to transformation, and finally back to transition for both parties if each fully commits to his or her respective role in the coaching engagement.

REFERENCES

Bartlett, II, J. E., Boylan, R. V., & Hale, J. E. (2014). Executive coaching: An integrative literature review. *Journal of Human Resource and Sustainability Studies, 2,* 188–195. doi:10.4236/jhrss.2014.24018

Boyatzis, R. E., & McKee, A. (2005). *Resonant leadership.* Boston, MA: Harvard Business School Press.

Gavett, G. (2013). What CEOs really want from coaching. Retrieved from https://hbr.org/2013/08/research-ceos-and-the-coaching

Glaser, J. E. (2016). *Conversational intelligence: How great leaders build trust and get extraordinary results.* New York, NY: Routledge.

Goleman, D., Boyatzis, R., & McKee, A. (2002). *Primal leadership: Unleashing the power of emotional intelligence.* Boston, MA: Harvard Business School Press.

McKee, A. (2017). *How to be happy at work*. Boston, MA: Harvard Business School Press.

McLeod, A. (2017). When coaching standards don't deliver, what next? Retrieved from https://www.linkedin.com/pulse/when-coaching-standards-dont-deliver-what-next-dr-angus-mcleod

O'Neill, M. B. (2000). *Executive coaching with backbone and heart*. San Francisco, CA: Jossey-Bass.

Peltier, B. (2010). *The psychology of executive coaching*. New York, NY: Routledge.

Sappala, E., & Cameron, K. (2015). Proof that positive workplace cultures are more productive. *Harvard Business Review*.

Siminovitch, D. E. (2017). *A gestalt coaching primer: The path toward awareness IQ*. Toronto, Canada: Gestalt Coaching Works, LLC.

29

Life Coaching:
The Heart and Soul of
Professional Coaching

Fran Fisher

L ife coaching is the heart and soul of professional coaching. It is the mother from which all other types of modern-day coaching emerge. Regardless of the type of coaching (life, business, organizational, leadership, executive, career transition, relationship, etc.), the coach is essentially working with people regarding what it is to be human and what it takes to be the fullness of who they are and achieve their greater potential.

THE ROOTS OF PRESENT-DAY LIFE COACHING

The roots of life coaching reach deep into the soil of human history. The evidence is apparent in the contributions of wisdom from ancient Eastern philosophers such as Confucius, Buddha, and Lao Tzu. Most notable is this well-known metaphor for the fundamental coaching concept of empowerment:

Give a man a fish and you feed him for a day;
teach a man to fish and you feed him for a lifetime.
     —*Maimonides, Torah Scholar 1135–1204 AD (Goodreads, n.d.-f, para. 13)*

   Eastern practitioners of martial arts and the Greek athletic coaches encouraged both physical training and achievements in personal excellence. Socrates modeled and encouraged self-understanding versus imparting knowledge: "The unexamined life is not worth living." His Socratic questioning approach to human development guides modern-day coaches in how to ask evocative questions that raise the client's self-awareness and ability to access his or her inner wisdom versus the telling or teaching approach. Three most notable "roots" in recent times are the helping professions, leadership mentors and advisors, and the Human Potential Movement.

THE HELPING PROFESSIONS

Today, we can see influences of psychological practitioners Sigmund Freud, Carl Jung, Alfred Adler, Abraham Maslow, and Carl Rogers in the development of what we now call coaching. For example, Carl Rogers is known for his client-centered and *unconditional positive regard* therapeutic approach; his shift of the traditional therapeutic perspective from *the client is wounded* to *the client is whole*; and his position on the benefits of providing *safe space* for a client.

Life coaches honor the client as the expert in his or her life and hold a belief that every client is capable, creative, and resourceful. Life coaches are intentional about:

- Discovering, clarifying, and aligning with what the client wants to achieve
- Encouraging client self-discovery
- Eliciting client-generated solutions and strategies
- Helping the client to hold themselves accountable

At the center of your being you have the answer.
You know who you are and you know what you want.
    —Lao Tzu, Chinese Philosopher, 6th century BC (Spirituality & Health, n.d.)

LEADERSHIP ADVISORS

Top leaders throughout history have depended on a personal confidant, trusted advisor, consultant, or mentor for support and guidance. Leaders recognize the benefits of having a third-party objective observer, listener, or sounding board; someone who is not afraid to offer honest feedback to increase personal and professional effectiveness.

THE HUMAN POTENTIAL MOVEMENT

The Human Potential Movement of the 1960s, 1970s, and 1980s was influential in raising human consciousness and introducing personal transformational technology. Practitioners such as Alexander Everett, George Leonard, Werner Erhard, and Fernando Flores were a few of the high-profile influencers regarding concepts of personal responsibility, integrity, empowerment, and a new ontological (study of the nature of being) language for supporting effective personal growth and change. George Leonard (1995), coauthor of *The Life We Are Given*, says, "Never before has there been so much scientifically based knowledge about the transformative capacities of human nature" (Leonard & Murphey, 1995, p. xv) and offers three basic principles for lasting behavioral change: long-term practice, whole person integration, and authority and responsibility remains with the individual.

Drawing from the dissertation research of Susan Cannon (2000) that analyzed patterns and cycles in human consciousness across time, this shift in consciousness has been occurring for hundreds, even thousands, of years on these three fundamental levels:

- *Our way of knowing* is about how we think, gather information, and understand the world around us. The whole-systems approach has become the preferred method for studying the world.

- *Our way of relating* is about how we relate to one another, or the stance we take with another human being. The new paradigm emerging is a partnership system where people work to bring out the best, not to eliminate the competition. Power comes from within and enables us to achieve what we desire, motivated by possibility versus fear.

- *Our way of being* is about our fundamental capacity as human beings to create our lives, the questions we ask, and the answers we give ourselves about the meaning of existence.

This new empowerment paradigm is raising our awareness to the responsibility for creating our life.

COACHING PRINCIPLES ARISING FROM SHIFTS IN CONSCIOUSNESS

Notice how those emerging shifts in consciousness inform the following life coaching principles.

PARTNERSHIP PRINCIPLE

A coach–client relationship is a partnership of two experts. The coach is the expert of the coaching process. The client is the expert of who he or she is. In this context, the coach holds no hierarchy of expertise. Coach and client are engaged in a shared discovery process together.

HOLISTIC PRINCIPLE

A coach takes an all-inclusive, whole-systems approach in facilitating the client's learning and self-discovery process, inviting, as appropriate, exploration of their mental, physical, emotional, and spiritual thinking, feeling, beliefs, values, needs, wants, and so forth.

WHOLENESS PRINCIPLE

The coach holds a core belief that the client is a whole being, capable and resourceful, not broken or merely a collection of isolated parts. Parts, yes, but parts that are connected and can be accessed for learning and growth. Example: "What strength can you call on that moves you toward what you want?" versus "Have you ever considered turning off the TV and going to bed earlier?"

BALANCE PRINCIPLE

A coach facilitates the client in discovering and prioritizing his or her allocation of energy or attention that will move them toward greater life balance. For example, choices the client is making with right brain versus left brain thinking, who they are being versus what they are doing, values they are honoring versus values they are not honoring, feeding the fear versus trusting their inner wisdom.

EMPOWERMENT PRINCIPLE

A life coach holds true to an empowerment principle. Partnering with unconditional respect and suspending any personal agenda, the coach is committed to supporting the client in building his or her capacity for making better choices, achieving goals, and ultimately increasing the client's satisfaction and fulfillment.

You cannot teach a man anything;
You can only help him find it within himself.
    —Galileo Galilei, Astronomer 1564–1642 AD (Goodreads, n.d.-d, para. 3)

CREATIVITY PRINCIPLE

A coach helps clients shift from victim to creator, from living at the effect of their circumstances to getting their hands on the driver's wheel of life. Coaches ask, "What do you want?" They help clients discover their deepest desires to access energizing motivations, vision, resources, strengths, and empowering beliefs. They also help clients clear obstacles. Clients discover how to replicate their unique creative processes and sustain a mindset for being the creators of their own lives.

Life isn't about finding yourself. Life is about creating yourself.
    —George Bernard Shaw, Playwright 1856–1950 (Goodreads, n.d.-e, para. 1)

SUSPEND JUDGMENT PRINCIPLE

The coach is more effective when holding a safe space for the client to remain open and responsive versus reactive. A coach avoids asking the client "Why?" The word *why* will often trigger defensiveness (e.g., reasons, explanations, excuses, blaming). A better choice is to ask questions that start with *what, when, or how*, inviting the client into a judgment-free zone for exploration.

POWER FROM WITHIN PRINCIPLE

A coach facilitates a client in discovering and learning how to access his or her point of authentic *power* within. This perspective is based on the understanding and acceptance that we cannot change others, but, as a coach, we can help our clients shift their relationship, perspective, or attitude about challenges or issues.

Between stimulus and response, there is a space. In that space lies
our freedom and power to choose our response.
In our response lies our growth and freedom.
        —*Victor Frankl, Psychiatrist 1905–1997 (Goodreads, n.d.-c, para. 2)*

Spirituality Principle

A coach facilitates the client in achieving greater satisfaction and fulfillment in life and work, to clarify core strengths and values, to discover life vision and purpose, to define success, to find meaning in the day-to-day as well as the grand scheme of things: to call forth the client's innate greatness.

Eyes see only light, ears hear only sound,
but a listening heart perceives meaning
        —*David Stendl-Rast, Catholic Benedictine Monk, 1926 (AZ Quotes, n.d., para. 3)*

Acceptance Principle

A coach accepts clients and meets them where they are without judgment. With caring and empathy, the coach lets go of any need to "fix" the clients, change them, or move them from where they are mentally, emotionally, or spiritually. This environment allows clients to feel safe enough to strengthen their self-acceptance, opening possibilities for greater freedom, creativity, and the courage to take risks.

A CORE TEACHING IN LIFE COACH TRAINING

As the coaching industry began to grow in the 90s, an international coaching association called the International Coach Federation (ICF) accredited three coaching schools: Coach U, founded by Thomas Leonard; Coaches Training Institute (CTI), founded by Laura Whitworth and Henry House; and the Academy for Coach Training (ACT), founded by Fran Fisher.

The school training structures and approaches differed, yet they were aligned on a fundamental belief: *Who the coach is being has more to do with the effectiveness of his or her coaching than the skills or tools he or she brings to the process.*

Coach U

Coach U created a course called *Personal Foundation*, recognizing that personal development work is imperative to the success of a coach. With its emphasis on the overall health of the coach being critical to the success of both coach and client, the *Personal Foundation* course includes an assessment of one hundred habits to address that are grouped in four areas of life: Physical Environment, Well-Being, Money, and Relationships. The concept behind this program is that by strengthening these habits, one will reduce stress, increase energy, and attract better and healthier people and opportunities into his or her life, and by so doing, will have the knowledge from experience to help guide clients to do the same.

COACHES TRAINING INSTITUTE (CTI)

Before expanding the curriculum and branding their school CTI, the founders offered two foundational training modules: *Being* and *Doing*. In the *Being* course, participants were facilitated in exercises for raising self-awareness of their worldviews, limiting beliefs and biases, and unconscious personas or behaviors. They were also guided to use a life assessment tool called The Wheel of Life. The concept of this assessment is to raise clients' awareness of their level of satisfaction in each of the key areas of life. That awareness provides a launching place for coaching the client in goal setting, planning, and designing specific actions for moving forward to achieve meaningful change in the client's life.

ACADEMY FOR COACH TRAINING (ACT)

At the ACT, the founder placed her Living Your Vision® (LYV) program at the core of the curriculum. LYV is a personal growth transformational process that facilitates an individual in: (a) discovering his or her personal vision, purpose, and values; (b) designing a holistic Master Plan for his or her life; and (c) putting a plan into action and learning how to live true to the essence of who he or she is. With this process at the core of the coach training program, the coach can be more of his or her best self in life and in the role of coach and have this experience to help guide clients to do the same in their lives.

Other schools, also early adopters for accreditation with the ICF, offered curriculum based on the belief that a coach's level of self-development is directly related to the effectiveness of his or her coaching.

MY JOURNEY TO LIFE COACHING

The Human Potential Movement was my pathway to coaching, a "yellow brick road" that led me from a place of low self-esteem—with a core limiting belief that I'm not good enough and workaholic life patterns—to a land of enlightenment! The movement used humanistic psychotherapies like sensitivity training and encounter groups that emphasized the development of the individual. In the 1970s and 1980s, I slaked my thirst for healing and growth at the fountain of positive psychology with the leaders of the movement.

In 1990, my lifelong pattern of workaholism finally caught up with me *big time*! I was on the verge of a nervous breakdown. For 2 years, I had been working 18-hour days, 6 days a week. Not only were the hours crippling, but the job itself (in residential real estate management) held impossible deadlines and unrealistic profit expectations. I got to the point where I couldn't hold a glass of water without spilling it. Instead of checking myself into a hospital, I tried something else. I flew from Detroit to Portland, Oregon, rented a car, and drove to the coastal town of Seaside. There, I walked the beach for a week, reflecting.

In the stillness of my solitude, soothed by the sound of the ocean waves, I heard: "Fran, it is time to put *yourself* in the center of your life." It became apparent to me I had nearly killed my health and relationships trying to fix and resolve and manage and control the circumstances of my life and work. I was making things happen, oh, yes *indeed*, but I was living my life needing the approval of others versus accepting my humanness and trusting my inner wisdom. What I had been doing was no longer working for me.

While soaking in the knowledge from the human potential courses, I had learned many self-empowerment tools. What was left for me was to trust the wisdom and take a leap of faith. Without a backup plan, I gave notice to my employer and took a year off to heal. I practiced listening to my intuition and acting on it. I started putting my own needs first instead of last. I took the time to discover the essence of who I am and how to live more congruently with my vision, my purpose, and my values. I called this my "inside-out" process. Rather than let the *outside* world dictate my happiness and self-worth, I practiced accessing it from the *inside*.

Your visions will become clear
Only when you can look into your own heart.
Who looks outside, dreams;
Who looks inside, awakens.
  —Carl Jung, Psychiatrist, 1875–1961 (Goodreads, n.d.-b, para. 1)

During this time, I also began sharing my own transformational inside-out process with small business entrepreneurs in a way that helped them achieve greater life and work satisfaction, fulfillment, and profitability. The culmination of this sharing was a process I created: LYV.

In 1997, I founded the ACT located in Bellevue, Washington, integrating the LYV process into the coaching skills curriculum. Applying the LYV process allowed every student to experience a personal transformation as the first step in learning how to facilitate personal transformation for others.

In 1998, at the ICF International Conference in Orlando, Florida, I was inspired to develop and share this definition for coaching:

Coaching is the sacred space of unconditional love,
where learning, growth, and transformation naturally occur.
  —Fran Fisher (Author, October 17, 2016)

What I mean by *transformation* is this: Transformation is a shift in perspective. Transformation occurs when a client shifts his or her current limiting view of the circumstance or relationship to the issue, to an empowering perspective or state of being.

So when life coaches create a safe environment and invite a client to explore his or her innate empowering qualities, such as core strengths, beliefs, and values, coaches can guide clients to a more self-empowered state in relation to their situation, circumstances, or issues.

Bless those who challenge us to grow,
To stretch, to move beyond the knowable,
To come back home to our essential nature.
Bless those who challenge us
for they remind us of doors we have closed
and doors we have yet to open.
            —*Native America Prayer (Goodreads, n.d.-g, p. 1)*

COACHING PERSONAL EMPOWERMENT

The following example of a coaching relationship highlights that the personal empowerment perspective encompasses all types of coaching including Executive and Leadership Coaching.

ANDY'S "EDGE"

My phone rang at 10:00 on a Saturday morning. Andy spoke with a tone of urgency and anxiety. He was a Senior Human Resource executive in a mega-global corporation. I learned that he had been working with this company for 6 months, that he had moved his family across three states and purchased a brand new house, and that his wife had just given birth to their second child. The previous day, in Andy's first 6-month review, his supervisor told him that he was not demonstrating the edge that this corporate culture required of its leaders.

In a state of panic and shock, and with so much at stake, he was worried about losing his job. He indicated that he wanted to gain the edge, so he was shopping to hire a coach to help him. I asked him if he wanted coaching to save his job or to help him develop his leadership skills, which might include developing the edge that this company expected of him. He said he wanted coaching to support developing his leadership skills. The *edge* was something he felt he needed to look at because his wife was also asking for that same behavior at home.

I replied, "Okay, then. I'm interested in working with you. I would refer you to other coaches if you just wanted to save your job."

Early in the coaching relationship, I learned that the edge meant that he needed to be more proactive. Andy designed two new habits to partner with his wife more in childcare and to partner with her more in-home maintenance. She was happier causing him to be happier.

For work, he designed a new way to be better organized so that he had more time for three priorities: strategic planning, anticipating the needs of others on his team, and relationship building. Six months later he felt he had made significant measurable improvements. Unfortunately, his supervisor did not give him the review he felt he had earned and deserved.

Rather than becoming angry and resentful, Andy looked to see what he could learn. He decided to let go of needing approval from his supervisor. He chose to risk losing the job. Instead, he directed his intention on gaining greater personal and professional satisfaction by simply doing his personal best. Andy also realized that aspects of the edge behavior this culture required was not resonant with his natural style, nor did he align with it philosophically as a way of people treating people.

In the following months, Andy attained greater self-trust and acceptance. Rather than trying to continue to accommodate a behavior that he did not believe in, he honored his natural leadership style and trusted that if it was effective in the culture that would be great. If not, he would leave.

ANDY'S EPILOGUE

What happened next for Andy was unforeseeable and amazing. Within 2 weeks of Andy taking that bold stand for himself, his VP supervisor was replaced. His new VP supervisor was aligned with Andy in cultural philosophy and leadership style. Together they took a stand within that division to be catalysts for change. We celebrated his courage and willingness to stay true to his core values.

AN INTENTION OF AWARENESS

Andy's story is an example of how an executive coach, with life coaching skills, helped the client recognize and transform his core personal essence by shifting perspective. With life coaching, it is about raising awareness and measuring internal as well as external impact, such as the relationships and situations that surround the client. In the case of the executive coach, it is also about raising awareness and measuring those internal and external impacts while taking into account the organizational environment and culture.

This same view can be applied to other types of coaching. For example, a writing coach supports clients to become aware of their blocks and resistances in order to move forward with their story; as a result, the client becomes more aware of his or her internal dialogue. A health coach will provide guidance for exercises and diet recommendations, and also help clients become more aware of the choices they are making in regard to those tools. Across the board, coaches come back to that fundamental principle: listening, caring, and being fully present have more to do with the effectiveness of the coaching than the skills or tools the coach might offer.

What is required is a commitment to discover purpose and to grow
to a new level of personal potential and expression.
The same principles for leading apply to us in all areas of our life—
it's all about living our life congruent
with our principles, beliefs, and character.
    —Kevin Cashman, Author, *Leadership from the Inside Out* (1999, p. 68)

WHO ARE IDEAL CLIENTS FOR LIFE COACHES?

Life coaches typically desire to work with someone who has a yearning for more success and fulfillment, increased health and well-being, and enriched quality of life: someone motivated to do the personal work to get there, someone who wants to make a positive difference in life. Whether the coaching is professional or personal, invariably the work circles back to the core of the individual: what needs to change from within and then what can change in the world around them. There are many reasons why clients seek coaching. The following list offers a sample of typical client issues:

Achieving Goals	Getting Unstuck
Starting a business Increasing income Planning retirement Publishing a book Fulfilling a dream	In life In a job or career In fulfilling one's potential In managing work and life balance In clarifying what one wants
Attaining Greater Happiness	**Making Changes**
Discovering vision, purpose, and values Getting to what matters Igniting or re-igniting passion Finding more joy	Overcoming fears Changing limiting habits Reinventing self Making a transition (relationship, career, lifestyle)
Finding Balance	**Improving Self-Care and Well-Being**
Achieving peace or contentment Increasing work and life balance Taking control of life Learning to live more on purpose	Establishing better health habits Increasing confidence, self-worth, self-esteem Improving quality of life Overcoming overwhelm Reducing or managing stress
Fulfilling Potential	**Enhancing Relationships**
Clearing roadblocks Accomplishing goals Gaining confidence Unleashing creativity Pursuing personal or spiritual growth	Improving interpersonal communications Deepening intimacy Expanding circle of support Building friendships Learning partnership

LIFE COACHING TOOLS, TECHNIQUES, AND STRATEGIES

As successful life coaches continue to expand awareness and develop themselves in order to help their clients, they may begin to specialize in specific areas, often developing their own tools based on the processes they have found work for them. Most life coaching methods include these basic elements:

- Assessing (emotonal quotient, values, strengths, preferences, personality, innate nature, etc.)

- Examining the current situation

- Discovering what the client wants to be different

- Exploring what it will take to get there

- Choosing a course of action

- Designing concrete action steps

- Supporting follow through and accountability

- Measuring learning and progress
- Celebrating successes, large and small
- Identifying what's next

Working from these steps, life coaches will use a variety of tools, based on their particular niche or type of clients, such as:

- Beliefs > behaviors > results
- Discovering core strengths
- Values clarification
- Vision board
- Goal setting and planning
- Daily habit development and tracking
- Life wheel
- Journaling
- Visioning
- Inquiries for reflection
- Completion exercise or progress check-in
- Structures that support the client in following through with his or her commitment. For example, setting the alarm, posting reminder notes, working with a support buddy, daily reporting to the coach, tracking sheet, post or carry a symbol, plan rewards, and so forth.

USING THE LIFE COACH PROCESS WITH A CLIENT

The following story illustrates a life coach process that helped a client move from an outside-in perspective to an inside-out way of being in the world.

ANNE'S CHOCOLATE CHIP COOKIES

Anne was in her mid-40s, and married with children who were preparing to leave home. For many years, she had worked to augment the family income and she was becoming more aware of her discontent in her job. Anne described her job as unfulfilling and uninteresting, and she realized it had been like that for a long time. She was also realizing the same was true of her home life. That was why she wanted to hire a life coach.

Anne said her life was like a waking dream in which she couldn't see a reflection of herself when she looked into a mirror. She was completely out of touch with herself. We talked about the *inside-out* concept and she began to recognize that her real power resided within, not outside of herself. She decided it was time to reclaim herself. She declared that she was ready to commit to the process. I acknowledged Anne for how courageous and heroic she was being to take the action of hiring a coach.

In an early coaching session, she left the session with an assignment to ponder an inquiry: Where do I give away my personal power? At the beginning of the next session, I asked Anne to share a win from the previous week. She couldn't think of one. I held the silence for a long, *long* time. Nothing. I encouraged her, "Anne, even the tiniest win or accomplishment is okay. Surely there is something we can celebrate this week, no matter how small it seems to you." I felt it was important to support her in experiencing a success that we could build on for going forward.

Then she said, "Well, there is one thing, but it is too silly to mention." I pounced on it, "Anne, I *do* want to hear it, and I promise I won't think it is silly."

"I tried a new chocolate chip cookie recipe this week," she offered timidly.

"Congratulations, Anne. That's absolutely terrific! Tell me more about trying this new recipe."

And then the awesomeness of her story unfolded. It turned out that she had been baking her mother's chocolate chip cookie recipe since childhood, even though she had left home, raised her own family, and—*get this*—didn't even *like* that particular recipe! We spent the rest of that coaching session celebrating the fact that she had made a *new* choice that honored herself. I acknowledged her courage to make a different choice and act on it. She had carried a belief that if she tried a different recipe, it would dishonor her mother who had died 5 years earlier.

I asked Anne how it felt to try that new recipe. She said it felt vulnerable and exciting and yet, she did feel some pleasure. We celebrated her commitment to self-nurturing. Trying something new was a first step, a breakthrough in an old pattern of leaving herself out while giving her power to fear or judgment.

Anne's Epilogue

"I tried a new chocolate chip cookie recipe this week" was just the tip of Anne's iceberg issue. Underneath the surface was a lifetime of choices Anne had made from the outside in. She left that coaching session with an inquiry to ponder: How do I create the experience of pleasure?

Over time, Anne let go of her fear of what someone else would think and began making more choices that brought her joy. Building on those successes she found the courage to look for a different job and make the transition. She unleashed a desire for more color and texture in her life, so she built a new wardrobe and redecorated her home. She also developed a new, more passionate relationship with her husband. Taking actions one step at a time turned the iceberg upside down. Now, the "great mass" of Anne's choices comes from the inside. With that, she began to experience more joy, passion, and aliveness in her life.

Musicians must make music, artists must paint, and poets must write
if they are to be ultimately at peace with themselves.
What human beings can be, they must be.

They must be true to their own nature.
This need we may call self-actualization.
 —Abraham Maslow, Psychologist 1908–1970 (Goodreads, n.d.-a, p. 1)

THE FUTURE OF LIFE COACHING

The coaching field has increased exponentially over the past 20 years. Life coaching is now a household term, and tens of thousands have benefited from having a guide alongside them, digging deep in order to transform themselves and the world around them.

Where is life coaching headed? Developing coaching trends reflect the current individual, cultural, and societal pressures clients are facing today. Consider the possibilities of helping clients expand their knowledge of the brain and its handling of change, mindfulness training, discoveries in the areas of health and wellness, or finding ways to shift perspectives on character and transparency in leadership. Life coaches will continue to look for innovative and compassionate ways to guide their clients on a journey to self-empowerment and transformation.

REFERENCES

AZ Quotes. (n.d.). *David Steindl-Rast Quotes*. Retrieved from http://www.azquotes.com/author/18142-David_Steindl_Rast

Canon, S., & Cannon, S. R. (2000). *Constructing images of the future for the United States at the year 2020 with Seattle-area cultural creatives* (doctoral dissertation). Retrieved from ProQuest Dissertations (9976883)

Cashman, K. (1999). *Leadership from the Inside Out* (1st ed.). San Francisco, CA. Berrett-Koehler.

Fisher, F. (2016). *Coaching principles: Five ways to create sacred space for your client* [Blog Post]. Retrieved from https://franfishercoach.com/coaching-principles

Goodreads. (n.d.-a). *Abraham H. Maslow > Quotes > Quotable Quote*. Retrieved from https://www.goodreads.com/quotes/366-a-musician-must-make-music-an-artist-must-paint-a

Goodreads. (n.d.-b). *Find quotes: C.G. Jung*. Retrieved from https://www.goodreads.com/quotes/search?utf8=%E2%9C%93&q=Look+into+your+heart+by+Jung&commit=Search

Goodreads. (n.d.-c). *Find quotes: Victor Frankl*. Retrieved from https://www.goodreads.com/quotes/search?utf8=%E2%9C%93&q=between+stimulus+and+response&commit=Search

Goodreads. (n.d.-d). *Galileo Galilei > Quotes*. Retrieved from https://www.goodreads.com/author/quotes/14190.Galileo_Galilei

Goodreads. (n.d.-e). *George Bernard Shaw > Quotes*. Retrieved from https://www.goodreads.com/author/quotes/5217.George_Bernard_Shaw

Goodreads. (n.d.-f). *Maimonides > Quotes*. Retrieved from https://www.goodreads.com/author/quotes/194459.Maimonides

Goodreads. (n.d.-g). *Native American prayer > Quotes > Quotable quote*. Retrieved from https://www.goodreads.com/quotes/434095-bless-those-who-challenge-us-to-grow-to-stretch-to

Leonard, G., & Murphey, M., (1995). *The life we are given: A long-term program for realizing the potential of body, mind, heart, and soul*. New York, NY: Jeremy P. Tarcher, a member of Penguin Putnam.

Spirituality & Health. (n.d.). *Lao Tzu on inner knowing*. Retrieved from https://spiritualityhealth.com/quotes/center-your-being-you-have-answer-you-know-who-you

30

Advancing the Practice of Professional Health and Wellness Coaching

Darlene Trandel

The United States is in a health crisis. The Centers for Disease Control and Prevention (CDC) notes that chronic diseases are responsible for 7 out of 10 deaths in the United States each year and account for 86% of the nation's healthcare costs and 99% of the Medicare payments (CDC, 2015). Diabetes alone affects 29 million (9.3%) people in the United States and contributes $245 billion annually to healthcare expenditures. Globally, the chronic disease epidemic is occurring in all income levels. Four out of five chronic disease deaths are in low- and middle-income countries. Moreover, disease in these populations tends to develop at an earlier age (World Health Organization [WHO], 2005, 2016).

Most of these chronic diseases such as heart disease, stroke, cancer, type 2 diabetes, obesity, and arthritis result from poor lifestyle choices (Willett et al., 2006). They are the most commonly treated and most costly diseases. Chronic diseases, however, are the most preventable and better managed conditions.

Chronic diseases are straining individuals, governments, and companies. The National Center for Health Statistics notes that while identified causes of death are heart disease, cancer, chronic respiratory disease, accidents, stroke, Alzheimer's disease, and diabetes, the actual causes are poor diet (calorie-dense, non-nutritious, salty processed foods), physical inactivity, smoking, and addiction (CDC, 2015).

Despite access to abundant health information and the best intentions of individuals to implement the recommended lifestyle changes, efforts frequently fail. Knowledge is necessary for behavior change but is not sufficient.

THE NEED FOR HEALTH AND WELLNESS COACHING

Chronic diseases challenge healthcare systems. Lifestyle changes directly result in less risk and incidence of chronic disease and cancer (Willett et al., 2006). Professional health and wellness coaches (HWCs), along with allied healthcare professionals trained to use basic coaching skills, offer the promise in assisting patients to prevent or better manage their chronic disease in making sustainable healthy lifestyle changes. This new health profession, HWCing (professional health and wellness coaching), has the potential to be a transformational force in healthcare systems.

A SHIFT FROM THE TRADITIONAL APPROACH

The healthcare system manages acute medical emergencies and conditions using a prescriptive approach, that is, fixing, telling, and instructing. While the expert approach is necessary when facing an immediate health crisis, it has not been shown to be helpful in adopting and sustaining lifestyle changes.

Changing lifestyle and self-managing chronic disease is a patient responsibility. As chronic care is carried out by patients and/or their families in daily life, new patterns of thinking, doing, and relating, as well as increased motivation and confidence to make changes are needed. HWCing generates positive energy and emotion necessary to fuel motivation, self-confidence, hope, and optimism in making health changes (Moore, Jackson, & Tschannen-Moran, 2016).

Many HWCs bring a past healthcare background where the traditional expert approach was used. Changing the focus to partner with the client, respect autonomy, elicit goals, focus on the client's strengths and values, facilitate change, and foster possibilities can be challenging for the HWC. It also can be difficult for clients to work with coaches as they have been conditioned to being told what to do. Nevertheless, when this shift is made, the results can be life-changing (Moore, Jackson, & Tschannen-Moran, 2016).

DEFINITION OF HEALTH AND WELLNESS COACHING

The International Consortium for Health and Wellness Coaching (ICHWC) defines HWCing with the following critical elements: partnering with clients, seeking self-directed lasting change, aligning with values, enhancing well-being, displaying unconditional positive regard, believing in capacity for change, honoring each client as an expert on his or her life, and ensuring interactions are respectful and nonjudgmental (ICHWC, 2017e).

While some definitions of HWCing use the word "patient" as opposed to "client" and "provider" for "HWC," ICHWC chose "client" and "HWC" to recognize the diversity of backgrounds from which HWCs come and the variety of people served. In addition, ICHWC chose not to designate levels of HWCs, although some suggest two levels should be recognized: one for those with advanced clinical knowledge and competencies and another for those nonclinically prepared.

HWCs share the basic tenets of other coaching domains as well as those of the International Coach Federation (ICF), the world's largest organization of professional coaches across all domains. The ICF defines coaching as "partnering with clients in a thought-provoking and creative process that inspires them to maximize their personal and professional potential." The client is viewed as "creative, resourceful and whole" (ICF, n.d.).

The common core for all coaching domains includes: (a) setting the foundation (meeting ethical guidelines and professional standards, and establishing the coaching agreement); (b) co-creating the relationship (establishing trust and intimacy with the client and coaching presence); (c) communicating effectively (active listening, powerful questioning, and direct communication); and (d) facilitating learning and results (creating awareness, designing actions, planning and goal setting, and managing progress and accountability; ICF, n.d.)

DIFFERENT FROM OTHER COACHING DOMAINS

While HWCing contains core elements of other coaching domains, variations exist. First, coaching is practiced in health and wellness in two main ways. One is where the individual functions as a full-time HWC, such as working in a role specifically designated as HWCing. The other is where the health professional, such as clinician, dietician, and physical therapist, uses HWCing competencies to expand effectiveness in their professional roles. These two approaches look different and emphasize different skills. Moreover, a lack of clarity in the literature exists regarding how best to effectively integrate these roles in a clinical visit while ensuring the coaching process is honored (Wolever et al., 2013).

Second, there is a knowledge base needed by an HWC when coaching medical patients. While HWCs do not diagnose, treat, or provide medical advice, most agree health/disease knowledge is needed by HWCs to identify dangerous situations requiring the client to seek medical care.

Third, patients may be more vulnerable when confronting health problems than clients coached in other areas (Wolever, Moore, & Jordan, 2016). Patients might encounter emotional handicaps or physical disabilities associated with the health condition, as well as fears, anxieties, loss, insecurities, and death. More time might be spent collaborating with clients on their health vision; raising awareness of their strengths; overcoming obstacles such as physical, mental, or financial; grieving loss of body integrity; dealing with minor and major health setbacks; and reconsidering and readjusting health goals.

Another difference from other coaching domains lies in the area of outcome markers. HWCs use biomarkers, including blood pressure, weight, blood cholesterol, and glucose levels. Changes in biometric measurements can be viewed as a physiological counterpart of behavioral change that can be quantified.

Fifth, unlike other coaching fields where the client or organization typically reimburses the coach directly, the question of who pays for HWCing is not settled (Wolever, Moore, et al., 2016). The research is unclear on the interplay of costs, outcomes, and sustainability around coaching interventions. If HWCing is determined to produce better health outcomes and lower health costs, there could be pressure for predetermined goals that produce positive physiological/health outcomes that might undermine client-determined goals and the coaching process. This may be of particular concern where payment for value exists, such as in Accountable Care Organizations (Wolever, Moore, et al., 2016). Nevertheless, there are currently a few specific health conditions where health insurance coverage is provided for coaching.

A last difference is sharing with the client. While HWCs do not assume the traditional expert or educator role, there is a place for sharing information noted in the HWCing scope of practice (ICHWC, 2017b). The exact details as to how to share information is yet to be determined.

COMMUNICATION OF INFORMATION

While the HWC does not assume the traditional expert approach of many types of healthcare professionals, there is an element of sharing health information with clients. In the systematic review of the literature on coaching by Wolever et al. (2013), one of the key components of defining the HWCing process was content education. This component was mentioned as a coaching intervention in 91% of the 284 articles included in the review. Disease-specific information was the most commonly reported content education provided (40%), followed closely by lifestyle and/or health (37%), and 8% on behavior change processes (Wolver et al., 2013, p. 9).

The findings of the jobs task analysis (JTA) named sharing information as a task of HWCs (ICHWC, 2017a). In support of the research and the JTA, the ICHWC includes sharing of information as an HWC competency that occurs within the client-centered relationship, undertaken with client permission or upon request, or otherwise required by scope of practice (ICHWC, 2017b, 2017d).

While sharing information is one task, what might be included as best practice has yet to be determined. Miller and Rollnick (2007) provide principles to consider when motivational interviewing is used to share information. Specifically, when the HWC believes that objective information might help the client in advancing the coaching process or the client requests information, information is shared, after permission is granted by the client.

Information is shared without interpreting its meaning for clients. Clients are allowed to ask questions and to process, evaluate, and respond to the information to determine whether it fits with their values, desires, and perspectives, or how the information might be applied (Miller & Rollnick, 2013). Research by Engelmann, Capri, Noussair, and Berns (2009) notes when information is delivered, it is made available to the brain to absorb, process, examine, and apply. Therefore, to fully engage the HWCing process, the emotive and sensory parts of the client's brain should be actively involved in evaluating the information. This allows clients to create and own their solutions (Belf & Marx, 2015).

Coaches must have multiple communication skills and empowerment strategies to integrate content information into the client's change process. In addition, the HWC approaches clients as resourceful, creative, and whole, while respecting that they knows what works best for them. HWCs share information without giving advice and partner with clients to move toward beneficial healthy decisions (Wolever et al., 2013).

WHAT BACKGROUND DO HEALTH AND WELLNESS COACHES BRING?

Healthcare professionals and health-related individuals can be HWCs. Wolever et al. (2013) noted a higher number of HWCs reported having some medical or other professional background. Of those with medical backgrounds, the majority were nurses followed by physicians and pharmacists. Of the HWCs that noted allied health or other health backgrounds, the majority were mental health providers followed by dieticians/nutritionists, psychologists, social workers, and health educators/promotion. There has also been a recent increase in the number of HWCs who were exercise professionals.

DISTINGUISHING HEALTH AND WELLNESS COACHES FROM OTHER HEALTHCARE PROFESSIONALS

The role and approach of HWCs are often confused with other healthcare professionals. HWCs do not employ the traditional educator approach that analyzes problems, gives advice, prescribes solutions, directs the client's goals and strategies, teaches new skills, or provides education (Moore et al., 2016).

HWCs do not diagnose or treat; rather they encourage personal responsibility and autonomy, reflective thinking, self-discovery, and self-efficacy. Clients are urged to discover their own answers (Livingstone & Gaffney, 2016).

HWCing is distinct from counseling, which is problem-focused and assists clients to understand, accept, and overcome emotional issues and problems (Martin, 2016). The practice of HWCing differs from therapy, which treats diagnosable character disorders in mental health and attempts to heal psychological wounds, resolve problems from the past, and restore functioning (Jordan & Livingstone, 2013).

Taking a holistic perspective of health and well-being, HWCs often work in collaboration with clinicians who design and clarify specific disease treatment plans. From this vantage point, they see areas to assist clients to integrate information from multiple experts and decide what actions to take (Moore et al., 2016).

USE OF INTEGRATIVE TERMINOLOGY

Some HWCs refer to themselves as "integrative" HWCs and include an additional component of knowledge and practice of evidence-driven healing therapies in coaching service. While integrative HWCs do not diagnose or treat illness, they have a working knowledge of and vocabulary in both traditional and other integrative healing therapies (Smith et al., 2013). These healing practices include acupuncture, yoga, meditation, and massage.

WORK SETTINGS FOR HEALTH AND WELLNESS COACHES

In a 2015 survey by the National Consortium for Credentialing Health and Wellness Coaches (NCCHWC), Jordan and Arloski reported the majority (75%) of the respondents practiced in private practice settings, 10% in healthcare organizations, 10% in healthcare benefits, and 5% in wellness settings (Jordan & Arloski, 2017).

The diversity of HWC settings has expanded to include healthcare organizations, hospitals and clinics; insurance third-party payers; employee benefits companies; disease management companies; health insurance plans; fitness facilities, spas, and health clubs; physician practices; community wellness centers; on-site employee wellness programs; human resources departments; private coaching practitioners; HWC educational and training programs; and academic institutions and schools (Wolever, Jordan, Lawson, & Moore, 2016).

COACHING PSYCHOLOGY IN HEALTH AND WELLNESS COACHING

Coaching psychology is designed to facilitate and enhance change, growth, goal attainment, self-actualization, and well-being in all domains of life (Moore et al., 2016). Dozens of coaching theories, frameworks, and approaches are integrated and weave the scientific foundation that enables effective coaching practice (Dossey, Luck, & Schaub, 2014). The knowledge, competencies, and resources outlined are found on the ICHWC website (ICHWC, 2017d). Common theories and frameworks used in HWCing are described.

POSITIVE PSYCHOLOGY INTERVENTIONS

Positive psychology examines strengths, achievements, and skills that allow individuals to feel engaged, seek fulfillment, function optimally, and find meaning in life and relationships, which is a perspective used in HWCing. Problems and challenges are not ignored but viewed as learning opportunities.

Frederickson's Broaden and Build Theory (2003) suggests that positive emotions broaden awareness and encourage novel, varied, and exploratory thoughts and actions that build skills and resources, enabling resiliency in the face of negativity (Fredrickson, 2003). The HWC uses positive psychology-based coaching interventions that encourage positive emotions as an essential component of good health and well-being.

SELF-DETERMINATION THEORY

The Self-Determination Theory by Ryan and Deci (2017) posits that intrinsic motivation prompts people to engage an activity because of rewarding internal factors, making it more likely that they sustain the activity for their own internal reasons.

The three innate psychological needs forming the basis for self-motivation are competence, relatedness, and autonomy. HWCs influence the client's motivation for change by maximizing autonomy, competence, and relatedness. Autonomy is fostered when the client self-defines goals and destinations. HWCs use feedback and affirmations directed at the client's strengths to help the client feel responsible for and capable of action.

SOCIAL COGNITIVE THEORY (SCT)

The SCT provides opportunities for social support through affirming expectations, self-efficacy, and using observational learning and other encouragements to achieve behavior change (Bandura, 1989). HWCs support their clients to devise effective experiments for change and encourage them to find role models that will show them strategies and skills for success. In addition, the coach assists the client in developing a system of support to attain and maintain the changes (Jordan, 2013).

TRANS-THEORETICAL MODEL OF CHANGE (TTM)

The TTM by Prochaska and Prochaska (2016) holds that a particular change occurs across six stages including pre-contemplation, contemplation, preparation, action, maintenance, and termination. HWCs help clients consider what stage they are in and apply coaching interventions appropriate for the stage.

APPRECIATIVE INQUIRY (AI)

AI is the discovery of the best in people, their organizations, and the world around them (Cooperrider, 2012). HWCs employing this approach connect to their client's positive core strengths, values, and resources for learning related to their efforts in making the behavior change. Instead of having the client identify problems, causes, and fixes, the HWC coach uncovers and celebrates the best of what is and could be (Moore et al., 2016).

MOTIVATIONAL INTERVIEWING (MI)

MI is a collaborative conversation to strengthen a person's own motivation and commitment for change (Miller & Rollnick, 2013). The HWC strategically employs interaction skills by asking open-ended questions, providing affirmations, responding with perceptive reflections and summary statements in order to engage the client, define his or her focus, resolve ambivalence, evoke motivation, and move toward action. By increasing the client's awareness of the potential problems, consequences of the status quo, and benefits of the health behavior change, the HWC attempts to evoke the client's own motivation to change behavior (Miller & Rollnick, 2007).

ADULT DEVELOPMENT THEORY

Another adult development model commonly used in coaching is the Constructive Development Theory by Kegan and Lahey (2009), which is based on the idea that individuals naturally progress over a lifetime through several stages of consciousness, continually constructing and reconstructing reality, values, beliefs, and assumptions. HWCs support a process of self-inquiry and self-exploration to identify obstacles that are preventing progress toward the goal. The coach then helps the client to construct and test new perspectives that support change in mindset and behavior (Kegan & Lahey, 2009).

NEUROSCIENCE

As neuroscience continues to develop the understanding of human thought, emotion, and behavior, more light is shed in considering coaching mechanisms and interventions for behavioral change. Brain plasticity, a lifelong property of the brain, underlies normal brain function and the ability to learn and modify, or establish new behaviors and the mindsets needed to sustain them. Coaching can be thought of as a strategic and purposeful means of facilitating change and an effective means of shaping neural pathways and enhancing emotional regulation (Davidson & Begley, 2013). Imagining activates the same neural pathways as the real experience and the process of envisioning may as successfully invoke change as does the actual experience (Jack, Boyatzis, Khawaja, Passarelli, & Leckie, 2013). The HWC also uses reframing to help the client become aware of a new perspective and liberated way of responding.

ESTABLISHING NATIONAL STANDARDS, BEST PRACTICES, AND CREDENTIALING

As HWC grew over the past decade, it became apparent that national standards for role definitions and expectations, best practices, background, and training of qualified HWCs were necessary to ensure the credibility, consistency, quality, and safety of these coaches (NCCHWC, 2015).

Three factors pressed the need for national standards and certification. First new approaches for preventing and managing chronic illness and escalating costs were needed. HWCs bring an evidence-driven skillset to clients in attaining and sustaining health enhancing lifestyles and may cut the costs of acute care in hospitals and emergency departments. HWCing also engages and activates clients to prevent disease, adopt health-promoting lifestyles, and self-manage health conditions (NCCHWC, 2015).

Second, there's a need for a clear role definition. The NCCHWC estimated that approximately 15,000 to 35,000 people in the United States identified themselves as an HWC in 2015 (NCCHWC, 2015). Without role definitions, standards of practice or a certifying process, anyone can call himself or herself an HWC. Consequently consumers, employers, and health professionals were unclear about competencies, backgrounds, and training of HWCs. In addition, this lack of clarity seen in the reviewed literature makes it difficult to evaluate outcomes and effectiveness (NCCHWC, 2015).

Finally, there is a need for national standards for education and training. Credentialing has been primarily in the hands of the training organizations and differences were seen on the amount, quality, and focus of the curriculum; the length and type of program (i.e., hours to years and university degrees to certificates); the background and preparation of faculty; and the method of delivery, (i.e., live, web-based, or self-study).

The Long and Passionate Road to National Certification

The NCCHWC, a collaborative volunteer nonprofit organization, was formed in 2010 to support professionalization in the field. It took years of effort to achieve consensus about what an HWC does. All stakeholders agreed that establishing standards for the profession and assimilating these competencies in the health-care system would be valuable to patient care (Jordan, Wolever, Lawson, & Moore, 2015).

DEFINING THE ROLE/TASK OF THE HWC

The Consortium conducted a JTA to establish what tasks in the HWC role and what skills and training are required to perform those skills. In 2014, 15 practice professional HWCs participated as subject matter experts for the JTA, and together with a certification specialist and consulting psychometrician, identified specific tasks performed in coaching intervention from beginning to end, the frequency of performance, and the importance of the task.

To validate this JTA, a survey was sent to 4,026 HWCs with instructions to rate how often they performed the tasks named and how important each task was to their work. The sample represented almost 20 HWC education and training programs and practicing coaches in the industry. The survey yielded a response rate of 25.6% (1,031) with results supporting the JTA named tasks and ranking of importance (Jordan et al., 2015; Wolever, Jordan, Lawson, & Moore, 2016).

Four domains of job tasks were identified: (a) those that occur at the initial stages of coaching, (b) those most central to the process, (c) those that address the client's evaluation and integration of progress, and (d) legal and professional considerations. Using the best-practice processes, the validated JTA provided clear role delineations that needed to be included in a certification exam (Wolever, Jordan, et al., 2016).

DEVELOPING THE NATIONAL CERTIFICATION EXAM CRITERIA

To develop program training standards using best practice procedures with validated JTA results, the minimum eligibility criteria to take the exam was determined by engaging 19 subject matter experts. These standards served as directives for the national training and education standards (Jordan et al., 2015).

The following standards are recommended by the NCCHWC (now ICHWC) for practitioners to become certified: (a) minimal combinations of academic and professional credential requirements, (b) successful completion of an accredited training or education program, (c) completion of documented coaching hours, and (d) completion of the ICHWC national certification examination. In addition, the requirements necessary for an approved training and education program were established (Jordan et al., 2015).

A two-stage certification process was created for training and education programs to adjust their curricula to meet the new standards for accreditation as well as to consider the diversity of education, training, and background for students and currently practicing coaches. After an initial first stage of temporary program approval having transition criteria, only graduates from an accredited program will be eligible to take the national certification in the final phase (Jordan et al., 2015).

A PARTNERSHIP ESTABLISHED IN PURSUIT OF NATIONAL STANDARDS AND CREDENTIALING

In 2016, the NCCHWC (now called the ICHWC) and the National Board of Medical Examiners (NBME) collaborated to further develop a national board certification exam for HWCs (NCCHWC, 2016).

The first step was creating a blueprint to ensure that all the HWC domains defined in the JTA process were covered by the credentialing exam and to outline the coach certifying examination. The blueprint sought to increase the validity and reliability of the credentialing exam by linking the exam questions to the learning objectives in each domain and indicating the weight carried by each question. Practicing health coaches wrote certification exam questions that were reviewed by the NBME experts for best practices regarding question format and structure. Last, expert ICHWC–NBME teams finalized the certification exam; it was offered for the first time in September 2017. *The credential is called the National Board Certified Health & Wellness Coach (NBC-HWC).*

ETHICAL CONSIDERATIONS IN HEALTH AND WELLNESS COACHING

Work forged ahead to establish a Code of Ethics for HWCing (ICHWC, 2017c). The Code emphasized that coaches maintain the strictest levels of confidentiality with clients unless directed otherwise by law. If a relationship exists between a coach, client, and sponsor, an agreement should establish how coaching information is exchanged. If the HWC practices independently and outside a healthcare organization or setting, adherence is voluntary and HWCs are not required to maintain client records. If records are kept by the HWC, these records need to be managed, kept, and destroyed to protect privacy, security, and confidentiality.

HWCs are expected to follow statutes, regulations, principles, values, ethics, and standards of their profession. Unlike other licensed professionals (such as registered nurses and medical doctors), HWCs are not regulated by the states. In terms of liability, however, HWCs will likely be held to the highest credential or healthcare license they hold. HWCs who hold a professional license should consider obtaining malpractice insurance when acting in a HWCing role.

For HWCs working within a healthcare organization or setting such as a health plan or healthcare provider, the Health Insurance Portability and Accountability Act of 1996 (HIPAA) requires HWCs follow procedures that ensure the confidentiality and security of protected health information regardless of form (California Department of Health Care Services, 2017).

EVIDENCE BASE FOR HEALTH AND WELLNESS COACHING

The empirical literature supporting the effectiveness of HWCing is in an early stage of development. The number of peer-reviewed studies are increasing—nearly doubling every 5 years, but there are notable limitations in the literature, including a lack of a common definition of HWCing; variability in the coaching methods, providers, duration and frequency; few randomized trials and systematic reviews; lack of comparison groups between coaching and other alternatives; and difficulty in generalizing findings across organizations, practice settings, and disease conditions (The Evidence Centre for Health Education East of England, 2014).

EARLY RESEARCH

Some of the first meta-analyses and systematic reviews focused on MI, which was first described by William Miller in the 1980s on his therapeutic experience in alcohol addiction (Miller & Rose, 2009). MI is supported by over 250 randomized trials and several efficacy reviews and meta-analyses across multiple healthcare conditions including health-promotion behaviors, medical adherence, substance abuse, and mental health issues (Miller & Rollnick, 2013). MI may offer some effective interventional strategies to achieve behavior change, although the specific conditions in which MI might be more effective remain unclear (Rubak, Sandbaek, Lauritzen, & Christensen, 2005).

In 2009, Newnham-Kanas, Gorczynski, Morrow, and Irwin published the first review of coaching for improved health outcomes outside of MI. The most important finding in their annotated appraisal of the 72 studies is that studies did not offer a definition of the coaching intervention. Other limitations included the lack of randomization of participants into treatment and control groups, inadequate details about methodological procedures used for replication, inconsistency in applying the treatment protocol, and variability of health areas examined.

LATER RESEARCH

Attempting to operationalize a definition of HWCing, Wolever et al. (2013) used PRISMA-guided systematic review for 200 peer-reviewed empirical articles and more than 60 expert opinions. Key components included: (a) coaching was provided by health professionals with diverse backgrounds; (b) coaching process was patient-centered; (c) goals were partially or fully patient-determined; (d) the coach encouraged patient self-discovery and learning using behavior change theory in addition to teaching and sharing information; and (e) a mechanism for patient accountability for behavioral goals was established (Wolever et al., 2013).

Olsen (2014) reviewed a random sample of 215 articles, applied Rodgers' evolutionary method of concept analysis, and proposed an operational definition that included (a) health focus, (b) goal-oriented, (c) client-centered partnership, and (d) a process of enlightenment and empowerment.

CURRENT RESEARCH ON THE EFFECTIVENESS OF HEALTH AND WELLNESS COACHING INTERVENTIONS

Dejonghe, Becker, Froboese, and Schaller (2017) conducted a systematic review and meta-analysis of HWCing in rehabilitation and preventive settings. HWCing interventions were loosely defined and were provided to patients in the rehabilitation setting and to healthy people in the preventive setting. From the 767 titles screened,

14 randomized controlled studies met the criteria of follow-up at least 24 weeks after coaching termination. While about a half of the studies pointed to long-term effectiveness for reducing weight and A1C levels, Dejohghe et al. (2017) emphasized that the small number of studies meeting the criteria for inclusion point to the knowledge gap regarding the sustainability of HWC interventions.

Building on previous systematic reviews, Sforzo et al. (2017), developed a comprehensive compendium of HWCing research from 1990 onward to organize, describe, and evaluate the strengths and weaknesses of the literature. Components for HWCing previously identified by Wolever et al. (2013) were used: (a) the coach was trained on behavior change theory and coaching processes, (b) the coach was a trained health/allied professional; (c) goals were partially or fully client-determined health goals; (d) patient accountability was tracked; and (e) development of a relationship between coach and patient/client (one-on-one or at least three sessions). Of the 2,824 papers identified by patient type or wellness focus using quality analysis and outcome measures, 214 papers met inclusion criteria.

Overall, the papers viewed HWCing as a positive intervention in making healthy changes in lifestyle and management of chronic disease.

- The studies focusing on cancer patients was the least represented with 13 peer-reviewed articles, with the findings showing some benefits in quality of life and psychosocial factors.

- The diabetes category reported improved blood glucose (A1C) readings and weight reduction as outcomes.

- The heart disease group reported positive outcomes on risk factor improvement, specifically low-density lipoprotein and total cholesterol levels, glucose levels, blood pressure control, and weight.

- Most studies in the obesity, hypertension, and cholesterol groups reported a positive impact, but HWCing effects were not separated from other interventions/therapies.

    ○ Most studies in obesity reported a weight reduction; however, HWCing was often conducted with other interventions that were important confounders.

    ○ Reduction of blood pressure occurred in the hypertension group; however, other therapies/interventions were not separated.

    ○ In the cholesterol group, no single outcome was reported in more than half the studies indicating more study is needed.

- Wellness represented 29% of the studies, which was the largest and included wellness and other conditions such as nicotine addiction, fibromyalgia, glaucoma, multiple sclerosis, overweight, depression, and stress. The most consistent effects were improvements in exercise and nutrition behavior, blood glucose levels, and psychological outcomes such as quality of life, stress, and depression.

The study concluded that HWCing provided a probable benefit to cancer, diabetic, and heart disease patients and a possible benefit to those with hypertension, obesity, and cholesterol issues.

Storzo et al. (2017) acknowledge the Compendium has limitations, including the possibility of missing relevant studies, the inclusion of some studies that did not meet the five criteria, and coding errors.

RESEARCH CONCLUSIONS

HWCing is a rapidly growing field with a diverse and expanding base of literature. The number of systematic and multiple analysis studies of the existing literature support that HWCing holds significant promise as an adjunct treatment of lifestyle behavior change to impact the prevention and course of chronic diseases.

REFERENCES

Bandura, A. (1989). Human agency in social cognitive theory. *American Psychologist, 44*(9), 1175–1184. doi:10.1037/0003-066X.44.9.1175. Retrieved from https://www.uky.edu/~eushe2/Bandura/Bandura1989AP.pdf

Belf, T., & Marx, M. (2015). *From the toolbox: Do you give advice to your clients?* [Continuing coaching education, ethics]. Retrieved from https://coachfederation.org/blog/from-the-toolbox-do-you-give-advice-to-your-clients

California Department of Health Care Services. (2017). *Health Insurance Portability and Accountability Act*. Retrieved from http://www.dhcs.ca.gov/formsandpubs/laws/hipaa/Pages/1.00WhatisHIPAA.aspx

Centers for Disease Control and Prevention. (2015). *Leading causes of death*. Retrieved from https://www.cdc.gov/nchs/fastats/leading-causes-of-death.htm

Coopperrider, D. (2012). *What is appreciative inquiry?* [Website]. Retrieved from http://www.davidcooperrider.com/ai-process

Davidson, R. J., & Begley, S. (2013). *The plastic brain. The emotional life of your brain: How its unique patterns affect the way you think, feel, and live—and how you can change them* (pp. 161–170). New York, NY: Penguin Groups.

Dejonghe, L. A., Becker, J., Froboese, I., & Schaller, A. (2017). Long-term effectiveness of health coaching in rehabilitation and prevention: A systematic review. *Patient Education and Counseling, 100*, 1643–1653. doi:10.1016/j.pec.2017.04.012. [Epub ahead of print]

Dossey, B. M., Luck, S., & Schaub, B. G. (2014). *Nurse coaching: Integrative approaches for health and wellbeing*. North Miami, FL: International Nurse Coach Association.

Engelmann, J., Capra, C., Noussair, C., & Berns, G. (2009). Expert financial advice neurobiologically "offloads" financial decision-making under risk. *PLOS ONE, 4*, e4957 [Online publication]. doi:10.1371/journal.pone.0004957

Fredrickson, B. (2003). The value of positive emotions. *American Scientist, 91*, 330–335. doi:10.1511/2003.4.330. Retrieved from https://www.americanscientist.org/sites/americanscientist.org/files/20058214332_306.pdf

International Coach Federation. (n.d.). *Core competencies*. Retrieved from https://www.coachfederation.org/credential/landing.cfm?ItemNumber=2206

International Consortium for Health and Wellness Coaching. (2017a, February). *Health and wellness job task analysis findings*. Retrieved from http://ichwc.org/wp-content/uploads/2015/03/JTA-ICHWC-Feb-1-2017.pdf

International Consortium for Health and Wellness Coaching. (2017b, February). *Health and wellness scope of practice*. Retrieved from http://ichwc.org/wp-content/uploads/2015/03/ICHWCHealthWellnessCoachScopeofPractice-FinalFeb12017.pdf

International Consortium for Health and Wellness Coaching. (2017c, February). *ICWHC Code of Ethics.* Retrieved from http://ichwc.org/wp-content/uploads/2015/03/Final-Code-of-Ethics-Feb-1-ICHWC.pdf

International Consortium for Health and Wellness Coaching. (2017d, May). *Health and wellness coach certifying examination content outline with resources.* Retrieved from http://www.nbme.org/pdf/hwc/HWCCE_content_outline.pdf

International Consortium for Health and Wellness Coaching. (2017e). *What is health and wellness?* Retrieved from http://ichwc.org

Jack, A. I., Boyatzis, R. E., Khawaja, M. S., Passarelli, A. M., & Leckie, R. L. (2013). Visioning in the brain: An fMRI study of inspirational coaching and mentoring. *Social Neuroscience, 8*(4), 369–384. doi:10.1080/17470919.2013.808259

Jordan, M. (2013). *How to be a health coach: An integrative wellness approach.* San Rafael, CA: Global Medicine Enterprises, Inc.

Jordan, M., & Arloski, M. (2017). *What is health and wellness coaching? (Part 1).* Health and Wellness Community of Practice [webinar]. Retrieved from https://register.gotowebinar.com/register/372426959719795202

Jordan, M., & Livingstone, J. (2013). Coaching vs psychotherapy in health and wellness: Overlap, dissimilarities and the potential for collaboration. *Global Advances in Health and Medicine, 2*(4), 20–27. doi:10.7453/gahmj.2013.036

Jordan, M., Wolever, R. Q., Lawson, K., & Moore, M. (2015). National training and education standards for health and wellness coaching: The path to national certification. *Global Advances in Health and Medicine, 4*(3), 46–56. doi:10.7453/gahmj.2015.039. Retrieved from http://journals.sagepub.com/doi/abs/10.7453/gahmj.2015.039

Kegan, R., & Lahey, L. (2009). *Immunity to change: How to overcome it and unlock the potential in yourself and your organization.* Boston, MA: Harvard Business School Publishing Corporation.

Livingstone, J., & Gaffney, J. (2016). *Relationship power in health care: Science of behavior change, decision making, and clinician self-care.* Boca Raton, FL: Taylor & Francis Group, LLC.

Martin, A. (2016). *What counselling is not: The counsellor's guide.* Retrieved from http://www.thecounsellorsguide.co.uk/what-counselling-not.html

Miller, W. R. & Rollnick, S. (2007). *Motivational interviewing in health care: Helping patients change behavior.* New York, NY: Guilford Press.

Miller, W. R., & Rollnick, S. (2013). *Motivational interviewing: Helping people change* (3rd ed.). New York, NY: Guilford Press.

Miller, W. R. & Rose, G. S. (2009). Toward a theory of motivational interviewing. *American Psychologist, 64*(6), 527–537. doi:10.1037/a0016830

Moore, M., Jackson, E., & Tschannen-Moran, B. (2016). *Coaching psychology manual* (2nd ed.). Philadelphia, PA: Wolters Kluwer.

National Consortium for Credentialing Health and Wellness Coaches. (2015). *Re: NCCHWC announces launch of national certification for professional health and wellness coaches* [Press release]. Retrieved from http://ichwc.org/PR043015.pdf

National Consortium for Credentialing Health and Wellness Coaches. (2016). *Historic agreement in place to nationally certify healthy and wellness coaches* [News release]. Retrieved from http://www.ncchwc.org/wp-content/uploads/2015/03/5-25-2016-NCCHWC-NBME-Press-Release-May-25.pdf

Olsen, J. (2014). Health coaching: A concept analysis. *Nursing Forum.* doi:10.1111/nuf.12042

Prochaska, J. O., & Prochaska, J. M. (2016). *Changing to thrive: Using the stages of change to overcome the top threats to your health and happiness.* Center City, MN: Hazelden Publishing.

Rubak, S., Sandbaek, A., Lauritzen,T., & Christensen, B. (2005). Motivational interviewing: A systematic review and meta-analysis. *The British Journal of General Practice, 55*(513), 305–312. Retrieved from https://www.ncbi.nlm.nih.gov/pmc/articles/PMC1463134

Ryan, R., & Deci, E. (2017). *Self-determination theory: Basic psychological needs in motivation, development and wellness.* New York, NY: Guilford Press.

Sforzo, G., Kaye, M., Todorova, I., Harenberg, S., Costello, K., Sobus-Kuo, L., . . . Moore, M. (2017). Compendium of the health and wellness coaching literature. *American Journal of Lifestyle Medicine, 20*(10), 1–12. doi:10.1177/1559827617708562

Smith, L., Lake, N., Simmons, L. A., Perlman, A., Wroth, S., & Wolever, R. Q. (2013). Integrative health coach training: A model for shifting the paradigm toward patient-centricity and meeting new national prevention goals. *Global Advances in Health and Medicine, 2*(3), 66–74. doi:10.7453/gahmj.2013.034

The Evidence Centre for Health Education East of England. (2014). *Does health coaching work?* Retrieved from https://eoeleadership.hee.nhs.uk/sites/default/files/Does%20health%20coaching%20work%20-%20a%20review%20of%20empirical%20evidence_0.pdf

Willett, W. C., Koplan, J. P., Nugent, R., Dusenbury, C., Puska, P., & Gaziano, T. A. (2006). Prevention of chronic disease by means of diet and lifestyle changes. In D. T. Jamison, J. G. Breman, A. R. Measham, G. Alleyne, M. Claeson, D. B. Evans, . . . P. Musgrove (Eds.), *Disease control priorities in developing countries* (2nd ed., Chapter 44). Retrieved from https://www.ncbi.nlm.nih.gov/books/NBK11795

Wolever, R. Q., Jordan, M., Lawson, K., & Moore, M. (2016). Advancing a new evidence-based professional in health care: Job task analysis for health and wellness coaches. *BMC Health Services Research, 16*(205). doi:10.1186/s12913-016-1465-8

Wolever, R. Q., Moore, M., & Jordan, M. (2016). Coaching in healthcare. In T. Bachkirova, G. Spence, & D. Drake (Eds.), *SAGE handbook of coaching* (pp. 523–545). Thousand Oaks, CA: Sage Publishing.

Wolever, R. Q., Simmons, L. A., Sforzo, G. A., Dill, D., Kaye, M., Bechard, E. M., . . . Yang, N. (2013). A systematic review of the literature on health and wellness coaching: Defining a key behavioral intervention in healthcare. *Global Advances in Health and Medicine, 2*(4), 38–57. doi:10.7453/gahmj.2013.042

World Health Organization. (2005). Preventing chronic diseases: A vital investment. *WHO Global Report.* Retrieved from http://www.who.int/chp/chronic_disease_report/full_report.pdf

World Health Organization. (2016). *Rate of diabetes in China "explosive."* Retrieved from http://www.wpro.who.int/china/mediacentre/releases/2016/20160406/en

31

What Team Coaching Is and Is Not

Janet M. Harvey

O rganizations that seek to explore new areas—markets, technologies, processes—often look to collaborative teams to develop creative responses. Organizational leaders who commission teams often place great hope in the promise of synergy, that a team will fulfill the folk wisdom that promises: "The whole is greater than the sum of its parts." There is evidence (Woolley, Chabris, Pentland, Hashmi, & Malone, 2010) that some teams do exhibit "collective intelligence" greater than the general intelligence of its members.

Reliance on teams introduces new complexities into organizational life. Leaders with many teams reporting to them can see the scope of outcomes under their management triple or even quadruple. Self-governing teams can alleviate this stress, but the centuries-old command and control governance model produces leaders—potential team members—who have been rewarded for taking personal accountability for producing results rather than sharing accountability with a team of peers.

Tension arises in teams when the needs of individuals conflict with the needs of the team. This tension generates undesirable behavior that impedes progress and can spill over into the organizational culture, affecting morale and other indicators of organizational health.

Research into factors that impede teams and research on the best interventions to accelerate team work both point to the social and emotional intelligence of team members. A lack of social sensitivity is a barrier to high performance, while the presence of social and emotional intelligence moves teams forward. Numerous interventions have been designed to improve team performance, but large organizations still struggle to discover methods that are consistently effective.

Team coaching has demonstrated the potential to be consistently effective across diverse organizational cultures. The coaching process supports teams to produce excellent results and become self-managing. Not all teams are commissioned by their organizations to be self-managing, however. Before accepting an engagement, the team coach needs to understand the scope of the team's authority. Table 31.1 shows four dimensions of authority and how these are expressed in different types of teams.

Teams typically aspire to be self-managing. In today's technology-enabled, zero-geography workplaces, self-governance makes more sense than a traditional command-and-control structure.

From the first moment of engagement, a skilled team coach recognizes the team as whole—resourceful, capable, and creative—even if team members are not acting as a cohesive team. Over the course of a coaching engagement, the focus on the team as client calls forth from team members their best collaborative behavior and returns them to the organization with greater emotional and social intelligence and increased self-awareness.

BRIEF REVIEW OF ACADEMIC RESEARCH

Several fields of academic research have contributed insights about group process consultation, of which team coaching is one method. These fields include: organization development, leadership development, group dynamics, and organizational health and culture. Research about what hampers collaboration goes back at least 60 years. One study (Maier & Solem, 1952) highlighted the adverse effects

Table 31.1 Characteristics of Groups and Teams

	Traditional Work Group	Traditional Team	Self-Managed Team
Power	Part of hierarchy, management controlled	Linked to hierarchy, some power shift to team	Linked to hierarchy, increased power and independence
Leadership	Manager or supervisor controls	Leader has limited managerial power and is selected by the organization	Leader is selected by the team and provides facilitation
Decision making	Authoritarian or consultative	Consultative, democratic, or consensual	Democratic or consensual
Activities or tasks	Independent	Interdependent, coordinated by the leader	Interdependent, coordinated by the group members

Source: Adapted from McGrath, J. (1984). *Groups: Interaction and performance.* Upper Saddle River, NJ: Prentice-Hall.

on team performance resulting from the suppression of minority views. Another (Smith, 1956) explored the dysfunctional impact on team effectiveness of role ambiguity in the form of quiet members who gave no explanation for their non-participation. A study exploring group processes for decision making (Collins & Guetzkow, 1964) identified interpersonal obstacles as hindrances to productivity. And research about managerial problem solving (Zand, 1972) demonstrated the unfortunate effects of mistrust on teams' ability to cooperate, communicate, and make decisions.

There is less research to date on the impact of various methods of process consultation on team performance. Based on the evidence that problems in the group process impede team effectiveness, Kaplan (1979) hypothesized that techniques designed to remove these impediments can improve team effectiveness. According to Schein (2009), "the decisive factor as to whether or not help will occur in human situations involving personality, group dynamics, and culture is the relationship between the helper and the person, group, or organization that needs help" (p. 242). Although coaches are trained not to think of themselves as *helpers*, relationship skills are a major focus of coach training.

Two recent studies point to the importance of team members' social and emotional intelligence. A group of researchers led by Anita Woolley at Carnegie Mellon (Woolley, Chabris, Pentland, Hashmi, & Malone, 2010) explored whether a team's "collective intelligence" might exceed the average general intelligence of the team's members. They discovered that the social sensitivity of team members—specifically the ability to read each other's emotions and take turns talking—was a more significant predictor of high collective intelligence than the general intelligence of team members. Research by Harvard Business School professor Amy Edmondson found that teams in which members felt safe showed stronger social intelligence. Edmondson defines psychological safety as "a sense of confidence that the team will not embarrass, reject, or punish someone for speaking up" (Duhigg, 2016, p. 9).

TEAM COACHING: DEVELOPING THE ONE-TO-MANY RELATIONSHIP

Demand for team coaches is on the rise, and many one-on-one coaches now feel drawn to become team coaches. This is a noble aspiration, and team coaching is a highly rewarding vocation. It is a mistake, however, to think that a one-on-one coach can perform proficiently in a team coaching role without training and practice beyond basic International Coach Federation (ICF) certification.

Developing the one-to-many relationship with a team requires a thorough understanding of group dynamics. A team coach must also have a deep appreciation for unconscious assumptions, habits, and biases and how these manifest as behavior in a team setting.

Throughout the lifecycle of a coaching engagement, the coach adopts an attitude of *generativity*, looking to the team as the source of awareness, clarity, alignment, and creative action. To be generative is to embody the dynamic capacities to originate, create, learn, and produce desired results. A coach has three roles in relation to a team: to *challenge, champion,* and *collaborate.* Recognizing that *the team is the client*, the team coach always engages the whole team, listening to the collection of voices and viewpoints, asking questions of the team, and challenging team members' apparent assumptions.

DEFINITION OF TEAM COACHING

Team coaching is a relationship that reveals team-generated synergy toward a shared purpose that respects and leverages unique strengths of each member and accelerates both team and individual performance.

GUIDING PRINCIPLES OF TEAM COACHING

A team coach champions, challenges, and collaborates with the collective of members on a team by embodying the following principles:

- A team as a collective of members is an entity that is whole, resourceful, capable, and creative.

- Team members receive coaching, invite learning, and seek group awareness during interactions.

- Attention is solution-focused in a way that builds toward the future.

- Judgment is welcome as stimulus for imagination and possibility.

Table 31.2 shows the roles and responsibilities for everyone participating in a team effort.

Table 31.2 Anatomy of a Team Coaching Engagement

Sponsor Relationship	Member Relationship
• Identify perceived need • Conduct culture discovery • Negotiate conditions of satisfaction/ success for the group results	• Identify perceived strengths • Determine what is visible to the members of the team • Discover operating paradox
Contracting	Coaching
• Analyze the current situation • Match gaps to services • Negotiate an ROI/ROE formula	• Generate and sustain a visible, empowering field • Champion, challenge, and co-create
Measuring Success	Celebrating
• Establish baseline measures for key business issues • Collect data • Affirm ROI/ROE effect	• Harvest behaviors developed and observable impact • Acknowledge member contribution to conditions of satisfaction/success

Source: inviteCHANGE Advanced Group & Team Coaching Program, ICF Accredited.

TEAM FORMATION

In an ideal coaching engagement, the organizational sponsor of a new team will bring in the coach to participate in the team's formation. Research on senior leadership teams (Hackman & Wageman, 2009) found that upfront planning is a critical success factor. The team will be more likely to achieve its goals if the sponsor addresses the following design questions:

1. Is there a well-defined problem (or opportunity) worthy of allocating organizational resources to?

2. Who are the people with the expertise and collaborative skills to solve the problem (or capitalize on the opportunity)?

3. Is a collaborative approach the best approach?

If the answers to these questions are satisfactory, the sponsor convenes a team and grants it authority with clear boundaries based on the organizational purpose it is called to fulfill. Wageman's research also recognizes that turnover impedes team performance. For project teams to be most effective, it is important for all team members to commit to sticking with the team until its mission is achieved. For intact teams, that is, those that serve as ongoing organizational units, research suggests that a tenure of at least 3 years is optimal.

WORKING AGREEMENTS ARE CRUCIAL

Research supports the long-standing consensus among coaches that working agreements, or norms, are crucial to a team's success. Team members' assumptions about competence, autonomy, and belonging influence their behavior in a group setting (Ryan & Deci, 2000). Such assumptions are often unconscious and manifest as unhelpful behaviors that endanger the collective sense of safety and trust, impeding collaborative work. Working agreements can prevent a team from getting stuck and will guide participants out of predicaments that inevitably arise. According to Ruth Wageman's research (Wageman, Nunes, Buruss, & Hackman, 2008), "Norms for acceptable behavior are the single most important differentiator for superior teams."

Typically, before a team begins its work in earnest, it gathers for a session with the coach to agree about how team members will relate to each other and the coach. The coach sets the tone by encouraging participants to talk directly to each other, to listen, and be open about personal beliefs and assumptions. Because the team is the client, the coach is free to challenge the assumptions, biases, and preferences about power, decision making, and task assignments that arise.

The coach convenes the first session with four purposefully simple questions:

1. What brought you here?

2. What is your team expected to deliver?

3. What agreements will support you to accept responsibility for the outcomes you are expected to deliver?

4. What approach to delivering the outcomes expected of you will honor your agreements?

The process of discussing these questions and creating working agreements transfers authority clearly to the team. When the working agreements are in place, each team member commits to abide by them.

Over the course of this session, the coach will make sure the team identifies the primary business issues and opportunities it will address and any known threats that may impede their work. This conversation also supports the team to begin to remove any invisible barriers that may prevent the collective from exercising emotional and social intelligence in their work together.

THE COACH STAKES OUT THE HIGH GROUND

Working agreements are intended to create the psychological safety that every participant needs to be able to participate authentically and spontaneously. When a team first comes together, however, members will stray often from the team norms, and the team won't yet have the collective awareness to notice each other's unhelpful behavior. It falls to the coach to set a positive tone for all the team's conversations and to remain solution-focused—especially when conflicts between team members arise. Table 31.3 shows the types of support all participants need. Until team members learn to encourage each other and express approval for diverse points of view, the coach provides emotional support to model it for the team.

WORKING AGREEMENTS GUIDE COACH AND TEAM

The coach brings the team back to its working agreements throughout the coaching engagement, inviting team members to celebrate when they are abiding by their

Table 31.3 Support Types Essential to Healthy Team Dynamics

Support Type	Behavior Observed
Belonging	Expressing acceptance and approval; demonstrating belonging to the group
Emotional	Rewarding and encouraging others; listening to problems and shared feelings
Informational	Giving ideas, advice, and suggestions; explaining and demonstrating how to perform a task
Task	Helping another work with tasks; providing supportive actions

Source: Forsyth, D. (1999). *Group dynamics* (3rd ed.) Belmont, CA: Brooks/Cole, Wadsworth, Cengage Learning.

agreements—especially when their observation of the agreements has allowed something new to emerge—and reminding them to notice when they are dropping back into old behaviors. Continually bringing the team back to its working agreements is the most powerful intervention at the coach's disposal.

Working agreements sometimes change over time. When a team is formed, individuals bring concerns about personal safety—conscious or unconscious—to the discussion about working agreements. After a team has worked to create safety and build trust, team members begin to shift their focus from themselves to the team. When this happens, team members allow each other to be more provocative and more alert to opportunities to push the edges of their collective comfort zone. New creative energies arise from this shift. As this occurs, the coach challenges the team members to adopt agreements that will support increased social and emotional intelligence in the team dynamic.

EXPANDED COMPETENCIES REQUIRED FOR TEAM COACHING

Team coaching is founded on the ICF Core Coaching Competencies, just as individual coaching is. Team coaches need expanded perceptual abilities not taught as part of basic ICF certification. To cultivate expanded perceptions, a coach must have control over his or her own attention, a modicum of self-awareness, and a habit of self-reflection. These capacities can be acquired and strengthened through practice.

PERCEIVING THE COLLECTIVE FIELD

The interactions among team members comprise the collective field. A relaxed, receptive state of mind prepares one to perceive the collective field. The first thing to notice is that these interactions are multidimensional. In addition to the words exchanged, there are emotions expressed and unexpressed, alignments and resistances, deep resonance and confusion. To attune to the collective field, one lets go of cognitive knowledge and intelligence-based ways of relating in favor of receiving what is emerging from the team. Phenomena of interest include:

- Emotions (expressed and suppressed)
- Sensations
- Changes in the pace and intensity of dialogue
- Silence
- Dead spots
- Judgments
- Intuitions
- Emerging new ideas

The coach notices these phenomena and whether they forward or hinder the team's process. For example, if team members have been taking turns speaking but

Table 31.4 Coaching Competencies: Communicating Effectively
One-to-Many

ICF Core Coaching Competency	Expanded Behavioral Focus
#5 Active Listening	**Notice:** Synthesize patterns of meaning through multidimensional perceiving
#6 Powerful Questioning	**Name:** Make visible the invisible
#7 Direct Communication	**Negotiate:** Activate creative synergy
Source: inviteCHANGE Advanced Group & Team Coaching Program, ICF Accredited.	

suddenly start talking over each other, a skilled coach will ask about the emotions that are arising and what these may reveal. The coach also contributes to the collective field by inviting members to notice new strengths as these emerge.

A good place to start for ICF-certified coaches who want to learn how to expand their perceptual capabilities is the "Communicating Effectively" section of the ICF Core Competencies. Table 31.4 shows the expanded capacity that can be developed from each of the core communication competencies.

ACTIVE LISTENING: SYNTHESIZING PATTERNS OF MEANING

Team discussions move quickly, and it is not possible to track all dimensions of a conversation simultaneously. The coach must discern what to notice. Internally turning down the volume on the flow of words and ideas allows one to pick up on emotions, intensity, pace, and other dimensions. The coach's task is to listen for the influence of varied phenomena on the team's process. An interruption may be a disturbance to the exchange of ideas, but it may instead be the emergence of a new perspective. A moment of silence can indicate the team is stuck or that an important insight is being felt in the collective awareness.

When the coach notices behavior that affects the team's work, he or she invites the team to pause and notice whether the behavior is beneficial or impeding. Team members learn from their reflections what behaviors support the team to function at its best (Table 31.5).

POWERFUL QUESTIONING: MAKE VISIBLE THE INVISIBLE

Observing the collective field with neutral attention primes the coach to notice behavior that arises from unconscious and invisible impulses. Research about group dynamics points to the need for surfacing biases, habits, assumptions, and preferences as these occur in a team's conversation. The coach asks open-ended questions to challenge team members to become aware of the team's experience and its influence on getting work accomplished. These questions create the opportunity for team members to notice their own behavior and link their behavior to their own unconscious impulses. This learning can happen only in the moment. Likewise, the

Table 31.5 Competency Development Skills for Active Listening

Behavioral Competency	Development Skills
Notice: Synthesize patterns of meaning through multidimensional perceiving	• See, hear, feel, sense (body), and intuit reactions/reactive impulse. • Notice and synthesize reactions from/with/to the collective field as the client. • Reflect out loud, be curious without attachment, blurt direct experience.
Examples in application	• Being willing to venture intuition about what is present and not being said, "I'm wondering if. . ." or "I'm sensing that. . .". • Use metaphors, visual language, and/or simplified concepts that assist understanding observations. • Participate through body language that shows curiosity, acceptance, and empathy, not voicing opinions. • Noticing own tensions of presence in the group as an engaged observer, as well as the whole of the energy field.

Source: inviteCHANGE Advanced Group & Team Coaching Program, ICF Accredited.

coach asks questions to champion collaborative behavior, inviting team members to celebrate progress. The best questions evoke team members' commitments to their common purpose. See examples in Table 31.6.

Table 31.6 Competency Development Skills for Powerful Questioning

Behavioral Competency	Development Skills
Name: Make visible the invisible	• Allow and declare acceptance of discomfort. • Generate group ownership for what is noticed in a meaningful way. • Use language that lifts up and clarifies and/or simplifies complex thoughts, feelings, and experiences within the collective field.
Examples in application	• I am noticing some tension in the room; what are you noticing and what does it mean for the group? • What emotions and energies are in the room right now? • In noticing "either/or" thinking, what is a possible, "yes, and" perspective for the group to adopt? • What wants to be expressed on behalf of the group to acknowledge progress? • What contribution is this discussion making toward the group purpose?

Source: inviteCHANGE Advanced Group & Team Coaching Program, ICF Accredited.

The coach intervenes continually with questions. Over time, team members become more aware of their own limiting behaviors and learn to contribute more purposefully, setting aside personal biases, habits, assumptions, and preferences that fall outside the agreed-upon norms.

DIRECT COMMUNICATION: ACTIVATE CREATIVE SYNERGY

The practice of asking open-ended questions stimulates team members' reflections. This generates a space in the collective field for the team to make more conscious choices about how it works toward its goals. The coach reminds the team often of its power to choose, and this practice helps team members sustain attention toward their common purpose.

If a team is stuck, the coach may ask members to look for a common thread among conflicting points of view or nudge them to forward movement by asking them to recall the strengths they have already demonstrated. These interventions activate the team's creative synergy. See Table 31.7.

When a coach uses these three expanded competencies continually from session to session, and team members take on the discipline of regulating themselves, the team wakes up to its potential. The capacity for collective self-reflection emerges, and insights occur faster. Team members no longer take course corrections personally, and the team enjoys accelerated learning. Team members support and

Table 31.7 Competency Development Skills for Direct Communication

Behavioral Competency	Development Skills
Negotiate: Activate creative synergy	• Engage the power of choice for what the team wants based on what is noticed and named. • Pose and invite questions that harvest relevant past experience in order to access strengths and resources in the collective field. • Embody and invite improvisational approaches as an exercise to live what is wanted for learning and insight.
Examples in application	• Being and remaining radically curious, accepting, and solution-focused, no matter what is being said, for example, "What choices combine the diverse points of view expressed so far?" • Be curious on behalf of the team in order to reflect what is being experienced that generates group ownership and create choice that moves the team forward in a positive and desired way, for example, "What is your combined experience that will be influential with the key stakeholder you are profiling now?" • "Stand in the shoes of the decision makers and identify the most important questions to answer and the answers you collectively believe will have desired positive impact."

Source: inviteCHANGE Advanced Group & Team Coaching Program, ICF Accredited.

encourage one another and genuinely enjoy working together. A self-sustaining high-performance team is born.

COACHING IS CONSCIOUSNESS

Like the ebb and flow of ocean tides, stuckness and movement are both part of a team's process. Conflicts inevitably arise in collaborative work. Team members experience ambivalence from time to time. A team will also encounter situations that defy logic and rational thinking. The coach—who observes the collective field and appreciates everything that arises in it—holds a more expanded perspective in consciousness than the team members, at least until the team coalesces and becomes self-sustaining. From this more-expanded perspective, the coach urges the team to move beyond "either/or" thinking to look for "both/and" possibilities. This is a paradigm shift, and it requires team members to embrace and accept the collective experience they are having in the moment.

Humans tend to resist experiencing the discomfort of feeling stuck, not knowing, being confused, or feeling powerless to overcome an intractable situation. Teams frequently try one of three tactics to get past the collective angst. They may:

- Minimize the emotions present in the situation

- Eliminate perceived contradictions

- Separate the contradictions from what they see as the crux of the situation

These tactics perpetuate stuckness. It is essential for the coach to intervene in these situations by asking questions of the team about its relationship to its situation, not the situation itself. For example when a team's budget is cut, emotional stress usually rises. A team coach invites the members to consider what is negotiable by the team and shift from victim to creator mindset.

Going back to the metaphor of the ocean tides, the tides are regulated by the force of gravity and the movement of our planet in the solar system. Teams are governed by organizational forces that they have no control over and may not even be aware of. When team members willingly endure the discomfort of being stuck and recognize what they can and cannot control, they open the space for creative possibilities.

The other aspect of consciousness that applies to team work is that states of consciousness are contagious. One person who is cranky can drag down the whole team. Likewise, one person's exuberance can lift everyone's spirits. The coach serves as a model for the team, maintaining a positive attitude, being solution-focused and forward-looking no matter what is happening at the time. Over time, team members also adopt this practice.

THE PROMISE OF SELF-SUSTAINING TEAMS

It is an inspiring and rewarding journey for a coach to accompany a team from its beginning until it becomes self-sustaining. A self-sustaining team can deliver the

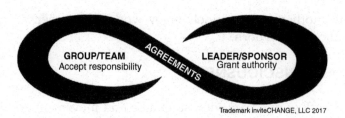

Trademark inviteCHANGE, LLC 2017

Figure 31.1 Team sovereignty.

results its organization needs without causing friction in the form of damaged relationships or other disruptions. A self-sustaining team can also monitor itself and correct course as necessary.

We could also label a high-performing, self-sustaining team as "sovereign." Sovereignty means to be self-ruling, independent, and in charge of the relationship within the conditions of our lives, or, in the case of a team, in charge of the relationship within its charter and organizational context. The infinity symbol in Figure 31.1 captures the reciprocal flow of energy among all contributors and suggests the possibility of unlimited creative potential for a team that can manage itself.

A sovereign team adds significant value to the organization it serves. Large organizations especially need to streamline decision making in order to innovate in response to rapidly changing conditions in the world. A sovereign team holds the promise of speedier implementation of new programs and products. A happy byproduct of a self-managed team is employee happiness. People enjoy their work more when they have some creative control over their work product.

The team coach also adds significant value to the client organization through building member capacity for sustained and positive collaborative work. A team coach who has guided a team through stuckness and movement earns the intrinsic reward of witnessing a team thrive.

REFERENCES

Collins, B. E., & Guetzkow, H. A. (1964). *Social psychology of group processes for decision making.* New York, NY: Wiley.

Duhigg, C. (2016). *What Google learned from its quest to build the perfect team.* Retrieved from http://www.nytimes.com/2016/02/28/magazine/what-google-learned-from-its-quest-to-build-the-perfect-team.html?_r=0

Forsyth, D. (1999). *Group dynamics* (3rd ed.) Belmont, CA: Brooks/Cole, Wadsworth, Engage Learning.

Hackman, J. R., & Wageman, R. (2009). Foster team effectiveness by fulfilling key leadership functions. In E. A. Locke (Ed.), *Handbook of principles of organizational behavior* (pp. 275–294). Chichester, UK: John Wiley & Sons.

Kaplan, R. (1979). *The conspicuous absence of evidence that process consultation enhances task performance.* Washington, DC: NTL Institute.

Maier, N., & Solem, A. (1952). The contribution of a discussion leader to the quality of group thinking: The effective use of minority opinions. *Human Relations, 5,* 277–288. doi:10.1177/001872675200500303

McGrath, J. (1984) *Groups: Interaction and performance.* Upper Saddle River, NJ: Prentice-Hall.

Ryan, R., & Deci, E. (2000). Self-determination theory and the facilitation of intrinsic motivation, social development and well-being, *American Psychologist, 55*(1), 68–78. doi:10.1037/0003-066X.55.1.68

Schein, E. (2009). *Process consultation revisited building the helping relationship.* Chicago, IL: Prentice Hall.

Smith, E. (1956). *Effects of threat induced by ambiguous role expectations on defensiveness and productivity in small groups* (Technical Report #l, Contract No. 1147 [03]). University of Colorado, CO: Office of Naval Research, Group Process Lab.

Wageman, R., Nunes, D., Buruss, J., & Hackman, J. (2008). *Senior leadership teams: What it takes to make them great.* Cambridge, MA: Center for Public Leadership.

Woolley, A., Chabris, C., Pentland, A., Hashmi, N., & Malone, T. (2010). Evidence for a collective intelligence factor in the performance of human groups. *Science, 330,* 686–688. doi:10.1126/science.1193147

Zand, D. (1972). Trust and managerial problem solving. *Administrative Science Quarterly, 17,* 229–239. doi:10.2307/2393957

32

Coaching and Spirituality: A Mutually Resourceful Relationship

Chad Hall

Spirituality describes those aspects of life and being beyond the material. Persons have varying approaches to spirituality and understanding these approaches serves the coaching relationship as coaches adapt to the spiritual beliefs and practices of clients in order to best serve them. Within the range of spiritual engagement afforded by the client's beliefs and practices, the coach can serve the client well by recognizing the numerous resources spirituality provides to the client and incorporating spirituality appropriately into the coaching relationship. Not only does spirituality provide rich resources for coaching, but also coaching serves as a resource for developing a deeper and richer spirituality.

WHAT DO WE MEAN BY SPIRITUALITY?

Mention spirituality to a dozen people, and you will likely get a dozen (or more) interpretations of the term. Some people link spirituality closely to a specific religion or faith tradition such as Christianity, Buddhism, Sikhism, or Islam. Others connect it to a more generic sense of God, a "higher being," or even a nonpersonal force beyond the material existence. Still others will be reluctant to talk about a personal God, instead favoring the personification of godly characteristics or behaviors such as Grace, Love, or Being.

Whatever one's interpretation of the term, spirituality describes a belief and approach that contends there is more to our world than the material stuff that surrounds us. This belief in "something more" differentiates spiritualists from materialists, who believe that physical matter is all there is and that everything we observe has a material origin and explanation.

As we explore the resourceful relationship between spirituality and coaching, we must keep in mind the variety of ways clients experience and express spirituality. Coaches should recognize that not every client sees the world through the same spiritual lens as the coach. Indeed, not everyone is spiritual, so the spiritual coach must make room for understanding and adapting to the client's spirituality, or lack thereof.

RESOURCES FOR COACHING CLIENTS

Spirituality provides rich resources for coaching clients. Whatever type of coaching one might seek—be it life coaching, executive coaching, transformational coaching, and so forth—one thing all clients have in common is a desire to move forward in some way. Whether forward movement is defined in material terms (increased income or physical health), in relational terms (stronger marriage, improved emotional intelligence, or more effective management), or in personal growth terms (time management, greater discipline, or character formation), spirituality offers resources that can positively inform and influence the client's direction and movement. Following are some examples that illustrate the resourceful aspects of spirituality.

MEANING AND PURPOSE

If we are to be fruitful in life, each of us needs a sense of direction and intent. As such, humans long to address issues related to meaning and purpose. Clarity of purpose provides orientation and direction for life's journey. Clarity of meaning infuses each mundane day with significance.

Positive psychologist Seligman (2011) notes that meaning is one of the five essential elements required for well-being: "Human beings, ineluctably, want meaning and purpose in life. The Meaningful Life consists in belonging to and serving something that you believe is bigger than the self" (p. 12).

Spirituality provides meaning-oriented resources that flow from the distinction between "inherent meaning" and "ascribed meaning." Ascribed meaning describes when a person notes a cause or value and assigns meaning to it so that it can, in turn, give meaning back to the person. In contrast, inherent meaning describes what occurs when one's belief in God or some other force behind the material world provides a built-in meaning and purpose to life. The built-in meaning and purpose are not subject to the person's opinion, but shapes the person and his or her opinions about reality.

At first glance, spiritually derived purpose may seem to have a significant downside with little upside. After all, a person free to choose (ascribe) life's meaning has the freedom and flexibility to construct a life unrestricted by what spirituality imposes. But such freedom comes with a great price: uncertainty. Ascribed meaning is fragile because it fails to address why something is right or wrong, good or bad. For example, we may believe it is wrong to hunt an animal to extinction or starve the inhabitants of a poor country, but in a world of self-created meaning we are unable to say *why* such things are wrong or why we should purpose our life toward stopping such wrongs. Clients who are driven to save an endangered species or alleviate hunger will run up against others who not only do not share their beliefs, but who directly object and oppose them. In the context of self-created meanings, how can your clients explain why their chosen meaning in life is any better than the rhino hunter or the dictator who gains power by trampling on the poor? Clients must appeal to something not only within them, but also outside of them, beyond the clients and their opponents, and even beyond this world they both inhabit.

While inherent meaning binds and restricts (one is not free to choose, unchoose, and re-choose that which is inherently meaningful), it offers adherents a purpose that is more indelible than purpose sans spirituality. Meaning that is built in has a greater durability for the person who endures life's many ups and downs. As a popular article in *Harvard Business Review* (Haque, 2013) contends, when clients connect their sense of meaning and purpose in life to something bigger and beyond themselves, they find the power to press on and to live more fully.

GRIT AND RESILIENCE

Several studies (Cornah, 2006) demonstrate a connection between spirituality and mental health, a connection that extends from simple wellness to life success. Spirituality is linked with reduced levels of mental illness, improved posttraumatic recovery, reduced depressive symptoms, and reduced anxiety. Coaches are especially interested in the connection between spirituality and persons' abilities to cope with and overcome life's stressors as they progress toward meaningful goals. This capacity to overcome and persevere is described as resilience and/or grit. In her wildly popular TED Talk, Angela Duckworth defines grit as "perseverance and passion for long-term goals" (Duckworth, 2013).

Resilience and grit require the individual to overcome life's setbacks and struggles (essentially "to get up when life knocks you down") and to press forward when the path is long and the reward is far off (essentially "to never give up"). As such, healing, forgiveness, optimism, and hope are essential to resilience/grit and spirituality offers ready access to these capacities. Spirituality provides healing from life's past and present hurts, including the capacity to forgive, which is essential for not holding on to the pains inflicted by other people. Spirituality also affords people resources for looking into the future and letting benefits that are currently far away fuel today's steps forward. The spiritual person's hope that things will be made right by a loving God or through a cosmic spiritual force such as karma offers a spiritually fueled optimism that can sustain life's most challenging moments.

Coaches are wise to invite clients to approach challenges from a spiritual vantage point. When we inquire about a client's source for healing, forgiveness, optimism, and hope, we help the client tap into (and grow) the necessary resilience and grit in order to keep moving forward.

IDENTITY AND GROWTH

Spirituality provides resources related to deep questions concerning identity. Questions about *Who am I?* get addressed in relationship to one's place in the creation and relationship to the creator. Each client is uniquely created and can more fully express the self when the client understands and appreciates his or her personal gifts, connection to others, and relationship to God.

Coaches can help the client more fully understand, appreciate, and enhance the client's identity through spiritual discovery. Central to this discovery process is an openness to learning the good and the bad about oneself. Many spiritual traditions have a dual emphasis concerning human nature, considering each person to be of infinite worth and respect while also deeply flawed. As the Christian faith puts it, each person is created in the image of God (*imago Dei*), but is also a rebellious sinner. Coaches who allow spiritually inclined clients to wrestle with their identity in ways that make room for both strengths and struggles will support client growth on the client's terms.

The coaching client who genuinely wants to address the question *Who am I?* is equally open to related questions such as *Who am I becoming?* and *Who am I intended to be?* Addressing such profound questions requires the client to not only look inward, but also to investigate external sources of wisdom, including that of spiritually laced assessments, sacred literature, and spiritual communities.

One popular tool for addressing issues of identity and growth is the Enneagram, which offers a spiritual lens for understanding and developing personality. The assessment offers users a sense of what is right with their personality as well as what can go wrong. Enneagram expert Cron (2016) even goes so far as to associate each of the nine personality types with a specific spiritual vice such as pride, gluttony, or sloth. When I have used the Enneagram with spiritually open clients, the "bad news" of their particular personality vice has actually turned out to be a form of good news in terms of deepening their self-awareness and offering a handle for better understanding of how they tend to trip themselves up. Clients who recognize a contrast between who they are and who they ought to be welcome this insight as an occasion of growth.

Sacred literature can also be a powerful resource for the client who is engaged in a coaching relationship. Research has shown that mindfulness is a powerful ally not only in reducing debilitating disorders and behaviors, but in also enhancing one's pursuit of a good and flourishing life. When mindfulness carries with it a religious or spiritual aspect, it can support spiritual growth and increase values-based behaviors (Symington & Symington, 2012). As coaches, we can invite our clients to consult and meditate on sacred texts in order to find wholeness, peace, and blessing.

Faith communities are also important spiritual resources. As Myers (2000) has shown, spiritual beliefs exercised within a faith community promote personal well-being. Clients whose faith is formed and expressed within a faith community can benefit from coaches who wisely welcome the faith community into the coaching relationship, and vice versa. Coaches can incorporate the client's faith community (church, synagogue, family, mosque, etc.) into the coaching relationship by understanding the significance of the community in the client's life, inviting the client to leverage the community for wisdom, accountability, and support when appropriate, and exploring successful participation in the community as a vital aspect of the client's life.

ETHICS AND DECISION MAKING

Ethics is concerned with right versus wrong, as well as with the larger questions of how best to live. Because spirituality addresses issues such as meaning in life, values, purpose, and morality, clients who are open to spiritual matters find guidance in how to live well. When coaching clients face decisions, especially challenging, complex, or otherwise difficult decisions, their sense of spiritual reality offers rich insights that illuminate their issue, guide their decision making, and provide a point of reference for locating the issue within their larger framework of meaning. One study (Fernando & Jackson, 2006) found that leaders who integrate religion-based spirituality in the workplace do so primarily in association with decision making. Religious beliefs offered leaders solace, guidance, and a source of inspiration for decision making.

One of the principal ways spirituality aids clients in making life's decisions is by narrowing options and eliminating some choices. This might sound counterintuitive since coaching is often concerned with expanding options and exploring new possibilities. However, research shows that too much choice can be a severe hindrance to human flourishing. As the research of Schwartz and Ward (2004) has shown, in a context of almost infinite options, people are less capable of making decisions, they are less satisfied with the decisions they do make, and they are more likely to blame themselves when a decision does not pan out perfectly. Schwartz recommends limiting choices in order to increase satisfaction with decisions and improving overall personal well-being.

Spirituality can serve clients by offering them a framework by which to limit options when options seem complex, cloudy, or otherwise overwhelming. For example, one of my clients was a successful leader for an oil and gas company. He was itching for something new in his career, but was plagued by too many choices. As a competent, charming, and ambitious professional who had proven to be a quick learner, he could have found success in almost any field. He was a devout Christian, so when I asked him how his career decision could best honor God, he applied a spiritual lens to his decision and found clarity. He began to speak of a sense of vocation, or "calling," in addition to other relevant factors such as salary, location, status, and competencies used. Within a few sessions, he decided to take a new role within the company that allowed him to live in a part of the world where he could work among a people group for whom he felt a special sense of call. While he recognized that his decision was not really one that begged a choice between "right and wrong," his faith allowed him to see which option was "more right."

Of course, spirituality can also aid decision making by expanding options when options are too few. Over the years, I have had many clients who faced a leadership crisis that had them feeling pinned down. Often these clients feel they have only two bad options. One such client faced a crisis when a trusted leader in his company resigned to start a competing firm and in doing so poached several of my client's best accounts. With a sudden reduction in income, my client felt he either needed to fire half his employees or incur additional business debt in order to stay afloat. Neither option seemed like a way forward, so I asked him to consider his faith as a way to illuminate the challenge before him. He chose to pray during our coaching session and also decided to invite others to pray that God would reveal to him a way forward. When we met for our next session a week later, he told me God had provided him a new option—one that involved bringing on a new partner who could not only provide a fresh infusion of cash to the business, but also could provide leadership perspective and skills that complemented and rounded out those of my client.

GRATITUDE AND SAFETY

Gratitude is a powerful force for promoting personal well-being. As Seligman (2011) summarizes, "Gratitude can make your life happier and more satisfying. When we feel gratitude, we benefit from the pleasant memory of a positive event in our life. Also, when we express our gratitude to others, we strengthen our relationship with them" (p. 30). Given the powerful positive effects of gratitude, coaches are wise to encourage clients to be grateful and to express both aspects of gratitude: the "for what" and the "to whom."

Clients experience a boost in positive emotion and shift to a more optimistic perspective when they take notice of what has gone right in life and connect life's blessings to a spiritual source. This gain in positive emotion can have powerful benefits to the coaching relationship since positive emotions prepare the human brain to be more creative and resourceful and since feelings of connectivity and security allow our brains to broaden our perspective and consider resources that will benefit us in the long term (Fredrickson, 2001). In other words, feeling and expressing gratitude to God for provision sets the client up to notice additional resources and provision that may have gone unnoticed or unclaimed during a more stressful state. Expressing gratitude also allows the client to experience a greater sense of connectedness to God, which, in turn, increases the client's sense of security. This heightened sense that God is actively providing for the client and securing the client's well-being only further advances the client's creativity and resourcefulness, providing a tremendous boost to the coaching relationship.

COACHING AS A SPIRITUAL RESOURCE

Not only does the client's spirituality serve as a resource in the coaching relationship, but the reverse is also true: A coaching relationship can resource spiritual growth and health. The nature of coaching is such that it supports client growth and development in all the areas of life that are important to the client as well as revealing newly important areas. Following are just a handful of examples of how coaching can resource spirituality.

COACHING APPROACH TO PERSONAL FAITH FORMATION

When we take a holistic approach to coaching, we offer opportunities for growth, development, and formation in all areas of life, including spirituality. In this regard, spirituality is not simply a resource to help the client find success and fulfillment in other areas of life (a means), but is also an area of life that can benefit from focused attention owing to its own intrinsic value (an end). When spirituality is the client's agenda, the coaching relationship supports new awareness, new actions, and new growth for the client.

In *Faith Coaching* (Hall, Copper, & McElveen, 2009), my coauthors and I explore why and how coaching serves as a strong catalyst for spiritual formation. In sum, coaching works well for spiritual growth because it provides a structured process by which the individual takes ownership of his own development. Unlike approaches to spiritual formation that treat every person the same, coaching takes into account where the client is in the spiritual journey and then promotes discovery of what is next, what the client is ready and willing to experience, and what is the best way forward for the client. Coaching resources spirituality by offering a safe and challenging relationship in which to explore various aspects of one's spiritual life as well as how spirituality manifests in important areas of life such as family, work, personal development, and health. Coaches who encourage clients to integrate spirituality into every aspect of life promote a robust faith life.

Coaching for Spiritual Leaders

Coaching and coaches can also serve as a resource for spirituality by extending the coaching option to spiritual leaders. Pastors, priests, rabbis, imams, chaplains, and others who serve to promote spiritual health and well-being can, and do, benefit from coaching. Leadership in any context is challenging, but perhaps nowhere is it more complex than in faith communities. My own experience as a pastor and later as a coach to clergy persons has taught me that serving a faith community requires an abundance of hard work, care, emotional intelligence, grit, and energy. In this way, leading a faith community is not all that different from leading in business or community or education—indeed, any leadership role is fraught with challenges. What *is* different with spiritual leaders is that those they lead are also, in essence, their supervisors. Faith leaders are employed by those they lead, which makes leadership in these communities all that more challenging.

The pastors I have coached benefit from a relationship in which the coach is not a direct stakeholder in the outcome of their leadership. For most of these pastors, I was the only person in their lives who was deeply engaged in their lives while remaining untethered to the outcomes that occurred in the life of the pastor or the life of the congregation they led. For leaders of faith communities, a coach can provide a safe, yet challenging, relationship in which to explore their goals, challenges, celebrations, and difficulties. The coach offers support to those who always support others (Hall, 2005).

Coaching for spiritual leaders can occur at key transitions such as entering or exiting a particular place of ministry. Coaching can also benefit faith leaders throughout the sabbatical experience. Sabbaticals offer clergy an opportunity to unplug from the challenges of leadership, to hear from God in a fresh and new way, and to return to their community more whole and more effective. In my experience, having the support and structure of a coaching relationship has proven beneficial to both the leaders and the communities they serve.

COACHING IN AND FOR FAITH COMMUNITIES

Finally, coaching can resource spirituality when the "client" is an entire faith community. Most people experience spirituality in a community of like-minded (and like-hearted) believers. A community serves the individual, and vice versa. Myers (2000) has shown that people who actively participate in the life of a religious community are happier and have a greater sense of overall well-being. While there are many positive benefits stemming from participation in the life of a faith community, these communities also deal with the challenges that come from having an identity, vision, and expression that flows from the collective spirituality of dozens, hundreds, or even thousands of members.

A faith community can experience coaching in ways similar to an individual. Coaching clients often are of two minds on an issue, have conflicting interests and opinions, and are unsure what success looks like. These same conditions are multiplied greatly in the life of a faith community, which makes coaching all the more important for them. When coaching a faith community, establishing the relationship is even more crucial (and complex) than when coaching an individual. Some of the core issues to clarify include:

- Who will receive coaching? Will it be a certain slice of leadership, a group selected from the larger congregation, key teams, or a combination?

- What are the expected outcomes? When coaching an individual, the agenda can meander a bit in order to adjust to the client's growth. However, when coaching a large group or community, such twists and turns can prove disorienting and lead to disengagement. Therefore, it is important to start with clear expectations concerning the purpose and anticipated outcomes.

- How will decisions be made? Will the congregation move through the coaching relationship by making consensus decisions, majority vote, or delegating a smaller group or person to make decisions?

INCORPORATING SPIRITUALITY INTO COACHING

Since spirituality provides rich resources for our coaching clients, we coaches will do well to facilitate the appropriation of these resources for client well-being and success. The following paragraphs provide additional instruction and examples for bringing spirituality into the coaching relationship in order to serve our clients.

CREATE AWARENESS OF CLIENT SPIRITUALITY

Not every coaching client will consider himself or herself to be "spiritual"; however, many will. As a recent Pew Research Center poll (Masci & Lipka, 2016) revealed, Americans are growing less religious, but more spiritual. As such, even among those who claim no religious affiliation or even describe themselves as "atheist" or "agnostic," growing numbers still claim to "feel a deep sense of spiritual peace and well-being" (para. 2) weekly or more often. Such findings should encourage coaches to explore client spirituality as part of the intake process as well as during other appropriate times in the coaching relationship. How do we do this?

First, it is wise for the coach to be aware of his or her own spirituality. Being clear about one's own spiritual beliefs, convictions, practices, and so forth can help the coach resist judging or over-identifying with the client. This is similar to how knowing our own personality preferences makes room for others to be who they are instead of assuming others should be like us.

Second, coaches will do well to normalize conversation about spirituality. Instead of demonstrating timidity about what might be a sensitive subject, coaches should show confidence in asking direct questions about a client's spirituality. Central to a confident discussion of spiritual matters is a nonjudging attitude and response. When the coach signals to the client that any response is valid, the coach makes it safe to discuss spiritual matters as well as safe to not discuss them, if that is the client's preference.

Third, coaches should make it clear to the client that the client's spirituality will be as significant in the coaching relationship as the client wishes. Bringing up spirituality does not give the coach a blank check for holding the client to some ideal based on the client's spirituality. Instead, it creates a shared awareness of what the client believes at a deep level and may or may not practice deeply. Such awareness enables the coach and client to determine how best to incorporate the client's spiritual beliefs.

BE OPEN TO SPIRITUAL GROWTH

Spirituality is not just a resource for client movement on other topics; it is an aspect of the client life's and growth. While spiritual beliefs may prove resourceful for a client's forward movement on topics such as career, family, or important decisions, coaches should also be open to the possibility that the client may want to focus on his or her spirituality in a direct manner.

For example, I had a coaching client whose presenting issue was work–life balance. She found her high-pressure, high-stakes, high-paying job very fulfilling in many ways, but her success at work left too little time for her family, her health, and her own sense of peace. After a few coaching sessions, she recognized that her spiritual beliefs could help her better navigate the challenging season she was experiencing. As she explored this, she realized that she had very little clarity about her spirituality and that in order to live well, she needed to focus on strengthening her spiritual life, connecting more deeply to "what really matters," as she put it. Over the course of several sessions, we worked on deepening her spirituality. This included reconnecting with her religious heritage through sacred texts and community worship. Eventually she was able to articulate what a "deep spirituality" looked like in her life and we began to explore those deeper waters in our sessions and in her post-session homework. After a few months, she was pleasantly surprised to realize that the things that previously perplexed her had now faded into the background of life. The more she focused on knowing and loving God, the less she noticed supposedly negative aspects of life that had once bothered her.

LET THE CLIENT BE THE SPIRITUAL EXPERT

Coaches are accustomed to letting the client be the expert in his or her life and work, and this extends to the client's spirituality. When it comes to spirituality, we must not slide into the role of spiritual expert.

Professional- and master-level coaches go beyond and beneath the immediate client goals to explore "internal shifts," which involve new awareness about who the client is, in contrast to new awareness about the client's issue. Internal shifts are not simply of instrumental value to the client; they are of intrinsic value for the spiritually aware client. An internal shift involves a new way of thinking, believing, or perceiving the world and spiritual growth can be the catalyst as well as the result of such shifts.

Coaches can offer opinions or insights (especially when invited to do so by the client), but should be careful not to direct or instruct, lest coaches slide out of the role of coach and into that of spiritual director or religious teacher. We must draw out from the client his or her understanding of spiritual reality, how the client knows spiritual truth, the degree and manner in which the client integrates spiritual truth in his or her life, and other aspects of spirituality. We cannot assume we see things more clearly or know things more accurately than the client.

CONCLUSION

At its best, coaching is a relationship that invites the whole person into a relationship. This relationship serves to explore who the person is, what the person wants out of life, and how the person can make progress in becoming and getting what he or she wants. Since many people live in a world they deeply believe extends beyond the material, coaches serve clients best by inviting their spirituality into the coaching relationship and by extending the coaching relationship into the spiritual realm. When we do so, we find the coaching relationship is enriched through the many resources spirituality brings to life and to coaching. We also see that coaching can enrich one's spiritual life in profound ways and in various expressions.

REFERENCES

Cornah, D. (2006). *The impact of spirituality on mental health*. The Mental Health Foundation. Retrieved from https://www.mentalhealth.org.uk/publications/impact-spirituality-mental-health

Cron, I. (2016). *The road back to you: An enneagram journey to self-discovery*. Downer's Grove, IL: IVP Books.

Duckworth, A. (2013). *Grit: The power of passion and perseverance* [Video file]. Retrieved from https://www.ted.com/talks/angela_lee_duckworth_grit_the_power_of_passion_and_perseverance

Fernando, M., & Jackson, B. (2006). The influence of religion-based workplace spirituality on business leaders' decision-making: An inter-faith study. *Journal of Management & Organization*, 12(1), 23–39. doi:10.1017/S18333367200004144

Fredrickson, B. (2001). The role of positive emotions in positive psychology: The broaden and build theory of positive emotions. *American Psychologist*, 56(3), 218–226. doi:10.1037/0003-066X.56.3.218

Hall, C. (2005). Coaching from the sidelines. *Leadership*, 26(2), 62–65.

Hall, C., Copper, B., & McElveen, K. (2009). *Faith coaching: A conversational approach to helping others move forward in faith.* Hickory, NC: Coach Approach Ministries

Haque, U. (2013). How to have a year that matters. *Harvard Business Review.* Retrieved from https://hbr.org/2013/01/how-to-have-a-year-that-matter

Masci, D., & Lipka, M. (2016). *Americans may be getting less religious, but feelings of spirituality are on the rise.* Pew Research Center Fact Tank. Retrieved from http://www.pewresearch.org/fact -tank/2016/01/21/americans-spirituality

Myers, D. G. (2000). The funds, friends, and faith of happy people. *American Psychologist, 55*(1), 56–67. doi:10.1037/0003-066X.55.1.56

Schwartz, B., & Ward, A. (2004). Doing better but feeling worse: The paradox of choice. In A. P. Linley & S. Joseph (Eds.), *Positive psychology in practice* (pp. 86–104). Hoboken, NJ: John Wiley & Sons.

Seligman, M. (2011). *Flourish: A visionary new understanding of happiness and well-being.* New York, NY: Atria Books.

Symington, S. H., & Symington, M. (2012). A Christian model of mindfulness: Using mindfulness principles to support psychological well-being, value-based behavior, and the Christian spiritual journey. *Journal of Psychology and Christianity, 31*(1), 71–77.

33

Coaching in Education

Christian van Nieuwerburgh, Jim Knight, and John Campbell

T he use of coaching in education has continued to expand since the turn of the century. Globally, schools, colleges, and universities have been deploying coaching interventions and approaches with the aim of improving student outcomes (van Nieuwerburgh & Barr, 2017). The growing interest in coaching in schools (Campbell & van Nieuwerburgh, 2018) has led to experimentation across a wide range of educational institutions to identify the most effective approaches. As part of these efforts, "coaching in education" has become a field in its own right (van Nieuwerburgh, 2012), delivering a variety of interventions that are underpinned by educational and psychological theories and research (van Nieuwerburgh & Oades, 2017). As this field has matured, and educational institutions have identified multiple ways of improving outcomes for learners, two complementary approaches have emerged: the facilitative approach and the dialogic approach.

FACILITATIVE APPROACH

The facilitative perspective considers coaches and coachees as equals, placing the recipient of coaching as the key decision maker in the relationship. According to Sir John Whitmore, "the relationship between the coach and coachee must be one of partnership in the endeavour, of trust, of safety and of minimal pressure" (2002, p. 20). It is the role of the coach to encourage coachees to share ideas openly by listening with empathy, paraphrasing, and asking powerful questions. Facilitative coaches do not need to bring subject expertise to the coaching relationship because they work from the assumptions that (a) coachees have the resources required to improve and (b) sharing expertise could undermine the self-belief of coachees and inhibit progress by keeping them from identifying their own solutions. One of us (van Nieuwerburgh, 2012) has defined coaching as:

> a one-to-one conversation that focuses on the enhancement of learning and development through increasing self-awareness and a sense of personal responsibility, where the coach facilitates the self-directed learning of the coachee through questioning, active listening, and appropriate challenge in a supportive and encouraging climate. (p. 17)

DIALOGIC APPROACH

Coaches using the dialogic approach balance inquiry and advocacy. That is, the coach continues to position the coachee as an equal partner and the key decision maker, embracing inquiry by asking questions that empower the coachee to identify goals, strategies, and adaptations. As such, dialogical coaches ask powerful questions, listen and think with coachees, collaborating with them to set powerful goals that will have a direct impact on students' lives. In contrast to coaches who adopt a facilitative approach, however, dialogical coaches *do not* withhold their expertise when it might help coachees improve in ways that coachees identify. They work from the assumption that some issues facing educators are best addressed through implementation of research-validated, effective pedagogical strategies. Therefore, coaches who wish to adopt a dialogic approach must have a deep understanding of pedagogical strategies that can be shared with educators to help them improve their practice.

It is important to note that coaches adopting a dialogic approach do not *advise* their coachees—they share possible strategies, allowing their coachees to decide if they want to try a particular strategy as they plan to meet their goals. That is, coaching is seen as a partnership with educators to help identify goals and pedagogical strategies. Coachees are the ultimate decision makers, who choose appropriate strategies and modify them to suit their learners' needs, whereas the role of the coach is to support these educators in implementing the chosen strategies and gathering data on whether or not the strategies are effective. In short, as opposed to the facilitative approach, coaches using the dialogic approach do not keep their ideas to themselves and recognize that strategies will need to be modified to meet learners' needs and to align with the particular strengths of educators.

COMPARING COACHING TO OTHER INTERVENTIONS

Sometimes coaching in education is confused with mentoring and counseling, but there are important distinctions between these approaches in educational settings.

COACHING AND MENTORING

Terminology becomes blurred when coaching is conflated with other approaches that aim to provide "help by talking" (Burley & Pomphrey, 2011). Mentoring refers to an interaction between a more experienced and knowledgeable practitioner (the mentor) and a less experienced person (the mentee) for the purpose of assisting with the mentee's professional learning and career development (Bloom, Castagna, Moir, & Warren, 2005). "Mentoring in education" has been defined as "a series of one-to-one conversations in which a more experienced person asks questions, provides guidance, shares knowledge and gives advice to support a learner to improve their performance and achieve success within a nurturing relationship" (van Nieuwerburgh & Barr, 2017, p. 506). Mentors have specialist knowledge or expertise, and their primary task is to transfer that knowledge to their mentees while guiding them toward career and professional development. An important point here is that while the mentor–mentee relationship may be focused on the best interests of the mentee, it cannot be described as equal.

It has been argued that coaching and mentoring can be viewed along a spectrum (Downey, 2003), with one end representing a "directive" intervention and the other a "nondirective" intervention. Mentoring is closer to the directive end of the spectrum because the more experienced person is likely to advise or make suggestions while supporting the less experienced partner. The facilitative and dialogic approaches to coaching, on the other hand, are closer to the nondirective end of the spectrum, as the coach facilitates the coachee's self-directed learning by listening and asking questions rather than telling the coachee what to do. Table 33.1 shows how the facilitative and dialogic approaches to coaching relate to mentoring.

Table 33.1 Comparing Coaching Approaches to Mentoring

Characteristic	Mentoring in Education: Directive Approach	Coaching in Education: Dialogic Approach	Coaching in Education: Facilitative Approach
Metaphor	Master–apprentice	Partner	Facilitator
Decision-maker	Mentor	Coachee	Coachee
Coach's expertise	Expertise relates to professional practice and professional development	Expertise relates to the ability to coach effectively and to professional practice	Expertise relates to the ability to coach effectively
Coachee's knowledge	Requires the knowledge and expertise of the mentor	Has substantial experience but may require additional knowledge	Has experience, resources, and relationships
Thinking	Mentor does most of the thinking	Coach and coachee think together	Coach creates a safe space for the coachee to do the thinking
Discourse	Advocacy	Inquiry and advocacy	Primarily inquiry
Purpose	Fast-track learning and development	Improve outcomes for educators and learners	Improve outcomes for educators and learners

COACHING AND COUNSELING

Another relevant "helping by talking" intervention is counseling. The difference between counseling and coaching lies primarily in the focus of the conversation. Whereas counseling is often used to address difficult issues such as bereavement or trauma, or to resolve troubling concerns rooted in the past, the purpose of coaching is to achieve more of one's potential and, therefore, tends to focus on the present and the future. It is important to recognize that mentoring, counseling, and coaching all have important functions in educational settings.

EDUCATION-SPECIFIC COACHING MODELS AND PROCESSES

Our focus in this chapter is the use of coaching in educational organizations, so we now present two major education-specific approaches: the GROWTH system and instructional coaching.

GROWTH SYSTEM

Originating in Australia over 15 years ago, the GROWTH coaching system is based around three core elements that provide a solid platform for effective coaching (Figure 33.1).

Underpinning the GROWTH system is a theoretical perspective that draws from recent thinking and research in positive psychology. This confluence of theories including appreciative inquiry (Cooperrider, Whitney, & Stavros, 2008) and solution-focused approaches (Macdonald, 2011) provides a growing evidence base for what makes the GROWTH system effective.

GROWTH Framework

The first element of the GROWTH system is a framework for conversations that provides a structure that enables progress toward clear actions and outcomes

Figure 33.1 Three core elements of the GROWTH system.
Source: © Growth Coaching International.

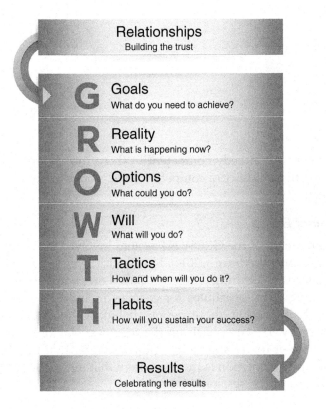

Figure 33.2 GROWTH coaching framework.
Source: © Growth Coaching International.

(Figure 33.2). The model is an extended version of the widely used GROW model popularized by Whitmore (1992). The extended components are based on emerging research. For example, Golwitzer's (1999) work related to implementation intentions supports the value of Tactics and Habits steps in goal attainment, and these steps have been incorporated into the GROWTH process. Specifically, Golwitzer's study highlighted how identifying specific next-step actions helps to increase the likelihood of implementation. Further, research supporting the value of leveraging strengths in support of goal attainment (Jackson & McKergow, 2006) is reflected in the R step within the GROWTH framework. In addition to helping to start from the current Reality, the "R" refers also to Resources. Identifying strengths and past successes in similar situations helps to build a sense of resourcefulness and agency—a factor that is important in developing higher levels of hope and all its associated benefits (Lopez, 2013).

Communication Skills

A second component of the GROWTH system is based around core communication skills, including:

- Listening
- Being present

- Empathizing

- Being succinct

- Clarifying

- Questioning

- Giving feedback

Many educators are already competent in these interpersonal communication skills. Developing these skills to a competent level is not difficult; mastering them is a lifetime project.

Coaching Way of Being

A third core component of the GROWTH system involves the concept of "coaching way of being" (van Nieuwerburgh, 2014). The coach's "way of being" can have a very significant influence on coaching outcomes. Based on an understanding of Rogers's (1980) way of being, ideal attributes for coaches include: humility, confidence in one's coaching ability, caring about people, belief in the abilities of the coachee, respect, and integrity. This emphasis on the coaching way of being helps to give a focus to the quality of the relationship, acknowledging that this less tangible element of the coaching interaction is the ingredient that may have the most impact on the success of the coaching session.

INSTRUCTIONAL COACHING

Originating mainly in North America, instructional coaching has been the subject of more than two decades of research, primarily at the Kansas Coaching Project at the University of Kansas Center for Research on Learning and The Impact Research Lab at The Instructional Coaching Group in Lawrence, Kansas (Knight, 2007, 2018). Instructional coaching is a dialogic approach to coaching focused on improving students' outcomes (achievement, behavior, or well-being) by improving teaching practices and/or learning structures in the classroom. During instructional coaching, "instructional coaches partner with teachers to analyse current reality, set goals, identify strategies to hit the goals, and provide support until the goals are met" (Knight, 2018, p. 2). Instructional coaches move through three stages of coaching: identify, learn, and improve (Knight, 2018).

Identify

Instructional coaching begins with the teacher, in partnership with the instructional coach, identifying a clear picture of reality in the classroom. This usually occurs in one of four ways: (a) watching a video recording of a lesson (this is most effective when coach and teacher watch the recording separately and then meet to discuss the video afterward); (b) interviewing students; (c) reviewing student work; (d) discussing data (such as time on task, level of questions, instructional time, etc.) gathered by the coach in the partnering teacher's classroom, or some combination of these approaches. Once teacher and coach have a clear picture of reality, they discuss it, with the coach asking questions that empower the teacher to identify a goal. The most powerful goals are Powerful, Easy (or Simple), Emotionally compelling, Reachable (they can be measured, and a strategy has been identified for reaching the goal), and Student-focused. Lastly, during this stage, the teacher and coach identify a teaching strategy or some other change that the teacher can implement to reach the goal.

Learn

Instructional coaches have a deep knowledge of effective, evidence-based teaching practices. During the Identify stage, instructional coaches, when appropriate, suggest strategies teachers might implement to hit their goal. During the Learn stage, instructional coaches help teachers learn those teaching strategies through dialogical conversations that position the teacher as the decision-maker about how a given strategy will be implemented. Instructional coaches do not teach teachers; they are equal collaborators. Thus, they may share checklists describing a strategy while asking partnering teachers how they would like to modify implementation of the strategies to better meet students' needs or their own strengths as teachers. Also, in order to help teachers better understand teaching strategies, instructional coaches may provide models of teaching strategies. For example, they may share a video, co-teach, or make it possible for a teacher to visit another teacher's classroom.

Improve

During the Improve stage, instructional coaches partner with teachers to make adaptations until the goal is met. This stage usually involves (a) confirming direction; that is, ensuring that the coaching session is addressing the partnering teacher's most pressing concerns; (b) monitoring progress; (c) making adaptations, such as changing the way a strategy is being implemented, changing the strategy, changing the goal, or changing the way progress toward the goal is measured; and (d) planning next actions. Instructional coaches and teachers collaborate until a goal is met, completing several cycles when possible and appropriate.

SHARED FEATURES OF FACILITATIVE AND DIALOGIC APPROACHES

As noted, facilitative and dialogic approaches share many features. First, both approaches identify improved outcomes for learners as the primary driver of coaching in education. Second, the skill set required for adopting a coaching approach is remarkably consistent: the ability to listen actively, to ask thought-provoking questions, to summarize and paraphrase, and to provide a supportive and challenging environment for coachees (Campbell & van Nieuwerburgh, 2018). Third, the most important aspect of effective coaching in educational settings relates to the way that the coach interacts with the coachee. This philosophy is evident in the Partnership Principles developed by Knight (2011):

- **Equality:** In a partnership, one person does not tell the other what to do. The coach and coachee share ideas and make decisions together as equals.

- **Choice:** Coachees must be positioned as the final decision makers. Coachees are partners who choose their own goals and then select the best way of progressing toward them.

- **Voice:** Conversations with a coach should be as open and candid as conversations with a trusted friend. When coaches live out the principle of voice, their coachees will know that their opinion matters.

- **Dialogue:** In a partnership, conversations should feel like a dialogue to both parties. Coaches actively encourage their coachees to share their ideas by positioning themselves as thinking partners.

- **Reflection:** Coaching is a learning conversation, and it is the role of the coach to create a reflective environment. Often, when people are told what do to (and when and how to do it), they stop learning. A coaching conversation should be one in which the coachee is able to reflect in a way that is engaging, energizing, and valuable.

- **Praxis:** This principle relates to finding ways of applying the knowledge and skills gained during the coaching conversation. The coach encourages the coachee to think about how to apply the new learning in practice.

- **Reciprocity:** In an authentic partnership, both partners feel that they have benefited from the interaction. Coaching should be a mutually beneficial learning conversation.

Both the facilitative and dialogic approaches to coaching in education have been tried and tested over many years in hundreds of schools in the United States, the UK, Australia, as well as other parts of the world. While retaining the principles of coaching, and building on research-informed, theory-based practices, these approaches have been continuously refined for effective use in educational settings. However, a key question for educators remains: "Where can coaching be used in our setting?"

THE GLOBAL FRAMEWORK FOR COACHING AND MENTORING IN EDUCATION

To that end, the Global Framework for Coaching and Mentoring in Education (van Nieuwerburgh, Campbell, & Knight, 2015) recognizes the breadth and diversity of approaches and provides an overview of the context in which coaching is being used in educational settings all over the world.

This framework is described as a "playing field" to capture the sense that it is a shared arena for people to interact and learn together. The playing field is divided into four areas, each representing a focus: educational leadership, professional practice, community engagement, and student experience. By identifying the different contexts in which coaching and mentoring can have a positive impact in educational settings, the Global Framework supports practitioners by suggesting practical interventions; encourages educators to share insights, experiences, and practices; and raises questions that require further investigation. While it seeks to bring a consistency of approach and terminology to the field, the Global Framework aims to be inclusive, flexible, and open to challenge and ongoing development. Next, we explore each of the four areas in further detail.

EDUCATIONAL LEADERSHIP

One important way that coaching can have a positive impact in educational settings is at the leadership level. For some time, corporations have embraced coaching as a way to support leadership development (Hawkins, 2011). More recently, schools and education systems have introduced coaching into this arena (van Nieuwerburgh & Barr, 2017).

Broadly, coaching at the educational leadership level has been focused on two main areas:

- The provision of one-to-one coaching for leaders, mostly by external executive coaches

- The delivery of "leader as coach" professional learning designed to support leaders to incorporate a coaching approach into their management style

One-to-One Coaching

Typically, individual coaching has been made available for aspiring educational leaders to support their preparation for more senior roles. Additionally, coaching has been provided for newly appointed school and college leaders to support them as they transition into new positions (James-Ward, 2013). Leading a school, college, or university is a demanding job, and coaching has provided a way to demonstrate support for those preparing for the role as well as for those getting started in these leadership positions. While individual coaching is a relatively expensive form of professional development, it is viewed as a worthwhile investment since one-to-one coaching offers benefits that professional learning delivered in a workshop context does not. Individual coaching is viewed as highly personalized learning because it can be delivered flexibly when it is needed. Coaching is a structured form of longer-term support and challenge that encourages accountability. That is, through this approach, school leaders not only embed new learning but also have opportunities to reflect on the application of learning within their specific professional contexts. These features of professional learning, delivered through one-to-one coaching, address some of the frustrations of professional learning delivered as traditional training (Broad, 2005).

Leader-as-Coach Training

In human-intensive, knowledge-based organizations, the ways in which people talk to each other is increasingly viewed as central to the way in which work gets done and progress is made toward goals (Kramer & Amabile, 2011). In particular, the way in which leaders intentionally engage in conversations is seen as an important component of effective organizational leadership (Cavanagh, 2014). This focus on the conversation is not proposed merely as an additional technique that invigorates traditional leadership approaches but as a fundamentally different conception of leadership involving leaders who co-create meaning and connection through the interactions in which they engage with other members of their teams. In this context, the knowledge and skills required to lead effective coaching conversations provide an ideal fit for this new conversational leadership approach. Consequently, school systems and principals have embraced coaching skills training in an effort to bring the best elements of coaching into a broader range of conversational contexts. This requires a clear distinction between formal, one-to-one coaching, and the use of a coaching approach.

The use of a coaching approach refers to applying various transferable elements of formal one-to-one coaching to a broad range of conversational contexts. These "transferable elements" include: (a) a focus on goals and progress toward a desired outcome; (b) a focus on leveraging existing resources that can assist in progress; (c) a focus on assisting the conversational partners to learn their way toward their preferred outcome; and (d) a focus on strengths (Campbell & van Nieuwerburgh, 2018). When applied with skill and humanity, these elements of effective coaching interactions can bring a positive, organizationally significant impact to the conversations that matter most.

PROFESSIONAL PRACTICE

Frequently coaching is employed to improve the way teachers teach, with coaches and other change leaders working from a recognition that better teaching will lead to better learning (Sanders & Rivers, 1996). For example, Hattie's (2008) meta-analysis of meta-analyses (reviewing more than 800 meta-analyses) demonstrates that when teachers (a) are clear about learning outcomes and success criteria, (b) effectively monitor student learning, and (c) make adaptations to teaching and learning to ensure student success, student learning improves. Two approaches to enhancing teaching practice are discussed.

Instructional Coaching

Instructional coaches use a dialogic approach. They draw on the literature on instruction while positioning teachers as decision-makers. After collaborating with more than 100,000 educators from around the world, researchers and consultants from the Impact Research Lab have identified seven factors as being necessary for successful instructional coaching (Knight, 2015).

Coaches who are successful:

1. Employ a clearly defined coaching cycle (such as the instructional coaching cycle described earlier in this chapter) when they partner with teachers. First, they identify goals and then the strategies to achieve them. Further, coaches encourage teachers to make adaptations to these strategies when needed to ensure that teachers and their students hit their goals.

2. Understand how to gather data in the classroom.

3. Have a deep knowledge of a few high-leverage, research-validated, effective teaching strategies. These strategies are not always a part of the instructional coaching conversation. Frequently, when teachers partner with coaches, they quickly identify strategies they can easily implement to improve student outcomes for learning and well-being. This often happens when the teacher notices what is working well and builds upon that success. However, an

instructional coach's knowledge of effective instruction becomes essential when teachers need to utilize new teaching practices that they do not know.

4. Understand the complexities of working with adults, embracing a set of principles that position teachers as equals and professionals. Through their interactions, coaches should demonstrate that the collaborating teacher is as important (or more important) than the coach. The teacher is the person who makes decisions about practice in the classroom.

5. Employ effective communication strategies such as listening, empathy, and effective questioning to foster dialogue between the coach and coachee to create situations where teachers feel completely comfortable commenting on and shaping the direction of the coaching process.

6. Lead effectively by being both emotionally intelligent and responsive to individual teachers. This means that coaches are ambitious and organized in order to address teachers' primary concerns through dialogue about how teaching and learning structures can be adjusted to improve student learning and well-being. Ultimately, they see coaching as a mutually beneficial learning opportunity—they learn with and from teachers rather than judging them.

7. Are supported by their administrators. At a minimum, to ensure success, administrators need to clarify coaches' roles and responsibilities, establish and communicate a policy on confidentiality within coaching relationships, and protect coaches' time.

Peer Coaching

Educational institutions can also rely on their staff to support one another to set and achieve professional goals through dialogue (Robertson, 2008). Peer coaching is particularly helpful in schools as teachers can role model being "learners" (Kidd, 2009), and it encourages them to take more responsibility for making improvements through analyzing their own practice (Lofthouse, Leat, Towler, Hall, & Cummings, 2010). This approach requires educators trained in coaching skills to provide support for one another. A typical way that teachers might work together is to plan for a teaching session together, then organize for one person to observe the other during the session, and follow up with a coaching conversation. This way of using peer coaching derives from a Japanese approach to professional development called "Lesson Study" (Fernandez, 2002).

Training educators to become coaches can have multiple benefits. First, the educational institution will develop a pool of trained coaches who might be able to support each other and institutional objectives. Second, coaching skills can be incorporated into a broad range of educators' daily tasks. Third, teachers who have undertaken coach training together have reported that "collaborating with others and having time for reflection enhanced their learning" (Barr & van Nieuwerburgh, 2015, p. 190). And finally, learning to become a coach or mentor can lead to educators being even better practitioners (Centre for the Use of Research and Evidence in Education [CUREE], 2005).

COMMUNITY ENGAGEMENT

Perhaps the least explored area of the Global Framework for Coaching and Mentoring in Education relates to the use of coaching to improve community engagement. Primarily, there are opportunities to use coaching to support, encourage, and engage the parents and carers of learners in schools. Some schools have started to offer formal programs to help parents and other adults involved in the lives of their students (Sterling, 2008). Further, Bamford, Mackew, and Golawski (2012) proposed that parent coaching could have a positive effect on relationships between parents and their children. This can have a direct impact on students' learning and can also have a positive effect on parents' confidence (Golawski, Bamford, & Gersch, 2013). Further, if schools deliver coaching training to parents, it may also improve relationships between schools and their communities. Even more important, empowering parents to encourage their children by identifying and developing their strengths (Waters, 2017) can support educational institutions to enable their learners to flourish.

STUDENT EXPERIENCE

This area of the Global Framework is the one in which coaches work directly with students. In this context, students participate directly in the interventions that seek to enhance their success and well-being.

Coaching Students

In one UK study, non-school-based adults provided academic coaching to high school students that led to enhanced examination performance (Passmore & Brown, 2009). In another study, young people at risk of developing mental health issues who attended a coaching program reported that they were better able to face challenges (Robson-Kelly & van Nieuwerburgh, 2016). Further, research undertaken in Australia has shown that coaching delivered by school staff can increase the resilience, well-being, and hopefulness of students (Campbell & Gardner, 2005; Green, Grant, & Rynsaardt, 2007). So, making coaching available to high school and college students seems to have positive effects on their academic performance and well-being. Similar findings have been reported in a university-based qualitative research study involving doctoral-level students (Lech, van Nieuwerburgh, & Jalloul, 2018).

Students Coaching Students

An alternative approach is to train students to coach one another. A number of recent studies have suggested that students who are trained in coaching skills and then coach their peers can improve their communication, problem-solving, and study skills (van Nieuwerburgh & Tong, 2013; van Nieuwerburgh, Zacharia, Luckham, Prebble, & Brown, 2012). This type of facilitative peer coaching has also been used with university students (Short, Kinman, & Baker, 2010). Coaching skills have even been taught to elementary school children (Briggs & van Nieuwerburgh, 2010; Dorrington & van Nieuwerburgh, 2015; Madden, Green, & Grant, 2011), and this promises to be an interesting area for further experimentation and research.

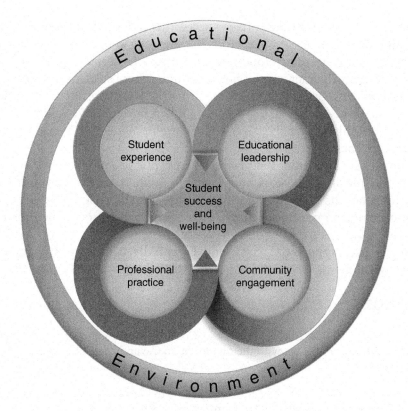

Figure 33.3 The Global Framework for Coaching and Mentoring in Education.
Source: © Growth Coaching International.

In our view, this area holds enormous promise. Students benefit from being coached and from coaching others. Even more important, we believe that the skills and learning acquired from these activities may play a part in students' lifelong success and well-being. As shown in Figure 33.3, the intended outcome of the work in all four areas of the Global Framework for Coaching and Mentoring in Education is student success and well-being. That is, we believe that improved educational leadership, better professional practice, enhanced relationships with the community, and positive student experiences will all lead to better outcomes for students.

The Global Framework recognizes that the various interventions discussed previously take place within specific contexts (e.g., a school, a district, or a region) which, in turn, are part of broader educational systems (in Figure 33.3 we have called this "educational environment"). In important ways, the educational environment will influence the ease of implementation and effectiveness of coaching initiatives. At the same time, thoughtful and effective implementation of coaching initiatives will impact positively on the educational environment.

CONCLUSION

While coaching in educational contexts is already having a positive impact, it has an even brighter future. The concept of coaching as personalized learning conversations resonates with educators. Many educational leaders in the United States, the

UK, Australia, and New Zealand have successfully adopted the essential elements of a coaching approach as part of their leadership styles, and educators are embracing coaching as a way of developing their professional practice and their interactions with learners. Further, elementary and high school students are coaching one another toward academic success and well-being. Finally, innovative educational institutions are successfully using coaching to strengthen links to their communities. We are optimistic that these powerful developments will become even more widely accepted and adopted.

Perhaps most important, the principles and practice of coaching in education are respectful toward educators and learners. By its nature, coaching focuses on positive outcomes. Its purpose is to unlock potential and allow people to flourish. Effective coaching in education must focus on improving outcomes for learners. However, the principles that underpin coaching require that we work toward both academic success and personal well-being. Essentially, we are working toward ideal learning environments in which people feel valued, appreciated, and empowered.

REFERENCES

Bamford, A., Mackew, N., & Golawski, A. (2012). Coaching for parents: Empowering parents to create positive relationships with their children. In C. van Nieuwerburgh (Ed.), *Coaching in education: Getting better results for students, educators, and parents* (pp. 133–152). London, UK: Karnac.

Barr, M., & van Nieuwerburgh, C. (2015). Teachers' experiences of an introductory coaching training workshop in Scotland: An interpretative phenomenological analysis. *International Coaching Psychology Review, 10*(2), 190–204.

Bloom, G., Castagna, C., Moir, E., & Warren, B. (2005). *Blended coaching: Skills and strategies to support principal development.* Thousand Oaks, CA: Corwin.

Briggs, M., & van Nieuwerburgh, C. (2010). The development of peer coaching skills in primary school children in years 5 and 6. *Procedia-Social and Behavioral Science, 9,* 1415–1422. doi:10.1016/j.sbspro.2010.12.343

Broad, M. (2005). *Beyond transfer of training: Engaging systems to improve performance.* San Francisco, CA: John Wiley & Sons.

Burley, S., & Pomphrey, C. (2011). *Mentoring and coaching in schools: Professional learning through collaborative inquiry.* Abingdon, UK: Routledge.

Campbell, J., & van Nieuwerburgh, C. (2018). *The leader's guide to coaching in schools: Creating the conditions for effective learning.* Thousand Oaks, CA: Corwin.

Campbell, M. A., & Gardner, S. (2005). A pilot study to assess the effects of life coaching with year 12 students. In M. Cavanagh, A. M. Grant, & T. Kemp (Eds.), *Evidence-based coaching: Vol. 1. Theory, research and practice from the behavioural sciences* (pp. 159–169). Bowen Hills, QLD, Australia: Australian Academy Press.

Cavanagh, M. (2014). The coaching engagement in the 21st century: New paradigms for complex times. In D. Clutterbuck, S. David, & D. Megginson (Eds.), *Beyond goals: Effective strategies for coaching and mentoring* (pp. 151–183). London, UK: Routledge.

Centre for the Use of Research and Evidence in Education. (2005). *National framework for coaching.* London, UK: Author.

Cooperrider, D., Whitney, D., & Stavros, J. (2008). *Appreciative inquiry handbook* (2nd ed.). San Francisco, CA: Berrett-Koehler Publishers.

Dorrington, L., & van Nieuwerburgh, C. (2015). The development of peer coaching skills in primary school children: An exploration of how children respond to feedback. *International Journal of Information and Education Technology, 5*(1), 50–54. doi:10.7763/IJIET.2015.V5.475

Downey, M. (2003). *Effective coaching* (2nd ed.). New York, NY: Thomson.

Fernandez, C. (2002). Learning from Japanese approaches to professional development: The case of lesson study. *Journal of Teacher Education, 53*(5), 393–405. doi:10.1177/002248702237 394

Golawski, A., Bamford, A., & Gersch, I. (2013). *Swings and roundabouts: A self-coaching workbook for parents and those considering becoming parents.* London, UK: Karnac.

Gollwitzer, P. (1999). Implementation intentions: Strong effects of simple plans. *American Psychologist, 54*(7), 493–503. doi:10.1037/0003-066X.54.7.493

Green, L. S., Grant, A. M., & Rynsaardt, J. (2007). Evidence-based life coaching for senior high school students: Building hardiness and hope. *International Coaching Psychology Review, 2*(1), 24–32.

Hattie, J. (2008). *Visible learning: A synthesis of over 800 meta-analyses relating to achievement.* New York, NY: Random House.

Hawkins, P. (2011). *Leadership team coaching.* London, UK: Kogan Page.

Jackson, P., & McKergow, M. (2006). *The solutions focus: The SIMPLE way to positive change (people skills for professionals).* London, UK: Nicholas Brealey.

James-Ward, C. (2013). The coaching experience of four novice principals. *International Journal of Mentoring and Coaching in Education, 2*(1), 21–33. doi:10.1108/20466851311323069

Kidd, W. (2009). Peer coaching and mentoring to improve teaching and learning. *Practical Research for Education, 42,* 50–55.

Knight, J. (2007). *Instructional coaching: A partnership approach to improving instruction.* Thousand Oaks, CA: Corwin.

Knight, J. (2011). *Unmistakable impact: A partnership approach to dramatically improving instruction.* Thousand Oaks, CA: Corwin.

Knight, J. (2015). Teach to win: Seven success factors for instructional coaching programs. *Principal Leadership, 15*(7), 24–27.

Knight, J. (2018). *The impact cycle: What instructional coaches should do to foster powerful improvements in teaching.* Thousand Oaks, CA: Corwin.

Kramer, S., & Amabile, T. (2011). *The progress principle: Using small wins to ignite joy, engagement, and creativity at work.* Boston, MA: Harvard Business Review Press.

Lech, A., van Nieuwerburgh, C., & Jalloul, S. (2018). Understanding the experience of PhD students who received coaching: An interpretative phenomenological analysis. *Coaching: An International Journal of Theory, Research and Practice, 11*(1), 60–73. doi:10.1080/17521882.2017.138 1753

Lofthouse, R., Leat, D., Towler, C., Hall, E., & Cummings, C. (2010). *Improving coaching: Evolution not revolution.* Nottingham, UK: National College for Leadership of Schools and Children's Services.

Lopez, S. (2013). *Making hope happen: Create the future you want for yourself and others.* New York, NY: Simon & Schuster.

Macdonald, A. J. (2011). *Solution-focused therapy: Theory, research and practice* (2nd ed.). London, UK: Sage.

Madden, W., Green, S., & Grant, A. M. (2011). A pilot study evaluating strengths-based coaching for primary school students: Enhancing engagement and hope. *International Coaching Psychology Review, 6*(1), 71–83.

Passmore, J., & Brown, A. (2009). Coaching non-adult students for enhanced examination performance: A longitudinal study. *Coaching: An International Journal of Theory, Research and Practice, 2*(1), 54–64. doi:10.1080/17521880902783124

Robertson, J. (2008). *Coaching educational leadership: Building leadership capacity through partnership.* London, UK: Sage.

Robson-Kelly, L., & van Nieuwerburgh, C. (2016). What does coaching have to offer young people at risk of developing mental health problems? A grounded theory study. *International Coaching Psychology Review, 11*(1), 75–92.

Rogers, C. (1980). *A way of being.* Boston, MA: Houghton-Mifflin.

Sanders, W. L., & Rivers, J. C. (1996). *Cumulative and residual effects of teachers on future student academic achievement.* Knoxville, TN: University of Tennessee.

Short, E., Kinman, G., & Baker, S. (2010). Evaluating the impact of a peer coaching intervention on well-being amongst psychology undergraduate students. *International Coaching Psychology Review, 5*(1), 27–35.

Sterling, D. (2008). *The parent as coach approach.* Rio Rancho, NM: White Oak.

van Nieuwerburgh, C. (Ed.). (2012). *Coaching in education: Getting better results for students, educators and parents.* London, UK: Karnac.

van Nieuwerburgh, C. (2014). *An introduction to coaching skills: A practical guide.* London, UK: Sage.

van Nieuwerburgh, C., & Barr, M. (2017). Coaching in education. In T. Bachkirova, G. Spence, & D. Drake (Eds.), *The SAGE handbook of coaching* (pp. 505–520). London, UK: Sage.

van Nieuwerburgh, C., Campbell, J., & Knight, J. (2015). Lesson in progress. *Coaching at Work, 10*(3), 35–37.

van Nieuwerburgh, C., & Oades, L. (2017). Editorial. *Coaching: An International Journal of Theory, Research and Practice, 10*(2), 99–101. doi:10.1080/17521882.2017.1355828

van Nieuwerburgh, C., & Tong, C. (2013). Exploring the benefits of being a student coach in educational settings: A mixed-method study. *Coaching: An International Journal of Theory, Research and Practice, 6*(1), 5–24. doi:10.1080/17521882.2012.734318

van Nieuwerburgh, C., Zacharia, C., Luckham, E., Prebble, G., & Browne, L. (2012). Coaching students in a secondary school: A case study. In C. van Nieuwerburgh (Ed.), *Coaching in education: Getting better results for students, educators and parents* (pp. 191–198). London, UK: Karnac.

Waters, L. (2017). *The strength switch: How the new science of strength-based parenting can help your child and your teen to flourish.* New York, NY: Penguin Random House.

Whitmore, J. (1992). *Coaching for performance.* London, UK: Nicholas Brealey.

Whitmore, J. (2002). *Coaching for performance: GROWing people, performance and purpose* (3rd ed.). London, UK: Nicholas Brealey.

34

Executive Coaching

Jeremy Robinson

WHAT EXACTLY IS EXECUTIVE COACHING?

How is executive coaching different from other types of coaching? What are some beliefs or misunderstandings people have about coaching (some of these people who have these misunderstandings are also coaches)?

As I seek to answer these questions, I'm reminded of the famous Zen saying: "Things are not as they seem; nor are they otherwise."

Let me start with a story. In 1999, I was lucky enough to have been invited to an event near Orlando, Florida, that became known at the First Executive Coaching Summit. Along with 35 colleagues, we co-wrote the first white paper on executive coaching, which when published was called "Executive Coaching Summit I: Documenting the Emerging Field of Coaching in Organizations." In this white paper, we defined what we as a group thought executive coaching was and what executive coaches did. The article summarizing the Summit's finding was written by an executive coach named Agnes Mura. The piece was published in the *International Journal of Coaching in Organizations* (IJCO; Mura, 2003).

The group had gathered as a brainstorm idea from Laura Whitworth, cofounder of the Coaches Training Institute (CTI). Whitworth noticed a growing demand for executive coaches by companies and organizations and convened a team to hold a summit. The group gained the sponsorship of the International Coach Federation (ICF) and decided to convene 2 days before the ICF conference in Orlando. Originally, more than 100 leading executive coaches responded to the invitation to participate in the 2-day summit. From this list, 36 were chosen by the convening team as applicants having the most extensive experience in the field, and who were also coaching in organizations at the highest levels of executive responsibility.

The task of summit attendees was to identify characteristics that set executive coaching apart from all other types of coaching like sports coaching, personal coaching, business coaching, spiritual coaching, life coaching, among others.

The summit group agreed to the following definition of executive coaching:

> Executive Coaching is a facilitative one-to-one, mutually designed relationship between a professional coach and a key contributor who has a power position in the organization. This relationship occurs in areas of business, government, not-for-profit and educational organizations where there are multiple stakeholders and organizational sponsorship for the coach and or coaching group. The focus of the coaching is usually focused on organizational performance or development, but may also have a personal component as well. The results produced from this relationship are observable and measurable, commensurate with the requirements the organization has for the performance of the person being coached.

In breaking down "quick points of the definition" in her article, Mura listed five keys:

- A relationship exists between coach and high-level individual(s) of the organization.

- The relationship occurs in and is sponsored by differing kinds of organizations with multiple stakeholders.

- Coaching is for the benefit of a person with high levels of responsibility and broad scope of impact.

- Focus of the coaching may be both organizational and personal development.

- Outcomes are observable and measurable, and match organizational performance requirements. (Mura, 2003)

As I re-read the work these colleagues and I completed almost 20 years ago, I'm struck by the fact that there are still myths and misunderstandings surrounding what executive coaching is and is not.

For example, many people believe that if an executive hires me to coach him or her, then I'm providing that person with executive coaching. It would seem to make sense logically. This person is an executive. This person pays me out of his or her own funds and I'm coaching them.

But I'd say no.

The important distinction is personally contracted coaching is not an organizationally sponsored engagement.

Some readers might argue that I'm quibbling here but I'd reply that they are missing the point. By definition of the first Executive Coaching Summit and other organizations to which I belong that have defined executive coaching, executive coaching is always defined as an organizational sponsored initiative. It helps even more if we take another step forward and describe executive coaching as an organizational sponsored *engagement.*

By describing executive coaching as an engagement, we let others know that we are handling an organizational initiative that has an arc to it and also has a number of organizational sponsors, whatever the level of coaching (more about different types of coaching a bit later in this chapter).

In describing "Managing the Coaching Engagement" in our book *Becoming an Exceptional Executive Coach*, my colleagues and I wrote the following:

- Engagement management describes the entire arc of the coaching process. As the coach, you are responsible for managing this process in its entirety, from initial introductions to the closure meeting.

- You are the expert about the coaching process; your clients are the experts about themselves and their situations.

- As the process expert, you are responsible for anticipating the flow and providing the client and sponsors with guidance about each step and expectations for it.

- Doing process checks with the client and sponsors will help you stay attuned to their reactions and needs, allowing you to address any concerns that arise.

- While there may be pressure to define coaching goals early in the process, it is more important that goals feel right to the client and motivate action, even though it may take longer.

- The essential challenge of engagement management is alignment: you and the client, the client and sponsors, and you and sponsors. This can be tricky but it is what makes executive coaching challenging and gratifying. (Frisch, Lee, Metzger, Robinson, & Rosemarin, 2012)

As we recount in "Becoming an Exceptional Executive Coach," all these pieces involving the client and sponsors, and you and sponsors are crucial to the coach being successful as both engagement manager of the project and coach of the client (Frisch et al., 2012).

Before the sponsor has even contacted us as a potential coach, there has been what we think of as "pre-engagement events" that have led to the request for this coaching. We don't know what triggered the coaching request. Was it a new opportunity this coaching client is facing? Was it a problem, or perhaps a mixture of opportunity and problem? Whatever the impetus, it is likely that a series of people have been involved in making the decision to consider executive coaching and these people may include the client's manager, an Human Resources business partner, and others in either leadership development or other areas of the organization. As a coach, our job is not only to coach the client but also help him or her be successful by leading this engagement to closure and a successful outcome.

Ultimately, in all executive coaching engagements, our goal as both coach and engagement manager is to help our client increase alignment with all the stakeholders involved in this coaching process, especially the client's boss. To be coaching a client independently of and segregated from an organizational engagement is to risk coaching a client out of that organization.

Why do I say that?

Because such coaching has no alignment with key coaching stakeholders. It risks being a random growth-oriented initiative that has nothing to do with the events in the organization that led up to the organizational request for coaching on behalf of this client.

Communication by the coach to other key stakeholders is essential for success of the executive coaching engagement.

We work in the service of the client's privacy and trust. Many of my colleagues and I tell the coaching stakeholders the following.

THE COACHING PROCESS IS PUBLIC AND THE CONTENT IS PRIVATE

What do we mean when we say this?

First of all, we mean that the person in front of us (or on the phone) is our client. The organization is the sponsor.

The coaching process that is public to stakeholders is the information about dates of coaching meetings taking place, their duration, the psychometric assessments administered, the 360-degree survey being undertaken, dates of various events in coaching such as the date of delivery of a coaching development plan, the date of the three-way coaching development plan meeting between coach, boss, and client—all of these events are public to the coaching client's boss, boss's boss, and Human Resources business partner.

Also public to stakeholders are the coaching goals articulated by the client, the client's boss, and other key stakeholders. As these goals shift throughout the coaching engagement into what we have called a Designed Objective, these goals are also public to stakeholders involved in coaching. Further, the key coaching deliverable, a Coaching Development Plan, co-written by the client and coach and added to by the client's boss, is also considered public to organizational stakeholders.

The coaching content, the conversational content between client and coach is private to the coach and the client throughout the coaching process. This means that the coaching client owns the right to what he or she has discussed at each meeting, absent the coaching goals that are public. This means that the coaching assessments taken by the client, including the 360-degree assessment, are the property of the coaching client. The coaching client may choose to disclose the results of these assessments and the 360-degree assessment, but the coach does not have a right to reveal this information unless told to do so by the client.

In operating this way as coaches, we believe that we create clearer and brighter boundaries about coaching for our clients. This leads to greater transparency to our organizations about what's going on in the arc of the coaching engagement.

This helps me as a coach stay true to the pledge that I make to all my coaching clients at the start of each engagement. My goal always, first and foremost, is to do no harm to you or your career.

The more clearly we define our roles and responsibilities as coach, client, and coaching stakeholders, the less likely anyone is to misunderstand the coaching engagement and to violate the trust that the engagement requires. Trust is the magic ingredient in improving stakeholder alignment. As the engagement manager, the coach can be the facilitator of building trust. It's plain to understand that to do so, the coach needs to proceed in the spirit of helping "thee not me." But that does not mean the coach is entirely selfless. The coach needs to make sure he or she is paid for the work and that all other events during the engagement are communicated about and are worked out as discussed. When we arrive at sponsoring organizations, we will find the clients in transition in their work journey and similarly when we leave these clients, they will still be in transition. Yet while we've been there we will hope to have provided real benefits including:

1. Helping clients meet behavioral goals and business results, and increase inspirational energy.

2. Bringing greater alignment in understanding and communication with their manager and other key stakeholders.

3. Helping clients have a greater sense of clarity and purpose of work related to their lives and life-long aspirations.

Sometimes, if we're really good at what we do or if we're lucky, we receive the gift of *the extraordinary client*. This client may not be extraordinary personally. But the journey that this client may need to embark on in the coaching engagement may make the client extraordinary in that it requires the client to transform his or her life entirely. If and when we receive such a gift, we get touched by the larger possibility of executive coaching as *transformative experience*.

Three years ago, I received a call from a colleague in NYC who had news about a former client of mine. She called to make a coaching referral and along the way of making this referral, she told me the story of what had happened with this former client's family. The coach was now referenced as an important person in this man's family's life. The client had changed the way he interacted with his children and wife. Up until his coaching, I learned, he'd been considered a loving father and husband, but was emotionally distant from his family. Post-coaching, he'd become the involved father and husband the family hoped he'd be. Obviously, hearing this was very gratifying, and proof that the work I'd done with this client had "stuck," something I often wonder about after my work is finished.

This client had seemed to be particularly challenging. Enormously intelligent and emotionally unavailable, the word I would have used to describe him would have been "robotic." But the "good news" was that his successful career in the business world had hit an impasse because of his difficulty teaching and being empathic with his direct reports and his problems being seen as a leader by his peers. This was good because his boss was telling him that despite his enormous capabilities to do his job, he'd need to be a much more successful communicator and role model to get to the next level. The boss needed him to be a leader, not just an independent contributor. And this client was very ambitious. An ambitious coaching client who applies that drive toward his coaching can often achieve impressive results.

His manager proposed that they hire an executive coach to help him change. Oddly, the manager told me after coaching had ended that he had been extremely skeptical that anything would change as a result of this coaching.

The client was very open to the coaching because he was in pain about his career hitting a plateau. I assigned him to read and study *Primal Leadership* by Goleman, Boyatzis, and McKee (2004). The book had a powerful effect on him. I did psychometric testing with him, including an Emotional Intelligence Bar-On Assessment. Testing revealed far below average empathy scores and above average self-actualization scores. It was clear to both of us we needed to use his drive to achieve business results to move his ability to be empathic with others. I pushed him very hard. I shadowed him in team meetings. We went through lists of all his organizational stakeholders, going over details of his relationship with each, often brainstorming how he might find a more tuned-in way of relating to each. I performed a deep 360-degree feedback study during which time I interviewed 15 of his stakeholders, plus his wife. I was pleased how committed to coaching he'd become. I tried to model an appreciative style that I wanted him to copy with his direct reports and his stakeholders, even as I was firm with him when he made missteps or said something brutally critical of others. I felt he was a good man with many loving qualities who was locked up in a shell. I was very appreciative when he made efforts to push out of that shell and became an empathic teacher to his direct reports. The good news of his changing started to surface at approximately the 4-month mark of his coaching and it continued to be experienced through the organization as our coaching was extended to 12 months. The client liked what was happening. He felt more effective with people. I understood it as his being more related with others. I was happy that I was able to reach his heart by going through his very powerful brain.

When the coaching ended, the manager repeated his pronouncement that he was surprised the coaching had worked. I was hopeful that the changes would stick with the client, but I was uncertain as to what extent they would. I knew it was most important that the client liked how he felt now that he had made these changes. That was the most hopeful part. It was a good diagnostic sign that the client continued to feel empowered by the changes in behavior he had made. That told me he had taken ownership of the coaching. The coaching was now his to drive.

Sometimes I tell people with whom I'm discussing coaching that I want coaching to line up as an unfair advantage favoring me and the client from the start. When the boss withholds a promotion to an otherwise extremely capable client due to a set of behaviors that the boss would like to see the client change, that can work in the favor of coaching. It feels to me that in these cases, we have the wind at our backs in coaching. My job is to successfully identify behaviors that will yield the greatest results for the client's coaching and keep him on track identifying and changing them. In the process, I need to model different ways I'd like the client to be so he can mirror it back to others. I want my client to see and feel the differences between behaviors that are not working and ones that will be more effective. Incidentally, these same behaviors will probably make clients feel better about themselves. *So at this moment we have the phenomenon of the client liking his or her behavior change.* Liking behavior change is a crucial element in a client choosing to hang on to this behavior post-coaching.

I also have the advantage of having worked at behavior change for a long time, first as a psychotherapist and now as a coach. So I have a lot of "flight time" helping people get to a new behavioral destination. I think my clients intuitively experience this. I make them feel comfortable, I like and accept them but I work with them to change. This is the paradox of coaching, as it is of any human endeavor involving behavioral change. Change requires a degree of self-acceptance to become more self-aware and then see if the changes are taking effect.

My colleagues at iCoach New York and I have identified seven different types of executive coaching, which we have identified as a seven-stage continuum of coaching (Figure 34.1).

The different types of executive coaching we reference are:

Type 1: Targeted Skills Coaching

Type 2: Feedback/Development Plan Coaching

Type 3: Feedback Coaching with Follow-up

Type 4: Transition/Assimilation Coaching (sometimes called Onboarding coaching)

Type 5: Leadership Effectiveness Coaching

Type 6: High Potential Coaching

Type 7: Leader's Agenda Coaching

Executive Coaching Types 5 and 6 are what is most often thought of when the term executive coaching is used (Frisch et al., 2012).

Type 7, Leader's Agenda Coaching, has been masterfully documented in Karol Wasylyshyn's book *Destined to Lead: Executive Coaching and Lessons for Leadership Development* (Wasylyshyn, 2014). Wasylyshyn's book includes eight chapter case studies of her work with disguised CEO or senior executive clients, including her interventions and commentary about coaching actions and interventions with each. Every coaching supervisee I've asked to read this book has found it inspiring and enormously useful in thinking about their executive coaching cases, no matter what the level in the organization. For myself, I'm enormously grateful to Wasylyshyn for her pioneering work as an executive coach and colleague.

EXECUTIVE COACHING IN HISTORICAL CONTEXT

Sometimes looking back on something helps us anticipate what might come next. Looking at executive coaching in its historical context also gives us ideas about where we want to continue to grow the practice of executive coaching. I believe that the first time any of my colleagues recall hearing the term executive coaching was in the 1980s.

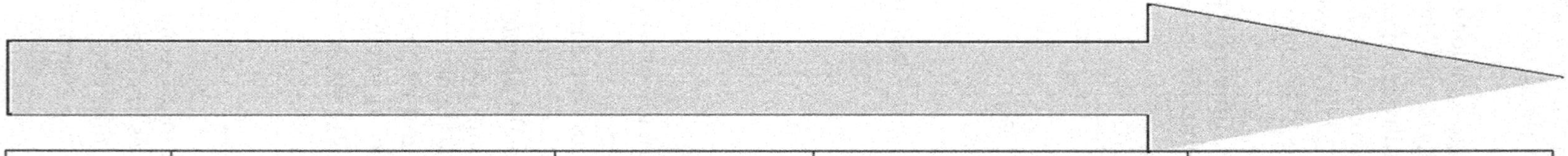

Type I	Type II	Type III	Type IV	Type V
Targeted skills coaching	**Feedback/development plan coaching**	**Feedback coaching with follow-up**	**Transition/assimilation coaching**	**Leadership effectiveness coaching**
One-on-one skills training, e.g., presentations, listening, giving feedback, etc.	Interpretation of 360 survey, self-insight questionnaires, simulations and other feedback from leadership training or other experience toward action planning for on-the-job development plan	Scheduled follow-up meetings/calls focused on progress in implementing previously drafted development action plan	Short program/limited number of sessions aimed at helping a newly hired/promoted executive make an efficient and productive transition to the new role; may draw upon insight, feedback, and transition planning tools	Full coaching engagement of 3–6 months minimum focused on improving current managerial or leadership performance; issue or obstacle that needs to be addressed through coaching

Type VI	Type VII
High potential coaching	**Leader's agenda coaching**
Full coaching engagement of 3–6 months minimum focused on readiness for future opportunities, often linked with the organization's talent management plan	Open-ended timeframe driven by the leader's agenda; almost always, a C-level executive or member of the senior executive team; less emphasis on stakeholders, tools, and formalized development planning, more emphasis on personal discussion and insight, with the focus on the executive's unique leadership challenges. Note: this is NOT consulting on business challenges, except as a vehicle to help the executive grow

©iCoachNewYork 2017

Figure 34.1 Coaching continuum: Individual development interventions arranged by difficulty and the likelihood of internal to external coach delivery.

Organizational Heads of Executive Coaching—whether they're called Human Resources business partners or Heads of Talent Management or more rarely, Heads of Executive Coaching—have today almost uniform agreement that executive coaching is most effective and a better use of dollars when provided for key talent and high potentials in organizations.

This means that many organizations that are sophisticated users of external or internal executive coaching now more rarely use coaches for executives who are derailing. We should note that this is an abrupt shift. When coaching first was introduced in the late 1980s and early 1990s many coaches were hired to coach executives who were about to be referred to outplacement programs.

Indeed, many of today's veteran executive coaches owe their beginnings as coaches to the work they were doing in outplacement programs at that time. By providing coaches to executives who were derailing, it was discovered that coaching could be enormously useful to both the executives and their organizations. Rather than being terminated, a good percentage of these people could be "saved" and retained.

As executive coaching became better known in the late 1990s and early 2000s, organizational leaders and executive coaches working inside and outside organizations began to wonder about the best allocation of money toward executive coaching. After all, they reasoned, if executive coaching is often effective (check the box) and expensive (check the box), why was it being applied mainly to executives who were derailing?

As CEOs and other leaders in organizations received coaching, they joined the chorus of those inquiring about the best use of coaching dollars. Executive coaching is a powerful tool. Why not focus its application to key talent and high potential employees? What would happen if organizations took that approach?

Discussions about applying executive coaching to key talent versus derailing executives began to influence organizations to spend coaching dollars more prudently—toward the development of the people in their organizations who would then in turn be most involved in the development of others.

As we remember, executive coaching was gaining media attention in the early 2000s. Because of the history of applying coaching toward derailing executives, some wondered if coaching was a form of "corporate therapy." *The Economist* magazine ran an article in November 2003 (which quoted this executive coach) with that exact title: "Corporate Therapy: Having an Executive Coach Is All the Rage" ("Corporate Therapy," 2003). This rumor about coaching as therapy, however, never really gained traction because almost all practicing coaches, especially those coming from the mental health field, were quite clear in providing boundaries and discussions with their clients regarding differentiators between psychotherapy and coaching. Coaching was about helping clients achieve business results. Executive coaching was not only a one-on-one initiative; it involved a boss and other key organizational stakeholders. Coaches spoke the language of business, helping organizational leaders calculate metrics around performance by eliciting business goals for coaching. Organizations learned that these business goals for the coaching client were often best determined by the coaching client's boss as well as by the coaching client.

Sophisticated coaches were clear in speaking to Internal Coaching resources that they were looking for clients with business goals, not executives who had "symptoms," like anxiety or depression. This became another way to triage those who were best suited for coaching. Yes, coaching could be therapeutic; it felt good to be in coaching. But it was a special kind of good feeling.

Executive coaching also needed to be differentiated from management consulting, another type of organizational intervention that was clearly not coaching. Management consultants get hired to provide expert information often from consultants who are subject matter experts (SMEs).

I recall trying to explain how executive coaching was different from his work to a management consultant client I was coaching in 2004. At first, I was at a loss for words. To help demonstrate the difference I asked this client (who was participating in a coaching program at a colleague's coaching school) to "coach" me in the middle of a session at which I had been coaching him. He demonstrated his style with me over 5 or 10 minutes as I willingly spoke about an issue I wanted coaching about. His "coaching" was giving me advice. After he did this with me, my words returned.

"Coaching is about providing inspiration," I reflected to him. "Consulting is about giving information." I thought then, and continue to think today, that these are important distinctions for us to have.

More troubling for coaches in the early 2000s was the idea that executive coaching was some kind of organizational "fad." It was a trend. In a few years or so, it would quickly be replaced. The reason I found this objection more troubling was the implication that coaching lacked substance, that it was superficial, or not relevant to the real needs of our coaching clients, that they were wasting their time.

I've never wanted to be involved in anything that wasted my time or anyone else's time. So this criticism touched a nerve.

Yet, as I write these words, I notice we no longer hear it said that executive coaching is some kind of fad or fly-by-night trend. The rumors as to coaching's imminent demise have died long before coaching has left the building. This has led me to wonder, what were the reasons people stopped asking, "Is coaching just another fad?"

The answers owe much to how coaching has evolved and become artfully practiced by many excellent coaching practitioners. Through the writings and practice of high profile executive coaches such as Marshall Goldsmith and Karol Wasylyshyn, business leaders came to understand that incorporating 360-degree feedback into coaching engagements would make engagements more effective.

By using 360-degree feedback studies in their coaching engagements, executive coaches gained much more entry and visibility into the clients' worlds. Moreover, the feedback we collected from the participant raters was more objective because it would not influence the performance reviews that our clients received at the end of the year. Raters didn't have to "elevate" what they observed. Our coaching feedback was done solely for the purpose of our coaching clients' development.

Stakeholders and clients of executive coaching saw something else. They saw that executive coaches were more sophisticated facilitators of feedback. Executive coaches took extra effort to explain to clients that when they talked to participant raters about providing feedback for their coaching that this was a different kind of feedback than these participant raters had provided before. Many clients told stakeholders that this feedback was for the purpose of "my growth as a leader." Stakeholders stood up and noticed. Their attention was aroused that these clients wanted feedback, wanted coaching, and wanted development in order to continue to improve their "game." It confirmed the title of the Goldsmith and Morgan article that, "Leadership Is a Contact Sport" (Goldsmith & Morgan, 2004). And this contact best occurred through feedback. Now, as feedback collectors and facilitators, executive coaches had increased their organizational remit. We now better understood our clients' business goals and helped them achieve targeted business results. We could do so by hearing from key stakeholders. Our coaching had moved from private to the client to public to others in the company. Coaches had become trusted and necessary recipients of key client information. Coaches had the keys to the feedback vault. When feedback is accurate and deep, it can help clients see around corners and anticipate obstacles and risks. Feedback in coaching meant another good new thing. It meant that those who received feedback became better organizational players because they had more focused information. Feedback may at times be painful but it began to be seen as a gift. The gift meant that feedback recipients had an advantage over others who had never received it. They were more self-aware. They could begin to understand the different ways they were seen, plus and minus. Knowing this gave clients further incentive to do something about it, thereby improving their organizational odds of success. Feedback pain equated to performance gain. The sound of coaching being effective started to register throughout organizations. Yes, executive coaching was expensive. But the dollars were yielding results. This was a further benefit to organizations in understanding differences between coaching and therapy. Almost all executive coaching clients found that they liked coaching. The only question was: How much did they like it? Clearly, coaching was inspirational!

Today, we see that although coaching is no longer spoken about as a fad; its acceptance and popularity pose other risks. What are the risks that I see today that might undermine the effectiveness of executive coaching?

The number one risk, which has been a potential problem all along the trajectory of the growth of coaching, is that the wrong people can become executive coaches for the wrong reasons. People may become executive coaches because they think it's a quick way to earn a buck. People on the question-asking portal called Quora, many of whom are intelligent individuals, ask questions about executive coaching that show they have not done any homework to find out what is required in terms of the self-discipline of being an executive coach; they just want to get into the field and "get clients now."

People who seek to become executive coaches need to understand that learning how to be a good executive coach is an apprenticeship, and probably a long one. It requires diverse personality characteristics. It requires a gift of being able to listen to people and help human beings change behaviors. It requires the confidence of being able to present yourself to business leaders as someone who can say something that is worth their time and attention. It requires you to self-regulate your emotions in a similar way that we coaches ask our clients to self-regulate emotions. Coaching requires constant course work in behavioral science and business subjects, and requires us to learn what it's like to stay present with our clients while at the same time working in the interest of "thee not me."

Good coaches are unbelievably attuned listeners who can ask both ordinary facilitative questions and very insightful ones. We have no problem with being provocative and direct with our clients in one moment or flexing to becoming tender and empathic in the next. It helps if we have good memories because we'll be required to absorb a lot of information in each engagement. It helps if we're pretty bright because our clients want good conversation partners who can hit the ball back conversationally. It helps if we are utterly committed to the process and the field of executive coaching which means having coaching supervision with a Master Coach, peer supervision, and having had your own coach. It is absolutely required that a coach be able to understand that he or she is not the client's friend although the coach may certainly have a warm demeanor.

Coaches need to live with paradoxical situations, and be able to tolerate complexity and uncertainty. If you have your own external coaching practice, you need to be able to tolerate what my late colleague Bob Lee labeled "CFA" otherwise known as cash flow anxiety.

CFA means we need to live through the ups and downs of being in business for ourselves. We need to have a savings account or line of credit to tide us through when business is bad or when business is good but we still are not getting paid in a timely manner. So we see that the personality factors required of a coach add up to the portrait of someone who can tolerate difficulties, such as financial frustration. It requires emotional resilience. We need to be able to persist with passion, as Angela Duckworth has defined "Grit" in her extraordinary book of the same name (Duckworth, 2016). We need to be able to have a strong sense of self and at the same time a "bullet-proof" ego that is able to adapt to CFA and other frustrations, while at the same time tolerate the provocations of a few provocative and overly aggressive clients, rejections from Human Resources leaders who don't include us on their coaching panels, rejections from potential coaching clients who are not wise enough to select us as their coach in beauty contests. We need to be competitive yet relaxed. We probably need a hard and a soft style. Almost every coach I've ever met loves the work of coaching clients. But some are unable to be resilient enough to endure and succeed at building a practice.

Have you ever watched one of those Wall Street mavens, perhaps even Warren Buffett, being interviewed on CNBC or some similar financial news network? They wax poetic about the "beauty of the market." They talk about how the market has wisdom, how it self-corrects, and so forth. The way they talk about the stock market makes it sound as if it's a living organism. They have worked successfully with the stock market for so many years, they begin to sound like experienced MDs who are able to diagnose the ailments of long-term patients just by checking a few vital signs.

My observation, after having coached for more than 30 years, is that the coaching market has a similar wisdom. That is what I mean when I tell people that the "coaching market self-selects and corrects."

It invariably self-selects out the con men, the egotists, and manipulators that some of our coaching schools are not wise enough to reject. It self-selects out the greedy, fast money guys and gals who come to coaching for the wrong reason and often leave quickly when they experience that coaching is not a quick game. Because the market selects, executive coaches find we need to learn the long game. We need to acquire some business vocabulary if we don't come from a business background. Maybe it wouldn't be a bad idea for us to read *The Wall Street Journal* or some similar publication. If we come from a background that has not included much learning in behavioral sciences like psychology, we need to make sure we find ways to make up for this deficit via supervisory or peer relationships with others who have studied the psychology of human development and personality.

Of course, we have unethical practitioners and bad actors in the executive coaching field as all fields have. But because development as an executive coach requires constant validation from clients and other organizational players, I do hope this self-selection process weeds out most who need to be weeded.

Looking back at the evolution of executive coaching, I find many reasons to feel optimistic. Right now, there is greater agreement as to what constitutes "good executive coaching practice" among external executive coaches and buyers and sponsors who are internal to organizations. By having decided to add 360-degree feedback facilitation and the use of psychometric assessment tools to our work, executive coaches have transformed ourselves into needed facilitators of information that clients don't just want to have; they need to have these data to manage and lead more effectively. This has been a career-saving pivot that has helped executive coaching be seen in this new light.

WHERE DO WE GO FROM HERE?

We need more good research and writing on executive coaching. Books like Wasylyshyn's *Destined to Lead* provide an invaluable casebook for the field (Wasylyshyn, 2014). Pioneering work that executive coaches are conducting now with group and team coaching needs to be encouraged with wisdom. The wisdom we provide to these endeavors needs to be for the clients of team and executive coaching to have clarity as to who is the client in these engagements and what are the terms of their confidentiality/privacy agreements. It goes without saying that coaches need to live up to these agreements. As we say, the coaching process is public and the content is private and owned by the client. This can get tricky when there is an entire team to provide information about to organizational sponsors. I don't think any of us want to return to the uncertainty of a decade ago when executive coaching was referred to in that *Harvard Business Review* article as "The Wild West of Executive Coaching" (Sherman & Freas, 2004).

REFERENCES

Corporate therapy: Having an executive coach is all the rage. (2003). *The Economist*, p. 61.

Duckworth, A. (2016). *Grit: The power and passion of perseverance*. New York, NY: Scribner.

Frisch, M., Lee, R., Metzger, K., Robinson, J., & Rosemarin, J. (2012). *Becoming an exceptional executive coach: Use your knowledge, experience and intuition to help leaders excel*. New York, NY: AMACOM.

Goldsmith, M., & Morgan, H. (2004, Fall). Leadership is a contact sport: The "follow-up factor" in management development. *strategy+business*, *36*. Retrieved from http://www.strategy-business.com/article/04307

Goleman, D., Boyatzis, R., & McKee, A. (2004). *Primal leadership: Learning to lead with emotional intelligence*. Boston, MA: Harvard Business School Press.

Mura, A. (2003). Executive Coaching Summit I: Documenting the emerging field of coaching in organizations. *International Journal of Coaching in Organizations, 1,* 19–26.

Sherman, S., & Freas, A. (2004, November). The Wild West of executive coaching. *Harvard Business Review,* Reprint R0411E.

Wasylyshyn, K. (2014). *Destined to lead: Executive coaching and lessons for leadership development.* New York, NY: Palgrave Macmillan.

35

Career Coaching: The ADAPT Framework

Steven Wendell and Janice Manzi Sabatine

This chapter outlines a meta-view of career coaching as a framework for the coaching engagement and utilization of theories, models, and tools. Coaching conversations are often referred to as a "dance" between coach and client. We expand on this metaphor to consider the micro–macro view of career management strategy as the "dance floor" that accommodates various coaching theories, models, and tools as the "dance styles" and "dance moves" with appreciation of client capabilities and preferences as their "dancing experience and preferences." The flexibility of this metaphor is particularly important given the abundance of relevant coaching approaches, the increasingly dynamic career paths of clients, and appreciation for the subtleties of the coaching relationship.

THE 21ST CENTURY CAREER LANDSCAPE

The career landscape in the 21st century has undergone a significant shift away from the traditional linear path of "climbing the ladder" at a single employer or within a single career path toward increasing mobility and career switching (Brown, 2001). This shift has led to an increase in employment options such as part time, contractor, adjunct, consultants, self-employed, and portfolio careers (Savickas, 2012). Numerous career models and theories have outlined some of the shifts in perspectives that are associated with this evolving employment contract status. The protean career is characterized by a person taking ownership of his or her career, being driven by core values, and success being determined by subjective psychological determinants (Hall, 1996). The boundaryless career spans across employers and organizational boundaries within an employer resulting in independence from the traditional organizational career arrangements (Arthur & Rousseau, 1996). Additionally, appreciation for the significance of happenstance or coincidence in careers has been highlighted in the Planned Happenstance Theory (Mitchell, Levin, & Krumboltz, 1999). Perhaps most significant is the importance of career adaptability described as "a psychosocial construct that denotes an individual's resources for coping with current and anticipated tasks, transitions, traumas in their occupational roles" (Savickas & Porfeli, 2012, p. 662) within the context of career construction theory and the related Career Adapt-Ability Scale (CAAS), which has been validated in 13 countries (Savickas, 2002, 2012). The CAAS assesses affective, behavioral, and cognitive elements across four domains: Concern (preparing for future career tasks and challenges), Control (taking responsibility for influencing one's future using self-discipline, effort, and persistence), Curiosity (exploring one's future self and alternative career scenarios), and Confidence (believing one can succeed in career aspirations and overcome obstacles; Savickas, 2012). The relevance of career adaptability in the 21st century is supported by a wealth of literature investigating the association of CAAS scores with career outcomes. A recent meta-analysis revealed association of CAAS scores with numerous subjective and objective career outcomes in addition to broader well-being and positive life functioning (Rudolph, Lavigne, & Zacher, 2017). Importantly, career adaptability capacities are considered malleable although only one publication so far has reported an intervention that raised the CAAS scores (Koen, Klehe, & Van Vianen, 2012). However, data from interventions based on the approaches in this chapter highlight the potential for career coaching (Wendell & Sabatine, 2016; Sabatine & Wendell, 2017).

The Internet represents another dynamic change. Previously, knowledge was a commodity held by experts that was accumulated through experiences and education. The prior sequestration of knowledge, models, and tools with individuals creates a filtering mechanism based on the expert's knowledge base and personality preferences. There is also an orientation toward single best solutions. The Internet opened the doorway for individuals to effectively explore a much wider offering of resources and potential solutions through self-discovery that can better align with their individual preferences. Additionally, the Internet is responsive to rapid growth and evolution of resources including career exploration, job search functions, and networking, to name a few. Therefore, staying current is a challenge for any individual or resource list. In addition, clients benefit from developing their autonomy to utilize updated resources throughout their careers. Career coaching combined with self-discovery is ideally suited to facilitate clients in utilizing these resources and establishing lifelong career management strategies.

ADAPT® FRAMEWORK

A useful framework for career coaching is the meta-view, Adaptability Development and Authentic Purpose Targeted (ADAPT) career coaching. ADAPT acknowledges the importance of *adaptability development* in the 21st century landscape, recognizes the importance of *authentic purpose* that is true to oneself, and references *targeted* to acknowledge flexibility rather than a stagnant or rigid plan. In addition to "adapt" as an acronym, the concept of "adaptable" is a dominant theme, which includes simultaneously encouraging adaptation to the models and tools. It encourages the coach to adapt to the client's preferences and career stage.

CAREER MANAGEMENT STRATEGY: MICRO VERSUS MACRO PERSPECTIVE

Clients seek career coaching for myriad reasons and a broad view of career management strategy is useful as context and for framing potential tools or assessments. It is useful to group perspectives on career management strategy into micro and macro perspectives (Figure 35.1).

The micro perspective is represented by a career management strategy that tends to focus on the work role to the exclusion of other life roles. This perspective may even dominate a client's view of his or her "real self" that may feel threatened when exploring career options. This micro perspective is typically dependent on shorter-term concrete and measurable goals. Traditionally, this is influenced by following established career paths that reflect a "climbing the ladder" orientation.

The macro perspective incorporates elements we call the "authentic life vision": "authentic," defined by Merriam-Webster, *not false or imitation, true to one's own personality, spirit, or character* (By permission. From Merriam-Webster.com © 2018 by Merriam-Webster); "life" being more holistic and incorporating career as only one of the domains of a person's life; "vision" representing longer-term fluidity as life events and perspectives inevitably change over time.

This typically vaguer perspective incorporates elements of the client's inherent "real self" influenced by personality type preferences, strengths, personal values, passions, and relationship of career to all life domains. The authentic life vision is

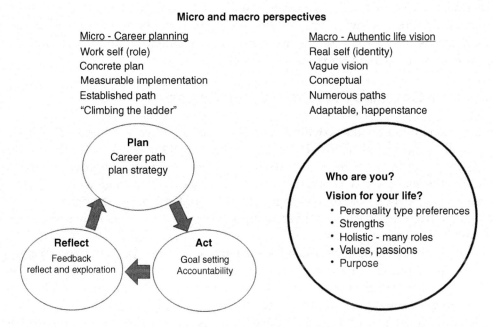

Micro and macro perspectives

Micro - Career planning	Macro - Authentic life vision
Work self (role)	Real self (identity)
Concrete plan	Vague vision
Measurable implementation	Conceptual
Established path	Numerous paths
"Climbing the ladder"	Adaptable, happenstance

Plan
Career path
plan strategy

Reflect
Feedback
reflect and exploration

Act
Goal setting
Accountability

Who are you?

Vision for your life?
• Personality type preferences
• Strengths
• Holistic - many roles
• Values, passions
• Purpose

Figure 35.1 Career management strategy: micro and macro perspectives.

broader and typically achievable through multiple career pathways, making it more adaptable and responsive to the inevitable happenstance that impacts one's life and career. Many career paths can align in the long term with honoring a person's inherent preferences and serving his or her values and purpose. However, the awareness from an authentic life vision benefits from integration into an effective career management strategy that includes the micro perspective to guide intentionality.

Individuals have tendencies to orient toward one or the other perspective and each have benefits and blind spots. Focus on the micro perspective may support more intentional career progress but may lead toward a career path that deviates from an authentic life vision or struggles with adapting to barriers. Conversely, focus on the macro perspective may be more fluid in adapting to barriers and take advantage of happenstance but may lack intentional progress of concrete actions and lead to paralysis or floundering career direction. In addition to clients having tendencies toward one perspective or the other, career coaches and their models or tools may also share these tendencies. Ideally, career coaching contributes to increasing the client's awareness and developmental growth in both perspectives while fostering a deep alignment between them.

COACHING ENGAGEMENT

PURPOSE OF ADAPT

A primary concern of the ADAPT approach is to align the coaching engagement with the client's perspective and preferences. The career management strategy with micro–macro perspectives provides a dance floor to let coach and client know where they are and where they might want to explore. It is also a flexible framework to integrate a variety of coaching models, theories, and tools. Ultimately, the goal is to enhance the client's awareness within, and alignment between, the micro and macro views to enhance the client's career management strategy. It should also identify areas or growth horizons for further development.

INDIVIDUAL COACHING PROFILES AND PRE-ASSESSMENTS

One consideration for the coaching engagement is whether to engage assessments that will be debriefed in the first coaching session. One concern is whether the assessment could obscure or supersede the client's agenda. Another concern is whether the client will have interest or the capacity to fully engage with the assessment. It may be more useful to engage with the client and allow the client's interest to emerge from the coaching conversation. This approach can be even more important with involuntary clients.

An alternative would be to use assessments to create a personalized coaching profile that is not initially debriefed with the client but helps the coach to understand the client's preferences and perspective. An example would be to combine the CAAS to gain some preliminary understanding of what clients might need with their adult development stage and personality type profile to assess how to best work with them and what approaches might be most aligned with their preferences. In addition to knowing the clients' profiles, coaches can assess their own adult development stage and personality type preference to understand how to best manage their own perspectives and preferences to meet the clients where they are.

CLIENT VARIATION AND PIVOT POINTS

Clients seeking career coaching vary widely, including those entering the work world, mid-career level, and those planning for retirement. Those entering the work world such as students or individuals re-entering work may not have developed career management strategies, reflected on who they are in relation to their career, or what they want from their life in the longer term. They benefit from exploration across all aspects of the micro and macro perspectives. Mid-career stage clients may come for coaching around advancement, creating a better fit in their current job, or considering switching careers. Clients considering retirement may be seeking help navigating a new purpose, dealing with a shift in identity, or setting up to semi-retire. Career coaching may also be ancillary to a client's primary coaching topic.

The ADAPT framework with the micro and macro perspective was conceptualized to provide a flexible framework and general principles that, like a dance floor, provide the space to explore a variety of career-related topics. Like on a dance floor, the particular dance style and dance moves may not utilize the entire space available, yet the floor will serve as an inviting reminder of what is available and help orient a person in relationship to this space. Similarly, the ability to transition and pivot around and between the micro and macro perspectives gracefully with your client partner should flow with ease as part of the coaching dance. This can be more challenging with clients that have involuntarily come to coaching as part of an organizational program and the flexibility to explore more widely provides greater opportunity to identify an area that resonates with their interests.

Coaching conversations provide many opportunities for entry points into the micro or macro perspectives and subsequent transitions between them. These transitions can provide critical linkage and integration between these viewpoints, and coaches should develop their awareness and preferred approach to powerful questions that "lead" the dance across the dance floor. The coach may explore how goals in the micro perspective honor personal values, or conversely, how personal values show up in goals. A coach may also explore how a client's career management strategy is aligned with personality type preferences or how the client can modify his or her strategy to better align with preferences. If initial coaching conversations are struggling to identify subtle entry points, inquiries around the client's career decision-making approaches or career planning strategies can shape the discussion toward a more direct entry point.

While coaching conversations often present natural transitions, tools can also provide valuable entry points or pivot points to a broader view while also elevating the client's curiosity and enthusiasm. This curiosity and enthusiasm can be enhanced by inviting the client to deconstruct or critique a tool, modify the tool, or use it in a novel way. For instance, the CAAS data can be useful to discuss with a client and can lead to a variety of discussion threads. A common Venn diagram primarily

Figure 35.2 Venn diagram for ideal career.

used as a static informational slide in career talks, referred to as the *Ikigia*, provides an example of how an informational slide can be transformed into a valuable tool when clients are encouraged to deconstruct or critique the diagram (Figure 35.2). This Venn diagram is typically used to represent the ideal career target (gray dot) that lies at the intersection of the four areas.

Typically, this diagram includes labels of profession, vocation, mission, and passion in several intersections but there are multiple reasons to remove these labels when using in a coaching environment including the potential judgment they may elicit. The variety of responses to this diagram range from inspirational to dismissal as unrealistic. When coaches invite clients to deconstruct and criticize the diagram through a series of powerful questions, clients can explore and stretch their perspectives on the big picture of how the topics relate. Additionally, this approach can stimulate client enthusiasm and engagement to further explore topics in both the micro and macro views. A few representative questions:

- Where will the gray dot be in 20 years?
- What if there were two gray dots?
- What might this look like for an entrepreneur? (two categories missing)

Two particularly useful areas to explore include:
How much they believe they know (are aware of) within each category?
What is restricting that knowledge?
Typically, this approach helps clients realize they are aware of only a fraction of the potential knowledge in each area and that it is restricted by past or current experiences and may be related to their current career field. For example, those in academic careers often have limited knowledge of opportunities outside academia and have skills they are unaware of since they haven't had opportunities to use them (Figure 35.3).

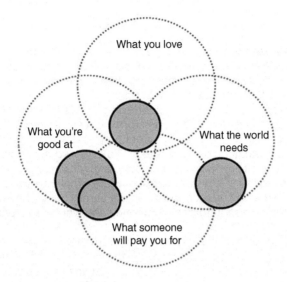

Figure 35.3 Venn diagram for ideal career: client awareness.

Such an approach generates substantial client enthusiasm for a variety of exercises, tools, and discussion. It can also be uplifting to clients feeling frustrated as they see there is much more to explore than their current limited knowledge. Exploring the client's perspectives on this Venn diagram can also be informative to the coach about the client's limitations and preferences in perspective taking and career decision making.

CASE STUDIES

NICHE MAKER—CAROL

- Coaching engagement: 1-on-1 career coaching, involuntary participation through an academic program.

- Narrative discussion and eventually a minimal introduction by the coach to the planned happenstance theory and 21st-century careers.

- No interactions or assessments prior to first coaching session.

Carol is a PhD student combining two divergent disciplines in a unique way that puts her into a unique niche (boundaryless career). She is very planful and is stressed from the inability to identify a future career fit and, therefore, no concrete path or direction is evident. She reverts to considering one of several more traditional career paths in one or the other discipline, but these prospects are noticeably deflating to her. The initial exploration of the macro perspective including strengths, values, and passions clarifies an excitement and fit for a niche career commitment.

She explored how her niche is an opportunity and the value of her niche to fill a need that hadn't yet been identified. She begins to see how she could create a new

---

(continued)

(continued)

niche career that doesn't yet exist analogous to nonexistent Venn diagram circles for *what the world needs* and *what someone will pay you for*. The outcome is unpredictable, but she begins to resonate with being a Niche Maker and to find comfort in accepting the ambiguity (growth horizon).

However, she repeatedly returns to expressing stress about not having a standard career path to use for guidance in forming a structured career plan (micro). She recognizes this is an unpredictable career path and that random events will have to occur for her to create her own new career. We explored the relevance of the Planned Happenstance Theory and what it suggests for characteristics and activities that enhance the chances of a pivotal happenstance. This now gives her something more concrete to focus on and incorporate into a career plan. She is more at peace with finding "comfort in discomfort" by accepting she won't see a path for some time but can still take concrete actions.

Carol can now incorporate planning (micro) from this new perspective to enact the characteristics and activities that increase the likelihood of happenstance occurring. She is interested in further exploring what she loves about being a Niche Maker and the characteristics that make her a Niche Maker (macro).

After that initial meeting Carol made a large colorful poster with the words "Niche Maker" and "Remember, it is not called Luck. . .it is called Planned Happenstance" (macro) and displayed it on her cubicle wall (Figure 35.4).

Figure 35.4 Niche Maker poster.

VISION BOARDER—SUSAN

- Coaching engagement: Group (coaching-based career course) supplemented with 1-on-1 career coaching. Susan began 1-on-1 coaching midway through the course, so she had exposure to a variety of content prior to coaching.

- Susan was provided with a packet of assessments including micro view associated (concrete and real world) work environment values, skills, interest oriented

(continued)

(continued)

> to a 'trait and factor' matching perspective, together with macro associated (metaphor and big picture) visioning exercises such as vision board, dream job, personal values. She was instructed to complete any two exercises.
>
> - Represents: Adapting to client-determined entry point for engagement, personality preferences, and preference for micro or macro view.
>
> Susan resonated with a vision board she created that had a picture of a black female doctor as a dominant feature. The topic of strengths was discussed after minimal exposure in the course. When she was asked what change she sees in the vision board, she reports the image of the doctor has been enlarged. What could further enlarge this image? She reports that learning to maintain awareness of her strengths and utilizing them more would further enlarge the image of the doctor. After a brief discussion about incorporating these responses into goals, she was challenged to craft these into goals for the next meeting (honoring her introverted preference to reflect "in-between" sessions and shifting macro view into micro goals).
>
> How did the image get there? She reports a staircase and visualizes adding stairs to the vision board. What do they represent? Challenges to medical school admission such as the MCAT exam scores, which she then indicates she sees a wall blocking the stairs for her. How can you get past this barrier? She explores moving the stair to go around the wall and the real-world version of this. She settles on building a steeper staircase. Who can help you climb these stairs? She reports classmates in a peer study group and a prep course. She also reports that the stress of the MCAT prep is like carrying a heavy backpack. What would lighten this load? She reports emotional intelligence, journaling, and mindfulness exercises have been helpful, but she hasn't been consistent lately. Continued discussion led to modification of her vision board to include some meditation images as a reminder to stay consistent and adding pictures of her classmates with some supporting her climbing the stairs.

GROUP AND 1-ON-1 CAREER COACHING

The combination and integration of group and 1-on-1 career coaching enhances efficiency and effectiveness. This approach may be difficult to achieve in a coaching practice composed mostly of individual clients unless the number of clients and overlap in client needs match a coordinated program offering. Internal coaching or programs delivered to organizations are more likely to be amenable to this combined approach. The *Foundations of Successful Career Planning and Development* course at the University of Pittsburgh provides an example of group coaching supplemented with 1-on-1 career coaching. The group format in the course includes topical class sessions that introduce topics with minimal "primer" background information and assignments to complete assessments (such as Myers–Briggs Type Indicator[R] [MBTI[R]]) or self-discovery exercises on the topic. Students submit written reflections and provide verbal reports in the subsequent class on the self-discovery assignments (honors MBTI introvert and extravert preferences). When necessary, assessments such as the MBTI are debriefed and discussed in class. The group discussion and topical "primer" material is facilitated by a professional coach mindful to avoid the "sage on the stage" role. The group debriefing of assessments and group discussion of self-discovery assignments provide significant efficiencies. In addition, the group discussion provides many additional benefits such as crowd-sourcing discovery of current resources and knowledge. After initial class sessions covering foundational topics including reflection exercises, 1-on-1 career coaching is engaged.

The topic selection, group discussion facilitation, and combination of group and 1-on-1 coaching align with elements of integral coaching (Hunt, 2009). It includes exploration in all four quadrants: Individual (Internal, External) and Group (Internal, External) of the AQAL (all quadrants, all levels, all lines, all states, and all types) to support change (Wilber, 1980, 2000). The self-discovery, role modeling, and discussion of perspectives around the challenging topic of careers in both a group and 1-on-1 format is also intended to support the potential for increased self-authoring and adult development (Baxter Magolda, 2001; Kegan, 1994). In addition, the topics, assignment reports, group format, and individual coaching collectively reflect the top five components identified as critical to career intervention strategies (Brown et al., 2003).

SELF-DETERMINATION THEORY (SDT)

SDT (Chapter 20) is an important framework that provides additional insight into an optimal coaching engagement consistent with the ADAPT framework. SDT asserts that meeting three basic psychological needs supports self-motivation and well-being. These include *autonomy*—engagement in interesting activities that align with core values, *competence*—the sense that one has the capacities to achieve valued outcomes, and *relatedness*—feeling cared for and connected to others (Ryan & Deci, 2017). SDT also asserts that motivation can be differentiated into *autonomous motiva-tion,* which is characterized by inherent drive when serving a person's interests and core values, and *controlled motivation,* which is characterized by external pressures and obligations (Ryan & Deci, 2017). The ADAPT framework outlines coaching approaches that are consistent with SDT and support increased capacity for autono-mous motivation by addressing issues such as values clarification. However, a deeper understanding of SDT is particularly relevant to facilitation of group coach-ing and facilitating client's goal setting.

INTENTIONAL CHANGE THEORY (ICT)

ICT (Chapter 19; Boyatzis, 2006) is an additional model that provides important insight into career coaching that is aligned with the ADAPT framework. In the ADAPT framework, emphasis in the early coaching sessions is placed on designing a personal vision, which aligns closely with describing the ideal self per ICT. Such a vision-based coaching approach has been shown to stimulate a positive psycho-physiological state that promotes numerous relational and motivational resources such as identity expansion, increased vitality, and activation of learning goals (Passarelli, 2015). Self-assessments and feedback, as will be described further in the micro perspective exploration section, assist the client in describing a real self. Supporting clients during career exploration and planning to recognize and acknowledge where their ideal self and real self overlap, where they are already exhibiting characteristics of their ideal self, may increase their sense of competence, one of the psychological needs supporting self-motivation and well-being (Ryan & Deci, 2017). Conversely, contrasting a desired future (vision or ideal self) with what might stand in the way (path from current situation or real self) may also be an effective method for stimulating motivation and commitment to goals (Kappes & Oettingen, 2011). The emphasis in the ADAPT framework of exploring supportive relationships and support structures again aligns closely with ICT, which proposes that supportive relationships are foundational to developmental change.

CAREER MANAGEMENT STRATEGY: MICRO–MACRO EXPLORATION

We now attempt to add more substance to the framework by providing sub-categories under the micro and macro perspectives that include a combination of tools, perspectives, and proposed best practices to support career coaches in their exploration with clients rather than to create content that could be passed on directly to clients.

MACRO PERSPECTIVE EXPLORATION

This exploration reaches beyond the client's current work world, which has its own value but may include biases and blind spots. It includes reflections and assessments of inherent qualities/traits, personal values, with a holistic perspective across all life roles. Looking for patterns or themes across this exploration can contribute greater clarity to an overall authentic purpose or mission statement. Expression of purpose and personal values throughout the career management strategy is an important contribution to career satisfaction and fulfillment.

INHERENT PERSONALITY PREFERENCES AND STRENGTHS

Personality type preferences and styles such as the MBTI and DiSC® provide insights into inherent preferences that permeate all aspects of our lives. Like writing with your preferred hand, honoring these preferences and styles can be more satisfying and productive. These preferences can be applied to selecting a career or modifying work duties and environment. They should also be honored in how the client approaches career management strategies and in identifying growth horizons.

The VIA Character Strengths and Clifton Strengthfinders identify inherent strengths such as judgment, creativity, fairness, or futurist, relator, strategist, respectively. Like preferences and styles, utilizing these in the workplace can be more satisfying and productive. Collectively, they contribute to clients' understanding of who they are. The VIA character strengths may also be useful for identifying and articulating personal values.

HOLISTIC LIFE

It is crucial to align career management with a holistic consideration of all areas and roles as part of a fulfilling life. The Wheel of Life is a common tool and many examples are available on the Internet. This is typically a large wheel composed of 10 concentric circles with pie pieces representing various domains of our lives. Career is only one of many domains, others being areas such as romantic partner, family, recreation, and so forth. The concentric circles provide a ranking in satisfaction in each domain, providing a useful tool to visualize satisfaction across all domains. While it is tempting to promote balance across all domains, some clients could feel unwelcome pressure to "do it all." Further, the metaphor of driving a car with perfectly balanced wheels may fall short as even these cars can get stuck in a traffic jam, which could represent a work environment surrounded by individuals with unbalanced wheels. It is also possible to have a perfectly balanced wheel where the degree of satisfaction in all domains is very low. It may be better viewed as a tool to promote awareness and support exploration of the client's integration of their career into their holistic life satisfaction. Goals from other domains can be included in a career management strategy to develop a more satisfying life. It is also useful to explore changes that might occur in the future across the domains as these may influence longer term career plans. Creativity in exploring this tool can lead to interesting perspectives and uses such as seeing whether life partners can accurately predict each other's wheel ratings or how they integrate their wheels.

PERSONAL VALUES

Personal values and beliefs are difficult to define with precision. They are generally stable and show up across all areas of life. Examples of potential values may include authenticity, autonomy, learning, and service. Clients may select values from various lists or the career coach may begin to recognize potential values as themes coming up repeatedly during coaching sessions. Interestingly, coaching at the micro level around career goals with questions such as "what personal value does this goal honor?" may help identify or clarify personal goals.

Exploring personal values provides a substrate for clarifying a client's sense of life purpose. It is also helpful to explore the alignment of personal values with elements of the micro perspective including career plans and specific goals.

SKILLS, INTERESTS, WORK ENVIRONMENT VALUES

Assessments that explore skills, interests, and work environment values add value directly within the micro level by influencing career planning and goal setting. However, they can also contribute granularity to the macro level authentic career vision. Some caution is needed when considering these assessments and reflecting at the macro level since they are more likely to be influenced or biased by past work culture in a variety of ways. This is also true of instruments such as 360-degree feedback instruments.

MICRO PERSPECTIVE EXPLORATION

The micro view is typically oriented toward shorter-term processes and actions to implement career progress with some directionality. Ideally this includes cycles of reflection, career exploration, goal setting, accountability, and feedback leading back to reflection. Typically, a full cycle is completed annually and may coincide with an annual job appraisal. However, the process should be dynamic, and engaged in and revised frequently. The engagement with the career coach and exploration across the micro and macro levels represents an initial expansive reflection and exploration from which a subset of tools, assessments, and specific reflective exercises should be incorporated into the ongoing annual reflection and exploration cycle.

INITIAL REFLECTION AND CAREER EXPLORATION

The reflections and exploration from the macro level, such as the MBTI, generate stable results that should be considered during an initial reflection but are not necessary to repeat. The wheel of life and some forms of visioning exercises are the exception. Reflections at the micro level include career exploration and assessments of skills, interest, and work environment values.

While career exploration is understandable for those entering or re-entering the workforce, it is also important to those content in their current career. Awareness of increased options and future career trends contributes the ability to tweak current job duties. The Internet provides access to an overwhelming wealth of information about careers from broad initial overviews such as O*Net (www.onetonline.org) to increasingly more specific resources including online career panels, resources available through professional associations, and detailed personal career stories. Many resources and articles about overall workforce trends and career-specific future trends are also available. Informational interviews, which involve brief conversations with individuals working in specific jobs of interest, are particularly helpful for exploring detailed realities of working in a specific career. In addition, they often contribute to building networking contacts in the career field. Increased awareness of the incredible variety of career options can become overwhelming. One of the advantages of macro level assessments such as personality type preferences and an authentic life vision is to provide a screening filter to focus on careers that appear to align with these parameters.

The micro level assessment of skills, interest, and work environment values provides additional layers for this screening. Skills assessments contain lists of skills and/or questions to identify skills utilized in examples of greatest successes. Interest assessments typically ask a series of questions around most enjoyable daily tasks or activities or those that put you in a positive mood. Work environment value assessments typically include a list of items or a card sort exercise that include items such as job security, fast paced, autonomy, and travel. While each of these assessments typically involves self-identification, seeking input from others can provide important information that may not be self-evident to the client.

Ongoing career exploration expands options for planned or unplanned career transitions and awareness to better navigate current career paths. Combined with assessments from the macro level, it enhances the potential alignment with purpose and overall authentic life vision including relationship to other domains of the wheel of life. Incorporating the micro level assessments provides granularity to satisfying career fit and potential to maintain this fit as these work environment values and interests naturally evolve over a lifetime. The skill assessments provide the additional benefit of identifying skills development goals that may improve a current work role or prepare a client for a future career or job transition.

CAREER PLAN

A traditional career plan typically includes an overview of goals for the coming year and detailed listing with primary goals, sub-goals, and a timeline. However, there are many different strategies that resonate with individuals including graphical representation, mindmapping, and cell phone apps. Career coaching should honor the client's approach and support the client to identify the growth horizon to the preferred strategy. Some areas for exploration include additional elements of a career plan including goal setting, accountability, feedback, and reflection. The following sections on Action and Feedback and Reflection provide details to consider during these conversations. Opportunities may also exist to explore goal categories for domains outside work that may have shown up on the wheel of life.

ACTION

Goal setting is an under-appreciated skill that requires developmental effort and warrants inclusion, ironically, as a distinct goal that should be explored in coaching conversations. The client's MBTI preferences will likely have a significant influence on his or her current perspectives around goal setting that should be acknowledged and accommodated by the coach. SDT provides some guidance to assist coaching around goal setting. Helping the client to link goals to interests and values will support autonomous motivation. The structure of goals including clarity of the goal and effective breakdown into smaller subgoals is a critical and challenging aspect of developing goal setting skills. Learning to utilize subgoals that are ideally balanced in their level of difficulty is important to perceptions of competence (Ryan & Deci, 2017). Although the promotion of SMART goals (specific, measurable, achievable, realistic, and time-bound) is pervasive, additional perspectives of goals provide distinct advantages. An important perspective on goal setting includes the differentiation between the use of performance versus learning goals based on whether the individual has the required knowledge and skills. Performance goals provide motivation to apply previously acquired knowledge and skills, while learning goals focus on acquiring the requisite knowledge and skills (Seijts & Latham, 2005). In some situations, the use of learning goals leads to higher performance than starting with a high-performance goal (Seijts & Latham, 2005). Accountability strategies can be useful to support goals that are subject to controlled motivation. Clients should be encouraged to explore their own creative accountability strategies to increase elements of autonomy. Strategies that include positive support and contribute to relatedness may prove most promising.

While career plans typically focus on career-oriented goals, considering goals from other domains on the wheel of life would be advantageous. Goals at the growth horizon of the career management strategy are also appropriate.

FEEDBACK AND REFLECTION

Formal feedback should be solicited annually and ideally framed as a progress appraisal. There are distinct benefits in using a three-pronged approach that includes a self-appraisal and progress appraisals from a supervisor and a mentor that is not in a supervisorial role (Hobin et al., 2014). The self-appraisal provides an opportunity to inventory accomplishments and enhance a sense of competency. This is also an opportunity to identify factors that may have inhibited or enhanced progress. Reflecting on goal setting and accountability strategies during the self-appraisal can provide valuable feedback for continued growth and adjustments. Progress appraisal feedback from mentors that are not in a supervisorial role provides valuable external perspectives that are more objective. A supervisor has a unique perspective to offer additional feedback and can assist with navigating factors that inhibited progress or augment factors that enhanced progress. In addition to reflecting on the progress appraisal, this is an opportunity to establish a regular reflection on additional elements such as the Wheel of Life, career exploration, and growth horizons in the career management strategy.

CONCLUSION

The significant shift in 21st-century careers and availability of self-discovery resources represent an opportunity for career coaching to facilitate clients' lifelong career management strategies. The ADAPT framework can be viewed as the dance floor to orient the models and tools of the career coach and suggest areas to explore. The ability of the coach to adapt to the client's perspectives and preferences in this dance can be enhanced by ongoing growth and comfort with additional models and tools, including many of those detailed in the other chapters of this book.

You are invited to participate in ongoing dialogue about this chapter through the following online forum: academiccareercoaching.com

REFERENCES

Arthur, M. B., & Rousseau, D. M. (1996). *The boundaryless career: A new employment principle for a new organizational era.* New York, NY: Oxford University Press.

Baxter Magolda, M. B. (2001). *Making their own way: Narratives for transforming higher education to promote self-development.* Sterling, VA: Stylus.

Boyatzis, R. E. (2006). Intentional change a complexity perspective. *Journal of Management Development, 27*(7), 607–623. doi:10.1108/02621710610678445

Brown, B. L. (2001). Changing career patterns. *ERIC Digest.* Retrieved from http://ericdigests.org/2001-2/career.html

Brown, S. D., Ryan Krane, N. E., Brecheisen, J., Castelino, P., Budisin, I., Miller, M., & Edens, L. (2003). Critical ingredients of career choice interventions: More analyses and new hypotheses. *Journal of Vocational Behavior, 62,* 411–428. doi:10.1016/S0001-8791(02)00052-0

Hall, D. T. (1996). Protean careers in the 21st century. *The Academy of Management Executive, 10,* 8–16. doi:10.5465/ame.1996.3145315

Hobin, J. A., Wendell, S. K., Zellers, D. F., Clifford, P. S., Lindstaedt, B., & Fuhrmann, C. N. (2014). *I have a plan. . .Now what?: Science careers.* Retrieved from http://sciencecareers.sciencemag.org/career_magazine/previous_issues/articles/2014_04_16/caredit.a1400094

Hunt, J. (2009). Transcending and including our current way of being. *Journal of Integral Theory and Practice, 4*(1), 1–20.

Kappes, H. B., & Oettingen, G. (2011). Positive fantasies about idealized futures sap energy. *Journal of Experimental Social Psychology, 47*(4), 719–729. doi:10.1016/j.jesp.2011.02.003

Kegan, R. (1994). *In over our heads: The mental demands of modern life.* Cambridge, MA: Harvard University Press.

Koen, J., Klehe, U. C., & Van Vianen, A. E. (2012). Training career adaptability to facilitate a successful school-to-work transition. *Journal of Vocational Behavior, 81*, 395–408. doi:10.1016/j.jvb.2012.10.003

Mitchell, K. E., Levin, A. S., & Krumboltz, J. D. (1999). Planned happenstance: Constructing unexpected career opportunities. *Journal of Counseling & Development, 77*, 115–124. doi:10.1002/j.1556-6676.1999.tb02431.x

Passarelli, A. M. (2015). Vision-based coaching: Optimizing resources for leader development. *Frontiers in Psychology, 6*, 1–14. doi:10.3389/fpsyg.2015.00412

Rudolph, C. W., Lavigne, K. N., & Zacher, H. (2017) Career adaptability: A meta-analysis of relationships with measures of adaptivity, adapting responses, and adaptation results. *Journal of Vocational Behavior, 98*, 17–34. doi:10.1016/j.jvb.2016.09.002

Ryan, R. M., & Deci, E. L. (2017). *Self-determination theory: Basic psychological needs in motivation, development, and wellness.* New York, NY: Guilford Press.

Sabatine, J., & Wendell, S. (2017, October). *Strategies and two-year results for a vision-based coaching supplement to a graduate student career course.* Presented at Institute of Coaching in Leadership and Healthcare Conference, Boston, MA.

Savickas, M. L. (2002). Career construction: A developmental theory of vocational behavior. In D. Brown (Ed.), *Career choice and development* (4th ed., pp. 149–205). San Francisco, CA: Jossey-Bass.

Savickas, M. L. (2012). Life design: A paradigm for career intervention in the 21st century. *Journal of Counseling & Development, 90*, 13–19. doi:10.1111/j.1556-6676.2012.00002.x

Savickas, M. L., & Porfeli, E. J. (2012). Career adapt-abilities scale: Construction, reliability, and measurement equivalence across 13 countries. *Journal of Vocational Behavior, 80*, 661–673. doi:10.1016/j.jvb.2012.01.011

Seijts, G. H., & Latham, G. P. (2005). Learning versus performance goals: When should each be used? *Academy of Management Executive, 19*, 124–131.

Wendell, S., & Sabatine, J. (2016, September). Preliminary results from a coaching-based graduate career course and supplemental individual coaching study indicate positive outcome measures including enhanced career adaptability. Presented at Institute of Coaching in Leadership and Healthcare Conference, Boston, MA.

Wilber, K. (1980). *The Atman Project: A transpersonal view of human development.* Wheaton, IL: Quest Books.

Wilber, K. (2000). *Integral psychology: Consciousness, spirit, psychology, therapy.* Boston, MA: Shambhala.

Index